YOUTH

The Years from Ten to Sixteen

BOOKS BY ARNOLD GESELL

THE NORMAL CHILD AND PRIMARY EDUCATION (WITH B. C. GESELL)

EXCEPTIONAL CHILDREN AND PUBLIC SCHOOL POLICY

HANDICAPPED CHILDREN IN SCHOOL AND COURT

THE PRE-SCHOOL CHILD FROM THE STANDPOINT OF PUBLIC HYGIENE AND EDUCATION

THE RETARDED CHILD—HOW TO HELP HIM

THE MENTAL GROWTH OF THE PRE-SCHOOL CHILD

INFANCY AND HUMAN GROWTH

GUIDANCE OF MENTAL GROWTH IN INFANT AND CHILD

AN ATLAS OF INFANT BEHAVIOR—TWO VOLUMES, 3,200 ACTION PHOTOGRAPHS

INFANT BEHAVIOR—ITS GENESIS AND GROWTH (WITH THOMPSON)

THE PSYCHOLOGY OF EARLY GROWTH (WITH THOMPSON)

BIOGRAPHIES OF CHILD DEVELOPMENT

THE FIRST FIVE YEARS OF LIFE:—A GUIDE TO THE STUDY OF THE PRE-SCHOOL CHILD

WOLF CHILD AND HUMAN CHILD

TWINS T AND C FROM INFANCY TO ADOLESCENCE (WITH THOMPSON)

DEVELOPMENTAL DIAGNOSIS: CLINICAL METHODS AND PEDIATRIC APPLICATIONS
    (WITH AMATRUDA)

A GUIDE TO THE STUDY OF THE YALE FILMS OF CHILD DEVELOPMENT (WITH AMES)

THE EMBRYOLOGY OF BEHAVIOR

HOW A BABY GROWS

FEEDING BEHAVIOR OF INFANTS—A PEDIATRIC APPROACH TO THE MENTAL HYGIENE
    OF EARLY LIFE (WITH ILG)

INFANT AND CHILD IN THE CULTURE OF TODAY (WITH ILG)

THE CHILD FROM FIVE TO TEN (WITH ILG)

VISION: ITS DEVELOPMENT IN INFANT AND CHILD (WITH ILG
    AND BULLIS)

STUDIES IN CHILD DEVELOPMENT

INFANT DEVELOPMENT

YOUTH

The Years from Ten to Sixteen

BY
ARNOLD GESELL, M.D.
FRANCES L. ILG, M.D.
LOUISE BATES AMES, Ph.D.

From the Gesell Institute of Child Development
and from the Yale Clinic of Child Development

New York

HARPER AND BROTHERS, PUBLISHERS

Library of Congress catalog card number: 56–6023

GRATEFUL acknowledgment is made to Old Dominion Foundation, Inc., for a grant-in-aid in support of the underlying research and the writing of this volume.

Contents

PART THREE

MATURITY TRENDS AND GROWTH GRADIENTS

Preface and Acknowledgments

A little over a half century ago G. Stanley Hall wrote a notable book with a formidable title: *Adolescence: Its Psychology and its Relations to Physiology, Anthropology, Sociology, Sex, Crime and Education.* This monumental work in two volumes was almost encyclopedic in scope and content. It provided a storehouse of factual knowledge combined with venturesome speculations concerning the evolutionary history of the psyche and the influence of that racial history on the psychology of modern man. Hall regarded adolescence as a new birth by which the highest and most recent human traits come into being. Through his highly suggestive writings he established adolescence as a distinctive field for scientific exploration and interpretation.

The founders and investigators of psychoanalysis also had a special interest in the evolutionary background and racial origins of mental mechanisms, conscious and unconscious. Their observations and theories are mainly based on clinical studies of adult psychopathology, supplemented by data from cultural anthropology. The Freudian concepts of the id, the ego and the super-ego figure prominently in the interpretation of adolescent phenomena. The role of primal instinctual impulses is stressed.

A vast and various literature on adolescence has accumulated since the pioneering publication of G. Stanley Hall. The diversity of this literature is only partly indicated by the Readings and References listed elsewhere. Many of the current studies are topical in character and deal with special physical, physiologic and behavioral aspects. There are an abundance of cross-sectional and group surveys, and numerous reports of measurements and statistics. Increasing emphasis is placed on the necessity of longitudinal studies.

The biological approach is dominant in many of the areas of research.

xi

The extraordinary growth of the present-day medical and life sciences promises much for a deeper comprehension of the adolescent as a functioning organism.

The problems of adolescence, however, are compounded and complicated by environmental factors which impinge with special force upon the youth of today. The comparative study of widely differing cultures and ideologies has become a matter of social as well as scientific urgency. The social approaches to the study of the adolescent personality accordingly have assumed new significance in an age of cultural crisis and global cold war.*

Our own orientation to the study of adolescence is detailed in the opening chapters of the present volume. This volume completes a trilogy which began with the publication of *Infant and Child in the Culture of Today* (1943) followed by *The Child from Five to Ten* (1946). Together the three books encompass the first sixteen years of the growth cycle. Each book is devoted to a distinguishable segment of the cycle. In content and construction, however, the series constitutes a single work, based on a systematic survey of the patterns and sequences of behavior traits observed in relatively homogeneous groups of normal subjects. Our developmental approach has led us step by step to chart the forms of behavior revealed at successive stages of maturity. Several thousand behavior items were available for codification and comparative evaluation in various fields and channels of development. Maturity traits and trends for twenty-four consecutive age zones are summarized.

A developmental psychology of infant, child and youth must of necessity begin with more or less orderly description. A purely functional psychology can scarcely explain human nature in general or adolescent youth in particular. Functions do not operate in a vacuum and a developmental psychology of youth must take into account the actual patterns of behavior which take form in a given culture. So we have traced the course of development of a group of normal youths in the concrete setting of their home, school and urban community.

The growing behavior patterns reflect the interaction of organism and environment. The primary aim of our study was to define the formative sequences of behavior manifestations; for they contain the clues to the underlying mechanisms of growth and the directions of development.

---

* For a critical appraisal of various methods of approach in the study of adolescence see D. P. Ausubel, *Theory and Problems of Adolescent Development*; also M. Sherif and H. Cantril, *The Psychology of Ego-Involvements*.

We use the terms growth and development interchangeably. The terms apply equally to mental and physical attributes. In a monistic sense they apply to both attributes in unison, for the mind is part and parcel of an indivisible organism. It is part of a patterned and patterning system—an action system. The individual develops as a unit.

Accordingly, development becomes a key concept. The concept has special import for the interpretation of the adolescent years because they mark the crucial transition from childhood to adulthood. Development is an integrative concept. It helps to resolve the dualisms of organism and environment; of heredity and habit; of structure and function; of mind and body. It allows us to think of the adolescent youth in terms of his individual growth characteristics and growth potentials. It leads to a more adequate recognition of the influence of constitutional factors on growth career. It acknowledges the importance of inheritance.

So much for general theoretical background. But the bare concept of development bakes us no bread. The concept remains elusive and vague if it is not related to the concrete life situations which occur from day to day in the affairs of home, school and community. We made a systematic survey of the developmental stages of behavior from birth to age ten. The early findings established a foundation and a perspective for the later studies. A fortunate combination of circumstances enabled us to maintain continuing contacts with many of the same children whose development we had followed from infancy or early childhood at the Yale Clinic of Child Development. Most of the studies of the youths from ten to sixteen years of age were made under the auspices of the Gesell Institute of Child Development, founded in 1950.

As will be detailed in the text, we ranged far and wide to get an intimate picture of how boys and girls grow up in the complex culture of today. They told us much in their own words, spontaneously and responsively. They talked freely about their interests and activities, their problems, difficulties, achievements, attitudes and ambitions. Their parents, particularly the mothers, generously gave expert supplementary information. Teachers from different grades drew on their specialized experience to assist us in exploring the characteristics of different age zones. The data yielded by standardized examinations and periodic observations were enriched and improved by all these participants in a mutual program of developmental research. We owe them all a great debt of gratitude. If our findings prove to have vitality it will be because of the sincerity of the participating contributions.

The findings are summarized for ready reference in three categories, namely *Maturity Traits* (behavior patterns and guidance problems which occur at a given age zone); *Maturity Trends* (growth gradients and sequences for a cycle of seven age zones); *Maturity Profiles* (a series of delineations characterizing the developmental import of each age zone). It is assumed that this triple arrangement will be used as a frame of reference, and not as a scedule of norms. So used it should have orientational value. Many of the problems which parents and teachers and society itself face in the youths of today look different and less insoluble when viewed in the perspective of patterned changes which often or normally occur as the growth cycle unfolds.

The gradients of growth, however, have their limitations. They must be interpreted judiciously, because of a wide diversity of individual variations. The gradients do not constitute a psychometric scale; but they do afford a useful indication of how the growth process trends toward its goals.

An awareness of the growth process is a first step toward guidance based on understanding. Such an awareness is also an aid to self-insight. This applies to youth as well as to elders. Accordingly we have addressed to youth a brief postscript on "The Value of a Philosophy of Growth" (Chapter 19, p. 495).

The literature on the biological and social aspects of human development has attained impressive proportions. The Readings and References listed in Appendix C only partly reflect the scope of this literature. We are particularly indebted to the recent studies of physical and physiological growth. The published research findings were checked against our own data by Richard Walker, M.A., who rendered valuable assistance in the preparation of the manuscript. Specific data on vision are based on the findings of Richard J. Apell, O.D., who is conducting developmental studies of visual behavior as an organic part of the research program of the Gesell Institute. The methods and principles underlying this special work are detailed in a volume entitled *Vision: Its Development in Infant and Child* (1949).* The basic research in this field received generous support through The Bureau of Visual Science of American Optical Company.

In further acknowledgment it should be recalled here that the early investigations of the Yale Clinic (1911–1948) paved the way for the

---

* A. Gesell, F. L. Ilg, and G. E. Bullis. New York: Paul B. Hoeber, Inc. Medical Book Department of Harper & Brothers, 1949, pp. 329.

present adolescent study. We owe much to all the staff members and students who participated in these investigations, which were generously supported by Rockefeller funds and by a grant in aid from the Carnegie Corporation of New York.

In retrospect we sense once more the friendliness which greeted us at almost every turn of our protracted investigation. We wish to pay a special tribute to the parents with whom we were privileged to discuss the development of their sons and daughters. We gratefully acknowledge the helpfulness of their parental insights and their truth-seeking spirit. And as for the daughters and sons, they were indeed far from expendable in our study. We thank them for their co-operativeness and candor. We owe them some return in a better understanding of the nature and needs of adolescence.

Gesell Institute of
Child Development
310 Prospect Street
New Haven, Connecticut

"It is all a marvellous new birth, and those who believe that nothing is so worthy of love, reverence, and service as the body and soul of youth, and who hold that the best test of every human institution is how much it contributes to bring youth to the ever fullest possible development, may well review themselves and the civilization in which we live to see how far it satisfies this supreme test."

G. STANLEY HALL

April, 1904

Part One

❦

THE STUDY IN OUTLINE

CHAPTER ONE

Orientation

Origin of the Study

THE BASIC theme of this book is *growth*—the growth of mind and personality. The book itself is a product of growth which traces its origins to previous studies. For a period of over twenty years the authors have been making systematic observations of normal child development. It has taken that much time to keep pace with the kaleidoscopic procession of behavior patterns which begin to unfold even before birth and which assume such variegated forms throughout infancy and childhood.

The present volume entitled *Youth: The Years from Ten to Sixteen* completes a trilogy which began with the publication of *Infant and Child in the Culture of Today* (1943), followed by *The Child from Five to Ten* (1946). Together these three books encompass the first sixteen years of mental life and growth. In content and construction the series constitutes a single work based on the unifying concept of development.

Having charted the behavior characteristics of the infant at advancing age levels, we adopted similar methods of investigation to explore the development of the preschool child, the school child, the pre-adolescent, and the young adolescent. Growth is a patterning process; it takes time. We were particularly interested to determine the influence of age on the organization of behavior under the conditions of contemporary American culture.

The progressions of the cycle of development lured us step by step from one stage to the next. In spite of the gradualness of the child's behavior growth, we found that each year of maturity brought forth characteristic

3

traits and trends. The relative equilibrium of 5-year-oldness gives way to the impulsiveness of Five-and-a-half and the creative thrusts of Six, and these in their turn lead to the inwardness of Seven, the expansiveness of Eight, the self-motivation of Nine, and the balanced poise of Ten.

Ten marks a turn in the spiral course of development. The behavioral beginnings of adolescence appear at about eleven. The adolescent cycle continues through the teens well into the twenties. The years from ten to sixteen therefore are significantly transitional in the long march toward maturity. Too often, perhaps, these years have been called troublesome, turbulent, and erratic, as though adolescence were an unsettling kind of intrusion. Our studies of the first ten years of life predisposed us to think that a youth is a child achieving a larger growth; and that adolescence despite its apparent irregularities is a consistent ripening process. We had come to the conclusion that the foundation and most of the framework of the human action system are laid down in the first decade.

The basic orderliness of the behavior patterns and sequences of infancy and childhood intensified our inquisitiveness as to the growth characteristics of adolescence. We felt an increasing compulsion to pursue the cycle of development into the teeming teens, using systematic methods of investigation comparable to those applied in the survey of the progressive age levels from birth to ten years.

This basic survey embraced some forty areas of behavior in the following major fields of child development: (1) Motor characteristics; (2) Personal hygiene; (3) Emotional expression; (4) Fears and dreams; (5) Self and sex; (6) Interpersonal relations; (7) Play and pastimes; (8) School life; (9) Ethical sense; (10) Philosophic outlook. Several thousand behavior patterns were identified and were codified into longitudinal *growth gradients* to show the sequences and directions of development. The behavior traits were also summarized in a series of *behavior profiles* to show in cross section the maturity characteristics of seventeen successive age levels as follows: 4, 16, 28, 40, 52 weeks; 15, 18 month; 2, 2½, 3, 4, 5, 6, 7, 8, 9, 10 years.

How do the mechanisms, the patterns, and the laws of growth manifest themselves in the intricate transitional years from ten to sixteen? Answers to this question became the goal of our new investigation, which is essentially a continuation of the developmental survey reported in the two earlier volumes.

The concluding paragraph of the preface to the volume on *The Child from Five to Ten* reflected our own orientation to the present study:

". . . But one more word about the children themselves. . . . They still have much to teach us, if we observe them closely enough. Indeed when the child of five reaches the age of ten he becomes so articulate that he can actually tell us something directly about himself and about ourselves. Perhaps at this significant transition age of ten, near the brink of adolescence, we must begin to take children more completely into our confidence!"

Setting of the Study

A fortunate combination of circumstances enabled us to maintain research contact with a large number of the selfsame children whose development we had already followed up to age ten. These children, along with siblings and age-mates, constituted a nuclear "core group" of 115 subjects, seen repeatedly throughout adolescence. To these were added fifty children seen at only one age. Altogether, from sixty to eighty-eight children were observed at each age. Statistical and other details concerning the subjects, their families, and the scope of the study are summarized in the Appendix. With few exceptions the families lived in New Haven, Connecticut, and its suburbs. Some who moved away returned periodically for the day-long visits required by the investigation. All had demonstrated a genuine interest in the methods and aims of the research.

The socio-economic status of the families was generally favorable; the method itself—requiring contacts over a span of years—tended to select families of stable position in the community. A preponderance of the fathers followed professional, semiprofessional, managerial, and skilled occupations. The children were representative of a high average to superior level of school population in a prosperous community. All told there were about 550 contacts with these children, over a span of twelve years. The early observations were made at the former Clinic of Child Development of the School of Medicine, Yale University; and, since 1950, they were continued at the Gesell Institute of Child Development, Inc., New Haven.

From the beginning the whole program was carried out in a congenial setting which combined co-operative research with a guidance service. The parents, particularly the mothers, made an invaluable contribution through the periodic interviews in which the progress of each child was defined and discussed in relation to his maturity as reflected in his behavior at home and school. As a result of these recurring reviews the parents acquired a deepened developmental insight into the child's nature and changing needs. We were, of course, dealing with normal children, and we shared with the parents a vivid interest in the child's behavior in terms of his individuality and growth characteristics. The parents were eager to observe the developmental examination, with the advantage of one-way-vision arrangements. The subsequent conference with the examiner (F.L.I.) became a give-and-take situation, in which parent and examiner could exchange questions and comments, based on the examination just witnessed.

The developmental examination also served as a touchstone for the recall of previous behavior and for tentative anticipation of behavior yet to come in an ensuing year. The developmental approach thus had a unifying, stabilizing effect upon our project. Investigation, interpretation, and guidance reinforced each other. The underlying motivations were mutual.

Subjects of the Study

In their own way the youths themselves responded to the aims and spirit of the research. They realized—some quite articulately—that they were contributing to a serious group enterprise. Few betrayed any anxiety. Many expressed pride and curiosities. Occasionally there was reluctance or definite resistance to keeping an appointment. We respected this attitude, knowing that it would prove temporary. We are especially indebted to our young subjects—the boys and girls who were so essential to our project. We need not assure them that they have been taken very seriously and that their contribution to research is uniquely appreciated.

The subjects of the study represented a fair sample of a defined section of the United States population. Most of the children fell in the high average to superior ranges of intelligence as measured by standard tests. In parentage, in cultural and socio-economic status the group was relatively homogeneous.

We should have selected a much more heterogeneous group if our study had been concerned with statistically defining a hypothetical "average" child for each of the ascending ages. On the contrary we were specifically interested in defining the basic sequences and directions of development as shown in the changing behavior of actual children. We assumed that these sequences are not fortuitous and that they would show a significant relation to maturity levels and chronological age despite diversities in individuality.

By virtue of their intelligence, understanding, and interest our subjects became important allies in the gathering of data about themselves. A wide-ranging personal interview with each child became a standard part of the investigation. To maintain privacy and mutual confidence the interview was conducted altogether apart from the developmental examination and was restricted (without observers) to one interviewer (L.B.A.). The scope of the interview is reflected in the gradients and discussions.

Here again our approach was naturalistic rather than methodologically rigorous. We depended upon the spontaneity and co-operativeness of the interviewee; and did not press or probe through private barriers. The questions and answers were pitched on an informal conversational plane. Often a simple phrase or hint released a flow of response. The tone of the interview invited sincerity and candor.

The data of the study have benefited accordingly. We were repeatedly impressed with the capacity of adolescent and pre-adolescent to perceive his own behavior traits and to recognize his own developmental problems. Perhaps we should give more attention to this kind of awareness. It has implications for research and for the mental health aspects of personal hygiene.

Method of the Study

The effectiveness of the methodology of any study of complex human behavior is necessarily dependent upon the manner in which the data are gathered. We have, therefore, stressed the underlying motivations and attitudes of all the participants of this study—the parents, the boys and girls, and the investigators. Without a suitable setting and favorable interpersonal relations, we should scarcely have been justified in undertaking our intimate survey of long range. Our naturalistic approach placed a premium upon congenial rapport with the subjects to insure optimal behavior both spontaneously and in response to the formalized test procedures.

Ordinarily a half day sufficed for observing and recording the behavior responses in the formalized test situations. Usually the boy or girl came attended by one or both parents, or at certain ages would choose to come alone. The greetings and preliminaries were quite informal, but they were not overlooked as indicators of individuality and adaptability from age to age. The standardized behavior tests took the form of a diversified developmental survey. The examinations were observed from a one-way-vision station by parents, staff, and by a trained secretary who made a continuous record of the behavior.

This somewhat comprehensive examination was not conducted as a series of proving tests to derive a score of successes and failures. It was designed rather to reveal characteristic modes of behavior which would yield clues to maturity status and maturity changes. The entire visit both in its planned and unplanned features was regarded as a life situation, which in its details and totality disclosed vital information of developmental significance. Immediate impressions of the responses to the developmental examination were discussed and formulated by a conference of the participating observers. The personal and parental interviews as already indicated were conducted independently.

The Developmental Survey

The developmental survey of behavior characteristics ranged over a wide area and combined both incidental and controlled forms of observations. The observation began with the first moments of the visit and the examiner's welcome. There was then a brief conversation which might hark back to the previous visit. The youth's adjustments to these informal preliminaries were duly noted. He was then conducted to the examining room, where he seated himself before an ordinary table, and for an hour or more responded to a shifting and varied series of test situations which were arranged in smooth sequence by the examiner who sat nearby. There were no visible onlookers and the examination proceeded in a quiet, friendly atmosphere without urgings or pressure. After the first examination, the procedures were taken as a matter of course and with a feeling of familiarity because many of the test situations were repeated from year to year to sharpen the evidences of developmental change and of persisting individuality.

The examination began with a few simple paper and pencil tasks. Without formal preliminaries our subject was simply asked to write his name, address, and the date, and the examination was under way. In the first two minutes he revealed himself in various patterns of response: body attitudes, hand postures and co-ordinations, eye movements, facial expressions, and tensional outlets; shifts of the paper and reorientations of the head to the paper; spontaneous speech and interpersonal references to the examiner, and so forth.

There were other paper and pencil "tests" such as writing numbers in series, writing with the opposite hand, drawing of geometric forms, completing an incomplete line drawing of a man. These tasks were not exacting, but they furnished permanent objective records which were comparatively studied in relation to age and to associated behavior patterns.

Other test situations, which are listed in the Appendix, include the following: (a) interpretations of Rorschach ink blots; (b) imitation of finger-hand gestures and right-left orientations; (c) five-figure form-board; (d) the Wechsler-Bellevue Scale of Adult Intelligence and other intelligence tests; (e) free and logical verbal association; (f) reproduction of designs; (g) thematic interpretation of pictorial materials; (h) free construction of mosaic designs; (i) somatotyping.

In all these varied tests we were not primarily concerned with the end results of success or failure. Instead the test situations were utilized to record and later to identify those modes of performance and patterns of behavior which most characteristically expressed the stage of the child's maturity. In later chapters these symptomatic behavior characteristics will be designated and duly listed as *maturity traits*. They will also help us to define directions of development at successive age levels.

The Interviews

The personal interview with our subject and the interview with his parents were an organic part of the investigation program. Both interviews were carried on independently. Leading questions were kept at a judicious minimum. The procedure was informal and favored free and easy conversation. There was no rigid standardization but the questions embraced the nine basic developmental areas considered in the present volume, under the following headings: Total action system, Self-care and routines, Emotions, The growing self, Interpersonal relationships, Activities and interests, School life, Ethical sense, Philosophic outlook.

Personal interview. The subject was at once reassured by telling him that the questions were not mental tests and that we were not looking for right or wrong answers. We were simply interested to know how he thought and felt; he need not answer if he so chose, and he could add anything he wished to talk about. In the context of the total interview the questions were formulated briefly and directly. For example, when emotions were under discussion the subject was straightforwardly asked, "What do you do when you get angry?" "Do you ever cry and what about?" "How about competition?" and so forth. Intellectual areas were sketchily explored with similar directness. The child gave us his ideas about time, space, war, ethics. As he grew older (ages fourteen, fifteen, sixteen), phases of the interview might reverse direction, and he would ask for the opinions of the examiner. In general, the children found the interview to be an interesting experience, and they were gratified to feel that their ideas were important enough to be recorded.

We have sometimes been asked if this very awareness of our interest did not have the effect of distorting the responses of our adolescents. Were they really telling the truth? Our subjects responded to our interview with the truth as they experienced it; each responded in accord with his inner picture of himself as a person. We could consider each response as an "item of behavior," significant in itself apart from the opinion of anyone else and significant too in relation to the parents' report and to our own observations. It reflected the subject's views of both the world and himself.

The Parent Interview. This interview was an important phase of each yearly visit. It was a two-way arrangement which invited eager questions and comments. Parent and interviewer had reciprocal reasons for defining the individuality and progress of the boy or girl whose behavior had just been witnessed in the standardized setting of a developmental examination.

Our study was organically geared to a guidance service. The parents, therefore, were given free rein to report their own observations, live anecdotes and problems, and any noteworthy happenings which had occurred during the year past. There was a mutuality of motive in this two-way exchange inquiry and interpretation. And since we were dealing with the parents of normal children, the conference could admit the humorous as well as the serious aspect of domestic problems. The revelations of the developmental examination led to concrete discussion of the child's behavior traits and potentials. Sometimes the traits of his earlier childhood came into consideration because our developmental guidance service oftentimes traced back into infancy and the preschool years.

The periodic guidance service had a stabilizing effect on the research. It focused attention upon the nature and needs of the child's development. The parents were in no sense on the defensive. They made a considerable contribution to our study through their constructive insight. We were not handicapped by undue reserve nor by a lack of candor, which might readily limit the possibilities of research.

Analysis of the Data

From the foregoing account of the ground plan of the adolescent study, it is evident that we spread a wide net to gather our data. The records were voluminous. For the children whose development we had followed since the earliest years the documentary files for a single individual assumed the proportions and detail of a biography. The wealth of data accumulated through some five hundred contacts presented a formidable mass of concrete items which challenged analysis and interpretation. The data on physical growth and maturity were in some areas supplemented by published research findings (see Appendix A).

Our task was to reduce these numerous items to a meaningful pattern. Our method involved the delineation of a series of growth gradients and maturity profiles. These, in the form of "sketches" of behavior, are arranged in a sequence which itself forms a pattern, a panoramic outline of the growth process. Such sketches could not be developed just by means of graphs and computations, for they do not denote averages, nor do they have a fixed location in time. Rather each profile presents a kind of composite prototype illustrating symptomatic behavior significantly related to a given period of development. Few of our subjects showed all the extremes of behavior we describe; the majority, rather, veered in the directions of these extremes as the course of growth progressed. Our approach, therefore, was in part clinical, based on naturalistic observation and on comparative appraisal of the progressive annual inventories.

Our discussions of growth make free use of the terms *age* and *year,* and our maturity profiles themselves are titled, Year Ten, Year Eleven, Year Twelve, etc. This is natural enough, for we start with age. But such terms must not be mistaken for a precise accordance with calendar time; in our research we could not attempt to be more precise in adhering to calendar time than is Nature.

Our method of discerning the growth patterns underlying the data involved a process having two steps. The first step was a crosswise comparison. All our records were sorted according to age. This was a strict sorting—all subjects who had passed their twelfth birthday but not their thirteenth were grouped together. These age groupings were studied—for the most part by classification and counting methods—to determine the most outstanding and consistently occurring behaviors for the age. This was a first approximation in defining a state of maturity, such as "12-year-oldness."

From this first approximation a pattern emerges; the general sequence of growth becomes apparent from age to age. But this is not enough. The outlines of the maturity profiles are blurred, for not all our 12-year-olds are twelve in a behavior sense. Girl A, aged twelve years ten months,

already shows the "inwardizing" of behavior found more often among
Thirteens, while Girl B at the same age still shows the exuberance of
Twelve. Boy C shows more features of earlier patterns. To picture the
features of Twelve most vividly we had to make allowances for the
subjects. The child was systematically compared with himself at successive stages of development. Girl A, then, could be used to help us define
Thirteen, as contrasted with Twelve. The decision of the child's maturity
level puts a premium on the clinical insight of the researchers—but it is
an insight based on both the preliminary findings of the first step and the
examiner's long-standing acquaintance with the child's history and individualities of performance.

To organize the great profusion of data it was necessary in both our
cross-sectional and longitudinal analyses to block out the developmental
sequences for over forty areas of behavior, ranging from eating and sleeping to parent-child relationships and ideas of time and space. Countless
behavior items were critically examined and checked against the several
sources of information: the parents' report, the behavior tests, the interview of the child, the clinical impressions. This entailed a painstaking
process of matching and fitting, of condensing and winnowing.

Fortunately, developmental data are to a large extent self-corrective.
They must fall into valid natural sequences to make sense, for they reflect
the inherent order of the growth process itself. They also reflect the concrete impress of cultural factors in relation to the advancing stages of
maturity.

Scope and Plan of the Book

The present volume invites the reader to interpret the manifestations
of adolescence in terms of the psychology of growth. Toward this end we
have formulated the findings of our study from three converging angles
of approach as follows:

1. *Maturity Profiles*
   Portrayals of the maturity characteristics of seven yearly age zones
   from ten through sixteen years.

2. *Maturity Traits*
   Behavior patterns and symptoms in nine major areas for each age zone:
   (1) Total Action System. (2) Routines and Self-Care. (3) Emotions.
   (4) The Growing Self. (5) Interpersonal Relationships. (6) Activities
   and Interests. (7) School Life. (8) Ethical Sense. (9) Philosophic
   Outlook.

3. *Maturity Trends*

   The sequences and gradients of growth for the sector of years from ten through sixteen.

Taken together the *Profiles, Traits,* and *Trends* constitute a flexible frame of reference which may be used to consider the maturity status and the developmental progress of a given child at a given age.

Needless to say, this reference frame is not a measuring scale of intelligence. It is concerned with the directions and forms of development rather than with abilities as such. *The governing concept is that of growth: growth as a patterning process.* Even a young adolescent becomes somewhat more understandable when he is considered from the standpoint of growth, of immaturity, and of relative maturity.

But growth is subtle, and often it is elusive. It takes time. We can scarcely perceive it without the perspective which comes with the passage of time. For our present purpose, we adopt the year as a fundamental unit of time for systematizing our observations of adolescent growth. Growth and age are inseparably linked—not in a rigid, mechanical fashion but in dynamic interplay.

Every passing year from ten to sixteen has a profound influence on the directions and dimensions of development. Each year leaves a significant impress upon the traits and trends of behavior, because mind and personality grow in obedience to deep-seated laws and cycles. Every child develops in a manner which expresses his individuality. Nevertheless, the basic mechanisms of growth are so firmly entrenched that each age zone takes on a certain characteristicness when it is compared with adjacent age zones. Our task is to delineate this characteristicness, age by age, in a way which will make the basic sequences of adolescent development more understandable.

We shall envisage these sequences in terms of yearly age *zones* rather than exact birthdays. Year Twelve, as a behavioral unit, is not just a point in time. It has duration. There is no gap between Twelve and Thirteen, or even a dividing line to show where one stops and the next begins; they shade into each other. Traces of Thirteen behavior may begin to appear soon after the twelfth birthday in some adolescents (girls especially). In others, no reduction of Twelve's exuberance may occur until after the thirteenth birthday. The latitude implied in a concept of age *zones* allows for many individual variations and sex differences. It keeps the primary emphasis on levels and patterns of maturity rather than on precise timing. Ages and stages fall into a continuous spectrum, but each su,-

cessive zone brings forth a quota of distinguishable maturity traits and trends.

A separate chapter is devoted to each age zone (Chapters 4–10). For convenience of reference the maturity traits of a given age period are discussed in a double-column section under nine headings, corresponding to nine major developmental areas. These areas encompass both individual and social aspects of behavior in relation to home, school and community. The discussions are written in an informal, concrete vein, and are designed to suggest methods of guidance as well as angles of interpretation.

The significance of specific maturity traits depends upon their relation to the general level and developmental pattern of a given age zone. When a total constellation of traits is viewed as a whole this pattern begins to emerge. We find that the maturity make-up of a typical 11-year-old is indeed different from that of a typical 12-year-old, who is in turn different from thirteen. Each age in terms of maturity has a core of characteristic-ness, which we attempt to capture by means of a maturity profile. The profile is of necessity a sketchy, cross-sectional outline; but it is based upon actual observations and illustrative details derived from the research records. Frequently we quote our subjects verbatim; for they reveal much in what they spontaneously say, and in how they say it.

The series of maturity profiles aims to characterize those maturity traits which are fairly representative of the seven age zones under the cultural conditions covered by our study. Accordingly the profiles may serve to orient the reader. They are not offered as psychometric norms. It is *not* our purpose to describe an "average child" at ten, eleven, twelve, thirteen, fourteen, fifteen, and sixteen years of age. Such a statistically ideal, normal average child does not exist, at least not in New Haven. The profiles, however, are sufficiently valid to offer clues to the nature of the organizing processes of psychological growth. When the profiles are read as a consecutive series they picture the general currents and contours of development over this cycle of seven years. In this way we get a panoramic view of the progressions of the cycle.

Part Three of the present volume (Chapters 11–19) provides another approach from which the trends of maturity can be examined in greater detail. A separate chapter is devoted to each of the nine major areas of behavior development. Instead of focusing upon a single age zone we look at the sequences of growth in longitudinal perspective, and tabulate the growth gradients for some forty distinguishable fields of behavior. A growth gradient is the series of stages or degrees of maturity by which a child progresses toward a higher level of functioning.

Our analysis of the raw data was described earlier as falling into two stages. The Growth Gradients were the first to be assembled, and they codify our findings for the strict age groupings. The presentation of Maturity Traits reflects the second stage, in which we took advantage of the information gained in the first stage to resift our original data—with a more clinical orientation. The two sections may show slight differences in emphasis in reporting some "items" of behavior, but with respect to the fundamental trends and the total patterns they are concordant.

The tabulated gradients reveal the *sequences* and the relative aspects of observed behavior traits. It is in this relative sense that our findings can be generalized beyond the particular group of subjects we studied. Had we reported statistical averages for precise age groups, then the application of our findings would indeed have to be narrowly confined to the adolescents we saw. But our gradients were not designed to be used as a measuring scale to derive a mental score. They are offered as a tool for evaluating developmental status. Treatment of growth as a process, a sequence of changes in direction, allows scope for wide variations in individuals and in cultures. Specific features of behavior will vary from group to group; sequences and underlying mechanisms of growth will show significant similarities. The emphasis throughout is not on the absolute abilities of the child but upon the stages of his maturity and his mode of maturing. For initial orientation we sum up this emphasis in italics:

The maturity profiles, the maturity traits, and the maturity trends are not to be regarded as rigid age norms nor as models. They simply indicate the kinds of behavior—desirable or otherwise—which tend to occur at certain stages and ages under contemporary cultural conditions. Every child has an individual pattern of growth unique to him. The profiles, traits, and trends are designed to suggest the various maturity levels at which he is functioning. The "ages" denote approximate zones rather than precise moments of time.

CHAPTER TWO

Development: A Key Concept

MAN WAS not made in a day. It took vast ages to bring his capacities of growth and learning to their present form. In some condensed way infant, child, and youth must retraverse these immense ages of the past. The organism must gather up and activate a heritage of potentials in response to a surrounding culture. This is the developmental task of the individual.

The race evolved; the individual grows. His growth career is in no sense a literal recapitulation of his racial history, but it does reveal deeply seated stages and sequences. It takes fully two decades to manifest these stages, advancing from infancy and childhood through youth to maturity. The total span from ten to sixteen embraces a late-middle portion of the individual's long epoch of immaturity. To appreciate the broad significance of these transitional years, it is necessary to consider their relative role in the larger totality of development.*

The Cycles of Human Growth

The modern infant comes into the world endowed with prodigious powers of growth. The vast complexities of his nervous system reflect the vastness of his evolutionary past. They embody and express his growth potentials. Five lunar months before he is born he is already in possession of his full quota of nerve cells. These billions of nerve cells continue to

---

* The terms *growth* and *development* are used interchangeably throughout this volume.

16

organize and mediate the patterning of his behavior throughout his life span. In the course of about twenty-five years he becomes an adult—but this does not terminate his mental growth, which may continue into the decades beyond the twenties.

"Grownups," however, vary enormously in the depth and range of the psychological patterns of the maturing process. This fact deserves recognition on the part of parents (and teachers) who may sometimes be so preoccupied with the problems of child development that they overlook their own personal problems of adult development! Fortunately, a knowledge of the growth processes of infant, child, and youth can lead to improved self-understanding. The phrase "growing up with your child" takes on increasing reality. It suggests that the guidance of psychological growth is a two-way transaction which requires a double awareness of the attitudes of the growing child in interaction with the attitudes of the growing adult. Two cycles of growth thus come into an interplay which changes profoundly with the advancing age of the child—and of the parent.

These two cycles do not run precisely parallel. They are widest apart during the infancy of the child. But they converge as he grows older, because the velocity of growth is greatest in the very young and slows down with increasing age. The junior cycle thus comes full circle. This seems to be Nature's arrangement for bringing two generations into mutual relationships, which in the human species has led to the prolongation of the period of dependence between birth and maturity.

The cycles of development apply equally to the physical and mental aspects of an organism. The child comes by his mind as he comes by his body—through the organizing processes of growth. We may think of him in terms of his physical make-up, his body build, his nerve cells, brain, and muscles. We may think of his mind and personality, as evidenced in his behavior characteristics. Mind and body, environment and experience are somehow combined and integrated through profound developmental forces, which always produce a unique individual.

The total organism of the child may be envisioned as a *growing action system*, structurally and functionally. This action system has the remarkable property of changing with time, and yet perpetuating a core of individuality. To sense how this complex system takes form one must consider the underlying stages of development. In our systematic investigations we have now surveyed the behavior trends for some forty developmental levels from birth through sixteen years. When these successive age zones are viewed in perspective there appears a rhythmic pattern in development. An underlying theme repeats itself.

The human infant dramatically displays behavior patterns and modes of growth which bear resemblance to those which appear in the years of childhood and youth. At 28 weeks of age, for example, the infant is typically in a phase of relative equilibrium; he tends to be self-contained, outgoing, and amiably adjusted to the household. At 32 weeks he is in a more precarious phase, sensitive to his environment and timid toward strangers. He is emotionally more withdrawn; his "equilibrium" is less stable. His action system is undergoing indubitable transformations pointed toward remoter goals. At 40 weeks he again proves to be in better equilibrium. The routines of daily life are (temporarily) fairly well established. He is able to play by himself for an hour or more. He likes to have people around.

This sequence is a sample segment of an extensive pattern, one that appears again and yet again during the years of development. Viewed as a whole, the preschool period—age two to age five—suggests the full turn of one subcycle of growth. Years two and five, in some sense, are similar. Not that abilities at the two ages are alike; the difference in skills is vast. But in mode of adjustment to the world around him, Five shows a poise and equanimity highly reminiscent of Two. Then, as Two becomes Two-and-a-half and as Five becomes Five-and-a-half or Six, a change occurs —a change *in the same direction* in each case. Behavior "loosens up," perhaps even "goes to pieces"; life becomes charged with equally attractive, yet incompatible, dual alternatives; "No" and "Mine" become prominent items of vocabulary. Through the succeeding years the pathways continue parallel. Three and Six-and-a-half bring increasing amenability, ability to bargain, a sunnier view of life; "Yes" and "We" are used more often. Three-and-a-half and Seven bring inwardizing thrusts, sometimes moodiness, even anxieties; Four and Eight reverse these thrusts, projecting them outward in expansiveness and boisterousness. Four-and-a-half and Nine try to bring inner and outer thrusts into unity, to focus and refine abilities down to a sharper point, to achieve greater self-sufficiency. With ages five and ten a resolution is (temporarily) achieved as growth forces are integrated. The subcycle completes another turn at a point of age which is both an ending and a new beginning. Two, five, and ten are such nodal ages. They reflect the economy of development.

It is of the greatest significance that these cycles do not just "happen" to resemble each other. Consider the course of development prior to two years of age. A similar sequence has appeared more than once in infancy in the accelerated rotations of the early cycle. Look ahead, beyond ten years: the developmental progression repeats itself once again from Year Ten to Year Sixteen. Viewed from a distance great enough to obscure the many smaller points of difference, the panorama is very similar, the land-marks appear in the same succession. Eleven, like Five-and-a-half to Six, is "loosening up," "snapping old bonds"; Twelve is more positive in mood, smoother in relationships; Thirteen pulls inward; Fourteen thrusts out; Fifteen specifies and organizes; Sixteen again achieves a more golden mean. (And we would venture to guess that the process does not stop with age sixteen, and that sixteen is another nodal age.)

These rhythmic sequences make sense. They compose the process through which growth is achieved—not by addition, bit by bit, nor by a smooth homogeneous enlargement, like an expanding balloon. Growth combines integration and differentiation. It is more nearly comparable to an intricate weaving and braiding process in which multitudinous strands are interwoven into co-ordinated patterns of behavior. Words like *strands* and *weaving* are, of course, purely figurative. They enable us, however, to visualize growth as a patterning process involving varied alternatives in varying prominence. The process itself is inconceivably complex, but the underlying principle is readily understandable.

Man is built on a duplex plan: his organs—eyes, hands, brain, heart— are paired or bilateral in construction; his movements depend upon a synchronized control of flexion and extension. Similarly, his emotions, his sensory-motor adjustment, his visual behavior patterns, his language and thought, his interpersonal relationships involve countless dualities which call for modulation and regulation. The whole pathway of development is beset with opposing alternatives. To an important extent these dual tendencies have their origin in the culture, but the seat of tension and choice is in the organism itself. The culture inflects and channelizes, but it does not generate the progressions and trends of development.

The problem of development, the task of the action system, is to bring the opposites into effectual control and counterpoise. This control is not a static balance, but a channeling of two-way tensions and conflicts in such a manner that the individual achieves integration, choice, and direction. This is accomplished through his mechanism of *reciprocal interweaving*, a mechanism which pervades all aspects of growth, structural and func-tional: The growth process counterbalances one extreme of behavior by offsetting or pairing it with its opposite.

A tight-rope walker maintains a balance by leaning first left, then right, then left in rapid reciprocation. He returns toward a golden mean after each shift, and this enables him to step forward even though he fluctuates from side to side. He brings flexors and extensors into repeated counterpoise; he modulates his movements. If he is unable to modulate he cannot walk a rope or even a plank. This simple analysis of motor control affords a hint as to the long-range growth of higher forms of self-control. It helps us to understand why the growing individual passes through successive phases which are marked by varying trends of behavior—outgoing in one period, withdrawing in another, relatively balanced in still another. Growth gains are consolidated during recurring periods of relative equilibrium. But there is a tendency for stages of increased equilibrium to be followed by stages of lessened equilibrium when the organism makes new inner or outer thrusts into the inner or outer unknown. This is the basic method of growing and outgrowing.

This mechanism is so fundamental that it governs the passing growth events of the day, the succession of behavioral phases of the years, and even the major rhythms of the grand cycle of human growth. The cycle moves onward in time and space. The consolidating stages of increased equilibrium stand out as they recur at progressive intervals, as though the cycle pursued a spiral-like course.

If we had more precise knowledge of these advancing phases in the curves of the spiral we would gain a deeper insight into the general ground plan of growth. We would also be in a better position to compare a child or youth with himself as he travels through the periodic sectors of the ascending cycle. At all ages, development serves as a key concept for interpretation and for better understanding.

Stages and Ages

In order to describe and discuss sequences of behavior changes—which are governed by primarily "internal," individual timing factors, we must somehow relate the events to more "external," universal measures. The most fundamental of these measures is that of chronological time—"clock time" or "calendar time." The units of this measure are by no means identical with developmental time—the durations of the inner "stages" of growth. Twelve-year-old behavior, for example, does not automatically begin on the twelfth birthday. Calendar time does not measure developmental time, but it does approximate it. The units under consideration change, for they must vary with the increasing age of the individual.

In describing growth changes for the infant, we can talk in terms of days, then weeks, then months; for the preschooler, in terms of three-month, then half-year periods; for the mature individual, in terms of decades. During adolescence, the year as a unit of age has special significance—for individual and for cultural reasons.

Age is both a biological and a sociological concept. For a billion years the rhythms of dawn and dusk and the changing seasons have exerted an impress on the life and growth of plants and animals. When man became perceptive enough to mark the progress of days and seasons, he began to think in terms of age and anniversaries. In due course he even noted that in a tree each year of growth is registered by annual growth rings. He has found similar telltale growth rings in the scales of fish and turtle and the horns of mountain sheep.

The annual revolution of the earth about the sun—the calendar year— has become a fundamental measure of time in his appraisal and record of human affairs. The concept of the year is so firmly embedded in his orientations that it is incorporated in manifold regulatory laws, customs, mores. Countless sanctions and prohibitions of family and community life are governed and delimited by age.

Accordingly, society sets up its yearly age standards and eligibilities along the road to maturity—admission to kindergarten and first grade, to clubs and camps, to the stepwise ranks in Boy and Girl Scout organizations; the religious rite of confirmation; work certificates; the license to operate an automobile; the right to make a contract; marriage; suffrage and citizenship; military service. Age qualifications expressed in years permeate the administration, the legal safeguards, and the traditions of our culture.

Paradoxically enough, it appears that society has simultaneously undervalued and overvalued the yearly unit as a criterion of growth. The significance of the individual year should be critically considered for the period of adolescence. Depreciation of its value is clear enough when the whole epoch—about a decade in length and encompassing a momentous variety of changes—is subjected to loose, sweeping generalizations. The term *teen-ager* has become almost a misnomer. As a cliché it is too closely associated with the delinquencies and glamours of the seven years from thirteen through nineteen. As a stereotype the comprehensive term *teen-ager* obscures the annual progressive changes in normal growth. We shall use it sparingly.

On the other hand, the precision of age-designated qualifications is often a false precision. Developmental events do not always fall at a convenient spot on the calendar. Besides the failure of growth events to coincide with calendar anniversaries in typical time of occurrence, there is the failure of human beings to be typical. By the time of adolescence, individuals may range widely in age of attaining any particular status or skill. A law that specifies that a chronologically 16-year-old is ready to drive a car does not fully meet the actual situation. Additional, behavioral tests do serve as further insurance of at least a minimum knowledge and skill, but currently fail to assess maturity and responsibility. Improving the selection procedures for this and other eligibilities should be recognized as an important challenge.

In the chapters which follow, then, we shall have to talk about developmental "units" in the language of chronologic or physical time. Our approach and our methods have certainly depended upon physical time. They are based on the premise that every year of adolescent growth makes a difference—a distinctive developmental difference, which calls for some kind of formulation. Though a developmental year, unlike a chronologic year, cannot be measured with mathematical accuracy, it is still possible by methods of systematic comparison to trace the developmental trends over a series of years and to ascertain the trends which are more or less characteristic of each successive period. No hard-and-fast lines can be drawn to separate the age zones of development. Ample allowance must of course be made for individual and sex variations. The data of our study, however, are primarily intended to bring into convenient view the *directions of development* and the relativities of age, maturity, and immaturity. For this reason they are presented in year-by-year age chapters and in gradients labeled by yearly ages—from ten to sixteen. The labels for the developmental stages might actually have been alphabetical—Stages A, B, C, D, E, F, G—but the practical advantages of defining these ages in flexible relation to chronological ages are obvious.

Individuality, Experience, and Growth

The process of development is unitary; the concept of development is unifying. Into development go genetic factors of individual constitution and innate maturation sequence, and environmental factors ranging from home and school to the total cultural setting. Concerning the innate factors, we postulate two closely related propositions: (a) Every individual develops in accordance with a unique pattern of growth; (b) This unique pattern is a variation of a ground plan of growth which is more or less characteristic of the human species. It is the second of these, the innate ground plan, with which this book is primarily concerned.

No one, of course, has actually observed this ground plan. We have recorded behavior—as observed by us and as reported to us. We have compared the recorded behavior of the same individuals at successive points in time. Thus, in a sense, we have observed development. We have considered experience, individuality, and growth—and found them to be interdependent. *Experience* is, obviously, related to the environment, but it is also dependent upon innate factors, for no two individuals experience the "same" situation in the same way, nor does one individual experience the "same" situation in the same way at different times of his life. *Individuality* likewise arises from an interplay, as innate potentials find environmental opportunity to unfold. And *growth* itself is the prime causative force. It is an ongoing process in time; new stimuli, whether stemming primarily from innate or from environmental sources, do not simply "add onto" the organism some new features but are themselves selected and transformed by the existing status of the organism.

Our study concerns itself mainly with growth factors—with the emergence and unfolding of behavior traits, as a key to the evaluation of maturity status. It could do this only by controlling or making allowance for factors of individuality and experience. The succeeding chapter (Chapter Three) discusses some manifestations of individuality which appear to be of significance. The maturity profiles and the chapters on maturity traits make passing reference to concrete relationships of individuality and environment to development. Maturity ceases to be a mystical concept when we use it to define the orderly sequences of behavior growth. In obedience to natural laws the behavior patterns fall into dynamic constellations, indicative of a ground plan.

Confessedly there is no calibrated yardstick with which to "measure" behavior patterns or underlying ground plan. Nevertheless, we can assemble specimen patterns systematically, match them for best fit, and arrange them into meaningful series of similarity and sequence. Lacking absolute units of measurement, we can use a method of orderly comparison, which enables us to explore the behavior values of age and the age values of behavior. This leads to the formulation of *gradients of growth* for specific areas of behavior and for the unitary, over-all cycle.

A growth gradient is a codification of the series of stages of maturity by which the individual (here, the youth) progresses toward a higher level of functioning. The gradients list "negative" as well as "positive" behavior symptoms. They also cite individual variations from the central trend. The descriptive language used cannot always be formulated precisely—it must connote as well as denote. Fortunately, the gradients could often include, in quotes, the comments of the boys and girls themselves. These serve better than any statement we could make to epitomize the quality of response at a given level.

Clearly, however, these growth gradients and maturity profiles are not psychometric norms. They do not measure specific abilities. They are not to be construed as normative standards nor as diagnostic criteria, except under clinical auspices and safeguards. However, they constitute a kind of "comparator"—an instrument for comparing something with a like thing. They are orientational devices which permit us to identify and assess levels of maturity.

The overruling emphasis is on the sequences and patterns of maturity rather than on age assignments. Our research interest was to gain a better understanding of the *dynamic trends of the growth process* operating over a period of time.

With all these cautions and reservations we hope that the reader will look upon the growth gradients as convenient tabular summaries, which suggest how behavior characteristics may change with advancing stages of maturity. Common sense will protect the gradients from misinterpretation and misuse. Constructively applied, they sharpen and deepen perspective. They afford a glimpse of the undercurrent forces which pattern development; they bring into focus the stages which precede and which follow observed behavior; they reveal an over-all trend toward increasing maturity. The management of adolescent behavior problems requires a developmental outlook and a discerning faith in the normal potentials of growth.

CHAPTER THREE

Individuality

━━━

THE GROWING child and youth reveal their individuality in the characteristicness of the manner in which they progress from stage to stage of maturity. Growth is the patterning process whereby the mutual fitness of organism and environment is brought to progressive realization. The potentials of growth are primarily determined and delimited by genes. Because of this, the potentials of the environment are also selectively determined and delimited by the potentials available in the individual organism.

The range of individual differences is as wide as humanity itself. In infancy many of these differences are subtle and elusive, but even then they are impressive in their scope. By the time of adolescence the differences which have become apparent stagger description. The vastness of the problem of individual differences, however, need not dismay or deter us unduly. We may at least observe the manner in which the adolescent discloses and develops his individuality as he moves from one stage of maturity to another, for we can approach the study of individuality from the standpoint of developmental characteristics.

Later chapters in this volume are concerned with a first approximation to what we have called the "general ground plan" of growth. They deal with concrete behavior traits and trends and with detailed gradients of growth which, in patterned sequence, are related to the psychological maturity of adolescents. The developing individual tends to approximate this sequence pattern, but he tends also to depart from it, to show indi-

vidualities of timing and of style even in his manifestations of the most
typical behavior. The ground plan becomes most significant when allowances are made for variation, when factors of age are tempered with
factors of individuality.

The number of possible ways of comparing and contrasting individuals
is as great as the number of traits that humans possess. We can do little
more than suggest a few significant lines of comparison, to serve as
examples of how innate growth or maturation shapes, and is shaped by,
individuality.

Constitution and culture. Bodily and temperamental traits combine
in such a multitude of ways that it is difficult to classify any individual
with a single formula. The deepmost aspects of individuality are biochemical, metabolic, and physiological. Every person has a more or less
unique metabolic pattern, reflected in his body chemistry and his endocrine functions. The fact that some of these metabolic and biochemical
conditions (like color blindness) are heritable is highly significant.
When not specifically transmissible, many functional characteristics may
nonetheless be constitutional.

*Constitution is the relatively fixed and inherent make-up of the individ-
ual as determined by innate endowment and growth career.* Since the
organism is unitary and indivisible the concept of constitution applies
equally to psychic and to somatic characteristics. Constitutional factors
express themselves both in the prenatal and postnatal phases of the development of the individual. He comes by his individuality as he comes
by his mind and body, namely, through the organizing processes of
growth.

This insures him from becoming a mere creature of the culture into
which he is born. A culture has been described as a large-scale molding
apparatus which "in each generation produces its type of individual." It
"consists of patterns of agreed upon behavior." Whether the culture be
totalitarian or democratic, it determines by incessant impact and group
domination innumerable uniformities in human behavior. In spite of all
the cultural forces which make for standardization, the individual preserves a measure of the individuality with which he is endowed.

This endowment comes chiefly through genes. As a member of the
human species a child develops in accordance with a general ground plan.
As an individual descendant of his parents and grandparents he develops
in accordance with distinctive variations of the ground plan. He embodies

mental and physical traits transmitted from his ancestors. Many of these traits are undefined, but some are startling in their family resemblance. The individual comes into this mixed species and family inheritance through innate processes of growth which are called *maturation*. Maturation is mediated by genes. Through learning and experience he adapts to his cultural environment by a process of *acculturation*. The two processes interact and interfuse, but the mechanisms of maturation are so fundamental that they are not transcended.

Growth is a unifying concept which resolves the dualisms of heredity and environment. Environmental factors support, inflect, and modify but they do not generate the basic progressions of infant-child-youth development.

These progressions are largely determined by genetic constitution. The order of progression is less subject to variation than the rates of development. Hence our recurring emphasis on the *sequences* of the developmental stages. The general tempo and the specific timing of the cycle of stages varies with each individual. The over-all tempo may be slow or accelerated; the progress steady or irregular with spurts and plateaus; the advance may be evenly or unevenly balanced in the major fields of behavior. Constitutional factors are pervasive but not static; for as experience is assimilated by the individual and becomes part of him, it becomes a part of his constitutional action system.

Some variations of individuality may be briefly considered under several headings as follows: (1) Sex differences; (2) Physique and temperament; (3) Mental traits; (4) Intelligence; (5) Giftedness; (6) Style of growth.

Sex differences. The most far-reaching constitutional factor divides the whole of humanity into two groups nearly equal in size. It is the factor of sex. Many of the behaviors commonly associated with being a male or being a female are at least in their outward expression a product of culture—of customs and expectations and also of subtle pressures from parents, age-mates, and society at large. But the earliness and persistence of many sex differences indicate that the traits have a constitutional basis, and that the encouragements and prohibitions of the culture do not so much engender as reinforce them. The manner of expression of such traits is patterned by society; but their sources lie deep in the organism.

Girls, for example, generally mature earlier than boys in total physical development, and also show an earlier interest in the opposite sex. Girls are more interested in the person, in social relationships; boys are more interested in objective reality, in mechanics, science and engineering, sports. Girls tend to prefer indoor activities and recreations; boys prefer outdoors. This difference is plainly exhibited in magazine reading, boys electing sports and science; girls, fashion and romance. Girls begin dating at an earlier age. At every age they express more planfulness about marriage than do boys and give more deliberate consideration to the personality traits of a potential spouse. They seem to have a "typically feminine" cast of mind, quite apart from their degree of mental ability, which makes them more sensitive to moral and personal issues. In our group, girls proved to be earlier and more articulate than boys in making ethical distinctions between right and wrong. They seem more "knowing" in sizing up and responding to the implications of life and conduct.

Sex differences can easily be overstated; the lines of demarcation are not sharp. Every individual has a combination of both so-called masculinity *and* femininity traits—in body chemistry as in behavior. There are many such composite traits, and they vary enormously from individual to individual. On the whole, boys and girls meet most stages of development in a highly comparable manner. But girls in general are slightly precocious when compared with boys, especially in physical growth and in social development, but also in many other areas. A tempering of the gradients of this book, then, toward expectation of slight acceleration in girls, slight retardation in boys, will help to make the age assignments more appropriate.

Physique and temperament. W. H. Sheldon approaches the problem of adult individual differences and deviations from the standpoint of varieties of physique and temperament. There are three major body types: the roundish endomorph (soft body, short neck, small hands and feet); the squarish mesomorph (firm body with rugged muscles); the spindly ectomorph (slender and delicate in construction). Pure types are rare. Individual differences in physique are usually manifested in mixtures of the basic body types. Similarly there are three temperamental types. The temperamental traits combine in widely variegated degrees in different individuals. The extreme endomorph tends to have a good digestive tract. He is good-natured, relaxed, sociable, communicative. The pronounced mesomorph is active, energetic, assertive, noisy, and aggressive. The fragile ectomorph is restrained, inhibited, tense: he may prefer solitude to noise and company. He is sensitive and is likely to have allergies. Temperament denotes the distinctive mental character of a person.

Though all individuals present complex mixtures of components, the "typical" endomorph, mesomorph, and ectomorph tend to express the ground plan of growth in characteristic ways which are now being investigated at childhood and youth levels. In the area of emotions, for example, the endomorph tends to show his feelings easily at any age; other people are too important for him to withdraw very far, even in the most "withdrawing phases." The mesomorph, at an age generally described as "less competitive," is non-competitive only in a comparative sense—compared, that is, with *himself* at other ages. The ectomorph is quicker to withdraw when troubled, takes more pains to hide his feelings. He may show an alertness and fast reaction, but in many areas he tends to show immaturities. He seems to need more time to grow. Our observations indicate that the gradients of growth take on added meaning when interpreted in the light of constitutional individuality.

Mental traits. A random listing of some of the psychological variables will suggest the wide-ranging scope of individual differences: native mental energy and intellect; native gifts and talents; degrees and kinds of mental imagery—visual, auditory, motor; dominance and dexterity in handedness, postural attitudes, and demeanors; voice; tensional outlets; emotional expression; reactions to novelty, frustration, and success; modes of learning and profiting by experience; patterns of visual behavior evidenced in command of eye movements, near and far vision, focal and peripheral awareness; visual skill in seeking, finding, holding, discriminating, and interpreting images and symbols; personal perceptiveness of aesthetic and ethical values. Some of these traits are highly distinguishing.

The balance of peripheral and focal awareness, for example, has a pervasive influence on behavior—the more peripheral individual responding readily to a multitude of stimuli in his surroundings, being distracted by "the dropping of a pin"; the more focal individual bringing his energies to bear upon a single narrow zone of concentration. The individual ratio of peripheral and focal awareness manifests itself over a wide range of behavior, from specific trends of visual perception to patterns of reaction in social relationships.

Intelligence. Variation in human intelligence has been an area of particular interest to psychologists and educators. Probably more research effort has been expended on this aspect of individuality than on all other aspects combined. Such study continues today—now focused not only on general intelligence but also on the more specific "intelligences," on verbal, numerical, and spacial abilities, form perception, and a number of other such factors. The results of these efforts have been highly fruitful, for intelligence has been found to be of significance in nearly every area of human endeavor. It would be surprising if intelligence did not show relationship to the course of total development. The methods of psychometrics accordingly make abundant use of the factor of age.

Indeed, intellectual growth itself has sometimes been considered to be *the* course of development, with "mental age" as its main measure. The limitations of such an approach are all too often demonstrated in a real-life situation. "Mental age," as the term is generally used, is actually a score obtained on a test; it is a valuable index of brightness. But a normal 10-year-old with a mental age of fourteen does not necessarily act like a 14-year-old; he tends to act more like a *bright* 10-year-old. Within the normal range, intelligence is not so much related to the *speed* of the course of development as to its *fullness*. The superior child tends to portray the developmental characteristics of his age with a special vividness. The growth of general intelligence is not markedly affected by sex differences nor by such physical factors as physique or age of onset of puberty. Total growth is more comprehensive and conservative than any single index, such as mental age. The maturity index has special import both for present status and future potentials.

Giftedness is one of the most intriguing manifestations of individuality. It is also one of the most significant from the standpoint of social welfare. It represents a human resource in growth potentials which needs to be discovered, encouraged, and conserved. This can be done within the framework of a democratic culture, without prejudice to the more modestly endowed. Indeed, more concern for the gifted will tend to benefit all children. Giftedness embraces many areas of behavior: promising aptitudes, exceptional talents, superior intelligence, leadership, creative personality, social insight, and a high order of capacity for continuing growth. A gifted youth does not necessarily embody all these attributes, but he is likely to be versatile rather than channelized and to have a wide range of interests and inquisitiveness. He may have exhibited unusual promise in the dynamic qualities of his spontaneous behavior during the preschool and infancy years. Giftedness has an hereditary basis which tends to reveal itself in the acceleration of intellectual growth as measured by intelligence quotients.

Superior potentials may be foreshadowed in early life in the arts and sciences, in music, language, and engineering, because giftedness and genius are subject to the laws of development. The precursor signs observed in the elementary grades often come to fuller manifestation in the high school years. Giftedness is a growth phenomenon, and as such it responds to cultivation through guidance and understanding. The studies of Terman and Cox, however, have shown that "youths who achieve eminence are characterized not only by high intellectual traits, but also by persistence of motive and effort, confidence in their abilities and great strength or force of character." This no doubt applies in some measure to all fields of eminence—to poets, writers, artists, scientists, and to leaders in industry and government.

The current culture is naturally placing a premium on scientific giftedness. The annual Science Talent Search, now aided by 15,000 Science Clubs of America, has demonstrated conclusively that a potential scientist can be identified by the age of sixteen. Symptoms of interest and ability show strongly by the age of ten, and often earlier. To what extent these foreshadowings should be stimulated is always an educational problem, which demands an appraisal of maturity traits in relation to the evidences of exceptional ability.

Style of growth. Every individual has a distinctive style of growth which is revealed when the progressive course of development is viewed in perspective. Some individuals, for example, develop in a smooth, gradual, step-by-step fashion; others seem to move in spurts, hardly changing for long periods of time, then acquiring new behaviors in a sudden flood. Again, some individuals show wide swings of behavior as they proceed from stage to stage of maturity, high-lighting the extremes of each phase, while others, by contrast, show only a slight gravitation toward the "prototypes" of behavior along their over-all course. Growth patterns such as these are often characteristic of the individual from earliest infancy throughout life.

Another dimension appears when the growth course is viewed over a longer time span. A majority of individuals appear consistent in over-all rate of development, showing a more or less constant amount of earliness or lateness in reaching critical or nodal points in the growth cycle. Others show variations in this respect. One pattern is that of rapid early development which does not later fulfill its apparent promise. It may seem as if the individual failed to clear a crucial hurdle in the early stages of development, and, though his growth proceeded in many ways, he remains handicapped by a lack in some particular aspect of organization. Another variation is exemplified in the immature individual. Slowness of development is sometimes a feature of generalized retardation, in which the individual never reaches an adult level of functioning. But sometimes it is a more benign immaturity, in which later stages of growth are either accelerated or prolonged, allowing the eventual achievement of average or even superior status. The "superior-immature" individual, the child of above-average intelligence who shows a total functioning more character-istic of a younger developmental level, presents special problems and a special challenge to the educational system.

In the foregoing discussion of *individuality* we have made meager use of the term *personality*. The two terms are not fully synonymous. Person-ality is the total psychic individual as manifested in action and attitude. It is the crowning product of the human growth process because it embodies all of the experience which the individual has assimilated—the remembered, the forgotten, the repressed. It represents a life history, a veritable biography. The present volume is more concerned with the underlying, innate individuality which gives form and foundation to the developing personality and its life history. Every adolescent youth de-velops in accordance with a unique pattern of growth, which is the key to his individuality. The genesis of this individuality will have further con-sideration in the chapter on the Total Action System. The gradients of growth and the related text will suggest the nature and trends of individ-ual differences which may occur at advancing stages of maturity.

Individuality is always in the making, even though it is also enduring. At every stage we encounter the factor of age, because time and growth are inseparable. In Shakespeare's poetic language, Time is a nurse, a breeder, a begetter which molds

> . . . the chance of things
> As yet not come to life, which in their seeds
> And weak beginnings lie intreasured.
> Such things become the hatch and brood of Time.

We turn now to consider what comes to life during years ten, eleven, twelve, thirteen, fourteen, fifteen, and sixteen.

Part Two

MATURITY PROFILES
AND TRAITS

A series of *Maturity Profiles* portrays the maturity characteristics of each yearly age zone regarded as a whole (Chapters 4–10).

The double-column text discusses the *Maturity Traits* in concrete relation to nine functional fields (listed on the opposite page).

A separate chapter in Part Three is devoted to each of these fields, to bring the *Maturity Trends* into longitudinal sequence for the cycle of years from ten through sixteen (Chapter 11–19).

Classification of

MATURITY TRAITS (Chapters 4–10) and
GRADIENTS OF GROWTH (Chapters 11–19)*

1. *Total Action System:* Physical Growth; Sex Interests; Health; Tensional Outlets; Response to Our Examination and Interview (*with* Richard J. Apell, O.D., and Richard N. Walker, M.A.)

2. *Self-Care and Routines:* Eating; Sleep; Bath; Clothes; Care of Room; Money and Work.

3. *Emotions:* In General; Anger; Worries and Fears; Humor; Affectivity; Self-Assertion; Expressing Feelings

4. *The Growing Self:* In General; Self-Evaluation; Wishes and Inclinations; The Future

5. *Interpersonal Relationships:* Mother-Child; Father-Child; Siblings; Family; Same-Sex Friends; Opposite-Sex Friends; Crushes; Parties

6. *Activities and Interests:* Outdoor Activities; Indoor Activities; Clubs and Camp; Reading; Radio, Television, and Phonograph; Movies

7. *School Life:* In General; School Subjects and Work; Teacher-Child Relationship

8. *Ethical Sense:* Right and Wrong; Sense of Fairness; Response to Reason; Honesty; Swearing, Drinking, and Smoking

9. *Philosophic Outlook:* Time and Space; Death and Deity

* Comparable *Maturity Traits* and *Gradients of Growth* for the years from one to ten are detailed in two earlier volumes by Gesell and Ilg: *Infant and Child in the Culture of Today* (Harper), *The Child from Five to Ten* (Harper).

CHAPTER FOUR

Year Ten

ı..

MATURITY PROFILE

YEAR TEN holds an interesting and highly significant position in the scheme of human growth. It marks the culmination of a decade of fundamental development which began with the prenatal period. A decade of adolescent development looms in the vista ahead.

During Year Ten the metaphorical spiral which symbolizes growth takes a somewhat leisurely turn toward far-off adult maturity. Ten is a year of consummation as well as of transition—an amiable, relatively relaxed interlude in which the organism assimilates, consolidates, and balances its attained resources. Accordingly, a classic 10-year-old embodies both the specific and the generic traits of childhood. Only mildly does he foreshadow the tensions of later youth. In a frank, unself-conscious manner he tends to accept life and the world as they are with free and easy give-and-take. It is a golden age of developmental equipoise.

Of course this stage is transient and it is not altogether unruffled, as we shall presently show. But in sketching any maturity profile we shall accent salient and representative traits, assuming that the reader will make ample allowance for individual differences and qualifications. We are not attempting to describe a specific child but an illustrative composite who in his age zone and cultural group reflects the trends and integrations of development. We seek thereby to characterize the processes and patterns of maturing. We permit ourselves a measure of literary license to animate the facts—not to exaggerate them. For convenience of diction we shall use **variously interchangeable** terms relative to ages and stages, such as *age*

37

level, age zone, maturity level, Year Ten, 10-year-old, or plain Ten. The pronoun *he* will often have to serve for both genders. The broad purpose of the profiles is to indicate the kinds of behavior which suggest how mind and personality take form in the growing years from ten to sixteen.

In development no year stands alone. Each year bears a dynamic relation to the years adjacent. Thus Year Ten becomes more meaningful when viewed in relation to the traits and trends displayed at nine and eleven. The transition from nine to ten is generally smooth, gradual, and steady. The day-to-day changes mostly go unnoticed. A few shifts may occur suddenly and dramatically. In due course an advance in maturity becomes apparent in demeanor, attitudes, emotions, and ideas. Possessions once cherished are given up. Boys may give up their play guns and early comics; girls, their paper dolls. There is a widening catholicity of tastes and interests, which makes itself felt in interpersonal relations at home and school and more privately in the child's interior growing self.

Ten is fond of his home and loyal to it. He is in some ways more closely attached to his family than he was at nine. The roots of attachment cling deeply to both parents. The mother has special prestige. Boys recognize her authority and obey her more cheerfully than earlier. Girls are confiding and accept her guidance. For the most part both boys and girls get along well with father and enjoy his companionship. A boy likes to go off on an excursion alone with his father in a bond of camaraderie.

Ten readily participates in joint family activities like picnics and auto trips. His good will makes for family harmony. He gets along least well with siblings in the six-to-nine age range. They raise problems too complex for naïve good nature. With children of preschool age, however, he proves to be a companionable caretaker and protector. He has a nurturing capacity which comes to natural expression in his understanding attitudes toward a young child—and toward an animal pet which he may be rearing. Girls show similar trends. They dream of becoming a mother, nurse, teacher, or veterinarian. A 10-year-old boy likes to read to a 5-year-old. The engaging manner in which this interpersonal relation is manifested is in character for both age levels. Five and Ten have basic attributes in common.

Ten is fond of friends. He likes to tell who they are and mentions their distinguishing merits. He may report them by full name, age, and birthday, and father's occupation. He combines specific interest in concrete detail with diversity of interest. This is rather characteristic of Ten's general psychology as reflected in his intellectual processes and attitudes, his predilections at school, and his outlook on life.

Cub Scout activities have a great appeal, but he also joins informal spontaneous groups and temporary fluid gangs. He tends to be tolerant rather than exclusive as to membership of these groups.

Girls are reported to show somewhat more tendency to "get mad,"—"not speaking," "not playing." They also prefer smaller and more intimate groups. Most girls have one best girl friend for an extended period. The interrelations in such a friendship are often extremely complex and intense. They embrace a wide variety of social and cultural values which are intimately discussed. The interactions of these friendships may operate as a beneficial mechanism in personality formation. The ego develops through these reciprocal adjustments between friends. Perhaps girls are more advanced in this respect at this age. They are at least different. The boys tend to be more inclusive and less incisive in their boy-to-boy friendships.

Ten-year-old boys candidly but not vehemently express either disinterest in or active disrelish of girls. One misogynist laconically said, "I don't like girls. Period." Another, speaking more mildly for his 10-year-old confreres, summed up with, "We *sort of* hate girls."

Girls of comparable age with slightly different accent say, "Oh, we don't like boys. They can be plenty mean." (Pull hair, chase, push, act rough, and throw food at parties.) Another milder spokesman said, "We are not interested in boys *yet*."

Although there is no sustained antagonism between the sexes, they often separate by choice in group games and folk dancing—boys in one group, girls in another.

Ten takes to schooling. This is not surprising in the light of his general characteristics of amenability, easy give-and-take emotionally, and concrete matter-of-factness. He likes to learn. He is not overconcerned about the personal peculiarities of his teacher if she is fair in management and informative in instruction. He accepts a reasonable amount of homework without resentment.

Despite a certain impersonality of attitude he much prefers a friendly atmosphere in his schoolroom. These are the things he likes in a teacher: "When we make a joke she laughs." "She lets us whisper." "Doesn't yell when she's mad." "Good disposition." "Patient."

Assimilativeness is a cardinal education trait in the ten-year zone of maturity. It is both a mood and a capacity. Accordingly, Ten loves to memorize, even at length; he likes to identify facts, to spot the cities on a map, to seriate familiar items, to take them down by dictation. He is less inclined to correlate and to conceptualize or generalize his facts. This hospitality for discrete facts and memorizing of material appears to be a developmental phenomenon which ultimately promotes his mental welfare. His spans of attention may be short and as choppy as his composition sentences: but they are numerous, they are various, and they denote a wide-ranging zeal for knowledge. Wide ranging is a developmental antecedent to deep delving. No wonder that he wants to talk, to look, to read, to listen more than he wants to "work." This is active receptivity. Ten is an optimal age for TV education.

Ten might almost be called an athletic age, not because of competitive interest in sports but because of sheer delight in the sheer physical activity of running, sliding, climbing, jumping, skating, bicycling. He feels as never before the urge of his gross musculature. His stamina is at a higher level. But true to his equable nature he also enjoys less strenuous exercise. He is fond of just fooling around with the other kids in his neighborhood. He feels most at home near his home. Much of this quieter activity seems aimless, but it has a logic all its own in the shifting interpersonal adjustments which it stimulates.

His organized group life is more serious. He venerates the symbols of his scout organization. He gravely forms secret and mystery clubs. They may be short-lived, but they can be touched with idealism and austerity. The mottoes so testify: "Have will power." "Share hardships together." The clubs, however, prove fluid. They have more aspiration than duration.

Simple comradeship rather than competition motivates his group associations. He tries to be as good as others but does not especially want to outdo his mates. At school he doesn't like to be singled out for praise. He says "It makes me feel funny if I'm the best." He is concerned if a close friend fails to get a passing mark. At the same time he doesn't want to get a better mark than his friend.

The basic developmental equipoise of Ten reflects itself in his prevailing attitudes, his emotional climate and moods. One of our subjects said, "I don't like to be cross." This is fairly typical because in general Ten is content with himself, with his lot, and the world; so much so that it is somewhat startling to learn that he is given to sharp bursts of anger and may strike out with primitive childish violence. These bursts tend to be brief, explosive, and shallow. They are soon over; the basic goodness of Ten's make-up asserts itself in a quick return to relative equipoise. Anger episodes at later ages prove to have a greater complexity because of the different maturity status of the organism. At ten, boys as well as girls still cry in the throes of anger; but they do not harbor grudges or nurse hurt feelings.

There are bursts of happiness and bursts of demonstrative affection, which have a pattern similar to that of anger and show the same tendency to give way to a stabilizing even tenor. Earlier fears, worries, and anxieties likewise lessen. The very volatility of his feelings serves to safeguard the maintenance of his amiable qualities of self-contentment, casualness, and companionability. As he grows older, his emotional problems may well increase. Meanwhile, if he were self-conscious, he might feel grateful for the developmental equipoise which is now strengthening him against the impacts of the future.

Although Ten is characteristically contented and casual in demeanor, he is by no means indifferent toward moral responsibilities. In matters of conscience he is rather concrete; he is more aware of what is wrong than of what is right. He is seriously opposed to cheating and holds for stern codes against dishonesty. He may have strong convictions about swearing and drinking. In solving his ethical problems he tends to defer to his mother, for his conscience is not robust enough to take over on its own. Nevertheless, it actively grows, for he will ply his mother with exploratory questions and tests to work out in his own mind whether something is right or wrong and how wrong.

Conscience has to be informed to grow; it is in a state of relative immaturity. Hence Ten's preoccupation with wrong as contrasted with right. Development often proceeds from the negative to the positive with the first emphasis on the negative. Hence also his strong tendency to alibi and to shift blame upon a sibling. He is usually truthful about big things, less so about smaller things. He declares that he especially hates war and Communism, all of which suggests that his conscience will in time encompass general as well as specific issues. Moreover, he lives so fully and spontaneously in the here and now that he has few burdens to place upon conscience.

For similar reasons, he tends to be matter-of-fact in his philosophic ideas and attitudes relative to time and space, death and Deity. His thinking is concrete and his notions are rather static. His sense of time is chiefly a sense of times as registered by the hands of the clock. "Space is to put houses on." He shows increased ability to manage time in his daily affairs. He is less driven by time. His attachment for home and neighborhood serves to keep him spatially within bounds. Indeed it is something of an adventure "to go downtown alone," to meet his mother by appointment. He enjoys a sense of achievement in this conquest of psychological and geographic space, although he may not yet be capable of a more complex errand. He still needs emphatic warnings as to the traffic hazards of the street.

Since Ten is frank and open-hearted, he unconsciously reveals the patterns of his maturity by demeanor, gesture, manner of speech, and by what he says. "I am happy," he remarks, "if after supper I go out and play." He enjoys simple neighborhood play; he has gotten parental permission. He is glad to be near home.

Asked to state a preference or make a choice between two alternatives, he shrugs his shoulders and says, "Sometimes *yes,* sometimes *no.*" "It could be *better,* it could be *worse.*" He is not dogmatic, or neutral. He tends to be liberal in his judgments. The shoulder shrugs are characteristic. They seem to suggest that he can carry water on either shoulder or on both. They are not evasive but tolerant in temper. With a properly inflected shrug he tosses off criticism. That too is an expression of his accustomed disposition.

His frequent and concrete references to his teacher, to his friends, and especially to his mother tell us much about his interpersonal orientations. He is not self-centered. Yet in moral situations he is becoming aware of a conscience. "I give attention to my mother, but I kind of know inside what to do." This self-scrutiny is destined to deepen in the near future. Year Eleven will bring forth new symptoms of self-awareness, self-penetration, and assertion.

The patterns and the degrees of self-awareness change from year to year—not of course in rigid conformance with the calendar but in obedience to the mechanisms of growth. Only by comparing the over-all transformations in the developing self from one year to the next can we appreciate what the growing-up process is like for child and adolescent. Even though there is no abrupt shift from one age to the next, each year yields its lawful changes in maturity traits and trends. The nature and the logic of the changes become evident when neighboring ages are compared.

Compare the maturity status of Ten with that of Nine. Ten is not only a taller, bigger, and stronger Nine, he is more advanced in the dynamics and the organization of his total action system. The maturity profile outlines resultant changes in his behavior characteristics. At the nine-year level he was inclined to be intense while now at ten he is relaxed. He was striving where now he is surprisingly casual. His former earnest, self-motivated zeal to acquire skill is replaced by unconcerned poise and self-assurance. At ten he is less channelized, less preoccupied and perseverating. Instead he is more easygoing, more eclectic, with multiple, varying, specific interests combined with catholicity of tastes. For the time being he seems to be less ambitious.

As Nine he frequently indulged in self-appraisals and more or less conscientious self-criticism or even self-competition. As Ten his personal and interpersonal emotional climate has somewhat changed. He is relatively unself-conscious. He is perhaps more popular with his elders than he was during phases of his 9-year-oldness—more popular, but not necessarily more worthy!

Here we should like to emphasize that the developmental maturity traits ascribed to Nine are not derogatory, nor are they necessarily harmful if not present in excess. On the contrary, they may well have an essential function in the dynamics of development. A discerning culture will make good use of the natural qualities of Nine. Ten had to be Nine in order to become Ten. The season for intense channelization was in the nine-year zone. Poise comes later, for it is always counterpoise. And how can one be unself-conscious without also being capable of self-consciousness? Poise and control imply modulation of rival tendencies. Developmental potentials come in paired opposites which are progressively woven into reciprocal balance. Year Eleven will bring new dualities which will demand new choices of the child and the culture.

MATURITY TRAITS

1. Total Action System

The taut-string quality of the 9-year-old is at ten giving way to looser, softer structure. This is expressed in Ten's general demeanor as well as in the changes in his bodily structure. He meets situations face on with sincerity and without embarrassment. He is not fearful of asking questions to put himself on the right path. He is full of good effort without being overanxious.

There is a certain poise in him as he works at a table or sits in a chair. His head movements are marked, as he shifts from side to side either because of his shift of gaze or possibly his shift of thought.

He prefers to be active, and the outdoors is his greatest love. He loves most to play outdoor gross motor games and to ride his bicycle. But he is not overly active. There is a congeniality in his activity that bespeaks smoothness in whatever he does.

HEALTH

General health is veering toward the "good now" or "better than before." Some enjoy very good or excellent health. The asthmatic or hay-fever children tend to show a definite improvement. Many of the somatic complaints so common at nine (stomach-aches, sick headaches, dizziness, leg pains) are now lessening or disappearing. Even though some of these sensations may persist, the urge to go out to play overpowers the demands of the symptoms. A few of the boys with a greater tendency to immaturity (always more common in the male) may have prolonged coughs.

TENSIONAL OUTLETS

There may be an increase of fingers-to-mouth activity including fingernail biting or playing with hair, but on the whole, tensional outlets are less evident at ten than they were at nine. The drawing in of lips so common at nine is now less evident and will soon give way to a greater tendency to extrude or pout the lips. If thumb sucking still exists, which it does occasionally with boys, a real effort to resolve this habit may be made by the boy himself. The habit may have become so automatic that it occurs only during sleep. A method evolved by one thumb sucker was to wear a glove and pin it securely to his pajama sleeve. Increased fidgeting, hopping on one foot, never being still, does not usually occur until mid-ten and is then more common in girls than in boys.

VISION

The visual behavior of the 10-year-old tells us much about his inner functioning. Ten accepts a visual examination of as long as an hour or more, without fatigue—and without much penetration of what is happening to him. He may be said to co-operate without being co-operative. He is complacent visually and rarely reports visual symptoms (such as blurring, doubling, eye-watering), even though tests show that the majority of 10-year-olds depart in some way from theoretical "ideal" vision. But it is always necessary to differentiate what is real trouble from what is a passing (often necessary) phase in development.

Ten is best in his fixation mechanism. He can locate. His eyes have a way of roving around a room or landscape, picking up this or that visually. But his general behavior often suggests that he does not wish to penetrate deeply or to define sharply. And certainly his visual focusing mechanism shows an unreadiness to take on this next step of definition and penetration. His "skeletal" or fixating mechanism is in control; his "visceral" or focusing system is loose and blubbery. It will take another year for this sharp precision mechanism to develop. It is no wonder if, in his thinking, Ten appears to memorize better than he achieves keen insights. It is no wonder he prefers *status quo*, here and now, and doesn't want to reach out into new lands—and especially doesn't want to wear glasses. He will wear them if he has to, but he would prefer not to.

Ten functions better binocularly than monocularly. He has neither the refinement nor direction that a differentiated monocular pattern would give him. Nor does his visual mechanism allow him the freedom to project out widely into space. This may have some bearing on his tendency to stay close to home and to play with his neighborhood group. It may also be why he wants the stimulation of movement, of bike riding and running, which thrust him bodily "out in space" when his own visual mechanism can't accomplish this act as well as it will soon come to do.

PHYSICAL DEVELOPMENT AND SEX AWARENESS—GIRLS

Girls at the tenth birthday appear to be about even with the boys in size and in sexual maturity. But, unlike the boys, the majority of girls will show the first slight but unmistakable signs of approaching adolescence during their tenth to eleventh year. Their childish body forms now undergo a slight softening and rounding, especially in the hip region. There is a softer padding of the whole chest area and often slight projection of the nipples. The waist is more accented, the arms rounder, less modeled in contour. Even with the slimmer girls, who may not show the bodily softening, there is a filling out in the face area which gives it a more oval shape. The features, especially the chin, seem a little less sharp and pointed, less elfin than at nine.

The majority of girls are on the brink of starting their more rapid height growth within this year, and some light, downy pubic hair appears in a number of girls, but very few have begun to menstruate before eleven years.

Partly because of their more rapid sexual (and social) development, girls are much more sex-aware than boys—though less outspoken about it. Girls are less prone to tell "dirty jokes," with sex and elimination connotations. They are aware enough to have become reticent about talking of sex, even with their mothers. Yet they may be curious enough about their father's and mother's relationship to ask rather personal questions—such as did their father really "do that" to their mother. The more aware girls are embarrassed when their brothers peek in on them, or when they see their fathers in the process of dressing or undressing.

Ten- to 11-year-old girls are very much aware of their own breast development, and may be disturbed if there is no evidence of this. Often they complain of soreness and tingling in the nipple region. Those who are advanced in breast development feel unsure of themselves, and don't know whether they want to put their shoulders back or huddle up to hide their changing contours.

Girls more than boys are apt to be embarrassed about receiving sex information. Many seem to have forgotten the knowledge they received at a younger age. But they are very interested in securing books about sex and babies. They tend to hide these books, and later to confess that they have read them many times.

Girls receive the knowledge about menstruation in different ways. Some are casual about it. Others look forward to it, and indicate that they will be proud when it arrives. But there are also those who are horrified at the thought and will accept the idea only when they realize they can't have babies unless they menstruate. Girls often ask about sanitary napkins, and remark that people make such a mystery about them.

PHYSICAL DEVELOPMENT AND SEX
AWARENESS—BOYS

Boys and girls are of comparable height, but the rate of boys' growth is slower. The boys appear not to have changed much in the quality of their physique. But on closer inspection and in comparison with his 9-year-old self, each 10-year-old boy shows subtle changes. There is a more solid look to Ten, even though this is not necessarily reflected in his weight. There is a slight rounding off and softening of body contours, especially around the chin and neck and in the chest area. No visible traces of sexual maturing appear except in a very small proportion of boys.

The 10-year-old boy's sex awareness is not much ahead of his physical maturity. He questions very little and when he does it is apt to be an offhand question—often asked at an inopportune time. But though sex information is taken very casually, most boys are interested in reading books of simple text describing the starting, growth, and birth of a baby. Many boys already know of intercourse, and a large number learn of it during Year Ten. They are interested in the father's role, and recognize the possibility that they too will become fathers some day. They casually refer to their future children, mentioning what they might wish to tell them or save for them.

A few boys are more self-aware, more self-conscious than most. These are the boys who want the door closed when they take a bath. They will no longer dress before a mother or sister, but curiosity leads them to peek at their sisters whenever they can. These are often the boys who are picking up the slang words, the short words referring to sex and elimination. They are quick to hear them spoken by the older boys and to see them written on the bathroom walls at school. The boys who use these words often do so without knowing their meaning, however, and may be quite shocked when they are informed what they are saying. Their ability to memorize makes them agile at storing up limericks, which most often have sex or elimination implications. The more knowing boys begin to differentiate which ones can be said before their mothers or "ladies" in general.

Still fewer boys now show a strong attachment for a girl. These infrequent couples may wish to hold hands and to write love notes, but usually they are embarrassed when people refer to "girl friend" or "boy friend." Such attachments, most Tens seem to feel, are for younger ages—or older ones.

2. Self-Care and Routines

EATING

Appetite. Even the poorer eaters are now realizing they are eating more than they used to. With some, appetite may fluctuate from very good to not so good. But with others appetite fluctuates with the food that is being served, e.g., a big appetite for steak and a poor one for fish. Such adjectives as "big," "tremendous," "too good" are used to describe Ten's appetite. Many Tens can eat at any time of the day and rarely lose their appetite for supper by having an after-school snack. Just the mention of a food produces a strong response either for or against. A few Tens, especially girls, have a poor appetite for breakfast but they may make up for it with a snack at bedtime. Appetite rises during the day, and many a Ten likes to know ahead of time what he is going to have for supper.

Preferences and Refusals. Ten likes more foods than he dislikes, in fact he may like most everything. His eyes sparkle as he tells of his favorite foods with an "I just love . . ." Some have not only favorite foods but favorite meals. Meats such as steak, roast beef, hamburg, and hot dogs head the list, with potatoes a close second. Potatoes —baked, mashed, or French fried—are at the heart of a 10-year-old's meal. Some particular cooked vegetable such as peas is preferred. Raw vegetables such as carrots, celery, and tomatoes may be even more preferred. A few Tens are branching out into more adult tastes for lobster and other seafoods. They are aware of their expensive tastes and some even worry about it. Ice cream and cake is the most preferred dessert. There are those who crave sweets and desserts and others who rarely touch desserts. Those who crave sweets are ready to beg, borrow, or steal candy. Ten is the age when the child begins to give evidence of his purchases by the candy-bar wrappers stuffed in his pockets.

Refusals are dramatically expressed by an "I just hate . . ." or by the telling gesture of feigning to vomit. Though Ten is adaptable and ready to try new things, he is very definite about real refusals. Liver, onions, and fish head the list of disliked foods, though these are not as unmistakably rejected as asparagus, spinach, and even cooked tomatoes. Gravy is now accepted and even liked but "mixed-up things like stews" are still off the 10-year-old's acceptance list.

Snacks. Between-meal eating is indulged in by the majority of 10-year-olds. Cookies, bread and butter, and fruit are preferred, with a drink of soda or a coke. Milk is drunk by a few.

Table Behavior. There is much less complaint about Ten's table manners. As one Ten reported, "I wouldn't say they were bad and I wouldn't say they were good." The chief specific complaints are poor posture, elbows on the table, and the fork held with a fisted grasp. This latter posture is more typical of boys, and gives the impression of all arms and hands. There is a tendency to encroach on their neighbor with a lifted elbow. The napkin may still be forgotten temporarily, but can be delicately brought to mind by erring Ten himself with a cryptic phrase such as, "It's snowing." One reason why there is less talk about table manners is because Ten has proved himself up to any standards away from home or when guests are being entertained. A goal has been reached which allows for relaxation when the family is alone.

SLEEP

Bedtime. Ten is not yet aware when he is tired and ready for bed. He still needs to be reminded. And as always with Ten, his response to this reminder is inclusive; alternatives are possible. "Mostly I go quite well, sometimes not." "If I'm tired I go right away or if not I hang around." In general, bedtime is from 8 to 9 with a majority going at 8:30.

Boys go to bed more easily and fall asleep more rapidly than do girls. They are, however, more ritualistic in their preparations, and more often like to be tucked in by their mothers. Girls more often have difficulty in falling off to sleep. Listening to a radio program, reading, or just lying awake thinking are common presleep activities. Their thoughts are not altogether pleasant ones, though a few are projecting into a life of heroism and success. Most are asleep by 9:30, with the boys asleep earlier, and some of the girls later.

On the whole Ten sleeps through the night. He has the sense of sleeping well. He is now reducing his time of sleeping to 10½ or 9½ hours, the boys sleeping longer than the girls.

Sleep. Ten still may have nightmares, though he reports a marked reduction, or that he doesn't "have them any more." In fact he reports as many pleasant dreams as unpleasant ones. Often he weighs them equally, "sometimes good and sometimes bad." He notes that the bad ones are more apt to come when he has a cold, after an operation, or when he's frightened by things he's read or seen. The good ones often remind him of real life, as though he were really there doing nice things.

Morning. Waking up or getting up is not usually a problem for Ten. Many are even early risers, especially boys. Seven A.M. is a common waking hour. Ten can go about his business—dressing, letting out the dog, making his breakfast—with much less reminding than he needed for going to bed. Some girls, usually the very ones who resisted going to bed, may resist getting up. They sleep late and may need to be dragged out of bed.

BATHING AND CARE OF HAIR

There is something about soap and water and being a 10-year-old that does not mix. The otherwise nice and co-operative 10-year-old stands his ground when it comes to taking a bath. He positively dislikes water, particularly when applied to the face for pur-

poses of cleanliness. He even goes so far as to consider cleanliness disgusting and may disdain or jibe at a friend who has clean hands.

There are, however, some 10-year-olds, boys and girls, though few in number, who have always been neat and meticulous. And there are those so repetitive and patterned in their activities that it would not enter their minds not to take a daily bath. (Beware of these very children! When they finally break away from habit, they may break completely.) Others already give glimpses of a future time when cleanliness acquires social significance. They may show a spell of washing but then they revert with a hate and resistance to bathing more vigorous than ever.

If parents recognize Ten's antipathy to washing, they may more readily adopt suitable measures. They will come to know that Ten needs to be reminded to bathe, that he may even have to be driven to the bathroom, and that filling and washing out the tub may be their job, not his. At times Ten will accept a bathing schedule if it doesn't interfere with his other activities, especially his radio or television programs. If left to his own devices, he would slip through three or four weeks without ever thinking of bathing. Considering Ten's incapacity for knowing or acknowledging when he needs to take a bath, parents may well consider the wisdom of the return of such an institution as the Saturday night bath or might settle for a twice-a-week schedule. Though Ten resists so strongly, he enjoys his bath once he is in it and may play in the tub for a whole hour. He prefers a tub bath to a shower, though a shower often facilitates the weekly shampoo with girls, who need most help with rinsing their hair.

As for self-care in other ways—the combing of hair, brushing of teeth, and care of nails—all these are in the hinterland as far as Ten is concerned. Short, unpermanented hair may solve the girls' problem. The chewing of carrots and celery may be as important to the care of teeth as brushing. And those who do not solve their fingernail problem by biting will just have to succumb to a manicure by a parent after the weekly bath.

CLOTHES AND CARE OF ROOM

Choice of clothes, especially daily clothes, is now coming within the interest of most 10-year-olds. A few mothers continue to lay out the child's clothes, but if Ten doesn't approve of his mother's choice he will change her selection. Though Ten is fairly good at choosing, he may not have sufficiently considered his choice in relation to the weather or the garment's cleanness. He's apt to put on the same outfit several days in a row. Therefore he needs to be checked, and fortunately he responds fairly well to suggestions.

Love of old clothes predominates, and dress-up clothes may be so distasteful that a 10-year-old boy may refuse to go to Sunday school because forsooth he has to wear a white shirt!

Ten does not wish to draw attention to himself either by dress-up clothes or bright colors. Blue and yellow are more often chosen by both sexes in preference to brighter colors. Some Tens hate new clothes so intensely that they will not wear them at all. Mothers regretfully report that "new clothes are handed on unworn." A well-stocked wardrobe at nine with expandible seams and hems might solve the problem of dislike of new clothes at Ten.

The care of clothes is now at a dismal low. Outer garments are slung and flung hither and yon. As one girl reports, "We sling our things down somewhere, but," she adds with 10-year-old co-operativeness, "we have to hang them up afterward." Dropping of clothes "just where he stepped out of them" is all too commonly reported by parents. Is this a part of Ten's on the spot, focal tendency which has not yet built up awareness of the impressions he makes on others? Is his quality of "niceness" also related to his self-contained, focal behavior? We might think about this as we pick up what he has dropped and so reduce our higher aspirations and less effectual demands. A spurt of spontaneous tidiness may come later on. Until then, as stopgap aid, we might settle for use of just a *single* chair as a repository for his clothes, plus a weekly cleaning out of his room, to insure a periodic fresh start.

Buying of Clothes. Ten is beginning to help in the selection and purchase of new clothes. Girls more than boys enjoy shopping with their mothers. Boys are more apt to dislike both trying on new clothes and wearing them. Whether or not the child goes to the store with his mother, she needs to consult his taste. No serious clashes occur and some sort of a compromise can usually be reached. The mother, however, is granted the final decision.

The one piece of wearing apparel that the child wishes full freedom in choosing is his footgear. Though he may shop for nothing else, he wants to select his own boots and shoes carefully.

Hand-me-downs are not as a rule

scorned; in fact, they may be cherished because they bring that well-worn feeling. Girls like to have mothers make their dresses and feel proud of their mother's accomplishments.

Care of Room. With Ten's interest in the old, the tried, the casual in clothes, you could not expect him to live in extreme order in his room. He himself says, "My room's a mess. If it was neat I couldn't tell where anything was. Books piled all on top of things. More *friendly*, more natural that way." But there comes that inevitable time when messiness brings on its own downfall, when it has gone too far and a spurt of total cleaning is the only thing to make a room livable again. Messiness alternates with cleanliness, but Ten never finds places enough for storing all his treasures or hoarding all his useless odds and ends.

Ten needs a room of his own where he can come to terms with his own untidiness and achieve a fuller sense of himself through his specially chosen possessions and accustomed surroundings. He will create order in time; he will discard; he will expand in new ways. Even at ten, pennants, banners, or pictures (football and baseball heroes for boys and horses for girls) are beginning to embellish the walls. A bed may be left unmade, but a pennant is fastidiously placed at just the right angle.

MONEY

Ten has usually come through that money-mad state that often occurs at eight and nine years. And he spends less of his money on comic books, his burning passion at nine. As yet his relationship to money is at a tenuous, beginning stage. But if parents could look back on Ten's response to money when Ten has grown into later adolescence, they might find even at this earlier age a clear indication of his individual money sense. That one Ten would be satisfied with 15 cents allowance, and another would be capable of budgeting $1.25, shows how wide the individual variation can be.

At any age the size of the child's allowance is related to his money sense. At ten he usually wants more than 25 cents, but is rarely up to asking for 50 cents. Many families settle on 35 cents. Sometimes payment of the allowance is contingent on the successful carrying out of jobs or the accomplished fact of the weekly room clean-up.

Some Tens save nothing. Others save everything. The purpose of saving may range from a bicycle to a trip to Europe. Enjoyment of the feeling of money on hand is the earmark of the child who shows promise of manipulating money well.

Spending likewise shows a wide range. Many Tens squander their allowance on worthless objects for themselves or others. Ten's appetite and love of sweets draws him to the candy or pastry counter. And he does love to "treat all the kids." But his generosity can also be more planful as he selects presents for others, and his Christmas responsibilities are definitely on his mind.

WORK

Ten is not what you would call a worker. He feels little drive toward work. Even when he is paid for a job, such as the emptying of the wastebaskets, his response the first week may be terrific, but then comes the inevitable petering out. Ten can dabble at many tasks—laying the fire, burning papers, mowing the lawn, shoveling snow, baby-sitting at home—but he has no sense of continuation. Some days he's good about doing a job and some days not. Under pressure and demand Ten's nice qualities may be overshadowed with feelings of fatigue and resentment. Parents need to be quite flexible in their demands on Ten, and to realize that he works best when he is working along with a congenial adult.

3. Emotions

What a bevy of complimentary adjectives pop into the heads of friends or parents of the 10-year-old as they describe him. Nice, happy, casual, unself-conscious, straightforward, sincere, relaxed, companionable, poised, terribly nice and friendly, frank and open —all tell the same tale.

With many, the change from nine to ten years is imperceptible. It comes so gradually that it is only through reviewing the past that the quality of the present can be discovered. But sometimes the shift into this pleasant terrain comes suddenly. "She suddenly snapped out of many difficulties; like a metamorphosis." Or, "He's on the happy side this year. He was on the other side last year." It is almost as though there were a real divide between 9 and 10 years and that Ten has come into the foothills of a new terrain, of the whole new cycle of growth from ten to sixteen. Some Tens have a very precarious footing in this new terrain; they may be preparing to enter but have not as yet entered. One boy prayed he would be "good and gracious," but time had to elapse before he could achieve this. Another

found his toehold in saying he was sorry, for the first time in his life.

On the whole, life is good for the 10-year-old, so good that he doesn't even have to think about it. He can be taken a little aback when asked specific questions about his emotional state, and frequently answers that he doesn't know, that he can't say, that he has never thought about it. He often qualifies his statements or includes a range of possibilities with a "well, it depends—" or "sometimes I do and sometimes I don't." On the whole, life is better at ten than it was, especially since he can "do a lot more things." He is a man more of action than of thought. Simple occasions give him great happiness for the moment of their execution. Playtime outdoors after supper, no homework, a visit to an amusement park, each stimulates a brisk happiness in Ten. Good luck is pretty much on his side, though bad luck may have its occasional days, but "it all depends."

Fears are at a low ebb. Former fears of dogs and of the dark may show their nascent resolution by the fact that Ten reports spontaneously that he does not fear them. Snakes he more frankly admits he is afraid of. Of course he might not like to meet up with a lion in the dark or be all alone in an old castle, he tells us. He worries nearly as much as he fears. There are always lessons and homework to worry about and getting to school on time. But his worries are on the whole rather specific and individual. One boy may worry that he might lose his wallet; another that there isn't enough gas in the family car.

The most universal emotional expression at ten is, surprisingly enough, anger. This contented, co-operative, nice little 10-year-old suddenly explodes into unmistakable anger. He is quick to strike out, kick, or even bite. If more controlled he boils over verbally, he may cry or noisily go to his room in a furor of name calling and foot stamping. But Ten is selective about his expressions of anger. He himself says, "Depends who I'm angry at. If angry at my sister, I shoot paper clips and elastic bands at her. And if one of my parents punishes me and I don't think it's fair, I just go in the other room and boil up. At school you just take it—sometimes I feel it's unfair at school. And I talk about it to my friend." Ten is not only selective about his expressions of anger but also about his ways of bringing himself back to equilibrium. Some outlet for his anger can be managed even if it's only telling about it to his dog, or planning some revenge which is never carried out. It is the short-livedness of his anger, the hot-point quality, which distinguishes Ten. It's all over in no time. He has an efficient exhaust system.

Though Ten might cry when he's angry, on the whole he feels he's "too old for that." He stoically says he wouldn't cry if he "got cut or couldn't go someplace," but he might if his father died. The very ones who formerly burst into tears now "collect themselves and speak calmly." Though boys may have cried just as much or more than girls in the earlier years, the female's greater tendency to tears becomes clearly evident at ten years. Sadness is occasionally at the basis of tears but not very often. Anger is a more potent cause.

Ten isn't too concerned about his own hurt feelings. His feelings may get hurt but not deeply. If they are hurt, many are still young enough to "cry and go home," but some can pretend it didn't happen. Ten restabilizes quickly. He may or may not let other people know how he feels, but in general he tends to cover up any difficulties.

As with expressions of anger or happiness, Ten has sudden bursts of affection for his parents; such simple physical expressions of warmth as hugging and kissing. He says very naturally that he likes his parents the best of anything in the world and he can often accept their demands or suggestions without conflict. He is so happy and contented in his family and his home that he would seldom wish to change his lot with others even though they had more possessions than he. But he may have a hankering for a bicycle like that of some friend or for the radio of another. Some boys covet the strength of other boys.

Perhaps Ten's greatest difficulties are in relation to his siblings—the eternal problem of close comparison. But fortunately his busy active life affords him more latitude from his brothers and sisters.

In marked contrast to his feelings toward his siblings are his feelings about competition with contemporaries. Though he likes the pull and tug of combat he doesn't like to be best. He feels funny if he is singled out from all the others for praise and he thinks how "all the other kids will feel." He wants to do his best, and would prefer to be as good as all the others—but not win.

The average 10-year-old is not very skilled at high-class humor. But he is watchful for possible puns, and has a ready stock of "corny jokes." Much of what is funny to him lies within the realm of April Fool jokes and is often not funny to the adult. He pounces (sometimes too heavily) on words with a possible double meaning—"Virginia, you must be a state." The telling of a joke is a finer art than Ten can often master. He may tell the point too soon or he may miss the point, or even worse he may have no point to tell. And yet he hopefully asks, "Get it?" His humor will have to change a great deal before it is appreciated by the adult.

4. The Growing Self

Ten has reached the happy state of being casually sure of himself, of being content in himself. He can range out into a wide sphere of interests yet can concentrate on each interest of the moment. He can think ahead to marriage in the most general terms—"it all depends on peace or war," and yet insists on specific qualities in a wife—"I want her to be a good cook." He has multiple interests. He is eternally resourceful. He moves from one point of interest to the next, giving each his full attention for the time he can sustain it. He likes to complete a task but he doesn't wish to enlarge or to elaborate upon it.

He prefers to cover the whole terrain with little rootlets. This is no time for deep growing. This is the time for wide expanding, for various experiencing. He wishes to try everything.

Ten moves through the quicker, sharper, more superficial world of thought rather than that of deeper feelings, though he does have a general feeling of well-being. He says himself that his self is "the way you think inside; not what you say." These thoughts he relates to his head, his brain, or his mind, which are where he is most apt to say his self is. Though he is aware of his heart, he is not yet ready to delve into its depths.

He has some idea of both his own greatest assets and his greatest faults. Some specific ability such as reading, spelling, or ice skating may be according to him his greatest asset, though his sense of fairness and being a good sport are uppermost in many a Ten's mind. His faults he relates more specifically than his assets: that he sticks out his tongue as he practices at the piano; that he forgets to brush his teeth; that he picks frosting off the cake; or that he writes 1952 when it's 1953.

He is, on the whole, happy in himself, in his age, in his parents, and in his home. The best time is "now," ten years of age, to most Tens because "you're not too young and you're not too old." A few, less well grounded in the present, might wish to be much younger or much older. And as is often true with Ten, the reasons are very specific—for wanting to be younger ("Little children's clothes are nice and cute") or older ("Then you can buy your own things"). One Ten managed to take in the whole gamut of past and future in one sweep: "The best time is when you're a baby to eight years old and from twenty-one to thirty. From one to eight you can do most anything you feel like and don't have to go by rules. And from twenty-one to thirty you go out places and stay out longer and you aren't going to college and you don't have to work for your money till you're about thirty. Between twenty-one and thirty you get money from your mother."

Ten's wishes are like the rest of him. He thinks either in broad general terms of peace on earth, good health, and happiness or as related to specific material possessions as a bicycle or a tractor. The joys of living on a farm with dogs and horses all your own may entice many a 10-year-old. Some girls, unable to achieve this coveted state right away, can bear to postpone it by planning to marry a farmer. A desire to have babies or care for them is also one of the strong wishes of girls.

Many Tens have heard and thought enough about college, career, and marriage to have some rather definite ideas about their choices. But these choices are strongly influenced by their parents—not through the parents' persuasion but because Ten often identifies with them, admires, and wishes to copy them. Therefore the college chosen is often the college of his mother or father; the husband preferred should be "like daddy" or just fatherly, and be of the same profession as Ten's father. Boys are generally less articulate on the subject, especially about their future wives, whom they may not even have thought about.

As for a career, again Ten may choose that of his mother or father. However, it is often difficult for Ten to choose one profession out of the many possibilities that come to his mind. But with both sexes there is the drive to help people and animals. A doctor, a nurse, a mother, a veterinarian loom large as possible choices. And the tendency for Ten to be inclusive makes the girls want to play life both ways, to have both a career and marriage.

For, as one Ten reported, "I wouldn't want just to be married and be a wife."

5. *Interpersonal Relationships*

If ever the word *family* acquires its true meaning, it is when the child is ten years of age. Ten not only accepts but likes his lot. In fact, no other father or mother seems to surpass his in his own eyes. His home is just about right, and even his siblings, if they aren't too close to his age and don't needle him all the time, become family assets. This is the last age for some time to come when the child enters into a family excursion with casual thoughtfulness, adaptability, and full enjoyment.

Mother has again become that center of the universe which she was at five. Both boys and girls get on well with her. They not only depend on her, but look up to her and admire her. Girls especially confide in her, confess to her. They may tell her so much that they are accused of tattletaling. But they want to feel that their mother is their friend and that they can trust her.

They accept the fact that she wants to improve them and they try to respond in a casual sort of way. In their turn they are spontaneously helpful, and boys especially like to surprise their mothers with some thoughtful gesture as bringing her a breakfast tray. Both boys and girls are very demonstrative in their affection for their mothers and boys really do like to be tucked in at night.

Fathers in their own way are also

very important. A home really isn't a home without a father, according to Ten, though at some earlier ages he could have gotten on quite well without one. Father may surpass mother in Ten's eyes and frequently is both adored and idolized. Girls especially show strong feelings for their fathers and may be cut to the quick by any reprimand from them.

It's the companionship with father that has now become such fun. And father may enjoy it as much as does his 10-year-old. Going on trips, hikes, playing ball or watching ballgames, swimming, skating, or just palling around—these are the activities Ten enjoys most with his father.

Ten not only respects his parents but he also respects their place as parents. His oft-repeated quotations of "Mummy says—" show that he accepts his mother's word as law. He believes that parents should love their children, but he disapproves of over-indulgent parents. "As long as they are fair." That's all he wants—"not too strict and not too easy." He may attempt to test his parents, but if they aren't going to yield he accepts their demands and is really glad not to be allowed to go too far.

Rumblings of 11-year-old discord may sometimes occur between 10-year-old girls and their mothers. But even though they have arguments, it's very important to make up. The following conversation between a 10- and an 11-year-old girl shows the assured quality of Ten:

11-year-old Mary—"Don't you hate your mother? Mine's just rotten today. I'd like to see her dead."

10-year-old Barbara—"Don't you realize you'd never see her again? You can be angry at your mother, but you don't need to hate her."

As nice as Ten is, he still doesn't, as a rule, have the stamina or the perspective to get on with younger siblings, especially with those in the age range of six to nine. True, he has no real desire to be an only child, but he is guilty at times of wishing the troublesome sibling would "just disappear" or "go live somewhere else for a while."

Ask him how he gets on with his brothers and sisters and he will tell you, "Well, sometimes we get on and sometimes not." It's usually the younger sibling who taunts and pesters him until Ten is forced as it were to retaliate physically. When the parent steps in to stop the fight, poor Ten, because he is older, usually gets the blame. Often he rightly feels that decisions are "not fair."

Ten gets on best with much younger siblings. He is good about caring for and helping with those under five. These younger ones are often reported to "adore" the 10-year-old. Ten especially enjoys reading to them.

Ten gets on a little better with older siblings than he did, and better than he's going to again until the older one has gained the broader outlook of fifteen years of age. Older siblings may play with 10-year-olds and take them places, but often they consider Ten a nuisance, especially when he tattles on them. Poor Ten may not have been really tattling—he just has to tell his mother everything.

Friends, friends—how Ten loves his friends. He wants to bring one home from school every day, but most of all he likes his neighborhood pals. He wants the one who is available at all times. He wants to be out of doors anyway and he naturally seeks out his friends. Fortunately, he is so adaptable that he might play baseball with one friend, go bike riding with another, and work inside with still another. And there is always so much to talk about with them. It's surprising to hear how much Ten knows about his friends. He reports fully about each one, giving full name, age, grade, birthday, physical disabilities, bedtime hour, father's profession, and many other interesting facts. One of the qualities Ten likes best in his friends is that they can be trusted.

There is more "getting mad" or "not playing" between girls than boys, though the expression of this anger by "not speaking" doesn't last very long. Some Tens report they used to fight with their friends, but that they haven't even had an argument for a long time. Ten can be quite diplomatic. One 10-year-old girl was known to add a note to the bottom of her birthday card invitation: "Please don't tell anybody. I couldn't ask everybody and I didn't want to lose any friends."

Boys are more apt to form large play groups than are girls. These groups are usually fluid and one child may move freely from one group to another according to his activity inclinations. Certain sports such as baseball demand grouping. And Tens also group spontaneously to form a mystery club or a U and R Club (Your and Our Club) and eagerly participate in formal organizations such as the Scouts. In his own spontaneous grouping Ten usually tries not to exclude others who he knows would wish to join. He doesn't want to keep them out by building up a wall of secrecy (as

he will at eleven). He simply, in his casual way, doesn't let the others know about the existence of his club.

It is true that the majority of girls are "not interested in boys yet," or as the boys say, "we haven't gotten to girls yet." Both sexes, however, by their use of the word *yet* are quite aware that a future of boy-girl relationships lies ahead of them. Some girls are still included in the boys' play, but only if they are good at sports. These are often the tomboy girls—but these very girls often become the most feminine ones in their early teens. Boys do "act rough," chase girls, pull their hair, push them down. It's no wonder that girls avoid them. Gentleness will come with time.

6. Activities and Interests

Play is paramount in the lives of many 10-year-olds. School and routines are even considered interruptions of the more important life of play. Ten is happily busy in whatever he does and he now has the skill, stamina, and rebound needed in gross motor activities. His day and his activities almost seem to plan themselves. There seems to be a happy meeting ground as enjoyment of the same activity draws Tens together. Boys like to organize for baseball and even welcome the tomboy girls to make up a sizable team. Bicycling is more often enjoyed in groups of two or more. Now that they are quite safe on their bikes and can cycle without fatigue they can take longer trips. They even pick out rough roads in order to enjoy "that bumpy feeling."

The sheer joy of exercising their bodies is shown in other preferences as sliding, skating—both ice and roller, swimming, climbing, boat rowing, and above all running. Some 10-year-old girls are known to be the fastest runners in their school. Racing is fun either on foot or on a bike.

Boys and girls separate in their choice of other outdoor activities. The girls are busy at jacks, hopscotch, jump rope (now double dutch), and roller skating. The boys may join in at times but their stronger male preference will often lead them along the road of hunting and fishing which stretches ahead into the future years. Boys and girls share an interest in horseback riding (whether they actually do have opportunity to ride or not), but the girls often show a far greater desire and even passion for this sport. As one 10-year-old girl expressed it, "I'd rather have a colt than a baby."

Animals in general and pets in particular are of great interest to most 10-year-olds. Many show capacity and interest in caring for a dog or a cat, but they can scarcely be expected to be fully responsible. "Back to the farm" is an oft-repeated wish which will increase in intensity at eleven when possession of a farm of their own is more coveted.

The 10-year-old is recognizing the growing-up process, and feels himself on the verge of more mature interests and ready to give up earlier, less mature activities. This shift is so recent that he often feels a little superior about it. Thus he will say, "I just don't think those boys (9-year-olds) will ever get over playing guns." His mother felt the same way about him only six months ago. Or the very girls who enjoyed doll play most may now classify it as "babyish."

However, there are still many boys who persist in playing cowboys, Wild West, or whatever the current gun game may be. And there are girls who may have given up paper dolls but who love to play house with real dolls, dressing them up and putting them through play activities similar to their own 10-year-old experiences. The play is intermittent, with intervals as short as two days or as long as two months, but there is a new and more mature sense of running a family in this activity.

Though indoor play is usually second best to outdoor play, Ten can occupy himself happily indoors especially with friends. Boys and girls enjoy playing together such table games as parcheesi and Monopoly. A great deal of time and effort goes into Ten's collections. He will collect most anything and may have a number of collections. When asked if she had any collections one girl exclaimed, "Do I! Have collections! Well—stamps, postcards, books, horseshoes, and just odd things." Added to these, Ten might collect coins, shells, storybook dolls, china animals, boxes (Ten loves boxes), stones, pictures of stones, birds' nests, snakeskins, airplane models, model soldiers, or just candy and gum wrappers. He still isn't too selective, nor is he ready to display and classify. Mostly he just wants more and more of what he is collecting.

Girls are busiest at writing plays, dressing up, and then giving the plays. Some sew, either for their dolls or occasionally for themselves. A few may knit.

Those boys who are skillful with their hands are busy drawing gadgets, architectural plans, jet planes, and rockets. Others draw elaborate pictures of battles, or violence, or cars and trains, with running commentaries. These may be somewhat less mature boys who are still trying to find themselves in the depths of 9-year-oldness. Ten likes to construct—whether he is making model planes or boats, working with his Erector set, or creating his own forms through carpentry. He needs a place in the basement, or a workshop where he can have his tool bench, and especially a place for his chemistry set if his interest in chemistry goes beyond the concoction of explosives. Electric train play with boys is like doll play with girls. It may be strong with some. With others it may return at shorter or longer intervals, or not at all.

The boy who is "not too good with his hands" may be the very one who still enjoys his trains. He is interested in other boy things but he approaches them from an imaginary realm rather than through the reality of construction. As one boy said, "We pretend we have special gadgets that haven't even been invented yet and maybe not for a hundred years or maybe not even never."

Clubs of all kinds are strong. Of all ages Ten is one of the readiest to respond to the call of the group. He is the most enthusiastic Scout member. He makes up clubs of his own—secret clubs, or mystery clubs patterned on the FBI or other interests of the day. Such clubs demand high standards from their members. Ten is out to improve himself. For one club the motto may be *"No sulking."* For another club it may be *"Have will power"*; or *"Share hardships together."* Ten shows his age, however, by choosing as his club password "potatoes."

But clubs are fluid—here today and gone tomorrow. Some even remain in the planning stage. The hut or tree house hasn't yet become the clubhouse though there is a dawning sense of wanting a place to meet. Eating may turn out to be the club's strongest motivation. Or a club may be formed for the purpose of excluding another child, using a name with the cloak of secrecy to make the exclusion legitimate.

SEDENTARY LOOKING AND LISTENING ACTIVITIES

Ten's relatively active life comes to a standstill at times. He is nowadays blessed with a wide provision of entertainment, information and thought-provoking media—television, radio, books, and movies. He most often takes them in this order of preference, though he may repudiate all in favor of outdoor active play. However, he may listen or watch practically all day long, for as one Ten tells us, "I have all the programs memorized so I know just where and when each program is. I can just turn it on and go zip—get any program." On the whole the passion for television he showed at nine is slightly diminishing. It is "no longer a matter of life and death," according to one mother. "He's tapering off—thank goodness!" voices another. Or he himself may report that he watches or listens "just about never." If he does watch and listen, he chooses blood and thunder, mysteries, cowboy, comedy, or family programs. Some, both boys and girls, know that they will have nightmares if they watch or listen to mysteries, and avoid them. During convalescence there may be a marked rise in interest in soap operas all day long. A decreasing number of Tens are interested in the late afternoon blood-and-thunder or cowboy programs. They are giving these up along with comic books. And a slowly increasing number are interested in the later evening mystery programs which may conflict with their 8:30 to 9 P.M. bedtime. Television may or may not be preferred to radio.

Reading shows as wide a variation of interest as television and radio, though more Tens are interested than are not. The avid readers have been avid since seven years of age and the uninterested readers may never read more than they have to.

As long as the word *secret, mystery,* or *horse* is in the title, Ten's interest will be attracted. He may show only one area of intense interest. One girl, when asked what she read replied "*The Black Stallion, Son of Black Stallion, The Black Stallion and Satan,* and *Island Stallion.*" There was no doubt about her interest.

Besides horse and dog stories, even "sad ones that are going to come out good in the end," Ten likes biographies of famous people, adventure, and mysteries. Some restrict themselves to stories about children of their own age and time. Others like to experience children of their own age growing up to become famous people. Historical books are interesting but sometimes they lack enough adventure.

The newspaper still receives only a glance from Ten. He picks up the headline and looks for pictures of accidents or war pictures. He keeps up with the funnies, and finds excitement in the Lost and Found columns.

Comics, happily for many parents, are showing their first signs of giving up their hold on him. He may show this by no longer having high stacks of them, not keeping track of them,

and no longer spending all his money on them. But there are many who are increasing their stacks, know each one they have or have borrowed or lent, and who are still dishing out their own funds to pay for them. A few, less willing to part with money, will spend an unusually long time near comic-book racks in stores in their attempt to select a comic book. Having read them most through, they may find little need to purchase them. Doctors' and dentists' offices may be favored for this one asset—comic books in the reception room.

It is rather surprising to find Ten not too interested in movies. He may show this by not being very selective about his choice, not caring what he sees, or by preferring not to go at all unless he thinks it will be a *good* movie. He may get tired sitting so long. A sad movie may move him deeply and produce a good cry. Or it may be too much for him, and he may even need to bury his head in his mother's lap. He would prefer sometimes to go with his mother, but he will also go with friends of the same sex—as often as once a week, or once every two weeks. But most Tens go only occasionally. Cartoons, Westerns, and slapstick comedies are his favorites, with murder mysteries showing a rise. A number of Tens can't take murder mysteries in any form, whether on radio, television, or in movies, but the overpowering realism, stupendousness, and duration of a single movie may have an especially powerful impact upon a susceptible 10-year-old.

7. School Life

Given the chance, Ten can really like school. He likes his teacher and he likes to learn. But, more than liking to be taught, he wants to be kept interested and motivated. You may hear him say to his teacher, "Gee, I've learned an awful lot from you!" He hates to miss school because he feels so much will be said so that he "won't ever be able to catch up."

Ten has time under good control. He isn't driven by time as he was at nine. His morning preparations at home are made at an easy, leisurely pace. He is the responsible one. He's not only in control of time but also of his belongings. He doesn't lose them or misplace them as he did at nine. His memory related to everyday living is greatly improved. He can bring things to school—an airplane he has made, or some of his collections—and can show them to the others without disrupting the class procedures.

His teacher is important to him, even though he isn't teacher-centered. He usually respects his teacher and often accepts her word as law even more than that of his parents. He quotes her at home and holds to his evidence which may consist of his having miscopied something his teacher has written on the board. He is most aware of his teacher's outward physical appearance. He reports about her size, her hair. The girls often comment to the teacher herself about how nice her hair looks.

Tens don't like a partial teacher. They want her to like all the children, to be their friend. They express affection naturally toward their teacher, and boys may take the teacher's hand. A teacher may also express affection or give needed support by putting her arm around a child at certain times. A man teacher can still put his arm around a girl in a fatherly way. Often

Tens are known to inadvertently call their teacher "mommy" without realizing they have done so. They respond well to firmness at school as at home, although they demand their rights. And if there is to be any punishment they want it to be immediate and on the spot. They greatly dislike long-term deprivation. In a group of Tens who need very firm handling a man teacher is to be preferred.

Ten likes his teacher to schedule time and activities for him. Then he's the first to remind his teacher if she has forgotten something in the schedule. Rather than starting the day in a more formalized way he likes to start it with stories. The teacher might read from a favorite story such as *Robinson Crusoe* or *Treasure Island.* Or about the childhoods of great men which are so well portrayed in the Landmark Series. Ten wants to know about the funny things great men did, how hard they worked. And he will build up a real bond with these men when he realizes, for instance, that George Washington had difficulty in spelling.

Ten not only likes to listen to stories but he likes to tell his own, about something he has seen or heard or read about. He can talk on and on and run what he is talking about "into the ground." Talking can indeed be one of his favorite activities. Some Tens plan with their teacher to come to school on Saturday just to sit and talk, because they never get enough of it.

Ten likes to read, too. A thirty-minute reading period after lunch is a good way to relax. He is so quiet and absorbed as he reads to himself that you can hear a pin drop in the room.

Ten's interest span is short. He needs a certain amount of liberty in moving around the room. He can move quietly. He wants to get up to sharpen his pencil, go to another child, or go to the library. He handles these excursions well, without the need for permission. There is some note passing, especially between the girls. The contents of the notes are often about their work, or what they are going to do at recess, but sometimes with the more socially aware children there may be some reference to elimination (not sex) or especially to the "behind."

On the whole there is fairly easy acceptance of one sex by the other. They help each other, laugh and talk together without being aware of the other as an opposite sex. Boys accept the girls if they don't bother them. Girls on the whole have more likes or dislikes for the boys but base their judgment on some relatively superficial reason. They may dislike a boy because he's fresh and laughs at them. But there is no real sex antagonism present. In group games as with square dancing or the Virginia reel the boys are apt to separate into one group and the girls into another.

Ten takes his studies in his stride but he has his specific preferences of attack. He loves spot geography. He may know the forty-eight states and their capitals but he is vague about government, crops, soil; he adores to place states, rivers, mountains, cities, oceans on a map.

He loves to take dictation. His handwriting is often loose and sloppy. He has lost the precision he had at nine years. When he writes a book report he combines his ideas in short, choppy sentences, but with enough punch to catch the reader's interest. These book reports more often than not are about horses and dogs.

And how he loves to memorize! He masters long poems like "Paul Revere's Ride" and recites them with good expression. More time should be spent on memorizing and less on penetration in thinking. For Ten has difficulty in combining or connecting two facts. He likes to take things simply as they are. His catalogue of memorized material will stand him in good stead later—for the penetration will come.

His difficulty in connecting facts is especially evident with his arithmetic. Even when two facts are pictured out for him, he doesn't see the relationship. And yet he wants to figure out things that have reality for him. He enjoys shopping and the handling of money. And toward the end of the fifth grade he loves the challenge of oral arithmetic. He has his arithmetic facts well in hand and he enjoys the exercise of putting these to use in a long, strung-out arithmetic problem of a fluid step-to-step movement ($5 + 6 - 2 + 3 \times 5 = ?$).

In fact Ten likes oral work in general. Or he likes to grasp visually through pictorial material. This is an excellent age for educational TV. He sees well and he listens well. Then he wants to talk about it. Sometimes his curiosity is so great and his listening so facile that he becomes more interested in an adjoining group's activity than in his own. Groups in the classroom work better under partial segregation with some physical barriers between them.

Sufficient time needs to be spent out of doors or in a gym, for Ten wants to exercise his muscles. The boys more than the girls want organized sports. If given a chance, the girls may choose to group in twos or threes and chat rather than to participate in sports.

Because Ten's interest span is short, his teacher needs to plan for timely shifts, especially to break into the more sedentary demands. Singing is one of his favorite "break-in" activities. He loves to sing, is sure of his voice, and joins well with a group. But don't give him any sissy songs. Dislike of such songs may well be a strong indication that 10-year-old boys are becoming aware of their manliness.

8. Ethical Sense

Ten is no longer confined to the child world. He is coming out into the adult world, the world of grownups, of citizens. Although he is casual in himself, he is aware of some of the responsibilities that going out into the world demands. But his awareness is so nascent that he is apt to think too stiffly, without any leeway. His parents report that he has a strict moral code, a strong sense of justice and of nobility —even to the point of indignation or smug self-righteousness. He is concerned when little children are pushed around (unless it is a sibling and he is doing it). He might not accept an honor if he feels he is not worthy of it.

Although his father and his mother are the chief sources of law, he doesn't restrict himself completely to what he has learned from his parents. He is a relatively free man, ready to make some of his own decisions. Making a decision may become an enjoyable game to him, one with uncertainty and a margin of chance. He can afford to take a chance because he's willing to accept the consequences. Part of his decision is reached through what he has learned from his parents, what he

knows they might expect. Another part might be through his own "thinking things out." And there is always his conscience ready to jump in and tell him when his decision is a bad one.

Ten is more concerned about what is wrong than about what is right. The negative comes before the positive. Often he is rather puzzled and wonders about how one should decide. But since Ten may be ruled more by what he wants than by what his conscience dictates, he is willing to do what he chooses, receive a bawling out, and then judge whether his conscience was right or wrong.

Though Ten sounds very ethical, when it comes right down to actual practice he does not always come up to the mark. On the whole he is truthful, especially about big things, but he can steer a course between real truthfulness and downright lying by just not saying anything. Or he can alibi or tease a bit. And sometimes white lies are, according to him, necessary to save other people's feelings or to get what he wants. But when his mother is there and his relationship with her is good, Ten just naturally tells the truth. He can hardly help himself. His thoughts spoken to his mother are like a homing pigeon coming home to roost. And it's easier to tell or confess if he's alone with her—and after the crime is slightly distant in time.

As for taking the blame, that's not so easy. Ten's mother is blamed less by him than earlier, almost not at all. But of his siblings, any one of them nearest at hand is apt to be blamed.

Ten is definitely concerned about fairness, particularly in his parents' treatment of him and his siblings. He is polite and obedient for the most part, but when he feels certain exactions are not fair he is ready to argue it out with his parents. Sometimes, however, what is fair and what he wants are not clearly separated. He judges cheating and stealing as awful and he rarely has motivation toward either, since he is content in himself and not desirous to excel.

He has more definite ideas about swearing than drinking. He doesn't mind grownups drinking as long as they don't drink too much. (Except for the puritanical Tens who declare that their mothers and fathers never touch liquor, though this may be quite untrue.) But as for swearing, he is more critical. Girls are especially outspoken. They think swearing isn't nice and it makes them "feel awful" when they hear it. Boys also condemn it but confess to past misdemeanors and at times to a hankering to do a little swearing themselves.

9. Philosophic Outlook

TIME AND SPACE

The casual attitude of Ten gives us a clue that he has things well in hand, that he has an inner source of motivation and potential for action. This ability to achieve is particularly evident in his control of time and space. He is now more the ruler than the ruled. He controls time more than he is controlled by it.

His concepts are still rather static and specific but they serve his purposes very well. Time is specifically the clock to him. Time is hours, minutes, seconds. He may also conceive of wider time, but it is still specifically related to days, past or future, time as told by the sky or the sun, time of the

year as recorded in seasons, or time of the century. One Ten sums up the wider view for us: "I try to imagine what happened years ago and what differences are now and what they will be several thousand years from now." It is evident that it is a boy speaking, and—who knows?—perhaps a possible future scientist.

Time at Ten is often related to happenings—"time things happen," "what you do." A sense of relativity may invade the time sense. Ten projects himself in feeling toward what he is about to do. Thus he might choose to be early to school, late to the doctor's office, and just on time when playing with a friend.

Although Ten does not yet have much feeling for the passing of time, he may grasp the idea that time might vary, that sometimes there is not enough time, and again too much time. He may have too much time during a vacation period and not enough time to do his homework. Thus he has the varying experience of: "Sometimes I'm crowded and rushed and sometimes I'm not."

Ten's own management of time is so improved that it is a great relief to everyone concerned, especially to his parents. He is pretty good at getting places on time, especially getting to school and coming home in the late afternoon. He doesn't use his watch as he did at an earlier age, because he has usually lost it. He may even prefer to look at a clock or to ask the time of someone else. Maybe it's the coming of dusk that gives him his clue. But within him is growing an orientation toward time—a new sense of responsibility, a responsibility to the requests of others, to the school, or to the home. When a task is demanded of him he is often a stickler for the exact amount of time that is requested of him. If he practices the piano for half an hour, he starts on the dot of time and ends on the prescribed dot. Practice begun at 6:17 ends at 6:47.

Ten's conquest of immediate space has the same success as his conquest of immediate time. It may seem like a simple task, but his ability to meet his mother downtown at a specific place is an achievement of no small note for a child of this age. It declares the beginning of a new freedom. He still needs the tie of the specific place and the single demand, but he arrives and completes his mission.

Space is rather specific in Ten's mind for "space is where things are" or "space is to put houses on." The architect-minded and home-oriented Ten frequently mentions houses and home. Even when he thinks of outer space, he may relate it to "a place where nothing is—no buildings—nothing." As time might be defined by Ten as the length between two points on the clock, so also space may be defined as "the space between two different things." And with all of Ten's thinking he includes both the very specific "here and now" and the wide concept of a generality. Thus in a nutshell Ten says, "Space is occupied by one thing or another or just nothing, air or whatever is up there."

DEATH AND DEITY

Ten, like Five, is related to the "here and now." He thinks in terms of reality. He wants facts. Neither death nor Deity absorbs his interest. He accepts the fact that all people die and that from his observation and experience death comes much later than at his age. You die mainly when you grow old. Therefore he queries—why think about it now when there are so many other things to think about? In his own words he sums it up, "Well, I think it's just something that's gotta happen so I don't worry about it." The important facts to Ten are that you die and get buried. "All this mournfulness and putting flowers on a grave" may have little meaning to Ten. "A man's dead and that's that."

He used to be bothered about death and what might happen after death when he was younger, but now he accepts what he knows, though he is interested in what might happen. He knows that after death the body disintegrates in time or "mummifies," but he doesn't dwell on this in his mind. Other changes that may occur after death he might try to speculate about. Ten might think the dead "just sit there and watch what's going on." He may conjecture that, "They don't have to be fed. They don't talk." Or he may be concerned that the dead "don't feel anything. They can't understand each other's feeling." As for heaven, that's a little beyond him because he "hasn't been there." But if there is a heaven, most Tens would rather think that both good and bad people could go there. For in Ten's eyes "the bad aren't as bad as they appear."

Ten's ideas about God are beginning to receive the same tests of his own experience and of known facts as his ideas of death have passed through. However, many Tens are still strongly influenced by the concepts of their parents and the religious culture they have come in contact with.

Even though Ten may believe in God, he doesn't "think much about it." He may even isolate God as a fact as he says, "I know He *is* whether I think about it or not." Those Tens who believe are more apt to think of God as a spirit or an invisible man than as a real person. They no longer blame God for things that happen to them either as a cause of illness or misfortune.

Rather, God can become a partner. God may become someone Ten can talk to. He may still say his regular prayers, but then if he "wants to talk to someone especially about something" he makes up his own prayers. The finding of some lost object such as a lost music book as he thinks about God can be very real proof to Ten that God must exist. Anyway, he does feel that God makes him better, that He affects him personally.

His belief in God does not, however, necessarily make him enthusiastic about Sunday school. Some who used to go no longer do so. Some may still attend because their parents make them or because they enjoy singing in the choir. However, as at all ages, there is that small nucleus of girls who especially love Sunday school and are faithful attendants.

CHAPTER FIVE

Year Eleven

‗‗

MATURITY PROFILE

AT HIS classic best the 10-year-old presents such an ample picture of equipoise, that he seems to be a finished product of Nature's handiwork. In a measure this is true, for childhood at ten comes to a kind of consummation.

But soon new growth forces assert their creative energy and childhood gives way to new dispensations, which go by the name of adolescence. Year Eleven truly marks the beginning of adolescence for it brings forth so many tokens of the growing-up process which in the course of another decade will take the child to the margins of maturity.

What are these tokens? They are new patterns and new intensities of behavior. The erstwhile complaisant 10-year-old begins to display unaccustomed forms of self-assertion, of curiosity, and of sociability. He is restive, investigative, talkative. He wriggles. He wriggles a great deal. He is not ill at ease, but he likes to be in motion and on the go. He is unceasingly hungry. His vast appetite for food is matched by his appetite for experience. He is increasingly inquisitive about adults, for he is growing up and will be one himself some day. He observes them with a new keenness; he may even mimic them to deepen his understanding. He does not like to be alone. He has all sorts of devices and ruses for exploring interpersonal relationships with his parents and his peers.

He loves to argue, but, as one mother commented, *you* cannot argue with *him*; he will not let you. Another mother with benevolent humor summed up by saying that her 11-year-old had "two life hobbies—eating and talking." With her humor she could also say, "She is difficult, but she is wonderful!" With her insight she could recognize that this self-assertiveness might not be sheer impudence, but a callow attempt to gain a bit more maturity and prestige.

With his bubbling spontaneity he makes multiple forays and thrusts into his personal environment, blithely unaware that he is "difficult" and "rude." He feels impulsions and moods which he has never experienced before. The even tenor of the yesteryear seems to be vanishing, but to the amazement of the household he can on occasion be "divine" away from home. Without condoning all his intensities and inconsistencies, we can readily acknowledge the profoundness of his inexperience in the new emotional areas of interpersonal behavior. He is a veritable tyro in these more complex realms. Emotions are structures which need to undergo growth and organization. Since he is in the foothills of adolescence, and the terrain is new, there is much to grow and much to organize.

The emotional life of the 11-year-old often has peaks of intensity. He can fly into a rage on short notice. He is subject to bursts of laughter and to variable moods. The moods come and go in ripples and sometimes in diurnal rhythm: mopish and grumpy in the morning; bright and cheery in the afternoon; good days alternating with gloomy; peevishness when there is too much to do with no time for play and not enough time for sleep. His emotions rise with swift crescendos; his voice also rises precipitously, for he yells on occasion so intensely that he arouses counter-yells; he swoops through a room uttering threats. These outbreaks call for firm and skillful handling. They cause endless irritation if they are regarded too sensitively or too leniently.

Such behaviors actually reflect the immaturity of new emotional developments which are now in their beginning stages. There is after all a quality of innocence and of naïveté about many of the 11-year-old emotional reactions. If this quality is realistically recognized, the accompanying irritations will greatly lessen. His ardors and enthusiasms likewise can be accepted even if they are not modulated. His angers are not reversions to preschool tantrums. New emotional patterns are in the process of development; they are not simple throwbacks to an earlier age. They are growth phenomena which have their primary origins within the organism rather than in the patterns of the culture.

For the organism is indeed in a state of change, which is not limited to gains in height and weight, but which involves the entire action system of the child. Even physiological functions like temperature control become unsteady. The 11-year-old has a way of feeling either too hot or too cold. He fluctuates between extremes. He fatigues readily. These are not signs of mere physical weakness, but are part of an all-pervasive process of developmental reorganization which embraces his total behavior.

To appreciate the constructive essence of his richly diversified behavior traits, they must be envisaged in terms of inherent growth. Even his negativeness, his importuning, his "arguments," have a positive function which furthers his penetrations into reality. His exuberance, his free-ranging curiosity, his engaging, outgoing friendliness also reflect the new ferments in his changing organism.

By such evidences he is more than a precursor of adolescence. He is an adolescent in the making. To gain a more concrete picture of the maturity traits of Eleven we need only to observe the characteristic ways in which he meets various life situations at home, at school, and abroad in the community.

Take for example his responses to the Year Eleven interview, a situation which is highly congenial to his current psychology. At nine years of age a comparable interview would scarcely have been possible. Now at eleven he meets you more than halfway and takes delight in the occasion. His candor and communicativeness are so great that the interviewer simply needs to listen to his free-wheeling conversation. He is politely factual, detailed, earnest, sincere, friendly. But he also gives full rein to his impelling curiosity; he may even rise from his chair to roam about the room in a rummaging manner, to touch and explore the physical environment, to manipulate the typewriter, to ask miscellaneous questions, particular and general, about the uses and meaning of this and that.

If he stays in his chair, he expends quantities of energy in postural activity. He wriggles with great versatility. He twists, bounces, and moves all over the chair, swings a foot across the arm, retracts his leg, knocks his knees together, bends over and pulls at his shoes. Concurrently he grimaces, cocks his head, and interjects comments and bursts of laughter. His activity embraces the whole body, extending from head to foot. Yet the movements are not "nervous" in quality or import. It is as though the entire psycho-motor system of the 11-year-old was richly supplied with sparking facilities. So he reacts in a multiplex rather than a complex manner, that is, at numerous points, with light regard for their relationships.

This multifarious reactivity makes him seem dynamic and often imparts charm to his companionship. The interview, accordingly, was enjoyed by both parties concerned and spontaneously the occasion took on the character of a social visit. The visual examination likewise released the sociable inquisitiveness of Eleven. He was intrigued by the technical optical instruments and asked many enlivening questions about the devices and procedures. The developmental examination is more restrictive, but it too released similar demeanors, in the form of smiles, comments, rolling of eyes, and in postural permutations. The latter sometimes expanded into a wide-spreading relaxational stretch of torso and all four limbs. Demeanors are difficult to describe, but they contain many clinical clues to the maturity and status of the individual. Hence Eleven "acts" a little differently from Ten or Thirteen. Experienced workers with children become increasingly aware of such distinctive maturity differences.

The fact that Eleven is often on his best or better behavior away from home is not altogether to his discredit. It at least demonstrates latent capacities! In fact, even though he is reputed to be the instigator of turmoil at home, he has strong feelings of attachment and loyalty for his family. He has been known to say, "I'm a free person. Why do I have to do what the family tells me?" But he enjoys nothing more than to be in the thick of family life if things get dull. He is not an isolationist. If he is lucky enough to have a room of his own, he does not retire to it. He gravitates to the family group, as though magnetized by them. They may call him a pest if he renews his insistent interruptions, but he may also become the life of the party, because he has a talent for gaiety and laughter. It is well to have him around, whether for better or for worse. In his zeal, and in the callow naïveté of his conduct, he can be quite unaware of the extent to which he interferes with the smoothness of family harmony. Remember, he likes belonging to a family and he likes the idea of having relatives, including grandmothers and grandfathers.

Much of the ineptness of his behavior can be ascribed to sheer inexperience in making interpersonal adjustments within a culture which is changing as he himself changes. The quarreling with siblings, the rebelliousness against parents, and the resistance to imposed tasks and proprieties are largely manifestations of early adolescent self-assertiveness and self-absorption.

Eleven is more adept at challenge than at response. As he matures he will bring the two into improved balance. But at his present stage of development he tends to set up challenging resistances in order to evoke responses which provide a leverage to work against. This is not malice aforethought, nor simple obstinacy. It is a developmental expedient which he uses, often very clumsily, to define his own status and that of others.

He also has more amiable methods of approach for extending his knowledge of human behavior. He likes to initiate a genial interplay with another person in order to observe the reactions to his probing overtures. This kind of challenge is a natural, almost instinctive, manifestation of the dawn of adolescence. It is part of the total game of life. In our emphasis on book learning we tend to forget that children are not born with a precise knowledge of human nature. The adolescent must learn to project into the life of others, to sharpen and to satisfy his fellow feelings.

As early as age eleven sons and daughters begin to see their parents as individual people whose personalities are reflected in behavior. The parents in our study group report that almost suddenly the 11-year-old becomes very critical of them. Affection does not vanish; but there is an excess of fault-finding, argumentativeness, name calling, yelling, talking back, and dramatic rudeness. Mothers appear to attract sharper and more frequent criticism than do fathers. A mother can be more patient and perhaps more tolerant because she recalls that her child passed through a comparable stage of contrary behavior in the shift from 5-year-old goodness to 6-year-old verbal violence. The contemporary culture has not worked out adequate controls for outbursts of violence, but fortunately the 11-year-old, under normal conditions, retains strong feelings of loyalty and attachment for his home. His turbulence does not spring from antagonism to the family life.

Adjustment to school is in some ways simpler and smoother than adjustment to home. At school he does not have to contend with siblings, parents, relatives, and domestic chores. He likes to meet his peers, to mingle, to tangle, and to compete with them. He is sensitive to the dynamics of the group, but is not necessarily dominated thereby. True to his self-assurance, he can say sweepingly, "I disagree with school!" Actually, under normal conditions, he is a keen, enthusiastic pupil and an eager co-worker, with insatiable curiosity. He reveals his promising potentials when he details the attributes of a good teacher. She must be "smart," interesting, firm but fair, humorous, understanding—and (who is speaking?) she must not yell!

In his school work Eleven shows great concentration when he works competitively with one group against another group, and decidedly so when the opposing group consists of mere girls. His intellectual processes are factual and not very academic. His thinking is relatively concrete and specific. Accordingly he still likes his extracurricular comics. Being geared to action, he takes to TV. In school he favors information by story form, in which one action leads inevitably to another and another. He is eclectic rather than reflective, and pays less attention to contexts and relationships. Perhaps he is laying the foundations for later conceptual thinking. At any rate his curiosity is boundless both in and out of school.

The out-of-school activities of Eleven are diversified and fluid. There is a great deal of plain "messing around," which satisfies his inveterate tendency to stir up interactions with his playmates—teasing, taunting, brief embattled tussles, mock hostility, mock conciliation, and interludes of warm friendliness. This kind of playful activity, with its endless variations, fills much idle time and doubtless contributes to the organization of maturing social behavior, both in boys and girls.

Girls have their own devices for defining emotional patterns. One girl commented that she had a host of friends: "I like everybody, but we have to quarrel to break up the smoothness." Another girl remarked, "Couldn't I just say who *isn't* my best friend?" Loosely formed clubs furnish a stage for the discussion of interpersonal relationships. There is much plotting, scheming, including, and excluding—all presumably for the expression and maturing of the emotions!

Boys gather in similar self-organized clubs, which have a fragile existence despite the emphasis on payment of dues. Without supervision such clubs easily get out of hand. Fortunately, baseball is the top favorite sport of this age. It is an ideal agency for the socialization of the 11-year-old, both with and without supervision.

The reciprocal civilizing influence of the opposite sex has not yet come into play. Only occasionally are girls admitted to participate in a baseball game. Most of the boys in our group express a neutral opinion about girls. "We don't mind girls," says one spokesman, "but we don't usually play with them. I guess we would if we had to." Many girls are now in an extreme anti-boy stage. A concise spokesman for her sex simply states, "They're all pests."

Nevertheless amenities keep on germinating. Boys quarrel with each other, but the quarrel is only half of the pattern; making up is the other half. Girls get intensely "mad *at* each other," but in due course they manage to speak *with* each other again. This sequence of warm antagonism followed by conciliation occurs so frequently and so spontaneously that it can be regarded as a developmental mechanism for the organization of the emotions. The squabbles are more than childish; because the 11-year-old is becoming a youth, and his emotions are undergoing a fresh growth toward maturity. His friendships take on a new depth and quality. He is more discerning about the individual characteristics of his companions. He takes a special delight in a visit which culminates in spending the night with a chosen friend. Among girls there is considerable spending of the night with each other.

Such away-from-home experiences are part of a gradual process in which parents as well as child participate—the so-called process of adolescent "emancipation." The term *emancipate* harks back to Roman law which defined it as the release of a child from paternal power. In modern life it means the long, progressive detachment by which the child finally attains sufficient maturity to be self-dependent and on his own.

Needless to say, Eleven is still in the very early stages of this process. He has more self-reliance than he had during Year Ten; he claims and enjoys the right to make certain decisions of his own. It is a healthy sign of mental growth when he feels a new freedom of moral choice within himself. We give him credit for his good attempts. He does indeed try to tell the truth. But if it is too difficult to do so, he may make a dubious denial and protect himself by crossing his fingers—a bit of magic which reminds us that morality of conduct is subject to the innate forces of growth. Eleven has a conscience which is growing in many directions. We have already noted his zeal for fairness and his abhorrence of cheating. The warmth of his attitudes may be greater than their depth. He is impulsive and lacks perspective to such a degree that he is perplexed by and even unaware of his emotional turmoil. There is something poignant about his bewildered, exclamatory question: "What do you mean, 'my rude outbursts'?" He is unaware of his rudeness.

It is not strange that parents themselves feel confused and frustrated by some of the intenser moments of behavior which contrast so strangely with the pleasant poise of Year Ten. Teachers, too, occasionally are amazed to see the deterioration in conduct which may take place when their relatively agreeable pupils of the classroom revert to the uninhibited interpersonal freedom of the playground. To interpret the behavior of a dynamic 11-year-old with all its ebullitions, its paradoxical inconsistencies and fluctuations, it must be viewed in the perspective of the developmental cycle. Such perspective does not automatically solve immediate problems of management, but it does favor wise and optimistic measures of control.

In perspective, Year Eleven proves to be an epochal year of transition and beginnings. The total organism, physiological as well as psychological, undergoes elaborating transformations. The subtle alterations in body chemistry and in the structural growth of the nervous system are concealed from our inspection, but they manifest themselves unmistakably in changing forms and modes of behavior. Many of the behavior changes come so gradually that they escape notice; others erupt so drastically that the culture reacts with a startled awareness. The exuberance of growth expresses itself in positive as well as negative signs. Symptoms of maturing talent and giftedness emerge. Individuality becomes increasingly defined, both with respect to favorable and unfavorable traits.

A few superior 11-year-olds preserve at an advanced level the balance and the integrative harmony of the previous year. More typically, however, the 11-year-old demeanor and deportment show a drift from old moorings, responsive to the hidden undercurrents of development. The contentment, the self-containedness, and free give-and-take of typical Ten, yield way to the multiform dynamic impulsions which we have outlined—a new self-assertive expansion, restless searchings, and probing thrusts; proud, touchy defenses; variable moods, dark and gay; flashes of anger and affection; active and effervescent curiosities; eager identifications, with home, school, and friends; low moments of discouragement; high moments of desire and aspiration.

These are traits of transition which betoken the onset of adolescence. Artlessness, ardor, and sheer awkwardness combine in patterns which signify a vigorous process of growing up. This is an optimal time to become acquainted with the basic psychology of adolescent development.

The ensuing Year Twelve will throw its shaft of light on the developmental logic of the immaturities of Year Eleven. The constructive essence of growth will be revealed in the emergence of new patterns of reasonableness and responsibility which were latent, and indeed partly visible, in the growthsomeness of Year Eleven.

MATURITY TRAITS

1. Total Action System

The incessant bodily activity and expenditure of energy that is so evident and often so hard to cope with at eleven is the outer manifestation of inner changes and an inner seething. Though some boys maintain their 10-year-old poise, poise is not a hallmark of this age. Eleven tends more to burst, to bounce, to throw himself around. His activity, especially when he is in any way confined (as sitting in a chair in an interview), is so constant that one almost becomes seasick watching him. He bounces up and down in the chair. He rocks back and forth. He pushes the chair around on the floor if the floor covering allows. Suddenly he will jerk his head or whole body forward, tipping his chair with him. Or he will wave his arms over his head, and clasp his hands on his head. He stretches. His hands seem to be in constant activity. If he has in his hand an object, such as a ball or a glasses case, he repeatedly tosses it up and down.

As he grows restless he stands, stretches, wants to shift to another chair or to lie on a couch. His legs are no less active than his arms. Often he holds his knees wide apart and then bats them together. Or he fiddles with his sock or his shoe.

His face is as active as all the rest of him. There is a remarkable play of expression across it. His eyes sparkle and are very mobile as they shift from side to side, then suddenly dart toward the person they are talking to. The eyebrows may be lifted up and down. Lips are often pursed or the tongue protrudes, usually to one side.

Eleven frequently bursts into laughter, especially when he is unsure of himself. He talks with speed, often emphasizing certain words. There is a lack of restraint in his voice, and a tendency toward a nasal upward inflection. Eleven can be quite noisy and can readily outshout another. With this constant, bursting energy, it is no wonder that some Elevens need to tap dance around the house or have an urge to do tumbling acts.

HEALTH

Though Eleven's health may be quite good, there is a tendency toward an increased number of colds, or grippe, ear infections, sinus involvement, and occasionally even pneumonia. The tendency for an infection to spread, as into ears and lungs or even into the meninges as in mumps meningitis, is a quality of the age as it was at the earlier stage of five and a half to six years.

Eleven's whole physical mechanism is very labile. All of a sudden he may feel intolerably hot and fling off his coat. With any overexertion or overexcitement, the allergic children may develop asthma. Girls are likely to vomit with colds or overexcitement. Fatigue is more pronounced than it has been and may be evident in an increased need for sleep. A fairly common complaint at eleven is that their feet hurt them.

Many of Eleven's somatic complaints are valid, especially those about headaches, eye pains, and twitching (all of which are often temporarily relieved by aspirin). But some Elevens tend to be rather hypochondriacal. They go to bed at the least sign of a cold or the slightest injury. They hear about other's illnesses and develop similar symptoms.

TENSIONAL OUTLETS

The tensional outlets of Eleven involve their increased motor activity. There may be more specific blinking of the eyes, sniffling of the nose, or contortion of the face into grimacing. At times, a peculiar smile may appear when Eleven is self-conscious. Eleven may return to an earlier stage of falling down and dropping or breaking things without meaning to do so.

VISION

The visual picture has changed considerably at eleven as has also Eleven's awareness of his vision. He knows when his vision blurs, especially after a long period of reading. He often reports that he gets headaches and blurring when he looks from a near to a far object.

There is a general loosening up of the visual mechanism and an improvement in the focusing ability. There is less danger of nearsightedness starting to develop at this age than there was at nine and ten years. The improvement in this "visceral" focusing movement, occurring simultaneously with Eleven's increase in the "visceral" or feeling responses, is suggestive of some pervasive underlying relationship.

In the visual test situation, Eleven shows that he is developing fairly good skills in ocular co-ordination, binocular fusion, depth vision, and visual discrimination. The more common difficulties are likely to occur in the "near field" of vision, with unsteady eye movements, variable fixation, suppression of vision in one eye, and reduction in depth perception. When such difficulties are present, Eleven is more likely to report visual symptoms than he was earlier.

With focusing difficulties and the reporting of blurring, the help of convex lenses for nearby work is often indicated. But Eleven does not want to wear glasses all the time. In fact, he often thinks it would be "terrible," but he will accept them for close-up work with benefit. Eleven might be helped by visual training, but he is not a co-operative candidate and often the time and effort spent on trying to help him achieve better visual functioning isn't worth the effort. Nor does he profit sufficiently to carry it through.

PHYSICAL DEVELOPMENT AND SEX AWARENESS—GIRLS

In contrast to the 11-year-old boys, who appear to be a relatively uniform group in their physical structure, the girls at eleven show marked individual variations, especially when the extremes of the slender and the heavy girls are compared. Similar extremes are also evident in their sex development. Some show no trace of sexual development, retaining the less differentiated form of childhood, whereas a few physically advanced girls already show the rounded contours and the physiological functioning of full adolescence.

The middle group of girls, however, shows a fairly consistent picture. By the end of this year all but a few have some pubic hair. The pelvic area broadens, both in underlying bone structure and in the tissue over this, thus showing, in many girls, a prominence at both the upper and lower corners of the pelvis (iliac and trochanteric crests) with a hollow between the two and a narrowed waist above giving the classic feminine "vase shape."

The great majority of girls have started their period of faster height growth and nearly a third have reached the most rapid phase of this cycle. Already the average girl has achieved about 90 per cent of her adult stature and close to 50 per cent of what she will weigh at age twenty-one.

Breast development continues as the area surrounding the nipples elevates to form a conelike projection on an otherwise flat chest. Sometimes a hard lump near the nipple is the first evidence of enlargement. Often one breast develops faster than the other one. Even the girls without definite breast enlargement usually show a greater fullness and softening of the pectoral region.

Girls show an absorbed interest in these developments—not only of their own but of other girls their age. They experience sensitiveness of the breast region, especially around the nipples, and may complain of pain. They watch the changes in their breasts—the initial spreading of the nipples, and the slow enlargement of the breasts. They are aware when one breast is "ahead of" the other one. Their interest can be so intense that it becomes a nightly game of check-up. Many dream of the day when they will be advanced enough in their breast development to wear a brassière. An occasional girl may wish to wear a brassière and silk panties when she goes to bed, projecting into a time that is to come. Such a time may seem sadly distant to the most flat-chested girls, who feel left out and often inquire about "falsies." And yet the very few whose breast development is most advanced may also feel out of step and ashamed, and may cry when a brassière becomes a necessity.

By mid-eleven to twelve the tighter T-shirts are being replaced by blouses. Soon the coveted brassière is worn. Fortunately, the manufacturers have recognized the desire for a very small brassière, so even the small-breasted can qualify when contemporaries check up as to which ones are wearing brassières. Not all girls, however, are proud of their breast development. There are those who are embarrassed, who hunch their shoulders in a vain effort to hide the inescapable evidence of development. But by most girls this initial embarrassment will soon have been surmounted, and the urge to be a "sweater girl" at twelve and thirteen will be far more absorbing. Underarm

hair, though present in only a few girls, may cause similar embarrassment. This situation, fortunately, can be remedied by shaving, until others have developed it, too.

Though knowledge about menstruation may not have clicked into understanding before, it is now better comprehended—probably because of its very imminence. Eleven is generally looking forward more positively to menstruation than she was at ten. But there are still those who shun the thought. Eleven is interested in sanitary napkins and how you wear them. She may have once thought the dispensers in washrooms contained paper towels, but her friends' laughter soon informed her that she had the wrong answer. Some Elevens feel more comfortable if they have tried on a sanitary napkin and belt. They may plan to wear one all the time when they are twelve, to be prepared. They wonder if you also wear them at night. Only a small percentage of girls start to menstruate in the eleventh year. There are, however, momentary premonitory signs of a sudden sharp abdominal pain or nausea in the morning.

Girls are not as interested in "smutty" stories or in observing animal intercourse as boys are. They are interested in knowing more about human intercourse, though they are becoming more reticent in talking about it with their mothers. It is important to see that they do not harbor any false ideas. They need to be told about the separation of the urinary from the sexual system in the male.

PHYSICAL DEVELOPMENT AND SEX AWARENESS—BOYS

Eleven-year-old boys in their physical development make up a far more uniform group than do the girls because so few show outward signs of sexual maturation. In this year puberal changes appear in only the most advanced group of boys. About a quarter of the boys have started on their rapid acceleration of height growth, though even for most of these it is not yet far enough along to be very noticeable. Still, the average boy has achieved a little more than 80 per cent of his adult height, though less than half the weight he will have at age twenty-one.

A definite "fat period" occurs in some boys, with an accumulation of adipose tissue giving them a "blown-up" look. The accumulation of adipose tissue over the hips and chest, especially in the breast area, is quite embarrassing to some boys. These boys tend to avoid tight-fitting T-shirts, wearing a looser top shirt to cover up. When they are in swimming they may try to mask their chest contour by assuming rather unnatural-looking postures, such as stretching their arms up and out.

Even in this well-padded group, a striking feature shown by Elevens is an apparent increase in bone size. This is not a fragile "boniness" but a seemingly heavy growth of bone which brings the skeletal structure into prominence. Even where overlying tissue obscures a sharp outline, one senses an increase in the framework beneath. The chest area especially seems to reveal this growth, with shoulders, shoulder blades, collarbone, and rib cage more in evidence than at ten.

Genital size has started to advance more rapidly for the more accelerated quarter of boys. Some have developed short, downy pubic hair, and an occasional boy has already moved on to the next stage of longer straight pubic hair.

Many are not too willing to discuss sex matters with their parents. They may either not ask any questions or still ask them at an inopportune time, thus showing their immaturity.

Boys' interest in sex is more stimulated by the behavior of animals than is girls' interest. Boys are interested in comparing the "insides" of animals with the insides of humans. When they begin to comprehend the growth and birth of a baby they sum up their response with "amazing." They, along with the girls, are interested to know how the "seed is planted from the father to the mother," though it is difficult for some to comprehend this. Knowledge about animals helps them to understand. But they may still be surprised that human reproduction is similar to animal reproduction, and at this stage of their understanding both boys and girls are apt to think that it "sounds nasty."

And yet it is surprising to find that some 11-year-old boys are beginning to understand the difference between the animal and human level. They begin to realize that a human being exercises greater selectivity in his choice of a mate, and that love is often a basis of this selection. They begin to recognize the personal relationships involved, to see that living with a person includes more than mating. Eleven is beginning to realize that marriage is also an institution, but that you don't have to be married to have a baby. A year earlier he might have thought that the marital state was essential to having babies. He still has more to learn about the functions of marriage and the importance of the family for the birth and rearing of a baby.

Some boys are becoming more aware of girls as girls. They are more conscious of the girls' figures, and may remark about "the way they walk— they wiggle their rears!" Boys respond to a pretty girl. They are curious about why girls sometimes don't go in swimming. A few know about menstruation and are curious about sanitary napkins.

Some boys are curious about others who seem less masculine. Sometimes the more slender, immature, slow-growing boys, or the chubby, broad-hipped, non-athletic ones, may be called "fairies." The boys who use this epithet and those who receive it often have little insight into its significance. They comprehend it in a way, but they do not receive a strong emotional impact. Many of these slow-growing boys who suggest a trace of girlishness at eleven eventually turn out to be more dominantly masculine than the very ones who have thrown names at them.

Erections occur with some frequency among many 11-year-olds. The sources of stimulation for such erections may seem almost haphazard to the adult; they include general excitement of any kind, not necessarily sexual, physical movements, such as bike riding or rope climbing, conversations, pictures, literature, daydreams, and the individual's own body. Over the next few years responsiveness becomes more selective and specific. Masturbation is a phenomenon known to many boys and experimented with, casually or more purposefully, by perhaps half.

As at all ages, boys are more prone than are girls to tell dirty jokes and to use special words referring to sex and elimination. They are now more aware of some of the implications involved, and may know that "the kids who laugh too loud don't know the meaning of the words."

The sixth grade, when the child is bordering on twelve years, is a good time to help in his understanding about sex by means of well-tried films. Boys and girls are still able to watch a movie about sex together and discuss it afterward. It is wise for the parents of these children to view the same movie, either with the children or separately, so that they will know the source of the children's information. The question period after the viewing of the film should, however, be for children and teacher alone, and perhaps for the sexes separately, depending on the film. A shift from the questions more common in fifth grade about two-headed calves and Siamese twins is very evident in sixth grade. The sixth grader is thinking less about the freakish side of reproduction and now has a wholesome interest in questions about his own body, in his own personal development. A movie about menstruation is very helpful for girls. The sixth grader also asks many intelligent questions about heredity, about what makes blue eyes or red hair. Such books as Schoenfeld's *You and Heredity* are fascinating to the child who is asking this type of question.

2. Self-Care and Routines

EATING

Appetite. "She has two hobbies in her

life," one mother reports, "eating and talking." This particular 11-year-old can be joined by many other Elevens who "live to eat," who eat all day long, and who can be kept track of on their stealthy journeys for food by the sharp sound of the opening and closing of the modern icebox door. Some Elevens become so ravenously hungry that they are compelled to raid the icebox, the cookie jar, or other sources of food. They often have fads and eat large quantities of one food. Five bananas before dinner, the entire contents of a full cookie jar, a whole fried chicken, or three helpings of potatoes. Some fathers feel it is impossible, almost indecent for their sons to be so hungry and so uncontrolled. But likely as not with some Elevens a ravenous appetite might be followed by a poor or finicky one. Fluctuations seem to come according to mood—"Some days can't get a thing down—other days I'm hungry as a bear." The sight of a certain disliked food may also suddenly take away their appetite.

Eleven knows that uncomfortable sensation of feeling full. He may feel so full that he will have to refuse his dessert. This reminds us of himself earlier at six years of age. Also reminiscent of this younger age is the refusal, especially by some girls, to eat breakfast. Not only may appetite be gone at the day's beginning but nausea may be present. These children are not necessarily the before-bed snackers.

Eleven knows that there may be a relationship between how much he eats and how fat he is. But he is also aware of the discrepancy that it doesn't matter how much some other children eat, they will not put on weight. On the whole, however, weight gains are considerable and have a rather close relationship to intake of food. Dieting is discussed and planned for but it is still mainly in the talking stage. One group of 11-year-old girls decided they would stop eating sweet desserts (except ice cream and whipped cream!). "We meant to stop," they earnestly insisted, "but honestly we never got that far."

Preferences and refusals. Eleven's emotionality is expressed even in his responses to certain foods. He adores this food and despises that one. He dramatically throws himself into his reporting by grimacing about his dislikes, licking his lips about his likes, spreading imaginary sauces as he reports about his favorite meat. He bolsters up his own hates by including "a lot of the kids" who feel as he does. Undoubtedly there is a great deal of group talk about food at this age.

Though preferences and refusals are strong, there can be a changing around. The food liked today may be the food refused tomorrow. Often these shifts are hard to fathom. Eggs may be refused after the child learns that a baby chick grows from the yolk. A scrambled egg, however, may remove this association. Parents need to have respect for some of these seemingly irrational refusals until the child works out new relationships of thinking.

Though food refusals are not much of a problem with Eleven, when he does refuse he does so with vigor. But at the same time he accepts a certain social responsibility when he eats away from home or when guests are present. He says he's pretty good at eating things he doesn't like. He at least makes a gesture of accepting. "Sometimes to be very sporty I take one pea [gestures] and put it on my plate."

SLEEP

Bedtime. Bedtime and Eleven are not congenial. He can be surrounded by clocks and watches but he never sees them. Nine may be his theoretical bedtime, but 9:30 is more often his actual bedtime. There is much dissatisfaction with a too early bedtime, and Eleven is ready to fight a battle for his 11-year-old rights since he is fully informed as to when "the other kids" go to bed. His bedtime may vary according to the things he has to do, e.g., his homework, a TV or radio program, a book he is reading. And he utilizes any excuse he can find to delay it.

Many Elevens should go to bed earlier than they think desirable. When they are allowed to stay up later, they wilt the next day. But there are other Elevens who could stay up all night without being too tired the next day. They are usually the readers, and if not caught will read until 12 or 1 A.M. Eleven should be allowed a certain amount of latitude in his bedtime especially over the weekend, but there usually comes that inevitable time when his parent has to "crack down." Greater latitude during a vacation period allows Eleven to assert his demand to feel "grown-up."

Most Elevens stay awake for at least a half hour before they drop off to sleep. Some show anxiety when they are in a room alone. They often would like to share a room with a sibling. Things they don't want to think about such as robbers may come to mind. But on the whole Eleven daydreams— possibly about airplanes, his "best crack-ups with the controls jammed." Or maybe about his "red stallion, Flame. He's a killer." Or possibly he tames wild animals which have gotten loose and then he keeps them for house pets.

Sleep. When Eleven is asleep, however, he's usually dead asleep. He can sleep through thunder and lightning. You could blow horns in his ears without waking him. He himself says not even an atom bomb could awake him.

Morning. The 10-year-old ease of getting up in the morning is no longer so common. Some mornings Eleven may feel like getting up, but other mornings he feels "kinda dead about it." Often he is peevish and cranky when he awakes. Even the early risers like to relax in bed for a while. More often than not, Eleven has to be awakened twice or more and finally be yanked or dragged out of bed. Even the most co-operative Elevens may need the stimulus of hot and cold water on their faces to wake them up.

BATH

With so much of Eleven's behavior growing more difficult, it is both surprising and gratifying to see a decreased resistance to bathing. Eleven still, however, finds bathing a bother and wishes to bathe only if he has the time. Though he is less often dragged to the bathroom, he still needs to be reminded, urged, prodded, or poked.

There are some self-motivating forces within him to bathe but these appear only off and on. Eleven bathes for a special reason. He may bathe for two or three nights in a row on his own and then not again for ten to fourteen days. Boys often prefer showers because of the ease and speed of taking them. Girls are beginning to enjoy the physical sensation and warmth of the bath and happily include the esthetic accompaniment of sweet-smelling soap, lush towels, and possibly cologne after the bath. Some Elevens scrub vigorously, but may restrict this excess to the legs, forgetting their ears, face, and neck.

But Eleven is by no means independent in his bathing. He often needs help in drawing his tub. Girls still need help in rinsing their hair, though the use of showers facilities this process.

This is the age when the dawning awareness of a new social self seems to be centered in both the hair and the teeth. Both boys and girls are suddenly very aware of their hair, though only at times. Teeth, earlier neglected, are now brushed more often. Some are said to be good about their teeth, a few proud of their teeth, and an occasional Eleven might feel guilty if he hasn't brushed his teeth. This new awareness of self may extend to the fingernails. At least there is an awareness of their being dirty, but not sufficient to clean and groom them.

CLOTHES AND CARE OF ROOM

Along with a sporadic improvement in bathing and combing of hair, Eleven shows a greater interest in clothes. The more immature boys can readily be spotted by their marked dislike of dressing up, their clinging to the same old blue shirt which they would like to wear day after day, and the complete absence of any interest in their hair. (Many of these boys might be better placed in school with 10-year-olds whose behavior they exemplify.) These are more often the slender boys, the boys who mature slowly, but they may be the ones who go far in the end.

At the other extreme are the clothes-conscious boys, those who love to dress up in their best, who are already beginning to wear flashy clothes, bright-colored shirts and socks, who slick their hair down. These boys are more often on the bigger, more robust side. They are the early daters and the social boys.

In general it is the 11-year-old girl who is the more aware of clothes. She is coming out of her dungarees into fluffy blouses and full skirts. She "loves" to dress up. She often has a definite idea of what she wants and what she will wear. The scales are tipped in her favor when she goes on a shopping trip with her mother because her mother has come to realize there is no sense in buying clothes she will not wear.

Interest in clothes does not mean that Eleven knows what to choose daily or how to care for his clothes. Both boys and girls oft repeat the question, "What shall I wear?" Decision is difficult for Eleven. Girls may end up in "outlandish costumes" when left on their own, though they may also have trouble in accepting their mother's suggestion. Girls often crave a different dress, a new dress, and if allowed would add dresses to their wardrobe which they would neither wear nor care for.

The best dress, the best pants are hung up and cared for by Eleven, but otherwise their clothes are slung around the room. This is very reminiscent of himself at five and a half to six when he undressed all over the house, dropping this garment here, that garment there. Eleven has a way of invading all parts of the house. He is not easily contained. Shoe trouble may return at eleven when he can't remember where he left his shoes the night before. Fortunately, Eleven is apt to have alternate pairs. But he doesn't realize it is his fault that he can't find his clothes. Rather does he utilize his difficulties as adequate reasons to be annoyed with the world.

Eleven is more apt to change his clothes from day to day, especially his underwear and socks, but some mothers need to be on hand to snatch the dirty clothes before they are put on again.

Eleven's care of his person though spotty is far better than the care of his room. But he's beginning to slick it up a bit with a banner here, a picture of George Washington there, a picture of a horse or possibly a ballet dancer. He is not quite so deep in his collections as he was. But he needs major clean-up sessions when he will release cartons of "junk"—at least to the attic. Mothers will profit by these clean-ups for often they unearth "that favorite fountain pen" or "the comb I lost."

Bedmaking is a chore for Eleven. He seems unable to make his bed in a simple way. He gives it his own touch which is a bit jangly. And what does it all matter, because Eleven spends very little time in his room? He wants to be with the family group. He likes to work at the dining room table. Even though he dawdles and gripes, his laughter rings out too. He's like a big puppy dog, all over the place.

Parents would do well to keep Eleven's door shut so they wouldn't be disturbed by the mess. Then they can stage a glorious clean-up campaign at intervals with high hopes and the spirit of adventure and conquest.

MONEY

Ten's more casual attitude toward money may be transformed into a real interest at eleven. Boys respond the more strongly. Money can mean a great deal to some but it arouses little interest in others. Elevens may either be said to be "money mad" or to "care nothing in the world about it."

An allowance becomes very important to Eleven. He often speaks up if his allowance hasn't been increased. His demand may now be for 50 cents, partly inspired by knowledge of what his friends are getting. Some Elevens are given the opportunity to budget a larger sum, perhaps a dollar a week, and a very few are given a monthly allowance of four or five dollars. This larger amount imposes quite a demand on scatterbrained Eleven, and the arrangement should be given up if it is found to be unsuccessful.

Though some Elevens can't hold on to money, it is surprising to see how many are known (aptly) as tightwads. Bank accounts may reach the high levels of $20 to $30. Saving is not usually this successful, but most Elevens do save some of their money. Those who are best at saving their own money, however, may be quite good at spending other people's, especially their mothers'. Counterbalancing the hoarding 11-year-olds are those who are generous, even too generous. They treat their friends, they love to give big gifts for special occasions.

But spending, on the whole, is becoming a thought-out process. Eleven is beginning to save for a purpose, even if it is "only fireworks." Boys are more apt to think of their own desires and needs. A boy will save his money for a model plane, a violin, or a bicyle. Girls, on the other hand, are thinking more of other people, and will more often save their money to buy presents.

Money can be used to motivate some activities, such as improvement in spelling, but unfortunately there are causes for poor spelling deeper than money can reach, and such stimulation as a rule produces only momentary good results. The opposite may also be tried; that is, deducting from an allowance when certain jobs are not carried out. This also is only a passing stimulation. One method that can be used effectively to encourage saving is to offer to match Eleven's savings when they have reached a given amount. He can then start toward a goal ordinarily beyond his means, such as a bicycle, and can reach it before his interest is expended.

WORK

Eleven not only hates work but he resists doing it and acts badly when required to help. His energies are spent in seeing what he can get away with, how he can trick his mother into thinking he has done something which he has failed to do. He reports that he is *supposed* to clean his room or that he is *supposed* to take out the trash, and by his admission it is evident that he avoids his chores. Or by his unpleasant response he often forces his parents into the unpleasant necessity of having to command. Eleven reports that he *has to* do the dishes, that he *has to* take out the garbage. His unwilling and unreasonable attitude is not pleasant to live with or to work against. Parents may well question the wisdom of their demands at

this age and often wonder how they might shift their techniques or demands so that Eleven could become a less disquieting member of the household.

Even compromise or bargaining may not work well with Eleven. If he carries out a task, he is apt to give it his own truculent or unreasonable twist. He may find it difficult to set the table as prescribed but rather selects the highest or furthest away dishes so that one is quite startled by the changes when one sits down to the meal that follows. Or the making of a bed becomes a tussle with ingenuity as he repudiates making it in a simple, everyday way. Whatever is demanded of him, he almost always needs to be reminded.

There are times, however, when he does things for fun. There are times when he spontaneously carries out certain tasks very nicely. He needs to be motivated from within rather than demanded of from without. This is especially true when his mother is the demander. But he will accept the challenge and the demand of tasks away from home. There should be more exchange of 11-year-olds between different homes with the added incentive of being paid for the job according to its worth. Eleven becomes surprisingly co-operative under the stimulus of the new and distant. Girls especially enjoy baby-sitting in the afternoon in other people's homes.

Eleven would act better in his own home if he were allowed a little more choice. One mother solved her problem by listing a number of small jobs such as "sweep the walk," "water the plants," "empty the baskets," etc., of which Eleven might choose two or three out of ten or so possibilities.

Eleven enjoys the choice and can surprisingly enough carry out these jobs with the spirit of the game.

3. Emotions

There may well be an odd, vague, uncomfortable feeling in the minds of the parents of 11-year-olds. It is as though some force of nature were grabbing hold of their offspring—as though he were acting under some influence quite apart from those of the tangible environment in which he lives. A further disquieting factor is that parents often sense that they have been in this same place before. They recognize the feeling of sudden drops, high peaks, and jungle-like confusion. The change in terrain comes gradually and imperceptibly. It is not until they turn a sudden corner and face it squarely that they recognize in retrospect that time when their now-approaching-the-teens child was entering a similar phase at five and a half to six years of age. The feeling is the same in memory—that sudden sweep from high to low, that unaccountable shift in mood, the same rudeness, the same devilish unreasonableness.

But there are differences, too. The once small child has now become big and strong. He now sets himself on an equal footing with the adult and though he may again act like an untamed lion he brings a new complexity of emotions into his forays. (Alas, how many adults are still in this 11-year-old jungle!)

The sympathetic parent, especially the mother, who has been able to grow through each stage with her child, knows that this should for her be a time of diminuendo, of back-peddling. The time when the child was more receptive to direct influence and help from the adult is, for many, past. This is a time when the parent acts best who hopes his child can find himself.

This does not mean that the parent should step aside and lose contact with the child. Rather he needs to recognize the fuller stature of his parental role, to see himself as the caretaker of growth forces which need a steady but responding environment to grow in, one that can control but will not force.

We can see Eleven a little differently at a distance, we who are a little removed from him. The home cannot help but lose its sense of perspective when Eleven shows that sudden blare of emotions out of all proportion to the thing at hand. How differently we speak of the 11-year-old than we did of the 10-year-old. Words come into our minds to describe him best—fidgety, disagreeable, resentful, argumentative, insolent, and sulky. We also know his states of confusion and uncertainty. We see him "flub-dubbing" around without knowing what he is doing. We feel his harum-scarum personality darting first this way and that.

We may be so caught in an awareness of the disruptive forces now at work that we too often overlook the positive forces—forces which may not have a chance to express themselves if the negative tendencies take over too completely and are allowed too free a rein, as can often happen.

The expression of these positive forces is more often seen in boys than in girls. Some boys seem to hold on to 10-year-old behavior the way they earlier held on to their baby teeth, though the second teeth were already erupting. The newly released emotional forces of Eleven, combined with the continuing equanimity of Ten, can produce a resultant "warming-up" force which makes them more sympathetic and thoughtful, more reserved and controlled. They have an alert, eager, bright-eyed expression. They are interested and pleasant. Even the boys who show the turmoil of eleven may restabilize themselves after a fit of temper by generously giving away some prized possession. An 11-year-old girl in a similar state might play a mean trick.

If we think of the 11-year-old only in his difficulties at home, we will do him a real injustice. Give him the gay atmosphere of a lively living room and he will rise like cream to the top. But it is away from home that he can act most positively. During a personal interview (or just chatting with a good listener) he laughs repeatedly with real gaiety. He is confiding and alert. He tells you about his waves of happiness. He knows what it is to be overwhelmed by some simple kindness expressed by his friends.

Eleven is aware that he has a disposition. He knows how he feels, but he often doesn't know why he feels the way he does. He knows he wakes up in the morning feeling cross, peevish, and mopey. He also knows that he may brighten and feel more cheery as the day progresses, especially if something nice happens.

An occasional Eleven can tell you why he feels so peevish in the morning. He feels he has too much to do, no time to play, and that he wakes up tired. If only he could get more sleep. This is more easily said than done, but Eleven's life could be improved if it

were tailored more to his needs and capacities. He needs a simplified program, more time for play and sports especially, and if possible an afternoon rest period, when some Elevens would really sleep.

When he works he works intensively and sometimes to the point of exhaustion. He gives generously of time and effort if it is his spontaneous idea. His is the law of immediacy, whether in carrying out a project, wearing some new garment, or going on a trip. Eleven is so spontaneous and immediate in his expressions that there is no doubt about how he feels. A grimace of distaste is expressed before words are found. He can be so spontaneous that he is often unaware of the havoc he is producing, and may report that life is better now because you have more privileges, even though parents are sure that things are much worse.

Though most Elevens are often feeling "real happy" over some specific event, ranging from the coming of a little sister to the eating of an ice-cream sundae, or having waves of happiness for no specific reason, many are beginning to feel times of unaccustomed sadness. A father's speaking crossly or a mother's sadness may inspire unhappiness in the child. A feeling of unpopularity with either boys or girls also may bring on feelings of dejection.

A far commoner emotion, however, is that of anger—a sudden, furious outburst, most uncontrolled, especially when directed toward younger siblings. As with Ten, the outlet of anger is expressed differently with a sibling, a parent, or the teacher. Though many strike out physically at a sibling or a peer, others are beginning to try to control themselves. Elevens may try not to strike out, though if an opponent tempts them too much they're apt to hit him. Still others, in the midst of their anger and planning what they will do, may forget what they were angry about by the time they are ready for action. The violence of their anger is often expressed through yelling, or through saying mean things.

Eleven can become red in the face, he is so angry. His anger may be out of all proportion to the cause, or it may be righteous anger when actions seem unfair and adult promises are broken. Nor is his anger so easily spent as Ten's. Eleven is more deeply involved and he needs to find ways and means to come back to equilibrium. He is more apt to carry out a planned revenge, to say mean things that hurt. He will hold a grudge, will pout and sulk. He involves others, who become angry with him. Or he can put himself in the shoes of another 11-year-old and can become angry through empathy.

Eleven is more apt to cry when he is angry than he was at ten. But his bursting into tears is as often over some trivial happening or when he is tired. Maybe a favored cover of a magazine was thrown out or his mother "looked cross-eyed" at him. Disappointments and hurt feelings bring on tears. Boys are just as apt to cry as girls. Eleven may even call himself a crybaby.

Relatively fearless Ten has become more fearful at eleven. He seems mainly afraid to be alone. This may account for his constant presence in the family circle and why he spends so little time in his room. He doesn't talk about this fear but he asks to have the light on in the hall and his door

open, or he looks in closets and under the bed. When his mother asks him what he's doing, he replies as nonchalantly as he can, "Just checkin', Mom." He keeps a flashlight by his bed. Some girls show a real fear of being kidnaped. Boys especially don't like the feeling of being shut in. A church service may stimulate this feeling.

Girls are more fearful of physical pain, of infections, and that something might happen to their mothers. Girls more than boys fear that no one likes them—and considering the turmoil of their social interplay it is no wonder they build up this fear. They also may be afraid when boys gang up that they may be the target.

Eleven isn't as nonchalant about his hurt feelings as he was at ten. He is more vulnerable than he would wish and often goes off by himself and even cries it out. Girls are especially sensitive to any criticism from their fathers. A few may want to retaliate for their hurt feelings but on the whole they contain these feelings within themselves.

It seems natural for Eleven to reach out for physical love when we realize the extent of his inner emotional turmoil. He needs some mast to hold to, someone who will receive him as he is. But the approach must be his and not his mother's. Boys especially are embarrassed by any public expressions of affection from their mothers, and girls may freeze up. But in private they snuggle close, can't go to sleep without that goodnight kiss, and even act so "mushy" that it may be the mother who becomes embarrassed.

Though Eleven is usually happy in his lot, his family, and possessions, he may covet some possessions of others such as a dog, a horse, or a TV set. But more important, Elevens may be jealous of others' physical attributes—beauty or strength which they wish for themselves. Girls are often jealous when their friends of the moment pay more attention to another friend than to them. And all 11-year-olds seem to be jealous of younger siblings, feeling they get all the breaks and the attention. Eleven is very aware of his friends' privileges and may be jealous of a later bedtime hour and the chance of going out at night.

He is not only jealous but competitive—very competitive. He says himself, "I'm up there fighting," or "Competitive—who wouldn't be? And how!" Some strive to be best in grades, others in sports. In any case, many Elevens are out to win.

Eleven's humor is expanding. He still is a good punner and likes slapstick humor, especially when things are so impossible they couldn't be true. He becomes the clown himself and has a ready audience in his 11-year-old friends. Elevens can be very silly over almost anything. Some slight remark about a girl will make a group of boys roll their eyes and laugh and laugh. The awareness of sex is also being expressed in smutty jokes, so natural to this age, though "dirty" humor still deals primarily with elimination, rather than sex. A group may roar with laughter at another child's expense (teacher told a boy to zip up his fly), then later be indignant, feeling she was grossly unfair to humiliate him before the whole group. Eleven moves widely and freely within the realm of humor and may fluctuate from uproarious laughter to a deadpan look. He is quick to catch the point and has his own way of quipping

and making light of more serious things. "Temper, temper," he may say to himself when he is angry.

4. The Growing Self

"Oh where and oh where has my delightful 10-year-old gone?" may be the refrain sung by many a parent of an 11-year-old girl or boy. Their very query suggests a loss. And there is indeed a loss of ease, of responsiveness, of getting on with others (parents especially), all of which seemed such an assured and established part of the 10-year-old. Now the parents may well ask, "What have I on my hands?"

When parents, or anyone who has to do with children, understand the laws of growth, they will come to know that a stage of turmoil inevitably follows a stage of calm. Otherwise growth cannot proceed. And the parent can help the growth processes even in the difficult stage of eleven by understanding what growth is trying to accomplish.

But it is not easy to understand the laws of growth at this particular stage of development, for so many of its manifestations appear to be so inconsistent. The 11-year-old is full of paradoxes. He's very "good" for a spell and then very "bad." He can be terrible at home, yet suave, giving, and charming away from home. He seems so sure of himself, yet he can't stand having you argue with him.

As we blame him less and try to understand him more, we realize how strongly the typically unpleasant qualities of Eleven—his belligerence, his selfishness, his unapproachableness—are expressions of his search for self, a self which he is trying to find and fashion anew in this new cycle of growth which takes place from eleven to sixteen.

Understanding on the part of the parent doesn't mean that the parent can entirely smooth things over. Not at all. The child must do his own growing. But the parent can provide the atmosphere which is conducive to good growth. When the wobbly 11-year-old self seeks affection to restabilize itself, may the parent be there to give whatever expression of affection is needed! When rebellion is expressed by extreme rudeness, thoughtlessness, and selfishness, may the parent ask himself, "Is Eleven rebelling against me personally, or is he rebelling against the complexity and uncertainty of his own inner depths?"

It is important for the parent not to stir up these uncertain depths. Better not to try too hard to point out the child's extreme rudeness and discourtesy toward his elders (and his contemporaries, too) but rather to work out ways and means to bridge difficulties of interrelationships. Eleven can more readily pull himself together on a businesslike, bargaining basis. You can say to him, "If you do this as your part in the family, then I shall do that as my part in the family." Such bargaining may involve, for example, the child's helping to wash dishes in exchange for the mother's helping him with his homework.

Eleven complains all too accurately, "Now, everything I do seems wrong. Ever since I was eleven." He says the wrong thing when company is present. He pushes too hard and breaks a gadget. He falls down and gets messy. And more often than not be doesn't realize what he has done and said, even when his acts and words are brought to his attention. He belliger-

ently replies, "What do you mean, my rude outbursts?" He seems to gather strength in himself by an "against" response, and this he executes with immediacy. He strikes out, hardly realizing why he is doing so.

This striking out—in actions, words, feelings—is all the more apparent to us because it is against people. He is finding his own self by reacting against other selves. He showed great interest in people, especially his contemporaries, at ten years of age, but now he is interested in constant interaction with people, any people.

Eleven exhibits an increased facility in mental and social activities, especially away from home. Feeling and insight are now as important to him as thinking. He may tell you that his self is in his head or heart, but in general he places his self in that part of his body which most actively expresses him. The horseback-riding girl may quite naturally consider that her self is in her knees. Another girl, desiring to become an opera singer, may tell you that her self dwells in her voice. Or a boy busy with his hands in woodworking and doing things feels that his self is in his hands.

Eleven is far more aware of his faults than of his assets. But even where faults are concerned, it may be difficult to pin him down to the acknowledgment of a specific fault. He may say, "I imagine I have a million, everyone has. I don't know exactly which is worse." In general, the faults he recognizes are those which imply that he has friction with other people. He says he talks back, he contradicts, he gets angry or tries to get away with things. Those few Elevens who recognize their own assets refer to their helpfulness, their kindness or friendliness to others—again evidences of their responsiveness to people.

Eleven, like his 10-year-old self, pretty much likes being his present age, but he feels and likes the idea that he is in the process of growing up. A few are very anxious to grow up. Very few, on the other hand, resist the idea. The best age is judged by the majority of Elevens to be from fifteen to seventeen years, because of parties and dances. Those girls who are more interested in dating are more apt to project to college as the best time.

A horse, a dog, and a farm—these are still the paramount wishes of many 11-year-olds, especially 11-year-old girls. The main difference from Ten is that Eleven wants a stable *full* of horses. Some Elevens are desirous of a new house rather than a farm. Though a few Elevens want a bike, a number are moving into a desire for forms of more rapid and expansive transit: motor scooters, motorboats, or sailboats. Girls desire clothes—whole closets *full* of beautiful dresses, but boys desire money, *lots* of it. The pursuit and presence of health, happiness, and peace are strongly desired by many. But there are a number of Elevens, especially boys, who don't have a desire in the world. Life is good to them, and they ask for nothing more than what they have. These are the very boys who actually seem better at eleven than they were at ten. They gather the feeling warmth that comes at eleven without experiencing the characteristic break-up and conflict. As we understand individuality better, we shall start to solve the riddle of different methods of growth.

Though Eleven may still be influenced in his choice by his parents'

profession, he is beginning to show a capacity to choose on his own. He has a certain awareness of himself, his capacities, his feelings, giving him a better basis for choice. He even knows that his mind might change. Eleven is quite articulate about what he wants to be. Many have settled down from the multiple possibilities they envisioned at ten to two alternatives: e.g., "a farmer or a doctor"; "a nurse or a ballet dancer"; "a model or a designer." Eleven shows a specificity of interest—"a *commercial* artist," "a *dress* designer," "a *night-club* singer."

At eleven, a boy or girl often dreams of becoming the center of the stage, of becoming an artist—a singer, a dancer, an author, a designer. He dreams of fame. He wants to be the top man. Thus if he chooses law, he wants to become a Chief Justice. If he chooses professional baseball, he wants to become the captain of the team. If he persists in his interest in farming, he at least wants to own his own farm.

Those Elevens who plan to go to college are less influenced by their parents than earlier as to what college they will attend. Some are not quite sure whether or not they want to go to college and may even fear that they won't be accepted. But Eleven does recognize that he needs training for many future careers. Many boys are already thinking of graduate school, of professional school after they leave college, and may know specifically which one they wish to attend.

Boys have thought far more about their profession than about marriage, and most certainly haven't thought much about a wife. A few, more articulate boys have thought about the outward appearance of their wife —"blond, pretty," "smart, pretty, and rich." Money seems to have an influence on the male's final decision.

The 11-year-old girl, on the other hand, is thinking far more about the qualities she desires in a husband than about her future profession. She has thought the problem through carefully and has even relegated good looks and wealth to second place. She wants her husband to be kind, honest, understanding, to have a nice disposition, and a sense of humor. She does want him to make enough money so that they can live and eat. (Trust Eleven to think of eating.) She also wants him to be reasonably intelligent and nice looking. But most of all she wants him to be someone to whom she can relate herself. This is the cry of Woman even in this nascent stage of awareness of her relationship to the opposite sex.

Most 11-year-olds, both boys and girls, want to have a family. A few still think in terms of a very large number of children or the restriction to one child, but most are thinking of two to four. They may desire one or two sets of twins. In any case, Eleven wants both boys and girls and he's apt to match them as twins or wants them to come alternately. He doesn't yet realize that life isn't as much under his control as he would wish it to be.

5. *Interpersonal Relationships*

Eleven, like Ten, is firmly placed within the family unit—but for what a different reason! He's right in the midst of any family activity, working at the dining room table, responding to everything that is going on around him, fearful that he will miss anything. His once-prized possessions in his room may no longer hold his interest. He spends next to no time in his room. But even with the family group he is fidgety and restless and is constantly punctuating the conversation with, "What are we going to do now?"

His once-adored parents have lost their halo, the evidence of their deification, and have come tumbling down to earth. Reference to his adored "mummy" has changed to "she." Fathers who are stricter with their all too demanding 11-year-olds may be dubbed "old so-and-so." Both boys and girls are less enthusiastic about discussing their parents with others and are more cagey for fear they are revealing too much. Though they quote their mother, they disagree almost at once with her opinion. They are aware that their mother doesn't know as much as they thought she did; they are aware of father's temper; they are aware of people's motives and of father's favoritism. These awarenesses afford new ammunition for them either to produce conflict or avoid it, or to wangle out of their parents what they most desire. Girls are more adept at the latter and have a facility for getting away with as much as they can.

The first-thing-in-the-morning conflicts are the hardest on the parents. Eleven argues about everything. As one parent reported, "She is exuberantly defensive." It is no wonder that the parent is forced into yelling at the child—and Eleven recognizes that father yells loudest.

It might be wise for parents of 11-year-olds to list the kinds of things they would like from the child and then to make another list of how the child thinks he might comply. The parents' list is quite long:

1. Be a little faster.
2. Work more around the house.
3. Take better care of room.
4. Help with animals.
5. Be neater.
6. Have better table manners.
7. Get on better with siblings.
8. Be better about going to bed and getting up.

The child's answering list is quite short in comparison and not very well defined:

1. He will be helpful when in the mood.
2. He will do most anything except wash the dishes.
3. He doesn't want you to yell at him.
4. He doesn't want you to tell his father.
5. Stop criticizing.

Eleven doesn't appear from this listing to be very capable of answering his parents' demands. He has again acquired the raw texture of the beginning of a new cycle of growth.

But life isn't all terrible with Eleven and his parents. He usually gets on better with one parent than the other. Girls especially have fun with their fathers—going together on walks, to the beach, to the zoo, or to the movies. Boys go fishing, boating, swimming, shooting, or to ballgames with their fathers. And they can invariably start a lively conversation about cars.

Mothers also have their special place—they are always there to be confided in. They are good about talking things over, especially with girls. And they are wonderful to be affectionate with. Eleven may be so affectionate that his expression of

this can be embarrassing to his mother.

His mood needs to be considered, although he can, to some extent, turn it on and off at will. He doesn't like to be demanded of or criticized, and the day-to-day demands are especially hard, though he may accept the challenge of a *project* (especially at a neighbor's house, unfortunately). Thus, a once-a-week room clean-up (his door shut in the meantime to keep the havoc out of sight) may be the answer to the room problem. And if his table manners are too terrible for father, Eleven had best eat early for a while.

Perhaps no other age gets on as badly as Eleven does with his siblings. He may control his physical expressions of anger, but he clearly says, "I'd like to hit him over the head with a baseball bat, but mother won't let me," or, "I'd like to give vent to my emotions and grab his hair. I feel like pulling it out by the roots." A younger sibling, knowing that Eleven will respond this way, deliberately tries to get a rise out of him by needling him, teasing him, joking with him, or getting into his things. Then the parent has to step in to save the younger sibling from destruction. If only Eleven could be separated from the rest of the household, especially on rising in the morning and around the dinner hour at night, much peace could be restored.

But in spite of all of Eleven's difficulties with his siblings at close range, there is no stauncher friend if a sibling gets into trouble. Eleven also thinks of himself (or, more often, herself) as a friend, almost a parent, when trying to improve a younger sibling, but would alas "murder him trying to get him to do the right thing."

Eleven gets on a little better with an older sibling, but, unfortunately, the older sibling is apt to call Eleven names such as "big fat slob," "stubborn mule," or "snip." Such names can fit him almost too well, which is perhaps the reason why Eleven responds to these salutations so violently. An older sibling knowing of Eleven's acumen, his keenness, his perceptive nature, and his drive to talk, would be wise not to bring a date around where Eleven could get at him or her. Some things are better left unsaid, especially in the midst of a budding romance.

Friendships are not as casual as they were at ten. Eleven does not just choose his friends because they are nearby and like to do the same things that he does. He chooses some even though they are at a distance and must be corresponded with to keep up the friendship. He likes friends who have "the same temperament" or who are "reasonable." That's probably why he gets on so well (most of the time) with his best friend. This is truer of boys than of girls. In general, boys are more apt to have one good friend and to go around with a lot of others. Their main purpose in life is to have fun together. A tree house may be the preferred place for the gang. And their interest in baseball is never-ending. Two friends alone are more apt to play games, read comics, or just sit around and talk. Bike riding is often curtailed because the bike has been dismantled and is in no fit condition to ride. Boys often spend the night at each other's houses. Throwing pillows may be the extent of their exuberance.

Girls have neither the strong single best friendship nor the grouping in gangs that boys do. They are more apt to have a fair number of good friends, three to five, among whom they shift. Girls are more influenced by their friends, are more one of the pack, and may actually be under the sway of a friend as though they were in a spell. They take it for granted that there will be stages of quarreling and stages of "not caring for anything." One Eleven defined the situation well: "We have to quarrel to break up the smoothness and then we have to make up about four hours after we quarrel." Eleven can't stand not speaking for too long. Her drive to talk is too great. Girls also like to spend the night at each other's houses and are more apt to have a group of three or four. They can become quite out of control in playing such games as recognizing their friends by the feel when the lights are out.

Whereas Ten often reported that he hadn't got to the opposite sex yet, Eleven is more apt to report that he's almost there or beginning to move in this direction. When a boy likes a girl, he's pretty sure that she likes him. But a girl often likes a boy without his being aware of this attention. Girls are apt to do a great deal of talking about boys to their girl friends. They can be quite aware of the quality of boys and may paint a verbal picture that is quite frightening. One girl described an admirer, whom she called an exception—"A shrimp, he weighs only fifty-nine pounds, and he's terribly skinny. He has a flat face with freckles and a pale dirty complexion. Just horrible all over." Boys do not usually have this type of perception, but they are aware of a girl's ability to talk. One 11-year-old boy reported that "you really have to keep away from that one. The talk of the town will spread to the talk of the city."

Girls enjoy the joking, teasing attitude the boys have toward them. "It's neat fun," they will say. They even enjoy the spitball and snowball fights and, as one boy said about girls, "There's not a better target around."

Birthday parties have worn off, although a few girls have parties for girls. There is a definite transition at this age away from what is classed as a more "babyish" party, though they still act like babies at their cook-outs and their Halloween parties unless the party is well planned and supervised. In mixed parties, which girls most often organize, they "play games and eat." It becomes an unfortunate occasion when a spontaneous game of boys throwing food at the girls arises.

A few Girl Scout troups organize dances. The boys may or may not know who has invited them. But in any case, as soon as a dance number is over, the boys gravitate to one side of the room and the girls to the other.

6. Activities and Interests

Play is no longer paramount in the lives of 11-year-olds as it was when they were ten. Play can be included in their relationships with people, but the people are now actually more important than the play. Elevens rarely choose to be alone and are forever in the midst of the family circle, even though they may get on badly with both parents and siblings. If forced to be alone, Eleven might imaginatively become two people, to play both sides of a chess or a baseball game so that he can experience that feeling of interplay which he so much enjoys.

Eleven's relationship with people is often far from positive. Sometimes his main activity, his main effort is directed against a certain contemporary. No one can be more cruel than an 11-year-old girl who doesn't quite realize what she is doing. And if her poor victim responds to her chastisement, she is inspired to double or triple her dose. Elevens need to be watched and to be given some idea of fair play. Rules have their place. But more important is to protect any tender, vulnerable Elevens by trying to keep them away from their more callous, taunting age-mates and to pull these callous, troublemaking ones into sharp line now and then.

The interests of Eleven are quite similar to Ten's. Eleven, however, doesn't have the strong urge to be out of doors and to be constantly exercising his big muscles that he had at ten. He is in constant movement, fidgeting all over the place, and he loves gross motor activities, but he is also a great watcher, explorer, and above all a conversationalist.

There is nothing he likes better than the project of constructing a tree house with all the multiple problems of how to get the lumber, nails, tar paper, or oilcloth for the roof. Who will "belong," and what the dues will be; what they'll keep the deck of cards in, and if wall hook-up tables will do. And then there is the question of hinges and a lock, inside especially, and an extra key for his best friend. This kind of planning and execution can occupy a whole summer.

The execution of such a project probably expresses Eleven better than anything else he could do. He feels the promptings of an emotional need to have this safe cozy place for himself and his best friend, plus the gang at times, where they can play cards, eat, collect dues, talk, and even sleep if their parents will allow them to. Probably every storekeeper in town knows about its construction and may have happily given his little donation if it's only a few dozen extra nails. All of this planning, buying, manipulation of funds, keeps Eleven in a glorious whirl of interacting with so many people—people who catch his enthusiasm, people who want to talk things over with him. This behavior is more common with boys, but many girls are just as enthusiastic and build just as good tree houses.

Though Eleven may seem clumsy and bumbling in his motor acts around the house, especially when he is coming into conflict with other members of the family, put him out on a ski terrain or on an ice or roller skating rink, and you may well wonder where and how he has acquired his new agility.

Both boys and girls like above all to go on walks, and to talk and romp around with their dog and their companion as they go. Everything can be of interest to Elevens. They watch any animals or birds they may see. They observe insects and discuss their habits. They visit cemeteries and read the poems on the stones. They are far more apt to walk than to ride their bikes because you can't romp on a bike the same way you can on foot, and anyhow it usually has a flat tire, or is dismantled, or some part is missing.

Collections are still going strong, and Eleven is most interested in the aspect of trading, especially of comic books and baseball cards. If the latter are on display, they are subjected to constant changing—this card being put up and that one taken down. If comic books are traded, it may become a group project, with batches from several members pooled, and swapped "as is" (each side holding a ransom, "just in case").

There are the definite cleavages of boy and girl interests as previously expressed at ten years. Some interests can become very intense with the added emotional force that Eleven brings, though the 11-year-old is also apt to drop an interest suddenly, when it has barely begun. Girls are still very interested in dress-up, may rifle their mother's closet, especially for shoes, and can look very rakish with rouge and lipstick a little too lavishly applied. Some are unusually adept at mimicking someone they know, in a very telling fashion. Some girls organize their interests and abilities into playing theater. They also like the games of secretary and librarian.

Many girls are becoming interested in sewing clothes for their dolls (and occasionally for themselves), and may be ready for a little hand sewing machine. Some maternal help should be available for unsnarling mistakes or the child will tire of it too quickly. Knitting is of less interest than it was.

Boys are more apt to use their creative imagination in games and inventions. They can think of all sorts of variations for war play and ballgames. A few are playing Ping-pong or tennis and others are target shooting with cork guns. Supervised B-B gun shooting is enjoyed but must be kept within lines of strict control.

Organized clubs are strong with most, though a few of the more mature may dub them "boring." If Eleven were consulted more and the activities were planned more around his interests, which he wants to shift rather frequently, he might enjoy organized clubs better. Many join and continue to belong because they think they should, but more often than not their hearts aren't in it. Their own private clubs don't carry very far either. Somebody's always absent or they forget to pay their dues. Paying dues may be far more important than electing officers.

Eleven has lost his idealized approach to clubs and his desire to improve himself that he had at ten. Now at eleven his clubs are for fun, for eating, "to be private from the boys," or just for play.

SEDENTARY LOOKING AND LISTENING ACTIVITIES

Eleven hasn't the urge either to listen to the radio or to watch television to the extent he once had. There is of course a considerable variation among children, but it is interesting to see how often Eleven is bored with programs he once favored. He may choose to put on his radio as he is doing his homework if allowed or as he is going off to sleep. Mysteries are still favorites, though they "don't make as much difference" as they used to. Comedies, family dramas, and theater productions are favored both on radio and TV. Boys as always prefer sports and some are regular news listeners or viewers. Though there is some interest in music on the radio, there is a much greater interest in listening to phonograph records. Eleven is swinging into the teen-age interest in jazz and popular music. He would like record albums of the latest musicals to play.

His reading depends a great deal on his basic personality. If he read a great deal at ten, he may read even more at eleven, and he sneaks in as much extra time as he can after he goes to bed at night. Sometimes electric-light bulbs have to be removed to break into this habit. Even those who formerly read very little are reading a little more at eleven. Their taste for books is similar to Ten's with a greater interest in animal, insect, or nature stories. (It is interesting in relation to this that Eleven's interests in pets are extending to guinea pigs, hamsters, turtles, and fish.)

Eleven often thumbs through the current pictorial magazine to keep abreast of the times. But he gives more time, effort, care, and real interest to comic books. There is a slacking of interest with a number of Elevens, but with some the interest has grown stronger if anything. Though they like books more, they "don't like comics any less." Eleven is becoming a little more selective than earlier in his choice of comic books and at least says he prefers the more innocuous animal ones—they are a good trading staple. If Eleven is not allowed to read comics at home, he can always find ways to get at them unmolested— at a neighbor's house, in the barn, even in the dentist's waiting room. Subterfuge can be very cunningly executed by some, with many small piles hidden in many different places. If one pile is found, and confiscated, that will mean that the others are at least temporarily safe since parents fail to suspect more. Banning of comics or increasing vigilance is not the answer to their control.

There is more attending of movies at eleven than there was at ten. A fair proportion go every two weeks, others go once every week, and most go at least occasionally. Many still accompany their parents, but an increasing number are going with friends. Eleven's chief desire is that it should be a "good" movie, which means (to the girls) one without fighting or murder. With a few Elevens, a certain movie may be so favored that it may be seen two or three times over.

7. *School Life*

The casual, adjustable, eager-to-learn 10-year-old has turned into a critical, demanding, sharp seeing and talking Eleven. When he's for you he's all for you, but when he's against you, you have to watch out or, better yet, see if you can put things right for him.

Though many Elevens are school enthusiasts, even liking school better than when they were ten because "it goes faster," all too many Elevens are speaking of school as one of their "problems." Such remarks as "I disagree with school" or "school is disgraceful" had best not be taken too lightly by a teacher or a school. Eleven should be heard and more fully understood. It is only then that a school can answer his needs and at the same time know what it can ask of him or give him as his responsibility.

It is very evident that Eleven comes to school chiefly because of the "kids." His need of his contemporaries, even when he gets along badly with them, is insatiable. He teases, chases, pushes, grabs, or hits his classmate, sometimes not realizing how much he can hurt, or at times with actual intent to hurt. But he also nudges or pokes with his elbow in a friendly way to get his neighbors' attention. He is often seen walking down the corridor draping his arm around a friend of the same sex.

Elevens cluster into small groups (on sex lines). There is nothing casual here. They may come together with intent as much for evil as for good. The group may suddenly dissolve to exclude certain unwanted members. Then the nucleus re-forms and may or may not allow the excluded one or ones to re-enter its confines. If Eleven is allowed to go his own way without sufficient adult guidance, his ways and actions are a little reminiscent of those of the jungle.

The teacher is probably the most important single factor in the school life of an 11-year-old. Eleven doesn't want to be held with an "ironclad hand," but he really prefers a "tough" teacher, one who can challenge him. He especially doesn't want a teacher who "treats us like babies." However, the same teacher may be criticized at other times for being "way up above our heads." Probably one of the most endearing qualities of a teacher to Eleven is that he or she "cracks jokes" or tells funny stories. Defining horse sense as, "Horses have sense because they don't bet on men," throws Eleven into stitches of laughter with an afterglow that will last for days and provide something to talk about and to think about. Or Eleven likes to be teased by his teacher on a personal basis at an opportune moment. "Did you trade minds with the yellow monkey you saw at the zoo?" motivates Eleven into action better than any kind of serious talk. But always a teacher has to balance in her mind whether her joking will upset Eleven or spur him on into action. She needs to choose the moment when she has his attention alone and not expose him before the group.

When Eleven's teacher can be described as patient, fair, humorous, not too strict, understanding, "makes things interesting," and doesn't yell, there is every reason to expect that Eleven will become very fond of her and will not be afraid to show or speak of his affection. Eleven often has a crush on his sixth-grade teacher. Boys express their affection more readily by doing things for the teacher—bringing her presents, staying after school to help, and even holding the teacher's hand at times.

What a change in the atmosphere of a sixth-grade schoolroom when the teacher is spoken of as a "real crab," "Ooh, she's terrible," "she yells and is too strict." Eleven can give us a fairly clear idea about what's wrong with his teacher if we will but listen. Here is the report of one 11-year-old girl:

"You know what I'd like to be? Not when I grow up but for just one day I'd like to be the teacher and give my teacher a taste of her own medicine. . . . I'd make her sit in a seat that you're cramped in. And then I'd give her work up to the sky. And then I wouldn't let her talk for one minute. Well, that's what she does to us. And I'd talk: 'Oh, no, you shouldn't do this, children.' And then I'd make her go up to the map and show me every little city. And make her spell very hard words. And then do around twenty-five examples of arithmetic problems. And before school I'd make her do twenty and then I'd call her marks right out loud before the class. And then I'd make her stay after school, and clean up everything and

do all the dirty work, and then she'd go home."

If a teacher or a school would right all these wrongs (if such they are), then the positive, the enjoyable side of Eleven would have a chance to grow in a healthier atmosphere. Not that life would become entirely smooth in the schoolroom, but it could at least be fitted to Eleven's growth potentials.

We might analyze Eleven's school behavior to see how his behavior reveals him more fully. When Eleven's teacher knows that the more usually peaceful atmosphere reminiscent of fifth grade may suddenly in the course of the sixth grade explode in her face, then she is on her toes, ready for anything that may come. She can be assured of one thing—that Eleven is still excited about learning, that he hasn't yet become "blasé" as he may be when he is thirteen and older.

With Eleven's difficulty in getting up in the morning and his tendency to cause friction in whatever he does, he sometimes comes to school in mental and physical disarray without having eaten his breakfast. Without food he is a little worse than usual. May it be hoped that the school provides at least a midmorning snack of milk and crackers. A truly community-minded school might take Eleven out of his home where he is such a disturbing factor at breakfast time and invite him to school where he could make his own breakfast. What a wonderful start for the day this could be—sociability, cooking for yourself, and the feeling of well-being that comes with a full stomach! Small groups could rotate and shift their members.

If Eleven had this better start he

might not resist the schoolroom housekeeping jobs as much as he does now. He might even like dusting, toward which he usually has an ugly attitude. But as always with Eleven, if he knows what he is to do (his jobs are charted) and if he knows he won't have to keep doing the same thing (jobs in rotation) and that he can shift if he wants to (free to exchange jobs with other children), he will cooperate to the best of his ability. Girls and boys bunch separately in small groups and somehow with a certain amount of leeway they do get their jobs done.

This same kind of leeway and control is needed in the total conduct of the class at work or at play. A wise teacher spots her potential leaders and will seat them at strategic places so that each may have his or her cluster of children who are under his influence. These leaders should be without authority and not known to the children or to themselves, but the teacher knows whether she can get them on her side and whether they will be at times a greater or better influence than she could be. (The teacher also knows that when she can't get an idea across to an 11-year-old, another child can sometimes explain it.) It is soon evident that there is less friction, less foolishness, and less giggling if these undefined groups are separated along sex lines.

Restlessness and wriggling in the seats is very common in sixth grade. Eleven needs to be allowed to move around the room and to talk, though he shouldn't be allowed to disrupt others' work and not accomplish his own. With a certain amount of freedom to move around the room there might be less note passing, less of

Eleven's vituperative attitude toward his fellow man in his cryptic remarks—"Donnie stinks," or, "He's a dope."

Occasionally, when a room seems to be distraught or chaotic, it may be necessary for the teacher to bring in martial law, to have each child sit up straight and face the front. This might not be necessary or even possible in a school that is truly geared to the 11-year-old where there might not be such formal seating. There could be other ways and means to bring the group together. Eleven wants to have opening exercises. He responds well to religious instruction or to a Bible story. Sometimes he wants to vary the exercises by singing a popular song.

Elevens would happily be responsible for the flag raising. They like to salute the flag and they pledge allegiance with vigor and enthusiasm. Elevens group well during this task.

Best of all Eleven enjoys gym and sports. Baseball is his favorite, but soccer, kickball, spud, volleyball, and football are close seconds. Boys and girls prefer to separate, but there are some girls who try their "dead level best" to be allowed to play with the boys. Boys have a hard enough time putting up with poor players of their own sex, but they won't tolerate poor players of the opposite sex.

When teams are chosen, the best players are chosen first and friends second. Games need to be supervised, for Eleven is a hard and critical taskmaster. He calls out, "You damn fool" when a comrade misses a ball, and he may further threaten, "You didn't *try* to get that ball; if you can't *try*, you're not going to be on my team." Parents may sometimes be ashamed of their 11-year-olds at home, but teachers can also be ashamed of these same 11-year-olds at school. Boys may get into a fist fight over anything—or without seeming to have any reason—and sometimes have to be separated. Or they will get even with another child by excluding him, by not giving him any candy. Eleven is not a fully socialized animal and needs help from a teacher or leader both to see what he is doing and to find a better way to do it.

Classroom teaching of an 11-year-old can either be an exciting or an exhausting experience (sometimes both). If a teacher can bring a warm, emotional, enthusiastic approach to the group, if she can be interested in what the members of the group are interested in, then, as one told us, she can "swing them ahead without allowing them to drag." She soon realizes that Eleven thrives on a certain amount of routine, that he likes to know what is expected of him, and what changes in assignments and scheduling occur from day to day. A long-term assignment of, say, six weeks, is accepted, though he needs to be checked on at intervals and may be expected to do a blitz with the help of his entire family in the eleventh hour.

Eleven is keen on competition of any sort. He'll even "work his head off to beat his best friend." A favorite method of competition is for one sex to be against the other. Not only spelling and arithmetic are used for competitive games, but history and other subjects can also be utilized. All except social studies, which just seems too complex ("boring") for the 11-year-old mind. In arithmetic, problems are also too complex, though he wants the mechanics of arithmetic. He delights in adding, subtracting, and

above all in showing his accurate knowledge of the multiplication table, which his teacher may come to loathe. Definition of words is quite as bad to Eleven as problems in arithmetic. He wants to use words in sentences, in context, and he likes to separate them into syllables, but he hates to define them. Teachers, fully aware of Eleven's dislikes, can still use geography and dictionary games in social situations to make them fun.

One of Eleven's greatest weaknesses is in seeing relationships, and it is obvious that if he doesn't see these relationships he won't remember the facts. Often he understands best if the teacher imparts her knowledge through a story. One danger in the teacher's telling stories, especially about historical events, is that she gets so carried away with this method that she might find herself shifting the historical truth.

There's nothing Eleven likes better than a good story—whether of adventure or nonsense. He's better at telling his book reports than writing them, but he's apt to go on too long. Therefore it is wise to restrict him to one incident. He prefers current events to past history and will be interested to locate places mentioned in the newspaper on his map. At all times Eleven wants his work to be related to his reality, to what it means *for him*.

Sewing and cooking for girls and shop for boys are among the favorite activities. Eleven especially loves to sing. Fortunately, more and more schools are providing better musical education. He likes drawing too, especially as it relates to his stories and projects. He likes to make long continuous friezes, preferring to project his thoughts imaginatively rather than to copy someone else's idea. Give him a project about markets and he will do an enthusiastic job in gathering information, making exhibits, drawing. (After all, food is one of his greatest enthusiasms.)

But even under the best of teaching and planning, Eleven fatigues rapidly. He shows his fatigue in his inconsistent learning pattern. One day he does remarkably well, the next day he appears to be stupid. He's out with illnesses periodically, more than he has been for the past three years. His body temperature varies very widely. Some Elevens are so cold they wear what seem like too many clothes, while others are too hot even though they appear to be practically naked. Elevens keep busy putting the windows up and down according to the way they feel. By the end of an afternoon at school Eleven shows his fatigue by becoming very scrambly and when he's finally let loose he's apt to run wild.

These fatigue patterns are similar to those he had at the earlier age of five and a half to six. Again at eleven, as at six, a half-day school attendance might be considered. The afternoon program could be optional and restricted to extracurricular activities. The teacher, working at such a high pitch, is quite as fatigued as the children, and she also would profit greatly by a half-day attendance with time enough to recharge her human battery for the next day's ordeal. If half-day sessions cannot be arranged, it would certainly be wise to allow Eleven's mother to decide when two or three surprise days off could be profitably taken during the year. Nothing could give more of an uplift and cut into the rising hatred toward

school of those Elevens who are having difficulty.

8. Ethical Sense

Eleven is not only emerging from the child world, but he is truly out in the midstream of the adult world, shifting this way and that in an effort to determine his own course. He wants to cut loose from the established authorities of home, school, and church. He wants to figure things out for himself. He is less strict in his moral code than he was at ten (or at least his code is changing). He has more freedom of decision within himself.

More often than not, Eleven makes a good attempt. He "tries to tell the truth"; he "tries to do right"; he "tries not to swear"; and he often *knows* what is right, though he doesn't always *do* what is right. He is at times puzzled about right and wrong and is apt to go by his feelings or by common sense. Those Elevens who are ruled too much by what their parents say or are too cautious about taking chances (such as going on other people's property) may be dubbed by their contemporaries as "yellow," or "chicken." Eleven is more conscious of the old problem of choice between being accepted by his peers and holding to his own ethical standards.

His chief concern in the field of ethics is about fairness. All the good that is in him rises to the top as he becomes adamant on this subject of fairness in all of his dealings with people. This is Eleven at his best—and under certain circumstances his best can operate.

Eleven does have pretty good controls through his conscience. His conscience may bother him and make him keep thinking about something he has done wrong. This concern may produce the opposite extremes of either retribution or confession to one's mother, but Eleven is trying to avoid trouble for himself and may not tell at all or may shade the truth in his own favor. There is a small group of girls at eleven who do the very opposite of what their consciences dictate. They do things to spite people, especially their mothers. They mean to do a bad thing, they feel glad they have done it, they like the feeling of abandon that comes with wrongdoing, and they truthfully say that their conscience doesn't then bother them. Most of these girls acquire greater depth of feeling in time, but some can produce increasing havoc as they grow older unless they are helped to realize what they are doing, how it affects all of their life, and how they can and must do something about controlling it.

The truth is not sacred to Eleven. He is more concerned about his own self-protection and is apt to tell things in a way that favors himself. Not that he meant to lie. It was just that he wanted to get out of doing certain things or to cover up not having done certain things. If Eleven is ashamed of something he has done, he may deny it when asked but protects himself by crossing his fingers as he lies. But on the whole he is good about telling the truth about big things.

In accepting blame, as in telling the truth, Eleven scores a "near miss" —he doesn't quite hit the mark. Some Elevens automatically blame others but more often they alibi, they cover up by criticizing others, though they don't actually blame them, and they manage to slip out of it a little.

Eleven is more tolerant about swearing and drinking than he was at ten. He seems almost to be trying to play it both ways. Girls still don't like swearing, but they might swear just to remind their parents that they, the parents, swear. And some might swear sometimes because it "sounds real grown-up." Boys may also be critical of others' swearing, but they swear themselves when they get mad— or maybe when they are hungry.

Drinking in adults is also condoned if the adults don't drink too much. Eleven recognizes the difference between hard and soft liquor, between mixed drinks and straight. He doesn't mind when adults drink cocktails, but he thinks it's very bad when they take a bottle of whiskey and drink too much.

Where Eleven really rises up in indignation is in relation to cheating and stealing. Maybe the heat of his indignation is fanned by guilty feelings over his own cheating or sore temptations to do so. At any rate, these acts are on his mind, and he often reports the misdemeanors of others to his mother. Boys more often than girls are reported to cheat at school. They copy at exams, or cheat at games if they are losing.

Boys may cheat more often, but girls are more apt to steal, especially in stores where the merchandise is out on counters. Sometimes they go in groups of three or four for the express purpose of shoplifting. There is usually one girl who is the leader and who has an undeveloped or non-conforming ethical sense. Many girls refuse to accompany the group, considering the plan as "horrible." Others want to experience the excitement of such a jaunt. One experience like this, especially if Eleven is caught, is usually enough to cure him of stealing for the rest of his life. If only stores, schools, and parents realized the prevalence of this tendency at eleven and twelve, they could help nip it in the bud. If the young stealers are caught right in the store, the impact is the strongest, and the whole incident can be handled in a serious but humane fashion. The parents should be notified, the law should be brought in. The girls should experience the fright that comes when one is close to the edge of something far more terrible and yet within the protection of those who love them and wish to help them. But at the same time they must learn the necessity of becoming responsible, worthy of the respect and the privileges given to them.

It is unfortunate when an offense like this is successful and then leads to further exploits and further successes. Often the friends of such an 11-year-old are the only ones who know, but sometimes the school is aware of the situation. The parents are too often the last ones who know, though they should be the first. When home and school, with their common interest in the child and his welfare, can communicate more freely, both will be able better to understand and cope with the problem.

9. *Philosophic Outlook*

TIME AND SPACE

Eleven is acquiring a more dynamic sense of time and space. He is beginning to feel the inevitable, relentless passing of time which no one can stop: "No matter what you do, even break all the clocks, you can't stop it." He knows that time never goes back-

ward. He also recognizes time as a measure of distance from one thing that happens to another thing that happens.

Eleven is quite good at handling time. He is more apt than not to get to places on time. He may be rushed for time, especially when he has too much to do. This "too much" in his opinion usually includes homework. He feels the difference between the slow dragging of time in the afternoon at school and the all too rapid flying of time when he is having fun.

The concept of space is not as easy for Eleven to define as time. He has some very definite ideas, even though he conceives of space as a "nothingness that goes on forever." Some are more specific and conceive of space as being "distance between anything," or they conceive of space being filled, even with nothing. ("Space is a place where there isn't.") A number of 11-year-olds recognize multiple possibilities. One speaks out clearly with, "Lots of kinds of space. Space is the room. Space where the universe is. Space between a word on the typewriter."

Eleven is in quite good control of getting around in his immediate space. He can go downtown alone on the bus and can get to his appointments with the help of a reminder from his mother as to date and time. Some Elevens are beginning to travel by train, if they don't have to change trains.

DEATH AND DEITY

Eleven takes death for granted pretty much as he did when he was ten. "If you die you die and that's all there is to it." But he is affected by the death of his grandparents and relatives and he's even more disturbed by the death of a favorite animal, especially a dog. He's interested in burial and may wish to go to a funeral just out of curiosity.

He's changing his concepts of what happens to people after they die. He doesn't think too much about it but at least he is less apt to think that they live like people on the earth. Maybe it's "like a long sleep," or maybe "their souls might keep going." Eleven has some idea of reincarnation—of a going away, coming back, and going away again. It's similar to what he thought when he was five and a half to six years old.

Eleven doesn't give much more thought to God than he does to death. A majority of Elevens think of God as a spirit or an imaginary person. It's surprising to see how many Elevens believe in God but do not feel that He influences their lives. With a growing God sense, Eleven is beginning to sort out what he has been taught and what he really thinks. Certain legends as about Adam and Eve, Gabriel blowing his horn, the existence of angels are being scrutinized more carefully in the light of Eleven's own knowledge.

But at the same time he's beginning to recognize a possible relationship of his being bad and a loss of some prized possession, especially when it happens twice in a row. And when he sees adversity happen to other people, too, when they have been bad or don't believe in God, then he begins to feel there must be something about the relationship of how you act and what happens to you. He prays when he wants something, like getting rid of a cold, even though he doesn't believe in God, and he feels in general that praying has a good influence on him.

Eleven is, if anything, less enthusiastic about Sunday school than he was at ten. Some wish to continue to go especially because they enjoy the choir. A number would prefer church (if it didn't last so long) to Sunday school. They want the religious experience that they often feel is lacking in the Sunday school situation. Many are disturbed at the way their contemporaries act, especially the boys, though their own behavior is not blameless. They might play pranks as a group by hiding all the hymnals and swearing the hymnals haven't come back from the binders yet. Or they might have one of their free-for-alls with spitball throwing and general disorder that is hard for many a teacher to control. (The lack of continuity in a once-a-week contact makes it harder for the teacher to build up a position of control.)

CHAPTER SIX

Year Twelve

MATURITY PROFILE

Y EAR TWELVE brings many changes for the better. This is what mothers report when they recall the strenuous, importuning self-assertiveness which so often marked the previous year. The 12-year-old, they say, has become less insistent, more reasonable, more companionable. Life runs a smoother course both for youth and adult.

But the contrast between Eleven and Twelve must not be drawn too sharply. Much of the harum-scarum behavior of Eleven has a developmental logic of its own. It leads into new areas of experience and thereby prepares for increasing discernment and discretion. Through sheer growth processes, aided by home and school, Twelve gains a new outlook upon himself and his contemporaries, young and old. He relies less on forthright pressures and challenges to realize his selfhood. He tries instead to win approval from others. He is less naively self-centered and can look at his elders and even at himself with some objectivity. These same qualities give scope to a growing sense of humor and to cheerful sociability. When in form, a 12-year-old youth proves to be excellent conversational company. Mutual understanding may even bring about a state of camaraderie for parent and son or daughter.

In all social situations Twelve shows a tendency to widen his awarenesses—a good sign of psychological growth. This was clearly reflected in his reactions to the interview situation during which he was asked a variety of questions. He was friendly, outgoing, co-operative, and ready to please. His spontaneous comments and his own questions revealed an awareness of the implications of the total occasion. "Quite a nice place you have here!" "Oh, this is fun." "Just see all of the attention I'm getting." "Tell me, is it interesting to work with children?" In the developmental examination likewise many orienting questions were asked all in a vein of eagerness and exuberance; for Twelve is predisposed to be positive and enthusiastic rather than negative and reticent. His responses to specific questions lacked the impulsiveness and immediacy characteristic of Eleven. Twelve was less voluble, more guarded and self-critical.

In many other ways Twelve shows that he has become less naive in his social relationships. His sense of self takes a more perceptive account of other selves, and this is one reason why he gets along better with all of his associates. He may even be able to direct a bit of his humorousness toward his father and to smile at himself. He displays increased tact in taking care of younger siblings. Well-balanced girls likewise are able to undertake responsible baby-sitting tasks. The mother-daughter relationship frequently shows a marked gain in maturity. The girl who at age eleven flared up with short temper at some slight inattention now meets a similar provocation with a gentle humor response effective enough to make the offending mother smile. One such girl, with twelve-year insight, detected a hidden purpose in her mother's presentation of a plan, and she, the daughter, countered politely with, "Mama, you are campaigning!"

These interpersonal patterns of behavior typify the essence and promise of Twelve at his best. He surely is "trying" to grow up. He protests above all that he is not a baby any longer, or at least that he does not wish to be so regarded. Perhaps his protestations arise in part out of a secret awareness of his remaining immaturities. As adults we should remind ourselves that he is in the very early stages of adolescence. Growing into maturity is not a uniform, steady process. It is uneven, particularly at the twelve-year level, when the child-youth is still so callow that he fluctuates at times between the extremes of grown-up helpfulness and childish lapses. We like to emphasize his high points of achievement because they most truly express his optimal potentials for further growth. Reliable records, however, indicate low points, even in the field of social behavior. Boy-girl parties are sometimes projected with enthusiasm, but, alas, they may not turn out too well. The agenda of activities so carefully drawn up in advance fails. Either the boys gang up and ignore the girls, or the boys act with ostentatious badness. They have been known to throw food and to spill liquids. Behavior within a group imposes tests which are difficult for young as well as old.

Nevertheless, the peer group plays a pervasive role in shaping the attitudes and interests of the 12-year-old. The group influences the operations of his conscience particularly in the expanding realm of his school life. His tendency is to look upon problems of conduct somewhat dispassionately, but from the standpoint of the group. He may even try to analyze a situation reasonably into specific pros and cons to determine his moral judgment or to define a calculated risk. His attitude is neither neutral nor priggish; he likes to exercise his intelligence and to keep unwarranted feelings under control. "I'm not bad, though I am not too good," says one; "if you're too good, kids don't like you, and it's also kind of silly." So he yields to the pressure of the group when his schoolmates conspire to rag an inexperienced teacher—by simultaneous group coughing and other disturbing devices. He is not faultless.

But he is by no means ill-disposed toward teachers. He likes to be taught. He develops a warm admiration for a firm, well-informed teacher who enlivens the school work with humor and can lead the class into the adventurous territories of new knowledge. The group loyalties and the unity of the class do not necessarily result in opposition to the teacher. On the contrary, the group prefers to make an ally of the teacher and to adopt her as a special member of the group. This enhances the psychological status and the influence of the teacher. The teacher becomes a catalyzer; the pupils supply the dynamics of their enthusiasm and curiosity.

A twelve-year school group is by nature spirited. Their enthusiasm is so abundant that it readily rises to a boisterous pitch. But the pupils can focus quietly on their individual tasks if permitted some freedom of movement. They have a growing ability to do independent work, although their ardor for group activity is more conspicuous. They seize every opportunity, even during an intermission, to engage in open, outspoken discussion. They like to debate political and civic issues. They are in their element when they plan the details of an uncharted group project, such as a dramatized historical episode, a puppet show, an intramural broadcast. The projects are not motivated by competition, nor by a desire for mere entertainment. The eager zeal which is displayed reveals the extraordinary educational potentials of the 12-year-old. These potentials include a sustained capacity for arduous factual learnings and training for basic skills.

The intellectual growth of Year Twelve should not be underestimated. Although Twelve often takes special delight in the sheer mechanics and precision of arithmetic, he shows an increase in conceptual thinking. He has an inkling of the conceptual import of words like *justice, law, loyalty, life, crime.* He can make an attempt at abstract definitions: "Time is how long things take"; "Space is something empty," but the emptiness is "something there's something in." He is becoming more literate, more articulate. His argumentation is less contentious and often more calm. He has a genuine feeling for reasonableness. His ethical sense tends to be realistic rather than idealistic. It is influenced by an attitude of tolerance, which is akin to capacity for humor. Both signify a growing sense of proportion and a counterbalancing of personal and social attitudes.

These attitudes hold great potentials for good; but they may come to grief in an unhappy home, an inadequate school, and a frustrating neighborhood environment.

We may, therefore, think of Year Twelve as being normally a period which favors the integration of personality. The basic traits of reasonableness, tolerance, and humor promote balances in the organization of behavior. There are four other closely related traits, which work toward the same integrative end: enthusiasm, initiative, empathy, and self-insight.

Many would consider outgoing enthusiasm as the dominant trait of the 12-year-old. If he is at all interested he is likely to be ardently interested whether it be popcorn, arithmetic, a friend, or a movie. His (or her) enthusiasm seems to depend on a fund of energy, which is available at all times to heighten any like or dislike. "It was just divine." "I adore mashed potatoes and gravy." "I *love* tomato juice, and I *hate* stewed tomatoes." "Wonderful." "Wonderfullest of all." "Oh joy."

Twelve tends to enter upon a self-chosen task with vim and spirit. He "dives" into a book with devouring zeal. Teachers report a great intensity of interest in mathematics assignments. He relishes the challenge of debate and discussion. His spontaneous and latent curiosities are immeasurable. He is spurred not so much by competition as by a natural urge to exercise his intelligence. He enjoys athletics and games mainly for their own sake. The enthusiasms which take hold of group and individual can be sustained over long periods in school. But out of school Twelve also has a self-protective method of compensating for excessive enthusiasm and effort. He reverts to casual, desultory relaxation, shapeless lounging, or sprawling and plain "hacking around."

Closely linked to enthusiasm is the capacity of taking the initiative. The 12-year-old exemplifies this capacity both individually and groupwise. If there is a job to be done, a picnic to be arranged, a meal to cook, a school project to be organized, he not only is ready to co-operate, but he takes over the initial steps. This executive ability does not spring from forwardness but from simple feelings of confidence and self-reliance. Good ideas call for execution when they are prompted by the good will and good nature characteristic of the 12-year-old.°

Empathy and good will are closely allied. Twelve has some skill in reading emotional expression and shows a tendency to project his own consciousness into that of others. He takes it for granted that other persons will enjoy good news of any kind; so he bursts with good tidings and takes spontaneous pleasure in sharing experiences. This too is a trait which has more implications for maturity than for immaturity. Sensitive to the feelings of others, he can show a marked degree of considerateness for his friends and for younger children. If he must step on adult toes, he does so lightly and may even deliberately choose the most psychological moment for a diplomatic approach.

There is a special kind of empathy directed to compeers. Boys and girls alike are keen to know how their age-mates think and feel about things. This awareness has great influence on their behavior. It also tests their capacity to take an independent stand. During the interviews it became apparent that there was a great deal of curiosity about how the other kids answered certain questions. Twelve is by no means overwhelmingly wrapped up in his ego; he is eminently sensitive to the attentions and interests of persons other than himself.

With this well-balanced outgoing interest in his fellow men, Twelve naturally gives evidence of increasing self-insight and self-control. He is more than dimly aware that he like everyone else has a life career and that he changes as he grows. He projects into his past and into his future. During the interview he may inquire with curiosity, "What did I say about that last year?" Asked about future education and vocation, the responses of Twelves showed a strong trend toward a single definite choice of a specific career combined with marriage.

Twelve sees himself in improved perspective. With the possible excep-

° The girl who recently sent a cherished good-luck charm to the President of the United States was twelve years old. Of similar age and maturity was the girl who in 1860 wrote a famous letter which persuaded candidate Abraham Lincoln to grow a beard. The writer of this letter received an appreciative reply signed, "Your very sincere well wisher." Twelve is also a common age for launching a juvenile newspaper. We know of a 12-year-old editor and mimeographer who for some time has been publishing domestic events and items in his *Family Times*. Recently he issued an "extra": *Another boy*. Since then the editor has been periodically reporting with factual concreteness the step-by-step development of his baby brother.

tion of fears his emotional behavior is coming under increased control. Tears and violence are usually kept in check. He takes pride in bearing physical pain with fortitude. He accepts just discipline; and sometimes he actually seeks self-discipline. He can atone for guilt felt. He tends more and more to perceive situations in their totality.

In appraising the development of child and youth, there is a principle of relativity which forbids us to consider one stage as basically better or worse than another stage. From the standpoint of growth each stage is sufficient unto itself and sufficient also unto the stage which precedes and follows. Each level of maturity has its inherent logic. The twelve-year stage, however, has a special distinction in the cycle of human development, for it brings into being an assembly of behavior traits which clearly foreshadow adult maturity.

The 12-year-old is not an adult in miniature. Nor is he a paragon. But he does embody modes of thinking, of feeling, and of action which prefigure the mature mind. His new outlook and attitudes signify *a capacity to mature* and they indicate the basic lines of the mental growth which extend into distant time.

During the next ten years or more he will continue to organize the behavior traits which we have described as symptoms of his emerging maturity. We noted an increase in conceptual thinking and use of ideas. We have stressed the balancing function of his attitudes of reasonableness, tolerance, and humor. These are developmental assets which promote the progressive attainment of maturity. They are reinforced by the dynamic assets of enthusiasm and zeal, initiative and intelligence, empathy and good will, self-insight and self-control.

A classic 12-year-old manifests the sum of these traits to an impressive degree. The traits are various but they are interactive and they constitute an organic constellation which has far-reaching importance for the cycle of adolescence. The several traits are manifested so ingenuously that they betray their innate origins. The culture inflects and shapes the outward patterns of behavior, but the inner predispositions come from innate growth. They emerge from instinctive compulsions—not with suddenness, but with surety. They cause the youth to feel differently about his own self. He reorients his interpersonal relations. It becomes natural for him to behave more maturely.

This affords ground for faith, even if complications and perturbations lie ahead. It is a most remarkable fact that these intimations of ultimate maturity should occur so early in the adolescent cycle. Thereby Nature gives us a glimpse into her secret mechanisms and latent reserves. Our task is to conserve the potentials so engagingly revealed by 12-year-old boys and girls when they are at their best.

Year Thirteen will bring us still closer to the problems of the maturing self. What shall we find?

MATURITY TRAITS

1. *Total Action System*

The seething, spilling-over, talkative, "bursting with energy" 11-year-old is beginning to calm down at twelve. He is more capable of organizing his energy, though he expresses this in seemingly opposite extremes: intense activity that pushes through to achieve a goal, and resting easy in non-committal, leisurely "hacking around." Enthusiasm is a quality characteristic of Twelve. With boys this enthusiasm is especially given to sports—to baseball in particular. Even among those who lack ability to play the game, an interest in it may pervade everything they think or do. Girls are often equally ardent in their interest and desire to care for young children. But however strongly enthusiasm for an activity may be expressed, both boys and girls seem suddenly to reach a saturation point and then almost collapse.

Just how they collapse seems closely related to how they will recover and build up energy again for further enthusiasms. Some Twelves, after intense activity, collapse hard and do not recover easily. As they did at eleven, they suddenly feel very tired, may develop a cold, and need to rest up for a day or two. Others seem to have a safety valve for more frequent, more gradual releasing of tension. The

ones who take it easy and "fool around" rather aimlessly manage this release process rather nicely. Too frequent attempts by others to goad them into more productive use of time seem to throw their revitalizing mechanisms out of kilter, and actually retard the return to energetic pursuits. We in the United States, especially in urban living, may be prone to demand too much action. We need to realize that an individual's control of relaxation can be just as important as his control of action.

The changed behavior of Twelve is very evident in a personal interview with him. He doesn't throw himself into the situation as much as he did at eleven. He becomes enthusiastic and may frequently interject such remarks as, "This is fun," but he now has the calmer demeanor of a co-participant, one capable of give-and-take. He is now more likely to remain seated in his chair, though that does not mean he is not still very active in wiggling around in it. His hands tend to be busy, reaching out to investigate objects, and fiddling with such attached ones as telephone cords. He has less need than he had at eleven to get up to investigate what he sees around a room. Instead, he now makes comments or asks pertinent questions about things he sees. This calming down of his "motor drivenness," this reduction of the need to go to the thing he is looking at, shows a new capacity in abstract projection which gives more scope and flexibility to his actions. He is less controlled by the object, more in control of it.

Twelve is more aware of what he says in our interviews and may groan —with delight, really—when he realizes that the interviewer is taking down even his initial exclamations ("Well . . ." "Ugh . . ." "Heh-heh . . ."). Though he answers promptly, he is more thoughtful than he was at eleven. His answers are clear, spontaneous, and interesting. He less often leaps into the middle of a thought; now gives an initial clue to the topic he is talking on. There is less clowning, dramatizing, and making faces than at eleven.

Twelve enjoys the interview. He likes to talk. He likes the interplay with the interviewer. Sometimes his eyes grow big and he regards the interviewer intensely as he is caught up in his own enthusiasm of reporting.

HEALTH

Though general health is excellent in some, and the more overt illnesses such as colds and bronchitis are in the minority, Twelve may not possess consistent good health. He tires less frequently than Eleven, but periods of extreme fatigue can occur when he hates everything and everybody that demands anything of him. This is the time when he would profit by a day off from school. The school needs to be aware of this kind of fatigue and to be ready to co-operate with the home, allowing an absence from school if it seems desirable. Twelve doesn't ordinarily wish to miss school

and will not take advantage of such an opportunity unless he really needs it.

Twelve, like Eleven, may still have sudden, unexpected, sharp, and short-lived pains in various parts of his body, localized most often in his head or in his abdomen. These probably portend the coming of puberty and are more common in girls. Twelve's feet hurt him as he complained they did at eleven, but now the pain is often localized in the heels. A shift in shoes may alleviate the pain. But greater care needs to be exercised in the choice of shoes, and Twelve may welcome a custom-built playshoe that he can fashion on his own foot.* Much later foot difficulty seems to stem from this time and much may be prevented if remedial measures are undertaken.

Colds are most likely to develop when Twelve has overtaxed himself with too many activities, but he also has the resilience with rest "to talk himself out of getting a cold." If he does develop one, he wants to get well as soon as possible and is not so apt to pretend that he is sick longer than he really is, as he was likely to do at eleven when he didn't wish to return to school.

TENSIONAL OUTLETS

The very reduction in the intensity of Twelve's tensional outlets suggests that he is on a more even keel. There are still those who under tension clear their throats, blink their eyes, show a nervous stutter. But the nail biting may be restricted to one thumb and stuttering may only occur in a particular, restricted situation, such as in the presence of the father. It is when

* Murray Shoe Kit, Alan Murray Laboratories, 616 Fairfield Avenue, Bridgeport, Connecticut.

Twelve is tired that nervous manner-isms most often occur, and they are no longer accompanied by that odd or confused look that was more prevalent at eleven.

VISION

Twelve is both aware of and con-cerned about his vision. During a visual examination he keeps asking if something is wrong with his eyes. Those who have had visual symptoms, such as blurring or aching eyes along with headaches, are even more con-cerned than most, and the visual ex-amination usually reveals an under-lying cause.

Twelve, visually, now has a better combination of the ability to fixate (which was dominant at ten years) and to focus (which was dominant at eleven). Difficulty in achieving this combination may produce a reduced power in focusing or a difficulty in discriminating, so that his responses to some focus tests may be vague. Each eye tends to respond differently in its focusing ability, but it is ex-pected that the eyes will regain their stability in working together and re-sponding more similarly by fourteen.

The Twelves who show difficulties in their combination of focus and fixa-tion without being aware of any symp-toms may be expected to develop symptoms by fourteen, and should then also be more ready to accept and profit by visual help (glasses or visual training).

The question of having visual help to improve visual co-ordination and efficiency at twelve is still as difficult to answer as it was at ten and eleven. Twelve will usually co-operate, espe-cially if his family feels he should, but

it isn't his own idea. He dislikes the idea of having to wear glasses all the time; he feels it would interfere with his activities. He will co-operate in wearing them to study or read, though it is a nuisance carrying them around. There is even less danger of his start-ing to become nearsighted than there was between nine and eleven.

PHYSICAL DEVELOPMENT AND SEX AWARENESS—GIRLS

Twelve is the age when the middle group of girls start to take their big-gest steps toward achieving the form and functions of young women. This is the usual period of most rapid adoles-cent growth in both height and weight. The height spurt seems to come a little sooner and a little stronger, and to distribute the body mass over more space. (By the end of this year the average girl has achieved over 95 per cent of her mature height.) Thus, despite an in-creased weight, many girls look less "chunky" than they did at eleven.

There is now a definite filling out of the breasts, a darkening of the nipples, and some growth of under-arm hair. Menarche occurs most often toward the end of this year. And one event less often remarked on, but common among both boys and girls, is the sprouting of a fine crop of freckles. (It is significant that freckles were especially evident once before—at six years, an age which has characteristics similar to twelve.) This is more evi-dent in some children than in others— and perhaps eventually we may be able to relate the individuals with large, splashy, almost confluent freck-les and those with the pinpoint variety to different types of body physiology.

The intense interest girls had in their breast development at eleven is calming down somewhat at twelve. Their self-consciousness may now be expressed by their choosing to wear tight sweaters, flaunting their developing form.

A stronger interest is now centered in menstruation. A few girls are still having real difficulty in becoming emotionally ready for this new biological event, which they see as a threat and a disruption in their lives. Others can better accept it, but within limits. They ask their mothers to keep it a secret and plan to tell only a best friend. Above all they may wish their fathers not to know. The earlier that menstruation appears, the more difficult it is likely to be for Twelve to accept. Acceptance is, after all, a matter of maturity. (Menstruation before the twelfth birthday may produce real anxiety and necessitate the wearing of extra pants or rubber pants.)

But a majority of girls nowadays are looking forward to menarche. They have been prepared for its coming, and, though naturally uncertain about just when it will arrive, they are ready in their attitudes and ready with the necessary equipment. The impact of its first actual appearance may produce some tears and vomiting, however much a 12-year-old girl is prepared with knowledge. But after this hurdle has been surmounted there comes a change of attitude, a more positive relationship to growing up.

The initial periods are generally light in flow and irregular in occurrence. Usually girls have very little premenstrual warning and are surprised to discover a few stains on their pants. There is an occasional occurrence of a period with some girls simply with any excitement, though this is rare. There may be a very heavy flow following a long lull of two or three months. Even in the midst of irregularity, however, there emerges a basic pattern which each individual establishes.

These early periods are not usually accompanied by such premenstrual changes in disposition as will occur in the next few years, though some girls are a "little crabby" before and during their periods. At first some may need maternal help in fastening their sanitary napkin in place. They need help in judging whether or not to wear an extra napkin, which may be removed during the school day. They need to be taught about the disposal of the napkins and checked in case they forget. And they need to understand why fastidious care is important, even to the use of deodorants, so they won't bring their condition to the attention of their classmates.

Mothers must recognize that although girls are more "knowing" than boys about sex matters in general, they can still be disturbed by misconceptions and also by their own feelings and other people's feelings toward them. Knowing, for example, that dogs conceive in heat, they may conclude that humans conceive while the mother is menstruating. They may be bothered by another girl's attention to them or by their own feelings toward an older person. They need to be able to discuss such disturbing ideas with someone. Fortunately, girls are much more likely than boys to turn to their mothers—to tell her of their thoughts and experiences, to ask her for information and guidance.

It is for the mother to be adequately informed and to answer questions as best she can. She can, without laboring her point, help the 12-year-old to view sex in its fuller perspective. Above all she can help her daughter to come to recognize that these feelings she has are natural to her new development, that physical sex acts she may have heard of, observed, or performed are also understandable as part of a growing-up process. The mother can help her to realize that it is the way she feels about sex that is most important.

If Twelve, boy or girl, has developed healthy attitudes and feelings toward sex, then he or she can move on into succeeding stages of growth. He needs help to know what he is going through, but he also needs to find his own way. Most individuals (in our culture) may well go through a perfectly natural stage when they view sex as dirty. A single homosexual experience may both satisfy the individual's curiosity and help him to choose the basic, heterosexual direction of growth. The child must do the growing, but the parents and other adults who are guiding youth need to stand by and guard him from permanent choice of dead-end pathways.

PHYSICAL DEVELOPMENT AND SEX
AWARENESS—BOYS

There is a wider range of differences in rate of physical growth among 12-year-old boys than among 10- or 11-year-olds. Both highs and lows stand out. The advanced group is far more advanced at twelve, while the less active group shows hardly any changes since eleven. The middle-of-the-road group, however, now shows definite

traces, of one kind or another, of beginning puberty. An increased growth of both penis and scrotum is noticeable in many. Long, downy hair generally starts to sprout near the base of the penis and a few darker, coarser hairs are intermixed. But even within this middle group of boys there are sharp differences in the way incipient puberty is shown. Some boys show genital size increase but no trace of pubic hair. The situation is reversed in others, while some show both. Within an individual physique, similar discrepancy appears, some parts appearing more, some less developed. The blossom of the puberal fat period may come into full flower only at twelve. (Many of the boys experiencing this could endure it better if they knew it was only a temporary phenomenon.)

Boys are becoming more interested in sex than they were. Some still allow their mothers to come into the bathroom when they are there and may show her any evidence of pubic hair with pride and amusement. Many appear to be embarrassed by sex talk and information from parents, however, and an occasional boy gets "red as a beet" at the very mention of the word *sexy*. Twelve is relatively less interested in the sex activity of grownups and more absorbed in his own sex interests. He has usually learned about (though not experienced) ejaculation. And he is beginning to realize more fully that sex activity occurs quite apart from the conception of babies and may, if he is a youngest child, ask his mother if she has had intercourse with his father since he was born.

Some interest in girls is almost inevitable for the majority of 12-year-old boys even though it may be as short-lived as it is sudden. Twelve is more fond of attending social gatherings, such as dancing school or parties. He shows a change in his care in dressing for the occasion, and he may still be wound up two days after it. The few who fall in love are curiously open in their expressions of love, telephoning freely, writing in books for everyone to read. But, in general, Twelve enjoys the group activity most, and would not dare try to kiss a girl except under the sanctioned ritual of kissing games, preferably with the lights out.

Erections often occur—both spontaneously, without apparent external cause, and under various kinds of stimulation. Mothers are now apt to find pictures of nude girls in their sons' pockets. Conversations and horseplay with other boys can be a potent source of arousal. And excitement of many kinds other than sexual, especially fear and rage, can induce erections. (This last phenomenon is usually already forgotten by late adolescence, but it can be a puzzling one to Elevens and Twelves.) Masturbation is usually a part of Twelve's knowledge or experience, if not of his vocabulary, and is engaged in with frequency by many. It may occur alone or in groups. Some boys are beginning to go to their rooms and lock the door, though this does not always indicate masturbatory practices by any means. A few less mature boys may return to doctor play with younger children. A few may have one homosexual experience with an older boy in experimental sex play or out of curiosity. Or an older man may insidiously lead Twelve on without his knowing what the older man wants. This adult seduction is a very rare event, but nonetheless Twelve should be warned about it (realistically rather than dramatically) and protected from it.

Sex is really interesting to Twelve, and he tends less to think of it as dirty than he did earlier. He wants information and he wants to be set straight. He can come to the wrong conclusions on his own, and might think that a "fairy" means a sissy, or that a "homo" is "crazy for girls." Boys would willingly go to a counselor with whom they could really talk freely and have their questions answered in a straightforward way. Twelve, it seems, would usually prefer to seek information from such a friendly but detached source rather than from his parents, however frank and confidence-inspiring they may be. If he does turn to a parent, it is more likely to be his mother than his father. But it is as if he feels that they both have known him too long and too intimately to allow him to take on a new role— that of an individual with an immediate and personal interest in sex. A counselor who doesn't think of Twelve as "just a child," and who is not himself uneasy in such a situation, will soon find himself bombarded with questions.

Lacking such a source, Twelve seeks out information elsewhere— searching magazines, newspapers, and dictionaries for sex words and stories; swapping information (and misinformation) with pals. Twelve-year-old boys often have bull sessions to discuss matters rather freely, at least as far as the pooled knowledge of the group will permit. There is a folklore of sex jokes, too, that they tell only to each other. Yet somehow the same jokes crop up afresh with each new generation.

2. *Self-Care and Routines*

EATING

Appetite. In the realm of eating, Twelve's stomach is described as a "bottomless pit." No matter how much he eats he never seems to feel full. He can go directly to the kitchen after a large meal of two to three helpings of everything to rummage around for cookies or other "stand-bys." He may neither think as much nor talk as much about food as he did, but he eats with real appetite at meal or snack time.

Many girls and some boys have a very small appetite for breakfast, but are starved by midmorning at school. Twelve would relish the planning and purchase of food for this important break in the morning. He would even raise the necessary funds. Educators might be amazed by the change in the atmosphere and rise in energy and motivation in a seventh grade when Twelve's hunger pangs are quelled.

Twelve more often than not has a big snack when he comes home from school in the afternoon. This snack seems in no way to interfere with his evening meal, when his appetite is enormous. Again at bedtime a large majority of Twelves feel unmistakable pangs of hunger that can only be quieted with a big snack. It is a pleasure to watch Twelve "rustle" up a meal in the kitchen. He is competent in cooking hot dogs or hamburgers and making elaborate double- or triple-decker sandwiches. He pours on jam, and ladles out peanut butter in thick layers until the contents are spilling and dripping from the edges of the sandwich.

Though Twelve's appetite is enormous, he may be beginning to restrict his eating to meal and snack time. He may also be aware of restricting the quantity of food he eats if he is overweight. He can cut out desserts and foods he doesn't like. Girls are more aware of their waistlines and they may be making a valiant effort to diet, though they often fool themselves by pulling their belts very tight. Twelve also may control his appetite by his thought for others and leaving something for them. Whereas he might have eaten a whole pie at eleven, he now leaves at least one piece for someone else to enjoy.

Preferences and Refusals. Surprisingly few Twelves have finicky appetites. Nor do their appetites fluctuate the way they did at eleven. Many Twelves speak of their "ideal meal" in which mashed potatoes and gravy figure strongly. Any form of meat, and sweets of all sorts are favored. Certain foods are still refused, especially root vegetables, fish, and creamed dishes. But Twelve isn't so averse to eating disliked foods. He adaptively camouflages the taste with a piece of bread or washes the food down with a swig of milk. And he is branching out in new directions with new favorites, such as mushrooms, artichokes, fried apples.

Table Manners. Parents complain less of Twelve's table manners than previously. At least his manners aren't as grossly disturbing as they were. However, his combined desire both to converse and to eat simultaneously forces him to talk with his mouth full. Or as he converses he may poise his knife or fork at an odd angle in mid-air. He is still tempted to eat with his fingers and he needs to be reminded about passing things or not reaching for things.

Preparation of Food. Twelve can be interested not only in cooking or baking his special, well-tried accomplishments. He may even be interested in the general preparation of food. He likes to "hang around" in the kitchen watching his mother cook. He may even be inspired to cook a whole meal himself, though he has to call to his mother frequently to make sure he's doing the right thing.

SLEEP

Bedtime. Twelve has in large part given up the 11-year-old fight about bedtime. To be sure he still needs to be reminded more often than not, but on the whole he doesn't object. There are still a few who resist; who need stronger pressures. But there are also those who go to their rooms earlier than necessary and who enjoy the slow preparation for bed as they read, listen to the radio, or finish their homework. With less resistance and better co-operation, Twelve proves that he has earned a shift in bedtime, which is moving toward 9:30 with a flexible extension to 10 or even 11 for special occasions or over the weekend. He can now "take" these exceptions and reduction in sleep without having to pay the price of exhaustion and illness.

Sleep. Twelve is happy to slip into bed but that does not mean that he falls right off to sleep. Though he doesn't mention any fears of the dark or of being alone, he often keeps a trusty flashlight by his side. Or his radio may keep him company. His thoughts before sleep may range into the fantasy realm of exploits with himself as hero. But he also mulls over the happenings of the day and the things he has left undone.

His sleep is not as deep as it was at eleven, when almost nothing could awaken him. At twelve he seems more restless and may talk out in his sleep. He dreams of nice experiences near home or of a future time when he is getting married. But troubled dreams, though fewer, still occur. Girls may dream that a prowler turns into their daddy or boys may dream that their mother is in danger of being grabbed by an ape. At times they awake so frightened from a dream that they are riveted to the spot. They cannot move in their attempt to run away, or even to turn over.

Morning. Twelve has fortunately lost the disagreeable disposition with which he awoke at eleven. He may lie in bed for a while before he gets up. But often he wishes to arise to read, draw, or to complete the homework he was too tired to do the night before.

BATH

The improvement in bathing that began at eleven continues at twelve. The idea that he *needs* to take a bath has entered the thoughts of the 12-year-old, especially when he is obviously dirty. He might even experience shame if he suddenly saw that his feet were dirty.

But Twelve does not restrict himself to bathing only when obvious need is present. He almost prevents this state of affairs by bathing quite frequently, even as often as once a day. But with the majority every two or three days is often enough. Showers are definitely preferred, not only by boys but also by some girls. Some like them so much they sneak in an extra one. Girls are apt to take tub baths, often indulge in a little soaking, even though on the whole the bath can be accomplished by Twelve with a certain amount of dispatch. Not that ears are washed. These are still the special province of the mother.

Some girls still need the help of their mothers to shampoo or especially to rinse their hair and also to set it. But those girls with nimble fingers are quite capable of grooming their own hair.

Though bathing may be under good control, a reminder may still be needed for handwashing. The very girl who has a beautifully done coiffure and is wearing lipstick may have to be sent from the table to wash her hands. Fewer reminders are needed for brushing of teeth. This is pretty much under Twelve's control though he may brush them only once, at night.

CLOTHES AND CARE OF ROOM

Twelve is becoming much more aware than earlier of his appearance. He is especially aware of what the crowd wears and almost never goes against the crowd. If scarves are the style of the day, girls want scarves. If corduroy pants are in vogue, these are the only kind boys will wear. They want to wear what they consider is "suitable." Twelve is particular about what matches and goes together. He wants his mother to check on the straightness of his tie, to tell him whether he looks "good" or not. Many girls are said to have good taste.

The fit of clothes is also important to Twelve. Fortunately for Twelve, the era of making the child grow up

into his clothes is past. Sometimes a whole new wardrobe is needed because of Twelve's rapid growth. Girls are especially fussy that clothes should not be baggy. And, alas, all too often an expanded waistline dictates a certain expansiveness. But Twelve valiantly pulls it in with a tight belt, so tight that it almost restricts her breathing unless the belt itself gives way.

Some girls are trying to look more glamorous in the type of clothes they wear, the style of their hair-do. They want to wear a little lipstick for a dance. Brassières, garter belts, and long nylon stockings are now on their minds—at least in the planning stage. They long to develop the need for a brassière and if only they could wear stockings just once to a dance! Many, however, do not wish to progress this rapidly and hold on to their bobby socks. Those who have tried stockings often return happily to the wearing of socks.

Their choice of jewelry is tasteful and nicely restricted to a charm bracelet or a string of pearls. But however elegant they look, however long they have preened before the mirror, they give unmistakable evidences of their age by a dirty neck or fingernails.

Boys are most concerned about not wearing "sissy" clothes. They are not yet ready for the flashier sports clothes, but they love bright plaid shirts and like to concentrate their new love of color and daring in a tie. They want to look "sharp." They may, however, be all dressed up for the occasion as with a "sharp" tie and proper pants, but that does not mean that they do not wish to wear their sneakers—even to church.

Buying clothes is not the chore it

has been. There are fewer issues about clothes between parent and child. Twelve knows more what he wants, both because of his growing good taste and his bowing to style and what the others wear. Twelve usually buys his clothes with his mother. Girls especially feel the need of trying things on to see how they look. If the mother brings home clothes she has picked out, she knows that she needs the leeway to return them if the child does not like her choice. But Twelve is adjustable, and, as he says, "We level it off if we have different ideas."

Beginnings, with Twelve, are better than endings. Choice of clothes is better than care of clothes. There are sporadic moments when the latter improves but on the whole it is the less usual Twelve who is neat and careful about hanging up his clothes, changing into clean clothes as needed, and disposing of dirty clothes. Twelve has a way of letting his clothes pile up to get wrinkled and "bent over." One mother of a 12-year-old boy in her exasperation pressed her son's bent-over trousers in their bent-over position and made him wear them. This didn't change things much, but he did "sort of hang things up" after that.

Twelve will accept a reminder about the care of his clothes. And one sufficiently strong admonition to "take a good look" at his room may arouse enough shame in him to set things right.

Not only his clothes clutter up his room, but also his collections, systematized or otherwise. And a new type of collecting is arising: mementoes such as ticket stubs, clippings, pictures of school teams. Twelve needs a bulletin board so that he can plaster it with all these bits and any special interest of the moment. With some it is pictures of dogs, with others horses. Pennants, football pictures, and movie stars' photos are finding their places on Twelves' walls. Fortunate is the Twelve whose walls readily receive the anchoring force of a thumbtack. Unhappy is the Twelve who needs to spend his allowance on Scotch tape to display his treasures on the wall. "It costs so much!"

Twelve spends more time on fixing up his room than in keeping it in order. But he does keep it nice when he thinks about it. And he can be reminded. However, with boys especially, mothers have to step in to clear up the room, at least once in a while.

MONEY

Twelve is usually not as intense in his interest in money and in securing it either through allowance or earning it as he was at eleven. Often allowances are given up, and Twelve has what he earns or is given what he needs. A number still have a 50-cent allowance, but more are moving up into the $1 brackets with some demand from the parents to budget. Bus tickets, school supplies, church and Scout dues, and occasionally haircuts are included. Movies and school lunches are more often extras paid for by the parents. Twelve is clever at saving money out of his alloted budget. He will walk or bicycle to school instead of taking the bus, or he will skimp on lunch or take his lunch, instead of getting a hot lunch at school.

Twelve does not just accumulate money as much as he did at eleven. It is more often saved for a purpose or spent—perhaps on a baseball mitt, a ukulele, or some records. The Twelves who handle money well always have money on hand. They are generous in lending and are especially delighted when their mother needs some money. They not only like others to pay them back but are also rather scrupulous in their own transactions in paying back. These careful Twelves do not as a rule spend money foolishly, but this is not true of all Twelves.

Quite a few are reckless squanderers with a burning desire to spend whatever money they have on hand. As one mother put it, "He can't stand prosperity." These are the children (and they may well become the adults) who are in terrible money trouble all the time. Money goes through their fingers like water. They are generous when they have money, but they are more often broke and in need of an advance or of borrowing more money.

WORK

Twelve is losing his earlier unpleasant, almost automatic resistance to work. He is now recognizing the fact that he *has to* and therefore he'd better get at it and do it. He may not volunteer and still needs to be reminded but he's often "good about helping" and even shows a little willingness now and then. He has, however, worked out with his mother the chores he *doesn't* have to do, such as making his bed, helping with the dishes, and setting the table. His mother also realizes that he helps best over the weekend.

He means to carry out a request or chore "in a couple of minutes," though his mother may think he delays longer than this. Often he does his best work when his mother is pressed for time or when she is away. Mother might plan to be away more often, or even, perhaps, to go to bed for a deserved rest so that fledgling Twelve might try his wings, especially at cooking.

Twelve is not only helping with the usual household and outdoor tasks but he is spreading to more difficult work. Girls are dusting, cooking, and trying their hand at ironing (handkerchiefs and such). Boys are washing the car, cleaning the garage, or doing rough carpentry.

Earning some money is part of Twelve's motivation. He prefers to be paid by the job rather than the hour. More boys are taking on a paper route, and both boys and girls are taking on baby-sitting away from home even in the evening. A few enterprising Twelves establish their own small-scale businesses, with wares for sale that they have made themselves. These may be miniature doll beds, plastic pins, or coffee and rolls to be sold at a neighboring construction unit. Through such projects Twelve may accumulate quite a sum of money, which often provides capital for further ventures.

3. Emotions

What a happy respite age twelve can bring. Gone are the harum-scarum ways of Eleven. Gone are the belligerent, disagreeable, argumentative, and moody expressions of Eleven. Not that these more negative aspects of behavior are *entirely* gone, but the good periods have steadily grown until they last longer and longer. The same child who at eleven had sudden flares of emotion at the least provocation may be good-natured, warm, and adjustable at twelve, with the ability to take a ribbing. Twelve stands out even more as "a delight" or "a joy" when he is compared to his 11-year-old self. He may still show the extremes of behavior, a "black and white" response, but these are better defined and not in constant conflict with each other. When Twelve loves, he loves wholeheartedly. A more exuberant girl may sign her letters to her mother with "Love, Love, Love (multiplied by 10,000)." Twelve's abounding enthusiasm may be equally expressed for pretzels, his parents, or religion. And his hatred, alas, can be quite as strong, and more often than not it is directed toward school. Twelve's extremes may be expressed in caution or daring; in uproarious laughter or complete absence of humor.

In spite of these extremes, Twelve shows a "miraculous smoothing out" compared to his earlier self. He seems to want to keep things in balance, to level forces of disagreement, to smooth over rough places. He may at times be spunky and impatient, but on the whole he is good-natured, pleasant, and will listen to reason. He shows a healthy caution in the midst of his enthusiasms and his anticipatory eagerness. This caution checks him from jumping into situations too soon, and saves him from the sometimes disastrous results he experienced at eleven. On the whole he feels that good luck is on his side. But at other times his luck is "about even," "in between," or it "balances." And he is ready to take the bad with the good.

Though he recognizes that growth brings more responsibilities, he also feels that more fun is added too. His 12-year-old mind happily feels the balance of forces. Along with Twelve's

more even-tempered disposition he often sustains a mood of happiness. He may be spoken of as a "merry boy," or may be heard singing all the time because of his happiness. At times there are sharp peaks of wild exuberance, especially over some future event, e.g., going on a ski weekend. He is especially happy over success in his school work and seems unusually capable of enjoying vacation periods. He is quick to see beauty on his nature walks and this perception produces added happiness.

Life can be terrible as well as wonderful. Most provocative of this state is homework over the weekend. But in the end he usually overrides his resistance, and buckles down and completes his assignment in short order. He is sad on occasion, especially when the death of an animal or of a human comes within his personal experience. He responds to a sad book, also.

Anger is still not under control at twelve though it is moving in that direction. More often than not it is aroused by a younger or slightly older sibling. Attack by hitting, chasing, saying mean things, or throwing something is more common than withdrawing. But an increased number are responding with silence, saying something under their breath or going off by themselves especially to their rooms to "think it over." A sophisticated Twelve may say himself, "I'm beginning to suppress my emotions," or (more likely), "Haven't really been mad lately."

Twelve might cry, especially if he is angry or moved to sadness, but on the whole he tries to hold back his tears. He may be just on the verge of tears, they may brim up into his eyes, but he stoically holds them back. Even when he is suffering pain, as being stung by a bee, he sets his jaw and is determined not to cry. He is more apt to cry at home than away, and if asked if he cries when he is at school he may say, "Don't be ridiculous."

On the whole, twelve is not quite such a fearing age as eleven but Twelve often does not feel too comfortable alone in the dark, either on the street or in the house. He hears creaking noises at night and fears an intruder. He thinks of criminals and killers and men bothering him on the street. Most Twelves will not tolerate a baby-sitter at night because they themselves feel capable of baby-sitting, but there are those who still need an adult near at hand.

Twelve's biggest worry is about school work, about exams, report cards, and not being promoted. It is for the school to question why Twelve worries so much. Is it because he is beginning to demand more of himself or is it because the school demands too much of him?

Twelve isn't immune to having his feelings hurt, but he tries not to show it. He may ignore any comment, walk away, blush, laugh it off, or try to figure out the reason for the remark. Not all Twelves are successful in this, for some strike out with a sarcastic remark, "I'm glad you think so!" slam a door, or hold a grudge. But Twelve seems better able now to pick the times when he wants to let people know how he feels and when he wants to keep his feelings to himself.

He has his own feelings enough in hand to be more aware of other people's feelings. He is often said to read his mother's emotions clearly. He watches her face to see how she feels. Twelve respects other people's feelings and is cautious not to tread on other people's toes. If he must, he tries to do it lightly.

Twelve is not as demonstrative about his affection for his parents as he was at eleven. He restricts his expression of physical affection mainly to kissing and this he definitely enjoys. He kisses goodbye. He kisses goodnight. Twelve talks about whether he is for kissing or against it. No 12-year-old party can be guaranteed immune from some form of kissing game—a most natural expression for Twelve.

There is little jealousy or envy in Twelve except where siblings are concerned. Girls who desire dates may be jealous of an older sister who dates. Twelves who haven't yet shaken off their 11-year-old ways may feel that parents pay more attention to a sibling than to them. This according to their standards is not fair. Twelve recognizes that other people may have more and better possessions than he has but he still considers himself lucky and ready to accept his lot. He becomes quite philosophical in his judgment—"Everybody has some bad and some good, so it evens up." Rather than envying, Twelve heartily disapproves of a friend who brags.

In his desire to hold things in balance, Twelve has lost the sharp edge of competition that he had at eleven. He prefers to be even with his peers, no better, no worse. He wants to do his best and to have a good time. He likes to win, but not all the time and he wants to give others a chance. Those who are good in athletics or in studies like to pursue their special line of ability with the sense of conquest.

Parents of 12-year-olds not only enjoy them in general but enjoy their sense of humor in particular. Eleven's expressions of irritability toward a parent can be spoken under the guise of humor at twelve. Rather than criticizing a father for his overweight, Twelve may remark, "What a physique!"

Twelve adores double meanings and seems to spot them with—or without—the least provocation. A teacher needs to be ready for Twelve's humorous thrusts. Thus, when she decides against letting a boy and girl sit next to each other and says she is going to separate them, some Twelve is sure to retort, "I didn't know they were married."

Dirty jokes are greatly enjoyed by Twelve. He not only understands them, but he tells them with great relish, and laughs uproariously. Though elimination jokes, especially ones relating to bowel movements, are still prevalent, the more specific sex jokes are most in vogue. These jokes can still be told in heterosexual company, which suggests that Twelve is still on the outside of this type of experience, looking in.

4. The Growing Self

Eleven was searching for his self. Twelve is beginning to find it. His parents speak of him as self-contained, self-competent, self-reliant. They, too, must feel this evidence of a new self. Twelve can't quite grasp this change in himself, but he does know that he feels different, that the re-experiencing of special occasions such as Christmas and his birthday seems different from what it used to be.

And his actions do indeed proclaim a change. There is a return of *joie de vivre*, according to his parents, which is reminiscent of himself when he was six and a half years old. At twelve he has become thoughtful, humorous, and a good companion even though there are times when he is nasty and cross and may become "hipped on one subject." His initiative is high, which helps him to plan ahead and allows him to have life more under his own control. He is now able to take over the responsibility of more and more of his life not only in relation to his home and family but also to the outside world.

All of these manifestations of positive behavior bespeak a new self-capacity, a total self in action. Some Twelves may still, as at eleven, identify their self as being in parts of their body such as their feet because they like to climb mountains or to dance. But most Twelves refer their self more to their total body which is alive and functioning. They speak of their self as, "It's all me." Or they will say that their self is in their brain because it "regulates the rest of me" or "controls everything." Sometimes they divide the self equally between the brain and the heart "because you can't live without them both." Or the mind is referred to as "the center of everything."

Twelve is concerned with his similarity to others both in his body and in his experiences. He may find it difficult to locate his self because, as he says, "Each part is like someone else's. No part is yours and yours alone. It may belong to you but it's like someone else's." This feeling of similarity may well come from his closer identification with his group. He is less isolated; less unique. One 12-year-old boy held the misconception that he alone made mistakes until he began to have common experiences of error with other 12-year-olds. Some Twelves feel this loss of the sense of uniqueness rather acutely. When, for example, they are baby-sitting and are treated as "the baby-sitter," they miss the feeling of their own individual uniqueness. But at the same time Twelve doesn't like the sense of feeling "peculiar" or "funny" when he is alone. This feeling is most apt to come on after some sudden change—turning off his radio or awaking in the night.

On the whole, Twelve doesn't delve deeply or want things very different. He is satisfied with his lot and feels that, "Everyone is the best the way they are." He might accept himself further by saying, "Better off to be what you are 'cause everyone has their own difficulties." He does not wish to hasten the growth process because he likes "what happens along the way." And he thinks that, "People should do what is suitable at their age." He doesn't "see that there is any reason to wish to be older because you are going to get older anyway. There is a certain time it will take." He may appear excited and expectant about what is going to happen in the near future, but he is well rooted in the present as it unfolds from day to day. He can wait to grow up.

Twelve is nicely aware of his assets. He seems able to pick the very ones which depict his age best—"being good-natured," "having a good disposition," "being kind," and "getting on with people." Likewise he knows

his shortcomings, the most outstanding of which are his becoming angry or fighting with his siblings.

When Twelve is allowed three wishes he may not desire more than two. A dog or horse is still desired by some. He may wish to move to some far-off place or at least to move to a new big house. Or if he could just have a bigger room of his own, a gym, or a swimming pool. He may be thinking of vacations and travel. And with Twelve's increase in intellectual interests he often wishes for better grades or that he might be smarter. Twelve's wishes are not only for himself but frequently for others. He wants to help his family or to take them on a trip. Girls especially wish for their father's success and health and that he won't have to work so hard. Those who are without siblings wish for them. Twelve not only desires peace in the world but he would eradicate diseases, famine and war.

Twelve is less sure of his future career than he has been. He is more apt to restrict himself to one possibility or may combine two, instead of giving two alternatives as at eleven. Perhaps he would raise horses and draw them. He vehemently states the things he does not want to do. He also recognizes that what he would like to do now might not fit into his ability later and he might not continue to want to do the same thing as he grows older. This recognition that there might be a change in choice shows Twelve's flexibility and scope. A few Twelves are still influenced by their parents' professions but most have ideas of their own. Raising and care of animals is less of an interest than it has been. Beside the usual desire to be a singer, dancer, nurse, or secretary, girls are now interested in writing and especially in writing and illustrating children's books. They are also interested in becoming teachers. Both sexes are interested in art or painting. Boys lean toward becoming doctors, architects, or scientists.

Twelve has a fair idea of which college he wants to go to, though many haven't thought that far ahead. Some are thinking of special schools for their final preparation. Girls more than boys desire coeducation.

Some boys have now thought enough about marriage to desire to be bachelors, though they realize they might change their minds. A few contemplate that they might marry their present girl friends (with whom they have a speaking acquaintance), but on the other hand think that they might change their minds when the time comes.

Girls are more assured in holding their sights toward matrimony, though they wonder about combining work and marriage. One of their main concerns is that they have something in common with their husband. Their usual tendency to balance, and to strike the middle way, appears when they name the attributes they desire in a husband. A husband should "neither be fat nor skinny." They may hope that he is "not too intellectual, but not too dumb" either. Twelve doesn't want her husband to be rich, but she also doesn't want him to be poor.

As for having children, boys are willing to wait to consider this issue when the time comes. A few girls at twelve still want many children, but on the whole they now desire two, three, or four, with both sexes included.

5. Interpersonal Relationships

It is difficult to catch hold of the subtle change that occurs at Twelve, but there is an unmistakable clearing of the air. Not that Twelve has changed completely, but, as his mother says, "He's over the hump." Twelve may first be aware of a change in his relationship with his parents. He recognizes that he gets on better with his parents, that he argues less. One 12-year-old girl attributed it to, "Father is less strict. He changed gradually." Then on second thought she added, "I think it was me."

Twelve's improvement occurs indeed, because he sees himself as well as the other person in a new light. He is now more a self in his own right, more a congenial member of the household. He can be with the family or away from them. He recognizes the change for the worse in his own behavior when he is tired. And he knows it is no time to clash with his younger brother before his brother's nap or before supper when he is fatigued.

Life is smoother and Twelve is beginning to take some initiative. But in daily routines, most of his acts are stimulated by hindthought, by the pressures of demand from his parents rather than by forethought. He rarely, however, becomes angry with his parents when he is demanded of, and is less apt to argue back. He knows ahead of time that he is going to act eventually but that he still needs that strong push to get him started. He knows that he will clean up his room after a long lecture; that he will "feel terrible" enough after criticism from his parents to act. Twelve is taking criticism to heart, but not necessarily enough to continue to repeat the desired act later under his own motivation.

Much of his parents' criticism (and there is less than at eleven) he accepts at face value. He knows that his parents think he is lazy, that he should take better care of his room, that his table manners should be better. But he has set up a camaraderie with his parents so that few major battles arise. A boy is "insolent in a polite way" toward his father. A girl turns a scolding by her mother into laughter by "her amusing reception of it; not with indifference but just kind of pleasant and funny."

Twelve demands less of his parents than he did. Sometimes he would wish to be more appreciated or approved by them, but he does less with them than earlier. He may complain that his father is so busy that he has little time for him, but actually Twelve needs his father less. Girls are at times flirtatious with their fathers and are often said to be able to handle father better than any other member of the family does. This is an age when girls more than boys are aware of the relationship between the sexes. This may be why they criticize their mothers for not wearing lipstick which they so long to wear themselves.

Fighting with younger siblings who are close to them in age (those in the six- to eleven-year range) is calming down. Twelve reports that once in a while he may have "breaks" in fighting or that he now gets on better. Twelve knows that this is the main area where his parents wish he would improve. He may also wish that his parents would improve by not spoiling younger siblings as much as they do. Those younger ones do bother him.

They get into his things and are prone to tease him. However, he is not so vulnerable as he was at eleven and is less apt to explode when he is teased about his liking a certain member of the opposite sex.

Siblings in the preschool age range he does well with. He seems to know how to play at their level and is often extremely fond of them.

Twelve is apt to admire or even idolize an older brother or sister. He may still squabble with those aged thirteen or fourteen, but his relationship with those who are fifteen and over is not only more neutral but often very positive. Twelve may confide in a sympathetic older sibling instead of his parents. Fortunate is the Twelve who has such a sympathetic sibling, for then his separation and emancipation from his family ties can be smoother and more gradual.

Twelve moves easily and freely among his peers. He rarely seems to be at a loss for friends when he wants them. He may rotate among as many as eight to a dozen friends, first "going with one and then with another." Girls especially go in twosomes. Nearby, handy friends can be drawn upon, but school friends allow for wider choice and greater selectivity. Twelve is fairly observant about his friends, knowing which ones still continue to quarrel, which ones don't seem as interesting because they are still "too good," and which ones are silly. One girl of twelve rotated back and forth between what she called the "nice girls and the horrid girls, the ones who talk about clothes." She knew she wanted to play with the "horrid girls" whenever she wore lipstick. This back-and-forth movement is natural to Twelve. He visits back and forth with his friends, first stays overnight at his friend's house, then has the friend over to his house.

Larger groups will form for athletic activities or possibly going to the movies, but on the whole Twelve likes a small group. The few informal, spontaneous clubs which continue may be on the verge of breaking up.

Twelve, for many, is an age of considerable boy-girl interest and activity. Some boys who were not interested in girls at eleven and won't be again at thirteen enjoy a short period of genuine interest in girls at twelve and are disappointed if they are not pushed by parents to attend the regular dancing groups. Each sex professes interest in the opposite sex. Those more newly interested will speak of the members of the opposite sex as "O.K." or "all right." But there are those who are more outspoken and speak of them as "darn nice." A few with more advanced interests have already been into and out of this interest. As one boy said, "I've been into girls for quite a while now so I just left them. I quit." But he, along with many others, will be "in and out," first giving a good bit of his attention to girls, then not bothering about them or being too busy.

It's usually common knowledge among a group which boy likes which girl or vice versa, but girls don't expect a boy to come out and say that he likes them. Talking together at school may be the extent of the friendship or dancing together at dancing school. A few progress to the point of going to a movie together, or writing letters to each other if they live at a distance.

Both boys and girls show a lot of shifting of interest from one friend to another. Boys get a girl in order to keep up with the other boys and they may give her up as quickly as they got her. None want to settle down to one friend of the opposite sex. Girls are perhaps the more talkative about the opposite sex among themselves. They may enjoy talking about boys as much as anything they actually do with boys. They may be "looking around," "keeping their eyes open," and they don't mind waiting until the boys come to them. "If they want us they can have us," one threesome of girls declared.

Parties can be fun, but alas if they are not planned for, if they are not held in leash, the results are often disastrous. Girls often leave the parties unhappy and disconsolate because they haven't been picked by the boys to dance with. And boys can wreck the party by throwing any available food or fluid and breaking glasses or bottles.

If Twelve's parents aren't able to plan for a party with him, assist with the games and the fun, and provide the necessary controls when needed, then it would be better not to have the party. Like six, twelve is an age when a party with both sexes invited is most desired. And it must be held at night. The controls can be easiest if they are brought in from the start, and what better control can be secured than Twelve's own interest through mental stimulation? Perhaps the name of a famous person is pinned to the back of each guest as he arrives, and he is set the task of guessing who he is by the way others treat him. Great hilarity can follow.

Of course there must be one game such as "Hide-in-the-dark," which seems essential to Twelve's craving for close, accidental, and exciting contact with the opposite sex. It doesn't have to end as a kissing game, but it has all the potential excitement of a kissing game. Some quieter game might follow, such as acting out slogans or simple sentences. Simple refreshments of fresh fruit punch and a mound of homemade cookies should be served at that magic moment when food alone satisfies the inner cravings of Twelve.

Such a party might end with the eternally satisfying play with balloons —blowing them up and batting them around. Within the span of two hours there may have been time for a square dance or the Virginia reel. No time can be left untended; parents should be on hand, even if not right in the room. (Strenuous as this may sound to parents, the saving of wear and tear on furniture, Twelve's feelings, and parents' dispositions make it well worthwhile.) The close can be most happily rounded off if it is possible to deliver the children to their homes, without the complications of their waiting to be called for by many parents.

6. Activities and Interests

Twelve has lost some of that insistent note he had at eleven when he was convinced that he had to "have this" or "go to that" immediately. He now wants to be a part of the group and he is heavily ruled by the group. But he can also enjoy himself alone. Though he likes organized activities, he enters readily into the shapelessness of "fooling around." He not only "fools around," but he "hangs around," he "sits around," he "hacks around," or he "walks around." He likes to let

life happen spontaneously at times and likes to flow along with it even though an experience may end up rather shapelessly. This doesn't bother him.

Twelve doesn't get into conflict with others the way he did at eleven, when he wanted his own way and to have things done according to his dictates. Rather, he now wants to hear what the other fellow thinks. Or he just wants to enjoy life. He likes variety and change. He's not one to repeat, and he lets you know about "the boring old schedule of doing the same thing over and over again." He gets "sick of" hearing the same jazz or Dixieland record played over and over again by his 14- or 15-year-old sister.

But Twelve isn't really bored too often, because he doesn't have time to do all the things he wants to do. He implies that he has little extra time by the phrase "when I'm free." One of the activities a certain type of more withdrawing 12-year-old girl enjoys when she's free is to walk around in the woods. She likes to look for little nooks where flowers might be hidden or to search out the dens of animals.

Both boys and girls can now be more readily separated into the more athletic and the non-athletic groups. The one sport that holds up with all Twelves is swimming. Perhaps their extra weight insures the buoyancy and ease of their swimming. They not only swim in the summer but choose to sign up for winter swimming courses in indoor pools. They dream of owning a pool of their own. "No water seems to be too cold for him," as one mother reported. And there is indeed no better place to "fool around" than in the water. But Twelve likes to receive instructions and spends good time and effort in trying to perfect his stroke when this is demanded of him.

The more athletic Twelves enjoy sports in season. The basketball and hockey seasons are now being added to the football and baseball seasons. Tennis, a more individual sport, is enjoyed even by the less athletic Twelves. Both sexes participate in roller skating and double-dutch rope jumping. These are still socially acceptable. Other sports such as sailing, golf, and fencing are now making their entrance in the sports interests of the soon-to-be teen-ager. Horseback riding persists as an interest, especially with a group of horse-loving girls.

Sports can be such a strong interest with some boys that little time is spent indoors. The less athletic boys, however, are spending more time indoors busily making things. Their products include little cars made of tin and wood (often of their own design), model planes, cars and even trains, photographs taken by themselves, radios, puppets, hooked rugs, knitted scarves. The girls enjoy the last three activities along with sewing. With both sexes there may be some difficulty in completing these products, but with a little help and spurring on from the parents Twelve usually comes through to fair completion.

Both boys and girls have a wide range of interests. Some continue to collect all varieties of things, but this urge is reported to be "not too vicious at the moment." The collection of postcards, especially those which picture many different lands, is a new favorite. Twelve spends much time looking over and talking over his postcard collection with his friends. Collecting copies of famous paintings is another preferred activity with a selected group. Both drawing and painting can be favorite activities at this age. And some try their hand at creative writing. The girls are more apt to write long stories whereas the boys are more interested in reporting in newspaper style. This is the age when letter writing is less of a chore, and the interest in having a pen pal from a foreign land is strong. Not a few friendships flourish through this back-and-forth exchange, though they may bloom only a short time.

Twelve enjoys some form of organization whether it is through his own initiative and effort or through those who control or stimulate his activities. Perhaps this is why the summer camp is so successful with Twelve. Perhaps the lack of organization with some Scout troops is also the reason why so many Twelves drop out, often with the complaint that they "don't do anything" in Scouts. Likewise, spontaneous clubs of the same sex are often dissolved at twelve. They don't seem to have enough substance to keep them together.

Twelve's best organization comes through an individual or twosome project in which he is heavily motivated, especially if to earn money. One boy may deliver coffee and rolls to a neighboring construction crew. Another may make plastic pins to sell. One project may provide money for another project and this one for still another project in true businesslike fashion. The money from the pins may provide money for a snow plow and this in turn may provide money for the real end desire, a radio and television laboratory.

Another project that often crops up among 12-year-olds is a local weekly news bulletin. Girls usually produce these by hand, but boys are more apt to use a hand printing press. The combination of their desire to do some creative writing or reporting and also to work the printing press is an ideal one. Often these news bulletins are started with great enthusiasm and plans for a long future—even some subscriptions. Each issue is numbered carefully according to volume and number, but all too few issues reach the local market.

SEDENTARY LOOKING AND LISTENING ACTIVITIES

Radio and television don't have the grip on Twelve that they have had. Some Twelves have their favorite programs but they don't have to listen to or watch them every day and often restrict their watching to convenient times. Mysteries are the most favored programs and these don't scare the listener the way they used to. That is probably why Twelve can take them or leave them. Though he would like to listen to adventures on radio or television while he does his homework (and this he often does quite effectively), Twelve is amenable to reason and will accept restriction to use of background music only. Classical music is preferred by some; jazz by others. But a large proportion of Twelves balance between the two in their choice.

Twelve often keeps his radio on after he is in bed. This he may do not so much for the specific program as for the sociability. For though he is less apt to be scared by the mystery murders he hears over the radio, he is more apt to be scared by unexplained noises he hears about him.

There is less time to read and there may also be less urge to read. Most Twelves do not find time to read more than one or two books a week. Boy and girl are entering the adult sphere of interest and may use the library regularly. A few are aware of the authorship of books and may wish to read other books by the same author. Mysteries lead as the favorite type of book for both boys and girls and adventures are a close second. *The Iliad* is often thought to be a fascinating tale of adventure to Twelve. Comic-book reading still persists, but without the avid concentration that demands rereading and hoarding. Twelve is less apt to spend his own money to buy comics, but he'll read them if they are around.

Movies, along with the rest of Twelve's activities, have come into fairly good perspective. In fact, he may be as demanding of a movie before he chooses to see it as he is about his demands of a teacher. He wants first to know all about a movie, what it is, who is in it. Also he wants to know if it is put on well and if there is good acting in it. If the movie doesn't pass in his judgment, if he hasn't heard "good talk about it," then he doesn't bother to go. Most Twelves go only occasionally when the movie has passed their tests that it is a "good movie," but others may still go once a week or once in two weeks. Twelve usually goes with a friend of the same sex or, less often, with his mother. A few boys go alone if they are interested in seeing the movie a second time or more or wish to see a favorite actress. If Twelve has a favorite actress or actor this may determine in part why he chooses to see certain pictures.

7. School Life

If Twelve has one outstanding characteristic it is that of enthusiasm. Enthusiasm can be so strong at this age that the child is carried away by it. He will literally be in such a rush that he might even knock down anyone who is in his path. This same 12-year-old enthusiasm can whip up a group to such a boisterous pitch of heated discussion that their teacher may need to step in to quiet them down.

The group is indeed very important to Twelve. His own identity can become lost within the group. The extremes, of first being drawn toward others, then being as strongly repelled by them, so common at eleven, are less apparent at twelve. Girls especially have a way of flocking together. And how they chatter together at every chance they can grasp.

Twelve likes to be at school a little ahead of time. It is not so difficult for him to get ready for school in the morning as it was at eleven. If he has homework he may have finished it when he awoke in the morning. Or without the demands of homework he likes to get to school early to finish any task left over from the previous day. The latter may be truer of boys than of girls. Catching up on the social activities of the others is far more important for the girls. After a weekend they will especially flock and chatter, telling each other about a dance or party; about going skating or horseback riding; about what they bought on a shopping trip; or about

the eternally interesting topic of boys.

Twelve is not as dependent on his teacher as he was at eleven. Twelves don't flock around the teacher the way they did, but will include the teacher in discussions or activities if she wants to be included. There should be a good flow between teacher and pupil. Twelve tends to like his teacher. He often speaks of her as wonderful. He still likes a teacher who tells good jokes and who understands him. But more than anything else he wants a teacher who can teach. He wants her "to know her work better" and "not to teach more than she knows." He thinks she "should know what she is talking about." And if "she knows just about everything you can put a question to her," then she is truly the "wonderfulest teacher of all."

Twelves can be challenged by their teacher. They are ready to be held in line, to be demanded of. If a teacher is not too sure of himself, is "soft," is not too good on discipline, then Twelves lead him a merry pace. They throw spitballs, they cough in unison at a prearranged time. The minute the teacher is out of the room they tell risqué jokes and laugh uproariously. But they act this way only with the teachers who do not hold a firm and challenging hand. They wouldn't think of acting this way with a teacher they class as "wonderful." If a seventh grade is out of hand, it would be wise to question the capacity of the teacher to handle 12-year-olds.

In the classroom, girls still tend to stay with girls and boys with boys especially in the early part of the school year. Each student is more on his own, more ready to buckle down than he was at eleven. But he needs to be allowed to move around, to get up to get books, sharpen his pencil, or secure paper. Sometimes he just stands by his desk to relieve his fatigue. If allowed a certain amount of freedom, he wiggles less in his seat and talks less to his neighbor. Note passing can also be cut down to a minimum because the need has been absorbed by allowing more freedom of movement. The increased restlessness that may occur at 11 or 11:30 A.M. might be related to hunger and could be relieved by a snack.

Twelve shows a wide variety of interests in his school work (though he still prefers sports). Arithmetic is often one of his favorite subjects. He likes the definiteness of arithmetic and he especially enjoys decimals. He likes to practice and he enjoys the ease with which he does his arithmetic almost without thinking. If there is an arithmetic assignment on the board he will often choose to do that first. And if he's in the midst of an arithmetic assignment which he hasn't finished in the usual forty minutes, he'd like to go on until he has finished it. It bothers him to have to stop with a feeling of incompleteness.

Twelve doesn't like to be held to too rigid a schedule. He likes to be allowed a block of time of more or less standard length but which can be extended so that he can finish. Sometimes when he is interested he likes to go on considerably longer than usual. He is especially carried away by certain topics in social studies. A good example might be one related to the Spanish Armada, Francis Drake, and the stealing of gold and silver from the ships. Such tales of adventure and outlawry might stimulate him to debate, a favorite activity with Twelve. Here is a fit topic: Was Sir Francis Drake justified in stopping these ships and taking their cargo from them? His enthusiasm may rise so rapidly that he may be ready to debate before he has built up his case. He is more concerned about carrying out his ideas right now than he is about how you go about it. His enthusiasm rises so rapidly that you have to guard against a rush. Perhaps the best way to stem the rush is to appoint different pupils to do different tasks. The appointment of a chairman brings with it a calming down and respect.

Twelve is quick to volunteer if a play is to be produced or read. He loves to read his part aloud. The use of a speaker's stand is especially congenial to Twelve.

Twelve's interest in and time for reading may be reduced from what it was earlier and in some confined to school assignments. He still loves tales of adventure and is partial to those which combine fact and fancy. He is beginning to enjoy a few lighter adult books especially where rollicking fun and real human drama unfold (*Cheaper by the Dozen, Life with Father*). Both sexes enjoy this type of human interest story, but on the whole the reading tastes of boys and girls differ quite sharply. It is only with condescension that the girls will read science fiction so favored by the boys. They know ahead of time that they won't like it. The boys won't even condescend to read stories about 17- and 18-year-olds involving romance and career which have started to interest some girls. Narrative and humorous poetry is enjoyed by both sexes, but a demand to memorize passages might spoil this enjoyment.

Boys are especially interested in astronomy and anything to do with outer space. Science fiction adds to the intensity of their interests. And they especially enjoy any simple but real experiments in science. They are curious to know what happens under certain conditions.

The extra subjects of art, music, shop for boys and home economics for girls are all favored. Twelve likes adequate provision for these activities. In art he often likes group creativity, and might enjoy painting scenery for a play with his entire group. In music he especially enjoys singing in harmony, and some are ready to participate in an orchestra. In shop, Twelve shows good co-operation, but he doesn't do a very finished job. He is more interested in accomplishing something in just a few sessions. Some fairly simple three-piece task like making a hamburger press would satisfy his desire for rapid accomplishment and also his interest in food and cooking.

Girls are eager and enthusiastic about both cooking and sewing. But their attention to the group may interrupt their attention to the matter at hand. When they cook, their primary interest is in cooking to eat. They would bake cookies at each session if allowed but they also enjoy the preparation of a salad, a drink, or some hot bread. They are becoming interested in serving.

The 12-year-old girl catches on quickly in sewing. She seems ready at first to continue on her own in the use of a machine. And she may start quite well, but all too soon she is in trouble. Invariably she has forgotten to check some basic step. Maybe the bobbin isn't threaded correctly, or the stitch is going in the wrong direction (even as Twelve's arithmetic process reverses—he may divide instead of multiplying). Twelve is not averse to asking for help when she is in trouble.

Athletics, as always, is the favored period. The boys enjoy the usual baseball, basketball, and football. The girls continue to play softball, dodge ball, and volleyball. They are still apt to stop and chat in the midst of the game and need someone to jostle them back into line. Twelve does a good job in selecting a team according to the ability of the individual though he is occasionally influenced by jealousy. He is competitive but not in the same ruthless way he was at eleven when he wanted to win at all costs. He is beginning to enjoy the game for its own sake.

Twelve is delightfully open and uninhibited in the classroom as well as in the home. He is outspoken about his dislikes. He speaks up if he feels his rights are being infringed upon. He especially doesn't feel it is fair to be held over in a class just before his athletic period. He wants nothing to shorten this period.

Girls are especially aware of their appearance. They may carry pocketbooks with them and are apt to primp before a mirror, combing their hair whenever they get a chance between periods. They flock together before a mirror when it is provided in the classroom. Lipstick may not be accepted by the group except for dances.

Twelves often follow the fads of wearing charm bracelets, pendants, gadgety pins, or long strands of beads. Just where the knot should be placed in the strand of beads may involve important group discussions.

Girls on the whole are more interested in the boys than vice versa. In fact, the girls are often chasing the boys. They want to sit near them. The boys' interest rises as the year progresses. They express their initial interest by poking. Soon they are snatching a girl's wallet or pencil box and are off to hide it. Sometimes the teacher needs to be sought to use her authority to redeem the lost article. Girls may play a similar trick on another girl, with all the girls except the one involved "in the know" as to where the article is hidden. Boys are apt to chase boys and are often after some prized possession such as the tag on another's blue jeans. Twelves like to grab or snatch anything that's loose. It will be another year before they will look upon these acts as childish.

Within a free-flowing, moving, but challenging school structure Twelve can have a wonderful time in seventh grade. His enthusiasm carries him in many different directions and he needs help in channeling it and giving it expression. He needs firmness and control. But when his freedom is too curtailed, when he is forced to move on before he's ready, when he is asked to conform in spheres that have no meaning for him, then he becomes frustrated and the negative side of the age comes to the fore. Homework is a point at issue. Twelve wants to work. He wants to complete a task. He will even ask for homework when it is not given. But as soon as it be-

comes a set pattern, as soon as it usurps his free time when sociability is so important to him, then he rebels and rightly so. Thus he may come to hate school.

The concept of a junior high school may also be another point at issue. Is Twelve ready to accept the bigness, the movement from class to class, the rigidity of the class time, that is demanded of him in junior high school? Do his problems increase? Is his enthusiasm dampened? These and many other questions must be asked before we can decide what kind of a school environment can best allow Twelve to give scope and form to his enthusiasm.

8. Ethical Sense

Twelve makes a level-headed approach to ethics. He seems to make his decisions more through considered thinking, through past experiences, through possible consequences, less through immediate feeling than earlier. He has spontaneous checks within himself, as through his conscience, but he is giving each problem that arises due consideration and weighing. He is basically a diplomat. He is not only tolerant toward others but also toward himself. He is still, however, not averse to seeing what he can get away with and he is also a lover of fun. And above all he does not wish to veer too far from the dictates of his group.

To some Twelves the decision and choice of right as against wrong is still arrived at almost spontaneously by how they feel, by common sense, or by the inner dictates of conscience. But, increasingly, it is thought of as a deliberate, weighed process. Twelve likes to figure out how many good points there are *for* a certain decision and how many bad points there are *against* it. But, if necessary, he can always think up an extra point for or against, and his choice of points is made not so much on a moral basis as in terms of personal advantage. If he knows that doing a certain thing would cause him to be kept after school, then he is less apt to do it. He is less tempted to do the wrong thing than he was at eleven. He has too much respect for himself. And though he may think primarily about what advantages he will secure from a decision, he is also aware of what others—grownups or contemporaries—think. Above all he does not wish to do anything to be classed as "too good" by his peers, for he knows that this might turn them against him.

Twelve's conscience stands guard over him and can, at times, be quite hard on him. But it doesn't, as it sometimes did at eleven, have that ruthless control that either dogged his every footstep or, through defiance, made him go to the opposite extreme of raising havoc. With this easier, looser control he may actually appear more conscientious than did alternately conscience-ridden and unrepentant Eleven. But, as he says, it's "half and half about getting away with things." His conscience can speak out clearly when he has done something wrong, but what he does about it depends on his evaluation of the severity of the situation. (One boy worried enough about cheating on a test to ask to take it over again; others would consider such an offense a trivial one.)

Telling the truth is generally not difficult for Twelve. He can be counted on to be truthful about big,

important things, though not always about little ones. He recognizes that there are times when you have to tell a lie, such as to protect another person. One can lie, according to Twelve, if there is a good reason.

Accepting the blame, along with telling the truth, is a part of Twelve's more positive growth, though he is not trying to acquire martyrdom by taking on any extra burdens. He says that if a sibling or friend were being wrongly accused he wouldn't let them down, but if they deserved the blame he "lets them have it." Usually he tries to be fair.

Twelve no longer argues just for the sake of argument the way he did at eleven. Then he was out to win and to prove his mother wrong at any cost. Now he argues to get his point, especially when he feels he's in the right! But he can show a politeness toward his parents even in the midst of argument. Twelve can be pretty fixed in his ideas and may not listen to reason too well. He can be convinced, though he may feel that his parents are ordering him more than convincing him.

Twelve spreads his tolerance to swearing and drinking. Everything has its place in moderation, he seems to feel. He isn't against swearing himself when he gets mad. But he doesn't think that parents should swear before children. This is not setting a good example to children, who are easily influenced.

Cheating and stealing are under much easier control for Twelve than they are for Eleven. Twelve, especially if he is a boy, may cheat in games or on exams, but then, if he considers it a serious offense, often wants to set things straight. (But cheating at cards and table games is often part of the game, the idea being to see who can get away with it most skillfully.) And he may say that some of his friends take things from the ten-cent store—as much for the fun of it as for the stolen articles. Some Twelves seem to have a hesitant admiration for these pilferers, but the majority do not seem themselves to be tempted.

9. *Philosophic Outlook*

TIME AND SPACE

It is not easy for Twelve to define time, probably because he has glimmers of concepts beyond his means of expression. Twelve thinks of the combination of the person and the place—the time a person is to be at a certain place, the time he is to leave. Or he thinks of time as "how long things take." In other words, time is a measurement; it is "what you measure life in [or by]."

The "never-ending" "everlasting movement" of time is not lost sight of, but Twelve wants to consolidate time along the way. He often refers to a "period of time." Time is the "passing of a certain period" or the movement from "one period to the next." People "use time to make a period," though "time is something that never began and never will end." This latter is a very advanced inclusive concept of time. It may be spoken of in another way as being the "whole span of life on earth." Space and place may be closely linked to time. A period may be spoken of as "a space of moments."

Twelve handles time well. He still has his rushed moments. He feels the contrast between the drag of time when he is responding emotionally to

a death and the speed of time when he's taking a joy ride in an amusement park. On the whole time drags very little because he fills it so full and because he often organizes time in blocks which he can handle.

Twelve valiantly tries to express his ideas of space. Many still conceive of space as "just empty nothing," or "wide-open space with nothing in it." And yet Twelve would give content to space as well as to the rest of his concepts and actions. He would fill it with "air," though he may balance between "air or nothing." He tends to look up as he thinks of space and speaks of it as "up in the air." Or he thinks further afield of "outer air outside the universe." In any case space is "something there's something in," even though it's "something empty."

Twelve not only tells about space but he experiences space. He might speak of it as "what we see all the time" or "what we live and sleep and eat and die in." Or he may experience the wonder, awesomeness, and endlessness of space. Standing on the rise of the Grand Canyon can affect him so deeply that he can't find words to tell of his experience. One boy of twelve expressed his ideas of space this way: "It's so big, marvelous. If you could walk on air you could walk for trillions of miles and never get anywhere, right where you were before. Makes me feel awful peculiar, small but at the same time wonderful."

Both immediate and far space are under Twelve's control. He moves with ease about the town, keeping appointments, going on shopping trips, or meeting people. He is fairly good in finding his way in strange places and knows that you ask a policeman when you are in trouble.

He has experienced the confusion of going in the opposite direction of where he had intended to go.

Distant travel, especially overnight travel, is a great treat for the 12-year-old. He may desire to go alone and even execute a change of trains or buses by himself. He knows about Travelers Aid. There is no need to feel lost or anxious. When he has reached his destination safely, however, he has accomplished what he set out to do and often forgets to notify his family that he has arrived.

DEATH AND DEITY

Though a number of Twelves are not too concerned about death, many are beginning to wonder about it. Some dread it and shudder at the thought of it, but many report that they are no longer afraid of it. Those who are still afraid may hope they may die in their sleep or may be frozen to death. Though they may not like to think about it, they still recognize that everyone must die sooner or later. They rationalize about it, saying that if you didn't die there would be too many people in the world. Or since they know that they will never know the answer about death, they give the problem willingly over to the philosophers.

But still there are those who would wish to work out their own answers about life after death and to think about their own feelings. Twelve has times of real pause, of looking up into the sky to wonder. What will it be like when he dies? Will he go on living or will everything be blacked out? The less wondering ones may accept what they are taught by their parents, or their church, that if you're good you go up to heaven and if you're bad you go down to hell. But going to heaven does "seem sort of silly" to a number of Twelves. Many feel there is a strong relationship between how you act when you are alive and what will happen to you after you are dead. Others do not feel this direct relationship. They are more concerned with death ending this life, even terminating any memory of what happened in this life, and they think about starting a new life after death. They think about the individual being born again and returning to the earth as another person. One boy wished he might return to the earth as Caesar.

There is indeed a very real religious concern in some at this age. Twelve looks back at a time when he didn't believe, when he wasn't interested. But now he's wondering about it, and has from time to time for the past year. Much skepticism is expressed— but this, in part, reflects Twelve's grappling with the problems, rather than disinterest. For often he can come to no definite conclusion. He says, "I don't know what I think," but he may even so spend quite a lot of time thinking about God and religion. Often his concepts are very vague, "something you can't explain," "something men think about," or "I just think He's there in your mind." Some are insistent through their reasoning, "There has to be something controlling everything." What God is is difficult to define—"half man, half spirit," "half spirit, half idea," or "just sort of an idea." He is not an impassive God to Twelve—He rules, He controls, He exerts power, He judges. But Twelve doesn't think that He is always watching him, for his reason tells him this would be impossible since He has so much else to do. Twelve is not always sure how his religious beliefs influence his life. He knows that his thoughts of religion give him a "good feeling." He also has some idea of how God might want him to act. He thinks that prayer helps "when you're in a mess" or "at crucial times"—such times as report card time, picking a winner or loser, finding a lost ball, or falling off to sleep.

There are the outright disbelievers at Twelve but these are in the marked minority. Even they are aware of what their friends think of their ideas or of how much their friends think about religion.

There seems to be little relationship between Twelve's interest in religion and his attendance at Sunday school. Many Twelves do not wish to attend and only do so because they are made to. Others go because of the social activities. A few are interested in the choir. Belief in God is more important to Twelve than attending Sunday school or church. A few of the more devout are now preferring the church service to Sunday school but on the whole the church service is "the most interminable" thing that Twelve has ever experienced, in his immediate opinion.

CHAPTER SEVEN

Year Thirteen

MATURITY PROFILE

E ACH YEAR brings an increment of maturity. The increment of Year Thirteen is rather complex because adolescence is now well under way, and many new phases of behavior will emerge. Some will be manifest. Other phases will remain obscure because Thirteen (during the course of a year) is not always too open and communicative. At home he may lapse into spells of silence, musing, and reverie. At school quite different facets of behavior appear. He responds with intense interest to the class assignments and discussions. He shows a great capacity to acquire knowledge through reading, listening, and looking.

Despite occasional moodiness he proves to be adaptable and dependable. He may even show impressive skill and protectiveness in helping with the care of a sister or brother of preschool age. He has a sense of duty. At times he seems overconscientious. He indulges in many private worries. He makes detailed criticisms of his parents. They in turn are perplexed and concerned about his recurring tendency to withdraw from the family circle. Perhaps these parents are themselves needlessly worried that their child will drift away from them. Many of the worries of youth may well be normal signs of a growth process which leads to self-insight. There is probably no reason to worry even about the articulate 13-year-old boy who told us, "Most of the time I worry that people won't like me. I suppose we all do. I worry that I'm going to worry. I worry that I should stop worrying."

We shall not ask him to stop worrying altogether because benign worry is simply one expression of the *inwardizing awareness* which is a cardinal maturity trait at this early stage of adolescent development. But this inwardizing is not confined to itself. It *takes in* the *outer* world. It is linked and interlocked with an *externalizing awareness*. The interaction of these two modes of awareness constitutes the major key to the psychology of the 13-year-old.

Two-way awareness is really a method of growth. It supplies a mechanism for assimilating the wealth of new experiences which now crowd upon the inner life of the growing youth. So much happens for the first time. But outer events and "experiences" do not always register their effects automatically. Many must be mulled over to become incorporated into the tissues of personality.

Accordingly, the 13-year-old withdraws from time to time into himself. He has brief intervals of self-absorption and rumination during which he releases and reviews with variations his inner feelings, tensions, and attitudes. This is not a morbid escape from reality. It is rather an experimental form of psychic play. The movements of the mind require playful, exploratory exercise quite as much as the muscular movements of the body to which in fact they are allied. This kind of inwardizing represents a positive, constructive function. It helps us to interpret some of the apparent vagaries of early adolescent behavior.

A 13-year-old boy joins the family group to enjoy an evening TV program. He is interested, but in the middle of the program his face suddenly assumes a detached and serious expression. He rises unceremoniously and without a word he goes to his room—to cogitate, to ruminate. We cannot penetrate his reveries, but they are not interminable, and on his own initiative and responsibility he presently makes a concentrated assault upon his homework. In a sense he is concerned both with inner and outer affairs.

Such behavior does not denote that the adolescent is making a retreat from reality. On the contrary, he probes more deeply into reality by turning things over in his mind. Such inwardizing behavior is serious business for him. If he were trying to escape reality, he would be more likely to resort to evasive and distracting humor or to frank opposition. Instead he seems at times to seek aloneness, not for its own sake but for inner satisfactions which it would be hard for him to put into words. He clarifies and organizes his experiences by inward rehearsals and self-examination.

His musings are many-sided. They involve choices, wishes, ideas, ambitions. They may lead to provisional and potential decisions in the realm of moral conduct. Such musings are far from idle; for they signify the effort of the adolescent to achieve a more mature self. Through voluntary reflective effort he finds that he is not completely at the mercy of instinctual emotion. His inwardizing leads to genuine thinking, and this in turn creates a sense of what he aptly calls will power. It is characteristic of a 13-year-old to be conscious of his increasing "will power."

Inwardizing behavior thus takes many different forms. It varies, of course, with the temperament and abilities of the individual. It may occur in brief episodes or in a long stretch during a lengthened solitary walk. A talented adolescent at this age may engage in extended periods of cogitation in his special fields of interest.

Some youths are more moody than others. But inwardizing mental activity can be regarded as a normal manifestation, unless it is carried to extremes of content and frequency. Indeed, inwardizing behavior deserves a certain respect which it does not always receive. When an adolescent is wrapped in his own thoughts, he can look sullen and glum without actually being either ill-humored or unsociable. Our misinterpretations then may do him poor justice.

Typical Twelve is blithe. Thirteen is reflective. This climatic difference came into contrast in the developmental interview. Like Twelve, Thirteen was usually co-operative, but not as spontaneously outgoing or as inquisitive. There was less conversation, less humor; his voice was low and sometimes he responded merely by a shrug; he sat with relative composure; tensional activity mostly confined to the hands. The interviewer felt the need of framing the questions carefully. The answering speech was slower, briefer, and subdued. Hesitancy seemed to be due to a self-protective guardedness and searching for the right words and phrase; for Thirteen in comparison with Twelve is a precisionist—a critic of his own performance as well as that of others.

His choice of words suggested a greater degree of maturity. He used expressions such as "to put it bluntly," "seldom," "harmonious," "conscious," "in my judgment." Occasionally he astonishes us by using the term "psychology"! All this is symptomatic of a growing intelligence. He takes a new pleasure in rational thought—in stating propositions and raising doubts He is able to think in terms of necessity, probability, and hypothetical conditions. He is becoming aware of reasoning powers as operations of the mind at his command.

He is beginning to apply these emerging powers to his emotional life, through self-appraisal and appraisal of his associates, young and old. He is aware of his changing moods and tries to bring thoughts to bear on them. He may express annoyance with himself: "I don't want to feel as I do." "Oh, I have been sort of mad at everyone lately." He uses words to bring his feelings under better control and to erect a bold front against lingering fears. He rarely cries from anger; he gives vent to rage by words rather than physical violence. He shows increased capacity to feel sadness. His varying moods are frequently pitched on a minor key. He may be shy with strangers. He is touchy. On occasion he protects himself by withdrawing physically as well as mentally from the focus of irritation. On other occasions he (or she) may take an unpleasant, antagonistic attitude, verbalized in a defiant manner, as though he were bent on defending his own ego by warding off the parent.

Thirteen is very sensitive to criticism and keenly perceptive of the emotional states of other persons. He shows new skill in reading facial expressions and in dramatic mimicry and impersonation, sometimes mixed with humor. In serious fun he enjoys matching his wits with a co-operative adult, sparring for advantage by verbal thrusts and counterthrusts. All this indicates that his emotional life is developing in close association with his intelligence and his social behavior. The whole vast field of interpersonal relations is subject to the basic joint mechanisms of inwardizing and externalizing awareness.

Interpersonal behavior comes to its first and most exacting tests in the home. Siblings still are a source of trouble particularly if they fall in the age range of six to eleven. But the trouble is less constant than formerly and tends to take place on a verbal rather than a bodily plane. Siblings under six attract interest and affection. Thirteen cares for them with pleasing protectiveness. Senior sisters and brothers often are regarded with admiration and respect and may become confidants. One girl remarked, "Well, I find Miriam [the older sister] very convenient. I can tell her things and she understands. But I think I have something against her. I guess it's just that she's an older sister." A 13-year-old boy commenting on his younger sister said, "We don't get on too well. Don't know what the trouble is. She pesters me and gets into my things. My parents think I could get on better. The baby is O.K. I prefer her and take care of her." Another boy commented on home pressures in general: "They try to improve everything about me: disposition and common sense, that I'm not responsible enough and that I argue."

Boys and girls alike at this age may withdraw from close confidential relationship with their parents. Somewhat in embarrassment, a boy ventures to suggest that he doesn't like to have his father put his arm around him. A girl may become extremely critical of her mother—"for her own good." The criticism is often sharpened to fine details, including the mother's clothes, jewelry, hair-do, make-up, conduct, and demeanor! The faultfinding is definitely at a more mature level than it was at age eleven, because it concerns the very problems which the daughter herself is trying to resolve. She is ceasing to argue for its own sake. In a quieter interlude she will initiate and seek a calm discussion of the issues. With increase of reasoning powers calm arguments assume an important function. Sometimes she may secretly long for calm discussion, wishing for a favorable opportunity.

As we might expect, Thirteen tends to be more discriminating than he was at twelve in his estimation and acceptance of companions. He has fewer friends. He is more likely to play by himself or with some one chosen friend. Girls, likewise, have fewer friends. They may even show less interest in boys than they did a year earlier. Boys show a similar trend. Illustrative comments: "Have not started on girls much. Don't dislike them, but just don't bother with them much. In Scouts we have dances. That's about all!" "As far as I'm concerned girls can be or cannot be just as *they* like. Most of my friends all have just about the same attitude. Don't find them repulsive. Just don't care." These firm declarations of neutrality foreshadow the rise in dating which begins in the years immediately following. Relatively few in the thirteen-year range date.

On the dance floor there are signs of change and impending change. Many boys have caught up in size with the girls, and their stance is becoming less awkward and less angular. Some girls, however, say that they cannot endure boys of their own age who act so ill at ease and clumsy.

Nevertheless, boys are not altogether careless about their personal appearance. If mirrors were equipped with meters they would show that boys as well as girls make good use of a looking glass to see how they really look to themselves and to others. Much time is spent in studying the reflected image, and comparing it with images conjured up from within. Improvements in attire, in make-up, postural address, and facial expressions are put to experimental test by the mirror. Thirteen desires to know how he impresses people. So he sets up a solitaire kind of interpersonal situation which brings into interplay the two mechanisms of inwardized and externalizing awareness. The mirror becomes a developmental device which fosters self-discovery and self-assurance. Alas, it also awakens agonizing concern if the reflected image proves too disappointing to the young beholder. But even so, it plays a constructive role in defining a realistic sense of self. As the individual grows, he must learn to live with himself and with the changing images of himself.

Movies and the TV screen hold, as it were, another mirror up to his nature. Here he sees an extraordinary variety of images of youths and grownups who have suggestive significance for his developing self. These images build up impressions of what he (or she) would like to be or would prefer not to be. In his reading of literature, comics, and cartoons he is also, consciously or subconsciously, identifying himself with characters and personalities.

But it is at school and on the street and playground that his sense of self experiences the powerful impact of the group, gang, team, and club. Here he encounters the flesh-and-blood images of his age-mates. He glories in being one of them. He tends to comply with the demands and the mores of his peers, but he is aware that questions of compliance or rejection are up to him. As a member of the school group he harbors a certain measure of independence and internal resistance to authoritarian teachers and principals. He feels a glow of expanding maturity when he sees the juvenile behavior of the neighboring 12-year-olds who chase each other down the corridor—"Kid stuff!"

Typically he is fond of school—a good school, with fair and efficient discipline. He appreciates a teacher who stresses factual knowledge and gives scope to panel discussions and pupil participation. He has a prodigious capacity to assimilate knowledge. When interest is aroused, he throws himself fully into the school tasks and into the special projects which he has helped to plan. His interests range far and wide over science and the liberal arts. He is hungry for facts.

Individual differences now declare themselves strongly. A few girls will form "a little club for creative writing," as an extracurricular activity. Independently another girl may make a scrapbook of favorite *New Yorker* cartoons, marking an advance beyond less sophisticated comics. Boys (and girls) of talent may begin to tinker with experiments and gadgets in connection with hobbies stimulated by school work.

Thirteen is at his best as a member of a responsive group in a well-conducted school. Such a group embodies great potentials in its eagerness and capacity for sustained attention. There is a readiness to learn combined with a desire to exercise independence of thought. It is not strange that teachers derive deep satisfactions in meeting the challenge of their dynamic eighth-graders.

The developmental significance of Year Thirteen can scarcely be summed up in a simple formula. It is a year of complex transitions which involve body, mind, and personality. The transitions often come unbidden and unknown in advance. The adolescent must meet them as best he can with and without the help of the culture.

Changes in body build and body chemistry exert effects on posture, co-ordinations, appearance, voice, facial expression, and inner attitudes and tensions. Each sex, each individual, has unique developmental problems which arise out of a distinctive physique and its distinctive physiology. The bodily changes intensify the awareness of growing up. The youth forms a body-image of himself, always wondering what impression he makes on others. With changing bodily conditions his moods change, fluctuating between secret despair and optimistic self-acceptance. He has to assimilate these somatic events which have an intimate claim on him. At the same time he is beset by countless interpersonal demands made by his father and mother, brothers and sisters, companions and teachers. Moreover, the claims of home, school, and age-mates often conflict and aggravate the confusion.

In the midst of all these pressures he preserves his self-identity and achieves a measure of independence. He meets his developmental problem by a heightened awareness of himself and of the world in which he lives. His sensitiveness and inwardizing characteristics are symptoms of a deepening and expanding sense of self. He has advanced far since the relative casualness of the 10-year-old. At thirteen years he is in a stage of momentous transitions. He is peculiarly in need of sympathetic understanding.

MATURITY TRAITS

1. Total Action System

The change which takes place between twelve and thirteen can be very profound. At thirteen there seems to come an inner mobilization and organization of forces. The tendency is to pull things together, to inwardize, to think about things. This narrowing down and compressing produces a great deal of energy, but how this energy is expended depends upon the success of the organization.

Thirteen almost seems to know that he needs to be more selective than he has been, that he needs to concentrate and to discard in order to achieve further growth. When he accomplishes this by withdrawing to his room many parents are both worried about his behavior and hurt by the feeling of being cut out. It is even harder to accept this change if Thirteen gives lavish time and attention to a friend over the telephone. It is often wise for parents to take their cue from Thirteen, not only allowing him to withdraw from them, but also withdrawing from him or at least standing by on the side lines, ready to help as needed.

Though Thirteen appears more quiet and withdrawn than earlier, he can be very active in his thoughts, storing up ideas and energy to be expended at a later date. Voracious reading is one way of satisfying this inner urge. Constant expenditure of this new-found energy on private enterprises is another. As one boy said, "Anything I hate to do is nothing." This same boy recognized his own change from twelve when he continued, "I remember last year I'd just sit around and get kind of sick of myself. This year I've too much to do."

This busyness of Thirteen can be so extreme that it may be hard for him to find time to "squeeze" in even things he wants to do, let alone household chores. But his energy can be bountiful. One parent reports, "No physical feat is too hard for her to undertake"; another, "She's never tired, always anxious for more activity." This is by no means true of all Thirteens; many are well on toward fourteen before this phase occurs. But when Thirteen is both mobilizing and expending his efforts in an organized fashion, especially on something that

has aroused his feelings, it is amazing to watch him in action. The death of a pet mouse might involve an entire evening as Thirteen fashions a beautiful little coffin, composes an epitaph or a poem to accompany the mouse to his grave, and finally buries him. And the mouse's demise might have occurred in the first place because of the time and loving attention spent by Thirteen in handling him. (Sally Benson, in *Junior Miss,* aptly describes a similar episode.)

In an interview the poised, withdrawn side of Thirteen is most in evidence. He is usually friendly but he is not spontaneous and communicative. He sits quietly with little movement. His voice is often low and difficult to hear, and he speaks more slowly than he did. He may answer with a shrug of his shoulders. He thinks hard before he answers questions and may bite his lips as he cogitates. His answers are sincere and honest, but he tells no secrets. At times he looks sad and grave, but as his interest is aroused he begins to warm up. At times he may laugh while drawing in his breath. Everything about him is pulling in in his attempt to choose, to discriminate, and to define.

HEALTH

Thirteen's health is in general continuing to improve. Fatigue is less marked than it has been at eleven and twelve. A few may still complain of stomach or chest pains. Skin sensitivity to wool, as evidenced by a rash on the inner surface of the arms, is present in some. Headaches are less frequent and have a more definite relationship to specific cause, occurring after a great deal of physical exercise or prior to menstruation. The presence of a fever as high as 103–104° which may occur without any evidence of a cold or other illness can usually be related to an unusual intensity of mental activity.

TENSIONAL OUTLETS

There is a further reduction of tensional outlets. Fingernail biting, hand-to-face gestures, or scratching of scalp persist in some. There are some small ticlike movements and twitches which may lessen with the taking of Vitamin B. A dry and scaly skin and scalp may also respond to Vitamin B.

VISION

About a third of our Thirteens reported specific or non-specific symptoms or complaints concerning their vision. About half of these were related to reading, and occurred in those Thirteens who love to read and who read excessively. The symptoms varied from individual to individual with reports of feeling tired when reading, of print running together or blurring, headaches after movies or television, feeling uncomfortable when riding in a car. However, few Thirteens recognized these complaints as arising from their visual mechanism.

During a visual examination Thirteen sits quietly and asks very few questions about the procedure, about his eyes, or about how well he is doing. He can, however, view his vision and its proper care with greater maturity than earlier. He will wear glasses if it is necessary. He may give good reasons why he would prefer not to, but he can accept the advantages of wearing them for near work—reading and studying—though he thinks of them as a nuisance. Thirteens who wear their glasses all of the time may dislike them for social affairs but know they might feel unsure of themselves if they went without them. By fourteen the girls especially will have a drive to be more free from their glasses and will work to secure this freedom. They will then be more ready to accept and co-operate with a visual training program.

Thirteen, in his inwardizing process, is reducing his functional farsightedness (or hyperopia). This trend, if continued, would result in a measurable nearsightedness, but fortunately Fourteen reverses the trend and the farsightedness is increased slightly. Those children who showed no farsightedness at eleven are in definite danger of becoming nearsighted at thirteen. And those who are already nearsighted are likely to show a further increase in this same direction. If Thirteen is somewhat farsighted and finds it difficult to focus from near to far through reading glasses, he might profit by duo-focus lenses (bifocals) so that in school he can shift more rapidly from the near work at his desk to the far work of the blackboard.

Thirteen is showing a greater power to focus than he did at eleven and twelve. Though he may fixate beyond the testing target, the visual findings indicate a better functioning of his two eyes together as a team. Most Thirteens, except the nearsighted ones, show a good mobility of their eyes as they follow a moving target and can accomplish this with a high degree of accuracy and ease.

PHYSICAL GROWTH AND SEX AWARENESS—GIRLS

Thirteen is a period of continued ripening for most girls. Weight and height continue to increase though at a slower rate. There is a general filling out of hollows for many girls, giving the hips, for example, a smoother appearance as the dip between the outer crests fills in. Yet at the same time there can be an appearance of slimming in the very girls who are filling out. This is most noticeable around the face, neck, and shoulders. This slimming down in the more ordinarily visible areas together with the increased height of Thirteen can give a "dual personality" to a girl's appearance. Fully dressed she appears actually to be slender. But in a more complete physical appraisal her hips and thighs reveal her fuller development.

Most girls have menstruated before their fourteenth birthday, and the average 13-year-old has achieved 95 per cent of her mature height. The secondary sex characteristics of breasts and body hair are developing steadily but slowly. But the main concern is menstruation if this hasn't occurred as yet. In some ways Thirteen is relieved when her periods finally appear, and perhaps comments, "Well, it's really here." A few may harbor some resentment ("I'm furious now") for fear their periods will curtail their activities. But this resentment is usually a passing emotion and many girls do not curtail their participation in sports.

There appears to be a relationship between onset of menstruation and a reduction in frequency of headaches. The menstrual periods themselves are not usually painful. Occurrence is still irregular, with a relatively long interval (as long as six months) between periods, but this interval tends to contract until, by fourteen, the periods

assume more regularity.

Though Thirteen is not so reticent about letting her friends and family know that she is menstruating, she is often not ready to purchase her own sanitary napkins. The situation is too embarrassing, and Thirteen is not yet beyond blushing.

Cleanliness is important to most Thirteens. They may be aware of the girls who are not fragrant, but they are not always good at the proper disposal of the napkins, sometimes even stuffing their dirty napkins or underwear into the corner of a drawer. Mothers may need to suggest that they go through their drawers to clean them out.

PHYSICAL GROWTH AND SEX AWARE-
NESS—BOYS

Where Twelve marked just the beginning appearance of traces of physical maturity features in many boys, Thirteen brings more definite changes. For the middle group of boys this is a period of rapid growth of genitalia. Pubic hair and axillary hair appear in about two-thirds. The hair at the corners of the upper lip starts to darken. The nose may seem to jut out like a promontory in both boys and girls; it will appear to fit with the other proportions of the face within another year. The voice deepens perceptibly in many boys and cracks in some. However, there are those whose voices sound higher and clearer than at a younger age.

By the beginning of thirteen most boys have started their sudden spurt of growth in height, but only a handful have reached the peak of this spurt. Boys are more concerned with their height at this time, whereas girls are less concerned, since the discrepancy in the heights of the two sexes is less marked. By the end of this thirteenth year, just about half of the boys will have reached their peak rates of growth, and thereafter they will grow more and more slowly.

Erections occur, not only with direct stimulation or erotic fantasy, but often spontaneously or under other forms of excitement. These may be rather painful. Boys may wonder why this happens when they are neither with girls nor thinking about them. Because of the unpredictability of this function many boys choose to wear an athletic support not just for athletics but all of the time. They feel more comfortable and also safer. Though only about half the boys have had ejaculations before their fourteenth birthday, most boys know about them.

Girls may shy away from boys at this age, because the boys are often too direct in their approach if they are interested in girls. The boys seem to lack finesse. They keep wanting to come to a new point in the conversation, but don't quite know what to talk about and may have to resort to discussion of school assignments. Boys tend to stare girls in the eye, and the girls sometimes have a hard job of softening this fumbling male intensity with their feminine small talk.

2. Self-Care and Routines

EATING

Thirteen's appetite has become well established, especially over the last two years. With some it is still as large as at twelve, but with others it is calming down somewhat. Whereas before they might have taken three to four helpings, some are now restricting themselves to one or two. They don't usually think about food except when they are eating; then they thoroughly enjoy it. Or if they hear some mention of food, they might start thinking about it.

Thirteen often snacks when he comes home from school in the afternoon or just before bed. He may be so hungry just before dinner that he can't wait and may eat a little something, which in no way takes away his appetite. But he is less apt to want the tremendous snacks he had at twelve, and is more apt to choose fruit or soft drinks. He may concentrate on one thing such as apples or oranges and consume large numbers of these. Some Thirteens are beginning to frequent the drugstore after school or after a movie to purchase a soft drink or a soda. (Sundaes are usually too expensive.) But it all depends upon what the group does and what the home influences are. Many parents report that their children are not the "drugstore type."

There is much less fuss at the table than there has been. Thirteen can now sit more quietly. There is no longer any battle about what he should eat. Most eat well, and they are usually allowed their refusals, which can be very strong. Certain foods, especially in the vegetable line, Thirteens almost seem to resent. They wish to have no part of them, not even to taste them. But these refusals are not many. There are the usual meat and vegetable preferences, and at thirteen there is an increased interest in fruits and salads. Desserts are more favored than they were at twelve. But candy is not craved the way it was. Some Thirteens are slimming down, but there are others who remain overweight. There is some talk of dieting, but on the whole there is a more controlled appetite, and lessened intake may solve the problem of overweight.

Table manners are said to be vastly improved. "He doesn't gulp his food the way he used to." "He now sits up straighter and doesn't bow his head down to the dish as he has previously." Nor does he "monopolize the conversation," though he still likes to talk.

SLEEP

Bedtime. Thirteen's need of sleep is lessening and therefore his bedtime is 9:30 if not 10 P.M. As he says himself, "My bedtime is 9:30, supposedly, but it depends on how long the supposedly is." Getting off to bed isn't usually too difficult, especially since Thirteen goes up to his room early. His greatest need is to be checked on by his parents as to whether lights are off, radio turned off, etc. To these demands he usually responds without too much resistance. He even likes bed and muses on the curious shift that "the older you get, the more you like your bed." Some Thirteens go to sleep almost at once and others listen to the radio or think to themselves for about a half hour. They are likely to plan ahead, to think of what they are going to do the next afternoon, or even the next summer. A few take unfair advantage of their parents and stay awake until 1 or 2 A.M., reading or listening to the radio. The majority, however, are asleep within half an hour and sleep soundly. *Sleep.* Many report that they dream even though they cannot remember their dreams afterward. Boys often

dream of sports, and girls dream of boys and of dances. Often they dream about what is on their mind and seem to be able to will a certain kind of dream which they wish to experience. Often their dreams are incongruous. A group of girls may come to a party dressed in variegated fashion from dungarees to a slinky dress of shimmering silver cloth. Or a male science teacher may be dressed in a two-piece flowery bathing suit, and be sitting on a fat woman's lap. A dream that starts out nicely about ordinary things may later become quite confused. A distressing dream may recur. Parents often report that Thirteen talks or mutters in his sleep and is often heard to yell at his siblings.

Morning. Awaking in the morning is not usually a problem for Thirteen. He is apt to awake on his own early enough so that he can lounge in bed and awaken slowly. If awaking at a certain hour is on his mind, he may awake too early. At times he will want to get up directly after awakening, and he may manage when he considers, "It's just a matter of will power."

BATH

The whole problem of cleanliness is now being taken more for granted, and less time and energy are expended on it than earlier. Parents frequently report, "He doesn't object but has to be reminded," or, "He has to be reminded but no argument." Thirteen hasn't the same enjoyment of water that he had at twelve. He has more the attitude of "let's get it over with as quickly as possible."

Thirteen bathes on an average of twice a week or every other day. He's more apt to shower in the summer and take tub baths in the winter, though boys are more apt to shower in all seasons. You can always count on Thirteen to bathe before a dance. With increased perspiring (related both to athletic activities and to development of new sweat-gland structures with stronger characteristic odor) Thirteen recognizes the need to bathe.

Girls shampoo their hair usually once a week and may need some help in rinsing. Increased interest in hair on the part of both boys and girls makes the care of hair, both washing and grooming, rather easy. Some mothers are quite surprised, when they stop to think about it, at how much time their 13-year-old sons spend looking in the mirror as they comb their hair.

Fingernails are not given the care that hair is. Parental reminding is usually necessary to cut both finger- and toenails. However, a few girls keep a fingernail file on their bedside table and groom their nails almost nightly. Care of teeth is pretty well established, though reminders to brush teeth are still necessary for some Thirteens.

CLOTHES AND CARE OF ROOM

A new kind of precision has come into the personal appearance of many Thirteens, both boys and girls. They are said to be "very particular," to "always look neat," or to be "very meticulous." Those who have previously been sloppy now look much better.

The group preferences will influence Thirteen's choice of clothes but he isn't a slave to the group the way he was at twelve. Now he is surer of his own likes and dislikes. He is fully capable of buying all but major purchases by himself. Even with the major purchase of a suit, dress, or coat, Thirteen is usually the one who makes the final decision, though one of his parents accompanies him. After all, he is the one who will wear the garment. Frequently, there is good agreement between parent and child, and it is still more surprising to see how often there can be disagreement and yet still respect for each other's taste. But generally Thirteen holds firmly to his (or her) choice, and persists until just the right suit is found—driving his mother almost crazy in the process. (At the other extreme is a certain group of boys who think little of clothes, prefer to be dressed in dungarees and sport shirts, and judge new clothes by their weight—the lighter the better. However, even with these boys when it is time to dress up they usually comply without fussing.)

Girls are especially aware of the clothes of others. They can size up pretty well which clothes will bring compliments and which won't. Though boys are more often conservative in their color choice, there are quite a few Thirteens who continue to choose loud ties and socks and also "sharp shirts" of bright colors. Thirteen is very aware of matching his clothes, and his good choice is evident in his final grooming.

Even with this more precise interest in his appearance Thirteen may not yet relate the care of his clothes to the way he wants to look. He may still "sling his clothes down," or "throw them around." Even a dress that Thirteen may be fond of can be left in a heap. Some hang clothes on the back of a chair or on a doorknob. Good clothes are more apt to be hung up properly. A very few are aware of the way clothes wrinkle if they are not hung up properly and will even press their own clothes.

Thirteen has improved about putting his dirty clothes in the hamper. He is also quite reliable in changing into clean underwear. In fact, his mother may even wish he wouldn't change so often. He is also becoming aware of which clothes should be sent to the cleaners.

His room is not only cluttered up with clothes, but with books and papers on the floor, along with dishes left from snacks. He recognizes the need of picking up, but he doesn't seem able to get around to it more than once a week, or once in two weeks. His mother may need to mention it, but no major battles need to be fought, because Thirteen can comply. When he finally gets around to it he may spend an entire Saturday on his room, starting with drawers and closets and finally ending up with a mess in the middle of the floor.

Thirteen spends quite a lot of time in his room. He may plaster his walls with pictures of movie actors or actresses or with pennants. He spends a great deal of time lounging on his bed, reading, listening to his radio, or doing his homework. And he often has his door equipped with lock and chain to insure privacy, especially from younger siblings.

MONEY

Though a few Thirteens are still down in the 50-cent allowance class, the majority receive $1 and even this can seem inadequate. Some include lunches and bus fare and are allowed to budget a larger allowance of around $2.50 a week. The earning power of the boys can be quite sizable, as low as $2 or $3 a month or as high

as $6 to $12 a week from a paper route. Boys as usual save their money for making specific purchases. These range from a camera to a power mower, snow plow, or a boat. The earning boys may pay for their own clothes. Girls are more apt to save for presents or perhaps the purchase of a dog.

Even the quieting down, thoughtful, inwardizing process of Thirteen doesn't resolve the financial difficulties of some. With them "money just goes," "it disappears." If they don't spend their money at once, they are at least "broke" by the end of the week. Somehow they always seem to need more, no matter how much money they have to begin with. Still others who don't lack funds have difficulty in organizing their budget or their money. They may have good intentions about budgeting but get all muddled about it. And they sort of leave money all over the house, in their pants pocket, or on the bedside table, or down in the kitchen. Someone needs to collect it for them and to sit down and go over their budget with them.

WORK

Helping in the home is gathering a certain pattern which parents can count upon, and Thirteen can carry through with a certain amount of willingness. As he rattles off four or five chores that he is responsible for and carries out, it almost seems as if that long-desired millennium has arrived. With Thirteen's greater willingness and proficiency, the demands upon him can actually be relaxed. His mother is more apt to demand of him as it fits in or when he has the time. There are still the "just a minute" ones, but on the whole Thirteen has worked out a routine, often taking turns in a job with a sibling, and he carries out his fair share.

Boys are especially enjoying handyman jobs which include repair of simple electrical devices and fixtures. They enjoy running errands and are adding caddying to their outside jobs. A very few are beginning to assist in a store. Girls are beginning to clean other rooms in the house besides their own and enjoy cooking breakfast especially over the weekend. Both sexes are doing considerable baby-sitting away from home and enjoying the earnings they secure.

3. Emotions

The changes that have occurred from twelve to thirteen though definite are rather subtle, and are at times not perceptible to Thirteen himself. Often he feels that, if anything, "things are a little better"—for his horizons are widening, both in the things he can do on his own and in his relationships with friends. But now, though special happenings can make him feel quite happy (being chosen for a part in a play, going to a party, passing a test), his emotions are generally calmer than at twelve.

Thirteen himself says he's "not too good-natured," and he often recognizes that he's nicer away from home than at home. Others may sense the changes more strongly than he does. Parents time and again report that he shows a real quieting down, that a more serious note is creeping in, that periods of marked moodiness occur. The exuberance and enthusiasm so prevalent at twelve have definitely calmed down. Even compliments paid him in the parent interview are given with caution and reserve: he is said

to be "fairly good," "quite cheerful," "pretty good." In many Thirteens the prevailing theme is a minor one, described variously as sullenness, moroseness, secretiveness, pessimism.

Thirteen, if his calming down hasn't gone too far into withdrawn behavior, usually has his emotions in good control. He feels more independent and acts more independently. He may separate from the family group and go to his room because he likes to be alone. He is content with himself rather than happy by himself. Very happy moments may come for no special reason, but these don't usually last very long. Other happy moments seem to come because Thirteen willed them into existence.

His feelings of sadness are more intense than they have been. These feelings may be a part of a mood, when he feels "gray and dismal as if things weren't too good," without any apparent reason. More visible causes, such as people or pets dying, friends moving away, may be at the basis of his sadness. But the thing that makes him feel most terrible is when his mother gets mad at him and has a big talk with him. He often knows that he should do something about his feeling so terrible, but he also knows that it isn't easy to act when he feels this way.

When he's angry, Thirteen seems to be able to control himself better than formerly. He doesn't often get really furious and explode the way he used to. He's more likely to be annoyed or irritated than angry. Even when really enraged he is able to exert some conscious restraint. Some Thirteens, the less controlled ones, will immediately say mean things when angry. But many say or do nothing; others walk out and go to their rooms to think things over and calm down. And now the response is often a "deflected" one. Seemingly restrained at the time, Thirteen may later take it out on someone else, especially his mother. Or, perhaps even more often, he turns his anger back on himself, "tells himself off." This seems to quiet him down gradually.

On the whole, Thirteen has recognized that he "can't do anything" when he's mad at his parents or his teacher. He has also come to learn that his parents are often proved to be in the right later on. But his teacher often poses quite a problem for Thirteen. Some Thirteens get so mad at their teachers, justly or unjustly, that they feel like being "terribly naughty." Those who don't have the courage to act aggressively may do the opposite of what the teacher demands of them. They will go so far as to depreciate a great person just because the teacher says he is great.

Thirteen is not often seen crying but he is at times found crying in his room. Sometimes he cries in anger, but also often when "things are just too bad." Both boys and girls may cry because they haven't been asked to a party. Usually these are the young, brilliant Thirteens who are competing with well-seasoned Fourteens. More often than not these more immature boys would be better off contending with others of their own age. The error of grade placement was probably made way back in first grade when the child's brilliance in reading and arithmetic overshadowed all else. And no one thought about the hardships of social life at eleven to thirteen and the devastating crying of Thirteen when he is excluded.

On the whole Thirteen is not a fearful person. He might say he has the "usual, normal fears that everybody has." But he often has fearful thoughts on his mind which he may try to belittle as he talks about them. You often hear Thirteen say he fears "nothing big like an atomic bomb," or that radio mysteries are "nothing to be scared of," or that he is "not afraid to stay in the house alone, but just gets awful lonesome." He reiterates that he's not afraid of walking down a dark street at night but that he just "walks a little faster." Thirteen is trying to convince himself that he is not afraid.

There is one special fear that a number of Thirteens have—the fear that comes when one is hemmed in, confined by a crowd or a subway or even a snow fort.

Though Thirteen may not be very fearful, he is a great worrier. He says himself that he "worries about most everything" or that he worries that he is going to worry. Each Thirteen seems to have something personal to fret about. A fair number worry about school work—the poorer students about their passing arithmetic, the good ones about making the honor roll. Some worry about their popularity, others about a sibling's popularity. Still others show concern over paying their debts or getting things done. A few go far afield and take on the burdens of international affairs. Thirteen's resolution of the state of world affairs can be quite simple. As one 13-year-old girl solved the problem— "If they used their heads they could settle it. They just want things. They never think about other people."

When faced with the question "What is your chief problem?" however, Thirteen is apt to say that he has no "major problems" or "all little problems that can be worked out easily." Girls are more concerned about popularity, attractiveness, and their future, whereas boys are more concerned about school or money matters. A few are held within the grip of the specific, such as staying up later on Friday night or concern over some physical inability or blemish. And there is still a fair number of Thirteens whose main problem is a brother or sister with whom they have now been fighting for many years.

Thirteen, though he seems so callous at times, has a very sensitive core within him. His feelings are easily hurt. Some boys can be especially hurt by something their father says to them. (This was truer of girls at eleven and twelve.) It's not only what people say to them, but also disappointments and failures, as in school work, that hurt their feelings. A number don't do anything about hurt feelings. Others pointedly ignore or snub the person who produced the hurt feeling. And a few are able to laugh it off, or try to crack a joke.

Thirteen is increasingly aware of his own feelings. Many show their feelings and don't care if others know how they feel. But many want to "hide" or "cover up" their feelings, or will let people know when they are happy but not when they are sad. Often they will let only their intimate friends and, on occasion, their mothers, know how they feel.

Expressions of affection do not come easily to Thirteen. He is more stand-offish. He seems to have pulled into himself, and is more inclined to think and resolve feelings within himself. He isn't very jealous of those who are better endowed than he or who have more possessions. "Once in a while" he might be jealous of "just little things," but on the whole he doesn't wish to change places with another.

Thirteen has reached the stage when he likes to compete in "things that matter"—to him. He is quite selective of what he wants to be best in. But he is not too disturbed if he doesn't win, even though he wants to and tries to excel—at least he says, "It doesn't break my heart," if he loses.

Humor has become rather crisp and sardonic in some Thirteens. A few are especially good at sarcasm. They like to repeat something someone else has said, in an exaggerated fashion. Thirteen's take-offs on his teacher's mannerisms are biting and can be very telling. One of his favorite occupations is to parody. Some of his sex jokes are quite advanced and often include a veiled mention of intercourse.

4. The Growing Self

What better way can an adolescent find himself than by pulling in all of his forces at intervals from the active scene of his life and communing with himself? The very substance and texture of thirteen provides for this means of growth. How each individual utilizes what the growth forces provide may vary greatly, but the terrain is the same. The rapid, shifting, conflictual movement of eleven has settled down through twelve to an apparently almost quiescent point at thirteen. But the quiescence is dynamic with inner resources. With new-found intellectual powers he is focusing his perceptions into sharp, even piercing, insights.

Thirteen is "willing to let time take its course." As one boy said, "I used to want to grow up fast, but now I would like to grow just slowly, just the natural way." That earlier hurry and anxiety for future experiences which he really wasn't ready for is now leaving him. He wants to live *now*. He wants to exist more fully. He is a natural existentialist, giving to life what he has to give; taking from it what he can absorb.

He is not complimented by his elders the way he was at twelve. But he is appreciated and (we hope) understood. How often a parent will say, "He definitely has a life of his own," or, "He lives by himself." At times the parents feel hurt by this withdrawal, feeling that Thirteen is shutting them out. Or they are concerned and worried that they should do something about his withdrawal. Too often they don't realize that this is a time for withdrawing, for being alone. These same parents could support growth more fully if they would provide the equipment and the place for Thirteen to withdraw to; his own castle, as it were, in which he can live his life more fully and richly.

Not all Thirteens withdraw physically in the home by going to their rooms. However, even those who are still a part of the family group are at times "lost" within the house. Or they do not wish to enter into the same group activities that they used to enjoy with the family. They may lead very busy lives, but they are more independent from the family group. They are even more independent from their own contemporary group. They may express waves of fads with the group, but on the whole they are not slaves to the group as they were earlier.

Thirteen is beginning to see him-

self more clearly. First and foremost it is his appearance that concerns him. This is his outward self. He is drawn to a mirror as to a magnet. Any stray lock must be combed into place. He is definitely interested in his clothes and grooms himself with meticulous care. This is all a part of the expression of his new-found discriminatory abilities, his intellectual awareness of form.

As for his inner self, that too receives his scrutiny. He is said to have good insight, to know what the other fellow means. Right in the middle of his own experience he can stand off at times and laugh at himself in an adult manner. His self-criticism is directed toward his inner self, his character. He recognizes his selfishness, his laziness, his too rapid anger, his poor understanding of the other fellow. He may catch himself in what he later considers false artifices. He knows when he tells stories, seemingly to make himself feel better. But he can be true to himself and will confess later, "I just hate myself when I try to get sympathy. I just told you that story so that you would say I was right and that Cynthia was wrong."

But Thirteen doesn't spend much time in criticizing himself. He is more concerned with being himself, getting on with himself, pleasing himself. The thought of being famous doesn't draw him the way it did at eleven. Now he "just wants to be able to please himself."

He is becoming aware of a new focal point, the brain, that seems more than anything else to be the place which is the seat of his self. He tells about the time when he thought his ring or braids were part of his (or her) self, but now these external detachable parts are not essential. They can change. His self may be expressed actively through his thoughts, his conscience, or his critical ability. But the place where all this action goes on is in the brain where "all conscious thought and all conscious movement go on." He is so aware of the brain that he sizes up his classmates and calls a more intellectual one "the brain." Or this can be his form of salutation over the telephone with his friends—"Hello, brains." But there are still those whose heart, stomach, hands or feet still dominate the self. The dominance of these parts and their heightened activity may be closely related to these special Thirteens' individualities. Or maybe these same Thirteens simply haven't yet reached the stage of thinking their brain is the center of all things.

The intellectual surety of Thirteen's self can be so strong that much interest and time are spent in verbal pursuits. An unabridged dictionary may become a treasured possession, especially with boys, and even the breakdown of words into syllables portends an interest in word origins. Thirteen feels his intellectual power and wishes to go out for scholarships.

With those Thirteens who are less secure in themselves, this age may be a very disquieting time. They may be hypersensitive to criticism. They may be so anxious, as when talking over the phone, that they have to write down first what they are going to say. They may be so uncomfortable in themselves that they take on an imaginary role to become someone else, to be some place else. These are the ones who have to escape from themselves to find themselves.

Thirteen's awareness of his assets and faults most often concerns his intellect. He may cite as assets his reasoning power, his brains, or his getting good marks. He knows he has the ability "to stick to things" and he speaks of his determination. Those Thirteens who are more aware of other people speak of their friendliness, their thinking before they say things, or not wishing to hurt other people's feelings. The opposite is often true when Thirteen considers his faults. He recognizes that he sometimes doesn't try to understand the other fellow, that he gets mad at others too quickly, and that he is selfish. He knows when he is putting things off and when he is lazy.

Thirteen may be so concerned with "right now" that it can be difficult for him, especially for boys, to voice even one wish, let alone three. Or if he can't be specific about his wishes he might wish to have as many more wishes as he wants. Though many still wish for material things such as fishing tackle, a better home, or a sailboat, some are now thinking of other people primarily and of themselves secondarily. One 13-year-old gave her wishes in order of preference. First she wished "that the people of the world would learn to live together." Second, "that I could design my own home with all the furnishings, materials, etc." And third, and perhaps most important, "that I had a boy friend."

A feeling for others in trouble, especially in physical trouble, is on Thirteen's mind. He wishes that there would be no disease, no illness. Or when disease or illness is present, he wishes that the person would get well. He wants "to clean out the slums" and "clear up Communism."

Thirteen has thought a lot about his future career. He has often discussed it with his father and may be influenced by him if his father's reasoning makes sense to him. He recollects the careers he has previously chosen and has now given up. The earlier choices of being a nurse, veterinarian, and lawyer are frequently given up. Some Thirteens realize that they first need experience to find out what they would like to do. One of the most common choices at thirteen, which undoubtedly is related to his own intellectual drive, is to become a teacher. These Thirteens who choose the teaching profession know pretty well what specific age grouping they wish to teach, anywhere from nursery school to their own age. Some new professions on the horizon are those of psychologist and sports announcer. Girls are thinking both of marriage and career, and, though a few would like to dovetail the two, the majority give marriage top priority.

Those Thirteens who plan to go to college have a fair idea of their choice, determined by what the college has to offer them. Many are beginning to consider the advantages of a small college. The pull of coeducation isn't as strong; in fact, both boys and girls may choose non-coeducation even though their interest in the opposite sex remains high.

Marriage is definitely on Thirteen's mind. Earlier notions of remaining a bachelor have almost disappeared, though some 13-year-old boys have not really given marriage their full attention. They haven't thought much about it and they haven't picked the girl out yet. In fact, they may not yet know what attributes they desire

in a wife, though some boys especially wish their wives to be smart. But the girls have given marriage a great deal of thought. They not only want their future mates to like things they like, but also to be like them. They wish to feel that others, such as their friends, would like their future mates. Here are the seeds of companionship.

As for children, Thirteen is less eager than he was for a large family. Quite a few have restricted their quota to two children, though there are still those who would desire three or four.

5. *Interpersonal Relationships*

If only Thirteen wouldn't snap back so, cut his parents short with a one-word answer, seem touchy, go off by himself—then his parents might know better how to approach him, how to deal with him. Thirteen doesn't want to queer his position in the family, but he knows full well that he isn't "as nice to my family as to my friends." He's not quite sure himself how things changed for the worse and is a bit bewildered as he says, "I don't know why we don't get on better."

Some Thirteens, however, get on "pretty well" or "O.K." with their parents. They often recognize that their mother is understanding and sympathetic, but they are reticent about asking her questions, especially questions about growing up. They might come to tell her about things that have happened, especially away from home, or they might come to her to settle an argument, *but* they don't often confide in her. They might want to talk things over with their mother, ask her advice about social things or complain about school, *but* they don't want her to go to school and fight their battles for them, no matter how much she could help.

Thirteen is often embarrassed by his mother, especially when he is in the company of his friends or some place where someone might recognize him, as at the movies or the beach. But if he's in a strange place, a distant city where he is safe in his unknownness, he will get on very well with her.

At home he is often critical of his mother in little ways. This is truer of girls than of boys. If it isn't her hair, it's that she forgot to put on lipstick when she went out. Or something is wrong with her clothes or even her handwriting which may lack the neatness that Thirteen himself has so recently acquired. Oddly enough, and happily so, Thirteen rarely criticizes his parents to others away from home. This criticism is reserved for the more intimate atmosphere of the home, where criticism has its place.

Parents may be said to be almost too critical of their 13-year-olds. This outlet of criticism can be so common and so persistent that they are said to "din" or "nag" at Thirteen. The more usual criticisms concern keeping rooms picked up, helping more around the house, and improving table manners. Fathers are more specific in their criticism than mothers. They may feel that Thirteen should try harder in school; that mother does too much for him; that he doesn't come when he's called; that he should stick to things better; that there should be more work, less fooling; that he should practice his music lesson more; that he should have a better disposition, better judgment, better common sense. Fathers can be quite biting when they speak of their daughters as dilettant-

ish, messy, and selfish. These criticisms don't endear their parents to Thirteen. In fact, a few Thirteens feel a little persecuted and some boys are so easily hurt that they burst into tears over any criticsim. All of these criticisms leveled against Thirteen may be accurate, but Thirteen can't change too much or too fast. One 13-year-old daughter, perhaps wiser than her parents, was heard to say, "I partly try to change but partly think that time will take care of it."

If only parents would recognize that time is on their side. This is an age of inward absorption, of withdrawing, of thinking things over. This shift in attitude, this inner concentration, may actually produce a social deafness. Thirteen truly doesn't hear when his parents call him, until they get his attention. The wise parent comes to realize that everything goes all right if he leaves Thirteen alone or stays on the surface with him. The parent further realizes that he needs to be tactful and reasonable with Thirteen in a grown-up sort of way. He needs to be careful of his criticism and to know that Thirteen is touchy. If he fails to recognize this, he will feel the impact of Thirteen's snappish answer, his antagonism or even open resentment. And he will produce a further withdrawing in Thirteen than would otherwise occur. Even information as important as being confirmed in church may then be kept from the parents.

Generally Thirteen's relationship, such as it is, is closer with his mother. He recognizes that his relationship with his father is "different" and "less close," though some girls have their first warm relationship with their fathers at this age. Thirteen often admires his father and is less apt to criticize him than his mother. He states that his father is often too tired, too busy, or not around enough to do things with him. But he does not say this in a complaining way. His father may go to sports events with him or to the movies or fishing and swimming. But where father comes in most handy is helping Thirteen with his homework. From Thirteen's point of view, "Daddy is easier to work with now." But from the father's point of view the improvement may lodge in the child—"She's beginning to think. It's a pleasure to work with her." And probably there is an ounce of truth in both opinions.

When and if Thirteen withdraws from the family group, it is more often to get away from his siblings than from his parents. Perhaps it is because Thirteen is so touchy that he is so constantly annoyed by his younger siblings, especially those in the six- to eleven-year range. He himself may be able to explain it by saying, "I'm going through a stage when everything bothers me." But, all too often, "It's hard to explain," or he really doesn't know why he gets on so badly with his siblings. He often speaks of a younger sibling as a "spoiled brat," a "pest," a "nuisance," or a "pain in the neck." This horrible creature does undoubtedly "annoy" him, "get on his nerves," "interrupt" him, and get into his things, though this latter is less of a complaint than formerly.

Thirteen on his part may not quite realize that he is all too often assuming an adult role, trying to improve his younger sibling, trying to make him do things a Thirteen knows how to do. He quarrels with his younger brothers and sisters most often over

"trivial things"; "just little things." Usually the fighting is in the form of "bickering"; often it is for fun, but sometimes it is in earnest and may need adult intervention. Then the parent may be forced either to threaten or actually withdraw part of Thirteen's allowance or to deprive him of some looked forward to event. The change in the atmosphere after such a bout can be quite startling, and the quietness in the home seems more intense because it contrasts with the previous noise.

Even with his sibling difficulties Thirteen would not wish to be without his siblings. He might wish to shift their age to younger or older. But he does feel that they help to prevent him from being spoiled. Boys especially would like a brother just their age, not realizing that this close relationship at home with a supposedly ideal brother would still produce many problems.

Thirteen's wider age separation from younger siblings under five allows him to assume a grown-up role more naturally. He often likes to care for them. He gets on fine with them. He plans surprises for them. And they adore him.

Also, he is getting on well with his older siblings, especially those fifteen or older. There may be some bickering, but squabbles can usually be settled without family interference. Thirteen may feel that an older sibling takes advantage of him because he is younger. But on the whole they are beginning to enjoy each other's companionship. Thirteen may feel at long last that an older brother or sister is really acting like a brother or sister should: "She's a real sister." Sometimes these older siblings are quite convenient. You can talk things over with them, maybe can even go on double dates with them. But when an older sibling criticizes until it hurts, Thirteen will retaliate in kind, though perhaps voicing his criticism only to his mother. As one Thirteen declared about his brother who had criticized his drawing, "Well, I don't like his attitude toward cops."

There is a considerable difference between boys and girls in their relationships to their own sex. Thirteen-year-old girls recognize a shift from being a part of a total group at twelve to having a number of separate friends at thirteen. As one girl put it, "Last year we had sort of a gang. Then I think I learned my lesson. You make more friends if you don't go in a gang." Friendship is important to a 13-year-old girl. She wants and needs someone to confide in, someone to tell secrets to, even though what she tells may not be very confidential by adult standards.

Girls often go around in groups of three. The threesome often shifts into a twosome, as two gang up against the third girl—either when she is away or when all three are together. Often this is meant only as kidding, but Thirteen can also be quite pointedly critical, even of her friends. As one girl aptly remarked, "With the best of friends there are always arguments; the better they know you, the more they can criticize." Adults might profit by the wisdom they once knew as 13-year-olds.

Some 13-year-old girls feel a loss of any close friends and remember that they felt more a part of the group when they were twelve. Or they might have had a best friend whom they have grown away from or have lost by moving away. The latter situation can be somewhat alleviated, for Thirteen can "correspond madly," according to her parents.

Boys of thirteen do not have the closely knit groups the girls have. They are more likely to cluster in gangs of four or five, with each member considering all the others to be his best friends. Boys don't seem to need the intimate atmosphere of imparted confidences that the girls demand. The boys are more concerned in *doing* things with their friends, and they more often group along activity lines. Friends are apt to be together mostly at school, though some do things together outside of school. There are always movies to attend, sports, hunting, and fishing to share. But boys less often stay overnight at each other's houses, especially since they may feel, "That's for girls."

Some 13-year-old boys get mad at their close friends in the gang, but on the whole they get on well, and if a controversy arises they can settle things peacefully. In fact, just the opposite of conflict often prevails in a group of 13-year-old boys. Each wants to be sure the other boy gets a chance, especially at sports.

Thirteen's general calming down is especially evident in his relationship to the opposite sex. Girls are unfortunately finding their male contemporaries too short of stature and too immature. They often refer to these same males as "drips" or "idiots" or "the awfulest dancer," though they must admit at times that some are "kind of cute." They also recognize that boys affect them so that they giggle and act silly, but they try to control this. Many Thirteens have one boy they are interested in and who may be interested in them, though they may shift to others from time to time. However, girls themselves recognize that some of their friends like boys and some don't. They also recognize that they don't talk about boys quite as much as they used to. Now they talk "about boys but also about everything."

A few girls date occasionally, more often with somewhat older boys, going to the movies or a dance, but they would never think of "going steady." Many girls would still like to play sports with boys. They definitely like to be around boys.

Boys not only seem to have calmed down about girls but some have even gone in the opposite direction. "My friends can have them, but I don't care," is a commonly expressed sentiment. Others may declare, "Oh bah, girls," or, "I don't give a snap about girls now," which rather indicates that there was a time when girls meant quite a bit to these same boys. A few have gone to the extreme of being a "woman hater" but on the whole the boys often show a neutral feeling toward girls. As one boy said, "Girls can be or cannot be just as they like. I don't find them repulsive. I just don't care."

Thirteen-year-old boys do very little dating, but they do enjoy a dance or a party now and then. Greatly to their surprise, the first girl they ask to any such function most always accepts. Not that the boys are very good party companions, for they usually herd together in a restless bunch. What is on their minds is evident in the terse comments tossed out from this male group—"Butt," "Rump." Their general behavior at a party has improved over last year, however, for, as they re-port themselves, "We don't have riots any more." But still, without supervision and good planning, they are apt to end up throwing things. And there always seems to be one boy who has his eye on the light switch, ready to douse the lights at what he considers an appropriate moment.

There should be almost as careful planning for a 13-year-old party as for one at twelve. However, Thirteens start more slowly and need to be given time to come into the spirit of things. It may be preferable that neither parent be in the active midst of the group but that some adult friend quick to catch the spirit of a party for this age officiate.

Girls are usually the more eager to attend these parties and often come early. Boys straggle along. It is some time before all the invited have assembled. There is that hiatus when the boys go off in a room by themselves and the girls start dancing with each other and you wonder if this is really going to be a party. It is at this point when organizational ability is needed, when the party needs to be swung into line. The thing Thirteen wants to do is dance. The difficulty of choosing a partner may be bypassed by a Cinderella dance, when the girls' slippers are lined up in a row for the boys to choose from. The addition of an orange held by pressure between the foreheads of each couple may be just the trick that breaks the tension.

The party can rise to quite a pitch, and the master of ceremonies will need, besides finesse, a loud voice. Games such as Spin the Platter (Truckle the Trencher, to some), with forfeits and prizes is just what Thirteen wants. Any kind of prizes will do —chocolate bars or anything. It's the fun of the games that's important. A birthday cake is not important, and may hardly be touched. It's the punch that counts, and calculation should allow for close to a quart per guest.

Two and a half hours is a good length of time for a party to last. And here, as at twelve, if the guests could be taken home without having to be picked up, the high note of the party could be better sustained to the very end.

6. Activities and Interests

Mothers may report that their 13-year-old son or daughter has put away "all childish things," but this is more a trend than an accomplished fact. It is true that Thirteen recognizes that he is "outgrowing" certain types of books, that he "used to" send away for pictures but he doesn't do that any more, or that he is now "bored" with mysteries which he once thought were so fascinating.

He recognizes and chalks up the change. But that doesn't mean that he won't enjoy a younger sibling's comic books even though he might not buy them for himself or keep them in his room. Some Thirteens are all too aware that they are holding on to childish things, a few even gloat over their continuance.

Sometimes it is just the difficulty of making a start. As one Thirteen says, "I think I should improve. One of those things that goes around and around. But I never get around to starting to improve myself." Another might report, "I like to do something silly and too young for me. I love to gallop around and pretend I'm riding a horse." And another, misjudging the interests of many adults, candidly reported, "This may be a shock to you but I love detective stories."

Whether Thirteen is more childish or more mature in his interests, he is always busy, and even passionate in the expression of his chosen activities. This passion may be expended over a dog or a horse, over sports, or over reading about movie stars.

Many 13-year-olds are "sports-minded," "sports crazy," or "wrapped up in sports." Even the less athletic Thirteens may sometimes play so hard they almost knock themselves out. They give their all. Though Thirteen has a continuing interest in football (touch football for girls), now basketball and hockey are coming to the forefront. Baseball isn't quite as strong as it was, but it is even stronger as a spectator interest on radio, television, or at an actual game.

Whatever individual sports were started at an earlier age (sailing, skiing, skating, tennis, golf) are now receiving a good workout and even a little polishing. Horseback riding holds its place for some girls, but on the whole it's not the craze that it was. Hunting and fishing are restricted to a few boys, but their ranks will be swelled in time.

The indoor interests of boys and girls are now showing a more defined separation because the pursuit of hobbies and the expression of greater interest in one specific line are growing more common. Boys' interests are more sharply defined than girls'. The mechanical-scientific interest in radio, both in construction and in working toward becoming a ham operator, is more widespread than earlier. Photography has perhaps shown the biggest leap and now often includes developing and enlarging. Many 13-year-old boys have earned enough money to equip their own darkrooms. Thirteens continue their interest in making models, especially midget racers, and enjoy designing cars and planes. Some boys now participate less in constructing but observe more. This ability to observe the lines of cars accurately may be even classed as a hobby. The eagle eye of a 13-year-old boy espies every quality and shift of line in a design.

Girls are interested in knitting, weaving, or sewing for themselves. They may dabble in photography or with radio, but they have none of the penetration and holding power that the boys have. They enjoy creative expression through drawing, painting, or writing. Or they will apply themselves to lessons in music, art, or dancing if they can give the time. But girls still need to spend a lot of time just "talking things over" with their friends, either in person or on the telephone.

Collections no longer have the fascination they once had. Stamps may be left lying around. Match-book covers may be hung up in festoons by the boys and foreign dolls may be held on display by the girls. But on the whole collections are not strong. Thirteen wants more than outward display.

SEDENTARY LOOKING AND LISTENING ACTIVITIES

Parents are often pleasantly startled by how little time Thirteen spends before the television screen. Some Thirteens have little or no time for television during the week but will watch over the weekend. Preferred programs vary. Radio listening may be preferred to TV, but this also is much reduced and only utilized as it fits in. Whatever is on at certain times determines what is listened to more often than not. Thirteen is apt just to tune in and see what's on. Sports may be the most preferred programs, and mysteries are still enjoyed. Music is often used as a background for what Thirteen is doing. However, a rising number prefer their music through records. They like both classical and jazz and are beginning to enjoy romantic popular tunes. They may buy their own records and will soon collect them the way they used to collect comic books.

Thirteen often wishes he had more time to read. Often he's too busy with other things. It may be his homework (if this is given) that cuts into his reading time. Or it may be a hobby like photography that "puts a dead stop" to his reading. Some Thirteens, however, are ready to read anything. Dog more than horse stories, mysteries, and adventures lead the list. Some boys restrict themselves to sports. But the classics are being plumbed by a few and historical novels are favored.

Newspaper reading is becoming more prevalent. A few read the paper thoroughly. But the majority concentrate on the front page, funnies, and sports. More time is spent on magazines. Some boys read science magazines from cover to cover. Others treat sports magazines as their Bible and save them religiously. The pictorial magazines are favored by both sexes. A few girls are enjoying movie magazines.

As at twelve, Thirteen wishes to select the movies he sees and usually restricts himself to what he calls "good movies." If the movie is not extra special, he would prefer to be out of doors participating in sports. Thirteen will attend with his parents though he prefers not to. He wishes most to go with a friend of the same sex and may meet up with and sit with some friend of the opposite sex after he gets into the theater. A few don't mind going alone.

Musicals and adventures are preferred. Girls are beginning to select romantic pictures. Historical movies are in the ascendancy. Some Thirteens have favorite movie stars and some girls have crushes on certain actors or actresses. Girls are more apt to feel themselves into a part. They may try not to cry and tell themselves they don't want to cry, but somehow or other they just can't seem to help it.

7. School Life

Such adjectives as sophisticated, more inhibited, calmer, conscientious, all give some idea of a real inwardizing change that is occurring at Thirteen years. The rapid, almost pell-mell enthusiasm of Twelve is now withheld and concentrated in more organized and sustained eagerness to learn. Thirteen stands off as he watches the antics of the 12-year-olds, chasing each other up and down the halls, snatching any loose pieces of clothing they can grab from each other to produce further chase and interplay. He calls it "kid stuff." He may not chase as he once did, but he jostles any nearby companion and is notorious for his inability to stand in line. He still snatches from classmates, but selectively. He snatches for a purpose, and wallets are the prize, for they document in pictures who is the current favored one.

Thirteen is basically happier in school than he has been. He says himself, "It's better this year, just nicer." But he qualifies his statement by adding, "Better because I'm probably more willing to learn, but it seems to me as if they teach better." Any eighth-grade teacher would probably agree with this statement, especially if this teacher had taught seventh grade. The open, wholesome lack of inhibition of the usual seventh-grader is refreshing. But his sudden surges of energy may not be sustained; restlessness intervenes. Whether there is a clock in the room or not, there comes the oft-repeated question, "What time is it?" Time is poorly spent so that even the best of seventh-grade teachers will finally grow weary and will give in to this demand and that demand just to keep the peace.

But not so with the eighth-grader. The time is better organized, concentration is more sustained, self-control is more evident. Thirteen has a better sense of responsibility. He is more dependable. A teacher can enjoy shared intellectual experiences with him.

However, Thirteen doesn't show these more sterling qualities immediately. He seems almost to hide them until he can show them fully formed. He feels that he is now entering the adult world and that he wishes to be treated as an adult. He is galled when he meets the cloak of authority. He wishes to feel independent as well as to be independent. He gripes whenever he feels restricted by authority. He wants the freedom of decision. But, alas, all too soon and too often he finds that he needs to come sheepishly back to his teacher for further help or advice.

Then it is for the teacher to make

this return possible, by treating him as man to man and not with the air of "I told you so." However, when he is resisting some task such as learning the complications of English grammar and strenuously feels that he "won't need to know these in life," he is only further upset by a teacher who agrees with him. At that very moment he is almost begging for authority, an authority that says (we hope rightly) that there are certain things you have to do in life whether you like it or not.

Thirteen (ideally) wants to get to school early. He likes to settle in slowly. He wants to visit with his friends. If he comes on a bus, he is calmer than he was at twelve when he talked, or even shouted, laughed, and was in general quite loud in his enthusiasm. But Thirteen can become boisterous with the piercing tones of a high shrill voice as he chats mainly with friends of his own sex in the halls or places assigned for early morning gathering. He has so much to talk about—future parties, what he's going to do over the weekend, who likes whom. Close proximity produces some form of physical contact, either in pushing each other or draping an arm on another's shoulder.

Some Thirteens would prefer to go directly to the classroom to have a chance to talk to their teacher. They often bring newspaper clippings or talk over generalities. Or they might want to finish some assignment not yet completed.

Thirteen doesn't settle down quickly. The group needs a bell to shock it out of its talking on its way to the classroom or assigned activity. Thirteen saunters into his classroom. There is a certain blasé attitude about

him. There would be less interruption to his day if he had his physical education at the beginning and end of the day. This is one of his favorite periods and would be a good initial period to get him started.

Boys often favor basketball over baseball. Perhaps it is its newness, but more than that the constant action, team interplay, and need for precision of shots give Thirteen the kind of exercise he desires. Tumbling is also a favorite. Optional athletics at the end of the day allow for the more athletically inclined to participate more fully, and for those who are less interested to go their separate ways.

Whether Thirteen needs to or should be asked to shower after strenuous physical activity is still debatable. If given a choice, he would most probably vote against it. He doesn't feel the need and he resents undressing and dressing again, and, if physically immature, he is reluctant to expose himself. He should not, however, be allowed to wear gym shoes in class all day. They are not good for his feet nor do they add to the fragrance of the classroom.

After gym class there is considerable primping, especially on the part of the girls who all carry their necessary equipment in their pocketbooks. A large mirror at the back of the classroom is rather essential for this activity. Eight to ten girls may primp at once. Lipstick may be applied, but most groups ostracize the practice until fourteen, except at dances. (City girls are more likely to accelerate the date of everyday use of lipstick.)

Thirteen's conduct in the classroom is definitely related to his attitude toward his teacher. He is very critical of her. He may approve of her because "She treats us like we're people." Or he may burst out with his feelings toward her, considering that she is "insulting," "always criticizing," "keeps interrupting," "too strict," "not strict enough," "boring," or "cracks jokes at others' expense." But he likes things said in fun and especially any comment implying that he was bad (so long as there is not too much truth in it). If after an absence he is greeted by, "I knew you were absent yesterday because it was so quiet," it makes him feel real perky inside. He seems to have an intuitive sense about when a teacher is a good teacher. "The good ones just seem to have something about them. They seem to know what they are talking about and can keep discipline." It is not hard for Thirteen to respect such a teacher.

But if he doesn't respect his teacher, he "tries to get away with things." Usually he isn't alone in his hostile feelings and he works with the group to play practical jokes on the teacher. It may be a thumbtack on her chair, which, fortunately, she usually sees ahead of time. Or it may be a capsule of perfume placed on the radiator so that it will melt and smell up the room. A similar container of perfume may be placed on the runners of the teacher's open desk drawer, in hopes that it "will smash and go all over the place" as she unsuspectingly closes the drawer. An undercurrent of belligerence definitely flows beneath the surface of such "fun." Adults need not be shocked to see it make its appearance. Rather they should be concerned about what they as adults did, or failed to do, to mobilize these belligerent forces.

School principals are often ill-thought-of by Thirteen, for they not only represent authority but also exercise it. One may be spoken of as "a big show-off, strutting around the halls like a peacock, always making stupid rules and always making speeches." Another may be said to "get in the way and mess up the classes." More often than not if Thirteen doesn't like the principal, he seems to feel that all the teachers don't like him either, for the principal is in authority over the teachers.

Previously the teacher was often identified with the subject she taught. Thirteen, however, is beginning to separate the two. He may like a teacher and not the subject she teaches, or he may heartily dislike a teacher and persist in an intense interest in the subject she teaches. This shows greater discrimination and independence of thinking on Thirteen's part.

Though the seating of boys and girls is usually mixed in eighth grade, there are times when they are best separated. On the whole, however, the group acts as a unit and its members are more poised than earlier. Though Thirteen has difficulty in settling down and getting started, once he has begun he can concentrate with unusual power. Sometimes he concentrates so well that he isn't disturbed by noises around him, but at other times he is disturbed by a noisy classroom and by a teacher who keeps interrupting. At times the class concentrates so well on individual work that dead silence prevails for as long as twenty minutes. This, certainly, is a newly acquired ability.

In his studies, Thirteen doesn't mind English but he doesn't like English grammar. He doesn't understand it. He doesn't really know what it's about and he doesn't see what good it will do him. But he often loves to write stories and may show a lively imagination. Sometimes he writes better than he talks. He especially likes to write about himself, about the story of his life, and he often enjoys hearing stories others have written about themselves. (A few more reticent Thirteens feel that it is an intrusion on their privacy to write about their feelings, and especially do not want their compositions to be read before the class. Their desire should be respected.) Thirteen's greater ease of expression makes letter writing less of a chore than it was. He can now be more successful in keeping up with his pen pals. This greater ease is evident not only in the words he chooses, but also in his actual handwriting. His writing is more uniform, but often very small, much to the discomfiture of his teacher. Thirteen's small handwriting is, after all, an outward expression of his good inward intellectual processes. He should be complimented, not criticized, about his small handwriting and even his stingy margins which show that he is conserving in all ways, even on paper.

In their reading, boys favor athletic or adventure stories, and girls, teenage stories about people their own age with such suggestive titles as *Summer Date*. Some girls persist in their animal interests, especially liking stories about horses. Thirteen is becoming more aware of style in what he reads. He like to pick out good descriptive passages, but this doesn't mean that he wants the writing to be too stilted, too subtle. He'd like it rougher. He's interested in what a person means, and if the author means a certain thing, Thirteen doesn't see why he can't come out and say it, just in a simple sort of a way.

Thirteens are above all else interested in trying new things. Those who like mathematics may like it especially if they consider it their hardest subject. They feel a sense of accomplishment when they have successfully solved a word problem. The boys especially like to check back over their work and to utilize the practical application of measurement and areas. The newness of algebra, or even geometry and trigonometry, is devoured eagerly by some Thirteens if these areas are made available to them.

They also enjoy the broadened outlook of world affairs in social studies. They enjoy reading the newspapers, clipping out items of interest, reading editorials, and looking at cartoons and puzzling out their meanings. They enjoy discussion periods, and now, recognizing more shades of gray, they can carry them a step beyond the black-vs.-white debates they waged the previous year. They like to delve into political history, to know more, for example, about the origin of the Solid South and its relationship to the Civil War. They are intrigued by study of the new facilities that are available since we are living in an air age. Passing rapidly beyond such obvious applications as transportation and mail delivery, Thirteens ferret out facts about more fascinating ramifications—rescue and disaster services, crop spraying, even the dropping of beaver in mountain lake regions for conservation purposes.

Thirteen persists in his interest in the solar system, the universe, and, closer to home, the weather. He's also shifting his interest in the macrocosm to an interest in the microcosm. Atoms and atomic energy intrigue him, especially their peaceful uses which offer so many more possibilities than just blowing things up. And he's becoming interested in natural and man-made substances, such as coal and plastics. It's the experimental part of science that intrigues him most. He wants to get in and demonstrate a thing for himself, and should have the facilities for doing so. And he is becoming aware of new branches of science, especially the field of psychology.

A future era of specialized course work and extracurricular activities is foreshadowed in Thirteen's increasing interest in hobbies. These should, as far as possible, be fostered on an individual basis, according to his special interests. Music, especially the playing of an instrument, is strong with some, but with others (especially boys) a regular music class is an anathema. Painting and drawing can produce similar extremes of response. Boys would often prefer study of radio if the facilities were available.

In shop, the boys "feel their oats" and may talk back a bit, but on the whole they are good workers. Thirteen can, in metal work, even carry through the demands of making a hammer, with the demands of sawing, filing, drilling. He plans well and doesn't want to quit. A woodwork project, such as a dresser tray for his father, receives a good finishing job.

The 13-year-old girls may assume a rather blasé attitude toward home economics but they show their eagerness as soon as they are into a project. They still can use an eggbeater backward and cut with the wrong edge of the knife. But they can often handle a total meal quite well. Their greatest

desire is to bake a chocolate cake with white icing and invite the boys to partake. Who is going to sit where is very important and best solved by drawing names. Thirteen is eager to go ahead on her own in sewing. She can now complete a whole garment— a dress or a skirt or a blouse without sleeves. As she goes ahead with increased speed toward the end, the quality of her work suffers.

In spite of Thirteen's reputation as a "griper," his protests need not interfere with his ability as a student. He may appear restless as he is settling down, putting his feet out in the aisle, wiggling, talking, sharpening his pencil, but when he once settles down he is good for a twenty- to thirty-minute period of intense concentration. He wants to finish his work and would prefer to finish at school than to take it home. He doesn't want any work hanging fire. This does not mean that he doesn't dawdle and waste time. But he does accomplish so well that it is a pity that he is given extra homework. If he does have homework regularly, he is usually conscientious and on his own, whereas he needed help at twelve. It is the long-term project that may suddenly catch him short of time. This may throw him in a tailspin or sudden panic, for his task seems interminable. He doesn't seem to see the end until he gets there. But he usually organizes and comes through, perhaps with some help.

At the end of a busy school day Thirteen likes to hang around the lockers if he doesn't have to rush off to catch a bus. He doesn't burst out of the building the way he did at eleven and sometimes at twelve. There will be three or four in a group of either boys or girls. A seventh-grade girl may join the eighth-grade girls to talk about an eighth-grade boy. The eighth-grade girls are more often talking about high school boys. It's a pleasant kind of chatter and teasing that would go on for some time if their teacher didn't almost sweep them out of the building.

8. Ethical Sense

Thirteen is moving in a more complex ethical realm than did Twelve. He is thinking less of what would be to his advantage and more about ethics in general and how they help you to relate to others and to yourself. With the greater definition of Thirteen, extremes of ethical behavior are brought out. There are the puritanical, almost prudish girls who are scrupulously honest, have an exaggerated sense of right and wrong, and who may not tolerate those who veer from what they consider to be an established ethical code. Then there are the Thirteens (more often boys) whose consciences don't bother them and who are more apt to veer from an established ethical code even under the cover of deceit. But the majority of Thirteens are finding it easier to make ethical decisions. They are now enjoying a new freedom which their sharpened ethical sense is giving them.

The problem of what is right and what is wrong is determined with a fair amount of ease. Most Thirteens can "tell pretty clearly" and can usually reach a conclusion "without any trouble." Some seem to know automatically and some boys, oddly enough, speak in absolute terms of "I always know." They recognize that various forces guide them: their conscience, what their mother and father

would think, or "what people would think." There is a new force operating, however, and this they call their judgment. Though Thirteen knows what is right and what is wrong, that does not mean that he will never do wrong. The fun of being bad still lurks around the corner, especially at school. And one couldn't really criticize Thirteen "for going into an old empty house," if he does no harm to it.

Thirteen pretty much accepts his conscience as a part of himself. He is aware that his conscience is *active,* that it is often *firm,* in fact *very firm,* especially about big things! He knows that his conscience doesn't bother him too much over little things and will even let him "get away with little teensy-weentsy things." It is when another person is hurt, when Thirteen is mean to somebody, that his conscience rises up in no uncertain terms to plague him.

Thirteen has come to fuller knowledge of what relative truth is. He tries to be truthful and wants to tell the truth, but sometimes he tells only part of the truth. Sometimes he tells "white lies," as much to protect a friend's feelings as to save his own skin. He especially dislikes telling his parents about any low grades he received, even though he knows his parents won't "beat him down." He is apt to evade a question, give an excuse such as that a paper hasn't been returned, or smooth things over by diverting his parents' attention. But he wouldn't avoid the truth if he knew that someone else would suffer.

Thirteen has made great strides in taking the blame when he is responsible. He is beginning to be willing to admit his own shortcomings. Sometimes he blames only as a joke. But there are still times when he isn't ready to take the blame and finds it easier "to push it off on others."

As at twelve, Thirteen rarely argues with his parents just for the sake of argument. He may argue for fun, but more often to get what he wants. But he doesn't argue much. He is now capable of discussion and has quite a few ideas on social issues. He feels he is open to reason but he really isn't very easy to convince or to have his mind changed. He may accept his parents' demands just because he feels he should, and even against his will, but remains unconvinced of their soundness.

The questions of smoking and drinking are now coming closer to Thirteen's own experience. He is now considering whether he himself would smoke or drink. Most Thirteens (especially boys) have tried out smoking, but in general they say they wouldn't smoke regularly, and may feel that such activities should be "delayed until around twenty or so." Toward drinking Thirteen is neither tolerant nor intolerant. He feels it should be considered on its own merits. Drinking depends on the person, and whether or not he knows his limitations. Thirteen is most concerned about overdoing drinking to the point of getting drunk—unless perhaps there were "some good reason for getting drunk, like a celebration." Boys are more casual in their thinking about drinking than are girls.

But when it comes to swearing, boys have very definite opinions as to whether they are for it or against it. Some swear a lot, especially to be one of the gang. Others reserve swearing as an adult privilege or may condemn it as a mark of being ill-bred. Girls are more aware of reasons why you should or should not swear. They want to excuse and justify their own swearing, though they disapprove of swearing in general. They might feel that children should at least have the privilege of picking it up by themselves and not from their parents.

Some Thirteens acknowledge their own slight infractions of the ethical code as relates to cheating and stealing but always claim good reason. Books do seem to be open on the floor during examination time and wind has a way of turning the pages. Or since your friends take little things now and then at a store, you yourself might pick up a miniature flashlight. Such are the all too plausible and seemingly reasonable thoughts of the 13-year-old. Most Thirteens, however, do not indulge in either cheating or stealing. They are aware of what others are doing but they do not usually report to an authority. Thirteen detests "squealing," and in many ways it is unfortunate to put Thirteen in a position where he is made responsible for this kind of reporting. Thirteen should be responsible to himself, and if he hasn't reached this stage it should be pretty obvious to the adult, parent or teacher. Such children need adult help and guidance. No time should be lost, for their behavior may well grow worse in coming years. Pressures from their friends will exert a less positive influence, for friends with attitudes similar to their own will be chosen. Demands from the larger group of their age-mates will continue, and more formal group pressures, as through student government, will have their place. But ethical problems are often dealt with too harshly by such a group, and might better have the wise supervision and individual guidance of an understanding but firm teacher or counselor.

9. *Philosophic Outlook*

TIME AND SPACE

Thirteen with his probing, defining intellect is less at a loss to define time than he was at twelve. He is now shifting from his more fluid concept of time in movement or the passage of time, to a more static concept of time. He speaks of moments, hours, years, "a pad of paper to write down happenings," "the marking of a space in life," or "the period or space between two events."

He may contemplate the starting or ending of time if he is philosophically inclined, but he's not sure about either end, whether or when time began and whether or when it will end.

Thirteen's life is a very full one, so full that he doesn't always have enough time for all he wants to do. He handles time quite well, but often arrives at that last-minute rush, the need to accomplish something in those last "decisive five minutes."

Thirteens live in the present, the "here and now," and in the near future. There are some Thirteens who become enchanted by faraway times and places, but most Thirteens realize that "only the present can be lived"; "the immediate past is gone"; and you can "never get it back again."

It is the "nothingness" of space that most concerns Thirteen. However he may express it, he is trying to tell about something which "doesn't exist but it's there." Some pin space down to air, atmosphere, or distance, but it

is more the absence of something that intrigues Thirteen. He might throw in a few stars or planets to occupy space or might think of the infinity of space that goes on and on forever. At the opposite extreme from those who have such expansive concepts are the close-to-home, reality-bound thinkers. They still conceive of space as room for things to grow in, to live in, or just to sit in (as when you save space for a friend at the movies).

The interest in travel so strongly expressed at eleven and twelve has calmed down at thirteen. There is less interest in visiting new or strange places. But Thirteen has become very efficient in his movement by train or bus to nearby cities, especially those he has visited before. With his increased movement in space he is coming to know what kind of a sense of direction he possesses. Girls are more often the ones with the poor sense of direction, and some of the boys have an almost faultlessly good sense, always knowing exactly where they are in space. Boys are also more aware of the points of the compass. All too often a girl is going in the opposite direction from where she wishes to go. Fortunately for adults who have the same difficulty, traffic engineers are now realizing this hazard and are marking roads according to direction of flow.

DEATH AND DEITY

Many Thirteens state quite frankly that they haven't given much thought to the subject of death. The thought of their own dying seems "so remote," and "not in the immediate future," that it hasn't drawn their attention. A few who have previously dreaded the thought of death now dread it less. Most feel there is nothing to be afraid of. It's "just an accepted fact"—an "inevitable event."

Some Thirteens think of death as a stopping place and ending. Boys may think of it more scientifically, that a "technical thing happens like the heart stops beating."

Those who think of death as "the end" are not much concerned with heaven or hell. They say they just don't know what happens. They want proof and they are fully aware that there is no proof. Death is "the end," and "most people are forgotten."

A few are concerned about what it feels like to die. Death doesn't seem as sad to Thirteen as it once did. His sadness may be expressed not so much for the deceased as for the ones who are left behind, the ones who were close to the one who has died. Thirteen may be interested in going to a funeral. He may be amazed that the body looks so real. He is aware of how others feel at a funeral and he says himself that he "feels better having had this experience."

There is quite a shift in Thirteen's belief about after death if he does have thoughts on this subject. He rarely thinks of returning to this earth as he did at twelve. He is slowly discounting the thought that there are two places to go to, and is considering that there may be "just one." He doesn't believe in "everlasting hell," though he might concede a "penitentiary for a couple of years, that's all," a sort of self-contained purgatory. He wonders if the tables might be turned in this one place, "which might be like earth," and where "those who get rich on earth might have to shovel coal and those who are working and starving to help the public might be the higher-ups."

But most Thirteens aren't quite so specific in their thinking. They may state frankly that they don't believe in hell, and that most people go to heaven even though they are bad, for "no one is really all bad." If punishment is to be meted out, maybe you're punished by yourself on this earth.

As with his lack of concern about death, Thirteen may not think much about Deity either. He realizes that he used to think much more about it. He realizes that his ideas have changed recently. Whereas, those who still believe used to think of God as a person or "half man, half spirit," they now think of Him most often as spirit. They will often strengthen their concept with the comment, "He's not a man." Thirteen thinks less of God "watching" him and more of His "knowing" what he is doing. But even though he believes in God, he thinks that He does not influence him personally, that He doesn't "enter daily life." One 13-year-old girl thought that, though God didn't influence her directly, He did "psychologically" in that she herself became the doer. God is a positive force in the lives of some 13-year-olds. Or He may more specifically stop them from doing a lot of things, especially may stop them from swearing.

Though the majority of Thirteens have some form of belief in God, an ever-increasing number are in doubt. They may be in transition—"certain times it seems doubtful; certain times seems very real." They may not believe what they have been told, but they haven't yet evolved their "own system." Or they may not completely believe in God because "there is no real proof." He "may exist," but they are "not absolutely sure." However,

Thirteen is often shocked by his own doubts when he thinks he doesn't believe in God.

The practice of religion is of importance to the believing 13-year-old. He is apt to pray most every night. He recognizes the influence on him of his own thinking. He might even believe that "when I think about things, that's the way it was meant to happen." He wonders whether religion and the church might make a different impression upon him if he took more interest in them and thought about them more. Thirteen is an age when many children are confirmed in the church by their own choice. The religious motive isn't always strong, but at least they "thought it would be a good idea."

The weekly or less frequent practice of devotion in some form of religious service is surprisingly common at thirteen. A number of Thirteens attend Sunday school even if they don't have to. However, there is an increasing number who attend because of a sense of duty or "when I can't talk my way out of it." If Thirteen doesn't want to go, he is as definite in his decision as he is about his choice of clothes or food. There is little gained by forcing him. He might prefer to attend church rather than Sunday school and, though he may not go every Sunday, he is apt to go on an average of once a month. He is not yet ready or old enough for the youth groups, but by fourteen he will be ready and eager, quite as much from a social as from a religious point of view.

CHAPTER EIGHT

Year Fourteen

██

MATURITY PROFILE

DURING this year the emotional climate undergoes growth changes. The shyness, the touchiness, and the gingerly vagaries of Thirteen give way to a robust, vigorous expressiveness. There is more laughter and more noise and singing in the house. There is less withdrawal. The household senses a new contentment and relaxation. Time and again the parents on their annual visit to the Institute report a decided change in the behavior picture, compared with that of a year ago. "He is a changed child—a different person."

The degree and patterns of change vary, of course, with the basic individuality; but in this profile we shall sharpen the contrasts of Thirteen and Fourteen in order to disclose the developmental mechanisms which are at work. There is nothing invidious in these comparisons. The new maturity traits of Fourteen are symptoms of the forward movement of a subcycle of growth. The inwardizing, self-absorption of Thirteen served to enrich the structure of the self which now becomes more fully integrated and in better balance with other personalities. Fourteen is therefore better oriented both to himself and to his interpersonal environment. He feels that he is coming into his own. He has a new self-assurance despite the pressures of mounting energy. Parents say, "He is full of beans," which is doubtless due to the joint influence of changes in body chemistry and to developmental reorganizations of his psyche.

He enjoys life. He tends to be friendly and outgoing in his interpersonal relationships both at home and abroad. His demeanor in the interview and examination situations was typically unconstrained and cordially co-operative. He was frank and communicative, but self-contained rather than confiding. He showed interest in the experience, and volunteered spontaneous comments and questions. He showed a definite awareness of the examiner as another person and often asked for her own opinions. He interjected bits of sociable humor. At thirteen, the interview responses tended to be more guarded and solemn, with much less conversation directed to the examiner.

Fourteen has a more mature attitude toward adults in general, and to his family in particular. He now uses the word *family* more freely and is beginning to think of the household as an institution. This at times makes him hypercritical. A son may regard his father as hopelessly old-fashioned. A daughter may exclaim in dismay, "Oh, Mother!" at a minor breach of propriety. Despite a tendency to feel highly embarrassed by parental conduct, the basic relationship with the family circle has become more genial and less tense. Disagreements are less tight and insistent. There is more mutual respect and confidence, based on increased understanding. Fourteen is developing a capacity to perceive how others feel, and to see himself as others see him. In an American household he may even bring his growing sense of humor into play; he ventures to "kid" and chaff his parents when they reciprocate with tolerance and insight.

He gets along well with younger siblings. Indeed, if they are about five years of age or less, he likes to take care of them, plays with them, and even buys them presents. With 11-year-olds he is not so amicable; but his difficulties are usually solved at the verbal level, by arguing and altercation. Most parents feel that Fourteen should treat junior siblings better than he does, and that he should also try to improve his behavior. In families of three or more children much is expected of the 14-year-old, which suggests that he has reached a higher level of maturity and responsibility.

Fourteen is interested in people, and is increasingly aware of their personality differences. He matches their traits against his own and those of his parents. He is somewhat intrigued by the word *personality*, and uses it more freely. But he is much less subjective than Thirteen in ruminating on these matters. He can be frankly objective in his estimates and comments, even in discussions with his teachers.

He is gregarious and seems to prefer a variety of associates. We ask him about his friends, and he promptly replies, "I have a whole gang of them." He can specify and appraise their several characteristics in great detail. His outlook on these diversities tends to be tolerant. "Everybody is pretty harmonious," he says. He is, however, sensitive to deviations from group standards. He is anxious to be popular with his age-mates. Interest in athletic teams, group activities, 4-H clubs, and similar organizations, reaches a high level of intensity. Devotion to a chosen group may go to passionate extremes, when the drive toward emancipation becomes excessive.

The psychology of the group frequently comes into competition with the concrete demands of home, school, and community. Fourteen has to pick his way, making many choices among diverging and converging pathways. Temperamental and sex differences come increasingly into evidence.

Boys in general prefer boy companions, as friends and as members of an activity group. One boy, with a touch of humor, declared, "I like people—every kind except girls." A census of our research series shows, however, that about a third of the 14-year-old boys do some dating. Steady dating is very exceptional. The girls wait to be asked. Even so a boy may exercise preliminary caution: "If I asked you, would you go?" About a half of the girls are said to date, but they do not "go steady." They are generally more interested in the opposite sex than are the boys.

Girls, however, take the most active interest in their girl friends of comparable age. These friends are numerous, varied, and selective. The close friendships so intense that they become quarrelsome are no longer typical. Friends are not chosen simply because they reside in the same neighborhood. They are drawn together by a reciprocal interest in their various personalities. Every school class is likely to have a congenial "gang," made up of popular and successful girls. Interests and activities are shared in connection with sports events, dramatics, school orchestra, picnics, parties, hikes, etc. Some girls of broad outlook go out of their way to be nice to unpopular or unattractive girls.

The eager, tireless communication which binds together a coterie of active 14-year-old girls is an impressive manifestation of social psychology. The communication occurs at every available interlude within a day, before and after school hours, whenever two or more girls may meet. When they cannot meet, the telephone brings them together. This is a peak age for interminable phone communications, gay, serious, and hushed. The conversations are punctuated with giggles, gossip, and all sorts of apparent trivia, which, however, are charged with meaning for the young persons on the line. Tape recordings would be revealing.

How much time is spent at the phone? "As much as mother can stand." "As much as we can get away with." But Fourteen has a sense of humor and might well be the author of the following rhyme which appeared in a high school anthology of poetry:

> The telephone was invented
> For the use of communication
> But now-a-days its basic use
> Is for teen-age conversation.
> In future years, I predict
> Our parents will combine
> And banish all our telephones
> To keep us off the line.

Talk, by whatever means, is now a preferred method among friends, to explore the intricacies of human personality. It is not an altogether idle pursuit. Rather it is an instinctive amateur form of applied psychology. Sometimes Girl A will suggest concrete improvements and alterations in the personality make-up of Girl B. As friends they analyze their traits, confessing, denying, and disputing. They talk not only about themselves, but about teachers, parents, principals, movie stars, disc jockeys, visitors, relatives, and about this boy and that boy. "Last year we used to talk about horses an awful lot, and the boys did not come into the problem, but now they're quite the main topic!" At this age, many boys have not given much thought to marriage; whereas every girl in our research group had definite plans and expectations. Moreover, the girls now lay special stress on personality traits as the most important qualifications of a husband.

Fourteen is alive; he abounds in energy, exuberance, and expansiveness. He is so optimistic about his own affairs and the world in general that he is sometimes swamped by his undertakings. Occasionally he may get into a curious entanglement which arises from the very abundance of his interests and impulses.

But we would not describe him as being essentially impulsive. On the contrary, he tends to be realistic and objective in his judgments. He shows a disposition to look at and to consider two sides of an issue. He likes to reason. He is capable of independent thinking and can take an intellectual pleasure in discussion. His use of language and the inflections of his speech unconsciously reveal the growth of more mature modes of thought.

On the basis of abundant verbatim records we have found that certain words and phrases are favored at a given maturity level. Such expressions convey symptomatic overtones. The following phrases from the conversation of Fourteen suggest the new patterns of thought and attitude which are emerging:

as a rule; now-a-days; as a matter of fact; necessarily; ideal; in my opinion; policy; unity; appreciation; suitable; on the whole; reputation; personality; adapted.

The primary intellectual abilities of the mind mature at different ages. Two verbal components of human intelligence, namely, verbal comprehension and word fluency, are said to mature to four-fifths of the adult level at about the age of fourteen (Thurstone). Our data point in the same direction. This zone of maturity yields signs of a marked increase in rationalism and logical thinking.

Fourteen is beginning "to use his mind" in new ways. Unless he is of a pronounced non-verbal type, he experiences pleasure in asserting a new command of language. He may take genuine interest in the composition of themes at school. He feels a trace of triumph and intellectual satisfaction when he puts to use a pertinent word or phrase for the first time in animated conversation. Such words are growth phenomena; they are not merely the product of conditioned reflex or rote learning. They betoken concealed but exquisite growth changes in the molecular organization of the brain. Words convey and catalyze *ideas*; they expand into propositions, paragraphs, and stanzas.

Fourteen is entering deeper into the ideational realms of thought. Words enable him to formulate two sides of a proposal or a choice; they serve to make him more considerate and controlled in emotional situations. They help to broaden his outlook for seeing things whole and in their totality. The latter capacity is in striking contrast to the marked focalization which occurs at the thirteen-year level. However, we may remind ourselves that the inwardizing, focal concentrations of Thirteen constitute a natural, incubative stage in the development of the more liberal and fluid mental processes of Fourteen.

The developmental characteristics of Fourteen make him a challenging subject for education. Consider his abundant energy and outgoing friendliness, the catholicity of his interests, his insight into himself and into his teachers, a budding awareness of ideals, a growing comprehension and command of words, and an exuberant inclination to reason. These qualities, intellectual, personal, and social, pose significant questions as to the best methods and arrangements of education. The basic questions apply both to boys and girls, whether separated or combined, even granting well-recognized differences such as the rate of physical growth.

The 14-year-old occupies a zone of maturity intermediate between the elementary or grammar school and the senior high school. Viewed in developmental perspective, he is definitely "outgrowing" the limitations of the lower grades. His mental maturation is proceeding rapidly, in preparation for the higher grades. But in this early phase of transition he may not yet be in a favorable position to meet the stresses and competition of a big, strenuous high school. He may need somewhat specific rearrangements in the educational system, to bring to full realization the promising potentials which he now embodies. Perhaps he peculiarly needs an educational unit with the controls of an adapted home-room setup. This is not a matter of soft pedagogy. It is a means of providing a more suitable congenial environment and a program which is more fully fitted to the basic maturity level of the group and the maturity patterns of the individual. Such arrangements would reduce excessive and misdirected competitions; and place Fourteen in a more favorable educational climate.

The individualizing of instruction, guidance, and counseling is of peculiar importance at this stage of a youth's career. Although he has strong identifications with the group, this is more than counterbalanced by his insistent interest in his own characteristics as an individual. He is keen to get new insights into his own development. He is very receptive to any suggestions which throw light on his individual traits, which means that he is also receptive to interpretive guidance. He seems to sense the push and the movement of growth forces. "Things are so different, this year and last year," he tells us. "It gets better as I go along."

His awareness of individual differences extends externally as well as inwardly. He sees himself in characters that he reads about in fiction and biography, or sees upon the screen and in actual life. "That's me," he exclaims, "that's me all over!" As an embryonic psychologist, one of our youths remarked, "I like to figure people out and put myself in their shoes and see how they feel."

Typically a 14-year-old is happy and self-reliant. But he is capable of

self-criticism, because of his new and fresh powers of reasoning. He indulges in lengthening trains of independent thinking, weighing pros and
cons. Too often, after self-examination, he rationally decides that he ought
to drop out of school. This well-deliberated decision poses new problems
for himself and for his well-wishers. He needs help to find himself—the
help of developmentally oriented counsel.

Year Fourteen is a favorable period for a re-evaluation of the individual.
The formative adolescent years, eleven, twelve, and thirteen, can now be
seen in better perspective. If in their entire sequence they show marked
deviations and difficulties of development, it is a time to think of long-
range plans and preventive measures. It is also a time when talents, giftedness, and leadership can be recognized and judiciously fostered. Many
boys and girls credit their schoolteachers with sparking their first interest
in science at about the age of fourteen years. Ideals likewise take root
and flourish in a new way.

Indeed, when all factors are considered, fourteen may be regarded as
a somewhat pivotal year in the grand cycle of human growth. The youth
is coming into his own. He is able, to a gratifying degree, to accept the
world as he finds it. At his typical best he presents a fine constellation of
maturity traits and potentials, which are in propitious balance. He is
exuberant and energetic; but reasonable in temper (notwithstanding the
loudness of his voice). He has a fair measure of wisdom and philosophy,
often expressed in wit and humor. His group loyalties are strong and
sensitive, but normally they do not distort his person-to-person relationships in the home circle, at school, and within the community. He has
many friends. He understands them pretty well, and has a sympathetic
awareness of the unpopular and unfortunate.

Emotionally he is not as precarious as he used to be. His spontaneous
attitudes make him tremendously educable in the realm of human values
and social obligations.

His educability is reinforced by a rising capacity to think logically and
propositionally. This capacity has not been too firmly established in the
evolution of the race. Therefore it becomes particularly significant in the
ontogenetic development of the individual. The instinctive basis of reasoning ability is repeatedly shown in the adolescence of individuals gifted
with exceptional intellectual power. Albert Schweitzer relates how in his
fourteenth year the joys of seeking for what was true and good came upon
him "like a kind of intoxication." He felt "a passionate need to think." As
a philosopher he holds the 14-year-old youth in high regard and pays him

a compliment: "If all of us could become what we were at fourteen, what a different place the world would be!"

MATURITY TRAITS

1. *Total Action System*

The tight, withdrawn ways of Thirteen have loosened up at fourteen. A profound change has occurred, not only within Fourteen but also in his impact upon the world around him. He now seems to be more of a self in his own right, more capable of easy give-and-take. He generates a friendly and relaxed atmosphere. There no longer seems to be the need to walk gingerly around him, to choose some special method of approach, as was often necessary in dealing with Thirteen. Fourteen, feeling more secure in himself, is more outgoing, more straightforward. No longer so much on the defensive, so fearful that people will pry into his personal affairs, he can talk freely in a genuine, agreeable way with other people—even with his parents!

In an interview, Fourteen's demeanor is quiet and relaxed. His posture is symmetrical; his feet are often placed flat on the floor. He shows few tensional outlets or shifts in interest from the task at hand. He listens well and he responds well. He has both the desire and the facility to communicate. Even when he does not talk much his smile shows his interest. Fourteen throws in incidental comments of his own. The interviewer too feels free to make spontaneous comments and to answer Fourteen's queries in an easy fashion. Fourteen may add humorous asides, may dramatize an answer, and

laugh in a pleasant, mature manner. He can turn his humor back on himself in a kidding way or express mild, good-natured sarcasm: "Very simple, eh?" (This same expression might have had a biting quality if voiced by Thirteen.)

Fourteen does not jump into an answer. He may hesitate for a while and only after a few orienting questions say, "Oh, now I get it." He shows a good, direct attack on a task. He wants to "work things all out." Though he may express some self-deprecation, he does not get panicky and, if he has to give up, he can do so gracefully. Even his excuse that he "didn't have enough sleep last night" is offered with insight and good humor.

One of Fourteen's chief problems is that he often wants to include too much in his thinking or to plan too much in his activities. This is all a part of his new expansiveness: a loose inclusiveness that can sometimes swamp him. This is why it might be hard for him to formulate an answer and why he may, in the midst of trying to solve a problem, comment, "This is driving me crazy." The tangles and overlappings in his social life are likewise part of this overinclusiveness. Thus Fourteen is apt both to arrive late for an interview and to have to leave early. He needs to be checked and planned with.

Fourteen is gathering a new sense of larger totals. His mobile eye movements give some idea of the multiple thought processes that are taking place within his brain. His very concept and use of the word *personality* suggest that he is judging others from a more comprehensive point of view.

HEALTH

Fourteen's health frequently is not just "good" but "really wonderful." He misses very little school because of illness; he can still attend even when he has a sniffle. Few Fourteens have the "habit" of being ill, as they might have had at eleven and twelve, and occasionally at thirteen. They can actually go to the other extreme of putting up with illness when necessary. One boy was quite willing to suffer a little asthma if only he could keep his dog, to which he was allergic.

TENSIONAL OUTLETS

Fourteen may have a few remnants of past tensional outlets, but these are only incidental. Fingernail biting may occur with some, but only during intense situations, such as viewing a movie. Headaches may occur when Fourteen can't adjust to the demands of his environment—or vice versa. An occasional Fourteen with a long-standing history of nervous tensions may have hands that tremble so much that at times he can't even play the piano. But this is the exception.

VISION

Visually, Fourteen is usually in good shape. His eyes handle the usual visual skills tests (fusion, suppressions, stereopsis, usable vision, centering) quite adeptly. His eye movements in following a moving object are good. The trend at fourteen is toward a more stable amount of hyperopia (farsightedness). It is often the Fourteen with supposedly perfect ("20/20") vision

and very little hyperopia who complains that his eyes bother him, especially when reading. A reduction in the reading program might alleviate the symptoms, but school demands will not always allow this. Fourteen then needs visual help—lenses or training—to build up the flexibility he lacks. Usually he is well motivated and cooperates better in a training program than he would have at thirteen or will at fifteen.

Fourteen combines his fixating and focusing mechanisms better than he has earlier. His responses are more like the usual adult patterns, and it is possible to predict more accurately than earlier what the eyes are going to do under certain test situations.

With the exception of those with very low hyperopia, Fourteens do not have as many visual complaints about reading as they did at thirteen. However, often they do not read as extensively as they then did. Reading, in addition to that required for school, often stays within the magazine realm.

Fourteen is more certain and dogmatic in his desire not to wear glasses, though he will "concede, if it is necessary." But if given the alternative, Fourteen is willing to do whatever is required to make glasses unnecessary. Even those who are nearsighted and really need their glasses will work hard in a visual training program, in order to become less dependent upon them and to be able to take them off for special occasions. The motivation to work and to improve comes from within, and is not just imposed by others as it was in preceding years.

PHYSICAL DEVELOPMENT AND SEX AWARENESS—GIRLS

Although there still are marked differences in rate of growth, the 14-year-old girl's body form seems typically to be more like that of a young woman than that of a child. Height growth is nearly completed during this year; after the fifteenth birthday few girls will add more than an inch to their heights. Weight growth too has slowed down, though this may continue long after height growth has ceased. Maturity features now approximate those of young adulthood. The breasts approach full adult size and pubic hair is full and dense.

For all their feminine softness, however, the body forms of many Fourteens give an impression of strength. Face and neck seem stronger. And the filling in of hollows gives a suggestion of greater compactness, even in the slimmer girls.

Very few girls have not menstruated by their fourteenth year. The majority are becoming well established in their menstrual patterns. Most are becoming aware of premenstrual symptoms which occur a day or two ahead of their periods. They may have cramps, a backache, or just a general state of emotional tension and nervousness. Their periods may be accompanied by slight cramps and they may at times feel badly enough to lie down for an hour or so. A few may feel dizzy or sick and may actually miss a meal or two. (These are often the girls who are characteristically influenced by emotional excitement.) At the other extreme are the girls who have no pain or other symptoms, and whose ordinary activities are in no way curtailed.

The menstrual cycle is now gathering greater regularity and is approximating a 28-day cycle, though in many it is longer (as long as 45 to 50 days).

The menstrual flow may be as long as five days or even extend to six to seven days. Fourteens tend to use sanitary napkins lavishly, often, according to their mothers, more than they need. This is no time to economize, however. An ample supply should be on hand, so that at least this aspect of Fourteen's adjustment to her new function of sexual maturing is made easier.

Girls may now feel an actual physical involvement in their response to boys. A 14-year-old girl may report feeling as though she were "falling apart" or "turning inside out" in the strength of her feeling. These feelings may be confusing to Fourteen, who has trouble grasping the nature and origin of these emerging but unpatterned sensations.

PHYSICAL DEVELOPMENT AND SEX AWARENESS—BOYS

Fourteen seems to be a transition zone for most boys. At thirteen, despite newly acquired features of maturity, the majority seemed to look like boys—more akin to their 10-year-old selves. By fifteen, most will look like men. Though at fourteen they are still far from mature in total development, they seem to have crossed a line. Actually, of course, this "line" may be crossed at thirteen or earlier, at fifteen or later; but most often it seems to lie in the zone between the fourteenth and fifteenth birthdays.

At fourteen the size increase in most boys is quite marked. This is the period of most rapid height growth for the greatest number of boys. The body form appears more heavily muscled. The adolescent fat period is a thing of the past for most of the boys who showed this at all. The larger physique, together with its newly developed maturity features, gives a strong impression of adolescent masculinity.

Pubic hair is now fairly dense and is darker in most boys. Hair on forearms and calves has become denser and sideburns have started to elongate. Deepening of the voice has become more noticeable. The voice change may occur slowly and steadily, or through a cracking process, or all of a sudden. The sudden change can be mistaken for a cold. It is as though Fourteen develops a hoarseness which never leaves him. With this sudden change of voice (which occurs in a minority) there are often accompanying sharp changes. Unself-consciousness may suddenly switch over into extreme modesty—almost as if the voice change shocked Fourteen into an awareness of his own sexual maturing.

The genital developments already visible at thirteen are quite advanced in many Fourteens. By the end of the fourteenth year, a large majority of boys will have experienced ejaculation, in one situation or another. By far the most common source of this first ejaculation is masturbation, a phenomenon that most boys have known about and a majority have experimented with since age eleven. Very soon after the first experience of emission, nearly all boys develop an individual, more or less regular pattern of sexual activity.

Nocturnal emissions may begin to occur in the period just before fourteen, though many boys do not experience these until late adolescence. Boys respond quite differently to the experience. Fortunately, nowadays more boys are informed about their possible occurrence, and are less likely to be disturbed by them, but even so some feel ashamed and hide their pajamas, while others take it naturally as a part of life.

Boys in general are definitely interested in girls. In some ways they do not seem so disquieted by girls as the girls are by boys, though they might blush if a girl called out to them on the street.

Fourteen is an age when further sex education is both needed and eagerly received. The same movies used in sixth grade can be repeated, but should be viewed separately by girls, by boys, and by parents. It is surprising what a change three years have made, and how differently the same films are viewed. Such movies often stimulate a barrage of questions, especially from the girls. Writing out such questions is often easier than asking them directly. The questions range over many topics, but most of them are personal and direct. Besides information requested about individual sex development, including the physiology and functioning of sex parts, many questions concern intercourse, both premarital and marital. Such topics as birth control, venereal disease, prostitution, and homosexuality are also raised. Fourteen not only wants information about these topics, he wants to discuss them, to work out some kind of evaluation of them.

Fourteens are trying to find their own way, to clarify for themselves how they feel, and to decide what paths are best for them. They can do this best on a basis of accurate information, presented in the context of a philosophy compatible with their own forthrightness. Unfortunately, they are too often left to make their own decisions when they are not adequately prepared to do so. It is the uninformed adolescent who is more likely to get into trouble. For example, a 14-year-old girl, with her expansiveness and her preference for older boys, may in some cases be rather vulnerable; in extreme cases a pregnancy may occur, either because she was incompletely informed or because too great license was allowed in social affairs. Parents need both to inform and to protect their daughters —not by prohibiting dates or setting unreasonable curfews, but by helping them to develop reasonable inhibitions and an understanding of the need for control when they are not yet ready to assume the consequences of their actions.

Without information many Fourteens do not know how to build up the necessary controls or understand why they need to build them up. With the freedom in dating we give our children today, we need at least to arm them with knowledge, to help them to the safety of their own self-control. It is also for the parent to judge how much responsibility his child is capable of taking. If the youth is not responsible, then other, outside checks must be imposed, either by parents or by society.

2. *Self-Care and Routines*

EATING

Fourteen is coming into the more adult realm of the aesthetics of eating, the enjoyment of eating. He still has a very fine appetite, especially if he is an athletically inclined boy, but this appetite is on the whole under good control. He is now especially aware of the smell of food, either the smell that repels or the smell that beckons. The aroma from a Hungarian goulash may repel him, whereas the aroma from food cooked over a campfire may draw him to it. He is also aware of the consistency of foods. It may be the sticky consistency of peanut butter which causes some Fourteens to dislike it. And it may be the firm consistency of an apple that so delights them.

Fourteen is still a snacker, especially after school. However, he hasn't that urge to eat that he had at twelve. He snacks on whatever his mother happens to have around, especially on fruit. He is less apt to snack before bedtime. He may say he's too lazy to prepare a bedtime snack, but this is because his appetite is less. If he does have a bedtime snack, he says he doesn't "sit down and make a feast" for himself.

He frequents the drugstore, but it may be as much in search of sociability as of food. There are, however, the two extremes at fourteen, the sweets eaters and the non-sweets eaters. The former have to tussle with themselves to restrict the elaborateness of the sundaes they order, but fortunately the depletion of their individual funds may solve their problem. The non-sweets eaters are more apt to order a soft drink and would prefer a piece of fruit to sundaes or candy.

Mealtime can be a very pleasant time for Fourteen and his family. He has his likes and dislikes, but the latter are minor. Some boys prefer pies to cake. And apple pie, so much a part of the American food culture, is the preferred one. One 14-year-old boy was heard to say, "I'd like to sit down and eat myself a whole apple pie but probably I'd get sick." Fourteen does know his digestive limitations.

There is some complaint about Fourteen's table manners but mostly in reference to his elbows on the table. He may use his fingers as a pusher but this can be easily remedied. In general the parental attitude toward Fourteen's table manners is non-complaining, and can be summed up in one mother's remark: "all that can be expected."

With Fourteen's increase in height there comes in general a slimming down. The need for dieting is less in evidence. There are always the few, especially the girls, who may nibble at food especially when they are bored, but on the whole Fourteen doesn't have that consuming interest in food he had earlier, especially at twelve. He himself cooks less than he did and, as a rule, only if he has to. He may have stopped making his own Saturday and Sunday breakfasts. But he feels confident in his ability to cook and still enjoys watching food being prepared. Some girls, however, continue to practice the art of cooking. Fourteen may tell you that he "likes to cook not so much for cooking's sake as for the enjoyment of seeing other people enjoy it." There is a streak of altruism entering Fourteen's life which is most pleasant to behold.

SLEEP

Bedtime. Fourteen is pretty much at the helm as far as sleeping goes. As one Fourteen puts it, "I usually go to bed myself. I know enough to go to bed." The hour of bedtime ranges from 9 to 11, with the commonest time at 9:30 or 10 P.M. Each Fourteen seemed to have his own variation of bedtime within the range of an hour. If he is tired he is apt to go to bed at his early bedtime hour. He is usually busy with his homework right up to his bedtime. He may listen to the radio or read a bit after he's in bed. Or he may daydream a bit, thinking of the near future or present. But on the whole Fourteen is most likely to fall right off to sleep.

Sleep. Most Fourteens report that they dream but also that they are apt to forget their dreams when they wake up. If they do remember them, they often report them as "rather uninteresting," "perfectly logical," and "just incidents." They often tell their dreams at breakfast and find that "people are usually reasonably interested" to hear their dreams recounted.

Morning. There is a great variety of waking times at Fourteen, and these times probably give many clues to personality. There are those who seem to need little sleep—who both go to bed late and get up early. These are often boys who live very full lives and who never have enough time to do all they want to do. Then there are those who are establishing a routine. They may awake on the dot of 7 A.M. They like the feeling of getting into a habit. Others have to establish the habit through the device of an alarm clock. And lastly there are those slugabeds who always want to sneak in that extra ten or fifteen minutes. They are the ones who have to be called not once, but twice or three times over. They happily sleep until noon on Saturday and Sunday or during vacation. May they be allowed this excess off and on so that they may handle the daily task of getting up a little more graciously.

BATH

When parents can report, "She's reached the clean stage now," it is evidence enough that girls, if not boys, at fourteen are more surely responsible for their own cleanliness. Though most girls bathe every other night or twice a week, an increasing number like to bathe nightly. They even miss their bath when they don't have time or are too tired to take one.

Boys don't come up to the level of the girls. In fact, many of them still have to be reminded and are even said to be "allergic to soap." They quite often need to be reminded to wash their hands before mealtime, and they have a way of slipping up on their bath. Fortunately, showers after athletics make home bathing less imperative.

Morning washing is all too often still an afterthought for some boys. They suddenly remember after they are all dressed in a nicely ironed shirt that they haven't washed their face. Then they splash water lavishly and wilt the beauty of their shirt, much to their mother's disappointment. They are still quite capable of forgetting to wash their necks.

Shampooing and care of hair is not the task it used to be. Girls may still need some help with rinsing when they take their weekly shampoo. Some need not shampoo their hair more often than once in two weeks, others with a tendency to oily hair want to shampoo it more often, at four- or five-day intervals. Fourteens are quite adept at putting their hair up in curlers or in pin curls.

Boys groom their hair well, including washing, and most are now responsible for seeing that it is cut every other week, though some parents still have to do battle to see that hair gets cut. A few boys are beginning to shave. This is accomplished very privately about twice a week.

Fingernails are now becoming a part of Fourteen's total care of himself. He may need a little reminding about both care of fingernails and brushing of teeth, but on the whole he is doing quite a passable job.

CLOTHES AND CARE OF ROOM

Fourteen earns a few gentle compliments from his mother: he is "pretty good about his clothes," he "hangs them up most of the time," he is "essentially neat," and he "makes a nice appearance."

He is indeed interested in his clothes, in a natural sort of a way. He likes variety. Boys will splurge on shirts and sports jackets. Some are on the more conservative side with the white shirt, the matched, single-color ensemble, and the patterned tie, while others may seemingly have strange preferences choosing a purplish-blue suit, a flashy tie, or an odd-colored shirt. Girls may realize that their basic taste in clothes may differ from their mothers', whether the tailored or more frilly clothes are chosen.

Both sexes are pretty well aware of what they need in the clothes line. They seem to understand the make-up of a total wardrobe. This is the age when boys are aware of the need for a topcoat. Some girls would go out of bounds in their purchase of clothes, especially skirts, if they got the chance. Oddly enough, it is the girl whose closet is most stocked who is most apt to moan, "I have nothing to wear!"

The purchase and choice of clothes is not too difficult for Fourteen. He takes care of the small purchases—underwear, socks, or shoes—by himself, but he likes a parent to help him decide about the bigger purchases. There is a fair amount of agreement between the parent and child unless their basic tastes differ quite basically. Then there may be a "big disagreement." And, by this age, the mother has or should have learned that her daughter won't wear something she doesn't like, and that any clothes brought home by mother on her own are likely to hang in her daughter's closet unworn.

A few Fourteens may demand or be given a small clothes allowance. It is, however, the unusual Fourteen who can budget wisely. Also it can be a great strain on Fourteen to keep track of his expenditures and not go broke.

Fourteen's care of his clothes is showing increasing responsibility. He says matter-of-factly that "we have a closet and I hang up outdoor clothes when I come in," as if the hall closet hadn't been there for some years past. He is more careful about hanging up his better clothes but still may have trouble in the proper use of hangers. He may even avoid the use of hangers and pile one piece of clothing on top of another on a single hook until the effect, according to the parent, is that of a "hunch backed person."

Fourteen is more apt now than formerly to report torn places and missing buttons and may even remedy matters himself. Oddly enough, it is as often the boys as the girls who mend their own clothes and sew on buttons.

Disposal of dirty clothes in a pile or hamper is becoming a habit pattern, and this pile can become pretty large if there is a daily change of shirts. Some Fourteens may relieve the laundry problem by washing and ironing their own shirts. They also may be quite expert at pressing their trousers or skirts. On the whole Fourteen is aware of which clothes need dry cleaning and may in fact run up the biggest dry-cleaning bill of anybody

in the family. But it is not surprising to see a 14-year-old boy all resplendent in a freshly ironed shirt yet unaware of obvious spots on his trousers. Shoes are being shined better than they have been, but their care still needs supervision by the parent.

The majority of Fourteens keep their rooms in passing fair neatness. Many even enjoy a tidy room. Fourteen still tends to leave clothes around his room but he does pick them up sporadically. He is less interested in decorating his room with pennants and pictures and may remove many of the trappings that he enjoyed so at twelve and thirteen. Girls who have a crush on a movie star may focus the theme of their decoration and interest on that one person. Different angle shots may be placed strategically about the room, even hang from the ceiling. Some Fourteens, like Thirteens, are apt to spend considerable time in their rooms. But on the whole Fourteen uses his room for sleeping and studying and would prefer to read in the midst of the family group. Those Fourteens who are not too good about keeping their room neat will nevertheless maintain order in parts, especially their desks. But Fourteen is apt to leave books strewn around. The best stimulus to urge him to clean up his room is the thought of guests coming or even just the cleaning woman. Fortunately, he is aware of what the other person might think of him. He's apt to slip up on his bedmaking, especially toward the end of the week, but a new week may bring the fresh start he needed.

MONEY

Parents are now feeling the fuller impact of how much it costs to rear a child, especially in this expanding, demanding age of fourteen. The weekly allowance of $1 plus extras, which totals around $2 with simple budgeting, may temporarily be sufficient. But with an increased demand for extras, and especially for clothes with girls, it is very difficult to work out even a monthly allowance. A few families find it easier to give up an allowance and give out money as needed. This method is easier with those Fourteens who are more conscious of money and are guided by what the family can afford. But with those who have expensive tastes but little desire to earn money to pay for these tastes the planning is more difficult. Their idea of money may be very inflated and it may be the one topic of discussion that produces the most quarrels with their parents, especially with their fathers. With these Fourteens it is necessary to set up boundaries and stick to them. Clothes-hungry girls need to have a clothes allowance, not for them to enjoy, but rather to control them within bounds.

Fourteen is more of a spendthrift than he has been. A number spend money foolishly and are usually "broke" at the end of the week if they are on an allowance. They may buy good books and records, but they have little money on hand.

Earned funds, however, are increasing. Summer jobs are often netting close to $50, which can be banked and left to gather interest.

WORK

Fourteen recognizes his own change in attitude toward work. He remembers how terrible he was two years ago and feels that he is "now quite good at it." He may not only do chores willingly but also automatically. Those who are less cheerful about work and more resistant may realize they are not acting up to their age.

Girls are now extending their activities in the home. They dust and clean, scrub bathrooms, and may be capable of cleaning an entire house. They may do their own ironing.

Boys not only wash the family car but may be able to change a tire and even keep the car in good mechanical condition. Some are beginning to do man-size jobs, such as ripping out a hedge or building a fireplace.

Regular jobs are usually summer ones, such as working at a garage or helping in a store. Baby-sitting may also take on a steady pattern over a period of months. But often Fourteen does not have the time to give to very demanding steady work, nor is he quite ready to take on fixed demands.

3. Emotions

The first acute throes of what is often thought of as adolescent behavior—which appeared so strongly in the withdrawal and touchiness of Thirteen—have now been gone through. A new, joyous, gay note is struck in Fourteen. No longer is it necessary for parents to skirt gingerly around their "pathetically edgy" sons and daughters. The atmosphere has cleared—laughter rings out in the house, singing, so long neglected, may be heard even in the morning. Fourteen has indeed taken a turn for the better. Fourteen loves living. As parents remark, "He's just full of it"; "He has burst out all over." If less exuberant he is "in general easygoing" or "happy in an adult way." It is the agreeable note in his voice, the humorous twist of a phrase that now makes him so much more pleasant to live with.

Not that he stays within the positive realm all the time. Actually, he seems to have two sides to his nature—though "he is easygoing, he gets moody," though "he takes things well in his stride, he is irritable and makes issues of little things," though she is "awfully happy" at times, she can also be thrown into the "depths of depression."

But on the whole Fourteen is enjoying himself in living. He recognizes that as he gets older "life gets more complicated, but it's lots more fun." He's moving with life and he says, "It gets better as I go along." He is becoming ready to accept his added responsibilities and he also recognizes that you come to "nasty places" every once in a while.

These "nasty places" don't come often, but when they do they are something to cope with. They are inner tangles that produce such outbursts as violent anger or distressed crying which are out of keeping with Fourteen's usual responses. When these moments come it is important for the parent or teacher to find out what lies behind the sudden flare-up or violence that seems all out of proportion to the occasion of the moment. It might, for instance, be discovered that Fourteen is mixed up in his studies and needs some special help. It is surprising how quickly you can get at Fourteen's difficulties and how quickly you can help him resolve them.

Fourteen tends to have moments of being "awfully happy." These are most likely to come when he's not in school, though he can be extremely pleased about being on the honor roll or having his team win. But it is his social life—going out on a date, getting something new to wear, going on a cookout—which gives Fourteen the greatest happiness.

Happy moods far outstrip Fourteen's sad ones. Rather than being sad, he is apt to be annoyed or moody. His moodiness can move into more active brooding or depression. But Fourteen is not likely to stay in these somber states for very long. He may drop into the depths occasionally, but is able to bounce back rather quickly.

Fourteen is less inhibited than he was about his temper and he is apt to get angry quickly, though not often. He shows short, explosive outbursts, especially against a sibling. He will suddenly "let off steam" before others, whereas at thirteen he more often controlled himself and withdrew to his room. If he now retreats to his room he may stomp off noisily. Fourteen is not one to keep things bottled up. He lets you know when he's "mad" or "annoyed." He's likely to "throw his voice around" and is especially likely to yell or shout at his siblings, or swear to himself in his room. But he less often strikes out physically, except at his siblings. If he's mad at his teacher, he can contain himself and remain silent. This is also usually true when he is mad at his parents.

Crying is not common at fourteen but when it does occur there is usually a good reason behind it. It occurs more often than not when Fourteen is angry or when he is in one of his tangled states. Crying doesn't necessarily make Fourteen feel better. It reveals more the state underneath that has produced the crying. It may well be a call for help and shouldn't be treated lightly.

Fourteen is not really a fearful age, though quite a variety of fears is reported. It is almost as though each child has his pet fear that has come to the surface. There are those who are afraid of bugs, spiders, bees, and moths. A fairly large number of both boys and girls are afraid of snakes. Some are afraid of high places, of deep water, of being out in the dark, of getting lost in the woods, of walking on a soft, mushy bottom in the water. They are afraid of being embarrassed, afraid of people, of being "left out," of social gossip, of "just what's going to happen" or "how things will turn out." This is an age when experience may resolve the fear. The reading of *Hiroshima* absorbed one girl's fear of atomic bombs; really being lost in the woods and finding his way out solved another boy's fear of being lost in the woods.

Worrying now has the same quality as fearfulness. Fourteen really isn't the worrier that he was at thirteen but he often has his pet worries. A few declare that they are too busy to worry. A large number worry about school work—getting homework done, getting good grades, passing examinations. Others worry about being late for school. Within the social realm they worry about friends if they haven't got them, worry about friends if they have them. They worry about what kind of impression they make on people, about their boy friend staying or leaving them, about family relations, about popularity. They worry about their reputation or lack of ambition or diseases they might get. But though the list is long, Fourteen's worries don't absorb him any more than do his fears.

A discussion of Fourteen's main problems shows that things don't disturb him too deeply. His main problem may be his body build—that he is too

fat, too short, or too tall. It may be something about his school work (especially exams) or it may be in the social sphere. But even when he complains, as one boy did about his 11-year-old sister who got on his nerves and made it difficult for him to concentrate, he adds, "but I don't mind it too much." And though Fourteen may complain about not getting on with his friends, he's apt to end up with, "but it's much better than it used to be."

Fourteen is not ashamed to show how he feels. He may still cover up feelings, but on the whole he is open about his emotions and likes to have people know how he feels. He is made of tougher stuff than was Thirteen. He is not as vulnerable as he was. He feels the impact of the other person, and his feelings can be hurt, but he's able to take it. He is less apt to hide hurt feelings, though he is capable of ignoring or trying to forget them. He may strike back immediately with a few words or may delay his thrust to a later date. But he tends more to be nonchalant—"so what?"—or to take things as a joke and laugh them off.

When Fourteen is asked if he is ever jealous or envious, he replies with ease that he's "not really jealous" or "only in a way." He may wish he had the privileges of someone else—"going out to dances," "having more freedom." He may wish he were as popular as some of his friends. He may wish he had the chance like some of his friends to work on a farm and drive a tractor. But as he thinks it over he begins to realize his lot isn't so bad, that he's "pretty lucky," that he "gets as many breaks as anyone," that he really doesn't want to change places with another person ("Oh, no!"). You can almost hear him and feel him hurrying back to himself as he says, "When I get right down to it, I'm just *darn glad* I'm myself."

With this good feeling of being himself Fourteen can enter into competition with a different feeling than he had at eleven. Then he was almost viciously competitive, demanding to win at any price. At fourteen he loves competition but in a different way. Fourteen likes to compete in what he's good in, more often in sports than in lessons. He wants above all to do well. If he wins, so much the better. He is especially happy if his team wins.

It is his witty, lightsome touch that makes Fourteen more fun to have around, at least in those moments when he is exercising this talent. His selection of gifts will be influenced by this new-found ability. (For father's birthday a recording of "It's later than you think.") Fourteen is reaching for the intangible, a new kind of sharing of experience. When he forms imaginary clubs and dubs them meaningfully "The Tennyson Brook Club" or "The Black Mark," it is the common experience of the members of the group which allows them to enjoy the humorous meaning of the names. Without explanation they will know that the babblers belong to the former, and the heavy receivers of demerits belong to the latter.

4. *The Growing Self*

By now, the most intensely inwardizing work of Thirteen has, we hope, been accomplished. The reflective process, the living with oneself, the thinking about oneself which characterize Thirteen are all a bit like an active hibernation process. Then comes the time when the inner bio-

logical clock is turning and the time for emergence into the sun arrives. And that time in many is fourteen.

The boy or girl of this age seems "so like himself." He feels like himself even though he might desire a few changes in himself—a little less fat, a little taller, a little shorter. He is now feeling his difference from other people, the quality of his uniqueness, even though he isn't quite ready to accept it fully. He still is influenced a bit by that idealized perfect form, the just-right proportions which he may have in mind. But he doesn't give too much thought to this because he's too busy just being himself.

As one father remarked, "He has finally absorbed himself in something outside himself." And so he has. That is one reason why he's so ready to take his world as he finds it. He is learning the art of how to master life. And in this mastery he comes to know that as one becomes capable of adapting within limits to the demands of the outside world, one learns, too, how to choose. Fourteen is beginning to know more clearly what he really wants and how he can discriminate. Thus he is capable of saying no because he is making a choice and not just being resistant. He can choose his friends and his literature, though he still tends to choose too much and to be swamped by his own exuberance.

Fourteen feels good in himself. You may hear him say, "I like myself the way I am." If he has not quite reached this state, he may seem almost too anxious to be a person in his own right. He may then overstep in his desire to take responsibility for himself and to plan his time on his own. He may still need more adult guidance than he thinks he does in talking over his plans before putting them into action. Because he is more completely himself he is able to look back on his former self with more perspective, more tolerance. Did he not once do the very things he now sees younger children do?

Those Fourteens who are immature or just resistant to growing up are often quite aware of how they are expected to act (girls think they should be boy crazy, wear lipstick and long stockings), but they would often be quite happy to be acting like a younger child, with twelve their favorite choice. Others who were slow in their social growth at twelve and thirteen are now eager to make up for lost time and become gluttons for social experience. The days, weeks, and months don't have enough time to include all of their planning. They tend even to overdo the characteristic tendency of Fourteen to go out of bounds. They spill out all over, and, in their attempt to organize their excess, they often produce confusion and tangles.

Fourteen may be quite aware of his outward appearance. His complexion often distresses him. He may desire some changes physically, but on the whole he gets on with himself and grooms himself according to inner dictates as well as outer appearances. His ensembles themselves, each nicely suited to a particular occasion, seem to thrust him into appropriate activity, rather than simply adding flash and sparkle as they did a few years early. A formal gown looks well on a 14-year-old girl. A tweedy jacket looks well on a 14-year-old boy. Their clothes seem to fit them, suit them, and express their personalities.

Fourteen doesn't like to brag about himself and may be very critical of his classmates who brag. But he can recognize in himself such good qualities as getting on with people, "good sense of humor," and "ability to appreciate things." A few still consider getting good marks their greatest asset, but more (especially among the boys) are concerned with their good athletic ability. Fourteen is willing to face his faults rather squarely, even though he isn't too good at their conquest. One fault many Fourteens have in common is their loud voice. This can be used in fun and sociability with their friends, or it can, all too often, be used to express anger. For Fourteen does not hide or control his feelings as he did at thirteen. And anger, especially toward his siblings, seems to rise easily to the surface. He is fully aware of this and of his parents' displeasure in his behavior. But it will take still another year for him to have the perspective needed to view his emotional episodes from a more adult point of view. When this shift in attitude comes he will find himself far less involved.

Whereas Thirteen more often than not thought of his self in relation to his brain, Fourteen thinks of the self in relation to his head or parts of the head. Mouth, eyes, face, as well as "brains" or "mind," give him a sense of himself. But there are also those who would place their self in their heart and a few in their stomachs, not only because they love to eat but because they "feel it right there, whether it's good poetry or hunger pangs." With still others their hands may seem the most important part of themselves because that's what they do things with. The concept of where the self is located seems to be more individual at fourteen than earlier and to tell us more about the individual boy or girl than about the age. The outgoing, fluid quality of Fourteen somehow encourages this individuality of expression to take place.

As he voices what he would wish for, Fourteen is not thinking of himself alone. Rather he is thinking of himself in the kind of world he would like to live in. First and foremost he wishes for a world at peace or for an end of wars. Then he wishes for a better world in general, in which there is a "unity of nations," "a union of all religions," and a "high standard of living" and "a better chance for people to grow up." More specifically he wishes that there were a more properly run government ("one that wouldn't allow taxes to go up"!) and a better educational system. He is especially desirous of happiness for both his family and people in general, and for himself in the present and in his marriage. He wants to be successful both in getting into and through high school and college, and wants also to achieve well in his career. A few are more concerned about personal attributes of intelligence, good health, popularity, but on the whole Fourteen accepts himself as he is, though he is becoming interested in finding out more about what he as a person is like himself. Money and what money can buy are more often wished for by boys than girls. But those who desire these material possessions are in the minority. Such wishes are expensive yachts, pianos, cars, and airplanes. This is the age when the desire to have a car and years enough to drive it is rearing its disquieting head. Many conflicts will be fought over this consuming passion before the prize itself is within the individual's possession and control.

Fourteen is in a delightfully fluid stage in relation to his future. Though he may wish he were old enough to drive a car or to have the privileges of college age, he really is having a fine time where he is. He plays around with the thought of his future but he "hasn't made up his mind," it "doesn't make much difference," he "hasn't decided yet." He often says he has "no idea" what he wants to be or will be. The future is ahead of him, "come what may." Medicine still entices a certain number. Fourteen is especially interested in any job to do with people. This may be expressed in social work, politics, psychiatry, psychology, diplomatic work, history as related to people, and on and on into any other ramifications that include people.

There is no hurry for Fourteen to decide about his future career. As a matter of fact he may be more interested in his immediate high school or prep school training than in college. Many want to go to college, though they often do not know where, and even these have definite moments when they're not quite sure if they want to go to college and "spend all that money" or not. Many are wondering if a vocational school might not be better. But within the American culture more and more individuals are pointed in the direction of college.

Fourteen is less intense in his thinking about marriage than he was at thirteen. It isn't even on his mind because it has become almost a part of his life. He says he's "planning to get married," he's "thinking about it," "probably will," and "most people do." There is a certain group of boys who "don't know," "haven't decided," or "want to grow up a little more" before they decide. Very few, however, are drawn toward bachelorhood.

Fourteen, on the whole, isn't in a hurry to marry. He recognizes he has much to do before that time will come. He even likes the thought of working for a while after college before he marries. But this does not prevent him from planning. It's almost as though he is capable of projecting himself and living in a future time when he will have his own home and family. Girls are so realistic in this realm that they are already rearing their imaginary children and desire husbands who will be handy around the house and capable of "fixing drains and putting up shelves." But girls want more than this practical side from their future spouses. They are now thinking more of love as a basis for marriage. However, both girls and the few boys who have thought about it are most interested in their future mates having a good disposition. Looks are something, intelligence is something, but in the end Fourteen is beginning to know that it's how well two people are related to each other and to their children that is of prime importance.

Fourteen is thinking quite realistically about his children. He hopes and plans to have them, but recognizes the uncertainties of life. Boys may be more aware of the inheritance factors and may desire a smart wife just because of this. The number of children desired ranges from two or three to four or five, with a preference for a mixture of boys and girls. And that age-old desire to have a boy first is already present in the minds of some 14-year-old girls.

5. Interpersonal Relationships

The change in the atmosphere of the home when a 13-year-older becomes fourteen can bring a wonderful relief and uplift to all concerned. The fearful parent, fearful that he will say the wrong thing, fearful that he will infringe on Thirteen's privacy, fearful that he will embarrass Thirteen, is fearful no more. He can be more natural with his 14-year-old. He speaks enthusiastically of the marked change that has occurred—the new ability of Fourteen to get on with his family. His parents are now able to talk with him. He is fun and you know you are going to enjoy what he says. The whole family relationship seems better.

The parental anticipation of a negative retort, criticism, resentment so typical of Thirteen has now shifted into a positive anticipation of fun, humor, kidding, and forthright laughter from the 14-year-old. The change can be a very welcome one, especially if Thirteen was morose and withdrawn.

This positive attitude and expression of Fourteen may not be in full flower with all Fourteens, but nearly all have at least some small shoots, such as being more agreeable. Even their arguing loses its tight insistent note and shows the flexibility of a disagreement. They may resist their parents initially but after thinking things over sometimes concede that their "mother had the right slant" after all, and they didn't. They come to recognize that the parent is right more often than not. Even the parents' continual desire to improve them seems "not to be such a bad idea." A word sharply spoken by Fourteen to his parent can be erased by an apology. A criticism may be withheld to save the mother's feelings.

But there are those Fourteens who

do have more out and out difficulties with their parents—especially girls with their mothers. Though many feel they are given as much freedom as they should have, others are champing at the bit and feel as though they are held in leash. They storm around and shout about their "big problem," their mother, though they often group their parents together as "they." "They" are often dubbed as "old-fashioned," "antiquated," even "living in the 1940's." Girls get into tangles with their mothers especially over the use of lipstick and hours of coming in at night. Boys have more troubles about going out at night. And there are the ever-lasting problems about homework, clothes, and helping around the house. There come intense moments when mother and daughter "fight like cats and dogs," and fathers are almost driven to whip their sons. But after considerable energy has been expended on both sides, parent and child can usually get together and work out a solution.

These intense moments do not occur often. They seem to be a part of Fourteen's tendency to get so tangled every now and then that something must be done to help him untangle. There is a trend toward an increased feeling of confidence in parents, even though he may keep any approval he feels to himself. Fourteen begins to feel a new understanding on the part of his parents, a desire to help him, and a real sympathetic attitude which seems new to him. This attitude on the part of the parents allows the child to confide in them and to discuss his problems, especially his social problems (more with his mother than with his father).

Fathers are often not as critical as they have been in the past, which may indicate that there is less to criticize. Fourteen recognizes when father puts the pressure on and when he lets up. Girls especially approve of their father's method of handling and, as one girl frankly stated, "It's most important for a father to have a firm hand and keep things in order." Fathers are on the whole said to be more strict and less understanding and sympathetic than mothers, but many daughters get on best with their fathers. However, they do not wish to accept affection from him any more than from their boy friends. Some girls, sensing their father's warm response to them at this time, may turn a cold shoulder toward him and may act very casually. This puts this type of father in a bad spot. He may even show some jealousy of the boys who escort his daughter.

Considering the extent and sharpness of a father's criticism of his 13-year-old, his criticisms seem mild at fourteen. He wants his son or daughter to be more lively, more outgoing, more friendly, more seeking of his company. He is shifting from his more specific demands such as the intellectual achievement he demanded at thirteen to the looser demands of the social poise he feels would become Fourteen. He seems to know spontaneously what Fourteen should be doing.

At long last there is some definite improvement in Fourteen's relationship with his younger siblings. He recognizes that his family's criticisms are still valid, but he really gets on better with his sibs than his family realizes. Of course there are little disagreements, little quarrels, and occasional moments when Fourteen is really mad at a younger sibling. But there are more times when he can have fun with them, can impart the benefits of his experience, can teach them things such as ballet for the fun of teaching and not to improve them.

However, younger siblings can be annoying, they do things on purpose just to irritate, and, what is most distressing to Fourteen, they take things without asking. Fourteen himself has some very definite ideas as to whom he gets on best with and what ages cause the most trouble. He reports all too truly on the extreme difficulties he has with an 11-year-old sibling and accepts the need "of managing and working around" them. If only parents were as well equipped and insightful in handling their 11-year-olds! And Fourteen is also well aware that Eleven gets on best with one sibling at a time.

Fourteen's relationship with his older siblings may be less favorable and his younger status is a disadvantage to him. Though most older sibs get on well with Fourteen, discuss his problems with him, and give him advice, the danger of a competitive urge is all too soon apparent. Older siblings will purposely not give Fourteen a break, may make him walk when they could have given him a ride. Or, when Fourteen is with his friends, the very presence of an older sibling may make him feel self-conscious. And Fourteen in his way is quick to see an older sibling's mistreatment of friends, especially those of the opposite sex, and is quick to express his disapproval.

It is the 14-year-old girl who is more perceptive in all of these interpersonal relationships, especially with contemporaries. As one so aptly remarked, "It's like jumping into a different world—things are so different last year and this year." The quality of this different world is elusive, hard to pin down. But Fourteen's use of the words "clique," "circle," "fitting into a group," wanting to "get in," even though she has to "push" her way in, "feeling like a parasite"—all these expressions and many more tell of a new social order, of the magic strands that hold a group together. The group, which may be as small as two or as big as seven, may prove to be an exclusive one, even though Fourteen wishes to show an acceptance of people as people.

Fourteen comes to realize that her selection of friends is far less determined by activity interests than it was earlier. In fact, she is at times shocked that she may have very little in common with a best friend except that she just feels "sort of pally." Reasons for choosing friends are so different from earlier. Fourteen likes a friend because she's so "full of life," "free and aboveboard," or "ladylike and yet a tomboy." Fourteen is apt to have "more friends and not just special ones," "a whole bunch of best friends."

A group of girls have much to talk about: "We talk about clothes, boys, teachers, what we think about dancing class or lessons, just a combination of everything." Discussions of the personalities of their various friends are beginning. (These will become a more precise art in another year.) Discussions also may touch on social problems, but these again will come to fuller flower in another year. Fourteen is ready to accept a certain amount of trouble within a group because she says "it's bound to be," but she is ready to do more than this. There are times when she knows she has to talk things out with a friend "in order to get along" and to restore a certain amount of understanding between them.

Those Fourteens who are on the outside of groups are rather sorry sights. They try to "get in" by joining up with all sorts of activities. But all too often they "meet the people and that's all there is to it." They walk down the corridors with another girl, hoping something might happen. At times this social predicament is recognized by a more popular (and a sympathetic) 14-year-old, and the unpopular girl may be included as an underdog. Then the latter may hold on tenaciously to her new-found place, even though she feels like a parasite. This kind act of inclusion may lead to considerable difficulty and often disturbs the unity of the group.

Fortunate are those outsiders who recognize that they are "not yet ready to enter into things enough to have wishes of their own" and who just stay on the outside. But they are accepting their place of growth, and happily play with younger children. Others continue to hold to just one friend and continue to enjoy half-humorous wrestling, calling each other "dear" with a certain amount of sarcasm.

Boys, as always, are more apt to "gang up" and to have plenty of friends without necessarily having a close circle of friends. They, like the girls, maneuver socially and know that they choose friends just because they happen to like them rather than because of shared activities. They are not too aware of how they select their friends—"can't say how I pick them"—but they know which ones they want to be with. They feel a nice satisfaction in their friends and often continue with neighborhood friends, whereas girls are more often interested in new-found school friends. They are freer in their feeling toward their friends and show a lot of good-natured, back-and-forth kidding. Situations that would have been too much for them at a younger age, such as being pushed down in the snow, no longer upset them, and they may report, "I think I can handle that now."

Boys have a really good time together. They enjoy each other's sense of humor. There is often a comedian among them whose every word is considered funny both by his friends and himself, even though an adult may fail to see the humor. The forthright laughter from a group of boys is the evidence of good fun that is often the by-product of a stag party. Even poker games may be part of the group's activities, with relatively high stakes involved. It is like expanding, exuberant, exaggerating Fourteen to choose high stakes of a thousand points to one cent. As the game gets under way, there is much ado and you would think that Fourteen was dealing in millions of dollars instead of just cents.

As do the girls, some 14-year-old boys sense the difficulties another boy may be having and are willing to protect him. A boy who is being black-balled by the others may be unobtrusively chosen as the tent mate of a boy who wishes to protect him on a scouting trip. And boys can help the "lame duck" with more sureness and trustworthiness, than girls can. They stay with their problem and are more apt to see it through. Some Fourteens are still lone wolves, but even they are expanding a little more and may stop by at a friend's house on their way home from school—a thing that would hardly have entered their minds a year ago.

The expanding and social interests of Fourteen include a *real* drive toward the opposite sex, boys being as interested in girls (though in a milder way) as girls are in boys. There are still the casual meetings on the bus, in the halls at school, at the drugstore, but these are often take-offs for further activity together. Most boys now consider girls "more fun than a nuisance." They report that very few of their friends aren't interested in girls. But they don't date very much and if they do they quite often date younger girls. They date mostly for parties or they may go to a party without having a date because "everybody goes all together." Suspecting they might be turned down by girls of their own age, they may protect themselves by asking cautiously such a question as, "If I asked you to go to the dance with me, would you go?"

Girls are now beginning to accept the subordinate role. They are more apt to wait to be asked to a party, if they do not go with the group. Girls are fairly sure which boy they want to go with and will blithely say to others that they are busy even when this is not the case.

Arranged parties are more fun than they used to be. The boys don't stand on the side lines so much. They mix better and they carry on more of a conversation, even though the girl may have to talk about sports. Girls prefer parties with older boys because they know that if the boys of their own age get the chance they will

begin horsing around and throwing food. And if they are allowed to choose a boy to dance with, they may find the boy they choose will run in the other direction. These actions bewilder 14-year-old girls because they wonder why such a boy came to the dance in the first place. Though he may say he came for the food, he really wants to be on the edge of the group, looking on but not really participating fully.

The kind of parties 14-year-old girls especially enjoy are the spontaneous ones, the ones that just come into being with very little planning. These occur more often in the summertime and with older boys. Knowing the penchant for boys to crash parties at this age, Fourteen doesn't let the idea of a party start to gather before about four o'clock in the afternoon. Certain individuals may be alerted and told to drop by casually later in the evening. These can be the most successful parties, especially when a room in the house is available, parents are on hand for the first half hour to make the group feel at home, and then withdraw to another part of the house as the party itself takes over and expresses its own development. Planning for games is generally needed. There might be piano playing, singing, dancing, or just talking. Parents notice the difference in these parties over the ones in previous years. There is an ease of mixing of boys and girls. There is almost no trekking to the bathroom. Girls are less interested in primping. Occasionally a couple might be lost temporarily out on the terrace or out for a walk. Then there might be a scurry, a shouting or tooting of horns, but the couple is soon found and brought back into the group. But couples are not a stable commodity at or before parties. The interplay and exchanging of dates is so rapid that Fourteen wouldn't think of inviting a couple as a couple. For, as one 14-year-old girl remarked, "How can you invite a couple to a dance because how do you know they'll still be a couple when you have the dance?" Eating is incidental and just a part of the sociability, except with the party-crashing boys who might wish to raid the iceboxes. Firm parental control and understanding can readily bring these infractors into line.

Individual dating is not as common with the boys as it is with girls. Boys may be in a good mood and take a girl out but it doesn't go much further. Girls know that boys date among a number of girls and vice versa. Each has an idea what kind of a person he or she would like to date. First and foremost the date should have a good sense of humor, and then such other qualities as intellect and ability to talk are helpful. Girls especially like boys who know their way around, and who might be "a little forward," and they prefer a boy to be liked by other boys. Both sexes dislike the conceited date or the wind-bag. Girls are beginning to recognize that looks don't matter. In fact, they are a little wary of the boy with too good looks. Likewise the girl who might be initially thought to be the most popular because of her looks and easy ways can turn out to be the least popular. Reputations and rumors get around. Fourteen is warned to "just stay away from so-and-so" or "he's a wolf—not worth being troubled with." Though Fourteen takes due warning, his (or more often her) kind heart wants to do something about it

—"somebody ought to tell him." And by slow degrees the right person is found to do the telling, and the maligned, sometimes unknowing 14-year-old may be able to accept the revelation with 14-year-old gratitude.

Activities in dating vary from the more usual parties at home to a movie, a sports event, picnics, or skating parties. Fourteens like to go on double dates as well as in larger groups, but there are also the two-somes especially of 14-year-old girls with older boys. Fourteen usually does not wish to go steady because "it ties you down and you don't have a chance to meet others and compare." If they do go steady, it usually doesn't last more than two to six weeks with an outside limit to four months. Some girls give their dates rough treatment, especially when the boys try to kiss them; or they just "drop them," "break it off," or "throw them over." Reasons for these shifts might not be too clear but things can shift rapidly when the heart is involved. However, the latter is usually not involved enough to get broken. Rather Fourteen is more often relieved to be rid of a too demanding relationship.

6. Activities and Interests

The life of a 14-year-old is all of a piece—an exciting, full, active, and happy existence. What Fourteens do specifically is less important than how they relate their activities to the whole of their lives. They have a capacity to think in terms of the whole year, relating their interests to the seasons. Thus, when asked about their interests in sports, they will often separate them into summer and winter types. The season that suits Fourteen best is usually the summertime. He often doesn't want to go to camp, because he isn't really interested in the life of a camper. He may prefer the casual, active, and social heterosexual life of the summertime.

It is school that usurps Fourteen's time in the winter. There is little time left, since he is at school for most of the day, has club activities after school, and homework at night. But he accepts all this as part of his life, and he fits in other activities around these more basic functions.

There is a considerable contrast in the interests in sports of boys and girls. Basketball is the favored sport in boys, but baseball and football are not far behind. The increasing muscular ability in boys needs to be put to the test. This is an age when the athlete begins to stand out more sharply and may be favored by his peers because of his prowess. But even when a boy knows he is "not top athletic material," or is "too light," he still often wants to be on a team of some kind. Intramural sports provide the kind of competition Fourteen enjoys.

Girls do not have the drive toward sports that boys have. What they do with sports is in large part determined by what the school provides and the kind of group spirit that surrounds a sport. Volleyball and field hockey are the more favored group sports. Tennis and Ping-pong are favored individually and there may be a return to an interest in bicycling.

Indoor activities have shifted considerably from the intense hobby interests of Thirteen to the looser social interests of Fourteen. A few of the boys continue their interests in radio—

working toward an operator's license or building models of various sorts. Likewise a few of the girls continue with their earlier interest in sewing, possibly designing and making their own clothes. Some of both sexes enjoy drawing.

But the greatest amount of time is spent in social gatherings, either of separate sexes or in mixed company. Group card games are on the rise with the semblance of an adult pattern. The structure of a gathering is loose, flowing, and shifting, with the power of restabilizing itself. When both sexes are present everything becomes a little more precarious. The social structure gets a little looser, more flowing, and shifts more rapidly. It is not uncommon for a boy to shift his attentions from one girl to another in the course of the evening. Because of this fluid structure, certain rules need to be laid down, preferably by the members of the group. And no control is more effective and welcome than nearby parents who can rapidly discern when the situation is getting a little out of control.

Verbal communication of some form seems essential to girls at most any age. Fourteen expresses this need in her talk fests, telephoning, and writing letters. Sometimes the telephoning demands are so great that an additional extension seems essential. This is, however, a family problem and needs to be solved as such. Rules for use of the phone should be laid down, though with a certain amount of flexibility. Fourteen should be expected to conform. It is to be hoped that Fourteen won't ask extremes of his parents, to the point that they will have to insert blotting paper in the mechanism to deaden the ringing of the bell after ten o'clock at night.

Boys distinguish themselves in their interest in cars. Many are beginning to drive under supervision. They want to "fool around" with cars. More opportunity should be provided for them, with strict rules about supervision. The problem of licensing will come up in a few years and a good preparation will not only make them more ready, but will also satisfy this terrible urge within them to be behind the wheel.

SEDENTARY LOOKING AND LISTENING ACTIVITIES

Television and radio are not a problem with Fourteen. Some watch or listen only occasionally or not at all, either because they have so much else to do, or because they don't enjoy the programs. The demand to have the radio on as they study has been fairly well relinquished in many, who report that they don't listen to the radio until their homework is finished. Radio in general is favored over television.

The programs Fourteens select vary considerably, reflecting their personal tastes. With boys the sports programs are chosen, whereas girls are more apt to choose the theater performances. Jazz is of interest to both sexes, and the disc jockeys know full well that their listening audience includes a good number of 14-year-olds.

Interest in records, strong at thirteen, is increasing at fourteen. Jazz and classical music vie with each other in popularity. Dance rhythms are of prime interest. Fourteen enjoys having his own records but he feels the expense of such a hobby. (And from now on there is one demand after another for money.)

The amount of reading Fourteen accomplishes is largely determined by his own individuality. Some do not have time for more than their school assignments. Others read a good deal and their interests are varied, especially since they are entering the adult sphere. They may track down a number of books by the same author. Or they will read or avoid reading on certain subjects—"anything in ancient history," or "nothing in politics." Their reading may be influenced by their moods, and the books themselves may create a mood in them. Trashy magazines make them feel bad. Other things make them feel gloomy, but much of their reading makes them feel good.

Newspaper reading is spotty with most Fourteens, though a few read the paper thoroughly. "Funnies" and the news are read most. Human interest stories, certain columns, and the society page are coming into Fourteen's orbit of interest. Sports for boys, and movie and television news have their continuing place. Magazine reading is steadily increasing. Fourteen likes to be informed of any special articles that might be of interest to him.

Movie going shows a variety of patterns. Most attend once a week, though a number go less often. They seem to know which movies they want to see, though a number just go for sociability. Usually they go with the same-sex friends though girls are no longer resistant to going with their parents as they were just earlier. There is some dating and double dating in relation to the movies.

Fourteen likes a happy ending. He often identifies his mood with the mood of the picture. He may feel good, sad, patriotic, or fearful—whatever the picture inspires. Girls especially may show an intense interest in certain movie actors, treasure any pictures they can find, and clip out any information about their favorites from newspapers or magazines.

7. School Life

Fourteen is ready for a change, in school as in other things—a sizable change that will satisfy his expansiveness. His decrease in suspicious belligerence especially readies him for new territory. He is quieter within himself, even though, compared with Thirteen, he is both less inwardized, and more noisy with the group. His greater inner quietness is linked with a paradoxical development—an increase in interest in himself, yet a decrease in "self-consciousness." His contemplation of his own personality is becoming less uneasy, dissatisfied, and defensive, more calm and judicious.

Fourteen often seems to bloom forth with new qualities that can make him a definite asset to any school setup he is a part of. He intermingles well, is more respectful, he has ideals. This is Fourteen at his best. However, he can also be disappointing to a teacher, for he may spread himself too thin, emphasize the froth of life, and fail to spend time and energy on his school work.

But school work, for Fourteen, is only a part of his full school life—sometimes seemingly a rather minor part, at that. He can be so busy with friends, before, between, and after classes (and sometimes during them too), that school work appears embedded in a much larger sphere of sociality. School provides at least the take-off point for much of Fourteen's social activity. He even makes plans to meet friends on the way to school. Fourteens who come to school on a school bus, however, still show a tendency to separate along same-sex lines.

Styles of dress vary with the season, the region, the latest fad—but, within the limits of "what is currently being worn," both boys and girls usually manage to show good taste and control in their dressing. They are less completely swayed by fads, and less dependent on the "protective coloration" aspects of group uniformity. So, though they stay in style, they do not swing too violently to the extremes. And they always seem to gravitate back to the old stand-bys—skirts or jumpers, and sweaters or blouses for the girls; plain shirts, sweaters and slacks, blue jeans, or khakis for the boys.

Few girls overdress or accentuate their sex through their dressing, as they might have done earlier. They usually carry pocketbooks, but do not use their primping equipment as much as formerly. They are using lipstick better than they did. Boys are wearing sport shirts less often, though ties are still only for special occasions. And they are now better about shining their shoes.

Sometimes Fourteens have a longing to return to their old careless ways of dressing—girls in blue jeans, boys with their shirttails out. It might be wise to allow a day to develop as a tradition when all of this pent-up desire could be expended legitimately.

Fourteen really enjoys such an opportunity and gives himself fully to the occasion.

Though Fourteen is expanding and ready for many new experiences, he is happy in the security of his own home room. If he is fortunate in his assignment to a room, he may be able to bring his individual problems to his home room teacher, whether they are as minor as lipstick or as major as a concern over his religious faith. Here too he may be able to form his group identity (unless the school is so factory-like, the classes so jumbled, that common ties do not exist). He likes this group to be close-knit, likes to identify the group with a name. Whatever any member of the group does may reflect on the whole group, for good or for bad. He likes to sit together as a group in the assembly; if someone separates, the group feels it and thinks he must be ashamed of them.

The home room is also an excellent place to exercise student organization and to plan for certain activities, both social and business. Fourteen loves to elect officers, though he still needs a certain amount of adult supervision. The athlete is most often chosen. At times other qualifications are needed for the job. It is here that a teacher can help by presenting the issues more clearly, to allow a better decision.

Fourteen often gets on better with his teachers than he did. He recognizes that they are more fun and he knows that he is nicer to them and vice versa. His criticisms of them are more valid, more closely related to fact, than they were. If a teacher is unsympathetic, indifferent, clear thinking, or full of originality, he says so.

A teacher of Fourteens needs to be especially aware of the group structure. Fourteen wants variety, but variety such as an announcement on the intramural radio acts as a disturbing interruption. The teacher must bring the group back where they started from to keep the thread of their attention. The buildup of atmosphere is essential to a better learning process. But there are times when the atmosphere is so fragile that it will suddenly break to bits. It is the skillful teacher who knows what to do in these moments, whether it means showing a film strip, going to a map, or some other quick shift to bring the group back together again.

In periods between classes or in time off for socialization, Fourteens waste no time in getting together to talk. Girls often act as though they are suddenly released, like a Jack-in-the-box. They scoot over to a friend to chitchat. They may have interesting information to report (someone smiled at someone in the hall). They look at the pictures in each other's billfolds. Boys are more apt to act like big dogs, cuffing each other. A soft start rapidly gathers momentum until plain loudness is produced. One teacher remarked that noise was so much a part of them at this age that they don't actually hear it. If they are asked, "Since when does the English language become more intelligible when it is spoken loudly?" they will still try to convince the teacher that loudness doesn't interfere with their hearing.

The immature student stands out in a group of Fourteens. He is the one who pushes, throws, talks too much. His laughter is the loudest and his jokes are made to draw attention to himself. He plays hooky. He is an-

tagonistic. He does not get on well
with the other members of the group.
He might trip or pinch others, or
hide another's book. It is this kind of
child who especially needs a careful
individuality study to determine what
he can do, where he can fit, and if
he needs some specific kind of help.

Boys and girls approach athletics in
different ways. Boys are more interested in testing themselves out. They
want to find out whether they like the
physical contact of football or not.
Many find individual sports, such as
bowling or tennis, more to their liking.

Girls, on the other hand, are more
influenced by the goal of artificial
awards. They often build up an elaborate point system. They are more
likely to show a lackadaisical interest
in softball. But they can be very interested in volleyball. They become
quite upset as a group if one of their
rank fails to get a certain award, such
as an anticipated letter. The individual
herself may or may not be so concerned. Fourteen doesn't mind failure
as much as she did.

The taking of showers after exercise is now accepted with less difficulty. A few parents still fear that
colds will be contracted. Also a few
of the more physically immature boys
complain. It is important to consider
whether these boys are not overplaced
in their gym group, whether they
wouldn't be better with a younger
group. It is also important to find out
which boys (if any) are causing the
trouble by making fun of these less
developed ones.

Boy-girl relationships come and go.
Some boys are still so self-conscious
about girls that they refuse to sit next
to them in assembly. Others seek girls

out in the halls, in assembly, in club
activities. Girls are more eager to
have boy friends than vice versa. As
one girl said, "You have no idea how
secure you feel when you have a boy
friend." The relationship between the
sexes at this age, as at any age, would
improve if the boys were a year older
than the girls. It is the boys' immaturities that so often make it necessary
for the girls to look toward the older
boys. About half the girls and a third
of the boys are now dating, but
"going steady" can usually be calculated within the span of a few
weeks. There is a definite attraction
toward each other, which can easily
be expressed through activities in
mixed groups: sitting together at
lunch, serving on committees, planning for dances. All of these are wel-
comed by Fourteen, for they provide
situations with some structure, in
which he knows how he is expected
to act and through which he can
communicate more easily with the
opposite sex.

Significantly, it is no longer possible
within the compass of our presentation to give an overview of curriculum
—for it has suddenly burgeoned out
with new variety and intricacy. We can
only mention a few suggestive items.
The more gifted students are usually
good in mathematics (algebra), creative English, and Latin. Though a
14-year-old may be warned against
taking Latin, he often wants to try
his wings. He sometimes seems to
want to prove himself, in much the
same way as he wants to test himself
in sports. Fourteen is a man of action;
he learns through trial and error.
When it is practical he should be
allowed a trial run, even though it

may end in failure. So long as such a failure is not viewed as a disgrace, it can produce far healthier growth in the 14-year-old who is not ready just to accept what others advise. Learning through error has its important place.

The whole field of social studies—politics, current events, reading the newspaper—may hold less interest for Fourteen. But he often likes to exercise his self-expression in public speaking, giving reports, participating in dramatics. And growing in his interest is the study of man—his biology, physiology, psychology. He is eager and ready to know more about himself.

Homework is accepted as a part of Fourteen's life, even though he may complain that it is piled on. He often needs less help with his homework than earlier and recognizes that he might know his lessons less well if he is helped.

Membership in after-school clubs is of real interest to Fourteen. Each student should be able to find his niche. There are the athletic clubs, the scientific ones, the dramatic ones, the music ones. There is a place for the non-athletic, less social boys in photography. There is the bowling club for the only moderately athletically inclined. A roller skating club can perform a real service for it is often sought by the ones who do not have a place socially but who can come to belong to a group through shared activity. Each school will have its own variety of clubs. It is probably fortunate when these clubs take the place of sororities and fraternities. All too often Fourteen gets caught in the web of a bygone era and finds it difficult to free himself from the intrigue and exclusions of such societies. Even some participating members state frankly that they wish they could do away with these groups.

Fourteen's life is indeed an active, full one. The more active it is, the better he likes it. The school needs to be ready to supply an active program and to help him fit into it. Fourteen may not realize it, but he often needs more help than he thinks he does. There are even times when it is essential to bring the parent into the school picture to unsnarl a point of difficulty. Fortunately, Fourteen will usually accept his parents' authority when he feels that home and school are working together for his better welfare.

Seeing Fourteen, with all his qualities of expansiveness, readiness for change, capacity for leadership, and receptiveness for knowing and doing more about himself, we would like to raise a question: Where does Fourteen fit best in the school system?

In a junior high school situation, with Twelves, Thirteens, and Fourteens grouped together, he comes to the top—not only because his grade puts him there, but also because he is capable of accepting the demands of such a position. Fourteen at the top of the heap comes into his own—both in self-development and in leadership. In contrast, in the first year of a four-year high school Fourteen can be submerged—lost in the obscurity of beginnings or scattered by the multiple attractions and distractions which abound. Many administrators, recognizing this, are strong in their advocacy of junior highs. Other educators feel that Fourteen is better off in a ninth-grade addition to an eight-grade school unit, for here too he can blossom in his own right. At any rate, there is considerable agreement that Fourteen would profit by some other status than being in high school. But in addition to the two possibilities already mentioned, there exists a third alternative, less often considered.

Since Fourteen is so total in himself, so ready for a change, might he not be placed in a unit of his own— a truly self-sustaining unit, just for 14-year-olds? (We refer, of course, to those who are fourteen by the developmental clock.) One town we know of * has tried this with most striking success. Their unit came into being because of practical necessity, but it was soon recognized as a stroke of luck and now would not be relinquished by students, parents, or educators, though space is ready and waiting in the new, nearby high school.

Why not include Twelve and Thirteen in this unit with Fourteen, as in the traditional junior high? Twelve speaks out clearly for himself—he is not ready. He gets all mixed up moving constantly from one class to the next, always racing with time. It is no wonder he runs in the corridors and chases his friends more than he would in a less complex setting. He still needs the closer supervision of one teacher instructing him in a number of different subjects. He needs the chance to move back into younger realms, as well as to push forward. Eleven-year-olds are good companions, and they in turn improve under the good influence of Twelve. And as for Thirteen, he can fit in with Fourteen but he's only on the brink of

* Clayton, Missouri.

giving up childish things and is better suited by a tempo geared to the 11- and 12-year-olds. He concentrates well but he isn't ready to be rushed. His belligerence increases as too much is demanded of him. He shows himself at his best when at the top of the heap.

The advantages of a self-contained unit for Fourteen seem multiple. No older, "wiser" students are on hand to be copied or to usurp all the power, position, and glory. Among others as wise or as foolish as they, Fourteens are not overshadowed; they find it easier to feel part of the group. Their time is more their own; more of it can be set aside for group and social activities. Girls enjoy the boys of their own age more when there are no upperclassmen to pull them out of their group and disperse their energies —at least during school hours. This containment of age and place is a restraint which can be accepted by Fourteen. It gives him a better chance to develop his own and the group's inner resources.

Other advantages come to the fore. Many boys are still hovering on the brink of decision as to whether they want to go into athletics or not. With competition not so stiff they can find out better what they are suited for. They become ready for, and definitely enjoy, intramural athletics toward the end of the year.

For those Fourteens for whom a full academic program is too demanding and too unsatisfying, a half-time work or apprenticeship arrangement could be instituted. Offered this kind of combination, many a student who might otherwise have planned to leave school as soon as possible could profitably continue. This is one way in which such a program appears to hold out real promise as a force against delinquency.

In turn it suggests one of the most important potential values of the separate unit: here is surely an ideal time and place for taking stock of the development of each individual. The educative process can be too concerned with teaching, and not enough concerned with considering "for what?" After all, it is the individual who is being taught; he is the "for what." It is therefore paramount that we know about him as a person—about his potentialities and deficiencies, about his individuality. At no other age in the ten-to-sixteen-years cycle is he more eager to know himself. At no other age is he more ready to set to work and do something about what he learns of himself.

Here is a place for serious study and appraisal of each student, a way station for overhauling and tuning up. Fourteen, already striving toward self-understanding and self-acceptance, would be an enthusiastic ally in a campaign which could not only contribute to present school success and personal happiness, but could do much to stem the tide of maladjustment and delinquency.

The idea of a separate school for Fourteen is still virtually untested. Where it has been tried it has worked most satisfactorily, and it certainly seems in theory to solve many problems posed by Fourteen's transitional status. It is no universal solution, and many telling criticisms may be leveled against it. But we believe that if Fourteen might be allowed to experience such a contained unit and then could speak for himself, the odds would not only be for his thriving under the experience but also for his convincing those in authority that it was a year never to be forgotten.

8. Ethical Sense

Fourteen is in a way less aware than earlier of his own ethical behavior because it is more a part of him. He has lost the intensity, the scrupulousness, the sense of feeling "terrible" that he experienced at thirteen. Just as his clothes sit well on him, so do his ethics.

He is now gathering his own concept of "morals." He recognizes the multiple influences that produce his own ethical code. As one girl explained, "You aren't exactly taught morals. But they are partly what you're taught, your own ideas, what you learn from experience, from reading, and what other people do." The diversified and easy movement of a 14-year-old makes it possible for him to mesh these various influences into his own sense of moral values.

And his moral interests go beyond himself, for he is now thinking of larger issues and of the relationship of one group to another. He is becoming aware of such issues as the treatment of minority groups, discrimination, and exclusion. He is basically in a very tolerant mood. He has both respect for and interest in other people. This change is evident in his attitude toward a cleaning woman. At thirteen he might have left things on the floor in his room and would have rationalized his behavior with a perfectly valid statement, "She's paid to pick things up." But at fourteen the crisp intellectual reasoning is softened by a new emotional inclusion. He is now more apt to be sensitive to her feelings. Fourteen's care of his room, oddly enough, improves when there is a servant in the house.

Fourteen is ready and eager to share experiences with those who are different from him in race or social class. This leads to a tendency to be over-enthusiastic and to go out of bounds, though he is gaining better perspective. Fourteen is one who can look at these problems with at least an open mind.

Fourteen doesn't have too much difficulty in deciding what is right and what is wrong. Though he usually knows what is best to do, he quickly adds, "but that doesn't mean I always do the right thing." He makes his decision from multiple influences. Some Fourteens "just seem to know," "have a clear notion," "go by common sense," or "just feel" what is right. Others are more influenced by impacts from their environment, the opinion of their family, other people or friends, or religious teaching. Still others are more calculating in their decisions. They weigh problems in their minds as to advantages and disadvantages, or who would be benefited or harmed. Some feel the tug and pull of two different forces; what would work out with their peers in the one direction and with their mother in the other direction. Their mother's opinion is important to them even if only to avoid trouble, but they might "temper it down a bit."

Fourteen's conscience doesn't always figure too strongly in his decisions. It is there to direct him if he needs it about big things, but it doesn't stay to plague him. For fourteen doesn't see much point in worrying about what he has already done. He is more interested in trying to fix it. This nonchalance of Fourteen makes him an easier person to live with, but also may get him into trouble in realms he is not yet capable of grappling with.

Just as Fourteen's conscience doesn't bother him too much, telling the truth doesn't bother him either. He might "stretch" the truth now and then and might question whether or not *anyone* is "strictly truthful." But he doesn't tell an out-and-out falsehood or just the opposite of the exact truth. If things are important, he will tell the truth. He is ready to stand up for something that he thinks is important whether it is for his own good or someone else's.

Where Thirteen preferred to avoid argument, Fourteen enjoys it and treats it almost as a game. He has had enough practice to know which way the argument usually ends or with whom arguing is most fun. Fathers usually win, either through the advantage of their years ("I start to drop my reasoning when I argue with daddy"), or their ability to terminate a dispute ("No argument!"). But mothers seem to be good bait for both sons and daughters and may well come out the losers. Such arguing is in good fun and sharpens Fourteen's wits. "On the whole," Fourteen will listen to reason about important things.

Smoking and drinking are now coming within the realm of Fourteen's own experience, for if he doesn't indulge some of his friends may. His attitude about these matters is quite casual and matter-of-fact. He is rarely disturbed by adults' drinking as long as it is "in proportion" and he is aware of the imminence of his own drinking experience. He is concerned about his friends being able to "hold" their liquor, but he doesn't condemn them for drinking. Likewise smoking is in the realm of a beginning experience. Many Fourteens, both boys and girls, confess that they have tried a cigarette or two. They know they do it because their friends do and they want to feel one of the group, or they wish to show off. Neither drinking nor smoking has usually come into the problem realm at fourteen, but there are indications as to which way the wind is blowing.

Fourteen is less concerned about swearing than formerly and he is less apt to swear than he was. At thirteen he swore both to release his own inner tensions and to feel a part of the gang. But now he hasn't the same needs. He doesn't have the same bottled-up tensions he had at thirteen and he has other and better ways to feel a part of his group. But he sort of takes it for granted that "everybody swears," "everybody does, except perhaps ministers."

Cheating is not usually a problem behavior at fourteen. He himself knows that he's apt to cheat or check with others only on subjects he is less adept in. And as he thinks over those who cheat, he may recognize the common denominator of low grades. If there is a great amount of cheating in a school, the teachers and teaching methods should be considered. There are some teachers for whom a student would never cheat. Fairness of a teacher is very vital to Fourteen, but also the fairness of students toward the teacher.

Fourteen is not moved to steal, though he may reminisce about the time he did steal, a few years earlier. He thinks about those who still do steal. Often he recognizes that these children are not poor and do not need to steal. And so in his accepting way he might give some such reason as, "I think she just can't help it."

9. Philosophic Outlook

TIME AND SPACE

Fourteen expresses his global, inclusive thinking even in his concept of time. He expands in his thoughts to include the world: "The world is run by time." He may expand further to include the sun, for time marked on clocks is reckoned by "how long it takes for the earth to go around the sun." Fourteen thinks of time in action, "the means by which we live," or "things grow, things die, anything can happen." Time is the "passing of minutes, days, and years," and "something goes on during all this time."

Even the more spatial interpretations of time may emphasize length or space: "length of a period in which events take place," or "space in which things happen." Fourteen is recognizing the inevitable relationship between time and space.

Control of time differs greatly at fourteen. There are those who handle time so well that they can even plan to arrive early for an appointment. But more commonly they arrive just in the "nick of time" or are characteristically late and seem to be in a constant state of rushing. If Fourteen had his way, he would both arrive late and leave early. Part of his dilemma is that he has overfilled his time, he has two engagements at once, he doesn't yet know how to synchronize time and space. And the hard part of it is that while some of his days are filled with an awful rush, on other days he seems to have "nothing to do."

Fourteen is oriented mostly to the near future, and he is enjoying the present. He does, however, "look forward to big things in the future."

Space is all-inclusive to Fourteen. It is "everything around us" and yet it is contained in "area": "space is area in which events take place." However, the nothingness of space still intrigues Fourteen as it did at thirteen. He even goes a step further and translates this nothingness (or everything) into "eternity" or "death."

Fourteen is exuberant about travel and often says he "loves to travel." But at the same time he'd "just as soon stay at home." He will become more of a traveler within the next year, more capable of sustained activity, more eager to leave home. Home is still a good and enjoyable place at fourteen.

If Fourteen does go to strange places, he adjusts better as long as he is outside. He is still apt, as he was at thirteen, to get lost inside big buildings. Girls especially have a very poor sense of spatial relationships.

DEATH AND DEITY

Fourteen is less concerned about death, and more concerned about life. He wants to live as long as he can; he wants "to live a whole life." He feels that "anyone with a good life ahead should not die before he reaches old age."

He seldom worries about death. He accepts it as "something that is coming." He even recognizes death as "a good thing." It may be "comforting to die" when one has been in an accident or when one is old. Animals are often "better off dead," especially when they have been injured. Fourteen seems able to face death without fear.

His thoughts of after death may include only the reality of being placed in a coffin and buried. This he knows. This he may have observed. But what happens after that he is not sure about. Fourteen is not a skeptic. He is just frankly unknowing. He thinks about the possibilities of what he has been taught, about heaven and hell, about how your life on earth might influence your life after death. He recognizes that various things might happen. He can imagine them. But in the last analysis, though he will concede "it might be true," he must conclude that he really doesn't know.

Very few Fourteens do not have some concept of God. They do not think of Him as a person, nor very often as a spirit. Some as at thirteen conceive of God as a "power over us" or as a "huge plant, factory-like, producing thoughts." Others conceive of Him as an "idea in people's minds." Still others are more vague and general in their concepts. They speak of, "Something that just is"; "Just Something there, you can't define it." They realize the inadequacy of the human mind and that it "cannot even get close to an explanation."

The boys especially are aware of unexplained scientific mysteries which lead them to "realize that there is something" beyond or at the head of it all. Quite apart from reason, Fourteen feels that it's a "good idea for people to have something they can have faith in," or that "everybody has to have something—a belief in something."

Though Fourteen is more often than not a believer, he doesn't feel much influence of his beliefs on his own behavior. He is not moved to pray each night as he did when he was younger. But he does think of Deity: "Something you could go to for help," or, "An outlet—a rather remarkable personal thing."

Fourteen is often an interested churchgoer and may attend two or more services on Sunday, or possibly may go to two different churches. He may continue in the regular Sunday school or may join a youth group if one of these is available. He attends the church service because he is interested and he enjoys the sermons, but finds pleasure in the sociality, too.

Fourteen is especially ready for the evening youth group activities. He is as interested in the social as in the religious side. He throws himself into the activity whether it's a basketball game, a discussion, or a dance. The facilities and opportunities differ greatly from church to church, but this is indeed an age when the church would find a strong response and should be eager to provide the necessary outlets.

CHAPTER NINE

Year Fifteen

MATURITY PROFILE

THE MATURITY traits of Fifteen are not readily summed up in a simple formula, or even in a series of adjectives. He has so many facets and phases that he himself at times seems muddled. His teacher and even his mother may respectfully regard him as somewhat enigmatic. Yet we also know that he keenly wishes to understand himself and to be understood by others. He says this in his own words and in the implication of his demeanors and his behavior.

The shift from the maturity traits of Fourteen to those of Fifteen is relatively gradual, but it yields a few striking contrasts. We pictured Fourteen at his typical best as a youth coming into his own—happy and self-reliant, exuberant and energetic, and fairly firm in emotional fiber, ready to meet the demands made upon him. Now one might logically suppose that these excellent and promising qualities would be enhanced and enlarged in the course of the following year. But it does not happen so, because development has a different logic. Fifteen frequently is "indifferent" and speaks with a soft voice, instead of exuberating with a loud voice. His outgoing energies are so frugal that he sometimes is considered to be lazy, or at least tired. He has a lessened interest in food, including sweets. He also gives an impression of apathy. This impression, however, may well be erroneous, for the apparent apathy is closely related to a quiet musing preoccupation with inner states of feeling. He gives focalized attention to these subtle states, which contrast with the more robust emotions of Fourteen. Some of the most significant maturity traits of Fifteen are concerned with an almost effortful refinement of the patterns of feeling.

This growing appreciation of the finer shades and shapes of feeling expresses itself in new sensitivities, irritabilities, resistances, aversions, and suspicions which crop up in the behavior of Fifteen. Feelings, whether negative or positive, do not come fully formed. They are fashioned through growth and experience. The new feeling awarenesses of Fifteen extend into intellectual, philosophical, and aesthetic realms. This is the thoughtful, quiet, serious side of Fifteen as compared with the enthusiasms of Fourteen. The logic of development makes consistent room for both trends of development.

The distinctive maturity traits of Fifteen revealed themselves rather naturally in the annual interview and examination. The demeanor of Fourteen, it will be recalled, in the same situation was typically unconstrained and cordially co-operative; he was openly frank and communicative. At fifteen one of our boys who had been a model of co-operation through all the years, including fourteen, was heard to say, "Oh, I'm not going to let them know too much." A number of boys and girls of fifteen proved to be monosyllabic and cold with a trace of hostility at the start of the interview, but most of these became friendly when the examiner did not press too eagerly the structure of the interview. Some, however, remained withdrawn and answered with vague, unrevealing replies. With others the situation became a conversational discussion period in which the subject asked the examiner's advice or opinion and thanked her on leaving.

Some of the subjects exhibited a rather new maturity trait. They made a noticeable effort to find just the right words and phrases to express their thoughts and ideas correctly, to give exactly the true impression of what they meant to say. A scrupulous respect for the spoken word, of course, has ethical implications, and ethics have a developmental background. This capacity to give focalized attention to details of thought and feeling is highly characteristic of the psychology of Fifteen.

The analytic preoccupation with minutiae and detail contrasts with the more global, over-all approach of Fourteen, and also with the greater integration of Sixteen. Fifteen tends to be more piecemeal and fragmentary in his immediate outlook. In his subjective musings he becomes a stickler for precision, and he seems at times to be a perfectionist. Whatever the individual differences in motivation, these various forms of self-examination are maturity traits. They denote a further organizing stage in the growth process. They are in the nature of growth mechanisms, even when they operate in the obscure and elusive realm of feeling.

The quieter moods of Fifteen therefore are part of the economy of personality development. His moods are not as intense and piercing as those at the thirteen-year level; they have a milder, modulating character. One of our fifteen-year subjects called them "little moods," and seemed to regard them as a legitimate and agreeable experience. They are essential to the refinement and directives of self-criticism. They may be a normal prerequisite to the higher order of self-control characteristic of Sixteen.

In passing we may note that the subjective mechanisms just outlined can operate in the direction of evil and of abnormality. A 15-year-old youth can nurture feelings of grudge, revenge, and violence. In this way various forms of conduct disorder and delinquency are patterned by insidious growth processes. Fifteen, for many reasons, is a vulnerable maturity zone. That is the darker side of the story.

The maturity traits of the fifteen-year age period can be envisaged under three headings, of which we have already dicussed the first: (1) Increasing self-awareness and perceptiveness. (2) A rising spirit of independence. (3) Loyalty but adjustment to groups of home, school, and community.

The refinement of self-awareness is fundamental, because it has far-reaching implications for his ethical sense and social perceptiveness. It influences his educability and it infuses his rising spirit of independence. It pervades the whole complex web of his interpersonal relations with groups and individuals.

A rapid review of these interpersonal relations will indicate how closely intermeshed are the threefold facets of self-awareness, independent responsibilities, and group loyalties. His developmental task is to reconcile them.

At fourteen a youth has begun to think genially of the household as an institution which has claims on his service and co-operation. But at the age of fifteen conditions tend to deteriorate. Some Fifteens without the formality of handing in a resignation virtually secede from the circle. They omit or skimp their greetings when they come home, they keep to themselves; they resist restraints and restrictions, however reasonable. Others engage their parents in a cold war of varying intensity. Still others vent their belligerence by dashing out of the door and getting away from it all, through an unannounced trip, perhaps to the neighboring drugstore.

The door slams on closing, to emphasize a defiant or a happy emancipation from home ties.

The spirit of independence is rising, but it is immature and expresses itself in crude forms, naïve and otherwise. Fifteen himself may smile at his outbursts of self-assertion as he grows older and recalls them in retrospect; but at the time of their occurrence he does not regard them as immature. His declarations show that he feels very serious about these matters, and the parents may think that he is drifting away from the family. The more extreme forms of defiance call for skillful guidance and strict measures of control.

Whether severe or mild, the manifestations of an independent spirit can be understood only in terms of individual development. The 15-year-old definitely feels that he is growing up. He does not wish to be considered a child any longer, and he hopes that his mother doesn't think that he is only a kid. He wants to cut loose and get away, especially tonight and tomorrow night. He does a lot of traveling in his fancies, when he withdraws remotely to his room. In imagination he attends a school in a distant town. Some girls have an overweening desire to go off to school. One girl in our 15-year-old group earnestly stated that she would like to be a rich woman and give scholarships so that all 15-year-old girls might go to school away from home!

When the independent spirit is at its height Fifteen would like to transcend the limitations of time and space; but usually he remains at home and attends a nearby school. He is obliged to conform to certain schedules determined by law and custom. However, he craves to have some free, loose, unbudgeted time at his disposal. This is a normal and even welcome symptom if it helps him to build up his self-reliance and self-assumed responsibility. In this broad sense the whole philosophy of independence hangs on a philosophy of individual development.

But the psychological development of the individual is profoundly affected by the pressures of groups. Fifteen, in his adolescent way, shows keen awareness of this fact—in his loyalties and adjustments to the groups of home, school, and community. He is gregarious. He likes gatherings. He tends to follow a crowd and enjoys spontaneous, informal groupings which include both sexes. He responds to the impact of a group of his peers seated about a table for panel discussion. Here he is challenged to pit his independent-mindedness against group pressures, a wholesome developmental experience.

Possessed of such strong social propensities, why does he choose to be a contending isolationist at home? He can scarcely tell us when he is in the very throes of a growth dilemma. He has been loyal to the family group for a long time. But now he has a new bias toward maturity; he wishes to "outgrow" undue dependence upon parental control. This presents a complex problem of feeling, which involves a conflict of attachment and detachment. He wrestles with the problem; he comes to two conclusions—he does not want to accompany the family when they attend the next public function at school and if he does accompany them he does not want to sit with them. Family unity seems to be at an all-time low!

We do not describe this situation to ridicule it. It has real poignancy for the 15-year-old at a certain brief stage of his emotional development. It is a transparent example of countless situations initiated by his instinctive feelings. His self-awareness is constantly changing; his spirit of independence is rising; rival groups are pressing him with rival claims. In the situation just related, he is protecting his status and public prestige with his compeers of similar age.

He is not trying to disown his family. His basic loyalty to the family group need not suffer because he now gives an increasing amount of attention to a few chosen friends. He tends to be more observant of personality characteristics, both within and without the family circle. The cultivation of a deepening friendship with another boy may be one of his important interpersonal achievements. At the same time his relations to siblings is greatly improved. He takes satisfaction in the admiration of the younger ones; he is more companionable with those near his own age, and he may idolize an older brother. He notes more analytically and seriously the personality traits of his parents. He feels a gnawing anguish when his mother and father do not get along with each other. His own ideas of marriage and career indicate that he is maturing rather than abandoning ideals of the family as an institution.

The pressures of school life bring into further relief the maturity traits of Fifteen. They also reveal the limitations and potentials of good and bad schools in relation to these traits. One youngster tried to sum it up in these words, "I like being away from home—but schools of course are just schools!" The pupil attitudes at the fifteen-year level are as various as the schools and as the pupils themselves. There are two extremes: school is wonderful—"we love it"; or school is impossible—"everything is wrong."

Between these two extremes are many patterns of resistance and acceptance and a host of variable background factors. Teachers have noted repeatedly what is generally called "the 15-year-old slump." This seems to be a kind of symptom complex—a limited period of discouragement based on confused self-criticism. Fifteen has a way of striving to clarify his thoughts and to define his feelings all at once. He finds this task too hard and he sinks by stages into a slump. The slump tends to be temporary. Discerning teachers recognize the symptoms and meet the challenge. Unresolved slumps, however, may lead to "drop-outs" which begin to increase at this particular age period.

On the other hand, many Fifteens gravitate toward a positive orientation. They enjoy the group life and the co-operative activities which the school affords. The school life becomes an outlet for the urge to loosen subservience to the home. Some pupils develop intense loyalties to the school and to individual teachers. Individual differences, academic and personal-social, declare themselves, giving scope to leadership, talents, and intellectual abilities. New interests and latent giftedness are revealed in reactions to special courses and extracurriculum projects.

There remains, however, a sizable group of "slow learners" with non-academic predilections. They are vocationally minded, and have a vague sense of wanting to do something practical and worthwhile. They do not reject school, but they are groping for a self-respect which they feel they lack.

Such feelings comport with the general psychology of the 15-year-old. He is serious-minded; he is essentially neither anti-school nor anti-home. In fact, in a sketchy preliminary way, he has begun to think about an eventual home of his own, a career, and the attributes of a husband and wife. This is not inconsistent with a tendency to detach himself somewhat from his present home. He is ready to learn more about the privileges and responsibilities of citizenship.

These pre-adult trends suggest that the school should be oriented not only to the individual developmental needs of the 15-year-old, but also to the community and the culture which lie in his path and in his prospect. This implies closer back-and-forth contacts between school, youth, and community. An educationally oriented community would enable the school to provide its youth with participating and apprenticeship experiences, never more needed than in our fast-changing civilization. The maturity traits of Fifteen call for this type of modern education.

The developmental task of Fifteen also demands a large measure of *self-education*. His former exuberance has given way to a more critical self-awareness and a growing sense of self-dependence. At the same time he realizes his increasing dependence on other selves. This creates a complex system of competing forces and a triangle of tensions. The educational problem for Fifteen is to resolve the consequent difficulties as well as he can on his own resources—with help!

His maturity traits and behavior characteristics take on added meaning when viewed in the light of education. For example, his recurrent tendency to mull springs from a desire to understand more precisely his own feelings or those of another person. He may withdraw from a room not to remove his presence, but to turn something over in his mind. In a dark mood he may shuffle off with his mind set; but more often his moods, as already suggested, are lighter and briefer. They function as substitutes for more direct experience. They enable him to mold his feelings, converting them into perceptions and judgments. Sometimes he dashes off because of sheer restlessness: he is readily bored by the too familiar and is keen for new experience.

He does not indulge in heavy moods. He prefers to cogitate. Sometimes he will abruptly terminate his thoughts with a Eureka snap of his fingers and a triumphant, "I've got it." He rather enjoys his ruminations. He can conduct them in a social gathering, suddenly bursting out with a quip or a bit of ironic comment. He is capable of scorn, coupled with exaggerated language. TV programs? "Most of the programs are lousy." Comics? "I just hate the thought of reading comics." Collecting match covers? "Juvenile!" But he can also entertain and express admiration for the ideas and the heroes of literature and of life.

His self-awareness and quest for independence are counterpoised by an increasing ability to identify with persons and situations. He may use dramatic mimicry to project and to vivify his impressions of teachers and other personalities with whom he is acquainted. He can make penetrating remarks indicating his impressions. His humor is dry and favors wit. Observations of the passing show and self-examination go hand in hand.

He is sensitive to his own limitations and prone to become confused about his potentials and responsibilities. With reduced self-assurance he craves guidance and interpretive counseling, particularly the counsel which does not emanate from the home circle. He is so interested in his own personality that he inclines to become a psychologist of sorts on his own. Perhaps he is at an age when he needs more objective knowledge of human behavior and human nature. By virtue of the wide ramifications of his self-awareness he is a most educable subject.

All things considered, Fifteen is a rather complex youth. He is surely more complex than happy, outgoing, enthusiastic Fourteen and he has not yet attained the smoother integrations of Sixteen. But he is in the process of organizing them and in the very process he discloses the multiplicity of his maturing traits and the resulting tensions of his inner life. In delineating his profile, we do not envisage him as an enlarged, super-version of Fourteen, but rather as Sixteen in the making. And when we take a closer look at the maturity profile of Sixteen, we shall doubtless find numerous patterns of behavior which only recently were at loose ends. Many reciprocal growth strands are being interwoven during the transitional Year Fifteen. So it comes to pass that Sixteen brings new culminations.

MATURITY TRAITS

1. Total Action System

We wonder sometimes, does age fifteen just happen to fit our idea of the sophomoric state, or is it rather that the state (derived from the Greek words "wise" and "foolish") was tailored to fit age Fifteen. Conversation and argument, the epitome of expression of Fifteen, give the dialectical exercise that this sophomore needs.

But one does not jump into one's full conversational powers in a short space of time, nor does every occasion permit immediate full functioning. Inner forces must be mobilized and the proper setting provided for Fifteen's unique potential in the art of disputation to be realized. To see Fifteen enter a room dragging his feet, indifferent in mood, remote in expression, one might never dream that such powers were hidden within him. And when Fifteen adds an antagonistic and disdainful note to his general indifference, one might just wish not to have much to do with him.

Fifteen needs time. He needs to be greeted with as much coolness and indifference as he lavishes on others. This can shock him into self-awareness. His politeness can then appear, and can be accepted with politeness.

Fifteen's quiet demeanor as he sits in a chair, being interviewed or examined, suggests that inner forces are taking over, that he is thinking or organizing within himself. Even his asymmetric posture, the one-sidedness to his action, suggests that he is defining a direction to his behavior.

Sometimes Fifteen seems unable to move from his detached state. It is as though he has nothing to communicate. He can answer only in monosyllables. His voice is so low that you can hardly hear him, and neither a faint smile nor an expression of sadness plays across his face. Nothing can be gained when Fifteen (more often a boy) is in this mood. But this same 15-year-old who seems so uncommunicative may come to life when he is working with his hands over a radio set or exercising his muscles on a football field.

As a rule, however, Fifteen warms up when given time. His behavior is especially revealing in the standard, more or less neutral interview situation. Fleeting emotions play over his face. One minute he is humorous, the next sarcastic or skeptical. His face assumes amusing and amused grimaces. He can be ironic about his own achievements ("That's great!") or can smile to himself as things begin to click into place ("Wait a sec!"). Sometimes his expression becomes sad; for a moment he might even appear to be on the verge of tears. His mouth is very mobile. He might draw in his lips, pout them out, raise or lower a corner. Similarly his eyebrows raise and lower, singly or both together.

His answers to questions come slowly, because he wants to phrase his reply just right. He may show his inner movement by his outward expressions. First he pauses, then laughs a little, gasps, starts to answer, stops, laughs again, and finally gives an answer quite different from the one he started out to give. He may show his tension by scratching his head or digging at his face.

But not all Fifteens warm up so slowly or have such difficulty in gathering their thoughts. Girls especially can carry on a friendly conversation with an adult, a conversation that flows back and forth. They like to discuss their personal problems, to receive advice. Boys more often bypass their more personal problems to discuss larger subjects. Several boys in our group were interested in the work of the Institute, in the developmental examination. They wanted to know what the tests proved and how these tests revealed their own personalities.

Both boys and girls are interested in their own personalities and are interested to receive information and insights. They are genuinely responsive in this type of discussion and often thank the interviewer when they say goodbye. It is when the interviewer seems to be prying too directly into Fifteen's private affairs that he withdraws and detaches himself.

HEALTH

Although many Fifteens enjoy good to very good health, the kinds of illnesses that often occur suggest the potential turmoil and depth of Fifteen's inner disquietude. Nosebleeds may occur, or there may be the first appearance of mononeucleosis, a disease of the bloodstream more common in later adolescence. Fifteen's acne may worsen to the point that it needs medical attention. Headaches may occur, sometimes apparently related to constipation.

There are not only these signals of more specific physical changes, there are also some evidences of psychic changes of severe character. This is the age when "black-outs" under the pressure of exams may be reported. An occasional Fifteen reports that he feels as if he were going all to pieces or that he "might just fade away." At such times he may stare into space and appear to lose contact with reality. Though perfectly "normal" 15-year-old behavior can be quite extreme, as other sections of this book emphasize, when symptoms become alarming—to parents or to Fifteen himself—it is time to seek psychiatric help.

TENSIONAL OUTLETS

Tension is high at fifteen and is expressed in a multitude of little ways.

Fifteen's hands may just wander over his face or twist his hair, but more often they exert pressure. He digs at his scalp, scratches pimples on his face, picks at his cuticle. He snaps his fingers. If he wears a ring, he twists it. Or he fools with a knife, sharpening it, whittling or carving, and inadvertently gouging the furniture or slashing his sheets. (His bed is a favored site for constructing things, and it suffers accordingly.) His hands seems to be eternally busy, always playing with something. It is especially irritating to parents when Fifteen fiddles with the candles or cutlery at the dinner table or plays with the sugar bowl or salt shaker. Some mothers keep a supply of nuts to shell on hand to keep Fifteen busy. These mothers are willing to clean up the mess of nutshells if this activity can take the place of other tensional expressions such as smoking.

Fifteen appears to have a low threshold for all sorts of stimuli. He is especially sensitive to noises and may have to shut himself in his room to study. The taking of Vitamin B in some form sometimes seems to raise the threshold of response to these various stimuli. Fifteen then becomes less nervous, less sensitive.

VISION

Fifteen tends to be quite well organized visually and his visual skills are usually good. Most Fifteens retain the same amount of hyperopia (farsightedness) they had at fourteen, and their power of focus remains as good at near tasks or even becomes better. There is a consistency in Fifteen's responses suggestive of the adult. In the reading situation, whereas at fourteen roughly half the group focused their eyes on a point in space closer to them than the printed page, and half focused beyond it, by fifteen the majority are focusing at a point somewhat closer to them. This is a further indication of their tendency to draw toward themselves or to inwardize.

Visual fatigue is one of the more common symptoms at this age, though this is not necessarily the result of marked distortions in vision. However, there do occur such distortions as poor oculomotor control, suppression of vision in one eye, or poor fusion of the images of the two eyes.

Fifteen tends to be very quiet during a visual examination. He volunteers little information and reports little even in response to direct questions about his visual activities. In some Fifteens the amount of reading has decreased even further since fourteen, and continues to be confined to magazines. But there can be a sharp increase in reading around fifteen and a half, when a new intellectual penetration is reached by some.

Even if Fifteen's visual examination should suggest enough distortion to call for visual help, this may not be the time to give it. Fifteen is often at too great odds with the adult, and his resentment of the demands may defeat any program he feels he could do without. Fifteen will consent to wear glasses if this is necessary, though he feels they are a bother, and may assert that he doesn't really need them.

PHYSICAL DEVELOPMENT AND SEX AWARENESS—GIRLS

Fifteen brings no new or dramatic changes to the physique of most girls, for most of the physical maturity characteristics have already appeared. It seems instead to bring a finishing off of growth features begun earlier. A more womanly form develops, with still further rounding of contours, a development almost of lushness in many girls' figures.

The menstrual cycle has settled down, usually to a span of twenty-eight to thirty or thirty-two days. The length of the period usually ranges between five and seven days. There may be a general lessening of the pre-menstrual tension, but there may also be an increase in premenstrual head-aches and skin eruptions, especially on the face. Fifteen tends to use fewer sanitary napkins.

PHYSICAL DEVELOPMENT AND SEX AWARENESS—BOYS

By fifteen the average boy has achieved about 95 per cent of his adult height. His body size is now so large that his face appears smaller in proportion to his total physique, though his facial features have ac-tually enlarged and strengthened sub-stantially.

His genitalia have reached virtually mature adult size. He has nearly full growth of hair on his forearms, and may have sprouted a few hairs on the chest area. Fifteen's facial hair is coarser, developing on the sides of the chin and in front of the ears and gradually merging to the adult form of beard distribution.

Boys are moving toward more es-tablished patterns of sexual activity, and their arousal is becoming some-what more channelized. They are somewhat less susceptible to stray, non-specific stimuli. Whereas earlier an erection might have been caused by non-erotic excitement—fear or anger—or by their own casual move-ments as they sat wiggling their legs,

such stimuli are less often sufficient. However, more directed activities such as dancing are beginning to bring sexual responsiveness.

Mothers less often report finding lurid sex novels lying around or hid-den under a pillow—but whether this reflects lessened interest or increased caution is uncertain. It may be, though, that unaided imagination is becoming a more sufficient stimulus, for daydreaming seems to be a much more potent source of arousal than at fourteen.

Masturbation apparently tends to increase somewhat in frequency at age fifteen. Fewer boys these days are so shattered by conflict over the alleged harmful effects of this prac-tice, but many are decidedly uneasy nonetheless. A few Fifteens are able to discuss the topic with their fathers in a thoughtful way, and these boys can be much relieved by his reassur-ance and by his suggestion that keep-ing active may not reduce the impulse for masturbation but may help reduce their concern over it and increase their control.

2. Self-Care and Routines

EATING

Though Fifteen has a good appetite, he has shifted markedly in his inter-est in food. He says himself, "Food just doesn't seem as interesting," and he reminisces about the time when his "favorite used to be eating." He can remember when food was terribly im-portant to him and how much he thought about food, especially when he was twelve or thirteen. Now occa-sionally reduction in appetite actually produces a loss in weight. He might even begrudge the time given over to eating. This shift is certainly not true of all Fifteens. There are those, boys especially, who still have very robust appetites at mealtimes, and between meals, though otherwise they give little time or thought to eating.

There is especially a shift in Fifteen's interest and consumption of sweets. Desserts may be omitted. "Sweet stuff" in general is not favored. Fifteen may remark that he hasn't touched a sundae for the past year; that he got "fed up on them even though they were scrumptious."

Fifteen is quite definite about what he likes and what he doesn't like to eat. He is fairly matter-of-fact in his reporting. Sometimes it is the fat on the meat or the slimy quality of the asparagus that repels him. Asparagus and fish are probably the most universally disliked foods. But he also recognizes that certain foods which he may like may not be good for him. The state of his acne may act as a barometer to disclose how much chocolate he has eaten. He recognizes the relationship and can control his intake. Likewise he is capable of dieting both in relation to quantity of intake or the specific foods he should or should not eat. He may wish to lose or to gain weight to be eligible for a certain sport.

The surest evidence of Fifteen's decreased interest in eating is that snacking is somewhat less intensive than it was. He recalls the time a few years back when he "used to be a real bug on bedtime snacks, but not any more." It might be that snacking keeps him awake, but he mainly doesn't snack much because he isn't hungry. Cooking is also far less interesting to Fifteen than it once was. He will cook if he has to or if he is hungry, but not from preference.

SLEEP

Bedtime. Fifteen is much more flexible in his sleeping patterns than he has been before. He can vary his bedtime according to his needs. Though he most frequently goes to bed around 10 to 10:30 P.M. he can go as early as 8:30 when he has an early morning appointment or a paper route. Or he can stay up until 1 to 2 A.M. for a dance without showing too great fatigue.

He is also now more conscious of his own needs for sleep. He knows when he is tired, when his "mind is slowing down." His planning to go to bed voluntarily at a certain time is not always carried out. He may still need reminders and can "putter around doing nothing" for quite a time. But he does know that he will become irritable if he doesn't have enough sleep. And, fortunately, with his more flexible sleep patterns he can make up sleep with a nap or extra sleep over the weekend.

Fifteen usually falls asleep without too much difficulty. He may think about many things until his "thoughts become vaguer and vaguer" and he drifts off. He may reminisce about how different his bedtime thoughts are from the time at eleven or twelve when he had wild adventures such as escaping from enemies.

Sleep. Fifteen is a good sleeper. If he is awakened for any reason, he can usually go right back to sleep. Dreams are an individual matter, but on the whole he dreams less now and often can't remember his dreams. Mostly his dreams come as he is waking up and almost "seem like subconscious thoughts more than deep dreaming in the night." Some dreams reveal a frozen state of inability to reach out, or to walk—a helpless feeling. At times Fifteen is self-conscious about telling his dreams because he fears they might be too revealing. One 15-year-old girl who dreamed she couldn't reach out and grasp her mother's garnets was heard to say, "Well, a psychologist could certainly make hay of that!"

Waking. Waking up and getting up don't pose too difficult a problem for most Fifteens. If allowed to sleep themselves out many would not awaken until 9 or 10 A.M. But if Fifteen has to get up, though he feels a little foggy, he manages. Often he sets his alarm clock to awaken himself, though a few need a more personal prodding. A fairly large number awaken spontaneously at the same time each morning, such as 7 A.M., even though they may have gone to bed quite late. But if they don't have to get up, they may happily go back to sleep again.

BATH

The shift into fairly dependable cleanliness at fourteen is showing further movement at fifteen. There are many responsible girls who take over all aspects of their cleanliness and upkeep of their physical person without reminding. These girls may bathe every day, but some still bathe only every second or third day. They use deodorants as needed. They shampoo and set their hair once a week. They care for their fingernails.

It is more often the boys who need to be reminded about cleanliness and who are apt to play a delaying game— "Well, I shampooed it last time," or,

"I had a shower at school today." But, on the whole, they are responsive to reminding and less resistant and resentful than they used to be. Fingernail care may be the "last gasp," but they do manage to use clippers and to show some awareness of keeping their fingernails clean.

A new note struck in bathing is that Fifteen can bathe in the middle of the day as needed, even as he can nap in the middle of the day. In such flexibility Fifteen shows that he has come a long way from the time when he was ten and had literally to be driven to the bathtub.

CLOTHES AND CARE OF ROOM

There is less talk and concern about clothes in general at fifteen. The spread and passion for clothes characteristic of Fourteen has come into better perspective. There is less demand for many clothes. Fifteen knows what he wants in style and color. That he likes what he purchases is paramount for Fifteen. He may ask for the opinions of others, especially of his mother, but in the end he both buys and wears what he desires.

Fifteen is not only aware of how his clothes look on the outside, but he is also aware of how they make him feel on the inside. As one 15-year-old girl remarked, "I can't have a good time if anything is wrong or I don't feel just right." There is often an expressed love for certain garments. "He loves his overcoat this year. You'd think he'd never had one." Or maybe it's a love for a special green wool shirt. If anything, the choice is away from the more flashy colors, often more toward green and yellow. One of the arguments boys may have with their mothers is about the more cheerful colors. Fifteens may show a tendency to shy away from gaudiness.

However, some 15-year-old boys can be very faddish about their clothes. They follow the group blindly, first wearing their collar up, then turning their pant legs up, or wearing their belt buckle in the back. These shifts in style may be made every week or two. Occasionally Fifteen may get an idea that he wants something completely out of the usual such as some odd-colored shirt or modified cowboy boots. At this point the parents may have to step in not only to prevent a too foolish spending of money, but also to help Fifteen view his choice more clearly.

Even the poorer shoppers are now more patient about trying on clothes. Parents accompany Fifteen only for big purchases. For the most part it is Fifteen who decides on purchases and his mother who agrees. A shopping tour is now more often accomplished with little dissension and confusion. Tastes of parent and Fifteen seem to be in good agreement. Fifteen is still influenced by what the others wear. But girls are also getting some of their ideas from magazines.

Fifteen makes smaller purchases by himself. Girls who may have worn stockings on occasion at fourteen are wearing them more consistently at fifteen. Choice of underclothes is especially important to girls, and what they wear on gym days.

The care of clothes is steadily improving. There are of course the persistently careless boys. Girls not only take good general care of their clothes, but may also accept the responsibility of washing out their underwear and socks or stockings and pressing their clothes. The cleaner's bills are not as big as they were at fourteen.

Care of room along with care of clothes is steadily improving. Clothes are less often slung around the room. There is a great improvement with some, but there are still the stragglers who persist in keeping a very messy room. Fifteen tends to be in between in the care of his room: it's "not a mess but not too picked up."

MONEY

The great variety of allowance patterns at fifteen is related to the variety in individuals' demands and to the variations in their sense of money. The weekly allowance of $2 to $3 is quite satisfactory for a number. Fifteen does his part by keeping careful track of what he has spent. A monthly allowance, ranging anywhere from $10 to $25, is becoming a bit more popular, but a few Fifteens would prefer no allowance at all, because it is so difficult to calculate ahead of time how much they will need.

There are those who bank fairly large sums, usually from what they have earned, but there are still those who are careless and who don't know the value of money. However, an improvement usually appears if Fifteen has begun to earn his own money. Recognizing money as representing a particular amount of his own time and work can do much to cure even a spendthrift.

On the whole, Fifteen is pretty conscientious about money. He is even inclined to be a little Scotch and is very protective of his funds. He is acquiring a good sense of values.

WORK

Fifteen still helps in the home, but he

is not the helper he has been for the past two years. He often doesn't have time and he also doesn't have the inclination. He may be dependent upon an industrious or inspirational mood. Work may interfere with his relationship with his mother. As one girl puts it, "Mother and I get on all right if there's no work to be done."

He works best away from home and can now find a number of jobs that will suit him. Boys work as handymen or caddies, set up pins in a bowling alley, or work in a store. They can surmount the displeasures of a job because it pays well. Painting may be one of their new abilities.

3. Emotions

The play of the emotions in some ways is like the weather, with its fluctuations of sunny days and gloomy days. There are seasons in the emotions too. Fifteen is a more quiet, thoughtful, somber season. It is again a time of controlled emotions. Fifteen speaks of his disposition as though it were an entity with different sides to it and something to which he is definitely related.

Often he not only feels as though he were under some somber, gray influence, but acts that way too. He may be gloomy, or moody, with a touch of cynicism thrown in. His mood may be so lingering that he's "in a slump." This minor mood, this trend to secretiveness, is like an intrusion upon the carefree exuberance of Fourteen. But Fourteen needed to be pulled in, to be calmed down, to view life in a longer perspective and one closer to reality. The outgoing forces of growth needed to be meshed with the ingoing forces. And the conver-

sion of a boisterous, noisy 14-year-old who throws his voice around into a quiet, soft spoken 15-year-old, whose hands wander over his face until you can hardly hear what he is saying, gives evidence of further changes occurring within.

Fifteen's moody, downhill moments do not always stay with him long. He speaks of his "little moods," "just slight depressions," his unhappiness that is with him only "some of the time." His withdrawing trend may be expressed in physical withdrawal, similar to his retreat to his room when he was thirteen. But it is without Thirteen's adamant intensity; Fifteen doesn't need to lock his door. He is often quietly busy and happy in his aloneness. He doesn't even have to go off to his room to be alone, for he can withdraw into himself in the midst of living room sociability as though he (or it) were not there. If he is asked to participate then, he may "clam up" or "freeze up," unable to say a word. He is said to be "unapproachable when his wall is up."

Fifteen may have times of feeling terribly tired, almost dead, times of general discouragement and feeling all mixed up. It is no wonder that he appears apathetic and indifferent at times. He recognizes his own lack of incentive. To protect himself he may give the general impression of being hard-boiled, may "try to enamel it over" so as not to show his feelings.

Sometimes Fifteen can pull himself out of these states by suddenly becoming annoyed or acting very gruff. Or if he feels it is necessary to make a good impression he will do so by sheer will power and control, even though it "kills" him. And always it is easier to accomplish this shift, this release of a mood, when he is away from home than when he is at home.

It is the quiet thoughtfulness of Fifteen that can at times be so disarming. If so minded, he states his facts so unobtrusively, with his "I believe so and so . . ." He is apt to act with quietness even when he is surely, relentlessly selling you something. A good companion to his quietness is his playful turn of mind and his enjoyment of ready wit.

Life is in some ways better for Fifteen, though he feels the added complexity and responsibility which comes with age. At least things are going pretty well and he is "quite happy." There are a number of happenings—being in a school play, making a little money, going on a successful boat trip —that may produce *real* happiness in him, but his is a quieter kind of happiness.

He doesn't get mad as often as he used to and is not so quick to fly off the handle. He is more apt to withdraw, walk away, or to ignore the source of his anger. Sometimes he just stays where he is and thinks things to himself without saying a word until his mad feelings have left him. Some Fifteens, however, are more apt to retaliate, especially against their mother, with a caustic or sarcastic remark. Anger toward a teacher might produce a set expression or a cold look, but Fifteen is aware it might not change the teacher's attitude.

Since Fifteen is more apt to cry in private, others may not know of this expression of his emotional state. He (or more likely she) is most apt to cry when he is unhappy and generally discouraged and may find that crying is a "sort of an outlet" or "a means to relax." Fifteen is also moved to tears

by what happens to other people as depicted in stories and movies.

Fifteen is not a fearful age, though quite a few still report fears of bugs, spiders, and snakes. He is apt to reminisce about the fears he used to have—fears of crashing into a tree, being mashed in football, and the like. He has his fearful moments, and may be more leery of high places, more uneasy when in a crowd, but he is not in the grip of fear.

Nor is he likely to worry as much as he did. He is apt to take life as it comes without worrying. He may worry about his school work, but, as he says himself, "If I worried more I would do better." The worry before a dance may be dispelled by the taking of a bath. Worries don't usually last longer than his anger or his moods and are usually under his control if he will make the effort to dispel them.

Though Fifteen may have certain specific desires (such as getting a driver's license, having enough money, or an improvement in his mother's health), he doesn't treat these as problems. School is probably his most persistent problem. But he's less apt to think of things as problems and is more aware that many situations are up to him to solve. Nor does he think much about luck except in cards. He has come to realize that "what happens is the way I do things," or "things depend on you more." With his increased awareness that so much that happens to him is up to him, he appears to be less sensitive, less susceptible to hurt feelings. He's apt to ignore a remark or criticism of a friend, though its impact often affects him "deep down."

Though Fifteen may be secretive and withdrawn, he is not always interested in covering up his feelings. He reports that he usually tries to conceal them but there are times when he even wants people to know how he feels. He is quite capable of communicating his state of mind. His set, cold expression, his apathy, his shuffling gait, his quietness, can all express more clearly how he feels inside than any verbal statement.

Fifteen is not one to be jealous or envious of others in a negative way. He may prefer others' physical attributes, their freedom, or their material possessions to his own, but he doesn't waste his nervous energy wishing for what he hasn't got. His envy is more apt to turn to admiration, and he is able to choose what is in his reach, what he would be able to emulate. One girl's ability to talk to boys is the envy of other girls, for instance.

Nor is Fifteen's competitiveness any stronger than his envy. He likes to be recognized, to come out ahead, but he's "not hot on the trail of competition." He doesn't really try very hard, sometimes doesn't even wish to bother.

A realm where Fifteen is perhaps at his best is in his sense of humor. He is more discriminating and may have discarded such forms as punning or the slipping-on-a-banana-peel types of humor. He now has a dryer sense of humor, full of witticisms not only funny to his contemporaries but also to adults. At times he utilizes irony or sarcasm with almost too deft a stroke. But the tendency to play practical jokes is at a minimum and indulged in only by the more immature 15-year-old boys, who now have more prolific ideas and carry them out with more ingenuity than they could at thirteen years of age.

4. The Growing Self

The endless search for and realization of one's self goes on from age to age. At some ages, as at fourteen, boys and girls are more ready to take life as they find it, more or less to accept themselves as they are. But Fifteen is more serious. He is coming to realize that what he is is more up to him. That may be why it all seems so hard and why he at times faces life with such indifference and even apathy.

There is no one more eager to find out about himself, to find clues to why he feels the way he does, why he acts the way he does, than Fifteen. But all too often he holds people off and will not tell them anything, fearing they will pry into his personality. Communication with others, the very thing he desires most, is all too often taken away from him by himself. And underneath his outward defenses he is all too often found to be muddled and confused.

Fortunate is the 15-year-old who can utilize his "refining" tendencies to become more subtle, more discriminating, more controlled, and above all more tolerant. Though Fifteen primarily looks out for himself, he has the capacity to project consciously out beyond himself, to be more aware, thoughtful, and considerate of others.

Independence and liberty are his constant cry. You would think he had never had either. He doesn't like to be restrained, to have questions asked about his whereabouts, his plans, the friends he is going to meet. He is expert at stalling in his answers to questions and ends up by telling you nothing or very close to it. He does not wish his inner privacy to be invaded.

He tends to maintain an apartness

either by going off to his room or by withdrawing into himself. He can be sitting in a room full of people without giving any evidence that he knows they exist. This is most apparent when he is with his own family group.

Those who have become more aware of themselves at this age are fearful that others might misjudge them. They don't want to do anything that might produce such a misconception. One 15-year-old boy went so far as to be afraid to drink milk for fear someone might consider him childish. But Fifteen may be his own worst enemy and give a false impression about himself. Girls who have a stiff, aloof carriage may give the misleading appearance of being snobbish.

Fifteen tends to settle into his age. Asked what age he thinks is best, he recognizes that you can have as much fun anytime and that "each age is what you make it." There are still a few who are looking back upon earlier, more carefree days. And there are those who are still looking ahead to the late teens and early twenties when cars and greater independence seem more alluring than living at their present age. But the better adjusted Fifteen is having fun now and doesn't wish to move on faster than time itself will dictate.

When Fifteen dwells on his assets he is more apt to think of his positive personality traits than of his social abilities. He speaks of his unaffectedness, his good nature, his tact, his determination. Likewise he thinks of his faults as expressions of a lack of certain desirable personality traits. He knows that he loses his temper, is impatient, insufficiently tolerant of others, or unaware of other people's ideas. And he may be quite aware of

the criticisms that others level against him—his lack of ambition, his laziness, his "don't give a damn" attitude.

Fifteen is gathering rather definite ideas about his self and how it relates to his own uniqueness. His self may thus be the way he thinks, or his speech and what he says. Or it may be his emotions, especially when he gets angry, or his eyes because they are a good means of communication.

One of Fifteen's most persistent wishes is to be able to get along with others, to like people without prejudice, to understand them, to be nice to them. He'd even like to study in a foreign land just to learn more about people, to learn the *real* story about them. And it is rather surprising to see how much thought Fifteen gives to his parents, even though he may not get on too well with them. He wishes especially for his mother to be in good health. He also wishes for his parents that they will get on well together and that they will be well cared for in the future.

Security is important to Fifteen. He wishes for it not only for himself but for his parents and for the world at large. He is concerned about world peace and is hopeful that the trouble in the world can come to some agreement. He is now relating himself to the time when he may have to serve his country in some capacity in case of war.

Though some Fifteens are still apt to wish for material possessions (a TV set, an electric guitar, a car, etc.) and for some changes in their physical person (big and tall, brains), many are aware of their shift away from these earlier desires. When they were younger it was easier for them to wish for a bicycle or wealth. But now they often realize that possessions and money aren't as important as they once thought they were. They are now thinking of what they can do themselves. They contemplate getting a scholarship or working their way through school to complete their college education. They are thinking in terms of accomplishment and may set their sights rather high, wishing to be first-rate in a chosen profession—not so much in a desire to be famous as to feel successful in themselves.

Fifteen wants to improve his attack on how he does things. He wants to improve his ability to study, "to think clearly and see things straight, in perspective," and to concentrate on something without being "taken away with things." He wants both to remain in control and to stay within bounds. Maybe it is because he wishes to improve so much that he falters and slides back in his discouragement and inadequate accomplishments.

Fifteen may not know what he wants to do as a future career but he is giving it thought. He was carefree about it at fourteen, but now the problem troubles him somewhat. He has a pretty good idea of what he doesn't want to be. Both the medical and law professions are losing a number who had once thought they would like to pursue these time-honored professions. It is the business world that is now attracting many of the boys. They are beginning to recognize the imminence of their future responsibility and are judging their potentials in a more practical way. Girls also are viewing their lives in a truer light and many are now planning to work only until marriage.

Some Fifteens don't want to be overly specific in their possible choices of future activities. They are thinking more of the general field they may go into—"something in the field of art," "something in music," "some sort of journalistic work," or "in dramatic work." Fifteen is thinking of work more realistically, and might reject certain professions, such as medicine because "you have to get up in the middle of the night." Going into architecture appears to be a major professional desire of both boys and girls, with psychology on the rise. No job, however, is beneath Fifteen.

Most Fifteens within our group are thinking about college. They are quite well informed about the different possibilities but they are in no hurry to decide until the time comes. If they don't get into a college of their first choice, they are already thinking of alternatives more in the vocational realm. Many are drawn to the smaller colleges. And whether the college is coeducational or not doesn't seem of too great importance. They would prefer that it not be too close to home.

Fifteen has thought more about marriage than he did at fourteen but he sees marriage in the larger perspective of time—"It will take its course," "marry in time," "not planning, but if I fall in love." A number of both sexes don't want to marry too young because there are so many things they want to do.

Whereas the 15-year-old girls are all contemplating marriage, there are a number of boys who don't look forward to it. They don't like the idea of being tied down. They don't like to have their interests interrupted. One father felt his son might consent to marry if a girl came "radio-equipped." Some Fifteens have looked into marriage and have discovered that a lot of people aren't happy in marriage.

But nothing would stop the girls in their quest. They are thinking a great deal about marriage in its wider implications. They are becoming ready to take on homemaking as a profession, though some would still like to combine work and marriage. However, they feel that circumstances will determine what would be best for them to do. Fifteen-year-old girls are more often thinking of love as a basis for marriage. Looks aren't too important, though they would not wish their husband to be "obnoxious" or "gruesome" looking. A lot of things, such as finances, looks, and race, don't matter too much about their future spouse, but the quality of his disposition does matter. Fifteen wants to have a husband you can have a good time with and who preferably has a good sense of humor. They are looking for such qualities as maturity or being sensible, considerate, and sympathetic. They would wish to be able to talk problems over with their husbands and would hope that he could agree with them more or less.

The boys on the other hand aren't as demanding of their mate. They are still thinking of looks—she should be at least "half-decent looking, but no beauty necessarily." They also desire a certain amount of intelligence. A few are aware that they would wish for a wife with character. But most of all 15-year-old boys are thinking of the housekeeping qualities of their future wives. They would like a certain amount of neatness and organization, and they hope that she can cook.

Fifteen is thinking primarily of his spouse in marriage. He would wish to have a delay after marriage before the children come. The number of chil-

dren desired hovers around three. Even the size of his family seems to be clipped down to a smaller size than earlier.

5. Interpersonal Relationships

Although Fifteen is much of the time a fairly happy person and gets on reasonably well with his parents, he sometimes shows all of the signs of waging a cold war with them. Sometimes his indifference, his apathy might be mistaken for a more positive antipathy. But his own words give an idea of why he doesn't get on better. His attitude is plainly voiced in, "They have the wrong idea," or, "They don't really have the upper hand."

There is often a considerable discrepancy between the report by Fifteen and by his parents, with either one or the other usually painting a prettier picture than exists in the other's mind. And often there is that flat summing up of a not too pleasant relationship—"I guess we get on O.K.," said by Fifteen, or, "I suppose we get on," spoken by his mother. Each feels the helplessness of failure and yet each hopes that things will be better.

The buoyant exuberance and boundless energy of the preceding year seems to have left Fifteen. The boys no longer manhandle their mothers. The yelling and shouting has collapsed into soft speech and resentment of noise. An earlier drive and motivation seems to have left many Fifteens.

They seem if anything to mobilize their energies best away from home, especially in new situations. School may not motivate them much better than home, especially when school exerts as strong or even stronger demands than home.

Some Fifteens obviously withdraw in the household. They go directly to their rooms the minute they come into the house, hardly greeting their mother. Others aren't as forthright about removing themselves, but show clearly how they feel. They may be sullen, disagreeable, and hard to live with. They show their resentment over any restraint but especially over restrictions on their going out and staying out.

Others, not feeling that this attitude which is obviously producing friction, irritation, and annoyance will get them any place, may choose a different tack. They become more secretive, on the defensive, and somehow keep their parents in the dark about their activities. A few, feeling that their parents, especially their mother, won't let them do certain things, will go ahead and do them and then tell her afterward. Fifteen's resistance to telling anything can be so great that, as one parent remarked, "It's like pulling teeth to get anything out of him."

Mothers fare better with daughters than with sons. Some daughters sustain a good, confiding relationship with their mothers. They will not tell them *everything,* but they do discuss essential happenings or things that are on their minds. A few, though a very few, are thoughtful of their mothers and even take pleasure in helping in the house. Those who are callous and thoughtless know full well how they *should* act. They know they *should* be more patient, that they *should* help around the house more than they do, but they seem unable to mobilize themselves into action. The "long quiet talks" fostered by their mothers

don't seem to change the situation too much. Rather do these talks produce embarrassment. Mothers are too prone to criticize their daughters' postures, not realizing that this poor posture is more confined to home and is related to Fifteen's inner attitude of apathy. And the maternal admonition to "be a lady" may in certain respects be a compliment, for it has recognized Fifteen as an adult member of her sex, but Fifteen does not always take it as such. The warning that Fifteen should not speak to strangers may even yet be a wise one, for some girls sometimes forget, even though they are aware that they should be cautious about whom they meet and how they act.

How different are the criticisms and the warnings of a mother to her 15-year-old son. She tends to overprotect him, to suggest that he wear his jacket, or not forget his raincoat. It might be wise for a mother to let her son accept the consequences of cold and wet, and hope he will learn a lesson, rather than for her to reinforce the pattern of rebellious indifference to his physical needs which some men have carried into adult life. And yet when a boy asks his mother, "You think I'm a kid, don't you?" he may sometimes wonder himself if he isn't and realize that he still needs a certain amount of mothering.

Mothers feel the precariousness of their relationship with their sons when they can report, "We're still on speaking terms." Even when a boy has all the freedom he needs or even all he wants, he still may not build up a good relationship with his mother. One boy's logic was a bit odd when he said, "I'm right almost as much as she is, so I don't listen to her." But his father was always right, according to his judgment, so he listened to him.

Fathers in general get on better with their 15-year-olds than do mothers. In some cases it's because Fifteen sees so little of his father that no true conflict is built up. But when father lays down the law, Fifteen usually complies. Some boys are apt to over-concentrate on such interests as radio at the expense of their school work. In one such instance a father was known to lock his son's radio room and not allow him to have the key until he had finished his homework.

Girls generally get on better with their fathers than boys do. But some fathers lose the respect of their daughters either because of their own ineptness or because of their poor understanding of their daughter's growing social needs. Some girls avoid their fathers, hardly speaking to them. Others frankly admit, "There is nothing between us," and show an impersonal attitude toward their father.

The family ties are loosening at fifteen. Boys all too often want to be free of both home and family. They want to get away—anywhere. They want to cut loose. They may enjoy the looser structure of a picnic or beach party or a family gathering, but they tend to freeze up with relatives whom they don't know too well.

The biggest problem boys have with their parents relates to going out at night. Some would go out every night if they could. They seem to have an uncontrolled desire to get away. No wonder the parents feel that they should stay home more. It is more difficult when either a son or a daughter doesn't make it too clear where he is going. Sometimes they are not sure themselves, but at other times they may be planning on a rendezvous which the parents might well not approve of.

The other all too difficult problem is the hour of return. Around midnight was a possible deadline at fourteen, but if one eats out after a movie, or goes to a party after a party over the weekend the time slips by to 1 or 2 A.M. Wise are the parents who establish certain rules, such as "no dating or parties except on Friday or Saturday nights," with the possible exception of a concert or some such activity in mid-week. And a compromise about the hour of coming home should be readily worked out according to the demand of the activities involved, with 1:30 or possibly 2 A.M. as an outer limit. An older teenager may well impose a far earlier hour closer to midnight on himself. Fifteen's excessive demands do not necessarily indicate that these late hours will continue into later years.

Some Fifteens seek to resolve their desire to get away by going away to school. If they are not yet ready for the independence this experience can provide, the change may be a little like jumping out of the frying pan into the fire. But many Fifteens are truly ready, and profit enormously by this experience when they are on their own. In fact, they begin to appreciate home from afar and discover how wonderful home really is. One 15-year-old girl who had been most eager to get away from home found herself thinking about home each evening around nine o'clock. She pictured her parents in her mind sitting before the fire, or possibly watching television. The very thought of that cozy home scene made her feel "all warm inside."

The improvement in sibling relationships that became more apparent at fourteen is now surprisingly evident at fifteen. It doesn't seem to matter what age a younger sibling is, Fifteen has a way of seeing improvement in him. You hear him say, "He's grown older"; "She's more intelligent"; or, "Her mind is developing." Fifteen feels that he gets on much better now with younger siblings and that he actually has fun with them. He might be too concerned about improving a much younger sibling's behavior, but he can sometimes check himself by thinking, "Probably it's none of my business." He willingly takes over putting a much younger sibling to bed when the parents are out. He can help the older ones in all sorts of ways. He is beginning to show an interest in what the siblings closest to his age either do or think. He is more like a contemporary with them. Part of Fifteen's good relationship to his younger siblings is that he now feels that they do look up to him "a little," a fact which he might not have recognized before.

With some Fifteens, however, the relationship with younger siblings is not so positive. They seem to get on better only because they don't pay any attention to these younger siblings. They appear to ignore them or they walk around them to avoid any conflicts.

Fifteen's relationship with older siblings is unusually good. Some pal around, go to the same parties, and confide in an older brother or sister. Relationships often improve after the older sibling has gone away from home and Fifteen sees him only occasionally.

Friends are important to Fifteen. Girls choose their friends for a wider variety of reasons than boys. With boys their friends of the same sex are most often selected through interests in similar activities. But girls more often choose a friend they admire, sometimes one who is achieving well in school. Girls would like to have a friend as a confidant to whom they could tell everything, especially if they have lost this more confidential, sympathetic relationship with their mothers. The feeling that whatever they tell their close friend won't be spread by her is important. Girls are becoming aware of emotional depth and warmth, and may speak of acquaintances as "shallow" or "very cold." But they might go with girls they don't like very well just because there is no one else around or "nothing else to do."

Though there is a trend in a number of 15-year-old girls to concentrate on one friend at a time, there is also a marked tendency to group. In fact, the groups are often rather large, often including six or eight girls or more. They often speak of a "gang of friends" who "all go around together." These gangs especially frequent places where they might expect to meet boys, such as coke bars. The noise of these places may be unpleasant to some 15-year-old girls who want to talk. They would rather go to each other's homes, have their soft drinks there, and settle into a good talk about all sorts of things, but especially about "how life will turn out."

The boys are not always as high-minded in their interests as the girls, and it is therefore understandable that the girls often choose older boys who are interested in the same things they are. Boys of Fifteen tend to "gang" more than girls and to form larger groups. They group more easily along activity lines, especially since they are so often sports-minded. And in true male fashion when asked what they do they say they "aid each other in this and that and the other." Here is the basis of future business relationships which thrive on a desire to do something for the other fellow.

The boys are less interested in the girls than vice versa and are more apt to choose their own activities apart from girls, though certain groups will also frequent the coke bars. When a single friend is wanted, Fifteen is apt to take anyone who is around. But if he shows strong interests, such as in radio or cars, he is apt to choose a friend with similar interests.

If parents of daughters have been concerned about a "going steady" pattern in dating, they can usually rest easy for a while during this fifteen period. Both boys and girls tend to have the same attitude of "take them or leave them," and they put this attitude into action. They often refer to the past few years when they did like someone of the opposite sex especially well and dated the same one for quite a stretch of time, "but not now." If anything, the trend is away from single dating and toward more intermingling in groups. One girl reports, "We date as a group," or another, "Everybody just goes all together and then pair off after they get there." A fairly typical 15-year-old boy shrugs and says, "What the heck; I just go with anybody who comes along; meet them around where the whole gang is." Another boy expresses the social pattern of his age and group in his comment: "Never been to a dance yet that required the taking of a girl."

A place for meeting, for having parties, becomes an important part of the life of a 15-year-old. It is understandable why coke bars or other eating places where fairly large groups can congregate are chosen. Sometimes a home can provide these facilities, though this would not be the natural choice of Fifteen who prefers to be away from home. High school or community club facilities would be preferred, a place where they could eat and talk and possibly do a little "necking."

This subject of so-called "necking" (which is really mostly kissing) is uppermost in the minds of many Fifteens and is often quite out in the open. Girls are all too aware of boys' designs on them and tend to respond in one of two opposite extremes. Some of the girls on the more prudish side are disgusted with some of the actions of their friends at parties, even shocked by them. Some girls feel very responsible for their friends when they go off with a boy from the group to "smooch." In fact, if a girl's behavior is too unbecoming she might be banned from future parties. The more tactful girl, knowing a boy is about to become "fresh" with her, will keep him busy, on the move, asking him if he doesn't want a coke, etc. Much discussion about kissing is carried on by the girls in their talks about life. Some girls feel you shouldn't kiss a boy if you don't love him (which would pretty much eliminate kissing at fifteen). Others spend all their time comparing how different boys kiss and how many times they kiss when saying goodnight. This is the kind of information Fifteen does not share with her mother.

Fifteens almost always have a good time at parties or in group activities.

At times they would prefer not to go, but usually find they have a good time when they get there. This is in marked contrast to the earlier years, especially from eleven to thirteen, when they went to a party with great anticipation and came home dead tired and in tears, or at least disappointed. The 15-year-old home parties with around five to seven couples can be very successful. They drink coke, eat sandwiches, dance, play charades, look at TV, or play records. These are usually not noisy parties.

Both boys and girls in reporting about other Fifteens say that about half date and half don't. Actually in our group most of the girls and about two-thirds of the boys do at least some dating. But some who have dated before now stop dating. A girl may "feel sure" of a boy and "suddenly it's all over." Girls have no exaggerated hopes about boys. They are learning that "they aren't wonderful" which they once thought and that "they aren't perfect." "They aren't reliable but they're fun, and only an occasional one is dependable." Boys aren't as outspoken about girls, their main complaint being that "they spend money."

Even when girls aren't dating, they usually have a feeling that there is "a horizon and a prospect." Fifteen "sort of lets things happen," but he does put himself in the position where things can happen to him. Fifteen is repeatedly concerned as to whether things "work out right" or "don't work out right." He is not a conniver. He plays his part and he accepts outcomes as they happen.

When Fifteens date they often prefer to double date, because "it's lots more fun." They may go to movies, bowling, or out to eat. And the pattern of dating is fairly "random" or "varied." Fifteen is ready to have a good time as long as it lasts.

All in all, Fifteen is really not too concerned about dating. Girls may say, "Those who do go out do it for something to do, but they're not really serious." And boys may be a little harsher in their evaluation of their friends' reported activities. "Still may be just talk. Bragging about this, that, and the other." Boys tend more to play the field, may shift between three girls at one time, and may even speak of their "harem." They are resentful at times when girls of their age or class in school date older boys. These are the "dating boys" who complain. But it is understandable that girls might prefer older boys, since they may have rather poor pickings among boys of their own age, many of whom are still obviously immature.

6. Activities and Interests

Fifteen doesn't show the wide, inclusive interests that he showed at fourteen. Earlier interests such as sports, the opposite sex, the playing of a musical instrument, any of which may have seemed at the time to have become a natural part of him, may have sometimes been dropped by the wayside. Fifteen is more apt to restrict himself, to concentrate on one channel. But he doesn't necessarily concentrate by going deeper and deeper into an interest. Rather, he may set up a repetitive pattern such as listening to a certain record until he achieves satiation. And not only satiation, but positive revulsion. The presence of satiety may well be one of the keys to Fifteen's action system. Following this gorging, rest or relaxation may be in order. That is why a number of Fifteen's activities need more to be thought of as rest or relaxation; or more positively approached as "recreation."

When Fifteen can say that he sleeps "for entertainment," it is evident how much relaxation means to him. Or he might "draw for relaxation." Various musical instruments he wants "to fiddle" or "doodle around with," but he may well not wish to improve his technique or to take lessons. He is definitely coming into the adult realm of the need for ease when he speaks of Sunday as "just a time to rest up."

Some of the sports-mad boys have now switched their interest into cars, but others are heightening their interest in sports, which have become their area of concentration. They maintain their interest in the major competitive sports and in swimming. There is a further rise of interest in golf, tennis, and sailing. The spectator interest is ever-increasing both in direct observation and through radio or TV. Wrestling, horse racing, and stock car racing are also being added to their spectator sports interests.

The imminence of a driver's license makes Fifteen all the more interested in driving. He drives whenever he gets a chance. Some 15-year-old boys show a mechanical interest in cars and tend to hang around garages to pick up any information they can. If they are fortunate enough to have an older friend with both a car and a driver's license, they enjoy "hacking around," usually with a group, in the friend's car.

There is a certain group of boys who show a continuing and persistent interest in radio. They often have their own radio room and spend hours in it, to the detriment of their studies. They are now coming into the diagraming of radio layouts. An early intense interest in trains may have led into an active interest in model railroads by fifteen. It is the "tinkering with things" that Fifteen especially enjoys.

Indoor games of various sorts are more indulged in by groups of boys than girls. Checkers, chess, and the various card games are favorites.

Girls' activities are quite different from boys' except for their common interest in meeting in social groups. There are the more definitely athletic girls who may participate in a wide variety of sports. But the more individual sports of tennis, sailing, ice skating, skiing, and horseback riding are the ones favored. One might be "mad about skating," or another might consider skiing the "most wonderful sport" she has ever participated in.

Girls in general are less active. They like to go on long walks with friends as much to talk as for anything else. Or they like to "sit around and talk" at each other's houses. They may prefer this to the noisy atmosphere of some of the general public meeting places. Much of their conversation dwells on boys, and often on plans for the immediate future. If they are not communicating directly, some are still apt to spend quite a bit of time on the phone. Girls are also quite good correspondents and hold up their side usually better than boys do.

It is the social life of dating, going to parties, meeting at drugstores and coke bars that usurps most of Fifteen's marginal time. This interplay with the opposite sex is of real interest to most Fifteens.

Work experiences depend upon the

community in which the child lives. Fifteen often wants to work but can't secure a job. Boys, especially, need the money. Girls do a very creditable job at baby-sitting. It is in the summertime that a few Fifteens plan their time around a work experience, but this is more common at sixteen.

SEDENTARY LOOKING AND LISTENING ACTIVITIES

Radio is generally preferred over television. Some Fifteens, especially girls, have their radio or record player on "constantly." Interest in jazz, sometimes specifically Dixieland, outweighs interest in classical music by a wide margin. "Dreamy stuff" is favored by some girls. Fifteen often likes his radio on as he studies and this doesn't seem to interfere with his concentration. Some boys seem quite capable of keeping track of the scores of a sports event without losing their concentration on what they are studying or reading. When Fifteen tells about the programs he views or listens to he doesn't name them specifically but classifies them in general categories such as "sports" or "theater."

Television is more frequently viewed for sports events than for other programs. Viewing, which often decreased at both thirteen and fourteen, may have reached an all-time low at fifteen. Some "can't stand it," "could do without it," or would be willing to sell their set if they got the chance. All in all, money-aware Fifteen may consider television "a waste of money."

Interest in and time for reading may increase over the past year, though Fifteen is quite aware that he doesn't come up to his former interest in reading, which was especially strong at eleven and twelve when he read far into the night if he got the chance. He doesn't wish to read a book unless he feels sure he's going to enjoy it. He might automatically resist required reading.

Boys often do read exhaustively on technical subjects. They also delve more deeply into encyclopedias and dictionaries than do girls. The reading fare in general has now come pretty firmly into the adult sphere. Even the tendency to read the dashing, daring, sexy novels may be decreasing now that fifteen is becoming more ready to accept novels of romance. Magazines may be favored over books. But Fifteen may feel guilty that he has spent time reading a short story in a magazine when he should have been studying.

Newspaper reading is becoming a more regular activity, though most Fifteens don't read the paper thoroughly. The news and funnies are the most favored. Sports sections are not read as avidly by boys as they have been. Comic book interest is barely evident. They might read one "just for the heck of it if there is one around." In typical Fifteen fashion, they reminisce about the time (eight or nine to thirteen) when they had a "mad passion for comics." They may have read them so much that they "hate the thought of them now."

Interest in movies is a pretty individual matter. Some go when there is "nothing else to do, which is seldom." Others won't go for a long time and then will go "all the time." Those who go away to school are apt to "cram in as many good movies" as they can during a vacation period. Fifteen will go with a variety of people and under a variety of circumstances.

Going with the same sex either in pairs or in a larger group is the most common. But double dating at movies is fairly usual, and "much more fun" according to some Fifteens, though an occasional Fifteen will consider it "crude to go to the movies on a date."

Fifteen is fairly selective in his choice of movies and often gets his clues from the reviews. But a number just go for the sake of going.

7. School Life

When Fifteen expresses a hostile attitude toward school, as he often does, he does not become the easiest person to teach. The very expression "the 15-year-old slump" suggests that an inner change has occurred in Fifteen, that something isn't quite right. Teachers are often surprised by this "slump" and may not take it into sufficient consideration. Many conflicts arise between teachers and students. The rise in drop-outs from school following this year, especially among the boys, indicates the crucial aspect of this year and the failure of the school to meet the challenge. But it is no wonder that teachers speak of Fifteen as an "enigma." Many teachers would welcome any light of understanding about Fifteen or help about ways to handle him.

Fifteens tend to move in groups, almost in crowds, but the clique or close circle of friends may not be as important to him as they were at fourteen. In schools where fraternities and sororities still exist it may be far less important for Fifteen to belong than it was when he was fourteen. He will join, however, and produce an alive and flourishing society, but there can be other, more satisfactory, ways of grouping. Fifteen prefers the new, the spontaneous, the changing. He likes the casual atmosphere of a clubroom where both sexes can meet together. He wants to gather with others at a table where he can sit and talk, have a soft drink, listen to records, and dance if the mood strikes him. He wants a place where he can drift in and out, flow with the crowd without the demand of too stiff a pattern. Fifteen is a good follower. That's why he moves so readily in groups.

The fringe students stand out on the borders of these groups, boys especially. These are the boys who are often busy with selected interests such as radio, who have high intellectual ability and little interest, at this time, in girls. But within the fringe are also boys who aren't doing well intellectually, who are misfits in the group. These are the ones who can't find their place, who tend to drop out.

Fifteen is an age when the demands of definition are too much for some. Fifteens want to define their thoughts, their philosophy, their place in life. But some give up the struggle and become discouraged. They seem to lack everything—purpose, skills, and social "belongingness." School becomes like a prison or jail to them. (They may even project this feeling into their drawings.) Within them is the feeling "I want to get out of here" or "I've got to break away." If they cannot be helped to find their place or some expression through activity, it is no wonder that they drop out.

At the other extreme, especially by mid-fifteen, are those students who have good personal and social adjustments, time for leisure interests, and capacity to express leadership in and of itself. This does not mean that they haven't gone through their own form of "15-year-old slump." But by mid-fifteen they are ready and eager to do better. They become interested in their grades. They are ready to work. The girls are more often interested in social studies and have a tremendous capacity to achieve, even at a college level. The boys have a similar high capacity and may choose to do real background research in such subjects as archeology or current events.

With Fifteen's tendency to rebel against authority in the midst of his own "confusion" and "floundering around," it becomes very important to plan for him more as an individual than as a part of a group. The group has a way of swallowing him up, and then his individual status grows weaker and he is in turn less of a person. The advantages of having a thorough developmental appraisal of each individual at fourteen when he is more interested and ready to do something about himself become even more apparent when trouble occurs at fifteen. He was eager to understand himself better at fourteen and to establish a tentative direction to his line of growth.

When Fifteen's family shows a lack of interest in his welfare, then it is all the more important for the school to strike a decisive note. The rebellious boys who are not doing well in their studies, especially in foreign languages and English, and who are prone to be absent from school are in danger of bolting permanently from school. These are the boys who would profit by a half-day work experience. If a boy undergoes any such experience in an apprentice capacity and in relation to the academic courses he is taking, it can be a very meaningful and satisfying one. And it is surprising to see how much such a boy improves in his concentration and interest in his studies when he has a successful work experience. The right job for each boy should and could be found—being a helper in a grocery store, an assistant in a garage, a worker on a farm or in a machine shop. Fifteen's interest can be high and his powers of sustaining are much improved over Fourteen's. The latter too often approached a job with excessive enthusiasm, and all too soon the job had to be scaled down to what he could produce. Fifteen is readier to learn the complexities of a job, whether they are the rules of safety with machines, the multiple operations needed in a machine process, or the complexity of some farm project, with the keeping of books and the calculation of profit and loss. The jobs within such a work-training framework should be salaried, both because of the service Fifteen renders and because he is in real need of funds and capable of handling them.

Since Fifteen seems to be in rebellion against authority, his adjustment often hinges on how authority treats him. Some of his opinionated remarks need to be slid over. And when he challenges a teacher, biting his lips and asking, "What will you do with me if I say what I'm thinking?" only deep humanitarian values of the teacher can prevent a clash or some act of defiance.

Fifteen is a real challenge to a teacher. Though she needs to learn how to "hold the line," a teacher respected by Fifteen gives him time to become receptive. Before a classroom period is begun she needs to be able to wait until her students have settled in their seats. Sometimes Fifteens calm down faster if she walks among them. At other times they quiet best if she stands and waits. A look from her may convey more than words. These methods of settling down may have to be practiced day after day. Once settled, Fifteens are capable of good attention. If they grow restless, it may be wise to allow them to shift from the assignment for a while. They will calm down faster with such an interlude.

Fifteens can be exciting to teach even in the midst of their slump if they are challenged in some new field. They ask many questions of why and wherefore. They are more able to think for themselves and are quick to pick up any error in a discussion.

Fifteens learn quickly in new fields and like the stimulus of a new lecturer to give them fresh material or a new slant on some topic. They want to have an opinion and to have sufficient information for their discussions. They especially like to have informal panel discussions where they can express their opinions. Feeling the weight of world problems as they do, they both need and like to talk. Religion and race are two of their favorite topics for discussion, especially if these topics are vital to their own experience. They often conduct such a panel on a testifying basis. If the discussion is about religion, it may become important for each one to report on his own church, its program, and its history. And also to report about his own beliefs. He wants to discuss and compare his own beliefs with what he has been taught. How, for example, does the story of

creation in the Bible compare with the theory of evolution?

A panel discussion allows for an easy give-and-take. He doesn't appear as discourteous as he does when he suddenly blurts out in the more formal classroom situation. When his opinion is at variance with someone who is reciting he may spontaneously burst forth. This need to express himself is more easily handled in a panel discussion.

Most of all Fifteen is interested in whatever affects his life. He will be interested in biology if he learns about things that touch his own experience. Take mildew, for example—he'd like to find out why clothes mildew, why house plants mildew. Or you can elicit his interest in literature by the discussion of some character. He likes to think about why the person reacted the way he did. He wonders if he would act similarly under a similar situation. And the final test of a person may be whether he would like to know him personally or not. (This topic is discussed more fully by Holden Caulfield in J. D. Salinger's *Catcher in the Rye*.)

Fifteen tends to identify himself with the situation, the person, the idea. Sometimes he unconsciously identifies himself with a teacher until his handwriting becomes a near copy of his teacher's and his way of pronouncing words is unmistakably similar to his teacher's. When Fifteen is too accepting, he may not be so challenging to teach, but he is certainly easier than when he is at odds with her. Then he speaks of her as being "crazy," a "real bore," or a "monster." He may consider any mention by the teacher of her personal affairs as a "waste of time." Sometimes these harsh judgments are only passing and Fifteen sees things in clearer perspective when he comes out of his slump. But at times the conflict between teacher and student can be so marked that a switch to another teacher is the only solution.

Though Fifteen might lumber along when by himself, he acts quite differently with the group, especially when he is dismissed from class. Sometimes it is wise for a teacher to hold back the dismissal until another class has passed through the halls. The teacher may stand in the doorway to stem the tide, or even resort to dismissal in rows to hold Fifteen in check, though this last is bitterly resented as babyish. Boys especially may be in a mad rush. They might plow right through a group without seeing anyone. They may still need to rush from one place to the other. But on the whole Fifteen is not rowdy in the halls. There is some pushing and loud talk. There is some meeting of boys and girls between classes with a trend toward "laying on of hands." But hall activity doesn't usually present a problem and is under fairly good control.

Boys generally do better scholastically than girls at fifteen. Some boys who have been doing poorly in previous years and have been hard to motivate are now willing to put forth more effort and to spend more time on their homework. They seem to concentrate better than the girls, whose energies are dispersed by the number of things on their minds. Some of these girls are busy every minute. Everything looms important and must be acted on at once. Such girls seem never to get everything done. They go here; they go there. They must make a telephone call. They must have an interview with a teacher, yet when they come to a prearranged conference they flounder and don't know what to talk about. They don't know how to start or to tell what's on their mind. Most of them really want to talk about vocations and especially about college. Suddenly in the midst of a discussion they may have to interrupt to make an important telephone call—important to them. Girls are surprisingly not disturbed by their poor scholastic achievement, which often hinges on the fact they haven't done the work. Such things don't bother them because they feel there are more important things to think about and to do. These more important things involve their social life.

Many teachers find that definite assignments are carried out best. And Fifteen is capable of doing a careful job. But the perceptive teacher will "try to pull out" if she can and let Fifteen make his own assignment. Homework can be quite a problem. Here the parents instinctively "try to keep out of it," but often realize that Fifteen may need to be helped over the hump of getting started. Fifteen often works better if his schedule is protected from interruptions such as telephone calls. Many parents find it helpful to lay down the rule of no telephone calls between seven and nine when they are studying. If anyone calls during this period a message can be taken to be acted upon after 9 P.M.

Fifteen profits by thinking over his homework period with his teacher. He finds it is best to tackle the subject that gives him the most trouble first.

Sometimes he concentrates better with a small snack or having the radio on. In a slack period he might profit by reorganizing his notebook or reading to himself. Fifteen's big problem is when he can't understand the subject, or when an idea isn't getting across to him. This discourages him. He also has difficulties in getting his own ideas across, especially in writing. Teachers need to be more aware of this difficulty. That is why panel discussions are often so effective, for it is often a contemporary who irons out difficulties.

A certain number of Fifteens desire and would profit by going away to school. Sometimes it's because Fifteen is ready and wants to be on his own. But at other times it's because he wants to "break away." Under this motivation he may find he is not ready to assume his own responsibilities and then may want again to break away from his new-found moorings. But the ready Fifteen is apt to say, "It's kinda nice to get in new places and not have to depend on your family so much." In a new milieu Fifteen often shows startling shifts for the better in both social adjustment and intellectual achievement.

Under a new stimulus Fifteen is less prone "to pick flaws" than he does with the old and the tried. "Picking" is a word that significantly describes Fifteen's method. He "picks out" some individual he feels hostile toward. He "picks" faults in a certain teacher's methods. Or he sees what he considers errors in the administration of his school or the system and picks them out for discussion. His list of objections may be long—students don't have enough privileges; the sys-

tem is not democratic enough; teachers don't give students enough responsibilities; students have to do too much for themselves. Or if he has trouble in finding any more obvious flaws, he might complain that a court should try the cases of cheating. Fifteen should be listened to, should be allowed to discuss his complaints but he shouldn't be allowed to disrupt the system.

Far better is it to harness Fifteen's capacity for "group spirit." Perhaps no activity stimulates this potential "school spirit" more than athletics. A pleasant crowding together is natural to Fifteen. If he isn't of an athletic build, he can be the manager of some sport, a cheerleader, or just a spectator. And he can sing.

The one thing he doesn't want to do is to go to any school functions with his family, and he certainly doesn't want to sit with them. He is happily saved from this discomfiture if a bus is chartered to transport him with his group to these various events. He behaves quite well in a bus. Occasionally a boy may throw some detachable article of a girl's clothing out the window but this can usually be retrieved and order re-established.

Fifteen is responsive to group loyalty. He likes to participate in a class project and see it through to completion. Sometimes he gives too much time and energy to some such project as a class play. The rest of his work suffers and he may be thrown off balance. Yet he wouldn't wish to give up his part, for he identifies so strongly with the group. Joining in to make a part of the classroom noise is another way of expressing his identity with the group. But if a tape recording of this classroom noise is made, hearing it played back makes quite an impression upon him and he becomes ready to change with the class.

Leaders often stand out at Fifteen. The same students may be chosen over and over again to lead a wide variety of activities. These are the students who act with ease in human relationships. At the opposite extreme unfortunately are the ones who get on badly and who are rejected.

Although Fifteen tends to be more individual in his choice of clothes, he is drawn with the group to wear more casual clothes such as dungarees if these are allowed. Certain fads are expressed and at times a group's attire is an expression of their defiance. This is a time for the school authorities to "hold the line" and to make certain justified demands. And Fifteens are capable of showing good taste. Girls don't wear much jewelry and are rarely seen to primp in public. Another evidence of taste is that boys rarely make "smutty" jokes or swear in mixed groups. However, the sudden appearance of a girl into a group will bring forth a whistle.

Boys and girls tend to move together as a group. They like to work together on committees. They tend to do less individual dating now and to date more in groups. Only an occasional pair goes steady. If a boy and girl are in love, the other Fifteens respect this relationship and do not tease them.

The success or failure in school at this fifteenth year is dependent on many factors. But if Fifteen is treated as being at the threshold of adulthood, capable of expressing his own opinion, then the chances of success will be more possible.

8. Ethical Sense

Fifteen has a more defined ethical sense than he has ever had before. He may speak of his ethical decisions as being automatic but most of all he demands that they be his own. He wants to think through to his own decisions and if he has chosen a wrong one he recognizes that he didn't think. Fifteen is more aware of conventions, of standards, of principles, of rules, and of religious codes. These help him to make his decisions.

Fifteen is pretty capable in judging right from wrong, especially from his own "point of view" or his own individual standards. Sometimes he has his doubts, or the problem seems a little vague to him. Then he tries to think it through to a logical conclusion. His parents may still be a strong force in his final decision and the question "Would Mom approve?" often acts as a decisive safeguard. Questions of right and wrong are becoming more specific, and relate often to social customs. An unknowing 15-year-old may act wrongly from ignorance. Then his contemporaries might laugh at him and he in turn accepts their lesson. But sometimes Fifteen doesn't want to do what he knows is right. Then he tries to persuade himself or to talk himself into some wrongdoing. His own resistance suggests that he possesses a good ethical fiber.

His conscience would be active if he did something very wrong. But there are certain smaller things he may try to get away with, such as going to a forbidden movie or meeting someone when this was forbidden. Fifteen doesn't necessarily try to hide his misdemeanors, such as charging something without permission, but he does wait until the course of events exposes them.

Then he usually tells the truth without flinching. It is not the truth that disturbs Fifteen, for he means to tell the truth. But he now recognizes that it might sometimes be kinder not to tell the truth. So he finds himself agreeing with people or complimenting them to be polite without speaking what he really thinks or believes.

When it comes to accepting the blame, you can usually count on Fifteen. He doesn't leap at the chance, but he does freely admit his share and has no desire to pass the blame off on someone else, as he well remembers he did when he was only a little younger.

Though many Fifteens argue with their parents for fun, some are more interested in getting over their "point" than in arguing for the sake of argument. Fifteen welcomes a good discussion but he is not too responsive to parental reasoning and may tend to close his mind to any influence his parents may wish to bring to bear.

Most of the boys and some of the girls have attempted smoking by now. Parents now realize whether they are likely to smoke or not and tend to invite them to do it in their own homes if this act becomes inevitable. Drinking is not yet within the problem zone, though some Fifteens will accept a cocktail if offered one at an adult party, and some girls as well as boys are beginning to enjoy beer. As for grownups drinking, Fifteen acts rather detached and speaks of it as "their affair."

Swearing is milder than it has been. In fact, Fifteen is rather selective of the swear words he uses. His tensions seem to be expressed through other channels than swearing. He may definitely dislike the use of any sacred swear words.

Fifteen is not prone to cheat, and he doesn't like to see cheating in others. He may notice that those who are in the lower ranks of the class are more apt to cheat, or that those who tended to cheat at fourteen aren't doing well in school at fifteen. He is now beginning to experience the shock that valuables left around at school might be stolen. He asks the age-old question "Why do they do it?" But most Fifteens are pretty honest, and as they recognize that certain children are more apt to be questioned about thefts, they decide that "it really doesn't pay."

9. Philosophic Outlook

TIME AND SPACE

Fifteen brings the fluid, inclusive concept of time characteristic of fourteen into more precise definition. Time becomes a method, a measurement. It is spoken of as an interval, an abstraction, yet "something very tangible." It becomes "space in seconds, minutes, and hours, a measurement of space."

Some Fifteens, however, cannot pin time down so abstractly. Though time is thought to be unchangeable, it still "marks the changing." It may be a "fleeting thing"; "you can't count on it, you can't figure it out," and yet it goes "on endlessly like a stream." Some Fifteens relate time to the revolution and aging of the earth. Still others would record it in history. There is in addition to the "history of time, also personal time." According to one Fifteen, "This is the thing that controls the fates of all men."

Fifteen is in better control of time than he was at fourteen. He recognizes his tendency to be late and so he "skins in" or sets his watch ahead so that he will be on time. He never has enough time, but knows that he does better when he is pressed for time. Fifteen doesn't like idleness. He "likes to have things come closely together, to fill in spare time." That's why Fifteen likes to do things slowly to the last minute, even though he might then be rushed. He'd rather be slightly rushed than sit around doing nothing.

Space can't be pinned down as easily as time. Fifteen has now learned something about matter, gaseous material, and gravitational force. He tries to relate these to space ("Space is an area in which there is nothing of material value, lack of matter," or, "Space is something that's got matter in it or a vast expanse of gaseous material"). But Fifteen is hard put to explain what he means about space or to understand what the other person means. "Space is, after all," he says, "something nobody knows anything about." "Nobody knows how big it is or how small it is." But this lack of knowledge does not prevent Fifteen from expressing his opinion or giving forth his information. Many wonderful arguments on the topic are batted about in science class, much to Fifteen's delight. This type of discussion whets his appetite for more.

Fifteen is showing a better directional control of space than he did at fourteen. Even the girls who earlier showed a poor sense of direction are now more aware of where they are in space, though they still don't know the points of the compass. Fifteen likes to travel, and he especially likes to be away from home. If he could fly, this would be his preference.

DEATH AND DEITY

The acceptance of forces beyond his own control, such as life and death, isn't easy to Fifteen. There are some Fifteens who are matter-of-fact about death—"If it happens, it happens." But in the midst of their very nonchalance they betray their inner concern. They say that they are not "shunning" the thought of death, that they "don't dread it or look forward to it." Death is "something always with you. Nothing you can do about it." They seem to accept the fact of death as a "stopping point," and may associate it with the color black.

Some try to look on the cheery side: "Somebody dies all the time, so I'll have company." And still others project death into killing and their own inhibition of this urge within themselves. As one boy says, "I wouldn't kill anybody because of fear of a moral God." Fortunate is the boy who has the counterforce to inhibit his urge to kill, even if it is only fear of forces beyond his comprehension.

What happens after death is "one big mystery" to many Fifteens. They frankly say they have "no idea" and that it is "beyond us to know." The thought of an "endless sleep" satisfies some. Even those who have previously believed in heaven now find this concept a little difficult to accept, though they would like to believe in some form of life after death. Their own spatial awareness finds it difficult to put everyone into either heaven or hell. "That would be an awful lot of people," muses one 15-year-old girl. And even when she reduced all the physical bodies to souls which "would not take up much room," she still had to concede "an awful lot of souls."

There are some Fifteens who cling to some thought of life after death with at least enough tenacity to allow the dead to remain in the minds or memories of people still living. This continuance may occur simply through those who were close to the one who has died, or it can occur more surely through a creative work such as the artist leaves behind him.

Fifteen is as unsure of his ideas about Deity as he is about death. He may solve his dilemma simply by saying he doesn't know, or even that he doesn't believe in God. And yet he hesitates. He says it's "kind of hard to say" or that he's "looking around for an idea of God." He recognizes his skepticism, but he also recognizes his oscillation. In a cynical mood he may come to the conclusion, "there is no God," and yet he is afraid to try this out. At other times, in a more positive mood, he may "feel extremely religious" and think "there probably is a God." But when his skepticism again gets the better of him he may conjecture that "religion is phony. People don't know. Then they make it up."

Though this uncertainty and searching are common at fifteen, some Fifteens can hold strongly to their beliefs. They will concede that "God is some great power that we don't understand"—maybe just "good conscience." They "know there has to be something there, otherwise it [life?] wouldn't have started." But in the midst of this positive statement that they "actually think there is a God," they will add, "but it's awfully hard for me to know what I think myself."

Fifteen is down to earth in his thinking. He is returning, at a higher level, to the concepts he had at nine and ten years of age. The cycle has gone a full circle round and he has returned to close reality. It is no wonder that the believing Fifteen not only conceives of God as a spirit, but also as a person. And no wonder that the skeptical Fifteen finds it hard to conceive of an incorporeal spirit, yet can't believe in a supernatural person.

A number of the more enthusiastic 14-year-olds who attended youth groups and church services regularly may now suddenly feel a break in their relationship with the church. For no apparent reason they no longer wish to go. There are those, however, who continue to enjoy the youth group activities, not only because of the social program but also for the worship service. These may be expected to continue their relationship to the youth group through the high school years.

The church service may be preferred by some to youth group activities. Fifteen might attend church more willingly if he were assured that he didn't have to sit with his parents. If he had his choice, he might prefer to stand in the back of the church. Though Fifteen doesn't attend church often, he does like to participate in special church holidays. He might even be willing to sit with his parents on such occasions.

CHAPTER TEN

Year Sixteen

MATURITY PROFILE

THE GRAND spiral of human development has its major and minor subcycles. The major subcycle which began with Year Ten comes to full circle at sixteen, and then takes a long swing of five years or more toward maturity. The 16-year-old youth if he rises to tiptoe can almost see the horizon of adulthood. He is himself a pre-adult.

Society accords him his higher status in various laws, customs, and expectations. The attitudes of parents, teachers, and counselors undergo subtle changes in recognition of his increasing maturity. We inevitably sensed these changes in connection with the interview, the examination, and the conversations at the time of his annual visit at the age of sixteen. The interchanges were as between equals. In his own attitude toward his elders Sixteen induces an impression of being more grown-up. When interpersonal attitudes spontaneously react upon each other in this manner, active developmental forces may be assumed. Sixteen has a more self-possessed mind because it is more ordered and under better control.

Fifteen, as we have already shown, was a necessary forerunner. He prepared the way for the broader and more balanced integrations of the behavior of Sixteen. With this advantage Sixteen displays greater self-reliance and deeper self-containedness. Wholesome *self-assurance* is his cardinal trait, and a symptom of his potentials. It was not so at the fifteen-year maturity level, when he often seemed to be dissatisfied, uncertain, and even rebellious. He then had a spirit of independence; now he has achieved instead a *sense of independence* He automatically takes a quota of independence for granted, and usually his self-confidence is so well founded that his parents take it for granted too—another example of the sensitive interaction of adult-youth relationships. At fifteen he resisted; now he simply hopes that parents will go their way and he his. Friction is reduced. "Don't worry about me," he says reassuringly.

He is more tolerant to the world in general. He tends to take life as it comes. Should an unannounced guest arrive, he may amaze you by the cordiality and the pre-adultish deftness with which he receives her, removing all tensions. At fifteen the same boy could not have done it. (We are describing a maturity difference, and not a temperamental one.) The heightened or deepened self-awareness at fifteen can interfere, temporarily, with outgoing patterns, whereas people are so interesting to Sixteen that they tend to evoke positive attitudes and social responses on his part.

Sixteen almost makes a specialty of his interest in people by building up multiple friendships. This is equally true of girls and boys; there is much companionship on a non-romantic basis. Sixteen is an age of informal parties, punch parties, beach parties, refreshments and records parties, and both formal and informal dances. Mixed gangs of a score or more may loosely organize for social activities without much worry about agenda or preliminary preparations. Two-thirds of the boys and about all the girls in our group date.

Boys cultivate their boy friends chiefly on the basis of mutual interest in activities, sports, or special undertakings. The majority also have friendships of long standing; but not intensively pursued. Most girls report they have "millions" of friends. Sometimes the girl-girl friendships are so intense as to annoy the families involved. The friends are mutually confiding: "She tells me everything and I tell her everything." Discussion of the traits of boy friends constitutes staple conversation.

Company of friends is usually preferred to company of family, partly because time is not available for the latter. Yet Sixteen likes to meet with his friends in his own home. Relationships with the family have actually improved; arguments are fewer. Parent-son and -daughter relationships show more mutual understanding. One daughter, however, is reported to speak up to her father and to kid him about his shortcomings. Another thinks that her mail should not be opened by her mother. Boys like to feel that they live their own life; but if a personal problem proves complex a boy will go to his mother for advice and discussion, assuming that she will treat him as an equal.

Sibling relationships vary with degrees of compatability, but in general they are satisfactory. Sixteen likes banter and laughter. Teasing of and by siblings probably retains some functional values both for teaser and teased.

Sometimes it seems as though Sixteen had forgotten the domestic circle. But his family loyalty and attachments have not actually weakened. They have simply yielded somewhat to give scope to broader socializing experiences beyond the home boundaries. Many boys welcome the opportunity to hold down a responsible job during the summer and odd jobs during the school year. The choice of employment opportunities is very wide. Many boys and girls are responsible enough to return to a summer camp, as counselors. Or they may attend special purpose camps, such as church camp, music camp, sailing camp, French camp. Girls may still show a certain reluctance about household tasks, but they are otherwise so busy that parents come to accept the conclusion that a 16-year-old girl simply doesn't have the time to help. Baby-sitting is a favorite occupation for remuneration outside of the home. However, it should be noted that Sixteen tends to rise to emergency demands in her own home when her mother is away. There is a tendency to function better without too prescriptive direction.

Sixteen is more solidly oriented to the future than he was at fifteen. Nearly all of our research group plan to go to college or to some special school such as a college of pharmacy or an art school. Choices appeared to be no longer influenced by college attended by parents. A sizable number of girls expressed a preference for a coeducational type of school.

Our Gallup Poll on matrimonial plans brought to light an interesting discrepancy. Eighty per cent of the girls, but only 18 per cent of the boys hope or plan to marry. However, many of the boys conservatively stated that they did not now know, and only a few definitely asserted that they would not marry. The girls as usual spontaneously emphasize having children, and often even go so far as to state how many children they will have, four being the preferred number.

We found our subjects more ready to talk about marriage in a frank, serious vein. When the boys were asked what characteristics they would value in a wife, they variously replied, "intelligent, pretty, economical, easy to get on with, a good cook, cheerful." One boy added "persevering." Girls replied, as earlier, that they want husbands who are "good-tempered, smart, unselfish, helpful around the house, and in love with me." Additional qualities now mentioned included the following: "Serious, reliable, faithful, steady, patient, not neurotic, knows where he's going." In these replies the girls instinctively stressed interpersonal relationships.

Girls of sixteen are rather domestically inclined; only one in six hopes to combine career and marriage. But two-thirds plan to work until they marry, "in order to have something to fall back on," or "in order to have something to do after things get dull." An equal-partner pattern of marriage is suggested in some of their testimony. The girls named ten different choices of career with artist, child psychologist, and teacher taking the lead.

Boys named as many as twenty-one different businesses and professions, notably, engineering, law, architecture, and medicine. The boys in our group were earnestly interested in questions of career. They take it for granted that they will have to do their share of the world's work. This attitude is part of their basic self-assurance. But Sixteen worries about military service; and its possible conflict with his preparations for a career is beginning to intrude upon his thinking. The tremendous political, technological, and scientific movements of the day are current events for him. They challenge him and they may fire his ambitions. Their impact, however, is almost explosive and they do not simplify his developmental task. Never in all history has the world turned more intently toward the resources of youth and education.

So far as Sixteen is concerned, it is fortuante that he is in a favorable phase of development, both as an individual and as a member of the contemporary culture. His maturity traits are more favorably balanced and ballasted than they were at the fifteen-year level of maturity. He has in reserve more resistance to totalitarian and mob influence. He is less engrossed with self-awareness; his spirit of independence is less impulsive. He has grown into a self-possessed sense of independence, which will normally protect him from excessive identification with anti-social groups and gangs. His concepts of family and career, his relationships to home, school, and community have made astounding progress since the age of eleven and have prepared him for the further advances of the next five years of adolescence.

Aided by the frank information supplied by our subjects and their parents, we can detect in Sixteen a constellation of traits which at a pre-adult level are foretokens of the so-called mature mind. First and foremost, Sixteen has his emotions pretty well in hand. He is generally on even keel. He is not touchy: he covers up hurt feelings. He is not given to worries and does not indulge unduly in moods. He seldom cries. He usually curbs his anger or circumvents it by walking away or indirectly by laughing it off. He likes laughter and indulges it abundantly, at favorable social gatherings. Time and again parents report he is now cheerful, friendly, outgoing, and well adjusted.

We must emphasize his mindfulness of people which contributes to his poise and ability to get along with them. He is interested in human nature and his observation is sharpened by increased powers of judgment, for he has been growing intellectually as well as emotionally. He is even beginning to appraise personal motives of people, both his peers and elders. Now that his self-awareness has diminished, he is more willing to see another person's point of view. He likes to feel that he takes a broader outlook upon things. On occasion he will make a startlingly adult comment on some moral or ethical situation, revealing a tolerant and perceptive attitude. One boy, describing an unfair punishment of a comrade at a preparatory school, remarked philosophically, "However, you are bound to meet up with things like that!" . . . Another, talking about a camp counselor, allowed that, "Some of them are wise guys once in a while, but that is to be expected." "Things don't come to you all at once. You can wait." Such statements, made with transparent sincerity, are symptoms of a maturing mind. They can be taken at depth as well as face value, for they spring from liberal impulses and signify that Sixteen has made a big advance in the organization of his own personality. Self-awareness, self-dependence, and personal-social adjustments have come into better balance and integration. This makes him at mid-adolescence a sort of prototype of a pre-adult.

Although he will not be inducted into the heritage of our culture by means of initiation rites, his developmental assets confer a special status upon him. From the standpoint of education and indoctrination, Year Sixteen has far-reaching implications for all youth, girls as well as boys.

Under the stress of a technological era, a democratic society will rely increasingly upon codes of individual conduct to preserve the rights and welfare of its citizens. With his broadened outlook even Sixteen has begun to recognize the importance both of written and unwritten codes of conduct. At the age of five he saluted the flag and spoke a pledge. He has since then encountered many a rule and regulation governing his behavior at home and school. He has had to accept the legal restraints placed upon driving a car. Other laws warn him. His parents and the parents of his comrades may have drawn up a co-operative code to promote the best arrangements for parties, dances, and other activities. Even at his present age Sixteen realizes that his country has serious claims upon its citizens. Recently these claims were formulated in a remarkable document, a definitive Code of Conduct for American Servicemen While Prisoners of War. The code is written in simple language which any youth can understand and it is considered to be far more than a military code. "It is an assessment of citizenship, a study in responsibility, a guide to better conduct in the future. It should be applicable to civilians no less than to soldiers." *

The advisory committee report which accompanied the issuance of the code has direct bearings on the developmental welfare of adolescents, regardless of military considerations. The code calls attention to the fact that a great many servicemen were teen-agers who knew too little about the United States, its ideals and traditions. The report stresses the need for spiritual and educational bulwarks against enemy political indoctrination. The basic responsibility for building good citizens—loyal Americans —lies with the home, the school, the church, and the community, in times of peace, "long before a lad enters the military service."

With this broad interpretation of the problems of training for citizenship, the principles of the Code of Conduct take on vast significance for the education and guidance of adolescent youth. In a sense all of us are mutually involved in the task of safeguarding our country and our way of life.

The 16-year-old lad symbolizes the complexity and the challenge of that task in a democratic culture. He was born with certain inalienable traits which are inherent in the very patterns of his development. At about the age of ten he ceased to be a child. Increasingly he has become an individual personality in his own right. He will continue to grow in obedience to the same deep-seated laws of development which have fashioned him thus far in a culture committed to respect the dignity and worth of the individual.

---

* *New York Times* Editorial, August 19, 1955. The opening and closing articles of the code read as follows:

Article I: I am an American fighting man. I serve in the forces which guard my country and our way of life. I am prepared to give my life in their defense.

Article VI: I will never forget that I am an American fighting man, responsible for my actions, and dedicated to the principles which made my country free. I will trust in my God and in the United States of America.

MATURITY TRAITS

1. Total Action System

The traditional ease and smoothness of life at sixteen is in reality so evident that one can hardly believe it. Sixteen's action system has indeed come into fine form, well integrated and freely moving. No matter in what field of endeavor he is expressing himself, he approaches each experience with ease and interest. And he accepts his part with co-operation and natural enjoyment. There is a readiness about Sixteen; he himself might say, "I'm as ready as I'll ever be."

This readiness, this naturalness in his own self-expression, makes Sixteen a pleasant companion. He accepts an interview as a real-life situation which he can enjoy and profit from. He sits in a relaxed posture and carries on a nice, easy conversation. He answers freely and informatively. He holds his attention within the framework of the interview and doesn't add extraneous material which might carry the interview off on a side track as he might have done at fifteen. He mobilizes his answers with ease. No warming-up period is needed as it so often was at fifteen. Nor is there the sharp and enlivened discussion that is more common at fifteen. In contrast, Sixteen's responses are often more on the superficial side.

But Sixteen likes to be challenged and he may accept an interview in such a vein. As one 16-year-old girl remarked, "Things seem so big to you at the time, but when you're interviewed you ask yourself questions and tell yourself, 'It's a great help because you find out just where you stand.'" Though not all are as articulate as this, the majority seem to enjoy an interview situation. If the interviewer thanks Sixteen for coming in, it is Sixteen who replies, "The pleasure is all mine."

HEALTH

Many Sixteens report wonderful or excellent health. They may miss school occasionally, but it is usually not for reasons of health. Sixteen might at times feel that there are other, more important things to do than going to school—going to an exhibition, for example.

Some still may have complexion difficulties, but they will do what they can in the way of diet and skin care to improve it. And often at Sixteen the complexion does improve.

Boys seem to be very aware of their lung capacity. They recognize it as an important factor in sports, and they may relate their long- or short-windedness to their cigarette consumption. Sixteen may at times test his capacity by holding his breath; to his dismay he might find that he blacks out and faints.

TENSIONAL OUTLETS

Much of the tight tenseness of Fifteen seems to have evaporated at sixteen. But remnants of tension are still expressed in some fingernail or cuticle biting, hair twisting, or foot flapping.

The irritation and anxiety that Fifteen inspired in his parents has also largely been resolved.

VISION

Sixteen can be approached in a visual examination like an adult. His responses are more precise and he recognizes his inadequacies. The examination can be conducted at a speedier pace than earlier. Sixteen is aware of his vision and enjoys talking about it. He is curious about the tests he is given and what the examiner is seeking to find out. He smiles as he performs the visual rotations, feeling that his eyes "must look funny" as he does this.

The visual performance is now much smoother. The visual skills do not show the distortions of earlier years. Motor co-ordination is good. There is, however, some variability on the fusion tests, indicating both a more flexible and a more unstable visual mechanism.

Most Sixteens still hold onto their hyperopia $(+.50\ D)$. It is unlikely that the nearsighted boy or girl will become more nearsighted at sixteen. There is a loosening up and flexibility in the relationship between fixating and focusing abilities. Sixteen shows a facility at shifting his focus from one point to another. That he can put his eyes to work too, and not just use them casually, is shown by the appearance of some functional astigmatism, which comes and goes in the visual examination. This response, akin to a grasp-and-release response, shows the increased latitude and range so characteristic of Sixteen.

Sixteen may not be much of a reader, but he does accomplish his reading with less effort. Often, however, he is either too busy with the demands of school, of a part-time job, or of social life, to do much reading.

If Sixteen needs glasses or visual therapy, he can decide on this without parental prodding. He is ready to accept what is required.

PHYSICAL DEVELOPMENT AND SEX AWARENESS—GIRLS

Sixteen-year-old girls as a group do not show much difference from 15-year-olds. The impression of softness and fullness given by Fifteen may diminish slightly, and many girls may actually lose some weight around sixteen. But the appearance of a 16-year-old girl seems somehow more her own. The growth forces that continue to shape it over the coming years will be slower, gentler forces than the dramatic, dynamic energies that have formed it over the past six years.

The menstrual cycle is pretty regular, but may have shortened its span to three weeks in some girls, while the duration of the period may have increased in a few to as much as a week or ten days, with considerable flow. Cramps are more common in the first few days of a period. At times these can be so severe that it is necessary for a girl to go home from school or to go to bed for a while.

Sixteen assumes a more adult feeling toward this biological functioning. Many can now purchase their own sanitary napkins without embarrassment.

PHYSICAL DEVELOPMENT AND SEX AWARENESS—BOYS

Sixteen brings continuation of growth toward maturity, not so much adding new features as shaping those already acquired. There seems to be a firming of the physique, a pulling of body parts into greater synchrony. Height growth is now 98 per cent complete for the average boy; over the next few years he will gradually grow another inch and a half. Many boys, however, have stopped growing altogether, while some, maturing later, may yet add another six inches to their height. Shaving about once a week is common with many boys. Leg hair is more plentiful and chest hair sprouts in some boys.

The boys who have been interested in girls have become even more interested, and some now show less desire for the more peripheral stimulation of nude pictures or lurid literature. But some are finding it difficult to control their sex impulses, and they masturbate frequently, seek erotic stimulation in pictures, read too easily procured sex novels (leaving corners of special pages turned down). Many seem to find increasing stimulation from rhythmic sources—music, dancing, their own movements. And daydreams seem to have become an even more potent source of arousal than at fifteen.

On the whole, there is little evidence of nocturnal emissions. Many boys have not yet experienced these, and among those who have they may occur slightly less often than previously. Frequency of masturbation continues at about the level it had reached at age fifteen. Physical contacts with girls, mostly in the form of kissing and petting, are becoming increasingly common. Fourteen-year-old girls report they have "trouble" with these older boys, and 16-year-old girls become very adept at distracting

them when these boys impulsively make advances. With the kind of social freedom given to young people today, it is unfortunate that some of the boys are not yet mature and moral enough to justify this freedom. They need the self-control, the sense of responsibility, and the imagination to foresee the dangers of injudicious petting.

Boys' awareness of the other person is becoming more insightful. The number who know about menstruation in girls increases greatly during Year Sixteen. And boys' judgment of others is likewise often perceptive and accurate. They seem to be able to spot the boy who exaggerates his prowess and the one who is less interested in or less adept with girls. Those boys who don't feel comfortable in social situations with girls, or who don't wish to participate in drinking or necking parties, might decide not to attend them because of their feeling that they might be wet blankets.

2. Self-Care and Routines

EATING

The 15-year-old with a poor appetite often shows some improvement at sixteen. Sixteen is less outspoken about his dislikes. In fact, his response to food is often rather bland. He may just eat to keep himself alive or just because the food is placed before him. He doesn't think much about food until he is "at a restaurant or near a meal." But there are those Sixteens, especially boys, who have persistently good appetites. The girls are often aware of this difference in appetite between the sexes especially when they are planning and cooking a dinner for "the boys."

Sixteens have their favorites in foods. They still may refuse certain foods because of unpleasant associations, as with tongue and kidneys ("I never could face eating them"), or because of the unaccustomed taste, as with mushrooms and eggplant. But with the tempering and broadening influences that come with eating out at a variety of restaurants with congenial friends, Sixteen is beginning to spread his tastes and is giving up some of his refusals and prejudices. Italian food is an especial favorite. Chinese food is also being approached with interest. The very Sixteen who will eat little or next to nothing at home may tuck away quite a meal at a social gathering in a restaurant.

Sixteen in general has his eating in balance. He does not go to either extreme. He may eat little for breakfast but makes up for this reduction during the other two meals. If he tends to be overweight, he recognizes that he just has to cut down on certain foods without necessarily needing to diet. He feels you can train yourself to give up a momentary pleasure of eating some special food to avoid "coping with what comes afterward, which is worse."

Snacking is not a problem at Sixteen. Some snack between meals and will often choose milk in place of a soft drink. Bedtime snacking is markedly reduced. But snacking at a restaurant after a movie or a date is fairly common. And the sociability is as important as the food. Sixteen's new taste for coffee is now being expressed. Whereas at fifteen he might have asked to try half a cup, or pretend to partake by having an empty cup and saucer at his place, he now is enjoying the taste of coffee and may choose it in preference to other drinks.

Though Sixteen isn't too keen about cooking, he knows he "wouldn't starve if he were left alone with a stove." Both sexes enjoy preparing food for various social gatherings of their contemporaries. And, as one girl remarked, "If you can read, you can cook. But," she added, "there also has to be a little oomph behind it."

SLEEP

Bedtime. Sixteen's bedtime is, according to himself, "all up to me" or "my own idea." He can now be trusted with his own variability. Girls are likely to go to bed later than boys, with the time ranging from 10 to 12 P.M. More boys are ready to go earlier, even as early as nine, either because they are tired and need the sleep or because athletic rules demand it. A straggling few, mostly boys, still need to be reminded to go to bed.

Each individual seems to develop his own ways of getting ready for bed. Some like to bathe early in the evening and study later. Others like to relax with music before they bathe. With boys, shaving may become a part of the bedtime preparation. Sixteen acts like another adult in the house, going about his own business. He knows that he needs the sleep and that it's up to him to plan to get it. When he has been out late over the weekend he knows that it may take him about half a week to recuperate by adding more sleep, and so he is ready to go to bed early at the beginning of the week.

Sixteen is apt to daydream a bit before he goes off to sleep. The girls daydream about their boy friends;

while the boys, if they stay awake that long, are more likely to dream about a new car or about some ancient model that appeals to them.

Sleep. Sleep at sixteen is untroubled. Many find dreaming "a pleasure" or "very agreeable." They often realize that their dreams come from something they have done or seen. They can often relate them to what they were thinking about before they went to sleep. Boys dream of girls, and girls dream of boys, and both dream about "just usual things."

Waking. There is a casualness about Sixteen's rising in the morning. He may use his alarm clock, though he would prefer not to. He likes to set his own inner biological clock and often finds that he can awake within three or four minutes of the time he has set himself. But he has no urge to hop out of bed. He is usually half awake when it is time to be called, but he likes to experience that friendly parental gesture of being called. He likes to awaken slowly and may need to be called a second time after fifteen minutes. A very few boys still need to be poked in the ribs or have their faces washed with cold water, but unlike their younger selves they know they need this harsher treatment and even ask for it.

Seven to seven-thirty is an average rising time. But Sixteen will happily sleep till nine or ten on vacation or until eleven on weekend mornings. This is one of the ways Sixteen makes up for his lost sleep, and fortunately his mother usually becomes reconciled to it.

BATHING

A certain group of Sixteens, especially girls, has "moved into bathing daily,"

as one mother reports. But this is not true of all. There may be a lapse between baths of two or three days, or even longer during the wintertime. But cleanliness is pretty much within Sixteen's own control.

Showers are especially enjoyed. And with the heavier athletic programs for boys at school, the bathing problem is readily cared for by the daily shower after sports.

Girls take easy, regular care of their hair and fingernails. Even their toenails are now receiving extra care, with modern footgear as revealing as it is. Boys manage to get their hair cut approximately every two weeks and most are accepting the task of shaving as often as is needed. A few need to shave every night, but others can wait three or four days or more between shaves. Occasionally a father may have to remark, "How can you stand that! You've *got* to shave!" Similarly with nails, there are still those boys who will embarrass their dates by having dirty fingernails, and who will allow their toenails to grow until they "look like chicken's claws." But most 16-year-old boys are accepting these demands of personal grooming as a part of life. They may cut their nails or their hair very short so that they won't have to take care of this again for some time to come.

CLOTHING AND CARE OF ROOM

Clothes are well under Sixteen's control, both in their purchase and their care. Sixteen manages to "look the way he intends to look," even when this is a "studied casualness or dilapidated look."

Sixteen knows when he needs new clothes either because his former ones are getting too small or worn out, or because a special occasion may demand a new outfit. Sixteen is usually reasonable in his demands, and this makes it easier for his parents to co-operate. Sixteen himself says he no longer teases for clothes, the "junior high way." Often when he used to tease he knew he didn't need what he was teasing for and didn't necessarily expect to get what he wanted by these methods.

Sixteen still prefers to have a parent accompany him for big purchases. But he would prefer to shop for shoes and such things by himself. Shoes may again be taking the forefront in his clothes interests.

A certain number of boys who hold good part-time jobs are now paying for their own clothes. Girls, with their less lucrative baby-sitting jobs, can pay for only a part of their clothes at best. Sixteen is also proud to wear hand-me-downs, and girls are delighted to have a mother who can sew. Some girls are seriously ready to learn to sew for themselves.

A clothes allowance, which may have been provided at fourteen and fifteen at a daughter's insistence, has often been given up by sixteen. The daughters themselves have often found that they either spend every cent of their allowance, usually ahead of time, or worry about spending every cent. Most Sixteens prefer to pay for clothes as they need them. A few girls who are still clothes-hungry can best be controlled, however, with a clothes allowance. They need to learn that there is a limit.

Most Sixteens are able to take fair care of their clothes. Girls see that their blouses are clean and their suits pressed. Mending is becoming a part of their responsibility, especially when their mothers toss clothes back to them and say, "They're not my clothes." And with good humor Sixteen tells us, "So I have to mend them." Some boys are as good at mending as are girls. But boys aren't as good at hanging up their clothes. They are still inclined to drape them around a chair or leave them on the floor. But they agree to improve even though they forget. They are at least willing.

The care of Sixteen's room is chiefly left up to him. There are some meticulous Sixteens, especially boys. But more often it is, as one Sixteen reported, "debatable" as to whether the room is nice or not. Parents don't say too much even when they don't think Sixteen's room is neat enough. Perhaps they have become reconciled to it, but they also know that Sixteen doesn't let things go too long. The time of clean-up comes eventually, even though a mother may feel that Sixteen can stand a mess longer than she can.

MONEY

The wide variety of patterns which were being established in the handling of money at fifteen continue at sixteen. Sixteen is given a little more latitude with money. He speaks of money allotted for "free spending" or to do whatever he wishes with. A few are establishing savings bank accounts and depositing or withdrawing money as they wish. The need for more money is ever-increasing and they know the feeling of "running out" or being "stony broke." But many a Sixteen would rather stay broke and not borrow against his future allowance.

Sixteen is realizing the value of

money from a more adult point of view. He is ready to shift his plans to adjust to the family finances. He is trying not to squander it on such expendable items as sodas. There are, of course, the spenders among both sexes who have a hard time controlling their desires to purchase whatever meets their fancy. And there are those who have expensive tastes, especially for records and clothes.

Savings may mount to several hundred dollars or more, with the prized car the goal of the savings. Or the savings may be spent for the extra insurance that will allow Sixteen to drive the family car.

WORK

Sixteen is often eager and ready to take on a job, part-time during the school year and full-time during the summer months. He is capable of taking on a variety of activities, such as ushering, camp counseling, clerking in a store, or working at a gas station. Most often he enjoys the work, but sometimes it is mainly the pay that holds his interest.

Sixteen is usually fair about helping at home and may do certain chores automatically. But a number of girls are not interested in doing chores and still find that this type of demand interferes with their relationship with their mothers. Certain tasks, however, they do very well and are best with unrequested help, as at a dinner party.

3. Emotions

Even though Fifteen gave all sorts of signs of things to come at sixteen, he all too often gave them first in their negative form. He glimpsed the fu-

ture and what he wanted to become ("I know I shouldn't be so messy"), but all too often he became discouraged, lost his incentive, and expressed himself more in rebellion than in cooperation.

It is hard to know where all of these disquieting emotional forces that Fifteen expressed so obviously have gone. The growth process itself holds the secret. Something new has been added. The perspective Fifteen was seeking has now opened up. It is as though everything has become related, and thus everything seems so much simpler. It is a similar experience that any traveler has to undergo: the preparation, the taking, and the completion of his journey. The initial step of seemingly endless time and effort given to the preparation for the journey is the most arduous. The journey itself with all the possible difficulties of inconvenience and changes has its own tolls. Then comes the final step of arrival. One is there and all seems so simple. It is almost as if the stages of preparation and undertaking the journey hardly existed in the light of the arrival.

And so it is with Sixteen. He simply states that he has an "even disposition," that he has his "emotions in hand." His mother says of him that he is "very even tempered" or that "he takes things in a matter-of-fact way." He himself knows that he is more outgoing and that he has broader interests.

He is coming to know that the secret of his own happiness is involved with others. He finds he is "thinking of the other fellow." And he also knows he is cheerful when he is with other people.

Life for Sixteen does indeed "get

better as time goes on." Perhaps his grim realization at fifteen that it was all up to him, that what happened depended upon the way he did things, is now bearing fruit. Sixteen doesn't think too much about why things are better, because he's too busy enjoying living. But when asked specifically he begins to realize that the reasons are within himself. It is his own personality that is improving, that is more outgoing, that has a more mature attitude.

His happiness is very real but not exuberant. He doesn't go to extremes. "Perfectly content" describes the pervasive quality of his happiness. He has his sad moments but these are infrequent. And, as one Sixteen says, "Why be sad? Why not make the most of what you have here in life and have the most fun out of things possible?" But he also cautions, "Don't throw everything over just to be happy."

Likewise, Sixteen doesn't wish to allow anger to take over. Fortunately he "just doesn't get mad" the way he used to. He is more "surface mad," "annoyed," "impatient," or "just disappointed." Sixteen is apt to "just sort of shut up," "walk away," or "forget about it." A few less mature boys who have their anger in less good control may choose to have a good fight to get it over with. A broken arm has been known to result.

Sixteen seldom cries. Boys almost never cry. But girls are apt to cry on occasion. They might cry over a real disappointment or at those rare times when they might feel sorry for themselves. But they admit that crying doesn't really make them feel any better. A sad movie will invariably bring tears from a certain type of empathic girl, more often on the rotund side.

Sixteen is as little influenced by fear as he was at fifteen. Those few fears that he has had in the past are not as strong. His fear of heights may persist; he "kind of enjoys the feeling, but it's kind of dangerous." He may be losing his fear of snakes, but a few Sixteens are still "skitterish" when in an open field. A more common fear at sixteen is of "new social situations." Sixteen may not appear to be a very strong homebody but he can be reluctant to move too far from home base and have to meet a lot of new people.

If Sixteen worries at all it is mainly about school, about passing, about exams. But he usually qualifies any worry with "but not too much" or "but not often." He has come to realize that if he "goes along with it [whatever he is worrying about], it usually turns out all right." And, after all, any thoughtful approach to life is a form of worrying according to one Sixteen.

With Sixteen's happy-go-lucky tendencies he doesn't view life as full of problems nor does he have any big ones to cope with himself. He does have "petty annoyances," "one-day problems or not even that long," or "just one this day and one that." Afterward he can hardly recall what they were because he often laughs them off the next day. If any exist, girls' problems are more apt to be related to social, interpersonal situations, whereas boys' problems more often revolve around a car or a job.

Though Sixteen appears insensitive to the remarks of others, it is because he hides his feelings. He becomes quiet or "shuts up kind of quick." He might say something sarcastic in return or "make as wise a one back as you can." But he is more apt to keep his feelings to himself and wait until they "wear off." Sixteen can also be receptive and may even like criticism. This often moves him to improve and, as he says, to "become a better person."

This trend to cover up hurt feelings is also true of other emotions. He may not wish to expose himself ("Don't want people to think I'm too touchy"), and he also doesn't want to bother people with the way he feels. But when he's with a good friend, that is different. Girls especially "let out" their emotions to a close girl friend.

The push of incentive that was so often lacking with Fifteen is definitely present at Sixteen. It is not necessarily a competitive incentiveness, though it may be. Sixteen wants to keep up in what he is good in. The boys more often want to do well in their studies or sports. The girls are as interested in their dress and an expression of their special talents as in their school subjects. Both sexes would like to be in the first ranks, might even wish to be first or on top, but they don't think of this in terms of beating others. They "really don't care."

4. *The Growing Self*

Sixteen is indeed becoming an independent self. He no longer needs to demand liberty and independence. He has grown into them. He has acquired a "sense of independence." He can now manage his freedom. He is still a little too aware of his newfound state and wants to express his independence absolutely or at least without the help of his parents. He doesn't want any suggestions or advice from them. He thinks he can handle his own affairs and this is very

close to true. He doesn't strenuously resist his parents. He only desires that they will go their way and he will go his.

Perhaps the best way he shows his poise and his natural self-confidence is in the way he meets people. He is pleasanter with guests. He has something to say to each one. And if it is he who is the host, the ease with which he introduces his mother to his friends brings a cordiality to the atmosphere that dispels all tensions.

When asked what age he thinks is best, his satisfied response, "right about now," shows that he is meeting life as it is. He wants to take life as it comes, to flow with it, and to accept it as it turns out. This is quite a mature approach.

His readiness is strengthened by his "ability to get on with other people," which he often considers one of his most outstanding assets. Conversely, his greatest fault he may judge to be his difficulty in getting on with people. He knows that he still argues, talks too much, "blows up" at people, and speaks out too quickly before he realizes what he has said. And other assets and faults are present. On the credit side, boys recognize their intellectual and mechanical ability. And on the debit side both sexes, as at fifteen, recognize their individual lacks of personality—their forgetfulness, laziness, stubbornness, or selfishness. The head with its brain and face is most often thought to be the place where the self dwells. The brain is judged important for it is from here that the total bodily functioning stems. And the face is also deemed significant because of its individual uniqueness. But the question "Where is your self located?" doesn't make too much sense to Sixteen. He is losing the facility to answer with a fair amount of ease the way he did as a younger child. He has to think before he speaks. He recognizes this question about the seat of his self both as "funny" and "tough." It is hard for him to say, to separate any part of the body from another part. He likes to take "a broader outlook on things."

Sixteen is no more facile in making three wishes than he is in giving his idea of where the self is located. Again he finds the question tough. He has to give it some time. But with thought he can produce three wishes, even though he is fully aware that life operates on more than wishes. Yet through the expression of his wishes he tells something of what he is concerned about in life. Above all else he is concerned with himself—with the improvement of his personality, with his success in school, college, his profession, marriage, and life in general. A few may want physical possessions such as a car. Another few may wish for world peace in more specific terms than they had thought before. "If one country could trust another, this could be the main step to the well-being of the world." Some are more concerned about the well-being of others, especially their families. But in our group of 16-year-olds the wishes for Sixteen's own individual expression and happiness are far more frequent than wishes for others. This stronger self-orientation need not be selfish. Rather might it reflect the truer realization of self at this age, which allows the individual to be more ready to act as a participant in life's experiences.

This new awareness of self helps Sixteen to realize that this is no time to choose a profession. He knows he must first "wait and see how things will turn out." He knows there are many possibilities and he knows he has gone through many changes within his own mind over the past few years. Some Sixteens are thinking within certain related lines such as journalism, advertising, insurance, and law. Others range from politics, to business, to farming. As one girl reported, she had a new idea every week. Time is in flux and fortunately Sixteen is ready to "wait and see."

Going to college is more certain in Sixteen's mind, but where is quite uncertain. There is a trend away from the choice of coeducational colleges in our group. Sixteen may consider two or three possible colleges at one time. Boys are more concerned about the financial aspect of going to college and may desire to try out for scholarships. They are also thinking about graduate study.

But it is marriage that more concerns girls. Some recognize that marriage may come before they finish college. In general they would prefer to marry after college or even after a short work experience. If something happens to their husband they may then have "something to fall back on." A fair number wish to combine some work with marriage for they "don't like the idea of sitting home doing nothing." Girls are also quite positive about their thought of children. Three is the number most often desired.

The boys on the other hand aren't so positively oriented toward marriage. They "don't think too much about it," they are "probably going to get married," but this "will happen later." The thought of military service is already beginning to usurp his thoughts so that at times he thinks of neither college, profession, nor marriage.

The girls are also concerned about military service for their possible future mates. But this does not interrupt their thoughts about what they would desire in a future mate. Love as a basis for marriage is less emphasized. Maybe it is taken for granted. Looks are also less considered. In fact, too good looks may count against a possible future candidate, since the girls are now relating boredom and faithlessness to a boy's good looks. Intelligence is important but not just knowledge. He should have "a sense of judgment" or "scope of knowledge." "Easy to get along with, friendly, social, understanding" would be added attractions. And a new important facet might be that "he knows where he is going" and that "he's capable of getting there." "Pretty steady and faithful" along with being a good father and provider shows that a 16-year-old girl has some idea of the basis of a good marriage. She is not approaching marriage blindly.

Boys, alas, haven't given their future potential mates as much thought. In fact, they seem to be giving them less thought as a partner than they have previously. But times will change and they will give more time and effort to the thought of marriage and their possible spouse.

5. *Interpersonal Relationships*

Though Sixteen usually gets on quite well with his family, he hasn't returned to his earlier active, participating state. He likes his home as a setting for his activities, but he doesn't necessarily feel responsible for this setting. He seems "remote from his family in a happy way," for he is often "lost in his friends and their activities." He is, however, grateful for the freedom he is given and is quite capable of accepting certain restrictions imposed upon him, especially in relation to the hour of returning home from a date. If he is away at school, he may find that he writes letters more frequently than he did and that he looks forward to hearing news about home.

Both sons and daughters get on quite well with their mothers with little or no friction. They recognize that she has an understanding, reasonable, and even sympathetic attitude toward them and their friends. But they like to hold their distance, to go their "own way." They recognize it's "a motherly way to be into everything," and that "mothers tend to be curious and ask a lot of questions," especially about their friends. Some mothers may even wish to continue to open Sixteen's mail, though most would not have done so at any age. Sixteen recognizes these "motherly" feelings as natural, but he is rather frank in letting his mother know how he feels and that he does wish to live his own life in his own way. He does not wish to receive direct advice, and "even suggestions are not good," according to Sixteen. It is not easy for some mothers and also some fathers to give up their position of protection, of advice as well as of authority. But they as parents do concede that Sixteen has a "good sense of independence." The wise parent is at least willing to put Sixteen to the test. And Sixteen is then more apt to return to his parents (especially to his mother) for advice and talking things over. He comes more as an equal and he shows his maturity by his poise and lack of excitement. And Sixteen does recognize that some of the seemingly "cruel" restrictions that his parents have previously put upon him were necessary. He realizes that even now he "can't do everything."

Sixteen tends to think of his father and mother together and often refers to them as "they." A daughter, however, often thinks of her father as "someone to cope with." She is aware if he is tired or if he would be disturbed by certain revelations. Both daughters and sons tend to see their father in a truer light and accept him more as he is. They are more apt to kid around with their fathers than with their mothers. Nevertheless, Sixteen watches his step with his father; he uses techniques. A daughter may purposely keep the fact that she is going out with a boy of a different religious faith from her father because she knows it will be disquieting to him. But Sixteen also feels freer to speak up to his father as he hasn't before. Conflicting principles may be aired. Fortunately, fathers, though they may still hold a very strict rein and feel the need of lecturing their offspring at times, are not usually provoked into open conflict with their sons or daughters.

Even the hours of returning home at night do not produce the difficulties they have at fourteen and fifteen. Sixteen may come in pretty late, but his parents are less apt to worry. They know roughly when he will return home—usually somewhere between midnight and 2 A.M., depending on the circumstances. And, feeling no pressure now, he may sometimes go to an early movie and come directly home afterward without having to stop for a snack.

The steady improvement in Sixteen's relationship with his younger siblings also eases this earlier point of conflict. Part of this improvement is because he sees less of his siblings. But he does enjoy their admiration. And at times he seems able to take on the more understanding parental role as he comments about a younger brother, "He's a little hard for all of us to manage." He might even out-mother his mother by saying, "Now listen, Mother, don't push Kate. She'll come along all right."

His relations with his older siblings are as good or better than they were. He would most probably consult an older sibling for advice. When they are together, their ease of give-and-take and interesting conversation reveals them as the adults which they really have become.

Both boys and girls seem to have plenty of friends. There always seems to be "one or more you can depend on." Girls are more apt to go around with a number of different groups than are boys. They like to keep up with their old friends as well as their new ones. They often speak of having a "bunch." Both sexes enjoy having the close relationship of a friend of their own sex. Boys are becoming more interested in sharing ideas and decisions with their friends as well as sharing in activities with them. Girls report that it is "just as much fun with girls as with boys, but both are important." With other girls they enjoy "talking, driving, shopping." And in their conversations they "go into everything, not just boys and clothes. But into politics and ideas, too."

Girls actually do not think of boys

all the time, as they sometimes did when they were younger. They like to date a "whole lot of different boys, some that you like more than others, some you like quite a lot, but nobody special." A 16-year-old girl's attitude toward a boy is "usually one of definite cordiality," but it mightn't matter if she never saw him again. Above all else she doesn't wish to go steady, to narrow herself down. She even enjoys a blind date now and then. Quite often she finds that a boy is more of a friend, someone she can talk to, who understands her and not one that she feels romantic about. She may even refer to her friendship with a boy as "platonic."

This is indeed a shift from Fourteen's absorption in the opposite sex or Fifteen's amorousness. Sixteen may knit argyle socks for a boy friend, she may kiss him goodnight, but her interest is often a sociable rather than a romantic one. And if he shows "a warming up," and gives signs of being excited, then she knows it's time to "brush him off."

The boys, like the girls, also want to "play the field" with the opposite sex. They find there are plenty of girls and they often date three or four different ones. They also generally do not wish to "go steady," especially if they have tried it when they were younger and found that it didn't work. They don't like that feeling of being "tied down." But they are surprised at times to see how fickle the girls are and how they "change just like that."

A number of the boys only meet the girls at dances. These gatherings seem to crop up fairly naturally either through the school or other organized groups such as church or Y. Girls favor dancing more than the boys.

But Sixteen, like Fifteen, likes the informality of a high school canteen to meet in. He also likes to go to the homes of his friends. Girls are most often the hostesses. Sixteens like the ease and casualness of the home, the drifting into the kitchen. And they especially like a gathering when it turns into a "good rip-roaring party with lots of people, with dancing, and singing in one corner and really good fellowship where everybody knows everybody else."

6. Activities and Interests

It is the enjoyment of his activities that distinguishes Sixteen. He is interested in the "here and now," the job to be done today. He isn't spending his time and energy resisting and rebelling the way he did at fifteen. His interests and activities are more within an adult pattern and have a natural place in his life. And in general he seems quite capable of going his way and doing what is significant to him.

Most of the sports interests he had at fifteen are being carried over into sixteen. The boys in competitive group sports are taking their positions and ability to play the game seriously. Tennis players may have groomed themselves well enough to enter tournaments. Those interested in sailing may enjoy the competitive aspects of the sport, but this makes them view their sailing skill even more objectively. They are interested in finding out what they did right and what they did wrong.

Though some girls are continuing to enjoy individual sports, and a few continue to love baseball, an ever-increasing proportion are doing less and less in sports. Some girls even seem proud of their lack of muscles and strength.

But boys, on the other hand, want to express their strength, to develop their muscles. They enjoy such strenuous jobs as cutting down trees and chopping wood. They want real jobs and they are now fortunately old enough to apply for them. There are multiple possibilities, according to a boy's special interests: he may be a clerk in a grocery store, an usher at a movie house, an assistant at a filling station, a clerk in a record shop, a mechanic in a radio shop. Many boys are able to arrange for these jobs part-time. Sometimes it would be fortunate if the school could arrange to release them for a half-time job. But in the summer many a Sixteen's whole life is planned around a full-time job, for which he is not only ready but eager.

Jobs are not as important to girls as to boys, although summer jobs are also sought after by girls. It is the social life, the life of "people and ideas," that is so important to girls. Just to be "out with people, to talk, to take a walk, to go for a drive" fills a large sector of their lives. Girls are very frank in their statement that, "A group of people who can't enjoy just doing nothing is no good." And there is nothing like a good party of friends to most 16-year-old girls.

The disadvantages of being without a driver's license have now in many instances been surmounted, so that complications of transportation are less frequent. However, other questions as to the fitness of Sixteen to drive, apart from his age, are now having to be considered and faced both by parents and by Sixteens themselves. Fortunately, there is a trend back into the home, a greater desire by the group to congregate there, and this brings easier, more natural controls.

SEDENTARY LOOKING AND LISTENING ACTIVITIES

Both radio listening and TV watching continue to fall off in many at sixteen. Sixteens do like to hear familiar music, whether it is classical or popular. Though some still wish to have the radio on as they study, others find that they become either too involved in their studies or in the music to take in both at once. Television is more consistently watched by boys, especially news programs. And sports events, including boxing matches, hold the male attention. But television otherwise is not a favorite pastime.

Music is most enjoyed through records. Many Sixteens have built up quite a collection of their own, and are now becoming interested in collector's items, perhaps including jazz of the 1920's. Sixteen might even baby-sit free in a home where he could listen to a good collection of jazz records.

Sixteen would be quite a reader if he had time. He feels awfully lucky if he can manage the time, but all too often something else has to be sacrificed and it is too often to the detriment of his studies. But, he tells us, if he had the time he'd read all sorts of books like *War and Peace, Anna Karenina, Pride and Prejudice, Tess of the D'Urbervilles, Of Human Bondage,* and all sorts of other books that he would like to think about and discuss.

There is time for magazines. And boys automatically find time to read certain technical magazines quite thoroughly. They are also better than girls at keeping up with the news through the newspaper.

Movies are of even less interest than they were at fifteen. Sixteen "takes them or leaves them" and may go only because it's something to do with the gang. He has no incentive to see a movie a second time. But he is interested in the theater and will juggle his funds to purchase a ticket. He is beginning to enjoy the fun of analyzing plays. And he recognizes a difference when he contrasts the reality of the stage and his feeling as a part of an audience with the separation and lack of vitality of the movies.

7. *School Life*

The integrating forces working within Sixteen can make him both a responsive and an interesting person to teach. He often speaks of his junior year as being "better than last year." And he also reports that he is getting a lot out of school.

This is the age when it becomes more evident in what direction he is heading. Those who are interested in college are now ready to buckle down to show that they can do the work, that they can grasp a subject and achieve well in it. Those who are drawn toward the more active, practical direction desire training in specific techniques of commercial or skilled trades. If this has not been available already, some may be ready to drop out and go their own way. There are other groups with less defined goals. One of these groups includes the slower maturers, mostly boys, who are not achieving very well but who wish to hold within the standard academic course. These students need to be given encourage-

ment, recognition of what they have done well, and, above all, time for growing. They may need special opportunity for expression in the arts or sciences or whatever the field is in which they function best.

The diversity of goals and of pathways toward them chosen by different Sixteens makes further account all but impossible within this compass. Our inability even to try to "encapsulate" the school activities of Sixteen is in itself significant. It reflects both the rich range of individual differences at this level of near adulthood and the multiformity of programs offered by school systems to meet this variety of goals and needs.

8. *Ethical Sense*

Sixteen's ethical sense is more flexible and at the same time more stable, and is fairly easy for him either to formulate or put to use. On the whole he can "usually tell" what is right and what is wrong, and boys, as earlier, feel they know "instinctively" or "automatically." Sixteen seems a little surprised to realize that his ideas are about like his parents'. As one boy sums it up, "I haven't found anything yet that was adverse to my parents' teaching." Or another says, "We go along together very well." But it is still important for Sixteen to determine what is right or wrong by what *he thinks,* by how it would relate *to him personally.* He recognizes that there are codes and principles laid down by parents and church, but what is important to him is how he "follows these from there."

Sometimes what he thought was right might turn out to be wrong afterward. Or if he is not sure and is without a strong opinion, he might be swayed by the crowd or his friends without necessarily making the best choice. But on the whole he does what he thinks, and he proves himself to be right "most of the time."

Though Sixteen says his conscience would bother him if he did a "big" wrong, he doesn't have many specific circumstances of wrongdoing to report. Similarly, he is pretty general about the truth and is undoubtedly quite truthful. In fact, he might be at times a little too truthful, a little too frank and open. Fortunately, both his parents and his friends seem able to take his remarks about their personalities or their acts. But Sixteen doesn't seem very inhibited or overly sensitive in what he says.

Sixteens are also frank in discussing their privileges with their parents. At times, these discussions can become rather heated, even though they are held in the realm of a "good healthy dispute." But Sixteen may say, "If I keep their [his parents'] point of view in line with mine, our qualms usually work out of their own accord."

The realms of smoking, swearing, and drinking seem to be on fairly even keel. There is at least little dispute about them. A number of Sixteens who have previously smoked have given it up. But there are the adamant smokers, few in number, who appear to be definitely entrenched in the habit. And they probably will be unless some strong force such as a future love affair should lift them out. Swearing isn't a problem. It is more an individual affair. Drinking alcoholic beverages has not entered the problem zone with the group of Sixteens we are reporting about. Boys report more drinking than girls but

they tend to limit themselves to beer. A few girls report that they might drink "just to be polite." Boys are apt to restrict themselves to soft drinks when they are at a party with younger girls. The girls unfortunately run into difficulty with the older boys (17- and 18-year-olds) who may insist on having hard liquor at parties. These older boys who drink too much may lose the respect of the girls who would be more tolerant "if they just got drunk alone with the boys." But even with this complication the driver of a car often recognizes that he is one who cannot drink.

Cheating is not a problem at sixteen. Often the questions asked on an examination don't lend themselves to cheating. And, as one boy warns, "Cheating isn't you, so why bother? What good is it going to do you?" Though stealing is not a problem, Sixteen may be concerned about the borrowed money that isn't returned. He recognizes that these debts may not be forgotten but are just not paid back. Sixteen would be a good age to put before discussion this seeming carelessness with funds. Is this seeming forgetfulness in the return of borrowed funds a subtle form of stealing? How can it be faced and curbed? Sixteen would bring his frankness to such a discussion and also a wisdom that is the intrinsic mark of his age.

9. Philosophic Outlook

TIME AND SPACE

Sixteen does not try to pinpoint his concept of time as much as he did at fifteen. His intervals include both a beginning and an end ("interval between one occasion and another" or "the span that elapses between events"). He sees relationships. As at fifteen he thinks of time as a measurement or a way of recording ("the measurement of the order of events" or "the way of recording events in a period").

But Sixteen lives in the present and looks to the future. His time concepts express his inner state ("days as they go by"; "moving onward of things, going forward"). Some are more inclusive in thinking, as "the passing of generations—people and events, happenings," or "the dimension through which we move from birth to death."

Sixteen lives well and fully in the present. He says he "likes to live right where I am." He likes the day-by-day occurrences of life. He looks to the near future and wonders "how the future will turn out," but this does not prevent him from living richly in the present.

The handling of time is pretty much an individual matter, but on the whole Sixteen is usually on time. He likes to strike a happy medium. He is now becoming aware of other people's sense of time and shifts his own manipulation of time to gibe with theirs.

As with time, Sixteen doesn't pin down space as he did at fifteen. Space also has its two sides ("distance between two things," or "interval between two points"). But it is the larger unknown concept of space that intrigues Sixteen. He speaks of "a limitless vacuum" or "a tremendous expanse of absolutely nothing."

Though space is empty and full of nothing, he projects his own human self into it as "loneliness" or he stresses the fact that it is "something you can't see or feel." Or he conceives of space as having "the power to have something in it." Space, like time, is something through which we move. But it is a kind of location dimension. It tells us "where the world and things are located."

DEATH AND DEITY

Sixteen may be influenced by the commonly accepted notions about heaven and hell, or it may be that this concept is congenial to his own thought process. But, in any case, he more often believes in a realm for afterlife than did Fifteen. He may simply think that the good go to heaven and the bad to hell. Or he may think that the heaven-bound individuals are those who are sorry for their sins, and the hell-bound ones are not sorry. But these "two conditions of afterlife, one for the good and one for the bad," may not necessarily be related to a place to go. It may even be "the state you are living in, an awful life is hell and a good life is heaven."

There are those who don't know, who haven't given the problem of death much thought, or who really aren't particularly interested in it. Others feel that nothing happens, nothing more than an endless sleep.

But even though Sixteen may not be too sure about his thoughts, his musings somehow do often lead him into believing that a person goes into another world after death. This world may be a testing ground, may influence what happens to him in the next world; or, on the other hand, it may not exert much influence. Some think that life after death would be a "better, simpler, nicer life." Others may conceive of "starting all over again—sort of peaceful and quiet, like before you were born." "When you are born again," according to one 16-year-old girl, "you completely forget the past."

Sixteen is more likely to have experienced the death of friends or relatives than when he was younger. He merely becomes very quiet when older relatives die, but may become stunned and deeply affected when a friend or contemporary dies. He wishes that people he knows wouldn't die.

Though some Sixteens don't have a concept of God that satisfies them or can't grasp or figure out what God is, others are finding their way into their own religious reality. Though a few think of God as a "person or figure," the majority state that they don't think he is really a man or in human form. Some think of him as spirit, but others think of him as "neither man nor spirit." He has become more of a guiding ruler, a supreme being, a force, a power, or just a feeling. Unlike Fifteen, Sixteen does not wish to pin down his ideas for, as he says, "If I had a definite concept He wouldn't be a Deity." He does know that you can't have a picture of God, nor can you see Him. But this makes God no less real to him. An occasional Sixteen feels that "God at times is there, nearby." But this belief in God does not necessarily mean that God is an influence on Sixteen's life. God does influence "at times," "to some extent," or, "He could when you need Him," but Sixteen has not yet built up a strong continuity of religious feeling within himself.

Part Three

❦

MATURITY TRENDS
AND GROWTH GRADIENTS

CHAPTER ELEVEN

Total Action System

THE FOREGOING chapters have described the maturity traits which characterize seven successive age zones. We are now in a position to take an over-all view of these traits and to examine their trends. This should yield some added insight into the directions and the goals of adolescent development.

Genes and Growth

In the following chapters we shall be chiefly concerned with the *sequences* of development and the gradations of growth. There are wide individual variations as to the precise time of emergence of specific maturity traits, but the *order of emergence* is governed by the mechanisms of maturation and is less subject to variability. Maturation represents the net sum of the gene effects operating in a cycle of growth. Genes are molecules which multiply by duplicating themselves. They are the chemical agents which initiate and direct the drama of development in its basic aspects.

Like other organisms, the human individual develops as a unit. Growth begins with a single fertilized egg cell, which contains some 30,000 inherited genes. The cell divides and gives rise to two cells which in turn divide. This happens time and time again, until the ultimate adult organism attains its full quota of some 26,000,000,000 cells. Each new growing cell contains a full set of genes, thousands of them.

The genes accordingly are distributed like a leaven throughout the growing organism. They are the sources of directive and constructive energy, during the whole cycle of growth from conception to maturity. They transmit countless hereditary traits, physical and functional, such as eye color, varieties of temperament, musical talent, blood group types, body types, etc. In conjunction with associated factors, genes determine the ground plan and the basic sequences of development in embryo, fetus, infant, child, and youth.

Microscopic sections of the embryo show its cells to be arranged in three germinal layers from which all tissues and organs are derived: the *ectoderm,* the *endoderm,* and the *mesoderm.* The mesoderm gives rise to the skeleton and muscles. Long before birth the infant-to-be is already equipped with a full complement of some six hundred pairs of muscles, including about forty-seven which are visceral. The endoderm gives rise to mouth, pharynx, and gastrointestinal tract; the ectoderm to skin and nervous system.

It is a remarkable fact that the 5-month-old fetus is already in possession of the full quota of twelve or more billions of nerve cells (neurons). This includes the cells of the brain cortex which later assume functions of perception, memory, and thinking. Also included are the rich networks of the autonomic nervous system which regulate metabolic, hormone, and temperature controls; secretions and excretions; cardiovascular, genito-urinary, and gastrointestinal functions, and also the cycles of activity, hunger, sleep, and sex.

Growth is a patterning process: Step by step it jointly organizes both structures and functions, and builds up an integrated *action system* directed toward immediate and distant goals. The demands upon the organism are peculiarly insistent during the years of adolescence.

The term action system is a serviceable one because it can be used flexibly to designate either structural or functional factors. It denotes the total organism as a going concern, particularly its propensities, its potentials, and behavior patterns.

The human action system is fearfully and wonderfully made. It took aeons of evolutionary time to bring it to its present level of complexity. From the standpoint of embryology we cannot readily separate structure from function nor body from mind. "Psyche" and "soma" are interdependent; each influences the other. The mind is not a separate indwelling entity nor a superadded agency. It is part and parcel of a unitary action system, which grows.

The growth characteristics of the adolescent action system are naturally significant. They reflect both the biological pressures of the species and the assertiveness of the individual. The developmental manifestations are legion.

By referring these manifestations to an actual, unitary system, we are better able to visualize the integrating nature of the growth process. At all levels of maturity the organism preserves its wholeness, and body and mind remain inseparable. We shall consider the role of the action system in two important fields of maturation, namely (a) Physical Growth and Sex Development, (b) The Developmental Aspect of Vision.

Physical Growth and Sex Development

Adolescence is pre-eminently a period of rapid and intense physical growth accompanied by profound changes which involve the entire economy of the organism. There are wide individual variations in the timing and degree of these changes; but the sequential order in which they occur is relatively consistent in both sexes. The individual tends to remain true to his genetic constitution, basically determined by genes. Even the hormones which play an elaborate role do not actually initiate metabolic transformations; they simply alter the rate at which changes occur. The cellular reactions are intrinsic to the cells themselves.

During the years from five to ten the rate of anatomic and physiological change is relatively gradual. Increase in stature advances on a gently rising plateau, but soon there is a marked spurt of height in girls (age ten to eleven) and later in boys (age twelve to thirteen). This spurt is closely related to the onset of pubescence and the endocrine regulation of genital structures and functions. The menarche (first menstruation) usually occurs in the twelve to thirteen age range. The first ejaculation (seminal emission) generally occurs in the thirteen to fourteen age range.

The entire organism is involved in extensive changes, including the following: increased food cravings and intake; increase in muscular energy, with a doubling of strength for the years from ten to sixteen; increase of puberal fat; changes in body conformation (widening of pelvis in girls, broadening of shoulders in boys); changes in physiognomy based on acceleration of the growth of the upper segments of the face; rise in blood pressure; quickening of heartbeat and breathing, followed later by slowing down and increased steadiness; voice changes; neural and biochemical changes manifested in heightened activity of sebaceous and sweat glands; increased susceptibility to acne and other skin reactions (pimples, pustules, blackheads, blotches).

Many of the physical changes of adolescence are so sudden and conspicuous that boys and girls alike become acutely aware of them. Although in earlier years a youth was quite careless about personal appearance, he now begins to visualize himself with and without the aid of a mirror. He projects into the future: "Will I always be too tall," "too short," "too fat," or "so skinny and so gawky?" "And what about that nose?" These are keen worries and call for sympathetic understanding. Fortunately in some matters of body size and disproportions the growth trends are predictably favorable and offer grounds for reassurance. The self is somatic as well as psychological. In its ego feelings we have ample evidence that mind and body are two facets of a unitary growth process.

To the physical growth symptoms already mentioned we might add a formidable list of tensional outlets. The outlets tend to vary in intensity and pattern at different age levels as follows: general bodily overflow, stamping, sniffing and grimacing at eleven; jiggling at twelve; scalp scratching at thirteen; pressurized fidgeting, cuticle picking, and knuckle snapping at fifteen. These tensional outlets usually prove to be temporary. They may be related to fatigue, or even to some ticlike behavior in childhood. Most of them are relatively benign unless they are linked with deep-seated emotional complications.

The criterion of healthy behavior is developmental. Behavior is normal if it promotes optimal development. Any type of behavior is abnormal if it becomes so extreme and detached that it prejudices the harmonious development of the total action system. This is especially true of those tensional outlets which have a sexual origin and may be carried to excess. No broad, permissive generalizations can be made concerning such outlets, including masturbation and its allied manifestations. The long-range personality factors always need careful consideration. Only candid knowledge and wise counseling can forestall unfounded anxiety, corroding guilt, and misinformation.

But the problems of sex education are basically cultural. They go far beyond instruction in the anatomy and physiology of puberty and reproduction. Puberty is a physical state—the earliest age of being capable of begetting or bearing offspring. The age is commonly designated legally as fourteen for boys and twelve for girls. In the period from eleven to fourteen the physical manifestations of sex may cause much concern, confusion, and uncertainty. First of all the concrete sex problems of the individual must be managed realistically in terms of authentic information and of personal hygiene. Youth, however, needs orientation as well as factual knowledge; he needs to develop increasingly mature and respectful attitudes toward the opposite sex; he needs to acquire a code of morality in all of his interpersonal relationships. By the age of fifteen, a youth begins to realize this rather clearly. Much depends upon his later judgment and self-control and the expectations of the culture in which he lives.

Does he sufficiently comprehend these expectations? He learns much from his own observations and from his social experiences in school and community. But he encounters many conflicting suggestions which produce confusions in his thinking and in his search for models and ideals. In the growing complexities of the contemporary culture youth is handicapped for lack of a more formal introduction to the meaning of marriage, the rearing of children, and the goals of family living. These are ultimate verities for the adolescents who in a few short years are destined to become parents.

A broadly conceived program of pre-parental education would protect important patterns of the culture and assist the individual to realize the wholesome potentials of a growing action system.

The Developmental Aspect of Vision *

Vision is a complex sensory-motor response to a light stimulus mediated by the eyes, yet it involves the whole action system. The development of vision in infancy, childhood, and youth is complex for the simple reason that it took countless ages of evolution to bring human vision to its present advanced state. Visual perception now ranks with speech as a distinctive human trait and it passes through comparable stages of growth. Vision, like sex, is not a separate isolated function; it is profoundly integrated with the total action system.

It could scarcely be otherwise, because vision has been the supreme sense in insuring the survival of man and promoting his intellectual and technological progress. All this is reflected in the elaborate anatomy of the visual apparatus, which links the muscles and the retina of the seeing eye to the vast networks of the somatic and autonomic nervous systems. Billions of neurons in the cortex of the brain engender and organize the photo-chemical energies which issue in vision. We see not with our eyes, but with our total action system.

* See also Gesell, A. (with C. S. Amatruda). *The Embryology of Behavior.* New York: Harper, 1945, pp. 289.

Gesell, A., Ilg, F. L., Bullis, G. E. *Vision: Its Development in Infant and Child.* New York: Hoeber, 1949, pp. 329.

This system is still undergoing active visual developments in the years from ten to sixteen. The developments involve three distinguishable components of the visual mechanism, namely, fixation, focus, and "fusion," which are correlated with the three germinal layers (mesoderm, endoderm, ectoderm) previously mentioned (page 278).

Arranged in hierarchical order, the major functional components fall into sequence as follows:

(a) The skeletal component (fixation) *seeks and holds* an image.

(b) The visceral component (focus) *discriminates and defines* the image.

(c) The cortical component (fusion, identification, and synthesis) *unifies and interprets* the image.

These major functions are interdependent; they develop conjointly, but not at uniform rates. Visual organization is so complex that there is a great deal of shifting and intermeshing of dominances at progressive stages. For example: (a) The 12-week-old infant stops his moving arm and looks at his hand (fixation); (b) at 24 weeks he focuses regard on a tiny sugar pellet; (c) at 40 weeks he identifies the pellet, plucks it and eats it.

Comparable though more subtle changes in visual behavior patterns occur during adolescence. At ten years the skeletal component (fixation) is relatively dominant; at eleven the visceral component (focus). At twelve years the two functions are in more even balance. At the thirteen-year level there is increased activity in the focusing field. At the fourteen-year level there is a steady improvement in the interplay of the two functions of fixation and focus. Such an improvement illustrates the developmental logic of the principle of reciprocal interweaving, which has to do with the intermeshing and modulation of two interdependent but opposing functions. This principle pervades the organization of the total action system in numerous areas of structure and function.

Fourteen is a favorable age period for appraising visual competence if there are untoward signs. Fourteen is interested in his own needs and cooperates well in any training program. Visual fatigue is a fairly common symptom at fifteen, but it is not necessarily due to any visual maldevelopment or reading difficulty. Ordinarily the visual skills are well organized and efficient for near tasks.

By Year Sixteen reading requires less effort. Visual performance is smoother, and begins to resemble that of the adult. There is a loosening with increased flexibility and interplay of the functions of fixation, focus, and fusion. This is shown in functional tests of eye following, mobility of accommodation, ocular pickup, convergence, associated postural and prehensive response, and visual adjustments to far, near, and intermediate space as registered by the retinal reflex.

The science of developmental optics is concerned with the growth and the organization of visual functions in their dynamic relations to the total action system. Developmental visual care goes beyond the symptoms of acuity and of refractive errors. It considers the whole child—his developmental maturity, the diagnostic import of his behavior patterns and behavior needs. Our studies have shown that the years from five to ten are especially significant from the standpoint of the early detection and developmental management of visual deviations and inadequacies.

There is another developmental aspect of vision which goes beyond the protection of visual competence. It has to do with the enrichment, the enjoyment, and the creative expression of visual experience. Such experiences lie within the scope of education, and also of self-development, for they are based on the higher growth potentials of the action system.

Consciously and unconsciously, visual behavior takes on new meaning in the ardent years of adolescence. There is a heightened intensity and receptivity in visual perception. The "eyes," because of the maturing brain cortex, are now more sensitive to color, to design, and to the dynamic balance of spatial relationships and configurations.

Vision thus proves to be a pivotal stimulus to the aesthetic sense of a youth. He becomes aware of the impressions of nature, and of beauty and ugliness in the works of man. This capacity to seek and to perceive beauty is an important feature of the process of growing up. It is a noteworthy sign of increasing maturity.

The aesthetic sense is closely allied to the ethical. It awakens new tensions of a very salutary nature. The youth feels a desire to do something creative. He finds a tensional outlet in the realm of graphic and plastic arts and crafts. He draws, paints, models, carves, builds, and contrives—manipulating with fresh visual awareness of relationships of space, shape, and dimension. He gains in confidence and self-reliance.

A youth should be generously provided with such creative outlets to safeguard his best potentials, to stabilize his growth, and to grant him the reassurance to which he is entitled. The culture might also profit thereby.

GROWTH GRADIENTS

1. PHYSICAL GROWTH

10 YEARS

Girls. Girls are of about same average height as boys but are growing faster. Most just about to start period of accelerated height growth.

Slight rounding of form, softening of features. Adipose tissue increases over hips, chest. Face and chin appear fuller, even in slimmer girls, when standardized photos of same girl at nine and ten are compared.

During Year Ten, slight projection of nipples, some light, downy pubic hair appear in many girls.

Boys. Average height same as that of average girl, but a smaller proportion of adult height has been achieved.

Though physiques differ widely, comparison with standardized photos of same boy at nine shows a more solid physique at ten, rounding of contours, especially around chin, neck, chest. (Not necessarily reflected in weight.)

No traces of sexual maturing, except in very small proportion of boys.

11 YEARS

Girls. Striking individual differences apparent, especially when slow- and fast-developing girls are compared: some still have childish body form, no trace of sexual maturity features; some are quite advanced into adolescence.

Middle group of girls, during this year, develops some pubic hair. Elevation of area surrounding nipple gives conelike projection on flat chest. Pelvic area broadens and fatty tissue is added, especially at upper and lower corners (classic feminine "vase shape").

Most girls have started spurt in height growth; some have reached apex of spurt. Average girl has achieved about 90 per cent of mature stature, closer to 50 per cent of weight for age twenty-one.

Boys. A more uniform group than girls, because few show signs of sexual maturation, and those who have started their growth spurt (about a quarter) are mostly not far enough along to show marked changes. A few do show some genital enlargement. Some have become quite tall, though these were tall to begin with. The average boy has achieved a little more than 80 per cent of mature height, less than 50 per cent of what he will weigh at twenty-one.

A "fat period" appears in some boys—a general padding of fatty tissue, especially in the hip region and around the nipples. This fat period starts to decline as the spurt in height growth increases, and is usually ended by age fourteen.

A feature striking in many Elevens, when 10- and 11-year-old growth photos are compared, is apparent increase in bone structure—a heavy growth of bone which brings skeletal structure into prominence, especially in chest area.

12 YEARS

Girls. For the middle group of girls, this is the period of fastest growth in height and weight. Height spurt usually comes slightly sooner and stronger than that in weight. With body mass stretched out more, many girls look less chunky than they did at eleven. The girls' greatest gain in strength also occurs at twelve and a half—about two years before the boys' greatest gain.

During Year Twelve the breasts begin to fill out, the nipples darken. Often some underarm hair develops. Menarche tends to occur most often toward the end of this year or the beginning of the next.

Boys. More differences appear within a group of 12-year-olds than among Tens or Elevens. The advanced boys are quite advanced; the immature ones show little change since eleven. As well as marked differences between individuals, differences within individuals are also striking. Though the middle group of boys now shows definite traces of beginning puberty, boys show this in different ways. Increased growth of genitalia may become noticeable, long downy pubic hair may develop near the base of the penis, or both may occur. Within the individual physique, some parts seem more, some less mature.

The prepubescent fat period is advanced in some boys, just beginning in others, and in still others will not appear at all.

13 YEARS

Girls. Growth is starting to slow down in many. Thirteen seems more a period of continued ripening than of sudden changes. Height and weight continue to increase, but at a somewhat slower rate. There appears a filling out of hollows in many girls; the hips particularly may appear smoother as the dip between the outer crests fills in. The filling in is most apparent in trunk and legs, while face, neck, and shoulders may actually appear slimmer than earlier.

Most girls who have not already menstruated reach menarche during this year, though some perfectly healthy girls do not until fourteen or even later.

Boys. The physical maturity features which made their first appearance at twelve become more definite at thirteen. Pubic hair with some pigmentation has appeared in a majority of boys; for the middle group, this is a period of rapid genital growth. The voice deepens perceptibly in many, cracks in some.

By the end of Year Thirteen, about half the boys have reached their fastest rate of height growth, and will thereafter start growing more slowly. First ejaculation usually occurs at roughly the same time as the peak in growth. A number of boys develop breast knots or tenderness of the nipples, usually lasting only a few weeks.

14 YEARS

Girls. Though many girls have not yet reached this stage, Fourteen's body form typically seems more similar to that of a young woman than that of a child. Height growth is nearly completed during this year, and weight growth has slowed down, though it will continue for many years.

Secondary sex characteristics are now quite mature: the breasts are near full adult size, pubic hair is full and dense.

Despite the feminine softening, the physique often gives an impression of strength; features seem stronger and more defined.

Boys. Thirteen, despite developing maturity features, looks like a boy; Fifteen looks more like a man. Fourteen years typically is a transition zone.

Size increase is marked. From thirteen and a half through fourteen is the period of most rapid height growth for the largest number of boys. The pubescent fat period, in boys who showed this earlier, is generally finished, and the physique appears more heavily muscled. Measured strength is actually nearly twice that of age ten.

Facial features are strengthened, body hair is more developed, with pubic hair denser and darker, hair on forearms and calves heavier, and sideburns elongating. Marked increase in underarm perspiration. By the end of Year Fourteen most boys have experienced ejaculation. Voice is often noticeably deeper.

15 YEARS

Girls. Few new features of maturity appear, but features which appeared earlier are brought to fuller development. Fullness almost seems to overshoot the mark with some girls; rounding of form continues almost to the point of lushness. A change in direction of development may appear in these girls in following years, with some slimming down of the physique.

Boys. Though still far from mature, Fifteen's physique is more like that of a man than like that of a boy. Height growth, on the average, is about 95 per cent complete. Strength is increasing at its fastest rate for the adolescent period.

Body hair is nearly fully grown, except in the chest and face areas. The beard, developing on the sides of the chin, before the ears, over the lips, is gradually merging to the adult form. Genitalia are virtually mature size. Head and facial features appear relatively smaller as body size increases, neck lengthens. Adam's apple often prominent.

16 YEARS

Girls. Sixteen-year-old girls do not appear strikingly different from Fifteens. Some have continued to grow in height and weight, but some have lost weight and seem to be in a process of refining maturity features acquired earlier. Physiologic functions are becoming more stable, more conservative, like those of the young adult.

Boys. Boys too are shaping features acquired earlier, rather than acquiring new ones. The physique seems firmer, more synchronous. The average boy's height growth is about 98 per cent complete, though some late maturers may yet add as much as six inches to their height.

Hairline pulls back at upper corners of forehead, squaring off the earlier rounded or bow-shaped hairline. Some now shave regularly.

2. SEX INTERESTS

10 YEARS

Girls. Many, by ten, have experienced some sort of sex play, usually of an incidental, transitory nature.

The majority, though not all, have heard about menstruation. Some show mild interest in father's part in reproduction. A few show no interest in sex and ask no questions.

Some interest in smutty jokes, usually related to the buttocks rather than to sex. Often report these to mother.

Some interest in boys, in marrying, in having children someday, but quite matter-of-fact and unromantic.

Boys. Many have been involved in childhood sex play. Most do little questioning about sex. Most are not shy about being seen nude within the family.

Most are aware that the mother is the origin of babies, and most now have heard of intercourse and the father's role. Interested in the father's "planting the seed," but may comment, "I should think that would be embarrassing."

Some use of "bad" words, interest in "dirty" jokes, especially about elimination.

May report these jokes to mother, often not knowing their meaning. May have little sense of which jokes can be told before girls or adults.

Some talk of their own (future) children—what they will save for them or how they will treat them.

11 YEARS

Girls. Most know about menstruation, reproduction, intercourse. Though many have "known about" these for several years, understanding is now clearer and more realistic. Separation between elimination and reproductive systems somewhat better understood, though Eleven's jokes still indicate considerable confusion between the two. Many understand explanations of the processes of menstruation and reproduction better if explanations are not too confused with talk of love, home, etc., but discussed as are other body functions.

Some resist or resent ideas of sex, especially own coming menstruation, but anticipation is generally more positive. Much interest in breast development—own and others'.

Boys. Considerably more interested in sex than at ten. Some questioning of parents, but much more information gathered from other boys. Often much interest in a variety of erotic stimuli—books, pictures, conversation, jokes (usually concerning elimination), animal behavior. Most still regard this as "dirty." Erections also often result from other, non-erotic stimuli—especially general excitement, fear, anger. Most boys know about masturbation and have had some experience with it.

12 YEARS

Girls. Much interest in menstruation. Many secretive about this, some fearful or resistant, but most accept as natural. Still some misconceptions about intercourse.

Much sex joking and double-meaning talk in school—more by boys than girls, but many girls interested in this. Strong emotional friendships, more likely to be with other girls than with boys.

Boys. Interest in sex continues to increase, with most boys' information picked up from other boys, and not always very accurate. Books on sex information are read with interest. Sex words, double meanings, and dirty jokes frequent, though not always understood. Some look up words in dictionary (which doesn't help much).

Details of own anatomy, pictures, animal activity of much interest. Some boys will discuss questions with parents; many prefer a more impersonal source, such as a counselor.

Frequent erections, masturbation. Kissing at parties, or at least interest in the topic. Whistling at girls, peeping, hitting, name calling, book stealing, and similar amatory advances.

13 YEARS

Girls. By the end of this year most girls have menstruated. Most accept this as natural, but some seem indignant. Interest in sex less overt, but in school much note passing, joking, laughing at double meanings occurs.

Boys. Many more are now modest about being seen nude. May request an athletic support, wear it all the time, because bothered by frequent erections.

Sex activity is mostly masturbation. Nocturnal emissions occur among some boys, though many have not yet heard of these.

14 YEARS

Girls. Interested in more complex aspects of reproduction—contraceptives, miscarriage. Not only more understanding themselves, but may ask how you go about explaining sex to children.

Interested in social aspects of sex—kissing, petting, "how far you go." Seem to take a quantitative approach: "She didn't *even* hold his hand." Many girls seem suddenly to blossom out and become very effective and sure of themselves with boys. But describe selves as getting "a funny feeling" at some movies or when they see a boy they like. Boys can be an all-pervasive interest with many girls.

Boys. Nearly all boys have had some masturbatory experience, many have had nocturnal emissions. Both these are a source of worry or guilt to some—most often those who are less informed by parents and less free to discuss such activity with other boys.

Boys' interest seems more definitely directed toward girls, though fewer boys are girl crazy than girls are boy crazy.

15 YEARS

Girls. Continued interest in social aspects of sex behavior, with increasing interest in ethical aspects. Discussions, with mother, may be so mature as to consider what to do about sex morals if you do not marry. Not only pros and cons of petting may be discussed, but also the morality of contraception.

Boys. Interests are becoming more channelized in many. The more random stimuli to which many responded earlier are less potent in arousing sex feelings. Interest is often becoming more social—in girls and dating, rather than in legs, breasts, etc., as earlier. Masturbation tends to increase in frequency.

Most boys now insist on privacy at home when bathing or dressing. Sex jokes are mostly restricted to all-male company.

16 YEARS

Girls. Most girls are well informed about sexual processes. Some still do not directly associate what they have learned with their own feelings and experiences, but most seem surprisingly mature in their feelings. The majority appear quite responsible and selective in their relationships with boys.

Boys. Interest in girls continues and increases in most. Social relationships generally are more frequent, and some physical contacts—mostly kissing and petting—have often occurred. Many boys find it difficult to control their impulses, seek stimulation from additional sources, and masturbate frequently.

Awareness of others also seems to be increasing—only now do many boys know of menstruation. Their evaluations of others' social and sexual activities often are quite perceptive.

3. HEALTH

10 YEARS

Health is generally quite good; greatly improved in many who had poor health earlier. Many report that there was a very bad time around six years for trouble with ears, throat, contagious diseases.

Some stomach-aches and headaches, and a little hypochondria (all more common at nine years).

11 YEARS

The majority of Elevens themselves report *excellent* health, though parents of some say they take to their beds on fairly slight provocation.

Somewhat unstable body mechanisms in some: feel hot easily, develop headaches, vomit if have stomach-ache. Colds and infections may spread to involve other areas. Some contagious diseases.

12 YEARS

Parents often describe children's health as "unusual," "remarkable," "incredible." Many miss much less school than formerly.

However, there may be sudden, violent headaches or stomach-aches. Fatigue less frequent than at eleven, but may occur in more intense bouts. Sore throats and colds often develop at such times.

13 YEARS

Health, in general, continues to improve. "Didn't miss a day of school this
year." Better able to carry on activity when illness is only minor: "Doesn't
give in to illness the way he did."

Some difficulty with colds, fatigue.

Acne and allied complexion difficulties beginning in some.

14 YEARS

Health is excellent in most, "really wonderful." Occasional use of health as an
excuse: "I get sick every so often, usually when I haven't done my school-
work and don't want to go to school." But this is less than earlier.

Major complaints are still colds and fatigue.

Complexion difficulties increase—pimples, pustules, blackheads, blotches. A
matter of real concern to some.

15 YEARS

Health is excellent in most. Some old complaints lessen; many mention "no more
hives," no asthma, etc.

Skin difficulties continue, and worsen in some, sometimes requiring medical
care.

16 YEARS

Health is excellent in most. Complexion starts to improve in many, especially
if aided by Sixteen's better ability to control diet, and care for skin.

4. TENSIONAL OUTLETS

10 YEARS

Stomach-aches and headaches are the chief tensional outlets, followed in frequency by nail biting and oral outlets—drawing in lips, stuttering, mutter-
ing. Hand-to-mouth behaviors, hair twisting, fiddling with things. A few
still suck thumbs.

Eating seems to be a tensional outlet for many. Some sudden, short-lived anger
outbursts. Some Tens seem to be in constant physical motion.

In examination: Relatively few tensional outlets are observed—many fewer
than in interview or elsewhere.

Mouth movements predominate: grimacing, lips snouted, tongue in or out,
biting of lip. Hand-to-mouth gestures.

May roll eyes or close eyes as they think; raise eyebrows. Head moves
jerkily.

11 YEARS

Many tensional outlets occur. Stomach-aches and headaches lead, nail biting again comes second. Facial twitches; hands to face. Still thumb sucking in some. Much general bodily overflow; moving around, waving arms. As at ten there seems to be constant physical movement of any or all parts of the body.

In more total behavior: anger outbursts, stamping around, "simmering"; spurts of intense activity.

In examination: More tensional outlets observed than at ten years. These increase in number and intensity as the examination progresses.

Mouth movements still predominate: mouth twitches, is pursed or snouted; tongue goes in and out, into cheek. Facial grimaces, eye rolling, eyebrow raising, frowning. Hands go to face, scratch face or head.

Initial comments in response to tests ("My goodness!"). Considerable erasing. Embarrassed giggling and laughter. Knees wave together and apart, one knee jiggles up and down. Some gross shifting of total posture.

12 YEARS

Stomach- and headaches, then nail biting still lead. Facial twitches. Much oral overflow, extending into giggling, vulgar laughter, loud noises, belching. Legs may be very active: Twelve jiggles or swings leg, fools with shoe, waves foot.

More generally: exuberance, enthusiasm; concentrated bursts of activity on one subject, then satiation.

In examination: Facial movements still occur: mouth twitches or grimaces, tongue goes in and out, lips are bitten. Some eye rolling or darting to one side.

But now hand movements predominate, especially stiff posturing of fingers and hands. Also drumming on table, twiddling pencil. Hand-to-face gestures; may rub or scratch ear, mouth, face, head.

Knees wave actively in and out, or jiggle up and down.

As tests are presented, may sigh, groan, blow, giggle, laugh, or make initial comments: "Oh dear!" or "Oh joy!"

13 YEARS

Fewer outlets at this age than earlier: many fewer gross bodily movements; more small tics and twitches, fiddling with things. As earlier, chief reported outlets are stomach- and headaches, nail biting.

General moodiness and withdrawal seem to take the place of more overt activity. Some periods of intense efforts related to one special interest.

In examination: Very few tensional outlets observed during the examination. Mouth and face movements have largely dropped out. But many hand-to-face gestures, considerable tapping fingers or pencil on table, fluttering fingers, erasing. Knee movements—in and out or up and down. Much slipping foot out of shoe.

Much laughter at own failures; negative exclamations: "Awful!" "Oops!"

14 YEARS

More tensional outlets than at thirteen—both more different kinds and greater frequency of occurrence. The following are all common: hand-to-face movements, nail biting, repeated sniffing or clearing throat, ticlike movements, tapping fingers, arm and shoulder movements, foot and leg overflow. More generally, getting excited or irritable, "exploding."

In examination: More tensional outlets than at thirteen, though fewer than from ten to twelve. Actual movements are fewer: some grimacing, whistling, raising of eyebrows, tongue in and out. Hands moderately active: drumming fingers, twisting fingers, fiddling with pencil, hands to face, erasing. Some waving of knees in and out, but less than earlier.

Tension is now more often released verbally or vocally; laughter at own failure or when tasks are difficult; initial exclamations; discussing, disparaging, or excusing own performance; conversing with examiner, asking orienting questions. Or yawning, groaning, sighing.

15 YEARS

Tensional outlets are frequent, but are generally less gross, more confined to small movements, especially of fingers and hands: nail biting, tearing of cuticle, twisting ring, fingering or twirling hair. Face and mouth movements are fewer (except in arguing), but hands may wander over face and head, picking or digging.

During moments of real stress, such as school examinations, blankouts ("Just can't think") and blackouts (actual fainting) may rarely occur.

In examination: Relatively few overt movements. Many subjects hold almost completely still—some seeming relaxed, but others appearing quite tense. Such movements as occur are quite minute.

Chief outlets are verbal: general, humorous, sarcastic, or critical comments about tests or about own performance.

16 YEARS

Tensional outlets greatly reduced in most. Some fingernail biting, hair twisting, foot tapping, but general tenseness lessened.

In examination: Most sit easy and relaxed. A little grimacing when mistakes are made, some hand-to-face movements. Main tensional release is in laughter.

5. RESPONSE TO OUR PROCEDURES *

10 YEARS

Examination. Ten tends to be sincere, friendly, naïve. Throws self whole-heartedly into situation. Interested and enthusiastic; takes self and examination seriously. Tries hard, but is not overanxious. Quick to admit own errors, and does so without embarrassment. Good, direct, uncomplicated relationship with examiner. Asks many questions of orientation ("You mean do it like this?").

Posture: Quite typically faces examiner at left, with right side of body turned slightly forward; leans forward to left, sometimes over left forearm. Typically, upper body is turned toward examiner, but arms may be symmetric (akimbo or on table). Lower trunk faces front, with legs symmetric (feet flat on floor or both on chair rung). Much head movement as Ten works, but not many changes of total body posture.

Interview. Extremely friendly response to interviewer. Generally trusting, confiding, frank. But also seems shy and vulnerable. Sits near interviewer or actually leans on her desk. Asks questions about interviewer, compliments her.

Very active—moves about room, asks about nearly every object in it. General bodily wriggling, much fiddling with things. Sits on end of spine, or all over chair. Pushes chair around on floor. Swings legs.

Comments on typing and number of carbons, examines typewriter. Wants to read own responses.

Inclined to go on and on with plot of story or details about his life. Tends to answer, "Sometimes I do and sometimes I don't." May not understand questions; needs examples to choose from. Asks, "How much more?" Short attention span; needs diversion.

11 YEARS

Examination. Usually friendly, cheery, eager, alert. Extremely aware of examiner. Amenable to suggestion and much pleased with any praise. Seem to take selves even more seriously than at ten.

---

* The Developmental *Examination* is the more standardized situation, centered around tests. Subject is seated at table, which is adjusted to elbow height. Examiner is on the other side of the table, at subject's left.

The *Interview* is more informal, centered around discussion. Subject is seated in easy chair near interviewer's desk and is free to roam around room at will.

Posture: Much movement, postures extremely varied. Most typically, both arms and legs are symmetric, whether together, apart, crossed, etc. But child leans a little to left, over left forearm. Does not turn left toward examiner quite as much as at ten. Tends to slant paper rather than turning trunk.

Some move from basically symmetric postures to more asymmetric ones as task becomes increasingly difficult. Often lean very low over paper, though occasionally lean back and hook left arm over back of chair to face examiner.

Interview. Friendly and polite, frank and confiding response to interviewer. Gives information freely, candidly; tells all. Quite factual and detailed.

Leans on interviewer's desk, manipulates typewriter. Comments about typing, interviewer's speed, carbons, number of pages. Wants to read interview questions and own responses.

Is all over his chair: feet over chair arm, lifts buttocks, bounces up and down, pulls arm off chair, pushes chair around on floor. May roam around room inspecting things, asking about them. Hands constantly active, swings leg, kicks at desk, knocks knees together, fools with shoe.

Interrupts interview with questions about objects in room or things in general. May request something to eat. Tires and wants to know how much more. Hard for some to give clear-cut answers: "Well, yes and no," "Hard to say." Prefaces many responses with "Well . . ." But once started may go on and on in endless detail. Dramatic emphasis on key words. Much grimacing—either ticlike or to express disgust. Much laughter; may tell jokes to examiner. Not much generalizing, just lists things.

12 YEARS

Examination. Continued positive relationship with examiner; still friendly, eager, exuberant. Very talkative; quite a bit of humor directed to examiner. Many orienting questions. Self-critical, much pleased with praise. Many, for all their vigor, speak in a low voice.

Posture: Considerable variability of posture—arms moving more than trunk, legs more than arms. Symmetric postures predominate, but often shift to asymmetry as examination progresses. Generally lean to left, on left elbow or forearm; head may be quite far down over paper. Toward end of examination may tend to sprawl.

Interview. Generally friendly, cheerful, enthusiastic, outgoing, co-operative, frank, and honest. Comments, "This is fun!" But less communicative then at eleven and also less interested in interviewer (though still such comments as "Quite a place you have here!"). Comments on typing, reads what has been written. May instruct interviewer which remarks to record and which not.

Most do not leave the chair now. Instead, *look* around room from chair, commenting on books and other objects in room. However, very active in chair—much wriggling; may move chair around on floor. Hands very active, much fiddling. Jiggles or swings leg, waves foot.

Groans, makes faces, dramatizes if questions are difficult, or just to illustrate points. Jokes with interviewer. Asks if he is going to learn about self.

Though some find it difficult to make clear-cut statements, answers are generally more cut and dried, with less embellishment than at eleven. And some can now generalize, not just list as they did previously.

13 YEARS

Examination.   Generally much quieter, more withdrawn. Less outgoing toward examiner. Less conversation. Voice low; may respond merely by a shrug. Some look rather sad, even negative. May move and speak more slowly than earlier. Attention relatively more directed toward task, less toward examiner. May work in a concentrated, unsociable fashion.

Posture: Quite variable, but less change of posture than earlier. Asymmetric postures now predominate: subject faces left, leans forward and to left, with right shoulder advanced. Arms and legs may be symmetric or asymmetric. As at twelve, tends to sprawl toward end of examination.

Interview.   Though most are friendly, they often appear withdrawn, look rather sad. Not spontaneous or communicative. Even when rapport is good, interview not very revealing. No secrets are told; answers are brief and guarded.

However, many seem to examine own thoughts and try to answer accurately. Some do become warmer as interview proceeds.

Most sit quietly, with little general movement. Hands are active, fiddling with things. May hold foot or swing leg. Few mention typing or ask to see what is typed.

Some interest in what tests show about their personality. Listen to interviewer's comments and may question her. Interviewer feels need to phrase questions carefully.

Little humor expressed. Not too explicit in responding: "It varies"; "It depends."

14 YEARS

Examination.   Many again are exuberant, friendly, sociable. May be quite enthusiastic. Most are attentive and try hard. Serious and sincere. But sometimes so disorganized as to disorganize examiner.

Much interested questioning: what are tests for, what do they prove, "Am I normal?" Some, boys especially, do not seem to feel fully at ease with selves or with examiner. May be self-conscious, gauche in gesture and comment, uncertain. Some are beginning to be critical of examiner.

Posture: Basically symmetric. Head low and centered, arms akimbo or elbows on table, chin in hands. Feet may be flat on floor or extended forward and crossed. Few changes of posture, minimal movement. As examination progresses, legs likely to extend. Eyes often roll upward, without corresponding head movement.

Interview. Again friendly and outgoing. Conversational and humorous. May spontaneously comment that they are enjoying themselves, like it here.

Enthusiastic and energetic, but energy now directed to expression of ideas rather than moving about room or in chair. Most sit quiet and relaxed, with only hands slightly active; some occasionally swing foot or wave one leg.

No attention to recording, but some do express interest in what they have said earlier or what others their age have said.

Volunteer information spontaneously. Usually quite frank, but not as confiding as earlier. Many try hard to express themselves accurately, but may have trouble in saying a thing just right.

Most are interested in interviewer's comments, frequently ask her opinion. But may wish to leave for other engagement before interview is finished.

15 YEARS

Examination. Many seem quite apathetic, indifferent, negative. May appear bored, jaded, sophisticated, skeptical: "All these tests are senseless." Most conform, but seem detached from situation, and detach selves further by speaking in nearly inaudible voice.

Rapport much poorer than earlier; probably the most difficult age for examiner to set up good relationship. Sparring between examiner and subject. Examiner feels that any gaucherie or lack of sophistication will be picked up immediately.

Though hostile at beginning, subject may become quite engrossed in and challenged by tasks. May become much more friendly and outgoing in examination situation—more than reported to be at home. Often will converse pleasantly if they start the conversation themselves, but likely to act bored if examiner starts it.

Posture: Mainly static; few postural shifts. May be symmetric or asymmetric. though asymmetric in majority. Face left, leaning on left forearm, or left arm extended downward beside trunk.

Interview. As in examination, may be monosyllabic and cold, even hostile, to start with, but most become friendly if interviewer is not too eager or complimentary and does not try too hard to structure the interview. Some, however, remain cold and withdrawn; answer questions, but so vaguely that they reveal little.

After initial coolness, interview becomes more conversational. Many seem to enjoy their own spontaneous commentary. Though a few reveal so little that the interview is soon terminated, with many the situation soon becomes a discussion period. May ask interviewer's opinion and advice, and thank her on leaving. Interested in what tests show about their personalities and in work of the Institute.

Most are relaxed and at ease, with few tensional outlets; hands occasionally slightly active. No interest in interviewer's recording. May try hard to express thoughts and ideas accurately, phrase things precisely, give exactly the right impression of what they mean. Occasional flashes of humor, often quite deft.

16 YEARS

Examination.   Where Fourteen was often disorganized and disorganizing, and Fifteen tended to be negative and withdrawn, Sixteen takes things easy. Examination is easier for both subject and examiner.

Friendly, humorous relationship with examiner; easy, natural manner. Tries hard but not too disturbed by failures. Has individual protection for failure: laughs, grimaces, says, "Interesting question!" With any new test may first be supercilious about how easy it is, then respectful and challenged as it gets harder, even slightly concerned if it becomes too difficult.

Posture: Tends to face front squarely, arms and legs in symmetric postures. Arms rather close to trunk; elbows occasionally on table top, hand at cheek. Feet generally together, toes out.

Interview.   Sits quiet, relaxed, at ease; almost no tensional outlets. Maintains a friendly, co-operative, conversational attitude. Answers questions thoughtfully but not in great detail. Also offers considerable spontaneous information. No attention to or comment about recording. May comment that interview is "helpful" or "enjoyable." Interview generally smooth, but a little superficial.

CHAPTER TWELVE

Self-Care and Routines

A ROUTINE is defined as a regular, established course of action, adhered to from force of habit. Who lays down the regular course? Who forms the habit? Who is responsible for maintaining the routine?

To ask these questions is to reveal the complexity of a subject which embraces a host of action patterns ranging from eating and sleeping to the washing of ears, to grooming, tidiness, table manners, etiquette, and household chores. Routines are designed to economize energy; but they have a mischievous way of generating friction and wasteful heat.

Here, as elsewhere, the maturity of the individual has a significant influence on his reaction to a proposed or imposed routine. There are other factors, but that of developmental readiness is never absent. Our growth gradients generally show year-to-year trends, which can scarcely be ascribed to pure habit formation. Fortunately, the usual trends are toward an increasing acceptance of responsibility which leads to increasing self-care. A condensed sketch of the age changes will bring these trends to light.

Eating behavior. The changes in eating behavior have far-reaching implications. In adolescence as in infancy nutrition is a most basic problem. Gone are the days when the mother worried that her young child did not eat enough. In reverse she is now concerned about the "terrible" intensity of appetite and the deepening of a bottomless pit!

Even the amiable 10-year-old has food on his mind; he looks ahead to the next meal, while he is ingesting the meat, potatoes, and the sweets of which he is very fond.

With Year Eleven appetite begins to variegate, and to fluctuate with moods and fancies. Eleven is ravenously hungry and he snacks at every chance throughout the day. But his tastes may be finicky and freakish, and on occasional days "he can't get a thing down." Yet he will eat huge quantities of one food in a single session. He can be gastronomically dramatic: holding his nose and pretending to vomit despised food, and licking his chops in approval of a favorite dish.

His table manners are versatile rather than routine in character: he finger-feeds, spears his food, messes his plate, tips his chair back, talks and talks and interrupts. Ironically enough, he may be sent from the table— the very table which has such strong appeal for him.

During Year Twelve appetite approaches a peak of intensity and capacity. Twelve talks less about food and is more comprehensive in tastes, with a predilection for mashed potatoes and gravy. Table manners are not as grossly disturbing as they were a year ago; but he is likely to talk with his mouth full, satisfying two urges simultaneously.

At Year Thirteen eagerness is not so strong; though some are reputed to "eat like a horse." However, there is less gulping of food, less head reaching down to the plate. Helpings decline from three and four to two, with an increased interest in fruit and salads.

Fourteen takes new and subtler enjoyments in the texture of his foods and the social and aesthetic aspects of a meal. This is reflected in attitudes and table manners.

At fifteen and sixteen appetites may continue to be hearty; but food interests are less engrossing. There is a marked reduction in snacks and also in the intake of sweets, reinforced by an awareness of acne and potential overweight. "Eating used to be the most important thing in my life, but no longer."

The foregoing summary is compressed in order to bring into perspective the latent and the active maturity factors as they operate over a stretch of seven years. Similar factors influence the routines of sleep; for the functions of sleep and of nutrition are closely interrelated.

Sleep behavior. The patterns of sleep behavior vary enormously in all its various phases: bedtime preliminaries, onset and depth of sleep, dreams, and activity during sleep, release from sleep, awaking, and wakeness. The individual variations of sleep are profoundly affected by the total maturity of the growing organism. Sleep does not readily yield to permanent routines. Neither Nature nor the culture has short-cut solutions for the manifold problems which arise.

The 10-year-old sleeps through the night, with good dreams and bad. The good dreams are reminiscent of the pleasant experiences of the day. The bad dreams may reflect past and delayed reactions to radio and television. Ten typically does not seem to know when he is tired. He responds to reminders of bedtime and of getting up.

Eleven often resists going to bed, especially when he is afraid to be alone. Once in bed he has difficulty in falling to sleep. In time he is dead asleep. Nothing awakens him. He has difficulty in getting out of this sleep. Sometimes he is yanked out of bed when he cannot wake up by himself. This suggests that the brain center which governs waking is in an immature (or protective?) stage of development. During Year Twelve the whole sleep cycle is more organized. He has given up pre-bedtime struggle; and he awakes in the morning without the peevishness and resistance which he showed the year before. At thirteen he wakes on his own.

At fourteen and fifteen the cycle is both more stable and adaptable. Individual differences declare themselves. Late sleepers seize the opportunity to sleep until noon when weekends permit. The average amount of sleep diminishes with age. Bedtime at age ten may be as early as eight o'clock. Each year (in our group) it is about a half hour later, reaching eleven o'clock by age sixteen. This means that the amount of waking time increases annually at a fairly consistent rate.

Bath. Taking a bath exhibits similar trends. Frequencies rise from once a week at ten, to twice a week at twelve, to once a day at sixteen. Ten, for reasons pretty much his own, resists bathing and washing—"hates it!" He needs parental help and supervision in caring for fingernails, hair, and teeth. Eleven is less resistant but requires prodding. Twelve and Thirteen sense the need of bathing, but may still need definite reminders as to hands, hair, neck, and teeth. Milder reminders as to details may be necessary for three more years, even though self-care is improving. Girls assume an earlier responsibility than do the boys. One mother who vividly recalled earlier phases of her daughter's development declared with a note of triumph, "Now at the age of fourteen she's reached the clean stage."

Clothes. There are stages, too, in the selection and wearing of clothes. When it comes to wardrobe and attire, however, it is not a simple matter to distinguish between maturity factors, the group pressures of age-mates, and the dictates of fashion. Looking back to the good old days when boys dressed like boys, a father recently commented that, as of today, "A boy of ten would rather be shot dead than appear in knee-length pants. He would be subject to the ridicule of his friends and enemies, and would come home from school—if he ever did show up at all—a psychopathic case!"

Clothes lies close to personality. Ten illustrates this fact in yet another way: he loves old clothes; he "hates" to dress up. New clothes may overstay in the closet unworn. Routine care of clothes is at dismal low level.

At eleven years there is a greater interest in clothes and appearance, especially in girls. "What shall I wear?" is a common question. Twelve-year-old girls wish to follow their peers in what they wear, adding touches of glamor. Boys of twelve often show a liking for bright colors, particularly in socks and ties.

Thirteen, true to character, is less dependent on the fashion commands of the crowd. He is more aware and more sure of his own likes and dislikes. He is also more perceptive of the proprieties and attractiveness of clothes in others. He becomes aware of how and why clothes wrinkle. The "routine" care of clothes may reflect this new awareness. Many girls of thirteen are meticulous about their appearance.

At fourteen, the individual trends become still more marked, and in girls the interest in clothes may reach a passionate pitch. At fifteen there is less talk and concern about clothes. There is a new interest in how clothes feel, as well as how they look. Care of clothes continues to improve fairly steadily in Year Sixteen. Care of room follows irregular trends from "a mess" at ten, to slicking up a bit at eleven, cluttering at twelve and thirteen, to fair and acceptable neatness in the next three years. Many boys, however, seem still to be indifferent to room tidiness at the age of sixteen. Individual variations are considerable.

Work and money. The household is a rather complex institution. It does not operate by itself. It requires work, and work requires effort. The school makes its definable demands in the form of homework. There is in addition a lengthening agenda of extracurricular activities, as related in another chapter. And how do the youths from Ten to Sixteen, in a favorable socio-economic environment, react to household tasks and opportunities of helpfulness? Much of course depends upon the expectations and the setup of the home; but our data again indicate the importance of the maturity factors in the attitudes of the boys and girls.

The 10-year-olds are often slow in responding to requests for help. They delay, dawdle, and object, but they do not openly rebel. They are reluctant. Eleven tends to resist more actively. Some merely sigh, groan, argue, and fuss. "Do I *have* to?" sums up their inner state and the outer stress. Twelve says, "Have to anyway. Might as well," in a spirit of resignation. "I do it, but I pout to myself." Nevertheless, one out of four of our subjects (age twelve) does baby-sitting—almost as many boys as girls.

Thirteen shows willingness to help; and may even offer to help without being requested or required. Fourteen and Fifteen take many tasks for granted, and show marked responsibility in tasks away from home. By age sixteen boys and girls take on substantial and very responsible jobs.

The trend toward increasing responsibility is paralleled by the rising scale of allowances and supplementary earnings. The weekly allowances for our 10-year-olds ranged from 15 cents to $1.25, the median amount being 35 cents and the mean 44 cents. Many at this age are very casual about money and forget to ask for their allowance. Some are quite irresponsible about saving. A few may worry lest the family money will run out.

The Elevens are more interested in money and become enthusiastic earners. Several are reputed to be "tightwads." The median allowance has risen to 50 cents. At twelve the median doubles in amount, a sum of $1. Budgets are getting more complicated and may include movies, candy, Sunday school, bus fare, school supplies, and school lunches. A few of the Twelves are rated by their parents to be "reckless," "all mixed up," "squanderers."

Thirteens, in general, however, are careful in their expenditures, and are rarely broke. About one-third supplement their allowance (median for age: $1) with earnings. At fourteen and fifteen individual differences in the handling of money are increasingly marked. The weekly allowance has risen to $2. Nearly half supplement their allowances with earnings and one-fourth of the Fifteens actually earn all of their own spending money. At sixteen, the available monetary resources begin to resemble those of an adult in their variety and management. Some supplement their modest allowance with earnings as high as $25 a month. This includes an allotment for clothes, although most Sixteens are not ready for a full clothes allowance. Many boys in part-time summer jobs earn as much as $20 a week or a few hundred dollars during a season. Many try to budget; some start a savings account; others confess, "Financial situation not good."

Although "routines" are intended to simplify life and to facilitate the mere mechanics of living, they frequently operate in the very opposite direction. Because of an unending need of improvement, they may attract an inordinate amount of adult attention day after day. Perhaps this is natural because these routines relate to the basic needs of food, clothing, and shelter—to say nothing of possessions, pets, personal hygiene, and interpersonal amenities. In all sorts of ways the demand for better habits gets involved with questions of obedience, propriety, duty, privileges, discipline, training, and character formation. Undue tensions and entanglements are bound to arise if the approach is too prescriptive or inflexible and relies too much on absolute methods of management. At an opposite extreme, a policy of indulgence and sheer permissiveness is equally futile and undesirable.

The household can insist on certain essentials and yet allow a margin of tolerance for imperfections. Far from being purely a habit-forming creature, a child is under the necessity of progressive rehabituation, because he is growing. Sometimes it almost seems as though his passing reluctances and resistances help him to a higher level of achievement; for in the long run he benefits from the guidance he receives in timely reminders and constructive approval. And as always he benefits from affectionate understanding.

We have seen how with increasing maturity the child and youth spontaneously takes on increased responsibility. His self keeps growing in scope and in independent insights. Genuine self-care depends upon self-motivation. He must see the logic and the advantage of the "routine" tasks which confront him. He does what is expected of him when he himself expects it of himself. Then and not until then does he display that blessed willingness which was prematurely hoped for in the previous year.

It is gratifying to know that the gradients of growth show an unmistakable trend toward self-care, willingness, and capacity. By recognizing that trend in advance rather than in retrospect, we place a premium on it.

GROWTH GRADIENTS

1. EATING

10 YEARS
Appetite. The majority "love food—eat tons—eat constantly," though many express this quite casually: "Sometimes I like to eat, sometimes I don't."

Even poor eaters have usually improved. They eat more, will try some new foods, will eat cooking other than mother's.

Many, however, do not eat a big breakfast.

Preferences and Refusals. Related with enthusiasm—eyes sparkle as they tell of likes, gesture of vomiting as they describe disliked foods. Variety of likes greater than of dislikes.

Favorites: "Any kind of meat" (especially steak, roast beef, hamburg and hot dogs, chicken, lamb chops). "Any kind of potatoes" (baked, mashed, French fried). Raw vegetables, especially carrots, tomatoes, celery. Cooked peas. Cake and ice cream.

Refusals: Liver (almost universally), fish, eggs. Cooked vegetables—carrots, onions, celery, tomatoes, cauliflower, cabbage, asparagus. "Mixed things like stew." Some dislike desserts, and some turn against that old favorite, peanut butter.

Snacks and Sweets. The majority do eat between meals, and even the self-styled abstainers may eat a little. Quote mother in relation to this: "I can have all the cider I want between meals—it's good for me, my mother says."

Favorite between-meal snacks are soft drinks, cookies, and fruit.

Marked individual differences in liking sweets. Some crave them, have a "terrific sweet tooth." Some are not interested. Others like them but try to cut down because of teeth or weight or parents' limitations. Ice cream is among the favorites; candy, desserts, and pie are not.

Table Manners. About half. of our group are described as having adequate manners, and they themselves say their manners are "not mentioned" by parents. Of the rest, some are described as "bad" or even "terrible."

Poor posture is the greatest complaint. Also criticizing food, holding fork incorrectly, talking too much. Some children criticize table manners of parents.

Mother may let up on them when father is not present. Children try to do better when father is there.

Cooking. Considerable enthusiasm about cooking, in boys as well as girls. About a quarter of our subjects do some cooking. Bacon, eggs, hamburg, or hot dogs are the chief foods cooked. Some even try cake or pancakes.

11 YEARS

Appetite. Eating is a real pleasure to most. They spontaneously state, "I love to eat," and their parents say, "He will eat most anything." But in a few, appetite has fallen off and they are "finicky" or "picky."

Children themselves are aware that they are eating more (or less) than last year, and comment on the relation between amount eaten and their own size.

Daily variation in appetite: hungry some days and not others: will eat certain
foods one day, then not on another. Considerable comment that they don't
like to eat or even look at food when they are full, or that some foods take
away their appetite.

Preferences and Refusals.   Very definite tastes: "I love . . ." or "I hate . . ."
The widest variety of preferences of any age, yet much uniformity in
preferences from child to child. With interest in cost of food, may say they
like to eat "expensive things." Most mention only one or two dislikes which
may be determined by texture.

Favorites: Meat—especially rare or raw (steak, roast beef, hamburg, hot dogs,
chops). Potatoes—any kind, but especially French fried or mashed. Spaghetti. Fried things. Corn and peas. Desserts—candy, ice cream, cake, pie.

Refusals: Liver. Vegetables: squash, turnips, broccoli, asparagus, cabbage,
onions—raw or cooked. (Dislike of cooked celery, carrots, tomatoes less
marked than earlier.) "All kinds of fish." Casseroles, creamed things,
mayonnaise.

Snacks and Sweets.   Nearly all eat between meals. ("I come home from school
and I'm STARVED.") Most parents do not prohibit this, but try to control
amount and selection to some extent.

Favorites are soft drinks, cookies, fruit, milk, "cookies and milk."

A few eat when bored or lonesome. More than at ten, but still only a few, eat
at bedtime.

Relatively little mention by parents of children's craving for sweets. Cake and
ice cream are still the great favorites.

Table Manners.   Those with good manners slightly outnumber those considered bad. Parents describe the largest number as "'fair," and they themselves say manners are not mentioned. A few report, "When I'm at home
my manners are perfectly AWFUL."

The most different specific complaints occur at this age, but the major ones are:
poor posture, elbows on the table, eating with fingers, criticizing food,
knocking things over, eating too fast or too noisily, talking too much.

Interest in own speed of eating, and in who finishes first.

Most try to do better in presence of company or at a restaurant, even eating a
little of a disliked food. Where Ten said, "She makes me eat things I dislike," Eleven may say, "I try to eat a little of things I dislike."

Cooking.   An age of enthusiasm about this for about half our group, as many
boys as girls. ("Love to cook—may sound funny for a boy.") Chief foods
cooked are eggs, hamburg or hot dogs, cookies, cake, and meat, but anxious
to try new things.

12 YEARS

Appetite. "Tremendous" is the parents' word for Twelve's appetite. "Enormous eater—always hungry—no end to his appetite." Amount consumed may strike some parents as awesome—or repulsive. Twelve is no longer called "finicky"; no longer mentions feeling full.

A few try to diet to lose weight.

Preferences and Refusals. Many more likes than dislikes. May have few or no refusals; some like "everything." More varied mention of favorites (fried apples, mushrooms, watermelon, artichokes). More ability to generalize, especially about dislikes ("Anything creamed—any kind of seafood—anything with fat or gristle"). Wants things attractively served.

Favorites: Mashed potatoes with gravy. Steak, hot dogs and hamburg, roast beef. Sweets—cake and ice cream. Peas and corn. Fruits. *Plain* things. ("Why have hash when you can have hamburg? Fancy food is ridiculous.")

Refusals: Fish, asparagus, cabbage, broccoli, squash, turnips, spinach, eggs.

Snacks and Sweets. By far the majority eat between meals. More eating just before bedtime than occurred at earlier ages.

Favorite snacks are cookies, soft drinks, candy, "crackers with stuff on them."

A stronger age than eleven for sweets. Some are said to eat them constantly, and, next to potatoes and steak, sweets are the most preferred food.

Table Manners. Twice as many of our subjects were reported to have adequate manners than poor ones; none were described as "terrible." For most, manners are considered "fair." Parents comment less on manners.

Poor posture and elbows on the table are the major complaints, along with holding the fork incorrectly, talking with a full mouth.

Tries to do better—to eat a little of disliked foods, to "leave some for others" of favorite foods.

Cooking. Less cooking. Girls' enthusiasm continues more than boys', but less "I love to cook" and more "Yes, I do, a little bit." Favorite things to cook are eggs, flapjacks or waffles, hamburg and hot dogs, other kinds of meat.

13 YEARS

Appetite. Our group divides between those who are still enormous eaters ("Eats like a horse—anything and everything—can't fill her up"), and those whose appetites are slightly less ("Not three or four helpings any more—only two, and sometimes only one"). Even the relatively small eaters usually come back for seconds, and mothers seldom worry now about the smallness of the amount consumed.

Food, however, even for some of the bigger eaters, is not the absorbing interest it was earlier. Less enthusiasm and more matter-of-factness about eating.

Unevenness of appetite—hearty eating in spells, or only for favored foods.

Some comment about dieting (some girls at this age look "potbellied"), but little actual dieting.

Preferences and Refusals.   Fewest likes mentioned, and thirteen is the only age at which more different dislikes than likes are named. Some odd dietary notions prevail—one girl "balances things inside" by eating sour apples, then sweet cake. More generalized expressions of preferences—"Fruits," "vegetables," "meats," "starches," "fats," "chocolate things."

Favorites: Steak (by far). French fries, hamburg and hot dogs, chicken, fruit, ice cream, desserts. Beans, carrots, peas, corn.

Refusals: Liver. Vegetables—cooked celery, beets, cabbage, spinach, stewed tomatoes, turnips, squash, parsnips, asparagus, broccoli, onions, and (by many) beans—baked, lima, and "those awful string beans."

Snacks and Sweets.   Between-meals eating is almost universal, and with some is almost constant—"I'm always hungry, every minute of the day." Pre-bedtime snack is very common, and often eating just before and/or just after meals. Favorites are soft drinks, cookies, fruit.

In general there is less eating of sweets than at twelve, but great variation. Some crave sweets, others are not much interested, prefer fruit. Some would like sweets but are "pretty good" about not eating them.

Table Manners.   Said to be improved. Less trouble at the table and much less fuss and confusion. Chief complaints are talking too much and poor posture. Fathers may complain more than do mothers.

Cooking.   Only about a third of our group now express interest in cooking. Interest seems less experimental and more practical than earlier. As in athletics, many show interest earlier, then later interest narrows down to those with some ability. Most frequently cooked are eggs, hamburg and hot dogs, cake.

14 YEARS

Appetite.   Appetite again (or still) is very large in the majority: "Eats everything—great quantities—never full—endless appetite." Considerably interested in food: "Food the best thing about the party [or the movies]."

Again, some try to diet.

Preferences and Refusals.   Likes again exceed dislikes, and are more generalized ("seafoods," "starches," "all the protein foods"), while dislikes are more specific. Some say they like "everything," or just "food." Some are becoming critical of meals served, type of food, how it is cooked, and report that disliked foods "nauseate" them. Liken their tastes to those of others ("I dislike good old spinach. Did you ever hear of anybody who liked it?" or, "Liver—all kids dislike that").

Favorites: Ice cream and steak (by far). Fruit, milk (much relished by many), turkey, chicken, seafood, potatoes (all kinds, mashed best), sweets, cake. Also hamburg, roast beef, sandwiches, pie. Some strong-flavored foods—catsup, horseradish, sardines.

Refusals: Similar to thirteen—liver, fish, hash, spinach, turnip, cabbage, broccoli, brussels sprouts, artichoke, cooked onion, celery, squash. "Odd-tasting" things—caviar, French pastry, head cheese, sauerkraut.

Snacks and Sweets. Nearly all eat between meals, some constantly, especially right before or after meals, after school, before bedtime. Some eat when lonesome or sad.

The social, away-from-home aspect of eating is beginning—something to eat at the drugstore or downtown.

Favorites are drugstore concoctions, soft drinks, fruit, and milk. Some eat a lot of candy, but more, though strong on desserts and sundaes, do not. Some just don't like sweets, but many believe candy is bad for teeth, complexion, or weight, and feel appearance and health are more important than sweet tooth.

Table Manners. Many no longer mention manners, though about as many as at thirteen are still "bad" or only "fair." Poor posture and eating with fingers are the main complaints.

May contribute little to mealtime atmosphere—criticize food, either talk too much or answer in monosyllables, argue with father. Disagree if he says they should be forced to eat disliked foods or complains of their manners. Argue as to whether elbows are permissible on table or not.

Cooking. An increase again, nearly half doing some cooking—boys as well as girls. Several comment that it is important to know how to cook, but earlier enthusiasm is largely lacking. Some say they can if they must but don't enjoy it much; others have to cook—like it or not—especially breakfast. Some like the social aspect—don't like to cook, but like to cook *for* others.

Foods cooked most are meats, eggs, cookies, cake. Some can get simple meals. Criticize their own cooking rather specifically.

Their statements may contradict themselves ("No cooking. Well, I might just make some cookies or something like that"), or may conflict with mother's statement (Mother reports no interest in cooking; girl says she likes to cook, gets whole meals).

15 YEARS

Appetite. Some, boys especially, still maintain peak appetite—"a bottomless pit." Others now eat less and think less about food. Parents are casual about the situation—"His eating is very good"; "No problem."

Some attention to dieting—to reduce, or to build up weight for football.

Preferences and Refusals.   More likes than dislikes. Dislikes are strong but few—many name only one food, and many will eat even these to be polite. Dislikes may be based on texture of food—asparagus ("slimy"), jello, sauerkraut, fat on meat. Some cite good effect of boarding school on choices ("Gotta get used to puddings at school").

Favorites: Meat—steak, hamburg and hot dogs, roast beef. Ice cream, fruits, desserts—especially pie. Raw vegetables. Less emphasis on potatoes and milk than earlier, but more on seafood.

Refusals: Green or root vegetables—asparagus, broccoli, cabbage, cauliflower, spinach, turnip, squash, cooked onions, carrots, stewed tomatoes. Casseroles, scalloped potatoes, mayonnaise, fish.

Snacks and Sweets.   As at all teen ages, the majority eat between meals—some, still, almost constantly. Some eat when lonesome or sad. Drugstore eating lessens, but pre-bedtime eating increases, if anything.

Favorites are soda, fruit, cookies, sandwiches. A minority likes sweets; but the majority is not much interested in sweets of any kind, preferring fruits, raw vegetables, and beverages to candy and pastries.

Some take food from refrigerator that was meant for next meal.

Table Manners.   Only one in ten in our group is reported to have less than adequate manners, and no one is described as "bad" or "terrible." Eating causes very little trouble to parents, either for manners or amounts or selection of foods. Very few specific complaints—holding fork inaccurately is the chief one. Some argument and discussion at the table, though not necessarily about food.

Cooking.   The number of those who cook, sharply decreases, though some boys still do. Meats and eggs are the main things cooked, though some bake or get a whole meal. As at fourteen, some girls like to cook for the enjoyment of seeing others eat, and may comment they would like a husband who liked good food. (Boys often specify a wife who liked to cook.)

16 YEARS

Appetite.   Our group is about evenly divided between very hearty eaters and those whose appetite is said to be medium or small. The former say they are big eaters and always have been. The latter characteristically comment that their appetite is very small recently—"Eating used to be the most important thing in my life, but no longer." The small eaters may say eating is "just a habit," or that they eat merely because the food is set before them.

More serious attempts to reduce the amount they eat and to cut down on sweets to improve figure or complexion.

Preferences and Refusals. More enthusiasm about food occurs than at fifteen. More favorites are mentioned, though fewer different kinds of favorites. Dislikes are strong, though greatly outnumbered by likes, and all but the most disliked foods are eaten.

Favorites: Steak, mashed potatoes, chicken, ice cream, sweets, fruit. Spaghetti and seafood increasingly mentioned; hot dogs, hamburgs, and sandwiches far less than formerly.

Refusals: Vegetables—broccoli, spinach, cauliflower, cabbage, turnips, squash, cooked onions, carrots, tomatoes, "weird greens." Peppers and eggplant are now mentioned. Liver, tongue, and tripe disliked by many.

Snacks and Sweets. Nearly all snack, though some are trying to cut down the amount. ("I eat between meals. Don't do it consciously.")

At home, between-meal favorites are fruit, sandwiches, ice cream, cookies, candy, cake, soft drinks, crackers and cheese. Away from home, especially when on dates, favorites are beverages (soft drinks, beer, coffee), ice cream, sodas and sundaes, steak, sandwiches.

Sweets of greater interest to many than at fifteen, but many try to cut down on amount eaten since "the pleasure is temporary and the bad results are lasting."

Table Manners. Very few are said to have bad table manners, and even these are not excessively bad. Though they can frankly describe their own manners as, "Not faultless by a long shot," they can also add, "Nobody complains." Some not only behave well but add to the social pleasure of the family meal. Parents' complaints are mainly: "Bolts food—shovels it in—mouth too full," and, "Leans on the table."

Cooking. Nearly a third of our subjects, and almost as many boys as girls, say they do like to cook. Boys, in fact, may express more enthusiasm than the girls, who seem to take it more for granted. Quite a few can get a whole meal, though most cook only a few things—usually cake, eggs, hamburg, or other meat. Many can and do get their own breakfasts, including cooking bacon, eggs.

2. SLEEP

10 YEARS

Bedtime. Average bedtime is 8:30, with a range from 7 to 9:30. Bedtime may be different on school nights and weekends.

Most have to be reminded of bedtime. Many resist and have to be urged. The
majority delay and "stall": one more bike ride, homework not finished, etc.
Listen to radio, read, think, or worry or daydream before falling asleep.
Boys may go to sleep quickly. Girls may lie awake an hour or so. Girls
asleep by 9:30 on the average; boys closer to 8:30.

Night. Most sleep through the night without waking, but nightmares are frequent and (at this age only) equal the number of good dreams. At least
a third of our subjects report nightmares—about "bad guys," robbers, animals, dragons, being chased or killed. A few wake or call out.

Morning. Average hour of waking is 7. Most get up right away or, if not at
once, within half an hour. Girls average 9½ hours of sleep a night; boys
10½. Rising causes much less trouble than bedtime. But there are marked
differences between those who wake early and get up as soon as allowed,
and those who need much help in getting up.

11 YEARS

Bedtime. Average bedtime is 9, with a range from 7:30 to 10. Some have a
varying bedtime, depending on TV, etc., but most are "supposed" to go at
a set hour. Many do not actually go as soon as they are "supposed" to.
Most have to be reminded or forced to go to bed. Much dissatisfaction with
earliness of bedtime. Many do not resist outright but practice a series of
"rackets" to delay. Many go upstairs without a fuss, but their stalling takes
place upstairs.
Most get to sleep after about half an hour of radio or of thinking and worrying
—a high point for the latter. Strong age for presleep daydreaming.

Night. More dreaming reported here (and at greater length) than at any
other age. Good dreams predominate now, but nightmares are still frequent, and violent. A few wake, most sleep right through. Dreams often
about ordinary things: homework, pets, fishing, cars. A few talk in their
sleep.

Morning. Average hour of waking is 7, and of getting up 7:15, since most lie
in bed a while. The average 11-year-old sleeps 9½ hours. About half wake
by themselves and half have to be called—usually repeatedly. Getting up is
very difficult for some. Sleeping very late on weekends is beginning in a
few.

12 YEARS

Bedtime. Average bedtime is a little after 9 P.M. Bedtime still largely determined by parents; children go because they have to, not because they think
they need the sleep.

Some stall, but many go to room willingly or even spontaneously. Might seek permission to stay up later. Some admit they are not "good" about bedtime. Delay in getting to bed occurs after they are in room—listening to radio, reading, doing homework.

Most lie awake half an hour or so—listening to radio, thinking, worrying, or daydreaming.

Night. Fewer nightmares occur and a little less dreaming. Dreams are mostly about daily life. A little talking and a very little walking in sleep.

Morning. Average hour of waking is around 7, and is a little earlier for boys than girls. The average child still sleeps about 9½ hours.

Many wake themselves or wake by alarm clock, but many are called by parents.

The majority do lie in bed for a while. Average hour of getting up is 7:15. Some are very sluggish about getting up (though difficulty not as great now in most as later).

13 YEARS

Bedtime. Average bedtime is now 9:30, with range from 8:30 to 10:30, later than this on weekends or in summer. Some have a range of bedtimes, depending on homework.

Less resistance and dawdling, unless special radio or TV programs interfere. Many know the set time and go. Most are reasonably satisfied with bed-time hour.

Many are "good enough" about bedtime so that occasional requests to stay up later are granted. Or if they do not go when supposed to not much is done about it. Not as much of an issue as earlier.

Some spend every evening in own room and then take responsibility about going to bed.

Some seem to get to sleep more easily now, though in many there is still a half-hour delay. May listen to radio. Less daydreaming—at least less re-ported.

Night. A few more nightmares than at twelve, but good dreams still pre-dominate. Less reporting of dreams. Many dreams are of daily activities, especially sports. A few predictive dreams. Some describe dreams as "crazy," "funny," "strange," "fishy."

A few wake from nightmares or talk or walk in sleep; some sleep soundly. An individual matter.

More pleasure in sleeping than earlier. As at seven, may express love of bed and of sleeping.

Morning. Average waking hour is still 7, and length of sleep is 9 hours. Hour of arising averages 7:30, though a surprisingly large number can get right up. Some take all responsibility for getting up—alarm used more than earlier. Others must be called by parents. Most either wake easily and get right up *or* usually find it hard to wake up and get up. Some are sleepy but realize bad results of late rising (late to school) so prefer to get up. May sleep very late on weekends.

14 YEARS

Bedtime. Average is now 9:30 for girls, but 10 for boys. Most take about 15 minutes to get into bed. Many now decide on bedtime themselves. Quite conservative about this, and some are influenced by the concept of "need."

A few need to be reminded, or even nagged, but in many the whole process is more as in the adult. Some, as at thirteen, are studying or listening to the radio in their own rooms, and go to bed when ready.

Once in bed, many—boys especially—drop off to sleep at once, while others may take about half an hour to get to sleep. (This is increasingly related to personality rather than age.) Radio after going to bed is less. Most, if awake, plan next day, think about school work or social affairs, or daydream about glamorous and heterosexual adventures.

Night. Individual differences are striking: differences between those who sleep lightly, waking at the least noise, and those who never waken; between early and late wakers; between those who need much and those who need little sleep.

About half dream, but very few nightmares. However, dreaming is less about everyday things and is apt to be "weird," "screwy," or confusing.

Morning. Average waking hour is 7 A.M. after 9 hours' sleep. Range is 6 to 8 A.M.

Much harder to rouse than earlier, but average time of getting up is 7:15. Conflict has shifted from problems of getting to bed to problems of getting up. Some seem to need more sleep, find it harder to get up, and sleep very late on weekends.

15 YEARS

Bedtime. Average is 10 for girls, 10:30 for boys.

Many take all responsibility, going to bed when sleepy or when through homework. Concept of "need" of sleep strong here. Others have set bedtime, but there is not much commotion if they do not go then.

Some already up in rooms, but most have been out with friends or downstairs with family in the evening. Some intend to go earlier, but "putter around" upstairs.

Less presleep activity than earlier. Go to bed, light off, lie and think a while or go right to sleep at once.

Night. Much less dreaming is reported and virtually no nightmares. Some sleep restlessly, but do not wake or report nightmares. Some are becoming interested in psychological implications of their dreams.

Morning. Most wake around 7, after averaging 8½ hours' sleep (boys slightly less).

On schooldays most get up within 15 minutes. Some very difficult to get up. Others set own alarm. Radio or phonograph may be turned on immediately upon waking.

Though bedtime is not a problem with most, getting up continues to be.

16 YEARS

Bedtime. Average bedtime for girls is 11, with a range from 10 to 12; for boys, 10:30, with a range from 9 to 12. (It is the conscientious athletes who make the boys' average earlier.) Bedtime during vacations is somewhat later for girls, much later for boys.

For most, the hour of going to bed is "all up to me." Very little pressure other than an occasional reminder is exerted by parents.

Many go to bed at once. Others listen to radio, read, or fool around for about half an hour in their rooms before going to bed.

Girls, if they do not fall asleep at once, are likely to daydream about boys. Boys are more apt to "think things over."

Night. Most sleep well, right through the night without waking. No nightmares reported, but more than half dream. (This is now more a personality than an age relationship.) Nearly all dreams are reported as good—about friends, sports, girls, "places I've seen."

Morning. Average hour of waking for girls is 7 (range from 6:30 to 7:30) and for boys is 7:30 (range from 6:45 to 8:30). Nearly all sleep much later on vacation mornings—till 10 or 11, if allowed to.

Only a minority wake by themselves. A few rely on an alarm clock but the majority still are called by their mothers. About a third of our group report that they get right up. The majority have to be called twice, or like to lie in bed for a while after waking. Getting up is still a real problem for many.

3. BATH

10 YEARS

Bath. Most bathe about once a week—under protest, since they dislike bathing, washing hands or face, brushing teeth. Most prefer being dirty to washing; have to be reminded, urged, even forced to bathe.

Mother may need to run, empty, and wash out tub; lay out clothes.

Many have to be reminded to wash before meals and even sent back to do so.

Hair.   Most are not much concerned about appearance of their hair. Shampoo is usually given by mother once a week, and is reasonably well accepted.

Cosmetics.   Use of cosmetics is not yet a problem.

11 YEARS

Bath.   Most bathe twice a week—oftener (and with less fuss) in summer.

Eleven shows less resistance than at ten, but needs at least to be reminded by mother. Many are "quite good" once reminded, but others have to be urged or prodded, and quite a few are still extremely resistant.

Many run bath for themselves, though mother may "start it" for them.

Back-of-neck and ear trouble persists. Care of fingernails and teeth has improved.

Most do not care about being clean, may be sent from table because of dirty hands.

Hair.   Boys often just won't comb hair. A few girls are interested in having hair clean, and a few are style-conscious.

Shampoo is usually weekly, mother still helping. Many think the end result is not worth the trouble, however, for the shampoo is often a real problem: "I simply *despise* to have my hair washed."

Cosmetics.   No use of cosmetics as yet, except when playing "dress-up."

12 YEARS

Bath.   Bathing is less of an issue, generally. Most bathe every other day or twice weekly. The concept of "need" of washing is beginning to develop, but mother still has responsibility for reminding. Some respond willingly, some still must be forced. Even those who dislike bathing enjoy soaking, once in.

Most run their own baths and take over the whole process, except shampoo and laying out clothes. Most are said to be "pretty good" about washing, combing hair, brushing teeth, with only a little reminding, checking, pressuring.

Girls may fuss with hair and wear lipstick but still be sent from the table because of dirty hands.

Hair.   Girls are getting to be very particular about hair: Is it combed just right? Is it clean? Is the style right? They may become quite discouraged about it, "won't come downstairs unless hair is perfect."

Usually still only a weekly shampoo, and mother still helps.

Cosmetics.   Though some now tease for it, most girls are not allowed to use lipstick except for parties. (This varies in different communities.)

13 YEARS

Bath. The majority now bathe every other day, but reminders are still needed. "Doesn't object but has to be reminded," is a typical parental comment.

Many feel that they do not have time to bathe. Others, generally girls, bathe nightly without reminding. A few are described as "very meticulous."

Most brush teeth without reminding. Most are better about grooming hair than nails or neck.

Complexion difficulties are beginning in many.

Hair. Appearance of hair is now important to both boys and girls, and more time may be spent on this than on other aspects of personal grooming. Boys may spend "hours" before the mirror combing hair, always carry a pocket comb. Girls are extremely careful about hair—brush, comb, put it up in pin curls.

Shampoo at least weekly, oftener if allowed, with some. Some now need no help.

Cosmetics. A "borderline age" for lipstick. Some use it for parties only, others every day—depending mostly on the custom of the community. Those who do use it are apt to get it on too thick.

14 YEARS

Bath. The majority bathe every other day, a few daily. Some now bathe without reminders, but some, boys especially, are still averse to any washing. Many still forget neck and nails, or will attend to hair but forget to brush teeth. Boys may wash faces after shirt is on.

Boys now, if not earlier, are modest about dressing and undressing before others.

Complexion difficulties continue.

Hair. With many boys, "hair is the only thing that counts." Girls take surprisingly good care of their own hair: wash, brush, set it, and may even cut and shape it. Shampoo weekly, and oftener if allowed to.

Cosmetics. Both girls and mother now generally say, "No trouble about lipstick." Most girls use it, and get it on reasonably well.

15 YEARS

Bath. Marked improvement occurs in most of the earlier "poorer" bathers. Most now recognize the need of bathing and washing. Many now bathe daily without reminding, though a few boys still need reminding or even urging.

Most are responsible about hands, face, hair, teeth. "No check-up" or supervision by parents for many. Girls may be extremely meticulous: daily bath, weekly shampoo, setting hair, caring for teeth and nails, using deodorant. Boys are better about hair than rest of appearance, and some still just keep clean "the part that shows."

Hair.   Even more care than at fourteen may be devoted to hair. Both boys and girls are very responsible about and interested in all aspects of care and grooming of hair.

Cosmetics.   Most girls now use lipstick.

16 YEARS

Bath.   The majority bathe daily, some every other day. Most take all responsibility about personal cleanliness—care of teeth and nails, as well as bathing. Only the occasional immature boy or girl needs to be reminded.

Most boys shave as often as necessary, without reminding. Boys and girls both are particular about clean underwear.

Earlier complexion difficulties are starting to clear up for many.

Hair.   Responsibility about hair is at an essentially adult level. Girls usually wash their own hair weekly.

4.   CLOTHES

10 YEARS

Buying Clothes.   Mother and child shop together. Though to some extent consulting child's taste, mother decides which clothes to buy, and most children accept this. Some hate trying on clothes in the store. But in general not too many arguments.

Daily Selection.   Most select their own clothes for wear in the morning, but mother usually checks, and may even lay clothes out. Some battles over what is "suitable" clothing. Several hate the idea of wearing new clothes or dressing up. Though some might mention that they are fat or thin, most are not particularly concerned about their own appearance.

Care of Clothes.   The majority are extremely careless about the care of clothes. Outer garments are flung down anywhere. Other clothes are dropped where they are removed, "just slung around," or at best piled on a chair. Most don't notice or mind if their clothes are dirty; and do not report tears.

11 YEARS

Buying Clothes.   Child exercises more say than earlier. Most accompany mother for buying the more important clothes. Girls may go alone to buy less important things, while boys more often let mother buy them. Some complain about stores: "Too confusing," "awfully hot," "get all mixed up."

If disagreement with mother occurs, the decision may go either way. The extremes range from: "Mother goes with me, but I decide," to, "Sometimes mother makes me get something I don't like. I get used to it, though."

Daily Selection. About half our group decide what to wear (except for special occasions), half still ask what to put on.

Children are beginning (if they did not earlier) to have very definite ideas about what they will or will not wear, and may refuse clothes they dislike ("If I don't like them I don't wear them, period"). But a few show only glimmers of this interest, and many prefer old clothes, or would wear "all colors of the rainbow."

Care of Clothes. Interest in care of clothes lags far behind responsibility in buying or selection. Eleven drops them on the floor as he removes them, "just steps out of them and leaves them," throws them *at* a chair or hamper, or piles them on chair or bed, but does not hang them up. A few put dirty clothes into the hamper.

12 YEARS

Buying Clothes. Fewer "issues" occur than did earlier, and shopping is a more co-operative venture: "We pick them out together." If real disagreement occurred, mother would probably win, but most work it out together. Each has more respect for the other's taste: "She knows if it's a good thing or not, but I know what the kids wear." Some respect mother's taste in general, but are stubborn about a few things.

At the extremes, some boys still allow mother to do all the shopping, some girls shop alone. Most prefer to have mother along. A stronger need than earlier is felt about trying things on before buying.

Wanting clothes like everyone else is at least beginning. Some girls start to strive for glamor, some boys to be "sharp."

Daily Selection. A marked change appears. Most girls and some boys take great interest in their own appearance—interest in style, fit, "matching" of clothes (though may be all dressed up and still have a dirty neck).

Many still consult mother about what they plan to wear—whether dress or shirt is clean enough. Girls are generally quite responsible about changing underwear and socks frequently. Boys more often like dirty clothes as well as clean; old as well as new.

Care of Clothes. Interest in looking nice seldom extents to *care* of clothes. Some can take responsibility for putting dirty clothes into the hamper, and a few hang up outdoor clothing, but mostly clothes are just piled on bed, couch, or chair.

13 YEARS

Buying Clothes. For many, this is the last age when mother generally makes the final decision. But mostly there is good agreement and appreciation of each other's taste, especially if mother recognizes the child's need to wear what others are wearing. Often shopping goes more smoothly with girls than with boys.

Less important items are frequently bought alone. Some mothers allow the child to go and scout around, then go along for the final decision. If mother brings things home, it is definitely "on approval."

Girls especially are showing more specific taste: color, style, what friends wear.

Daily Selection. Most select their own clothes for daily wear. Interest in personal appearance increases, some becoming quite "narcissistic." Many girls and even some boys are described as "meticulous."

Care of Clothes. Though the extremes range from, "Has never hung up one garment in his life, to my knowledge," to, "Even presses his own clothes," carefulness has generally begun, especially in girls, to extend to care of clothes as well as of self. Best clothes more often are hung up on hangers, other clothes hung on doorknobs or backs of chairs. Shoes still under the bed or "right where he took them off."

Some are good about selecting clean clothes, disposing of dirty ones. Put dirty clothes in the laundry, and may even send things to the cleaners.

14 YEARS

Buying Clothes. Many girls and boys are now allowed to make the final decisions, but prefer nevertheless to have mother along when shopping, and in case of serious disagreement will try to compromise. More disagreements occur with boys, who may speak of "winning out" or "losing," where girls more often speak of agreement or compromise.

A few shop alone, and some have a clothes allowance.

Daily Selection. Both sexes "love" certain clothes, and boys take pleasure in looking "sharp." Girls may have reached the "clean stage—"cold cream, deodorant. Boys may now be careful about shining shoes, changing shirts daily.

Care of Clothes. Many, but not all, hang up their clothes fairly consistently (though not always on hangers—may all be hung on same hook). Girls are **more** often careful than boys, and some are "fastidious" about care of

clothes as well as about their own appearance. Some show inconsistency--
hanging things up one day, not the next; "meticulous," then "sloppy."

Many are very careful about the state of clothes—dirty ones into hamper or to
cleaner's. Some girls take all responsibility about clothes care, wash out
their own underwear and sweaters. Responsibility ranges from a few (including girls) who do not even report tears in clothing to a few (including
boys) who sew on their own buttons.

15 YEARS

Buying Clothes.   Less variation appears. In most cases, mother goes along
to advise, but boy or girl decides. ("I buy what I want. She just pays.")
A few report, "We both decide."

Where this is not the case, some other arrangement about making decisions
has been worked out, and few arguments occur. Mother's decision, if
asserted, is accepted. Those who do have trouble are probably the less
mature ones. For these, "clothes buying is not a happy time." A few would
"buy anything to get out of the store."

Many have at least a partial clothes allowance, but others are not yet ready for
this.

Daily Selection.   Most make all decisions about what to wear, seeking only
minor advice. Many show a great interest not only in wearing the "right"
things, but also things which "go together," and take real pleasure in certain special articles of clothing.

The majority are meticulous about their clothes and their persons, but a minority
would still be actually dirty, even their hands, if not reminded. Boys show
a greater difference than girls between the way they look every day and
when dressed up.

Care of Clothes.   In general, clothes are well cared for, sent to cleaner's,
pressed, mended. Most hang clothes neatly on hangers, though exceptions
occur, especially among boys. Most are reliable about disposing of dirty
clothing.

16 YEARS

Buying Clothes.   Many go shopping alone for less important articles. Most
boys go with mothers for major purchases, but disagreement seldom occurs. Most know what they want, how they want to look, and are allowed
to make their own choice.

Girls do more of their shopping alone, but a good many prefer to have their
mothers along when shopping. They feel more secure, and believe she has
better taste and judgment than they do. Some girls scout around alone
first, then have mother come to help make the final decision.

Little disagreement occurs about either what to buy or how much. Little teasing
for clothes: "We just consider what I want and need."

Clothes allowances even yet are not very satisfactory for most. They are not
yet ready to plan wisely.

Care of Clothes.   Nearly all take the responsibility about having the clothes
they wear, including underwear, neat and clean. The majority take good
care of their clothes, most girls hanging them up as they remove them,
but a few boys still leaving them on the floor or draping them on a chair.

Most are careful to put dirty clothes in the wash, and some take responsibility
for sending clothes to the cleaner's, though boys are more apt to let mother
do this. Girls especially may wash, mend, and press own clothes. Some boys
are careful to press trousers and shine shoes.

5. CARE OF ROOM

10 YEARS

Rooms, on the whole, are very messy. Clothes just slung around all over everything, shoes on floor, desk piled high. Many say they *prefer* rooms this
way.

Spasmodic cleaning, parent-instigated.

Some pennants or pictures on walls but most rooms are not "fixed up" very
specially.

11 YEARS

Room is still very messy: clothes piled on bed or left on floor, desk piled high.
"A terrible mess," "awfully untidy." Parents express great dissatisfaction.

A few children say that they *try* to keep rooms neat. Most apparently do not
try very hard. Many report they want things left messy: "I don't like my
mother to move stuff without telling me, whether it is on the floor or not."

Many now have room "fixed up" elaborately: banners, posters, stickers; pictures
of athletes, movie stars, horses, on the walls.

Occasional spurts of cleaning, parent-instigated.

12 YEARS

Little improvement appears. "Messiest room in the house"; "A shambles. Top
of the desk littered—can of worms, half-eaten apple, candy wrappers, dirty
socks." Clothes still all over the room; litter of collections, systematic or
otherwise.

With some boys, mothers have given up and clean room themselves. With
others, and with girls, a weekly clean-up is usually instigated.

Much "fixing up" of room: pennants; pictures of movie stars or athletes, bulletin boards, wildlife charts, horse pictures.

13 YEARS

The bedroom—"my *own* room"—was important earlier, but now is even more so. Many spend most of their spare time in it. In some cases it is a little neater, but mothers still complain: "cluttered," "careless," "sloppy." Some Thirteens try to clean up spontaneously but complain that it gets messy again right away. Child may be satisfied but parent rarely is.

Some rooms fairly tidy except inside bureau drawers and closet and on desk.

Furnishings and decorations (banners, pictures, etc.) still very important.

"Hermits" who live in their rooms may have them quite elaborately equipped with food and provisions for entertainment.

14 YEARS

Care of room usually lags behind care for own appearance and for clothes.

Children themselves are mostly satisfied with their care of rooms; parents are less so. Our group is about equally divided between those who keep their rooms reasonably neat and those who do not. Girls are a little more often in the neat half than boys are.

Some are beginning to want their rooms to be neat, though they do not always achieve this. They may vary from time to time, or only *parts* of the room may be a mess.

15 YEARS

Marked improvement occurs. The majority now keep their rooms either "clean" or "passable." Girls still are generally ahead of boys, and individual variation still appears, with a range from "neat as a pin" to "a mess."

Many will pick up nicely, but just when they feel like it, not when mother insists. Some "could" but do not, as part of revolt against parents' demands.

16 YEARS

Continued improvement in care of room occurs. Many are reported to keep their rooms neat, or reasonably neat. Many make their own beds, vacuum, and dust, as well as keeping the room picked up. Some even keep closets clean, though many cannot extend neatness to the inside of closet or drawers. And many are variable, cleaning up the room only when it gets too messy, or "only on weekends."

A few, boys especially, are said to keep the room "immaculate." At the other extreme, for a few—again boys—the room is still "not too neat, but mother has given up. She doesn't interfere."

6. MONEY AND WORK

10 YEARS

Money. The majority depend on an allowance for money, though some do a little work in return for this and others supplement the allowance with earnings. Only a few have to earn all their money.

The weekly allowance ranges in amount from 15 cents to $1.25, the middle figure being 35 cents. Most are reasonably satisfied with the amount, though a few think it too small. Not required to do much with this allowance; most spend it as they choose.

Many are very casual about money at this age—forget to ask for their allowance, leave it in a pocket, or lose it. Parents say: "Irresponsible"; "Not interested"; "Money means nothing to him."

Some save a little; others save nothing. Some worry that family money will not last.

Work. Most are not good about helping at home: "I hate it"; "I'm tired and I don't want to help"; "Not too good at it." Parents say, "Never does a thing but what she groans." Slow about responding to requests for help: delay, object, dawdle. Most do not openly rebel.

Most work best away from home. Boys do better outdoors than indoors.

Some are paid for work, others are expected to work in return for allowance. Among regular tasks: set table, do dishes, make bed, clean room, take out trash or garbage, mow lawn, garden, shovel snow, sweep, dust, feed dog. Some care for younger siblings, but most do not yet baby-sit outside of home.

11 YEARS

Money. By far the majority still depend on an allowance, though some have to do a little work in return. Many supplement allowance with earnings. Many are now enthusiastic earners. Only a few earn all their money.

The weekly allowance ranges from 25 cents to $1.25, the middle figure being 50 cents. A few receive enough money to allow for saving or some school expenses. Most do not as yet.

Some now complain that they want a bigger allowance, or that other children get more.

A few parents discipline by depriving of allowance if behavior is bad.

Most are more interested in and more careful with money than at ten. More save at least some. Some receive extra money particularly for saving. Several now described as "tightwads."

Work.   Most are even worse about helping than at ten. Nearly all have to be reminded about tasks. Some merely sigh, fuss, groan, delay. Others resist, argue, rebel: "Like fish I'm nice about working. Quick and prompt? I'm just the opposite!"

Mothers say that tasks formerly accepted now become major issues, and may wonder, "Is it worth it?"

Tries to get out of tasks if possible. Works slowly, resentfully, messily. "In a minute" stronger than at ten; also, "Do I *have* to?"

Home tasks about the same ones as at ten years.

As at ten, better away from home. Some do a little baby-sitting away from home, in the afternoons mostly. Boys do outdoor work away from home.

12 YEARS

Money.   An allowance is still the main source of income for most but an increasing number supplement allowance with earnings, or earn all. Some earn several dollars a week.

Allowance is considerably larger now: middle value is $1. However, a good many budget, and allowance now covers many more expenditures. An allowance of $2.50 weekly might be apportioned as follows: 50 cents save, 50 cents Xmas club, 60 cents movies and candy, 10 cents Sunday school, 25 cents school supplies, 55 cents emergencies. Others have to pay own bus fare or for school lunches.

Some save fairly large sums to make important purchases. A few are reckless or "terrible" with money—squander it, or are "all mixed up." Many do quite well, at least try to make their money last.

Work.   Still reluctant about helping but most now resigned: *"Might as well* do it the first time she asks. *Have to anyway,"* or, "If she wants to she can make me." Most don't volunteer but will help if asked or if they have a schedule. Resistance may be silent: "I do it but I pout to myself."

About one-fourth of our subjects do baby-sitting. Almost as many boys as girls do sitting and Twelves sit at night as well as in the afternoon.

Boys' tasks at home include chiefly: mowing lawns, shoveling snow, odd jobs, burning papers, raking leaves, clearing out garage, errands, washing car, making own bed, emptying wastebaskets, washing dishes. Usually better at outdoor than at indoor work.

Away from home boys have a paper route, shovel snow and cut lawns, baby-sit.

Girls' tasks at home include: doing dishes, making beds, cleaning own room, vacuuming, dusting. A little simple cooking and ironing. Baby-sitting. Their chief work outside of home is baby-sitting.

If no boys in the home, girls do some outside work. Boys often do some inside work anyway.

13 YEARS

Money. The majority have an allowance. It is either large enough to include bus fares and school lunches, or parent pays for these separately. Allowance centers around $1 to $1.50, but range is from 30 cents a week to $4.

About one-third do supplement allowance with earnings. Most very flexible and effective about this. If they need more, they earn it. A few earn all that they have. Only one or two have no allowance or earnings and merely ask for what they want.

Individual differences, but in general a rather careful age: "Never broke," "always has money." Most are reasonably careful—save for presents and necessary big expenditures. However, even now a few forget to collect their allowance.

Work. Most are now much better about helping. Not enthusiastic but at least willing. "Quite good about helping though I may say 'In a minute.'" May say, "I do it voluntarily"; "I'm responsible for my room"; "I'm determined to improve about helping"; even, "Some of the things I like to do." May even offer to help when not asked or required.

Parents say, "She can do her share without resisting, dawdling, getting in the way."

Many, boys as well as girls, now have steady baby-sitting jobs. Also many are paid for baby-sitting at home. Tasks are about as at twelve, except that girls now often get a simple meal, and boys are starting to do caddying.

14 YEARS

Money. With a handful of exceptions who earn all their own money, and one who merely asks when she wants it, all now receive a regular allowance.

The median allowance is now $2 weekly, the range from 40 cents to $5. The larger allowances include bus fare, lunch money, etc.

Nearly half now supplement allowance with own earnings.

Individual differences in handling money are becoming increasingly marked. Thus parents' comments range from: "Careful with money. Thinks a long time before she spends," to, "Money means absolutely nothing to him. He buys foolish things."

Many at this age have an inflated idea of money, how much people should earn, how much things cost: "This thing was *only* $5."

Work. Helping around the house is now less of a problem. Tasks are by many taken for granted: "My responsibilities are—" May not be enthusiastic about helping but do it more or less routinely; less delay and fewer objections than earlier.

Most do not take as much responsibility as parents think they should. But some mothers feel that Fourteens are very busy with school and outside activities, and actually make fewer demands on them than earlier.

Nearly half of our subjects supplement allowance with earnings from outside work. Paper route, caddying, baby-sitting, and working in stores are most common activities. Most are very responsible about such outside work.

15 YEARS

Money. The majority still have an allowance. The amount still centers around $2 weekly, but the range is now 75 cents to $6.25.

Nearly half of these supplement their allowance with earnings. Also nearly one-fourth of our Fifteens actually earn all of their own spending money. Many like the independence of this: "Used to have an allowance but prefer to earn it myself." Some earn in summer, though no time to earn in winter.

Only two in our group have no allowance or earnings and merely ask for money as they want it.

Not too much saving in bank, but many have $10 or so at home saved for special purchases.

Work. Most now more or less cheerfully list tasks which they are "expected" to do. Seem mostly to take these for granted: "I have my own tasks." Most may not be enthusiastic workers but at least make little fuss.

Having to do work may still interfere with the delicate friendly relations between mother and daughter, but little "overt conflict," as one girl says.

Many state that they just haven't time to help much and many parents accept this.

Tasks are becoming increasingly complex and responsible. Girls get meals, do major cleaning, take over when mother is away. Boys undertake outdoor projects as well as routine work; may do painting, make electrical repairs.

Work away from home may be quite responsible and remunerative.

16 YEARS

Money. Almost as much variety as among adults in amount of money available and how it is handled.

Allowances vary from nothing, through 75 cents a week supplemented by own earnings, to as much as $25 a month which includes a clothes allowance. Some earn all their own money. Others neither earn nor have an allowance but ask as they want it.

Most not ready for a full clothes allowance.

Both boys and girls may supplement allowance with baby-sitting or similar earnings. Many boys in summer or part-time jobs earn sizable amounts of money—$20 a week or several hundred dollars during summer.

Many do try to budget. Success varies. Several say, "Financial situation not good." However, in many, more appreciation of value of money than earlier. Some do save money in a bank account.

Work.   Most boys do some routine tasks at home. This is by now usually taken for granted and doesn't make too much trouble.

Girls and mothers still have trouble about household tasks though less than formerly. Many girls are still lazy, uninterested, and not too co-operative, though may routinely do dishes, beds, or some other assigned tasks. Most do not help as much or as willingly as parents wish they would.

Many are so busy parents accept that they don't have time to help.

Many boys have really substantial jobs either after school or during the summer. May earn as much as $20 a week or so. May use part of money toward school or other expenses.

Both girls and boys may be camp counselors in summer.

Baby-sitting is a favorite occupation of many girls and some boys.

CHAPTER THIRTEEN

Emotions

THE VERY word *emotion* suggests agitation and excitement. And there is a tendency to think of emotions as though they were disembodied forces which in some mysterious way arise from their depths to seize the individual and place him at their mercy. Adolescence, accordingly, is considered to be a highly emotional period of development—"a crazy, mixed-up period." This extreme view exaggerates the dramatic and disturbing aspects of emotion. It fails to acknowledge that much of the emotional life of the normal adolescent is calm, deep, and constructive. The inconspicuous manifestations of emotion need greater recognition.

Emotions are not foreign intrusions; they are part and parcel of the unitary action system. This complex action system constantly assumes changing patterns of tension and of motor preparedness. An emotion is essentially a feeling of motor attitude, whether it be in the form of anger, fear, affection, or serenity. These specific feelings are responses to immediate situations. In their boundless variety they reflect the life experiences and above all the maturity of the individual.

Emotions grow. They are not fixed entities. They change with age throughout infancy, childhood, and youth. Even a baby can teach us something about the innate nature of these developmental changes, which continue into the years from ten to sixteen. Compare for example, the emotional maturity of a typical infant at 28 weeks and at 32 weeks of age. At 28 weeks the infant is generally in good equilibrium and presents an amiable union of self-containedness, contentment, and sociability. He discriminates strangers, but adapts to them. He has himself well in hand, both in attitudes and activities. At 32 weeks of age, however, he is not so self-contained; his face often wears a questioning, half-bewildered expression. He is less forthright; he shows a greater tentativeness in unaccustomed situations, and needs more time to adjust to them. He looks with new penetration at the movements of people around him. He is more conscious of sounds. He seems much more sensitive than he was a month ago. He is quiet, watchful, often withdrawn.

Such a remarkable change in the patterning of emotion is a common growth phenomenon in childhood and adolescence. This is a kind of change which cannot be ascribed to sheer environmental factors. The change comes from within. It comes naturally through hidden, innate processes of growth. Similar changes in sensitiveness occur throughout the adolescent maturation of emotions. The developmental trends of these basic changes are outlined in the growth gradients assembled in the present chapter.

The gradients show that the climate of emotion alters somewhat from year to year in concordance with the advance in general maturity level. There are certain persisting emotional characteristics which can be referred to inborn temperament. There are other individual characteristics which trace to recent and remote life experiences. But underlying and pervading these distinctive traits there are sequences and patterns which are intrinsically developmental. They are shared by adolescents of comparable maturity. Making due allowance for individual differences of temperament, it is possible to look for maturity signs which indicate whether or not a given youth, emotionally, is growing up. We may ask, even though we cannot answer, does he act his age emotionally?

Here we may recall our concept of "emotional behavior" (and also the sensitiveness of the 32-week-old infant). Emotion is essentially a personal feeling of motor attitudes evoked by the situations of daily living. As the action system changes from age to age, so do the situations and the responsive behavior. The direction, the shape, and the sequences of change are not fortuitous. They are consistent enough to warrant the conclusion that emotional behavior develops stage by stage, and is just as structured and patterned as walking, seeing, talking, manipulating, and thinking. At times, however, an emotion may be charged with an elemental wildness and primitiveness which demands special controls and interpretation.

For simplification we have characterized the maturity traits of seven age zones with key adjectives and phrases, which have many implications as to the general course of emotional development. "Ten" is casual and easygoing. Eleven is sensitive and self-assertive. Twelve is outgoing and balanced. Thirteen is withdrawn and inwardized. Fourteen, expansive and exuberant. Fifteen, restless and apathetic. Sixteen, friendly and well-adjusted. This is a compressed thumbnail summary, but despite over-simplification it gives a just impression of the over-all semi-rhythmic fluctuations which mark the advancing cycle of emotional growth be-tween the nodal ages of ten and sixteen.

The transformations which takes place during the cycle of seven years are remarkable in variety and extent. Each year releases new emotional potentials, resulting in readjustments between the changing organism and the expanding environment. Emotions thus become both symptoms and creative forces in the continuing drama of development. Their role goes far beyond mere expression. Their influence is not restricted to intense and vivid episodes. Mild, intimate, and secret states of feeling, which recur spontaneously or compulsively, also play a role in the patterning of adolescent personality. There are, moreover, voluntary forms of feeling, which a youth summons up in his ruminations and his efforts at self-control. These feelings are of moral and developmental significance. We shall have more to say about them in the following chapter on The Grow-ing Self.

As the self matures, emotional behavior matures. A rapid review of characteristic patterns of emotion at successive age periods will show an interesting alternation of outgoing and inwardizing trends, of expansive and withdrawn attitudes, of positive and negative responses. Emotional growth requires an interweaving organization of opposed tendencies both on large and on small scales, in brief and in prolonged stretches of time. The remarkable complexity and wealth of organization which is accom-plished between the years from ten to sixteen is truly impressive.

Ten is a good starting point for tracing the directions of this organiza-tion. Ten is a nodal age which marks the end of one cycle and the begin-ning of another. It is a relatively integrated stage of maturity, and com-paratively simple in emotional structure. "Ten" as an individual is gen-erally equable, contented, amiable. He does not think much about how he feels; he takes himself for granted; he does not make many demands on others. He does not go far afield to seek experience which might deepen his emotional life. On the whole he is not very competitive, envious, fear-some, or worrisome. Sadness scarcely touches him. He is benign.

But, as if to remind us that his emotions are nevertheless growing, he occasionally bursts out with intense, brief episodes of extreme joy, of affection, and of sharp anger. His anger is so unexpected that one wonders what seizes him with such frenzy. He verily yells, strikes out, kicks furiously, and even bites! The flare-ups, however, are soon over; he suddenly becomes quiescent and he harbors no grudge. There is something childlike about this evanescent response; but it may be a precursor of the more profuse emotional patterns which come into evidence in the following year.

The contrast in the emotional behavior of Eleven and Ten is unmistakable. The relative blandness of Ten gives way to variegated responses with many unaccountable shifts in mood, and with undercurrents of irritability, belligerence, and argumentativeness. Variously, he feels peevish, hurt, sad, jealous, competitive. But at times he also feels gay and cheery, affectionate, timorous, and worried. Undoubtedly he feels all sorts of emergent emotions which it would be difficult to describe. Although puberty may lie a year or more in the future, the ferment and the profusion of his feelings signify that adolescence, as a psychological epoch, has already arrived. His anger has new intensity and depth. It is less episodic and shallow than at ten. He is apt to call names as he strikes out. He does not restabilize quickly and he cries or sobs in a manner which reveals that he is keenly affected by the experience. He may have to retaliate before he comes back to equilibrium. This too suggests a positive developmental factor rather than a regression to infancy. He may show a renewed and heightened fear of the dark.

His emotional capacities are also developing in genial and favorable directions. In a talkative, effervescing mood he becomes engagingly candid while he pours forth the many pleasant things on his mind. Having started a project which appeals to him, he can work at it with sustained determination almost to the point of exhaustion. His multiplying interests have a new intensity—further evidence of developmental transformations in the realm of feeling.

Despite the vagaries and the impulsiveness of manifold experiences, ordering forces soon come into play. Things begin to smooth out both for the parent and the child. Twelve is in better self-control, as a rule, and he does not flare up as readily. He can go to extremes of exuberance and anger without being thrown off balance. He can inhibit fears. His efforts at emotional control are more obvious. He is more restrained in demonstrations of affection. He shows caution as well as daring. He is becoming aware of the feelings of others as well as of his own. In mysterious ways which no philosopher has yet divined he comes into possession of new types of humor. This too contributes to capacities of control; for the sense of humor is an acutely paradoxical mixture of inwardized and projected emotion. Sometimes, however, the projection is so immature in quality and propriety that the humor itself needs control.

Twelve in general tends to be outgoing, exuberant, and enthusiastic. At the thirteen-year level there is a calming down. In obedience to under-lying rhythms of growth the emotional life now shifts to increased in-wardizing trends. Thirteen is more withdrawn and more thoughtful both about himself and others. He is more deeply saddened by household dis-appointments and misfortunes. There is a minor strain in his moods. He even takes his feelings out on himself. He may retreat to his room and "tell himself off," in an attempt to master his anger. This is a favorable sign in the evolution and control of his emotional behavior. It means that he wants to resolve his feelings within himself. His greater sensitiveness and even his secretiveness indicate that his emotions are deepening and refining. For some time the subjective inwardizing trends remain domi-nant. This may well be a normal trend in a complex process of develop-mental organization.

In due course, at the fourteen-year level or thereabouts, outgoing, ex-pansive tendencies come to the fore. This shift, which derives from an inherent developmental cycle, can be quite pronounced in some indi-viduals. A full-blown 14-year-old is a spontaneous extrovert. He does not hold back and brood or feel sorry for himself. He is full of laughter, jokes, and humor. He throws his voice around somewhat noisily and lets people know how he feels. He permits unresolved fears and worries to come to the surface. His tendency is to enjoy life in an energetic manner. He considers himself to be pretty lucky and does not wish to change places with anyone.

Once again a withdrawn phase follows an expansive one. There is an evident calming down at the fifteen-year stage of maturity. The symptoms of change are somewhat enigmatical. At times Fifteen appears apathetic, indifferent, and unapproachable. At other times he is keenly perceptive and critical. His musings focalize on subtle issues. He breaks forth with abrupt movements which are associated with flashes of insight and feel-ing. His attitude toward school may be one of wholehearted enthusiasm or of hard-boiled resistance. His soft-spoken voice contrasts strangely with the talkative noisiness of Fourteen. His emotional life is far too com-plex for brief characterization; but it indicates an increasing self-awareness which comes to a higher expression at the sixteen-year level of maturity.

Sixteen in normal sequence attains a stage of improved integration. Typically he is well adjusted and functions on a more even keel. He tends to be friendly and positive, rather than negative and critical. He is inclined to be more tolerant and considerate. The better balance of his self attitudes and social attitudes foreshadows the adult maturity of the twenties.

Looking backward we find that the over-all emotional qualities of Sixteen are reminiscent of Ten; but the capacities and patterns of response at sixteen are markedly advanced over those at ten. When the years between ten and sixteen are viewed in perspective, we see a progressive process of organization, which reflects a combination of constitutional and cultural factors. The emotional self grows through an assimilation of experience, which normally leads to increased control. Thus anger, one of the most powerful of all emotions, is expressed with immediate combativeness at the ten- and eleven-year age levels. Physical violence rather than verbal violence is then the rule. At the thirteen-year maturity level this primitive violence gives way to withdrawal from the room and to verbal retort, with greatly improved control of temper.

Among our research group, eleven and twelve appeared to be the most fearing ages. Animals and darkness were the most common fears from ten to thirteen. Thereafter persons and social situations figured more prominently. At thirteen and fourteen worries exceeded fears. At all ages the main worries had to do with school. Ten was rated as one of the happiest ages; thirteen on the basis of self-reports is least happy. The tendency to cry varies with age and sex. The least tearful ages by our data are ten, twelve, and fourteen; the more tearful are eleven, thirteen, and fifteen. No boys of sixteen admitted to crying.

It is interesting to note that although both Ten and Eleven are prone to anger, Ten is not competitive in disposition, while Eleven is decidedly so. Sixteen is more competitive than Fifteen; but true to form he may make qualifications to the effect that he likes to be in the highest group, but not on top. He likes to win once in a while, but not all the time. Most of our 16-year-old subjects thoughtfully state that in their own opinion they are neither envious nor jealous.

The emotional life of the adolescent is not, of course, confined to the major emotions such as anger, fear, love, jealousy. It embraces countless situations in which unnamed feelings are aroused or suppressed. These "feelings" in fluid or fixed forms, intense or mild, are omnipresent. All activities of mind and personality are inevitably colored and reinforced by feelings of some sort—by moods and wishes, by desire or repugnance; by acceptance or rejection. Feelings, in this fundamental sense, are not mere by-products. They register and direct the reactions of the individual. They reflect and influence both physiological and psychological functions. They enter into the mental and moral processes of perception, judgment, evaluation, and decision. They operate almost ceaselessly in the formation of character.

Character depends not only on what we think and do, but on how we master and organize our feelings. Self-mastery is not limited to critical moments of high tension. As the adolescent enters his teens he often recurs to quiet, meditative periods of self-examination. He has earnest moments of high resolve and aspiration. He begins to define his self by matching it with that of other selves. He explores his potentials in terms of self-chosen heroes and ideals. Thereby he gives precision and status to his feelings. They contribute to the structure of his personality development. These calmer phases of his emotional life are frequently unnoticed or even misunderstood; but they are very important to him and to society.

During these phases he becomes self-conscious; he indulges an inner life by which he revives or creates states of feeling and manipulates them in his fantasy. This is not an idle or harmful pursuit under normal conditions; for self-consciousness, as a distinguished philosopher remarked, implies ethical freedom. A healthy-minded youth uses this freedom to refine conscience and to strengthen his feelings for aesthetic and spiritual values. Many of his emotional traits may be partially organized at a subconscious level; but they also need the insight and controls which come with active, self-conscious consideration. Under this concept, feelings become purposeful voluntary devices in the development of adolescent personality. An emotionally immature youth fails to cope with feelings in this realistic sense. He tends instead to surrender to them.

An adult is regarded as being emotionally mature when he can manage his own affairs in a responsible manner and can take adequate account of the attitudes and responsibilities of other persons. Presumably this degree of maturity may be achieved with the twenties, although it is significantly prefigured at the sixteen-year level. In no small measure the youth from ten to sixteen is engaged in the many-sided task of achieving emotional maturity under guidance and by self-education.

Emotional growth is a progressive patterning process, which pervades

the manifold situations of everyday life. This process involves above all
an intricate web of interpersonal relations. It extends to the routines of
self-care, to the interests and activities of home, school, and neighborhood, to the ethics of daily conduct, to the philosophic concepts and attitudes which emanate with the expanding self. Separate chapters are devoted to each of these areas which embrace the patterning of emotional
behavior. The growth gradients of each chapter are designed to give concrete indications of the sequences and directions of emotional development in the setting of our contemporary culture. The gradients seem to
give evidence of an underlying developmental anatomy of feelings and
emotion.

GROWTH GRADIENTS

1. EMOTIONS IN GENERAL

10 YEARS

Ten is seen by his parents as direct, matter-of-fact, simple, clear-cut, childish.
Generally easygoing and balanced.

Some fears persist, but Ten is less anxious, exacting, and demanding than he
was at nine. Seldom cries, and reports that he is "real happy."

Anger is not frequent, but is violent, immediate, expressed physically, and
soon resolved. Humor is broad, labored, not generally funny to adults.

11 YEARS

Eleven is described by parents as penetrating, sensitive, proud, selfish, competitive, belligerent, jealous, resentful, argumentative, contrary, rude,
unco-operative.

Yet with other adults he can be polite, factual, serious, honest, sincere, confiding, unguarded.

Dramatizes and exaggerates his expressions ("Never had a decent Christmas";
"Worst mother in the whole school, and everybody says so").

Response to anger is frequent, violent, physical, emotional, and verbal. Humor
is lively, "corny," often smutty. Many fears, many worries, many tears—
yet most think of themselves as happy.

12 YEARS

Twelve is viewed as expansive, outgoing, enthusiastic, overgenerous. Described
by parents as good company, friendly, understanding, thoughtful, likable,
reasonable.

Relatively uncomplicated—many fears, but fewer worries, less jealousy, little
crying. Great enthusiasm for things he likes; utter hatred for things he
dislikes. *Loves* or *hates,* no middle ground.

Deals with others, and can be dealt with, through his humor, which is now
funnier to adults, though drawing on insult, sex, and practical jokes.

13 YEARS

Thirteen is described by parents as thoughtful, inwardized, quiet, self-contained. This may go to extremes, and then he is described as withdrawn,
morbid, morose, moody, secretive, lethargic, indifferent, sullen, seclusive,
"in a minor key."

Extremely sensitive and vulnerable—easily hurt, irritated, or annoyed. In anger,
wants most to get off by himself, to his own room. Many cry on occasion.
Humor is less frequent and leans on sarcasm, but is more amusing to
adults.

14 YEARS

Fourteen is expansive and outgoing, energetic and enthusiastic. He is much
less withdrawn, and appears much happier than at thirteen. Loves competition. Anger is less frequent, and is manifested verbally rather than
physically or by withdrawal. Humor (other than parents') is much appreciated.

Fourteen actually may experience more inner confusion and turmoil than his
independent, self-assured manner might indicate.

15 YEARS

Fifteen is described by parents as more self-confident, determined, subtle,
discriminating, self-controlled than at fourteen. Behavior is much less
outgoing, and many are moody, restless, dissatisfied, apathetic. Prefers
to cover his feelings.

May be muddled and confused. Mature enough to be aware of many problems,
he has not yet worked through to solutions. Fifteen appears unhappy with
himself and with others—yet his own reporting shows him as happier than
he seems.

16 YEARS

Sixteen appears cheerful, friendly, positive, outgoing, well adjusted, matter-of-
fact, "even-keeled." He generally takes things easily, thinks things are
going reasonably well, takes a calm approach even to problems, doesn't
believe in worrying.

Some Sixteens are becoming quite analytical about their own emotions. Show
considerable interest in whether they can control their emotions or are con-

trolled by them. Anger is better in hand. Humor can be used as a social technique. Self-evaluation is frequent: "I get impatient," "I'm a little moody."

2. ANGER

10 YEARS

Ten is not a characteristically angry age. Many Tens say they try to keep their tempers, and more than at following ages say they don't get mad or don't do anything about it when angry.

But response to anger, when it comes, is violent and immediate. Most commonly its expression is physical: "beat them up," "sock them," "hit and kick and bite," "kick the place around." Next most common is some kind of emotional violence: "blow up," "explode," "boil over," "get so MAD I could kill people." More cry in anger than at any following age.

Already a few leave the room or go away by themselves when angry. Even this is usually preceded by some token of violence: "Stamp my foot and go to my room," "boil over and go to my room." Responding merely verbally also occurs, but less often than at following ages. Though verbal, the responses are none the less violent—Tens yell, screech, call names: "That old drip!" "You're a bitch!" Especially do they shout back if sent from the room.

A considerable number plot revenge, though they seldom remember to carry this out.

Most say their response depends on whom they are mad at. If at parents, some can't do much, some boil over. If at friends or siblings, there is usually physical violence. If at teachers, they "can't do anything," or "just tell the other kids."

In summary, *physical* and *emotional violence* lead at this age.

11 YEARS

Eleven's anger is aroused far more often than Ten's. (Nearly twice as many anger responses are reported at eleven as at any other age in our range.)

Physical violence is even more prominent than at ten, and is by far the most common response. Children fight, hit, slam doors. Emotional violence, too, reaches its high point, and the angry 11-year-old is likely to "blow a fuse," "blow my top." Nearly as much crying occurs as at ten.

Violent verbal retorts are common: yelling, swearing, calling names, saying mean or sarcastic things, talking back or snapping back. Leaving the room, though a less common response for Elevens, still occurs more than at ten or twelve, and occurs violently, as "stamping" or "slamming out of the room." Pouting, sulking, and planning revenge are also characteristic.

When angry at a teacher, the majority say, they just sit and take it, "sit and sizzle," "just burn up inside," or else write notes about her and pass them.

Thus, *physical violence*, some *violent verbal retort*, *emotional violence*, and *leaving the room* all occur conspicuously, and in that order, at eleven.

12 YEARS

This is the last age when immediate physical violence is the most characteristically reported response to anger. Twelve still may fight or strike out physically, or take some less common action such as throwing things (for which this is the leading age).

Verbal response to the situation is now more common than earlier. Twelves talk back, "tell her off," "just talk nasty." They may call names, and some mutter under their breath.

General emotional violence—boiling over or exploding—does occur, but less commonly, and there is less crying than earlier. Some just "sit and seethe," or "smolder inside." Some, though fewer than at surrounding ages, simply leave the room. Most can now do this without slamming the door.

If angry at a teacher, Twelve reports, "I tell her to shut up in my mind"; "I say, 'Shut up, you old mole,' or, 'Drop dead.'"

Thus *physical violence* and *verbal retort* are the leading types of response.

13 YEARS

Thirteen brings a marked change. By far the most characteristic response is to leave the scene, often to go to their own rooms (and close the door).

Some kind of verbal response is next most common. This retort is less violent than earlier—there is little shouting and screaming, and even less talking back. Mostly 13-year-olds merely say mean or sarcastic things. A few swear or argue.

Sulking is a common response, and quite a number do cry, but there is much less "blowing up" and "boiling over." Scowling, frowning, and making faces are characteristic of thirteen.

Behaviors not earlier reported are "deflected responses" to anger—taking it out on someone else (especially on mother), or even getting mad at themselves for getting mad at others.

A large number say that they never get mad, or that even when they do there is nothing they do, or can do, about it. Some say they "just sit and think about it."

Anger at a teacher most often results in practical jokes or making faces. In general, *leaving the scene* is the most outstanding response at thirteen.

14 YEARS

Anger responses, as reported, are greatly reduced in number at fourteen. Highly characteristic of the age is the remark, "I just sit and take it."

The usual responses at fourteen, and following, are verbal ones. Physical violence seldom occurs, and emotional violence, including crying, is much less frequent than formerly. However, verbal responses may be quite violent. Fourteen may yell, swear, call names, or just say mean or sarcastic things. Talking back and snapping back often occur.

Leaving the room when angry—often to go to his own room—occurs as often as verbal retort. Those who do may mutter around, slam the door, even lock themselves in.

Quite a few take it out on someone else (especially on mother), or try to make the person at whom they are angry uncomfortable. A few now do nothing immediately, but later talk the situation over, with some friend or with the person himself.

Fourteen, if angry at a teacher, will "sit and take it," "grin and bear it," or "talk to myself."

The leading responses at fourteen are *leaving the room* and making some *verbal response.*

15 YEARS

The number of anger responses reported is again reduced. Physically and emotionally violent responses still do occur, but are not characteristic of fifteen. A few do cry on occasion when angry, but this also is not usual.

Two kinds of response occur most commonly: leaving the room ("I just go away somewhere," "want to be alone") and responding verbally—saying something mean or sarcastic, arguing or swearing, or telling "what I think of them."

Quite a few sulk or plan revenge. But a fairly large number say that they try not to show anger, try to suppress it, or try to ignore the person. Some talk it over with the person who made them angry; others, less kind, "explain, but in a harsh tone."

If angry at a teacher, Fifteen reports, he may do any of a number of things: "sit and take it," "give her a cold look," "talk to myself," "say to heck with the homework."

Fifteen's main responses to anger are *verbal retort,* and *leaving the room.*

16 YEARS

Tempers are much better controlled at sixteen than earlier. The majority say, "I just don't get mad the way I used to," "I'm on a pretty even keel."

Many express a wish to be able to control their emotions. If they become angry, many "try not to show it," "suffer in silence," "grin and bear it."

Others sulk, brood, "look stony," "sit and glare," or "mutter," and a few "say
something mean," but others can "stay and talk things over." Only an
occasional Sixteen "blows up," slams doors, shouts, or cries when angry.
Thus, by sixteen, anger responses are less frequent and *generally not overt*.

3. WORRIES AND FEARS

10 YEARS

Worries. Fewer worries than fears. The main worries at all ages from ten to
sixteen concern school, and nearly all worries at this age center around
homework, lessons, and being late. A few worry about family finances and
the cost of food—a concern which drops out in later adolescence.

Fears. Many different kinds of fears are reported, but fewer altogether than
in the ages immediately following. Animals, especially wild ones and
snakes, are mentioned most; the dark is feared by many. Also high places,
fires, criminals, "killers," burglars.

A few are beginning spontaneously to mention things they are not afraid of—
chiefly the dark, dogs, and being left alone.

11 YEARS

Worries. The most worried, as well as one of the most fearful ages. As usual,
the most fears deal with school, homework, and lessons. Money, mother's
welfare, and own health are other frequent worries. Several also mention
family relations, father's driving, and world conditions.

Fears. Eleven and twelve are the most fearful ages in this age range. Animals
are the most feared—snakes, bugs, cows or bulls. The dark, especially
being left alone in the dark, is next most frequent, and high places are
often mentioned.

More at this age than any other tell spontaneously what they do *not* fear—
chiefly, the dark and snakes.

12 YEARS

Worries. Fewer worries than at eleven, with school still the main source.
Money and health have dropped out in favor of social worries—family
relations, that people may not like them, or that they may make a bad
impression.

Fears. Another relatively fearful age. Being alone in the dark or being out in
it are mentioned most. Next come animals, especially snakes, then crowds
and high places.

Some say their fears are "silly" or "disgusting," but they still have them.
Again many spontaneously list things not feared—chiefly dogs and heights.

13 YEARS

Worries.   At thirteen and fourteen, more worries are reported than fears. Most worries still center around homework and lessons, with more concern over grades than at any other age. Other main concerns are mother's welfare, own appearance, and, for girls, their relationships with boys.

Fears.   Much less fearfulness (our group reports about half as many fears as at twelve). The dark definitely leads, followed by fear of crowds and of high places. Animals are less feared than formerly, though snakes are still mentioned by many.

New, social kinds of fears are beginning: "people," "applying for a job," "performing in public," "family quarreling," "social gossip."

Fewer children need to mention spontaneously the things they do *not* fear. However, quite a few make such modifying remarks as, "Not exactly afraid of it, but don't like it very well."

A few enjoy scaring themselves with frightening thoughts.

14 YEARS

Worries.   As at thirteen, worries exceed fears. School is still the chief source of worry, though less so than earlier. World conditions are now a source of worries, though these are exceeded by more personal-social worries: "my appearance," or "that people might not like me or I might make a bad impression."

Fears.   The fewest fears are reported at this age. Animals (especially snakes), the dark, high places—all are feared about equally. As at thirteen, social fears are mentioned: applying for a job, performing in public, social gossip.

15 YEARS

Worries.   Worries and fears are reported in about equal numbers at fifteen. The chief source of worry remains school—grades and homework in particular. Some Fifteens worry about their own health, some about popularity, some about "everything."

Fears.   Not a fearful age, though slightly more so than at fourteen. Chief fears reported are animals (especially bugs), being alone in the dark, high places (more than earlier), and social problems.

16 YEARS

Worries.   The majority say they do not worry very much—"Don't believe in it;

it doesn't help any." A few, though, describe themselves as worriers, and report worrying about "almost everything."

The main concern is school—homework or examinations. Several worry about their own futures, or, more globally, "What's going to happen to the world."

Some incidental worries are about gaining weight, about health, or because "I'm so terribly shallow-minded." Some even say they worry because they think they don't worry enough.

Fears. Most state that they have no fears, and are reported by parents to have none. The main fear reported (by girls, not by boys) is of being alone in the dark, especially on a dark street. "New social situations" are next most often mentioned. Snakes are feared by boys as well as girls, and fear of heights still continues in many. Several now fear accidents—an airplane or car crash.

4. HUMOR

10 YEARS

Humor is mostly obvious, often heavy and labored, and not usually funny from an adult point of view (child reports a lot of mail when there is none).

Cannot understand why no one laughs. Asks, "Get it?" Explains joke.

Most cannot take a joke on themselves, or any kidding; are afraid someone will make fun of them.

Practical jokes. Jokes about each other's names. Considerable punning. Riddles.

When repeating jokes of others, apt to tell them badly, omit salient parts, miss the point. May repeat "dirty" jokes to mother, usually not understanding them.

11 YEARS

Humor is now lively, "corny," and often smutty. The majority are reported by parents to have a good sense of humor, and many like to amuse others, adults as well as contemporaries.

Eleven shows spontaneous interest in whether others, especially teachers, have a good sense of humor. Parents' humor, especially father's, is usually much more appreciated now than it will later be.

Most like practical jokes, laugh at misbehavior in school ("Throwing apple-cores and erasers is funny"), clown, say silly things, mildly insult each other ("Say it, don't spray it").

Cartoons and funnies, movie, radio, and TV comedies are much enjoyed. Puns and limericks ("God made the teachers in the night, and forgot to make them bright"). "Deadpan" humor (girl sees picture of microscope in book on biology and says, "Oh, it tells how microscopes have babies").

Smutty humor chiefly concerns elimination ("A blizzard of birds"; "Aren't you glad elephants don't fly?"; "European—Oh, no I'm not." Boys laugh coarsely at mention of horses and start to say, "Sh . . ."). Girls often object to the dirty jokes of boys at school, and say they like clean jokes.

12 YEARS

Humor is becoming funnier from an adult point of view. Most Twelves still appreciate adults' humor and many can carry on much quite humorous banter with adults.

May criticize parent under guise of humor ("What a physique!" to father, or semi-sarcastic jokes about father's reported athletic prowess when younger).

Practical joking continues (calling for taxi to be sent to other people's houses), and increases in many, though a few start to outgrow this. Clowning around and insulting friends runs high ("You look like Frankenstein. Anybody looking at you would die"). Some "kid" each other about the opposite sex—may even "kid" a dog about *his* girl friend.

Less interest in funnies, but much enjoyment of magazine cartoons. Some still pun, but some already groan, "Oh, no!" if others do.

Some make dry, humorous remarks against themselves or their own products, if praised (sarcastically, "Great!"; "Genius at work—I could sell this idea for a million dollars").

Smutty humor is now more about sex (butcher's sign in boy's room: "Legs and breasts, 39 cents"), though some elimination humor continues (woman who has lost her [son] Heinie). Much sex humor at school—notes passed, poems and jokes told when teacher is out of the room. Some quite uninhibited.

13 YEARS

A less humorous age for many, though what humor there is may be very good from an adult's point of view. Sarcasm is an important element of Thirteen's humor, and is enjoyed by most, though a few are much against this.

Others' mistakes in action or speech (especially parents') are enjoyed. Some are still amused by parents' efforts at humor.

Cartoons are much enjoyed, even quite sophisticated (*New Yorker*) cartoons.

Less practical joking in many, except in school. Clowning around and loud, foolish horseplay is still considered funny, especially by boys.

"Kidding" each other about the opposite sex occurs often, and some are beginning to take kidding better, though great individual differences exist.

Smutty humor continues, and can be very advanced and direct. Thirteen is the last age, for many, for enjoying such jokes freely in mixed company.

14 YEARS

Some of Fourteen's humor is excellent from an adult point of view, and many spontaneously comment that they like a sense of humor in others. But most are much distressed by any attempts at humor on the part of their parents, especially before outsiders.

Humor may be used against parents or teachers. (The "Mary-Helen Fan Club"—all girls called in by school principal for misbehavior.)

The incongruous is especially appreciated. Many themselves pun, though they dislike any punning on parents' part. Still much enjoyment of magazine cartoons.

Practical joking is definitely on the wane in most, except at school. Here, boys (more than girls) play many crude practical jokes on each other and on teachers.

Insult and ridicule are still favored humorous techniques. Fourteen's loud, "corny" humor in public places (especially busses) can be very tiring to adults.

Some show unconscious humor. (One boy remarked, "I like people—most every kind except girls.")

Smutty humor is definitely on the decline in group situations; dislike of "off-color jokes in mixed company."

15 YEARS

Fifteen, in some, is not a strongly humorous age, but what humor there is may seem quite amusing to adults as well as to contemporaries. Irony is increasingly used.

Some are very alert to adult humor—hidden or subtle meanings. Many spontaneously comment that they like others who have a sense of humor, and some are less distressed about parents' humor, though not always fully appreciative of it.

Some can now (unless upset or unhappy) take kidding, and some can make jokes at their own expense.

Cartoons are enjoyed, especially those with a slightly morbid flavor (Charles Addams'). Many appreciate humorous literature at an adult level (Donald Ogden Stuart's *Perfect Behavior*).

Practical joking is not now considered funny by most, though much sarcasm, insulting, and "slamming" of friends continues.

Most still enjoy the ridiculous, especially if it is not too obvious, like to recount humorous incidents or *faux pas*. Punning has dropped out with most.

16 YEARS

Parents often comment that Sixteen has a good sense of humor. His efforts are often amusing from an adult point of view, and he understands most adult humor, gets inflections, understands subtle cartoons.

Sixteen may use humor positively—trying to kid a friend out of a bad mood, responding to criticism with kidding. **May also use sarcasm to defend himself.**

Sample humor from school paper:

"Lost, billfold containing $100 bills. Wanted for sentimental reasons. The billfold is not worth much, but the money was given by a sweetheart."

"Available, slave. Sixteen-year-old white girl. Has not been worked hard. Good for twelve hours a day."

5. AFFECTIVITY

10 YEARS

Happiness. One of the happiest ages. By far the majority describe themselves as "real happy," "happy as anything." Sources of happiness are simple: "If after supper I go out and play"; "If I was going someplace nice"; "If the girls are nice to me at school"; "If we can take the dogs with us on our summer vacation."

Sadness. Most Tens, asked if they ever feel sad, reply, "Occasionally," or "Seldom."

Crying. One of the least tearful ages. At least half as many are said not to cry as are reported to cry. Most, however, say they "might" cry. Their main cause of crying is anger, next is physical hurt.

11 YEARS

Happiness. Our subjects report themselves as happy, sometimes with more qualification than at ten: "Often real happy," "I'm a pretty happy person."
Many different things can cause happiness: "When I got my radio"; "When I got my little sister"; "Invitation to go fishing"; "When mummy asks me to go to the movies with her"; "Going to the shore"; "Ice-cream sundaes"; "Throwing erasers and applecores in school."

Sadness. Even more than at ten, children typically reply that they seldom feel sad. Sadness is caused by such trials as having to take care of siblings, "father mean and cross to me"; having nobody to play with.

Crying. Eleven is the most tearful age between ten and sixteen, with the main causes of tears being anger and disappointment. Mothers report that children cry more easily now, and are apt to burst into tears at almost anything—if she "merely looks cross-eyed at them."

12 YEARS

Happiness. The majority report being mostly happy, but are quite moderate in their statements. Many say they are only *sometimes* happy, despite their parents' views of them as extremely happy and enthusiastic—"shows wild exuberance."

Again there are many sources of happiness: "Going on a ski weekend"; "Going out in the woods"; "Having fun with the girls"; "Good report card"; "Homework done"; "Nice spring day, go for a walk."

Sadness. The majority of our 12-year-olds say they are occasionally sad. A fairly large group describe sometimes feeling "in the depth of depression," "might as well be dead."

Things that make them sad are discord between parents, a pet dying, having to take a music lesson, having nothing to do.

Crying. The least tearful age in this age range, though many say they "might" cry or that they sometimes do. Now report that crying does not make them feel much better. Crying arises from anger, from hurt feelings, from sad books and movies, or, more specifically, "if somebody dies."

13 YEARS

Happiness. Though most still report that they are often very happy, this is apparently the least happy age. More than at other ages report that they are "not very" happy. Or they or parents describe their emotions as "even, moderate, calm."

Sources of happiness are: "Going on a trip or visit"; "Picked out for a part in a play"; "Passed exams"; "Lot of baby-sitting jobs to make money."

Sadness. This is, from Thirteen's own reporting, by far the saddest age. The largest number say yes, they are sad. More than at any other age describe themselves as getting into the depth of depression. Others say that they are sulky, have bad moods, are broody. ("I often feel as if everything is absolutely terrible"; "Yes, I do feel kind of gray and dismal, kind of moody.")

Things that bother them are disappointment, people dying, friend moving away, plans that don't come out.

Crying. Again a more tearful age, though a small Spartan group reports that they never cry. Anger is still the leading cause of tears but crying also occurs over disappointment or hurt feelings.

14 YEARS

Happiness. Happier again. They report that they are "real" happy, "pretty" happy, or sometimes happy.

Things that make them happy are success in sports, new clothes, "Boy asks you out," taking a trip, going to camp.

Sadness. Much more cheerful than thirteen. A great many admit to sulking and bad moods, but there are no "depths of depression" reported.

Kinds of things that bother them are too few dates, too much work, annoyance at teacher who marks too hard, misunderstandings with friends.

Crying. Less tearful, though a fairly large number "sometimes" cry. Those who do, probably cry less often than earlier, and most feel crying doesn't help much. Main causes of tears are anger, "things are real bad" or "feeling very badly."

15 YEARS

Happiness. Fifteen, according to his own reporting, feels happier than he is often observed to be. The majority consider themselves happy.

Things that make them happy are school politics, school play, "World history— wonderful teacher," good evening at a dance, looking forward to things.

Sadness. Fifteen is less happy than Fourteen by his own reporting, though his sadness is again likely to take the form of sulking, broodiness. The word "moody" is spontaneously used here more than at any other age: "More moody than I used to be," "moody and cynical," "kind of moody and cross."

At this age unhappiness tends to be more a general mood and few can give specific causes for their difficulties.

Crying. The majority still cry, but for the most part on rather rare occasion. For the first time anger is not given as a leading cause of tears, but is replaced by failure, criticism, or frustration.

16 YEARS

Happiness. The majority describe themselves as "pretty happy." A few, however, are very happy or even "perfectly content." Many say that they are much happier this year than last.

A few say they are occasionally very happy, and then at other times feel absolutely hopeless.

Sixteen does not give specific causes for his happiness.

Sadness. Most now feel happy more than sad. Many say that they are never or seldom sad. Others admit to occasional sadness, however, and several report a recent "black" period, or say that recently things did look pretty hopeless. More say that they have occasional moody spells.

Crying. No boys admit to crying now, nor are they said by parents to cry. Many girls do cry on occasion, though most admit that it does not make them feel any better. Reasons for crying include: real disappointment, watching a sad movie, "if sorry for myself" "if I get mad and want to be dramatic."

6. SELF-ASSERTION

10 YEARS

Competition. The majority state that they are not competitive, though the typical Ten comment—"Sometimes I am, sometimes I'm not"—occurs. More are aware than at other ages that it is "hard on the other kids" if they win, and some say winning makes them "feel funny."
Some like to excel in certain situations only, as "in sports, not in lessons."

Jealousy. About half admit to being occasionally jealous or envious—mainly of the possessions of other children (movie projector, TV, bike). Some report envy of attributes of others; some of children—especially siblings—who are "treated better" by mother or teacher.
As at most ages, some say they do envy others but would not change places with them. Some say they are not envious of anyone—that they have everything in the world.

Pride. Few are self-centered enough to think in terms of pride.

Revenge. Getting even and spiting others occur as strong motives in some Tens' reporting.

11 YEARS

Competition. A highly competitive age. More respond, "I like to be better than others—of course!" than at any other age. A few state that they like to be as good as the others but not better.

Jealousy. Over half (more than at any other age) admit to at least occasional jealousy. Possessions again are most envied—good dog, horse, electric train, TV. Some envy attributes of others; many envy the way others—siblings especially—are treated by parents and teachers.
Some, as at ten, say they are not envious: "I'm the luckiest little girl—I got everything."

Pride. Eleven is a proud age. Parents say, "She has her pride," and often report that it is best to let the child work things out for himself, with only a slight hint or slight help.

Revenge. A very strong sentiment, though Elevens may get over their anger before doing anything about their planned retaliation. "Getting even" is given as a main reason for fighting with siblings.

12 YEARS

Competition. The majority report that they are competitive only at times, or only in certain situations—"sports but not lessons," or "lessons but not sports." Conspicuous is the wish to be "in the middle," "even with the others, no better and no worse." Like to win *sometimes*, but not always—"I like to give the other people a chance too."

Jealousy. One of the least jealous ages, though still nearly half our subjects report occasional envy. Possessions—nice clothes, nice room, a horse—are still most envied. As at ten, and especially as at eleven, there is resentment of the way brothers and sisters are treated by parents or other children are treated by teachers. A few envy attributes of others: health, looks.

Pride. Twelves evidence a pride in self, but a less stiff and aggressive pride than at eleven.

Revenge. Very little vengefulness is reported.

13 YEARS

Competition. Though less so than at eleven, this is again a highly competitive age. The majority say that they are competitive, and many add, "Oh sure!" or, "Of course!" A modest few are content to "do my best, that's all."

Jealousy. More envy is expressed at thirteen than at twelve, though the largest number of any age say they may be jealous but would not change places with the person. Possessions are somewhat envied, but now children are beginning to envy popularity or privileges of others: "They get all the breaks"; "Get bigger allowances"; "Lots more popular."

Pride. Pride now in many has become more pride in accomplishment than pride of self. Want to do their best.

Revenge. Most either do not plan revenge, or plan it and forget it before doing anything about it.

14 YEARS

Competition. Again a strongly competitive age. Many such comments as, "Oh sure, competitive!" "LOVE competition! Everybody does." A few, as before, say they are content just to do their best.

Others, as at twelve, say that it depends on the situation: like to be good in sports but not in lessons, or in lessons but not in sports.

Jealousy. A slightly larger number than at thirteen disclaim any jealousy. The largest number of all say that they are jealous but don't say about what. Popularity, especially with the opposite sex (for girls), and privileges are the things now most envied.

Pride. Pride may now take form of wanting to do well, or "to do my best." Try to make a good appearance; try to control their emotions.

Revenge. Only a minority plan revenge, but there is more staying power here and those who do plan it are more likely to carry it out than earlier.

15 YEARS

Competition. A less competitive age. About as many say they are competitive as say they are not and many say it depends on the situation.

Individual differences are very conspicuous here—the tougher, more muscular individuals express much more interest in competition than others.

Jealousy. Fewer now will comment frankly on the subject of envy and jealousy. Of those who do, the majority say that they are not envious or jealous. Popularity and freedom are the things most envied.

Pride. Pride again may be somewhat aggressive—pride in own ideas, own opinions, own ability to win arguments.

Revenge. Again, only a minority plan revenge, but those who do are even more likely to carry it out than at fourteen.

16 YEARS

Competition. More interest in competition is expressed than at fifteen years. The majority, both boys and girls, say that they are competitive: "Very," "Sure," "Certainly," "Enjoy it." Others make qualifying statements ("Sometimes," "It depends") or say they would like to be in the highest group but not at the top, to win once in a while but not all of the time. Only a few state flatly that they are not competitive.

Jealousy. By far the majority say thoughtfully that they think they are never envious or jealous. Of the few who are, the largest number are jealous of younger siblings. This kind of jealousy can be quite strong at this age. Also mentioned are success in school, social success, and staying-out-at-night privileges.

Revenge. Only one of our Sixteens admits to planning revenge, and even she does not carry it out: "I plan revenge—big plan—but nothing ever comes of it."

7. EXPRESSING FEELINGS

10 YEARS

Hurt feelings. When their feelings are hurt, the majority of 10-year-olds either cry or "go away," sometimes both: "I start to cry and then I go home." A few already are able to "just ignore them."

Moods. "Sometimes I let people know how I feel, sometimes I don't," is the most characteristic response. Many let people know when they are happy, but not when sad. A large number, even at ten, say they hide their feelings and try not to let people know how they feel.

11 YEARS

Hurt feelings. When their feelings are hurt, the majority say they just go away. Many still cry. An increasing number, however, is able to "ignore them." A good many say something mean—either to the person, or about him, reporting, "I do something mean, if possible," or, "I insult them back."

Moods. Most Elevens (more than at any other age) say they cover up their feelings. However, many (also the largest number for any age) let people know how they feel and even *want* people to know. Another large number vary about showing their feelings, doing so at some times but not at others. "When you're happy it's O.K. Not fair to make other people sad."

12 YEARS

Hurt feelings. Very few now need to go away when their feelings are hurt, and a decreasing number cry. Saying something mean to the person or ignoring him are the main responses.

Moods. The majority vary from time to time about showing their feelings, but nearly as many say they keep their feelings a secret, or at least try to. It is a smaller group that not only lets people know their feelings but *wants* them to know.

13 YEARS

Hurt feelings. When feelings are hurt, none now "go away," and only a few cry. The chief response is to ignore the person—at the time, and often later ("Just avoid the person," "snub them"), or else to ignore the situation ("Just skip it"). Quite a few tell someone else about it. A few now can treat it as a joke. A few plan revenge.

Moods. Variability marks Thirteen's showing of his feelings. The largest number now either hide their feelings or at least try to, but a good many do allow their feelings to be known, or say they vary from time to time or from situation to situation. At this age particularly they let certain people know how they feel and not others.

14 YEARS

Hurt feelings. Feelings generally seem to be a little more hardy at fourteen, but if they are hurt the majority, as at thirteen, say they ignore the situation, laugh it off.

Moods. Most report that they vary about letting feelings be known, but more now allow their feelings to be known than cover them up. And many not only allow, but want their feelings to be known.

15 YEARS

Hurt feelings. Very few at fifteen admit to ever getting feelings hurt. Of those who do, the typical response is to ignore it, or "don't do or say anything." A few, however, plan revenge.

Moods. By far the majority now try to cover up their feelings. A characteristic comment is: "I'm not good at concealing my emotions, but the proper answer would be that you conceal them. You should, because it bores other people."

16 YEARS

Hurt feelings. Feelings are decreasingly vulnerable: "Much less sensitive than earlier." Most now, if their feelings are hurt, "just skip it," or "pretend I didn't notice." Only a few "say something right back." Some can kid with friends if they criticize or say something mean. And some even say that they welcome criticism because they can improve themselves.

Moods. Nearly all now say that they at least try to cover up their feelings, and that they think you should. Reasons for doing so are becoming more mature: "Don't want people to think I'm too touchy"; "Don't want to bother others with the way I feel." Some mention a relativity to their expression of feeling: might let a good friend know but not others; might let people know if happy, but not otherwise.

CHAPTER FOURTEEN

The Growing Self

AN APPRECIATION of the psychology of the self is very helpful in understanding the problems of adolescence. It might almost be said that the central task of the adolescent is to find himself. In much that he does and says, he seems to be engaged in an active search to discover what he is or what he ought to be. Sometimes he gives evidence of confusion in his arguments and questionings. He cannot penetrate the future with clear vision, and mere introspection only aggravates his difficulties. As adults we hold a certain advantage. We have reached a region of maturity, which for him is still a vague and far-off goal. From our vantage ground we are in a position to sense the nature of his perplexities.

Fortunately, there are deep organic forces which normally protect the growing self and which carry it stage by stage nearer to an ultimate goal. There is an innate, recurring desire to grow up. Even as a young child the adolescent felt and expressed his seniority over a yet younger child. As a teen-ager he is acutely conscious of his age status and his age prerogatives. His self constantly undergoes elaborations as he moves through the grand cycle of development with its manifold spirals and subcycles.

The Gradations of Growth

The self grows. That is its most significant characteristic. From earliest infancy the self takes organic shape under the pressures of growth. With astounding swiftness the boundaries of the self expand. The infant looks at his hand; later he fingers his fingers; he grasps his feet; he smiles at his mother; he hears his name and responds to it. In time *he* calls him*self* by his own name. Under the impact of older selves he becomes a person in his own right. He expresses his selfhood with *I, we, you, me,* and passionately if necessary with the possessive pronoun *mine.* Often he is at odds with himself; but with marvelous certitude he builds up an interior citadel of attitudes which is his very own. He as much as says, "I am I. This is me." By the age of five years he has a robust appreciation of self-identity. Psychologically, his self is the sum and essence of this individuality which he alone can experience. But it is not a fixed entity. It is a product of growth—a mixture of permanence and change. The child remains true to his inherent nature in the manner in which he structures his self and projects it into the future.

The fundamental growth characteristics of the self therefore are already revealed in the first five years of life. And the years from five to ten give many evidences of how the self will continue to mature in the years from ten to sixteen. The developmental advance proceeds with fluctuating patterns which foreshadow those of adolescence. At age zone *five* the child is self-contained, but takes a serious interest in his ability to imitate grown-up behavior. At *six* he is the absorbed center of his own universe, self-assertive and combative rather than imitative. At *seven* he is sensitively aware of his bodily self, but withdraws into his psychic self and may even fear loss of his identity. At *eight* he is typically outgoing, eager to establish contacts with his mates and with elders too. At *nine* he again concentrates more upon his own affairs, showing a distinct gain in self-dependence, self-criticism, and self-motivation. His marked zeal in perfecting a skill proclaims the growth of his self.

In broad outline the foregoing maturity traits reflect the general manner in which the self grows. Comparable phases and trends reappear at higher levels as the cycle moves from ten into the teens. The patterns which then emerge are new, but they resemble previous stages as though they were the recurrent motifs of a familiar symphony.

The 10-year-old, for example, in his self-equipoise is reminiscent of the 5-year-old. He is self-contained, relaxed, direct, easy in his give-and-take.

Eleven is more tense, questing, and egocentric; he searches and tests his self by conflict with others.

Twelve is in better balance; accepts others; sees both them and himself more objectively; but unevenly fluctuates from childish to more mature attitudes.

Thirteen withdraws and inwardizes in order to focus more deeply upon his own thoughts, moods, and images in a manner reminiscent of *Seven*.

Fourteen, more outgoing, seeks and defines his self by comparing it with others, by matching and by imitation; he is less inwardly centered.

Fifteen withdraws not physically but mentally to meditate, and to explore his self in relation to ideas, ideals, and the opinion of others.

Sixteen is more at ease and circulates more freely among age-mates and adults; seems more independent and self-reliant.

This condensed, thumbnail gradient enables us to see the growth of the self in fuller perspective. Although the day-to-day growth may be quite imperceptible, the year-to-year progressions are unmistakable. There is an uninterrupted advance from concrete to conceptual attitudes and from naïve egocentricity to a perceptiveness of the selves of others. With the aid of the culture the mechanisms of maturation assist the adolescent in his searches to find himself.

Many times the growing self seems to resent and resist the proffered aid of the culture; but even the resistance may have an experimental testing motivation which leads to constructive results in the end. The records of innumerable interviews show with few exceptions that the boys and girls are genuinely interested in achieving a better understanding of themselves—and of us. In the personal interviews we were gratified and often charmed by the naturalness and spontaneous candor of their comments.

Self-awareness and Self-appraisal

This readiness on the part of modern youth to engage in self-examination and self-appraisal need not be ascribed to a morbid form of introspectiveness. It is in part a cultural phenomenon, induced by the tremendous and insistent impact of a technological environment. Through radio, television, and pictorial publications, the growing self is confronted by a kaleidoscopic succession of images and voices. There are many occasions of bewilderment and confusion for the young spectator and listener as patterns of life are presented to him in the jumbled variety of audio and visual programs. Nevertheless, his sense of self is at least sharpened by the concentrated sights and sounds. He also has some self-protective mechanisms, which help him to accept the good and to reject the evil that comes to his senses. He can convert what he sees on the screen into symbols and models for potential imitation. But his evaluations are most basically influenced by his actual experiences at home, at school, and in the community. These experiences are vital because it is through inter-personal relationships that the self achieves its final organization.

The *diary* as a device for self-examination plays a meager role in the years from ten to sixteen. If kept at all, the entries are usually limited to dates and events, and the record runs a brief and irregular course. No boys in our entire group kept a diary. Half of the 12-year-old girls did keep one for a brief period. At the later ages the proportion fell to one diarist out of three or four. A 14-year-old girl probably spoke for her group when she said, "Diaries were really worth keeping in the eighteenth and nineteenth centuries but not nowadays because you don't really have the time to sit down and say what you really think about things."

Nevertheless, even the short-lived intermittent diary has a certain piquancy for the young diarist. It quickens the sense of self and of privacy. It may be hidden in secret places or, paradoxically, it may be brought to school with ostentatious secrecy to tempt the boys to try to take it away. The confessional Dear Diary apparently belongs to more advanced ages. One of our subjects terminated her diary because: "My sister might read it. And I think that anybody with sisters runs danger in keeping a diary."

The interview sessions from year to year yielded lively data on the development of self attitudes. Our questions ranged widely and included wishes, preferences, ambitions, assets and faults of behavior, and anticipa-tions as to career, marriage, and even attributes of spouse! We also pro-pounded a metaphysical query: Where is the self located? The general trends of the revealing responses are outlined to give an over-all view of the course of development in the years from ten to sixteen.

Outline of Growth Trends

Location of self. The awareness of the self is of slow growth. It does not come with dramatic suddenness although it has its high moments of pleasurable or painful excitement. Nevertheless, the child from ten to sixteen in terms of his own experience has some grasp of the idea of a *self* —of his own self. He knows that as an individual he can think of himself with reflective consciousness; that he has a self which is both subject and object; that he is the agent of his activities and the subject of his feelings. Increasingly he comes to understand what the culture means by such compound words as self-respect, self-control, self-denial, self-reproach, self-pity, self-reliance, and he realizes that in some way the self is related to what people variously call his mind, personality, character, soul, conscience, ego.

Accordingly, our juvenile subjects were ready to talk about the self despite its abstruseness. We found that they were not even deterred by the formidable question: "If you had to locate your SELF at some point or place within your body, where would that place be?" One 10-year-old replied quite interpretively, "In my fingers because I do more things with them." Brain, head, and mind were usual answers at all ages. The 11-year-old combined concepts such as "head and hands," "eyes and ears," "brain and heart." A 12-year-old more comprehensively replied with, "All of me." Thirteen, true to form, reflected intently and tended to emphasize thinking: "The way I think and my brain." Fourteen stressed emotion: "If in school some teacher reads good poetry, I feel it right here," said one, pointing precisely to the epigastric region. Another said, "In your heart and soul and what you feel. You can't locate it. It's in you, but it's not physical." Still another respondent, age fifteen, pleased us with a developmental comment, "I suppose my brains is myself and about the center of most everyone. I suppose when I was little, I used to say my stomach." Sixteen found the question "tough" or "funny." He could not answer with ease, because he didn't wish to separate any part from the whole. He tended to identify himself with his whole body. One boy replied, "It's located in the face—the most characteristic thing—the whole difference between people. That is what you think of when you think of others." Several significantly responded, "All parts."

Self-estimate of "faults" and "best traits." There were a few direct questions which required frank self-appraisal. By and large the subjects replied freely when asked, "What do you think is your best trait?" The replies both for assets and for faults showed an early developmental trend from specific and concrete behavior to general personality traits. As the self matures, the capacity to appraise matures.

Ten, true to character, is very specific and topical: "My spelling" is reported as an asset; "Picking frosting off cakes" is a fault! *Eleven* already displays more concern for personality traits: "I think I'm quite friendly." Faults: "I dawdle at practicing." "I'm very sloppy." "Careless." "Don't clean my room." *Twelve, Thirteen,* and *Fourteen* continue to report their bad manners specifically—"I lose everything"; "Poor table manners"; and "Talk too loudly." Fourteen shies away from bragging about himself and he is able to face his faults rather squarely. *Fifteen*, however, makes more mature responses as to his and her faults: "Self-conscious," "quick temper," "sarcastic." His trend toward more precise awareness is revealed in his remark, "I am unaware of other people's ideas." *Sixteen* is more apt to generalize and speaks of his "inability to get on with other people." He may confess broadly to "stubbornness" or "selfishness."

Assets as opposed to faults are more generally expressed in the terms of personality traits and social traits at the ages from twelve through fifteen— "A good disposition." "Determination." "Sense of humor." "Good nature." "Being tactful." Faults seem to reflect the negative pressures of the culture. The positive merits and assets are more suggestive of individual aspirations.

Expressed wishes. The content of the wishes reflected the changing evaluations of the growing self. Material possessions are definitely in the lead at ages ten, eleven, and twelve. They ranged from bicycle and gun to a house and a farm. But even self-assertive Eleven may desire "health, happiness, and peace" for all! Twelve's wishes may show concern about his family. He would like to see them take a trip. Thirteen shows a new depth of feeling and sympathetic thinking about people in general. Poverty, slums, disease disturb him. Fourteen wanted a better world to live in—"better government" and a better educational system. Fifteen expects more of himself. He wishes to "like people without prejudice and understand them." Sixteen has a balanced orientation to his self in relation to others. His wishes speak of happiness, success, career, and personality improvement.

Boys clearly lead in specifying guns, health of self, money, peace, and "to be older." Girls definitely lead in wishing a baby, a house, health of others, and marriage. The tally indicates that the girls' responses were more altruistic than those of boys of corresponding age.

Vocation and career. The young adolescent is interested in factual knowledge concerning vocations; but he shows a growing awareness of himself in relation to a life plan. He talks not so much in terms of the vocation but in terms of personality traits; and surprisingly early he relates the whole problem to marriage, family life, and children. This portends that he is already outgrowing the family of which he is still a dependent member.

Realism increases with age. The 15-year-old is definitely more mature

than the 10-year-old in his outlooks on a career. This is reflected not only
in more discriminating knowledge but in the serious manner in which he
(or she) interprets the demands of a chosen vocation. At ten or eleven
years of age there is a wide variety of choice in any one child and from
child to child. The choices tend to be somewhat fanciful or glamorous
rather than practical. Boys are going to be cabdrivers, inventors, hunters.
Girls say they want to be opera singers, dancers, acrobats. Every sixth
girl in our group expressed a strong wish to become a veterinarian!

At twelve the variety of choices narrows down, and the choices are
more decisive and realistic. One girl had a succinct plan: "Raise horses
and draw them!" By thirteen about two-thirds of the subjects make a
single choice, the boys often electing the profession of their fathers.

At fourteen the range of choice begins again to widen, reflecting the
expansive tendencies of this age level and a maturing breadth of insight.
One boy made a full sweep in his projection: "I'm going to be a lawyer.
Then after I've practiced for a while, I'll go into politics. State politics
would lead to national. I'd go into politics with a goal of cleaning it up."
A number of new careers are mentioned for the first time, indicating again
an expansive trend. Girls choose psychiatrist, social worker, career diplomat. Boys choose historian, mathematician, reporter, sports announcer.

The 15-year-old typically is somewhat withdrawn, but at the same
time is more aware of the complexities of the world's work. He states his
vocational interests in language which betokens a broadened appreciation
of fields of activity. Instead of saying, "I am going to be a doctor," he
says, "I'm going into medicine." Similarly, others say, "I'm going into
journalistic work," "something in the field of art," or "on the stage." High
purpose is voiced in serious inflections: "I want to make something of
myself." "I want to do something big." "I want to be somebody." And
that somebody, of course, is his own self.

Sixteen is more tentative and open-minded. He has a better appreciation of the complexity of the career problem. "I'm going to wait and see
how things will turn out." "Hard to know." "A new idea every week."
"Maybe something in medicine or psychological work." Thus, by sixteen
years there is ample evidence that the young adolescent has advanced far
beyond the general innocence of age ten and is moving into the idealistic
zones of the later teens.

Marriage and spouse. Questions of career naturally lead to questions of
marriage, since marriage itself is a form of career which may compete or
combine with other careers. Our 10-year-old respondents showed little

spontaneous interest in the matter, but equal numbers of girls said that they will work only till they marry and that they will combine career and marriage. But two-thirds of the total group of 10-year-olds declare that they plan to marry. This proportion rises to nine out of ten at fifteen years. Girls throughout the whole age range from ten to sixteen years definitely lead in expressing an intention to marry. They spontaneously mention children, usually specifying two, three, or four. Not until the ages of fourteen and fifteen is there an equal or greater interest expressed in spouse as compared with children. At these ages all the girls plan to marry, and a large number expect to combine marriage with a career. Almost half of the boys at fourteen years of age, however, say they "don't know," and a few flatly state they do not intend to marry. By fifteen years, three out of four decisively state that they plan to marry. As foreordained breadwinners they have less to say about career in relation to home and children; but the girls showed a marked awareness of this topic as early as age thirteen. It evidently figures in their ruminations.

Attributes favored in wife or husband. Responses to the question, "Can you tell me what kind of a person you want to marry?" also disclosed a sex difference in trends. All told, the boys at ages ten to fifteen mentioned thirty-one different traits. The corresponding total for the girls was forty-eight traits, ranging from "handsome," "likes boats," and "doesn't smoke terrible cigars," to "same tastes," and "someone you can talk problems over with."

At the ten- and eleven-year level the specifications are comparatively concrete and practical both in girls and boys. "Smart," "pretty," "blond," and "nice," are the favored attributes in a wife. The girls in contrast make more mention of personal qualities and personality traits without, however, overlooking such concrete matters as "a good provider," "not too important so he won't be too busy," "a good father," and "must like horses." Twelve, typically enough, balances the specifications of a husband: "neither too fat nor too skinny"; "not too intellectual, but not too dumb." The emphasis on personality traits and behavior characteristics appears earlier in girls and develops with increasing clarity. By the age of fifteen years the girls already show a maturing awareness of the attributes of character reflected in the adjectives they employ ("sensible," "considerate") and in the tone of their responses. "Want someone you can talk over your problems with." Here is an unmistakable sex difference which is based on deeper insight and a broader sympathy. In humane wisdom the feminine self may well display some precocity.

But the boys are maturing in their own masculine manner, and at four-teen years they begin to place more premium on personality traits of the spouse, such as a "good disposition," "understands what I think," "same tastes," "doesn't want everything just so."

By the age of sixteen many of the boys and girls reveal a considerable degree of maturity in their outlook upon marriage and family responsi-bility. Their responses are serious in tenor and import with slight atten-tion to glamour and romance.

When the voluminous interview data for all the ages are viewed in perspective, they do not suggest a stormy and uncertain course of de-velopment. For the period of pre-adolescence and early adolescence the organization of the self tends to be gradual and relatively steady in direction. There are great individual variations, but there are also devel-opmental mechanisms which serve to keep each individual true to his self, when the culture provides appropriate safeguards and directives. Our task is to gain a deeper insight into the private growth processes which form the very matrix of the changing self. In the present chapter it is important to emphasize the pervasive influence of constitutional growth factors upon the organization of the self. And it is these factors which demand more understanding and usually justify more faith.

Other chapters will indicate how the intrinsic developmental forces and the impress of culture combine to shape the specific biographic pat-terns of the self. Culturation and maturation operate in conjunction. This is conspicuously true in the vast field of interpersonal relations which bring old and young, parents and teachers, siblings and companions, into reciprocal interactive tensions. The resultant attitudes of the self are also deeply influenced by physical, physiological, and emotional conditions; by school life and by ethical and philosophical orientations.

Self-realization and Responsibility

The developmental psychology of the self leads inevitably to problems of religion, of morals, citizenship, philosophy, and finally of conscience. With the approach and the arrival of adolescence, the child and the youth inclines more and more to self-examination—not morbidly, but in response to impulses of growth and the stimulus of practical necessity. At first his self-inspection is sketchy; but it deepens with time. If sensitive by nature, he may occasionally even be awed by what he discovers within himself.

Whether he is articulate or not, he comes to realize that he is the pos-sessor of a self which is basic to his being and his welfare. Should he not be encouraged in this process of self-realization, which is indeed a growth process? Much can be done for him by skillful guidance based upon a sympathetic understanding of his formative self. Such guidance depends upon mutual confidence. It relies upon tactful, well-timed suggestions which evoke self-insight without undue introspectiveness and without excessive appeal to abstract virtue. Moral and spiritual values are fostered by making the problems of the self less metaphysical and more practical. The self can be pictured as a growing reality which needs to be safeguarded from within and nurtured from without. By adopting this point of view, methods of guidance can be made more effectual. We have not sufficiently recognized the potency of a developmental concept of the self for the young adolescent in relation to his mental health, his education, and his conduct.

Our studies have demonstrated that the young adolescent has a significant degree of awareness of his self as an organic part of his total being— as an agent of his actions, as a subject of his feelings, and as the source of his personal judgments and reasoning. He cannot put all these intimations into words, but *he knows that he has a self.* With growth and experience this conscious self takes on increasing reality and consequence. In a favorable culture he acquires a sense of honor and of self-respect. With time he learns that he himself as an individual must make the final distinctions between right and wrong. He finds that his self does not operate altogether automatically and that it is not entirely at the mercy of concealed forces. On the contrary, the self has the strange capacity to commune with itself both as a spectator and as a mentor with a small voice. This most mysterious of all self phenomena proves to be a profound reality for the growing adolescent. This is his conscience.

The concept of self, therefore, contains far-reaching implications for the interpretation of the nature and needs of youth. It can be made a key concept in a preventive mental hygiene of the adolescent and in the guidance policies of the various adults who are solicitous of his welfare. The concept, however, remains sterile if it is used in an absolute and abstract manner. To be effective it requires discriminative knowledge of the underlying stages of development. A major purpose of the present volume is to provide this knowledge in concrete form.

The years from ten to sixteen are years of transition from childhood to youth on the way to a maturity which is several years distant. The 10-year-old confronted by a moral decision may say, "I pay attention to my mother, but I kind of know inside what to do." A 15-year-old in a similar situation may say, "I do have my doubts sometimes. If it's a problem, I toss it over in my mind. If I can't decide, I talk to my dad." The task of the culture is to help where it can, not so much by exhortation and appeals to honor, as by reason and by a constructive analysis, which places problems of choice and decision in perspective.

The adolescent lacks perspective for the simple reason that he has not yet experienced the fuller maturity which comes with time. To compensate for this handicap he needs to take increasing responsibility upon himself, so that he can build up a perspective based on self-acquired morale and self-reliance. Independence of thought and decision should be judiciously fostered as a safeguard against anxiety and self-depreciation. It is a growing self, and its stamina will depend upon a cumulative capacity to perceive its own powers and limitations. "Character training" rests on self-training and upon a realistic acknowledgment of the self as the source of reason, volition, and integrity. Only on that basis can the human organism cope with its environment at a mature level.

For such reasons it is wise to recognize how the self grows and not to fall back upon purely absolutist approaches and appeals with each recurring crisis. It is the day-by-day growth which counts, if the culture encourages youth to guard well that "inside" sense of self. A Victorian poet summed it up:

> Self-reverence, self-knowledge, self-control—
> These three alone lead life to sovereign power.

GROWTH GRADIENTS

1. THE GROWING SELF

10 YEARS

Ten shows no great concern about self, tends to take self (and life) as it comes. Parents report that he is much happier and easier to get along with than at nine.

Easygoing and matter-of-fact. Very specific; doesn't generalize.

Shrugs off responsibility; can usually toss off criticism and bad grades. If asked a question, replies easily, "Sometimes I do, sometimes I don't."

Much interested in own future parenthood and in how he will treat his children.

Still describes self as "a pretty good boy (girl)."

11 YEARS

Often describes self as changing for the worse since ten: "Now everything I do seems wrong." Parents tell a similar story.

Seems to be engaged in an active search for self and finds it in conflict with others—parents and friends. Responsive to outside forces, but against mother. Jockeys for position with friends.

May oppose whatever is going on in the home; works against what is expected of him. Little sense of wanting things to be smooth for others. Described as egocentric and selfish.

Hypochondriacal. Clumsy. Very talkative, but cannot generalize. If asked a question, temporizes: "Well . . ." Then "amplifies, glorifies, clarifies" even the simplest statement. Tells plots of movies in endless detail.

Super-critical of both self and others, but resentful of others' criticism.

12 YEARS

Twelve seems to search for self by trying to win approval of friends, and by assuming (at times) new roles of more mature behavior. Especially aware of this when others fail to treat him in accordance with his concept of self—very insistent about not being "treated like a baby."

Has much better perspective. Can stand off and view parents a little objectively; less embroiled with them. May even be able to view self more objectively, to realize that he is not in all situations the center of the world.

With less egocentricity and better perspective comes a smoothing out of inter-personal relationships. Most are said to be much "better" than at eleven.

Enthusiastic and impatient; "can't wait" for all the wonderful things anticipated. Often seem shapeless in thought, action, and posture.

Very uneven: very childish and then extremely mature. Responsible, helpful behavior, which seems to be on a whole new level of mature, smooth functioning, may alternate with childish, obstreperous, "bratty" behavior. Shapes fingernails but forgets to clean them; fusses with hair but doesn't wash face.

Very critical, at times, of self and own appearance. Cannot accept praise grace-fully—clowns or comments ironically ("Exquisite!") if praised.

13 YEARS

Thirteen seems to search for self within himself; tries to understand himself—his own looks, thoughts, moods. Beginning interest, in many, in own personality (though may scorn personality tests—"What good are they?"). Agonies of concern about personal appearance: too fat, too thin, bad complexion, poor features. Great insistence on outward similarity to others; generally better groomed than at twelve.

Inner life important; "brains" an important concept. Some Thirteens imaginatively play secret roles: great actor, athlete, tragic figure whom nobody understands, Duncan Hines. Some pretend to great sophistication, try to appear very jaded and worldly. Often self-absorbed—indifferent, absentminded, dreamy, "doesn't hear."

Often an age of withdrawal, in one way or another. Quieter outside the home than at twelve or fourteen. Many comment that they like the feeling of being alone. Like to be in own room with door shut, even locked. Withdraw from family group, sometimes even from friends—"A regular hermit." Generally much less sharing and confiding with adults; "I don't want to be close to anyone." May construe a normal interest of others in his affairs as prying.

Many are thoughtful not only about selves but also about more remote problems: capitalism, underprivileged people, women's role in the world.

14 YEARS

Searches for self by comparing and matching self with others. Wants to be just like the others. Directed toward other people (rather than away from them, as at thirteen). Very anxious to be liked by friends.

Great interest in personality of self and friends. Interest in results of personality tests, concern as to whether or not he is "normal." May be quite dissatisfied with own personality, behavior, and appearance; may comment, "That's me," when he sees someone very fat, very thin, etc.

May understand that he behaves much better away from home than at home. Parents describe Fourteen as selfish and as lazy—yet also as busy every minute, trying to do much more than time allows, "Just squeezing things in." Extremely preoccupied with own activities, friends, life. Independently establishes relationships with adults outside the home as well as with contemporaries.

Much interest in appearing grown up and in having freedom. But very uneven again, as at twelve: very mature one minute, babyish the next.

Often has quite a concept of age changes in behavior of self and of friends. Spontaneously resolves to "do better" next year. Many seem to feel that "something wonderful" is right around the corner.

15 YEARS

Fifteen seems to search for self in relation to his own ideas and ideals, and what others think of these. Thrives on argument and discussion; is anxious to state things correctly, to convey exact meaning. Likes to analyze own thoughts as well as those of others. Interested in others' opinions of him (except those of parents), once his initial, defensive indifference to adults is overcome. Self-analysis is thoughtful, more objective than earlier.

Beginning to be more interested in his differences from others, as well as similarities—but still quite faddish about dressing like the crowd, etc.

Again withdraws, though not necessarily physically. Can be extremely uncommunicative with adults. Sophisticated, blasé, super-casual air: "Not going
to let them know too much." Determined not to be treated as a child;
demands freedom and independence. Goes out against people.

Uneven, but span of mood is longer—changes occur from day to day, rather
than from hour to hour. Inconsistency is not so much in level (babyish
or mature) as in mood. Posture often expresses general apathy and dissatisfaction; many lumber along, head and shoulders forward, mouth open.

Some take a longer-range view than formerly; "Things not too good right now,
probably better later." But now seems to realize that the "something wonderful" which he was expecting at fourteen depends upon himself.

16 YEARS

Many now seem to be less engaged in a somewhat frantic searching for self,
but have established a sense of self which is both reasonably realistic and
adequately adapted to the world's demands. The majority appear to be
independent and self-reliant; "I have to work that out for myself" is a
frequent comment.

A remarkable state of poise and equilibrium has been achieved by many. Some
even welcome criticism because they feel that they can "take it and make
myself a better person." Some protect themselves by prefacing their remarks with such comments as, "Sort of crazy"; "You'll think this is weird,
but . . ." but can then proceed to explain their ideas.

Changes from fifteen are described by parents and by Sixteens themselves as
being for the better. The typical comment, "Everything is much better,"
generally includes school, home, and social life. Sixteens describe themselves as happier, more confident, better adjusted; make such comments
as, "Things are very good right now"; "Best year yet." Parents consider
them to be more adult and less rebellious than earlier.

2. SELF-EVALUATION

10 YEARS

Assets. Tens evaluate their own assets principally in terms of abilities as in
school or in athletics (bike riding, roller skating), and in terms of individual personality traits—being fair, being a good sport.

Faults. Tens most often see their main faults in relation to particular situations. Often in relation to school—careless, don't do homework. Also in

specific actions in other situations—pick frosting off cakes, lie and swear, stick out tongue when practicing.

Problems. Many state that they have no problems, and those who do report problems mention only a few. The main problem reported is too hard school work. Other leading problems have to do with pets (mostly not having one), and with wanting specific possessions.

Location of Self. Ten most often thinks of his self as residing in his brain, head, or mind. "Brain" and "heart" are the leading single items mentioned as the seat of the self.

Diary. None of our Tens keeps a diary. Boys don't even mention the topic; a few girls say it might be fun to do so later.

11 YEARS

Assets. Personality characteristics are most often mentioned: helpful, friendly, good-tempered, systematic. Abilities (good in drawing) less frequent.

Faults. School behaviors less often mentioned than at ten. Specific bad actions most frequent: "I swear," "have bad table manners," "talk too much," "contradict," "don't clean my room." More general traits begin to be mentioned: "sloppy," "careless," "stubborn."

Problems. The smallest proportion of children of any age in our range report problems, but those reporting tend to mention quite a few.

As at all ages, the main problem reported is school work—too much or too hard. Teachers are more often mentioned as problems than at other ages.

Lack of money and of particular possessions are more often mentioned than at other ages. Personal appearance and lack of skill in sports are now occasionally mentioned.

Location of Self. As at every age, the brain is seen most often as the seat of the self. Several Elevens give multiple concepts: "Hands and head," "eyes and ears," "brain and heart." Many give qualified responses: "I guess," "I suppose." Many cite reasons for choice: "My heart because it keeps me living"; "My voice because I'm a good singer"; "My knees if it's horse-back riding."

Diary. About a third of our Elevens keep a diary, writing down things they do, rather than things they think. Of those who do not keep a diary, a few started one but did not keep it up, a few hope to start one later.

12 YEARS

Assets. A social theme is frequent. Most often mentioned are good disposi-tion, getting on well with others, good work or good conduct in school.

Faults. Continue to name mostly specific bad actions: "I lose everything," "sometimes lie," "have bad table manners." Often a social theme: "Fight with my sister"; "Get mad at my mother"; "Ignore someone when they tell me something important."

Problems. More problems are mentioned at twelve than at any other age, and the outstanding problem continues to be school work.

Trouble with brothers and sisters, and worry about parents not getting on with each other, are second in frequency of mention. Personal appearance is a problem to a few, and desire to be more popular or to get on better with friends (of same or opposite sex) begin to be mentioned.

Lack of particular possessions is still a frequent problem.

Location of Self. Though the brain still leads as site of the self, heart or "brain and heart" are mentioned almost as often, and "all of me" occurs conspicuously.

Typically: "The heart because it beats and keeps you alive"; "My heart, because most of my love is there for some people"; "My mind is more me, but I wouldn't be here without a heart."

Diary. None of our boys, but nearly half the girls keep diaries, and older girls often report starting their diaries at twelve. Some thoughts as well as activities are recorded. Most say they do not write in their diaries very regularly, or that it is quite a chore.

About half the girls who do not keep one either used to or hope to later.

Several girls bring their diaries to school and "try" to keep them from the boys or tempt the boys to get hold of them.

13 YEARS

Assets. Personality characteristics definitely lead: good disposition, determination. Health, brains, athletic ability also mentioned.

Faults. Still primarily specific behaviors: "Don't clean my room," "talk too loud," "crack my knuckles." Some mention of personality and character faults: "Lie," "worry," "bad temper," "lazy," "grouchy."

Problems. Fewer problems are reported than at twelve—perhaps because of increasing reticence rather than decrease of problems. School work is still most often mentioned, and is followed by difficulty with brothers and sisters.

Location of Self. By far the main response is brain, head, mind, or "the way I think." "My heart" and "all of me" are occasionally mentioned, as are "stomach" and "conscience." Considerable hesitancy in responding: "Suppose it's my brain; I don't know."

Diary. No boys keep diaries, and many fewer girls than at twelve do. Many girls report they used to but either forgot to write or got bored with it ("Oh God, I've got to write in my diary").

Several complain that younger sisters do or did read their diaries.

14 YEARS

Asests. Greater variability of types of assets mentioned: personality (good sense of humor, good-natured and determined), social abilities (get on well with others), and scholastic abilities.

Faults. Though the same types of faults are mentioned as at thirteen, the trend toward greater generality is evident. Actions mentioned are more general: "I fight too much," "mind wanders in class," "don't help around the house." And personality and character traits are frequently cited: "I have a weak personality," "have to do what the crowd does," "I'm conceited," "sarcastic," "critical," "a kleptomaniac," "can't keep a secret."

Problems. As at thirteen, relatively few problems are reported. Though school work is still the main single problem, the majority of problems mentioned are social ones: desire to be more popular, worry about personal appearance, relationships with brothers and sisters, desire to get on better socially. Wish for more independence or for a better character or personality.

Location of Self. Though the brain or head is still most often mentioned as the site of the self, many other responses are given: heart, hands, stomach, voice, face, conscience. In contrast to Thirteen's emphasis on thinking, Fourteen tends to include feeling: "My heart, because all my emotion comes from my heart"; "My stomach—I feel good poetry there, or if I'm hungry I feel it there."

Diary. As at thirteen, about a quarter of our girls, none of our boys, keep diaries. Many did keep one earlier, but stopped because they were too lazy or did not have time to write in it, or were afraid someone would read it.

15 YEARS

Assets. Though both are reported, individual personality traits (confidence, unaffectedness, good nature, common sense) far outweigh mention of more social abilities (being tactful, being a good sport, liking people). Intellectual assets again are mentioned: "My mind"; "Being able to think and reason."

Faults. Personality, character, and social faults have largely replaced mention of specific bad actions. "Being catty," "self-conscious," "untolerant," "silly," "sarcastic," "lack self-confidence." "Lack of ambition" and "my don't-give-a-damn attitude" mentioned. Also: "Don't get on with people—don't take their ideas instead of my ideas"; "not patient and kind with my mother and little sister."

Problems.   A definite increase in reported problems over the preceding year. School work has been a main problem at all ages, but is outstandingly so at fifteen. Wish for popularity or better personal appearance, as at fourteen, come second. The future is a matter of concern to some Fifteens.

Location of Self.   As at thirteen, brain, head, or mind are four times as frequent as the next leading response. The heart is less often mentioned than earlier, though it may be combined with another response: "My brains—they kind of make me think about what my heart is going to do."
Communication is an important concept, leading to mention of the eyes, "because you can communicate with the eyes." Or "speech and what I say." Hands are also mentioned.

Diary.   No boys and a minority of girls keep diaries, though many girls did so earlier but gave it up—mainly for lack of time. Most girls who do keep a diary do not write in it every night but only "when something exciting happens."

16 YEARS
Assets.   Social abilities and individual personality traits about equally emphasized as assets. Getting on well with others is the single leading item mentioned. Humor, patience, curiosity, determination mentioned as personality traits.

Faults.   Relations with others and personality traits are also about equally emphasized as faults. "I speak too quickly," "argue too much," "lose my temper," "am intolerant" are among the interpersonal difficulties. Being lazy, unreliable, moody, stubborn, forgetful are seen as personality faults.

Problems.   Nearly all Sixteens report at least one major problem, though the amount of concern shown about problems does not seem as great as earlier. A great variety of problems is reported, and sex differences are quite marked.
Girls most often mention popularity with boys as the chief problem. Also mention personality lacks: being on the defensive, being at the mercy of their emotions. Family relationships and personal appearance also present problems.
Chief problem for boys is getting a driver's license, getting a car, or getting

to use the family car. Other problems relate to school marks or to summer jobs.

Poor health is a problem to a few.

Location of Self. Mind, head, and brains continue to be the leading conceptions of where the self is. Heart occurs more than at fifteen, and for a variety of reasons: "Keeps me alive," "where you really feel things."

Several see the self in "all parts." Others mention the face—"because no two people look alike and the face is your most characteristic thing."

Diary. Only a few girls—and still no boys—now keep diaries, though those who do keep them usually write in them faithfully.

3. WISHES AND INCLINATIONS

10 YEARS

Likes. "My mother and father, of course," is the outstanding answer to the question, "What do you like best in the world?" "Horses" comes next in frequency.

Other leading preferences are activities (skating, drawing, playing) and objects (own radio, house in the country). Holidays, travel, money are also named. Some likes are really wishes: "to be a missionary, doctor, or actress"; "to be a hunter."

Dislikes. Things mentioned as dislikes tend to be either quite broad or quite specific. Most often mentioned are war, Communism, work. Also reported as disliked are school, teacher, "people who treat me badly," staying in on a rainy day, and specific foods—peanut butter, codliver oil.

Wishes. Asked what three wishes they would make if they could, Tens more often wish for material possessions (especially for a bike, a horse, a dog) than for anything else. Boys are much more likely to wish for guns, girls for babies.

Other main wishes are for health and happiness—both for themselves and others and for personal improvement—to be better, smarter, nicer.

The wish to live on a farm is strong for a number of Tens.

11 YEARS

Likes. As at ten years, "my mother and father" are mentioned most often as things liked best, and again "horses" is second in frequency. Few other likes are mentioned, except eating and travel.

Dislikes. School now holds first place as the thing hated most. Eleven's more specific hates often seem more pointed, less bland than those mentioned at ten, and include cruelty to animals, losing friends, going to bed at night, poison ivy, snakes, things that injure you.

Wishes. Wishes for material possessions are made by a majority of our group, and by far the most frequent specific wish is for a horse. (At eleven, as at every age, many more girls than boys wish for horses.) Dogs and bikes are also desired by many, and the wish to live on a farm is at its peak. Many who do not mention a farm do wish they lived in a different, better house.

A number wish for improved health (generally for others) or for happiness (for themselves). The wish to be "better" in some way is as frequent as at ten.

A surprising number of children (one in seven, in our group) have no wishes to make, usually reporting that they are perfectly satisfied.

12 YEARS

Likes. Mother and father still lead as best liked of anything, and animals of some kind—cats, dogs, horses—are next in frequency of mentions. Sports have come in strongly, and eating, dancing, and reading are other favored activities. Nice clothes and "my home" are among the things most liked.

Dislikes. School, homework, "my friends," "my brother and sister," and "people who boast" are now the thngs mentioned as most hated. New, 12-year-old hates are being sick, someone scratching on the blackboard, and eggs.

Wishes. Though declining slightly from the peak reached at eleven, and much more varied in types, wishes for material possessions are still decidedly more frequent than any other kinds of wishes, and a horse is still the thing most often desired.

A new awareness of self is shown in the frequency of wishes concerning future occupation, scarcely mentioned earlier and now actually at a peak for the ten to sixteen period. Wishes for self-improvement may be related to this. The happiness of others is as often wished for as personal happiness.

13 YEARS

Likes. A real change appears at thirteen years—great variety of likes occurs, and parents have dropped out in mention of best liked. Friends of the opposite sex are now most often mentioned, and are followed in frequency by eating, "my home," and automobiles. Items mentioned for the first time at thirteen include: a good time, the United States, peace and quiet, luxury, and popular music.

Dislikes. War and Communism, as at ten years, now lead the list of hates.

Teachers are again mentioned. New 13-year-old items often include sensitive, "heartache" kinds of hates, which contrast with earlier annoyances: thinking about refugee children, disease, poverty, people who are selfish, disaster. Also mentioned are the Dodgers, and "a license, because I don't have one."

Wishes.   Wishes for personal possessions have declined markedly in frequency since twelve, only a quarter of our Thirteens mentioning material objects. As earlier, a horse is still the most often desired possession, especially by girls. A new house is the wish of quite a few.

Peace, and happiness for others are now frequent wishes. The wish to be better (especially smarter) and wishes concerning future occupation are also frequent, though less so than at twelve.

The extremes of wishing for "all the wishes I want" and of being able to make only two wishes and not a third occur quite frequently. Both may reflect Thirteen's caution about committing himself too freely to specific wishes.

14 YEARS

Likes.   Fourteen's likes seem to be broad-ranging. Sports and friends of the opposite sex now lead in frequency, followed by travel and music. Likes first mentioned at fourteen include: knowledge, art and literature, just living, shelter.

Dislikes.   Communism is still most often mentioned as the thing hated most. Work, as at ten, is again hated, and certain friends are mentioned. The personal, intense feelings of anguish which some Thirteens had from *thinking* about things are replaced by more objective, external kinds of hates. New 14-year-old items, for example, are: off-color jokes in mixed company, "things I don't understand," ungodliness, being afraid of things at night, "bigger boys bothering me," and "people who come to your house and say, 'I don't care,' when you ask them what they want to do."

Wishes.   The wish made most frequently by Fourteens (by a third of our group) is for peace. Associated with this are wishes for the betterment of others, for others' happiness and health. Wishes for material possessions have continued to decline in frequency, and are varied and scattered over a number of items. They are surpassed by wishes concerning future occupation. The wish for money has increased—perhaps replacing the wish for "all the wishes I want," which has correspondingly declined.

15 YEARS

Likes.   Again, as at thirteen, great individual variation appears, with no two "best likes" alike. Among items mentioned are: reading, sailing, art, literature, just living. For the first time, security is named as a thing liked best.

Dislikes. Most 15-year-olds report that they have no "greatest hate." Earlier mentioned hates have without exception dropped out. Now such things as "impotent anger" and "people who try to be mean" are mentioned.

Wishes. Wishes for peace and for general betterment occur less often than at fourteen, while wishes for personal improvement have increased strikingly. Wishes to be better, smarter, or nicer, to have a good personality, to be popular, are expressed more often than at preceding ages. Personal happiness is more often wished for than the happiness of others.

Still fewer individuals make any wishes for material possessions than did at fourteen, and wishes concerning future occupation also occur less often than they have since twelve years.

16 YEARS

Likes. Great individual variety of likes, and many Sixteens find it difficult to indicate the thing they like best. Only one mentioned material objects ("car and radio"), while others have more general preferences, such as work, communication, "having other people like me."

Dislikes. Most Sixteens do not indicate a greatest hate. Those mentioned are now mostly in a quite new area: artificiality, hypocrisy, "seeing someone pushed around." A few are more like the pet peeves of earlier ages: English class, and getting up in the morning.

Wishes. Wishes for the betterment of others and for peace are outstanding in frequency.

The trend in wishes for personal possessions, which had showed a consistent decline following its peak at eleven, is now reversed, though the frequency of such wishes does not nearly approach its earlier level. The main cause of this increase is the desire of many, both boys and girls, for a car.

4. THE FUTURE

10 YEARS

Growing Up. Most Tens seem to take life as it comes, and cannot say whether life gets better or worse as they grow older. But more do think that it gets better than think it gets worse: "You get to do a lot more things," "feel more important," "don't have to tag along with your big brother."

Tens appear to be more closely rooted in the here and now then they will be later. As many consider "right now" to be the best age in life as name some older age (ranging between twelve and twenty-one); a few (more than at later ages) name a younger period as best.

The majority of Tens, including many who feel an older age is the best age, would not change their current age and are in no hurry to grow up.

College.   Just over half our group of Tens plan or hope to go to college. (Except at age thirteen, this proportion stays quite steady up to fifteen years.) More boys than girls plan to go. Only about half those who plan to go have picked out a college; quite often this is the one their father or mother has attended.

Career.   Plans for their future careers are rather indefinite among many of our Tens, and the careers chosen are much more varied than in the years which follow. Many Tens give several choices, often quite unrelated.

Choices are often still somewhat fanciful, as at younger ages: some girls say they want to be acrobats, inventors; boys choose to be cabdrivers, hunters.

Girls seem to be a little more mature: more know what they want to be, and more can settle on a single choice. Their main choices are: teacher, veterinarian, skater, actress, writer, nurse. Boys' main choices are: doctor, scientist, athlete.

Girls show marked individual differences as to whether they want a career or marriage. About equal numbers say they will work till they marry, will combine marriage and career, will work part time after they marry, and that "you couldn't do both." For all this variety, there is little spontaneous interest in the problem.

Marriage.   The great majority of girls and half the boys expect eventually to marry though a number hasten to add that they have nobody picked out yet. The remainder do not know if they will marry or not, apparently have not given the matter much thought.

More Tens, especially more girls, spontaneously mention their future children than mention their future spouses—primarily to tell how many children they want (two is the preferred number).

Wife's attributes: Boys name rather specific traits they would desire—that she be smart, pretty, blond, tall, economical.

Husband's attributes: Girls also seek specific and practical qualities—a good father, good provider, good-tempered, easy to get on with, honest, and having a liking for horses.

11 YEARS

Growing Up.   Despite wide variation in opinions, the majority of Elevens feel that life gets better as you grow up, and that things are better now than they were. (Parents' opinions do not always concur.) Several report that they have more responsibilities or that things are harder, but that they also have more privileges.

Though the largest number would not change their present age, nearly as many (more than at ten) say they are anxious to grow up, and the majority consider that the best age in life is one older than eleven. Twelve to twenty-two is the range of ages considered best, with "the teens" most favored, because of dates, clothes, parties, and dancing, and because the teens bring privileges without too many responsibilities. A substantial number, however, still feels that eleven is the best age.

College. As at ten just over half our group plan to go to college. A few more than at ten have selected a college, which is often their mother's or father's college.

Career. More Elevens than Tens have a definite choice of career, and only very few have no idea of what they want to do. More now can make a single choice, and, as choices become more realistic, the variety of occupations chosen becomes smaller.

Girls choose most frequently: veterinarian, teacher, actress, dancer, farmer. Boys choose: doctor, lawyer, engineer, architect. More boys than at other ages (about one in five) want to follow their fathers' careers.

About a third of the girls spontaneously comment about career vs. marriage. Of these, the majority hopes to combine the two, and the next largest group plans to work until marriage.

Marriage. Still more girls than at ten, but about the same number of boys, expect to marry. Spontaneous emphasis is still on having children, rather than on future spouse. Many more girls than boys mention children, but boys show an increasing interest, especially in the number of children expected—still most often two.

Wife's attributes: Pretty, smart, and rich are most often mentioned by boys, as well as such other qualities as nice, blond, "she likes me and I like her."

Husband's attributes: Handsome, good-tempered, and "making money enough to support me" are by far the outstanding traits sought by girls, along with a sense of humor and brains. Also mentioned are understanding, nice personality, "I like him," helps around the house, ambitious, unselfish, gentlemanly, a careful driver, good father, likes horses, and "not too important, so he won't be too busy."

12 YEARS

Growing Up. Most Twelves feel that life is better as they grow, or that increased responsibilities and increased fun about balance each other.

As at eleven, the largest number would prefer to be their present age, but nearly as many are impatient to grow up. Some older age is again most often named as best, with "the high school ages" generally named, because of the social life, parties, dates, and dancing. (One Twelve would like to be forty-five, with a good business and a good income.) Quite a few still feel that twelve, or some younger age, is the best age.

College.   As previously, just over half plan to go to college, and about half of these have a specific college chosen. Some now name several choices. For the first time, several mention choosing a college because of the course of study offered, and now only a few plan to attend their mother's or father's alma mater.

Career.   The trend toward a single, definite choice of future career continues. Many fewer now make several choices or express indecision. Boys are now more definite in choice, and more likely to give only one choice than are girls.

Plans continue to grow more realistic. Especially is there less stress by girls on caring for animals. Girls' main choices are now: teacher, singer, dancer, nurse, secretary, scientist, writer. Boys choose: doctor, scientist, aviator, lawyer, engineer, architect. A number of boys still plan to follow their fathers' careers.

As at eleven years, the majority of girls hope to combine career and marriage, and the next largest group plans to work until marriage.

Marriage.   The number expecting to marry is about as at ten and eleven, but now a number of boys state flatly that they will not marry. Children are still more often mentioned than spouse, and both are mentioned decidedly more by girls than by boys. Somewhat fewer than earlier show interest in the number of children desired, but the preferred number has increased to three.

Wife's attributes: Pretty, smart, and blond are qualities most desired. New traits mentioned are that she be a good cook, have a nice personality, and not be always fooling around with other boys.

Husband's attributes: Especially desired are that he be kind, smart, "able to support me," good-looking, understanding, tall, and have a nice personality. Helpful around the house, athletic figure, character, same religion, and "loves me" are also mentioned.

13 YEARS

Growing Up.   More than at any other age feel that life stays about the same, not getting better or worse—or perhaps "just a little above the same."

Nevertheless, many express impatience to grow up, and some older age is decidedly considered best. The ages preferred range up to twenty-five; "after that you start getting old." Now college age is most often chosen as best, "because of proms and things and dates," rather than high school age.

College. College is a matter of increasing interest to many. More than previously (about two-thirds) say they hope to go to college, several qualifying this with *if* they can get in. Many more than previously have chosen a preferred college. Parent's college is apparently no longer an important factor in this choice. A few choose on the basis of courses taught. And for girls, though not for boys, coeducation is often a requirement of their choice.

Career. Thirteen marks the peak for single, definite choices about future work. Earlier ages sometimes made multiple choices rather capriciously; later ages, with greater realism, recognize the difficulty of making a single certain choice. Thirteen tends to assert his choice without indecision.

Choices generally seem reasonably realistic. Girls want to be a teacher, singer, scientist, or lawyer. Boys most often choose to be a doctor, scientist, architect, veterinarian, teacher, farmer, engineer. Boys, on the whole, seem a little less mature in their plans; a sizable number still want to follow the same career as their fathers.

More girls show interest in the problem of career vs. marriage than at other ages, the great majority making some spontaneous comment about their plans. Many still hope to combine career and marriage, but many plan to work only until they marry, and a few want to work part time after marriage.

Marriage. An increasing number, especially of boys, plan to get married, and only one boy now plans not to. A surprising number of boys volunteer the fact that they have nobody picked out yet, but apart from this, little mention of the future spouse is spontaneously made. Boys have little more to say about future children than future spouse, but the great majority of girls do make some comment about them. The desired number of children is three or four.

Wife's attributes: When asked, boys most often report they want a wife who is pretty, a good housekeeper, smart, and nice, with a nice personality and not always fooling around with other boys. New qualities mentioned are that she be good-natured, affectionate, cheerful, able to follow leadership, and likes to have a good time.

Husband's attributes: Outstandingly preferred are a nice personality, "something in common with me," a good provider, some specific profession, good-looking, same religion, well liked, and "we love each other." Neat, well educated, a good dancer, nice, and tall are also mentioned.

14 YEARS

Growing Up. In contrast to the Thirteens, the majority of Fourteens feel that life is definitely better now. Several mention its increasing complexity, but feel this is balanced by the increased fun.

Many more (about three times as many) are impatient to grow up than prefer to stay the age they now are. As at thirteen, some older age is definitely considered best. The college ages are generally preferred, with social life the main inducement for being older.

College. Fourteen seems to show less concern about college than either Thirteen or Fifteen do. As in the years before thirteen, just over half our group plan to attend college, and half of these are uncertain about which college they would prefer. Parent's college is rarely important in making their choice. Coeducation is considered an important factor by some girls, who state a preference for a coed or non-coed college.

Career. Fourteens show less certainty in their choice of career. More individuals make multiple choices, and the group as a whole makes a greater variety of choices than at thirteen or fifteen.

New kinds of careers are now mentioned: by girls, psychiatrist, social worker, diplomat; by boys, historian, mathematician, reporter, sports announcer.

Leading choices for girls are: teacher, nurse, musician, scientist, social worker. Boys choose: doctor, radio or TV engineer, aviator, lawyer, architect, engineer. Few boys now choose their father's profession.

Fewer girls express interest in the problem of career vs. marriage, and now equal numbers plan to work till marriage and to combine marriage and career.

Marriage. Though all the girls in our group now plan to marry, fewer than half the boys have definite intentions along these lines; as many don't know, and a few plan not to. Children are less often discussed, and the number of children desired is scarcely mentioned spontaneously.

Wife's attributes: Personality rather than physical characteristics are now most often named, primarily: smart, economical, good personality, same tastes, good disposition, "understands the way I think," "doesn't want everything just so."

Husband's attributes: Above all a good provider is desired, as well as a good father, smart, good-tempered, tall, helpful around the house, with a sense of humor, and "something in common with me." Personality, religion, politeness, education, background, and love are also mentioned. Several comment that looks, money, and race don't matter.

15 YEARS

Growing Up. Most Fifteens seem to have a definite opinion as to whether life gets better or worse; few feel it stays the same. More than at other ages feel that life improves, but also more than at other ages feel it gets worse. The increase of demands and responsibilities is mentioned by many, but this increase, for some, is made up for by increased privileges or increased self-understanding.

The strong preference for being older is not so generally evident now. Though ages considered best are most often older ones, ranging from sixteen to thirty, many name fifteen as best, and nearly as many would continue at their present age as would rather be older. The advantage cited for older ages is now independence, rather than social activity.

College. More of our group than at any previous age plan to go to college, though half of these still do not know where. Many now name several possible choices.

Career. Many Fifteens are quite indefinite about their choice of future career —more so than at any age since eleven. Though the group as a whole names many fewer possible careers than earlier, individuals find it difficult to decide on a single choice within this range.

Many, instead of saying they are going to be a doctor, actress, writer, now say they are "going into medicine," "going to be on the stage," "going to take up journalistic work." And many of both sexes, though not too clear as to details, express a wish for tremendous success: "I want to make something of myself"; "I just want to be somebody."

Girls most often mention: teacher, artist, actress, musician, scientist, psychologist, sociologist. Boys mention: doctor, dentist, lawyer, writer, engineer, architect.

Interest in career vs. marriage is again strong in many girls. As at eleven and twelve, by far the largest number hope to combine marriage and career.

Marriage. All our 15-year-old girls plan to marry, and most of the boys, except for one boy who is undecided and a few who are determined not to. About equal numbers make spontaneous comments about future spouse and future children, and, for the first time, about as many boys as girls. Three or four is the number of children most often desired.

Wife's attributes: Pretty, smart, a good cook, good-natured, a good manager, and a nice personality are traits most desired. Traits desired for the first time by boys (though many were earlier by girls) include: sense of humor, same religon, neat, things in common, tolerant, friendly, well organized, good character, someone you can respect.

Husband's attributes: Increasingly often, personality, rather than physical qualities—sense of humor, good temper, affectionate, well liked, sensible, mature, understanding, intelligent, strong, honest, same ideas, "someone you can talk problems over with."

16 YEARS

Growing Up. Some Sixteens just can't say whether life gets better or worse, but nearly all who can say feel that life is getting better this year. They enjoy having more freedom and more responsibility and finding their place in life. Many feel that they are improving personally: "I'm more outgoing," "have more interests," "disposition is better," "attitude seems more mature." A few feel that life gets harder, that they run into more problems as they get older.

A definite satisfaction with the present age is expressed by the majority; the best age is "right about now." Asked if they are impatient to grow older, most make such comments as: "I like it where I am"; "I'll take it as it comes."

College. Still more than previously (90 per cent of our group) plan to go to college or to some special school, such as art school or pharmacy college, though many add the qualifying comment, "Going if I can get in."

More than previously have a particular college chosen. Nearly three times as many girls as boys express preference for a coed college; more than half the boys would prefer an all-boys college, only a third of the girls prefer a girls' college.

Career. Somewhat more decisiveness appears among Sixteens in their choice of careers than among Fifteens, though a few girls are undecided. A considerable variety of choices is mentioned. Boys most often choose engineering, law, architecture, politics, and medicine. Girls choose art, teaching, and child psychology. Journalism and science are often mentioned by both boys and girls.

The majority of girls plan to work until they marry, "in order to have something to fall back on," or "to have something to do after things get dull." Most girls are now, however, rather domestically minded—only a few hope to combine career and marriage, though some would work after marriage if they needed the money.

Marriage. Apparently a sudden change in matrimonial plans—most girls plan to marry, but the great majority of boys are undecided. Spontaneous comments about future spouse or children have decreased markedly from their earlier levels, though the few girls stating a preferred number of children show some agreement in desiring four.

Wife's attributes: Intelligent, pretty, easy to get on with, a good cook, are most desired. New traits sought are that she be athletic and persevering.

Husband's attributes: As earlier, good-tempered, smart, unselfish, helpful around the house, and in love with them are qualities sought by many girls. But a new group of desired traits is mentioned: serious, reliable, faithful, patient, not neurotic, knows where he's going.

CHAPTER FIFTEEN

Interpersonal Relationships

YOUTH has to find itself through interpersonal relationships. The personality patterns of a growing youth depend to a significant degree upon interactions with other personalities. The interactions are so diversified in form, content, and intensity that they do not readily yield to generalizations. However, there are ordering forces. The classified series of growth gradients which appears on pages 390 to 422 concretely suggests the directions of development and the problems of interpersonal control which confront both youth and adult.

The nature of these problems has already been glimpsed in the chapters on Emotion and The Growing Self. We have seen how emotional climate and weather fluctuate with ages and stages. Easygoing Ten and argumentative Eleven produce sharply distinguishable patterns of interpersonal relationship. Thoughtful, inwardizing Thirteen brings about new situations which contrast with the outgoing friendliness of Sixteen.

In last analysis it is the growing self which puts its imprint on interpersonal attitudes. The adolescent growth of self is a deep-seated process of searching and finding. Ten is still in the realm of childhood and shows no great concern about matters of self. He takes his self for granted and takes life as it comes. Eleven launches a real search for self by assertive contacts and contentions. Twelve tends to search for self by trying to win the approval of associates. Thirteen shifts the search inwardly into his own self. Fourteen identifies and defines his self by matching it with other selves. Fifteen explores the attributes of his self in relation to his own ideals and growing ideas. Sixteen takes a sabbatical leave from active search, having achieved a good measure of self-reliance. All these changing attitudes of a growing self are manifested in changing patterns of interpersonal behavior.

The patterns do not grow in a vacuum. They take shape in a complex cultural environment. They cannot be divorced from the previous life history of the individual youth. They are subject to the constant influence of other personalities; particularly the personalities of parents and teachers. A youth must reckon also with brothers and sisters, with aunts and uncles, relatives and strangers, schoolmates, boy friends, girl friends, team and club associates, and an occasional antagonist or ruffian. In the course of the seven years from ten to sixteen he encounters a great variety of persons, young and old. He is not always sure of himself, but he strives to organize his interpersonal experience as best he can. He asserts himself under stress, not always wisely and considerately.

To what extent the stresses arise from within and to what extent they are produced by the cultural environment will vary with the individual, his age and maturity. As early as the age of three he began to use the pronoun "I" with emphasis and to say "I like." Even then he showed a prophetic awareness of interpersonal relationships. You can actually bargain with a 3-year-old! Each succeeding year normally brings some advance in self-insight and in perception of interpersonal relationships. The years from ten to sixteen are no exception. The adolescent growth forces are continuous with those of infancy and childhood and they operate with similar sureness. We can have a reasonable degree of faith in their potentials.

Many parents, however, anticipate the problems of adolescence with trepidation. They have heard such wild stories about the excessive demands and defiant conduct of the teen age that they lose all the benefits of a more confident and trusting attitude. Some of the parents of our research group, on the other hand, testify that they found the adolescent years to be the "easiest" which they have experienced. These parents had been closely following the earlier stages of development and could recognize a similarity in the methods of growth which were later manifested in the adolescent period. The years from ten to sixteen require complex and far-reaching interpersonal reorientations, but the basic mechanisms of the growth process remain the same. The over-all trends of this process are favorable, particularly if original endowment and training have laid a good foundation in the first decade.

The patterns of American family life and the temper of the times combine to evoke an amazing variety of patterns of interpersonal behavior. To present a fair picture of these patterns, the growth gradients have been expanded to include many specimens which illustrate individual differences. The gradients are also designed to disclose the negative as well as positive manifestations of behavior in the forward movement toward increased maturity.

Parent-youth relationships often suffer severe strain, but they may take on a significant meaning when viewed in the light of their developmental implications. This does not mean that an emotional episode should be judged or indulged on the basis of a distant past or a remote future. In developmental guidance the immediate present has priority. The task is to recognize the growth forces which may reveal themselves in subtle, quiet signs or in dramatic manifestations of self-assertion, of confession, contrition, resistance, pride, and in other forms of counterthrust. Authoritarian discipine ignores the significance of growth.

Parents, Siblings, and Family

"Growth forces" is a somewhat abstract phrase, but these forces take on concrete reality when they are envisaged as progressive changes in maturity traits. A rapid survey of these changes may place them in perspective. The following summary is neither a timetable nor a series of norms. It does, however, indicate the trends in interpersonal behavior which emerge under contemporary cultural conditions.

Ten is a homebody. He is warmly attached to his mother; he may idolize his father. He likes to participate in the family activities. His amiable confiding nature evokes affection. But he has a strange capacity for anger which he vents on siblings, physically and verbally. He fights with them if they are in the five- to fourteen-year range of ages.

Eleven is a bit paradoxical. He is even more combative than Ten toward siblings and is resistant, if not rude, toward his parents. He becomes a disturber of peaceful family life. On the other hand, he is intensely demanding of family activities and keenly enjoys participating in them. Withal he has a callow exuberance which can be rather delightful. And despite anti-sibling proclivities he displays an ardent loyalty in behalf of a distressed brother or sister. The quality of his ardor helps to redeem him.

The family unity remains unimpaired despite the insurgencies of Eleven. Twelve moves into a calmer maturity zone. Twelve accordingly is more tolerant and sympathetic toward his mother and companionable with his father. He enjoys his family and its activities, but is beginning to seek the company of friends beyond the home fireside. As for siblings, he enjoys those under five and idolizes those over fifteen. He has been known to use quarrelsome language with those of intervening ages.

Thirteen is reticent, often to the extent that he wants to be left alone. So there are marked and sudden withdrawals from family activities. He is less close and less confiding in his relationships with mother and father. He is so touchy that he is easily provoked by a sibling; but he is no misanthrope. He displays real affection for the youngest siblings and gets on fairly well with those under six and over eleven.

Fourteen has reached a stage which makes him sensitive to the proprieties, standards, and appurtenances (automobiles, etc.) of his household and his parents. He is critical and readily embarrassed. He studies his siblings to get along with them better and to compete with them. He gets along worst with the one who is about eleven years old.

Fifteen feels that he does not have enough freedom and he suffers from restraint. This tends to make him argumentative and remote with both parents. He may find his chief interpersonal satisfactions with friends and with activities outside the home; so that family unity is apparently at low ebb. But Fifteen is also critical of himself as well as others. His attitudes toward siblings have improved. He is pleased with the admiration of the younger ones, companionable with those near his own age, and pals with one who is older.

A cycle comes to full turn at sixteen. Even with a discouraging record of turbulent interpersonal behavior in the past, there is a smoothing out of former tensions and of the superficial conflicts with parents and siblings. Sixteen is typically protective toward younger siblings and may attain almost an adult level of comradeship with an older sibling. Arguments with father may also approach an adult level and may be leavened with a maturing sense of humor. Sixteen has many interests outside and beyond the home; but still likes to return to its shelter and amenities.

So the home remains on its foundations. But we should report that parents are genuinely dismayed by the incessant tensions between siblings —tensions which take the form of quarrels, wrangles, squabbles, spats, and downright altercations in which blows as well as words are interchanged. Fortunately the milder encounters take a beneficial form in good-natured teasing and banter with a spirit of fun and humor. But the belligerent encounters, if unchecked, can become so dominating that they obstruct the normal functions of family life. This constitutes a problem for the mores and for the domestic policy of the individual household concerned.

Friends and Associates

The capacity to make friends is both an art and a personality trait. Most parents justly prize this trait when they see it exemplified in a son or daughter. Some parents are perhaps too inclined to let the matter take care of itself; others go to unwise extremes of promotion in the opposite direction. The youths themselves show great individual differences. Some make friends naturally with the greatest of ease. Some are inept and precipitate conflict by pushing themselves into situations where they are not wanted. Still others are so individualistic or exploratory that they drift in and out of friendship, concentrating, withdrawing, and then resuming relationship. But here again maturity and sex factors play a pervasive role, as evidenced by the growth gradients, for this complex area of interpersonal behavior.

The underlying factors are so lawful and specific that the growth sequences must be considered in four distinguishable aspects or panels, namely, (a) Boys with Boys; (b) Girls with Girls; (c) Girls with Boys; and (d) Boys with Girls.

The four panels are separately summarized for each age level in the following order: a,b,c,d. In this developmental analysis, the term "sex lines" will be used to indicate a shifting boundary which more or less divides the two sexes. It is an interpersonal boundary even though it divides.

Ten. Boys mingle easily with each other. They play with whoever is available. Ten has an instinct for forming fluid groups with all the accompanying insignia and trappings. Relationships tend to be amiable and even benign. Ten truly enjoys friends.

Girls set up relationships which are intense and emotional, showing a love of intrigue, secrecy, and conspiracy. But there is little fighting or argument. Difficulties are soon over. Girls at this age cannot stay mad at each other long.

Most of them are not interested in boys "yet." Most of the boys express either disinterest or dislike of girls. There is an incipient awareness of sex groups; but the *sex lines* cross rather freely, as with children of younger age.

Eleven. Boys are now less casual and more selective in choosing boys to play with and talk with. There is quarreling followed by making up; but not on the intense and complex scale more habitual with girls.

Girls watch each other "like hawks" and try to control each other. Verbal battles result in cool interludes of "not speaking." But the drive to speak is so strong and warm that making up becomes a frequent ritual for re-establishing interpersonal relationships.

At this stage girls display varying degrees of interest in boys. Some are distinctly anti-boy ("Boys are disgusting"); some are neutral; others "sort of like" a certain boy. The boys are mostly neutral about girls, but a few sort of like a certain girl. Both sexes tend to withdraw and cluster into their own sex group. Sex lines are crossed at a distance; boys gather and stare at an opposite group. Or they break out with teasing, taunts, and shouts of derision. Or they hurl spitballs, and snowballs if available. The girls enjoy and even stimulate this kind of interpersonal relationship.

Twelve. Boys make friends easily with their peers. The relationships are somewhat diffuse and shifting but amiable. Selective friendships can now be sustained at a distance by phoning, writing, and visiting.

The friendships of girls likewise are now more thinly spread. The former intense emotionalism is dropping out. "We go around with everybody." A friendship, however, may dissolve when one of a pair moves into an interest in boys.

Boys and girls mix and mingle in rather shapeless groups. Both now freely cross the sex line, back and forth; but usually without strong attachments, even though kissing games are popular. Only one-third of the boys profess an interest in girls. A boy or a girl may be liked without being made aware of it. But others may know. A few girls date, but usually in the form of a planned dinner or dancing party.

Thirteen. Boys are somewhat less sociable than at twelve. There is less group spirit and more interest in solitary activity. The tendency is to cultivate one or two close friends. They do not indulge in much controversy and settle things easily.

Girls are critical and argumentative with their friends; but they regard this as a desirable ingredient of friendship. Much is explored, dissected, and mended through talk and more talk. Friends tend to go in threesomes and twosomes.

The prevailing intersex attitudes have in general calmed down. If anything there is less mutual interest than at twelve. A few boys have become "woman haters." More typical is the comment, "Interested in them, but actually don't take them out." Boys do little dating, but are surprised to see how easy it is to get a girl to go to a dance with them! The girls, alas, may find a boy of their own age too short and immature as a dance partner. They tend to gravitate toward older boys.

Fourteen. Boys become more sociable again. They spontaneously fall into loosely knit, gregarious groups and friendly gangs where "everybody is pretty harmonious." There is much forthright laughter, good fun and humor, and a natural kindness toward each other. Close friendships are based on common interests.

Girls form groups which are more sharply defined. There are inner circles and fringe circles, which exclude as well as include. Friendships are more selective, and personalities are discussed with intensity and avidity.

Sex lines are crossed casually and opportunistically, at meetings, more or less by chance, at the drugstore, church, and in the hallway at school. Boys are less interested in girls than girls are in boys. Girls date more frequently than boys although they are assuming a more subordinate role. Some go steady for two weeks or longer, "but few hearts are broken."

Fifteen. Boys manifest some talent for friendships within their own sex. Several close friends may be chosen because of community of interests. They share these interests with enthusiasm and get along well.

Girls likewise are selective, choosing girls whom they admire. They may form a small coterie, just to talk many things over—life, for example, and interpersonal relationships. A girl seeks a trusted companion, the kind who can become a confidant.

Most of the girls and almost as many boys now date; but there is less going steady. Girls often form a "bunch," and may date boys as a group. Some boys show independence of attitude; a few are too openly enamored and pursue more than one girl. Fifteens like to congregate as an informal, mixed group, at a canteen or party, where they can eat, talk, and listen to records, and where they can pair off on suitable occasion.

Sixteen. Boy friendships are motivated by a desire to share activities with their peers and pals. They like to do things together, not so much for the project but for the heart-warming experiencing of co-operative interpersonal relationships. They prize one or two dependable friends of long standing. They seem to have plenty of friends and often prefer their company to that of the family.

Girls of this age consider friends as a most important factor in their lives. They cultivate new friends as well as old.

Nearly all the girls and most of the boys in our groups do more or less dating. Only a few go steady. Boys may "play the field," by dating three or four girls. Girls are capable of showing definite cordiality to a boy while sustaining a platonic type of friendship.

From the foregoing summary it is evident that the formation of inter-personal relationships between the two sexes is subject to deep-seated developmental forces. It is an intricate patterning process, which involves the individual in relation to his or her groups, as well as to the dictates of the culture. In the epoch from ten to sixteen, the relations undergo a remarkable series of relatively gradual changes. When surveyed in their entire sweep, the gradualness and the latent purposefulness of these changes become apparent. The interpersonal relationship between the sexes is a product of slow growth in the history of the individual, as it also was in the history of the race.

GROWTH GRADIENTS

1. MOTHER-CHILD

10 YEARS

The relationship between Ten and his—or her—mother tends to be straight-forward, uncomplicated, sincere, trusting. The child throws himself whole-heartedly and positively into this relationship. Many say that they like mother (and father) the best of anything in the world—"My mother's just about right!" Criticism of mother's behavior and embarrassment at it in public does not occur to Ten.

Mother is important as a final authority: "Mummy says . . ."; "Mummy doesn't like me to . . ."

Girls are very confidential with mother, and like to confess to her not only bad deeds but even bad thoughts. Both boys and girls are extremely affection-ate and physically demonstrative, sometimes embarrassingly so. Boys especially like to snuggle, and to have mother tuck them in at night.

Several boys are described as having a "mother attachment"—"trails mother everywhere, depends on her." But boys also seem more ambivalent than girls: "Trails mother, but you don't dare give him an inch"; "Wants to give mother things, but much turmoil—shouts and loses his temper."

Ten is aware of his mother's criticism, and may try to improve. But some—
boys more than girls—feel that mother is always trying to improve them.
The beginning of some 11-year-old resistance and "yelling" appears in some.

11 YEARS

Eleven, in sharp contrast to Ten, tends to be rude and resistant to his mother,
seems to "work against" her. May argue about "everything," the main
purpose being to prove mother wrong. Some seem to feel there is nothing
right about mother. Girls may observe her closely, then criticize. And
both boys and girls may resist or object to any suggestion that she makes,
vetoing it practically "before it comes out of her mouth."

Eleven strikes out against mother, verbally and even physically, "takes things
out on" mother. Great scenes can occur: stamping feet, yelling, talking
back, calling names—"dope," "stinker," "liar," "old meanie." Mothers are
sometimes reported to "get mad and yell in return."

Much exaggeration and dramatization—"You're the meanest mother in the whole
school, and all the kids say so!" Very mocking in reporting privileges
denied by mother.

Many report that mother is trying to "improve" them, and mothers do feel that
both girls and boys should help more with housework, pick up room better,
get on better with siblings. But though they expect a lot from mother,
11-year-olds are very reluctant to give any help, and to any request are
apt to reply, "Do I have to?" Many mothers give up trying to get Elevens—
especially boys—to help around the house.

Child seems extremely unappreciative of "treats" and always wants more than
is provided.

At times, a much more friendly, co-operative relationship does prevail, with
girls described as confiding, boys as "pallish." Some boys are very affectionate with mother. Girls may feel much better after confessing even
minor misdemeanors to mother. But, in spite of this, more things are kept
from mother than earlier.

12 YEARS

Twelve seems to have emerged from his 11-year-old battle with parents. Many
now express considerable humor and friendliness toward mother. They
have themselves better in hand, and so can often be quite patient and
tolerant, tactful, sympathetic, and objective with mother. May even
"handle" mother with humor.

Twelve is easier to reason with, less ready to fight, argue, shout, or rebel
openly. Many do feel that mothers are overly critical about their not helping with housework, keeping room neat, getting on with siblings, and
about table manners. And some are reported not to hear mother's com-

mands and comments. But Twelve generally seems reasonably helpful, and some boys, who might earlier have co-operated with mother's suggestions, may now even take the initiative in improving a situation—"Don't say a word, I'll fix this."

Some feel that mother does not give them enough privileges, doesn't fully appreciate them, or "treats me a little younger than I am." But, in general, Twelve is much less demanding. He is more willing for mother to live her own life in her own way. And at the same time, he shows that he really cares about her opinion and approval. His outlook on the parent-child relationship is shown by his still speaking in terms of "minding" and "not minding."

Twelve generally feels quite friendly, confiding, and companionable toward mother. Though most are less openly affectionate than earlier, they like to be "chummy." But their behavior is very uneven—babyish one minute, very mature the next.

Among many girls, there appear the beginnings of feelings that mother is "not very modern" in dress, make-up, hair-do, and deportment.

13 YEARS

Thirteen brings a withdrawal from mother. Mothers often worry that they are losing the close, confiding relationship they used to have, but 13-year-olds comment that they don't want to be close to anyone—just want to be left alone.

Thirteen is very reticent, gives grudging, one-word answers to questions. Some (especially boys) are reported to behave as though mother was persecuting them. The simplest question or show of interest from mother may be construed as prying. But some Thirteens can enjoy occasional thoughtful discussions with her if they instigate these themselves.

Most are much less influenced by mother's directives than earlier. If disagreement arises, girls may sulk and openly express resentment; boys may argue and talk back. Boys report, "Often she gets mad and gives me a big talking to." Still more violent friction can occur: "We yell at each other"; "Sometimes we brush it off, but sometimes it's terrible." Some boys are quite openly rebellious and hostile, and speak rudely, even profanely, to mother. A few boys, however, may be starting to try to influence mother through use of techniques other than direct demand or rebellion. And, fortunately, Thirteen's descriptions may give more hope than his behavior: "I yell at her if I'm mad. But the way I treat her is not a part of what I think of her."

If reminded to help around the house, Thirteen responds with less open rebellion, but more "in a minute" than earlier. Many know, and list, parents' criticisms, but have no intention of changing. Most feel criticized too much, and some mimic mother: "Mother says, 'Why do I always have to tell you, blah, blah, blah?'"

Criticism of mother is often quite extreme; there are times when nothing is right. Boys are most likely to be critical of the way things go around the house: "What! My egg isn't cooked yet?" Some feel that mother knows nothing, and there appears the beginning of the complaint, "She just doesn't think the way I do." Girls more often criticize mother's make-up, hair-do, clothes—"for her own good." May also criticize her personality. May be as faultfinding (though not as embroiled) as at eleven. Beginning to be embarrassed by mother in public. With all this, Thirteen may nevertheless worry about mother's health.

14 YEARS

Fourteen's basic attitude generally seems to be that mother is hopelessly old-fashioned, that she doesn't understand him, that they "have nothing in common." Complaints at thirteen were more specific and minute. Now they are more general: mother is just too antiquated.

Mother often feels put on the defensive, trying to please a child who demands everything, appreciates and gives little. From girls especially, the typical comment at any remark or activity of mother's is, "Oh, Mother!" Fourteen seems much embarrassed by mother in front of friends—by her actions, her remarks, her humor; walks at least several paces behind her in public. May criticize one parent to another.

Most feel that mother restricts them too much. "Parents tend to make children of our age much younger than they really are." Can slip back into quite childish behavior with mother: "I'm *not* a good girl!"

On the other hand, Fourteens often react passively toward maternal criticisms of them: "I just sit there when she criticizes"; "Don't like to be preached at, because usually I know what the person is going to say before they say it."

Fourteen generally has much more difficulty with mother than with friends or the outside world. Boys often feel freer to express anger, displeasure, or disagreement with mother than they would with father. Some may be unsympathetic if mother is tired or ill. Many know they wouldn't want friends to see how they treat her.

However, many are companionable. Some feel on an equal basis with mother, and boys may tease her affectionately. Girls can be reasonable and good company for mothers, and most girls report, "I confide in her." Many boys too may confide if allowed to do so spontaneously, though most mothers wouldn't dare to probe or ask questions—would be "so squelched." Some may even enjoy times alone with mother, may find her a good listener. Both boys and girls may apologize to mother after rude retorts or shouting in a rage.

Many mothers report that best results are obtained from praise rather than criticism.

15 YEARS

Fifteen typically reports, "We get on pretty well," or, "I guess we get on O.K." Mothers are more likely to say, "Well, we're still on speaking terms." Relationships are not smooth, and Fifteen and his mother even seem to disagree in reporting how they get on. A mother may say things are fine, her daughter say they are terrible, or vice versa. Boys, in reporting, may picture the relationship as better than mother pictures it.

Mothers tend to feel that Fifteen is selfish, critical, rebellious, and not very responsive, and report considerable sulking, moping, slatting around, arguing, and flaring up.

Girls more than boys confide in their mothers, but even girls are apt to feel that mother does not understand as well as does some friend. In fact, the most common complaint is that, "She doesn't understand. She doesn't think the way I do."

Fifteen feels strongly that he does not have enough freedom. Girls feel that mother tries too hard to make them ladylike. Mothers and daughters may get on beautifully—"if there's no work to be done." Boys are extremely resentful when mothers make them stay in at night, wear suitable clothing, study, help around the house, or tell where they are going or have been. Such demands seem quite unreasonable to them.

Maternal affection is not as a rule well received. Daughters may comment, "Those long, quiet talks just embarrass everybody," and sons are especially resentful of public displays of affection—"None of that stuff, Mom."

Fifteen often seems to feel a need to get away—a girl "can't stand" her mother, a boy has "just got to get away from her—I'm just waiting to get off to college."

Some Fifteens seem to realize that they are at their worst with their mothers. Some admit that they should be more "patient" with her, and a few are actually beginning to be more thoughtful. Fifteen's typical attitude seems to range from: "Mother's too old to know what it's all about; things were different when mother was a girl," to, "Mother is quite up-to-date and sympathetic—as much as a parent *can* be."

16 YEARS

Sixteen's relationship with his mother has improved markedly. It is generally described as "excellent" or "very smooth," and even those who are still dissatisfied with the relationship mostly report that it is "better than it was."

Some boys and girls do occasionally still get very angry at mother. But many, especially girls, resolve to do better, and silently criticize themselves when they do not treat mother politely.

To Sixteen, it seems that the improvement in relationships is because mother gives more privileges than earlier. Nearly all feel that they have more freedom, and some even feel that they have as much as they deserve, as they begin to understand the need for the restrictions which are imposed.

Many seem to feel that mother is satisfied with them. Most describe her as "reasonable." There may be considerable confiding in mother. Sixteen likes to "go places" with her, for fun. Relationship is again becoming more companionable, and some actually say, "We have good times together."

A few boys do feel that mother is too much "into everything" that concerns them. But, in general, the feeling is that mother treats them much more "as a grownup." And many Sixteens even feel that parents now know more than they used to.

2. FATHER-CHILD

10 YEARS

Both boys and girls, for the most part, are said to get on extremely well with their fathers. Girls are described as "adoring" their fathers, being "wonderful pals." "He's the shining light." And many boys are described as "admiring" or "idolizing" father. "Thinks his father is the end answer to everything." Children themselves spontaneously report. "We have fun"; "I think he's just about right"; "Best father in the whole world."

Many girls believe that they are more like their father than like mother. Several mothers say that they leave the disciplining of daughters to the father, since he is more effective.

A few boys do not get on well with father—he loses his temper at them.

Some, of both sexes, complain that father doesn't have time to do things with them. However, most spend a good deal of time alone with father—at ballgames, movies, on walks, or playing games, reading, wrestling.

11 YEARS

Some Elevens continue great admiration or even adoration of father, but in many this attitude is becoming much more matter-of-fact. Most do get on reasonably well, and there is still much companionship between fathers and children (in addition to "whole family" activity). Fathers take sons or daughters rowing, swimming, walking in woods, shooting, to games, movies, the zoo.

Father's role in many cases is now that of disciplinarian. Many Elevens say their fathers are *very* strict, and that fathers get angry with them. Fathers are generally less patient with the arguing and talking back of Eleven than are mothers, and particularly feel that girls do not help mother enough around the house. Fathers are apt to lose their tempers, and several Elevens complain that they are impatient and irritable—"He has a bad temper from being in the Army."

Both boys and girls have less to say about fathers than at ten. Most do not directly criticize their fathers yet, but many have some complaints, and there is some resistance. The majority complain that fathers do not have enough time to spend with them, and a few suspect that fathers don't *want* to spend time with them. Several feel that father gets on better with some other sibling, because his personality is more like theirs.

Several are, mothers report, definitely afraid of their fathers. Some fathers are quite harsh with sons: "He's not a fierce man, but if he's tired and you do wrong he'll hit you." At the same time, a few boys are beginning to talk very roughly to (or about) fathers: "Old so-and-so."

Girls especially are often better with father than with mother at this age, even though father may be less patient and tolerant than earlier. Girls report (with some pride) that when father speaks, "He means it!"

12 YEARS

Most Twelves get on well with their fathers. With boys and with most girls the relationship is now less adoring and more companionable than formerly. The earlier strong relationship is "toned down": "I'm on good terms with him but arguments come up"; "We get on normally, but I hardly ever see him." A few girls develop a flirtatious or hero-worshiping attitude toward father, and get along extremely well on this basis. And some, boys especially, who before had trouble, now get on better with father.

Fewer activities are shared, though in some cases—*if* father has the time—sailing, sports, reading, shooting, playing ball, watching TV, and discussing (sports, politics, war) are enjoyed together.

Most, boys as well as girls, are good about "minding" father. Some resent prohibitions, but still accept them.

Children of both sexes likely to report that they resemble father more than mother.

Twelve is quite aware of his father's criticisms of him: that he doesn't help enough around the house, is too lazy, doesn't treat siblings well, is not prompt or neat. Fathers are said to scold or "blow up" or be irritated about these things. Quite a few say that father is stricter than mother.

Some Twelves start to evaluate father's behavior as they did not earlier: "He has an awful temper, but he's nice"; "He's not henpecked, but he doesn't assert himself." Many feel that father (as well as mother) spoils siblings. Some (boys especially) begin to criticize father's treatment of mother, or mother's belief in what father says.

Some boys begin to run down or criticize parents jokingly. What would have been a criticism at eleven can be a humorous dig at twelve: "What a physique!" Some boys also show competition with fathers, in feats of wit, skill, or endurance.

13 YEARS

Thirteens do not show a "typical" pattern to the extent that the earlier ages did. Great individual differences exist: some get on better with father, some with mother; some think father is more strict, some think mother is.

A few girls are still very affectionate toward father, or are affectionate now for the first time. The majority take father for granted more than earlier. And some, especially boys, are described as resentful of father. But they do not flare out at father as much as at mother.

In general, 13-year-olds "mind" father better than mother, and his discipline is usually more effective. Thirteens are more afraid of father, and also feel that he doesn't nag so much, so they pay better attention. Less out-of-bounds rebellion occurs with father than mother. Some Thirteens are saucy and snap back, but most still do not. "I plan to, but then I don't dare."

Most confide in father less than in mother. They admire and respect him more, criticize him less, and behave better with him, but feel less close to him.

Often behaviors in father and child seem to complement and reinforce each other. Children themselves withdraw, and at the same time think that fathers are too busy for them. Father thinks boy is too interested in sports, and boy is disappointed because father is not more interested. Or, more positively, when homework goes better, girl says, "Daddy's easier to work with now," and father says, "She's beginning to think."

"Doing things together" tends to decrease. About half our Thirteens still do companionable things with father: ballgames, swimming, sailing, movies, discussions. Others report that he is too busy, or that he is cross and irritable because he works so hard. Father's help on homework may be accepted better, and with less bickering, than mother's. Some fathers take only occasional interest in Thirteen, and their timing may not be good: "When he does try to talk and take an interest he asks different things, and you don't feel like talking, and then that makes trouble."

Nearly all Thirteens feel that father is critical of them in some ways. "He says I'm a dilettante, messy, and selfish." Some know that father criticizes them to their faces but praises them to outsiders.

Thirteen's criticisms often include the complaint that parents favor or pamper younger siblings. And a few boys criticize the way father treats mother.

14 YEARS

Many Fourteens, both girls and boys, state that they get on better with father than with mother. (There are, however, many exceptions—father is too busy, too unreasonable, gets mad too easily.) Mother's estimate of the father-child relationship does not always agree with what son or daughter reports.

Some think that father is hopelessly antiquated, though this is more apt to be thought of mother than father. Fourteens seem a little more likely than earlier to think of parents together, as "They," and to think that They are pretty hopeless. Especially in public is Fourteen embarrassed by Them.

But many Fourteens feel that father does understand them better than mother, is more reasonable, does not have to have everything just so, does not nag, and is not so oversolicitous and fearful of their welfare. Even then, his standards may be felt to be hopelessly high: "Anything I do makes them criticize"; "They try to improve me in most every way." And father is still less confided in than mother, though he might be consulted, depending on the problem.

Fathers are usually firmer than mothers. May be unduly restrictive about daughter's dating. Fourteen admires, respects, and fears him more, and minds him better. Girls quarrel with fathers much less than with mothers, and boys are more respectful to fathers. With boys, father seems to know "when to put the pressure on" better than mother does.

Some criticize father to mother and mother to father, and are quick to play mother's authority against father's if the two do not agree.

Boys and girls resist any physical show of affection, or even too much verbal concern. Some fathers are annoyed because sons and daughters show so little appreciation, or because they do not fully answer direct questions (which are not always well timed). Fathers' complaints suggest that Fourteen is rude, insolent, selfish, messy, lazy, ungrateful.

A few Fourteens still attend sports events, etc., with father, but much less of this occurs than earlier. Many prefer father to mother for help with homework. And some enjoy discussions and arguments together.

15 YEARS

Despite many exceptions, the majority of Fifteens say that they get on better with father than mother. Though they confide more in mother, they show more respect and admiration for father. They feel that "he's more often right," "he understands me better," "his personality fits with mine."

Less hero-worship occurs than did earlier. Even a boy who has been a very enthusiastic son may report merely, "We get on O.K. Our relationship is good *on the whole*." But some have a fairly jolly relationship, with considerable humor involved—more than with mothers.

Difficulties, however, do occur—either sudden outbursts or more protracted hostilities. Some real blowups occur—"He starts yelling and I yell back"—and can develop into serious scenes with the whole family involved. Or troubles may be continuous; Mother reports, "They kind of avoid each other now," or, "They don't even speak." Some mothers still "protect" Fifteen from his father, but boys often resent this.

In spite of withdrawal or arguments, most manage to get on fairly well, except for the occasional blowups. The actual adjustment ranges from quite warm and friendly, to knowing what to steer clear of, to armed truce.

Many Fifteens feel that they are restrained too much. The biggest problem for both boys and girls seems to be time of getting in at night. Boys especially want complete liberty, and fathers say, "No respect for what you say unless it's with an iron hand." Gentle or halfway measures and rules do not work.

Companionship is less than before; absent in some cases. Fathers help less with homework. Boys do more with father than do girls—in some cases camping, playing golf, discussing sports, shooting.

Much arguing and discussing occurs. But many Fifteens are embarrassed by any serious personal talks with either parent, and "just clam up." Little physical show of affection is accepted by either sex.

Boys evaluate father's abilities and personality more than earlier: "He's not good in radio, but we go camping"; "He's not really fatherly"; "He's cross and gruff with my friends." The father-child relationship itself is often evaluated in terms of the past—"Better [or worse] than last year."

16 YEARS

Sixteen's relationship with his father is reasonably good—often reported as, "We get on pretty well." Many still say they get on better with father than with mother—some say because they see him less. But the relationship with father has not improved as much between fifteen and sixteen as has the relationship with mother.

Most Sixteens are still more respectful of father than of mother. ("Have to watch my step.") May mutter objections under their breath, but wouldn't dare speak out. However, some do speak up to father as they would not have dared to earlier.

Both boys and girls may enjoy discussing (or arguing about) theoretical matters with father. And his help on financial matters or really difficult school work is still valued.

Many girls still express the belief that they are most like their fathers. But girls also often feel that their fathers are unsympathetic, and too restrictive about dating.

3. SIBLINGS

10 YEARS

The majority of 10-year-olds fight with their brothers and sisters—at least younger ones (except infants), at least part of the time ("sometimes we get on and sometimes not"). Most say they would not want to be an only child, but several comment, "Once in a while I wish he'd just disappear," or, "Sometimes I'd just as soon go live somewhere else for a while."

A minority express stronger antagonism: "That spoiled brat! Sometimes I feel as if I hated the sight of her"; "I'd like to smash her face in!" Whether or not there is real rivalry and jealousy seems to be more a matter of individuality and situation than of age.

Fighting is most frequent with younger siblings. The usual pattern is that the younger one teases, "needles," taunts, or pesters until Ten retaliates physically. Then the younger calls for help, or parents step in spontaneously. Then Ten thinks parent is unfair. Most feel that younger siblings are favored, and also that they "get away with a lot of stuff I never got away with."

With younger siblings close to Ten's own age, though there is much good-natured playing together, fighting and bickering are very common. Fighting involves name calling ("Pig—fatty—dope"), "wrassling," and real physical fighting intended to hurt—pushing, kicking, hitting, biting. Good-natured "wrassling" becomes real fighting when someone is hurt. Much fighting occurs over possessions—"We both want the same thing."

Younger siblings feel that 10-year-olds are too bossy and try too hard to keep them in line. However, Tens do at times play nicely with younger siblings. In fact, younger ones often tease Tens to play with them. And many Tens are very good about caring for or helping with siblings who are under five. These younger ones are often reported to "adore" the 10-year-old.

Some Tens know they are not good to younger siblings: "If I want to play with him I'm nice, but if I want to be alone he's a GONER!"

Tens get on better with older than with younger siblings, and report that older ones sometimes play with them or take them places, but that there is still a lot of fighting. Many think that older siblings consider them a nuisance or tattletales, because they seek protection from parents.

11 YEARS

Eleven gets on badly much of the time with younger siblings (except with the *very* young ones). Fighting varies in amount from "occasionally" to "about half the time." And though physical fighting is giving way to verbal argument and name calling, violence still often occurs—hitting, kicking, biting, pulling hair. Much "needling" occurs, both physical and verbal: "She can't go by without touching him—just a little poke or jab. Then he reciprocates. Then a real physical battle."

Eleven's chief complaint is, "He gets me into trouble!" The younger one "starts something," Eleven "pays him back," parent punishes Eleven. Eleven resents parents' idea that because he is older he should put up with the younger one and not retaliate, feels that this is "siding with" the younger one.

Eleven is very critical of faults of younger siblings: thinks they are lazy, messy, careless, untruthful. He tries to correct and boss them, and this is resented. Often "yells" at younger siblings, even though he complains that older siblings yell at him. Possessions, too, are the cause of much difficulty: "He gets into my things."

Some lock the door to keep out very young siblings, "try to ignore" ones nearer their own age. Feel that young siblings tag along too much. Sometimes don't mind this, but often do. Occasionally, however, Eleven plays well with younger ones and may be glad of their company, especially when away from home.

Most Elevens get on reasonably well with siblings who are much older than they—eighteen years or older. About those just a few years older they say, "We fight some, but not as much as we did." Fighting with older siblings may now be more verbal than physical: "We don't hit each other, but we argue about everything." Still tease older ones and are teased by them.

Some playing with older siblings—especially sports. But older ones feel that Elevens tag along too much and don't want them around when older friends are present.

Many say they miss older siblings who have gone away to school, but are partly glad they are away.

Eleven may worry that brothers and sisters prefer each other to him, or gang up against him.

12 YEARS

Twelve seems to get on a little better with younger siblings than he did at eleven, though relations are usually less than the parents' ideal. Mostly, Twelve expresses a great lack of enthusiasm for younger siblings: "Oh, I guess he's all right"; "Guess I have to *say* I like having a sister." His expression may be as positive as, "We get on about as well as most, I guess —squabble some, have some fun together," or may be more negative: "We get on awful"; "He's a pest"; "She's terrible."

The amount of fighting admitted to ranges from "occasional quarrels" to "al-

ways fighting." One boy says, "Once in a while we have a break and don't
fight. On the average we fight once a day—sometimes three times, sometimes not at all."

Having the last word is very important.

Chief complaints are that younger ones tease and taunt them (especially in
front of friends and especially about boy or girl friends), hang around too
much, pester them to play games, get into their "stuff." "He hits me but
I'm not allowed to hit him," is common, as is, "He gets away with things I
never got away with."

Relationships tend to improve with increasing age between siblings. Many
Twelves are quite good with brothers and sisters who are four or under.
These are described as "O.K.," or even "fun." Relations with brothers and
sisters sixteen and over also is mostly good: "Idolizes her," "admires him."
This is a recent development with most. Their own statements about the
improved relationship reflect considerable docility: "He teases me all the
time, but only in fun. He never beats or hurts me"; "Get on fine now—she
doesn't seem to dislike me as much."

Most, however, get on very badly with 13- and 14-year-old siblings, at least
part of the time: "We're always fighting—sometimes with words, sometimes with fists." When not fighting they get on "fairly well." Boys enjoy
wrestling.

Several at this age say they like being an only child: "I don't know if I should
say this, but I have a dog and I like him as well as I would a brother or
sister."

13 YEARS

Most Thirteens, as earlier, get on quite well with older or much younger
siblings, sometimes expressing real affection for the latter. Most still have
trouble with those just a few years younger, but this trouble is usually
less constant than earlier, and often is just general trouble. Rather than
listing specific complaints, as earlier, they say, "Don't know exactly what
it's about." Fighting may also be less bitter: "We fight a lot. We enjoy it,
but my parents don't like it." Real hatred for a younger sibling is rare,
but occasionally is reported by parents. Younger siblings in these cases
may like, even "adore" the older one.

Worst difficulty seems to be with the 10- and 11-year-olds, with whom some
"argue and fight all the time," and with 6- and 7-year-olds, whom they
describe as "a pest," "a nuisance," "awful," "impossible," "spoiled brat."
Thirteen is critical of younger siblings: they lie, are messy, ask stupid
questions. The younger ones resent this, and give trouble when Thirteen
tries to "boss" or discipline them.

Fighting now is more verbal than physical. Occasionally Thirteen says very mean things to younger siblings: "Who could like that stupid so and so?" "She's just a queer." And these younger ones definitely talk back ("Oh, mind your own business"), or mimic and mock. A few Thirteens are mature enough to control younger siblings by use of "techniques," but most still just try to boss.

In several families, Thirteens are punished for mistreating younger siblings, as by deductions from their allowances. But parents may be beginning to side with Thirteen a little more, recognizing faults of the younger children. This helps out.

Insight into relationships with siblings is shown increasingly: "Probably partly my fault; he wouldn't pester me if he didn't get any reaction"; "Later she won't find it so attractive to bother me, but right now I'm sort of touchy"; and some humor: "We get on fairly well. For instance, when he's asleep."

Some admit the advantage of siblings as playmates if nobody else is around. And several comment spontaneously that they are glad not to be an only child, because if they were they might be spoiled.

A marked improvement occurs in relations with older siblings, even with those close to Thirteen in age. Not only may they not fight, but may even express positive affection: "We do a lot of palling around together"; "She's definitely my sister now"; "I can tell her things and she understands— definitely convenient."

Thirteen is described by parents as "devoted" to older siblings, admiring, proud. And though parents often report the relationship as being better than the children say it is, Thirteen himself says, "Get on better than we used to —real improvement this last year." Quarreling with older siblings is now only occasional in most.

14 YEARS

In his relations with siblings, Fourteen usually shows some improvement over years past, but generally leaves much still to be desired (by parents), especially in his relations with those closest to him in age. Most trouble is with 11-year-olds.

With much younger siblings—five or under—most Fourteens get on well: take care of them, play with them, even buy them things. But the trouble that occurs with those between six and thirteen is suggested in Fourteen's comments: "Nuisance," "pain in the neck," "that face of hers—it kills me!" And some simply say, "I just don't like her as well as I used to."

Fourteen's chief complaints about siblings are: "Argues all the time," "gets into my things," "tags along," "makes noises and moves around so," "when she isn't talking she's singing or dancing," "shows off and wants to be the center of attention," "wants me to do everything for her but doesn't want to do a thing for me."

Fourteen may recognize and comment that if one member of a family is out of sorts it spoils things for all. But, nevertheless, a great deal of arguing takes place. And though physical violence occurs less than formerly, it still does occur. Some merely threaten to hit, but some actually "get mad and hit him," "slug him whenever I get the chance."

Most parents feel that Fourteens should treat younger siblings better, and try to improve their behavior. Frequently they step in to prevent ill-treatment of younger ones. Some Fourteens, on the other hand, occasionally protect younger siblings from parents.

Marked individual differences exist in Fourteens' relations with older siblings. Some get on very well—go to dances, sports events together. But many get on badly. Fourteen especially criticizes the way older ones treat him or other members of the family. Many say they do get on better than they used to with older siblings because they don't see much of each other.

Fourteen sometimes comments that in families of three children there is constant pairing off of two against one. Many of both sexes say they would rather have brothers than sisters.

15 YEARS

Relations with younger siblings are definitely improving. Particularly do Fifteens get on well with much younger siblings who look up to, imitate, and boast about them. They admit they enjoy this admiration. Some help with the younger ones, putting them to bed, etc. Often Fifteen will not allow parents to criticize them: "She's a good kid; let her alone." Most are exceptionally fond of and good with infants (though one boy says, "The baby is kinda noisy. I just don't pay any attention. The dog is really better —smarter").

Fifteen's chief complaints are that the younger ones are spoiled, do not mind parents well, do not mind him: "He just plain won't mind, and then I blow my top." Other complaints are that they annoy Fifteen ("making so much noise when I'm practicing"), and tease to play with him (especially the 9- to 11-year-olds). Some are now willing, and able, to use "techniques" with the younger ones.

With brothers and sisters near their own age, Fifteens often become very companionable: "We hack around together a lot"; "We have more interests in common—a real change." Some arguing and fighting still occurs, but some say, "We always get caught when we're disagreeing, so I think our parents don't think we get along as well as we do."

Some seem to feel that siblings are improving: "She's a lot cuter than she was," "more intelligent than she used to be"; "used to be a nuisance, but not now."

Relationships with older siblings generally range from good to excellent. At worst, Fifteen says, "We get along O.K.—don't see much of each other." Moderate enthusiasm is more often expressed ("Now we're getting older we pal around more. We fight a little but not much"), and many express the greatest enthusiasm ("Very close. Real good friends. We talk things over"). Parents report, "He idolizes his older brother."

A few still squabble or fight occasionally, but many can now ignore a troublesome sibling, or can walk away from trouble. And several even report, "Haven't had a fight for months. We just marked our last fight and decided not to fight any more."

16 YEARS

By sixteen, most get on well with older and much younger siblings, and at least don't have much trouble with those just younger. Most report marked recent improvement, and many attribute this to their own increased age. Some can even criticize and thus improve their own behavior toward siblings: "I was too bossy with him."

The improvement is also probably due to the fact that Sixteens see less of siblings, and that friends are much more important to them. Sixteen enjoys the admiration of younger siblings, and may like to consult older ones, but generally spends little time with either.

A few are still jealous that parents favor and "spoil" younger ones. And some teasing of and by 16-year-olds still goes on—much enjoyed by the one who does the teasing.

4. FAMILY

10 YEARS

Ten feels a much closer relationship with his family than he did at nine. He accepts and enjoys his family and usually participates most willingly in any kind of family activity—picnics, rides, movies, trips together. "Every Sunday afternoon the whole family goes for a ride."

Most Tens are well satisfied with both parents—not critical of them, and do not like older siblings to criticize parents.

However, quarreling with siblings may upset family harmony: "We're not a very harmonious family. Every meal something happens. We eat and scream mostly."

11 YEARS

Many Elevens have a strong family feeling. Though rude and quarrelsome within the family, how they behave does not necessarily indicate how they feel. Eleven likes belonging to a family, likes the idea of having relatives, appreciates his own family, and prefers it to families of friends.

Eleven enjoys family activities, of which there are often many: movies, picnics, weekly rides, zoo, listening to music together. In fact, he can be quite demanding for family activity: "What are we going to do today?" Mothers report, "God forbid if we just stay home!"

Many are beginning to see their parents more as individuals, not just as parents, and some criticism of them occurs. Some rebellion: "I'm a free person. Why do I have to do what the family tells me?"

Eleven often appears quite unaware of the extent to which his quarreling with siblings, rebellion against mother, unwillingness to help, interferes with family harmony.

12 YEARS

Twelve is easier-going within the family group, and shows less rebellion, but also less intense interest. The majority are still well satisfied with their families and feel close to them: "Pretty good family—I'm lucky to be in it"; "I think we do well as a family."

Family activities and excursions interest Twelve a little less than they did at eleven. Beginning of some withdrawal: "I like to spend some time with my family, but some time with my friends." Or even, "I just have to get out of there sometimes."

13 YEARS

Thirteen often brings a marked and sudden withdrawal from any participation in family activities. May spend only the necessary minimum of time with family, as at mealtimes. "Just not a part of the family—withdraws and is hostile to individual members."

Thirteen has less to say about the family than earlier. Comments: "Of course we have our arguments"; "Fairly harmonious—of course everybody has their little spats"; or even, "I think I'm beginning to break away a little, but I take that as natural."

Each member of the family may have his own opinion or criticism of others: son may think father treats mother badly or that mother is too much influenced by father; mother thinks father is too strict with son; father thinks mother is too easy.

Boys may go out with father alone, rather than with whole family.

Many worry when parents argue.

14 YEARS

Many Fourteens are highly embarrassed by their families. They feel strongly the need of breaking away and establishing independence: "Sometimes if you're too close to your family it's too bad, because you never can leave them."

May be highly insulted and indignant if family does not have the very best TV, car, house, etc.

Fourteen is often less worried than earlier when parents argue, and may think it's silly.

Some admit that they wouldn't want their friends to see the way they treat their families: "I don't add very much to the family life—I ridicule everybody." "With my family I acquire a very nasty disposition, you might say. Well, what have I got in common with them?"

15 YEARS

This may be a low point for family unity. Fifteen withdraws, argues, may be extremely aloof, hostile, secretive. Several comment that they get very "mad" at their families. Strong feeling prevails that the family is too old-fashioned, unsympathetic, not understanding, too strict.

Great desire is expressed to be free and independent of the family: "They want us to stay home more, but they would have a job to make us stay home." Fifteen may even wish he could live in a hotel and not be bothered by a family.

For many, friends are everything, family nothing.

16 YEARS

In general, Sixteen has a much better relationship with his family. Fewer arguments occur, less hostility, more appreciation. Most are more satisfied with the amount of freedom given them. Several actually state that they appreciate their families more than they used to. Many feel that their families compare well with other families, though may comment, "I think I have a good family—*as families go.*"

Conformity may, however, be only on the surface. Though fewer arguments occur, some feel that the family just doesn't understand them and that points of view are very different.

And though relations may be smooth and friendly, of many it is said, "Does nothing with the family"; "Absolutely no time for the family." Company of friends is usually definitely preferred to that of parents.

5. SAME-SEX FRIENDS

10 YEARS

Girls. Most have a best friend, often several. Relationships among these friends are extremely complex and intense—much getting mad and not speaking. ("We just don't speak for a while . . . and then she'll come back with some ice-cream cones and we'll make up.")

Much anger, jealousy, and fighting if friends associate with other, disliked girls ("Laurel spits fire if I go out with Nancy"). Very possessive of friends and very demanding.

Apt to be very cliquey and purposely say things to put girls against other girls. "Let's go against somebody."

Much emphasis on secrets and whom they can trust: ("I can trust her never to tell *anything* no matter how mad at me she is or what"). A few describe personality of friend ("We're very much alike except that she hates to read and I love to read"), but most emphasize mainly trustworthiness.

Considerable spending the night with each other.

Boys. Some 10-year-olds have one or two "best" or "trusted" friends. Others have a whole "gang" whom they seem to like about equally: "To me they aren't best friends. They're *all* my friends."

Groups may be fluid. Or one boy may have two definite groups which do not mix. Some, though they have many friends, often prefer to play with just one friend at a time

Most "get on good." Not as much fighting and getting mad and not speaking as among the girls. However, some ganging up of two against one.

Boys, in telling of their friends, tell usually their full names, ages, where they live, and what games are played together. Some will shift kind of activity to suit taste and abilities of companion of the moment.

Chief activities seem to be baseball, football, wrestling, electric trains, riding bicycles, building tents or huts, going to the movies.

11 YEARS

Girls. A few have just one or two best friends; others have many. Some just loosely have "a whole gang" of friends; others arrange them in a definite hierarchy ("My best friend is Lollie. Then next comes Ruthie and on the same line with Ruthie is Eve"). Some may list all friends, criticizing each. One typical Eleven asks, "Could I just say who *isn't* my best friend?"

Relationships continue to be very emotional, intense, and complicated. Much getting mad, not speaking, threatening "All right for you," or waiting for the other to give in. All this is probably enjoyed at least by some. ("Whole gang of friends and I like everybody. But we have to quarrel to break up the smoothness.")

Considerable verbal, emotional, and physical conflict among girls: "She's always trying to strangle me"; "She's just plain nasty—mentions my braces and asks me why I lisp." Very vulnerable to mean remarks of friends in front of others. Very limited ability to laugh this off.

Some are strongly under the influence of a best friend and try hard to please her in everything. May, for instance, neglect practicing at friend's behest. A few very warm or even sentimental about friends: "She's awfully nice," or, "I'd never get mad at my dear pal." A few take up with some quite unpopular or unattractive child and are very loyal.

Jealousy about who else friend plays with, quarreling about very small, unimportant things. Much jockeying for position: insisting on paying for own treats, or on treating friends, too compulsive and insistent to be mere generosity.

Beginning of specific criticism of friends: "She's really too tough for me," or, "She swears a lot."

Spending the night with each other is a continued interest.

Boys. As at ten, some concentrate on one or two best friends, some are part of a gang, and some have both.

Relations in many are described as "O.K.," but in others are much less smooth than at ten, though not as complex as among girls. There is much quarreling and making up, getting mad, not speaking. "I let them start speaking, but if they won't I have to."

Rather specific criticism of friends: "he brags," "he blames me." And, conversely, warm compliments: "One real friend, a real pal"; "My greatest friend. Interesting to talk to and we both have the same ideas"; "About the same temperament as me."

Baseball, bicycling, sports, movies, and hut or tree house play are enjoyed by the gangs.

Beginning to spend the night with each other.

Several report that they have plenty of children to play with ("Roughly about ten good ones"), whereas their mothers say that they are lonesome, don't have many friends, or don't have much social life.

12 YEARS

Girls. Expansive in friendships at this age. Many no longer have a single friend but now "a whole gang" ("Go around with everybody. Try to be nice to all"). Sometimes just two or three separate off from the group, but it's "not against anybody." A few now have real trouble making friends, but these are in the minority.

Relationships less intense. Some getting mad and not speaking, but less. Less under influence of friends. However, "telling her off" is important.

"She lives near me" seems to be an adequate reason in many cases for friendships. Most report that they have a good time together, or "get on pretty good."

Some friendships break up when one girl suddenly moves over into great interest in boys leaving the other behind: "She goes around with older kids now"; "All she talks about is boys and clothes." Or, conversely, "She seems so goody-goody. I've changed. I was like her."

Spending the night with each other is strong.

Boys. The majority now seem to have rather a large number of good or best
friends: "I have four best friends," "three different buddies," "quite a few
friends, maybe twenty; of these, eight are my best friends."

With the diffuseness of Twelve, several report that, though they have many
friends, they have "no *special* friends," or, "A lot of special friends—like
them all alike." "Different ones at different times."

Neighborhood play with whoever is available has somewhat given way to telephoning to or specially inviting certain friends.

Some dissension and some complaining about friends: "Some of them annoy
me"; "We quarrel some"; "Some are silly—they brag and fool too much."
Most, however, with considerable shifting from friend to friend, get on
reasonably well. They are beginning to mention dependability of friends.

13 YEARS

Girls. Some still go around with a "whole gang" ("Four of us fool around
together"). But many Thirteens seem less well supplied with friends than
earlier: "Marcia was my best friend but she left"; "This year I don't seem
to have many friends." May also be less close with friends than earlier:
"Not really intimate," "nobody close now."

Unevenness seems to mark friendships now: "One day I'd love to do something.
Next day I don't feel like it"; "I have spells of liking them." However,
confiding secrets to friends is important: "I don't have any definite friends
but I do trust those I have"; "I do tell her my secrets."

In a group of three, any two, then the other two, may pair off and talk about
the third "just to decide how we want to do."

Beginning interest in discussion of own and others' personality and behavior.
Girls classify other girls as the "fast" set, the "intellectual" set, etc.

Some now said to treat friends much better than family.

Still a good deal of spending the night.

Boys. Some still play with a "whole gang" or have several "best friends."
But most are less sociable than at twelve. Many have only one best friend.
"Had a best friend but he moved away." Many have plenty of friends at
school but say that because of where they live they have nobody to play
with at home. In several cases, groups or gangs of three or four break up
and all members withdraw to a more or less solitary activity.

Those who still have a group of friends may nevertheless prefer to play with
them separately.

There seems to be more "getting mad" than at twelve. One boy reports, "The
guys at school are awful. All hate each other and hate everything. Act
awful. Not wise to themselves. Juvenile. A few good ones. If anybody hates
your guts just look out. They really get you."

Can now keep up friendships with out-of-town friends by writing and visiting.

14 YEARS

Girls. Preferred friends may now be schoolmates who live in other parts of town. May associate with girls in the neighborhood, because of proximity, but may not consider them best friends.

Friendships not so intense and quarrelsome as earlier. But much interest in each others' personalities and may try to change friends' personalities. Much talking about activities, boys, emotions. Typical comment: "Last year we used to talk about horses an awful lot and the boys didn't come into the problem but now they're quite the main topic."

Each school class seems to have its "gang" (not club) of the more popular and successful girls. Those outside very anxious to be accepted by them.

Girls very active with friends: movies, sports events, band or orchestra, baby-sitting, picnics, parties, hikes.

Perhaps the high point for telephoning: "As much as mother can stand"; "As much as they can get away with." They giggle, gossip, do homework, listen to records, over phone.

Some girls at this age go out of their way to be nice to unpopular or unattractive girls.

Boys. A few have a single best friend. But the majority have "a whole gang of friends."

No longer choose friends on the basis of availability. Thus preferred friends may be school friends who do not live nearby: "Quite a few friends at school but they don't live near me." The majority of boys mention sports as the thing they have in common with their friends. A few choose friends who are "smart." Or may have several different friends to share different interests.

Most seem to get on reasonably well with friends. "Everybody pretty harmonious."

Boys, like girls, are becoming interested in the personalities of their friends.

15 YEARS

Girls. "I have a whole gang of friends but one in particular," is the most common remark. In general these groups or gangs get on very well with each other.

The more outgoing girls like the sense of liking the whole class and getting on with everyone. More focal girls stress the pleasure of having one confidante whom they can completely trust.

Much interest in and discussion of the personalities of friends: what is good and bad about each. Quite critical remarks: "She's shallow"; "She's naïve"; "She exaggerates and wears too much lipstick." But many recognize that one friend cannot fill all roles—that one may be athletic, one fun to date with, another good to study with.

Double dating together can be a great bond between two girls. Many like to feel that they and their special friend are alike, and different from the others. Some girls still wear friendship ring (on wedding ring finger) for best girl friend.

Less phoning than earlier. Conversations are about: "How life will turn out, boys, girls at school."

Boys.   Many boys are popular with a large group of friends—"a whole gang." Parents report, "Tremendous amount of being called up"; "All come for him, call him, constant stream." But whether part of a gang or not, most are partial to one or two best friends. A few merely comment, "I can usually find somebody."

Most seem to get on very well with friends. "Get on swell," "have terrific times." Idea of mutual help between friends is coming in: "Aid each other in this or that"; "Counsels friends who are in trouble."

Interest in personality is increasing: "I fool around more with the brain type"; "I like the well-behaved type"; "I like friends who are happy and buoyant."

Very secretive about activities, with parents. Or with interviewer: "I have quite a few friends. All sorts. I just go around with whoever I'm with." Parents say, "He wants to be surrounded by his friends but he can't stand his family."

16 YEARS

Girls.   Most girls report that they have "millions" of girl friends, "always plenty of people to do things with." Most, in addition to individual best friends, do belong to some sort of group. This may be formalized as a club or sorority or may be informal.

Though nearly all girls do some dating, friendships with other girls are for many as important or even more important. Relationships between two girls may be so intense as to annoy families: girls may walk about, arms entwined; may stand for "hours" on the street, talking intently before parting, then fly to the phone the moment they get home to call each other up. If separated, may write daily, lengthy letters. May be strong rivalries between two girls over friendship of a third. May wear "friendship wedding ring."

Relationships tend to involve much confiding: "She tells me everything and I tell her everything." But also much quarreling and disagreeing: whether certain boys are nice, how to dress, how to behave in public.

Most girls show a great interest in their friends' personalities and like to analyze and discuss these at length. Girls often are extremely critical of their best friends. Girls like to compare themselves to their best friends and much interest in which of any pair is the dominant one: "We get along well but I think that I try to please her more than she does me. Perhaps I'm a little more tactful than she is."

Typical reasons for having a certain girl as best friend: "She always wants to do what I want to do and she's so friendly and not bossy and we get along." Discussing "boy friends" is of great interest; double dating may be a real bond between two girls.

Boys.   The majority do have one, or two, best friends often of long standing. However, many are still part of a rather large "gang." "Most of the boys at school have a certain 'bunch' they go around with." Most boys of this age seem to be well provided with friends. "Always plenty of people around when I want to do something."

Though a few are especially interested in the personalities of friends, the majority are interested more in shared activities. What they *do* with friends, especially sports, still seems to be the main bond. ("It varies with the different sports. You find someone you get along with in one sport and in the next sport he's not there.")

Most prefer friends' company to that of family.

Some boys have trouble keeping up financially with friends.

There is still much telephoning between friends.

6. OPPOSITE-SEX FRIENDS

10 YEARS

Girls.   Perhaps the majority are "not interested in boys yet," or are against boys: "Oh, we don't like boys. They can be plenty mean." Girls complain that boys pull their hair, chase them, push them down, act rough, and throw food at parties.

Some girls are willing to play with boys but are not personally interested in them: "I like to play with boys, but that's all."

However, about a third of our 10-year-old girls express positive, personal interest in boys or in some one special boy: "I fool around with boys. They walk home with me. I like some of them [smiles]"; "One boy that I admire from a distance . . ."; "Two boys I like. They like me. We fool around when the teacher isn't looking."

Most consider that girls who kiss boys are extremely forward.

Boys.   The majority of 10-year-old boys express either disinterest in or active dislike of girls: "I don't like girls. Period. Tattletales"; "We *sort of* hate girls"; "They're tiresome to have because they always get mad at you."

Some say they used to have a girl but now she likes someone else and they "haven't bothered to get another." Some still let girls play baseball or other games with them. A few express friendship, but nothing warmer, for girls: "I like girls but I don't love 'em"; "The nearest I do is *like* a girl. That's all. I haven't told her yet. I'm not that far in about girls."

Typical comment: "We haven't gotten to girls yet. All we're interested in is shoving them down on the ice."

11 YEARS

Girls.   Many girls are now in an extremely anti-boy stage: "They're stinking," "disgusting," "all pests," "some of them are very queer," "just horrible."

Some, however, are neutral: "Not too much interested in boys. I don't dislike them but feel neutral"; "I don't think we've got to boys yet." May emphasize the non-romantic aspect of any relationship: "I don't like those who go around saying they love you and you love them. All thinking about love. Not an interesting topic at this point."

Others, more advanced, are on the verge of heterosexual interest: "A little interested. We talk to each other about boys. But we don't play with them. *They won't let us.*" Or, "We each have ones we sort of like. I don't know if they like us and I don't know if they know that we like them."

The whole relationship, if friendly, may still be very peripheral: "Boys I like. I'm not sure whether they like me. They might. My sister finds out for me. She asks their sisters."

Boys do pester girls considerably: trip them up, snowball them, throw spitballs, hit them, strangle them. Girls, as a group, tend to feel that boys, as a group, are fresh, rude, disobedient in school.

Beginning of calling up and "kidding" over the phone; either boy or girl may initiate this. Usually do it when a whole group is around to enjoy the results.

Boys.   Most boys now express a neutral feeling about girls: "I don't hate girls but I don't like them yet"; "We don't mind girls but we don't usually play with them. I guess we would if we had to." However, nearly a quarter of our boys are warmer than this. They either are "interested in" some certain girl, or even "have a girl friend," though this latter may be "just to keep in step with my friend." Interest is usually reported very matter-of-factly and without the self-conscious, pleased smile which comes in later.

Several boys "had one but she moved away." A few, perhaps more mature, emphasize: "I like them as *friends*. Not as girl friends."

Reasons for liking certain girls include: "She walks lightly"; "She's altogether pretty."

Most feel that girls are no good at sports: "They have no judgment at all. Even a dumbbell could do better."

The boys in a school class are, as a group, rivals of and hostile to *the girls.*

12 YEARS

Girls.   Many now are on the verge of being interested in boys. Typical is the statement: "Yes, we're sort of interested in boys. But we don't go out with them. We just talk about them and have ones that we like." Or, "Well, I have one boy that I like. Just kind of like him but we don't go out together. He doesn't know it." A few think that the boy of their choice does "know it," or believe he likes them, because he calls them "stupid."

Others don't have a particularly favored boy but say, "I think boys are O.K."; "They're all right," or, "Nobody I like. I just have my eyes open at the moment."

Though the majority are friendly and even enthusiastic, some still express earlier hostility: "The boys are drips. Just drips. I mean they're *drips!*"

Interest is fairly general, but not much dating. What dating occurs is usually in relation to planned parties or dances, and parents usually transport.

A few admit that they flirt or are "boy crazy," but these are somewhat advanced for their age.

Girls are often larger than boys, and this presents a problem.

Boys. About a third, whether accurately or not, report that they used to have a girl but they lost her or gave her up and haven't bothered to get another. About a third "haven't gotten into girls yet." The remainder say that they do have one or more girls. However, some of these girls do not know it yet.

Enthusiasm of most boys for the girl of their choice is not excessive: "Just got her for something to do"; "Got one just to keep up with my friend. Then he gave up his so I gave up mine."

Some, however, seem quite enthusiastic and even spontaneously mention marrying—some current choice or just someone eventually. But still speak of going over to her house "to play."

Probably it is the somewhat immature boy who is now strongly anti-girl: "All you can picture them as is tattletales and squirts," or, "They're useless. Every time you want to do something there's always some stupid girl in the way. Like if you throw a spitball, there's some stupid girl has to stick her head right in the way."

Regardless of own status, the majority report that "most of the boys have somebody," even though she may not know it, or they may not actually be taking her out.

Many of the boys do enjoy dancing school and parties.

13 YEARS

Girls. A few rather mature girls do quite a lot of dating. Some girls, however, still say that boys are *idiots* and that they don't like them. The typical 13-year-old seems to be between these two extremes. She likes boys and talks about them to other girls but is not yet "boy crazy." Several say they don't *necessarily* like boys, but guess they are all right.

Many say there is one (or several) they like, but these preferred boys may not know about it. In fact, a good deal may go on in the girls' minds with no actual contact with the favored boy. Apparently, to many 13-year-olds, boys in the flesh are too much trouble, but they love to talk and think about them.

Many girls are more withdrawn from boys than at twelve. More critical of boys: "Last year I liked boys terribly much. But now I don't like them as much. Oh, they're bad! They like to play kissing games." Also, girls seem to get less attention than earlier. They often prefer just to invite other girls to parties; may pretend to make love to each other, call each other "Darling!"

Most association with boys occurs at school, at parties, or (still) in "playing together." Parents may still transport girls to and from parties.

A good many girls say cheerfully that they have no one now but seem to look forward to more success in the near future. Some admit that they giggle, talk silly, and act silly when boys are around. Explain that this is because they are excited and embarrassed.

Girls still have the difficulty that many of the boys their age are shorter than they.

Boys. Less interest is expressed in girls than at twelve years. More than half the boys say they have no girl of their own. The majority of these say, "No girl yet." A few have tried having a girl but it hasn't worked out very well: "I used to have a girl but I got bored." And several express neutral feelings as at eleven: "Don't find them repulsive"; "Like some as friends but not as girl friends. Don't like that kind of stuff too well."

A few say either that they have a girl friend, or at least "sort of like" girls. But with most, this has not gone as far as dating. Boys "play with girls," "sit with them at the movies," "kid" on the phone, dance with them at organized dances, but don't "really" take them out. Might get a friend to invite girl out for them, but won't "take a chance" themselves.

"Interested in them. Don't actually take them out" is perhaps as typical a statement as any. Or, typical of Thirteen's negativism, "I wouldn't say I don't like girls." A few, however, are "woman haters," or "don't give a snap about girls."

Things liked in girls are "a good personality," "manners," or, "she's quite special for a girl. She's a tomboy and quite interesting. Good mind. Pretty. At some things she can outlick any boy in school—skiing, for instance."

At school, between classes, boys snatch girls' bandanas, pour sawdust in their hair, grab their books, and pay other such attentions.

14 YEARS

Girls. About half the girls do go out on dates now, though few report that they are "going steady." "None of my friends going steady, just having fun. Not serious about anybody." And about half, though they like boys, report, "Not any boy right now"; "Haven't started dating yet."

Several say, "Just started really dating recently." Before that went to arranged parties and dances. Actually much variation, from girls who still have a secret crush on some boy who doesn't know it, to those who do quite a lot of dating.

Many girls are considered to be quite boy crazy. Think boys are "simply wonderful," "absolutely divine." Spend a lot of time talking about boys, though enthusiasm may exceed actual activity. Girls often ask boys to arranged dances.

Quite a lot of going to church groups or club meetings and hoping to get taken home. First age for much going to movies on dates.

Some girls still have considerable trouble about boys being shorter than they are.

Boys.   Only the exceptional boy at this age has a steady girl friend. Those who do date (about a third of our group) go out with several different girls, no one special favorite.

Boys are now interested in whether their friends do or do not date. Their estimates, however, vary. One boy says, "No one in our class goes out with girls. More interested in sports and their future." Another estimates, "Less than half the boys have girls. But only a couple of boys don't have an interest in girls." Still another comments, "I think the girls are much more interested in the boys than the boys are in the girls."

Dating is just beginning for many, as for the boy who describes his friend as *actually* going out with a girl. Some who don't date yet do enjoy hanging around drugstores and "kidding" with girls.

Some boys who did like girls earlier are now less interested than they were. Others have just not yet become interested, as the boy who says, "I like people. Every kind except girls."

Some report themselves as being more popular with girls than parents say they are.

15 YEARS

Girls.   With only rare exceptions, most of the 15-year-old girls do at least some dating. A few "go steady," but the majority "just go out with a lot of different boys. Nobody special"; "Just something to do, not too serious." Amount and intensity of dating varies tremendously from girl to girl. Some have their boy friends "underfoot" all the time. Some still date mostly during the holidays or summer vacations, or at planned parties and dances. Now much attendance at movies with friends of opposite sex, on single or double dates.

Girls enjoy boys but may "rave" over them a little less than at fourteen. May even be beginning to be critical: "Boys are not reliable, but they're fun"; "They aren't wonderful, they're spoiled brats"; "I love them but I know they aren't perfect."

Girls feel more at ease with boys now; no longer worry as much about what to talk about. Most can "manage" the high school boys, but feel that the college boys are "on the make."

Kissing now a subject of great interest to and among girls.

Much corresponding with boys who are away at school.

Hanging around soda fountain, with or without an established date, can be strong.

Great "mix-ups"—hard for the adult to follow—in a social group about who is whose boy friend at the moment. There can be much shifting and changing.

Boys. About two-thirds of the boys in our group are now dating. Of these, only a very few have one (or more) steady girl friends. The others go out with "just different ones." Most not only do not go steady but do not want to.

Non-daters may report, "Only about half the boys have girls." Daters may say, "Most all the boys I know have girls."

In many, the change has come since fourteen, the number of daters having approximately doubled since then. And even some of the later maturing non-daters comment, "I haven't even started yet. But maybe this year."

The majority of dates are for movies and dances. Considerable double dating, but not always. Some now object vigorously to the expense of dating: "Girls drive me nuts! They always want to spend your money and they talk too much."

Many are now much put out by the fact that the most attractive girls prefer older boys. Boys realize or suspect that other boys' stories of their prowess with girls still may be "just talk, bragging about this, that, and the other."

16 YEARS

Girls. With the exception of one girl, all of our 16-year-old girls do more or less dating. Only a few go steady, though some have tried this and given it up. Most prefer to "just date around. Not going steady, don't believe in it," or to "go out with different ones. More fun."

Some are by now very much at ease with the opposite sex; others are just beginning to date, still feel awkward, and don't know what to say to boys. Some girls slide flexibly from one romance to another; others take each new boy very seriously, and are really much upset when things go badly or break off.

Much telephoning.

Definite distinction between "old stand-bys" and "just friends," and those considered more exciting. May know that the boys who are "just friends" may listen to them better than those who are real admirers.

Most try to keep reasonably within parents' rules of where they may go in the evening and when they must come home.

Talking over boy friends with other girls and double dating may still be among the most important aspects of having dates. Many still feel that dreams of romance are more exciting than anything that takes place. But, apart from many snags, shifts, mix-ups, the majority seem to get much pleasure and satisfaction out of dating and out of talking about boys.

A few are now wearing fraternity pins, and may talk of marriage, though they admit frankly that they don't really expect to marry this boy and "probably he doesn't expect it either." Most now kiss their dates goodnight but criticize friends who are too promiscuous.

Many boy-girl relationships are still quite superficial and just for something to do. Others are very intense and almost adult. Considerable good evaluation, as shown by one girl after a broken romance: "I tried to hang onto something that wasn't there and tried to make him into something that he wouldn't be in a million years."

Boys. As at fifteen, about two-thirds of our group are now dating. Of these, only two or three go steady. Others have tried it but feel either that it ties them down too much or that girls are too fickle. The majority (nearly half) do date but do not go steady. They often have several different girls. May date several times a week—mostly for movies or dancing.

Approximately a third do not date as yet. However, several of these state spontaneously that they "have nothing against girls." These non-daters are definitely the immature boys.

Several mention that they are part of "a gang of about twenty-eight [or forty to fifty] kids" who do social things together.

Only a few boys complain of the expense of dating, or of the fickleness, cattiness, conceitedness of girls. Most seem to look favorably on girls: "Dating brings me a lot of pleasure and it goes pretty smoothly." Most boys seem to feel comfortable when out with girls.

7. CRUSHES

10 YEARS

A few girls have crushes on schoolteacher or camp counselor, usually some one adult in their immediate life. Others have what amount to crushes on horses or on the mere idea of horses. A few have crushes on each other.

Only one boy mentions what seems to be a crush (on General MacArthur). Boys more inclined to admiration or hero-worship.

11 YEARS

Most crushes at this age seem to be of girls for same-age friends. Enthusiasm for horses continues. Boys admire historical figures as Abraham Lincoln, or sports stars, but these do not seem to be real crushes.

A few girls and boys admire movie stars of the same sex as themselves.

12 YEARS

Girls' crushes seem to be still mostly for contemporaries, actual friends, or slightly older girls: "She has *everything*." A few girls already have crushes on boys. The boys may or may not know about this. Many still retain an enthusiasm for horses.

Boys may admire sports heroes. Some have crushes on older women, especially on pretty, young teachers.

Now a few boys and girls have crushes on movie stars, of either sex.

13 YEARS

Girls may have crushes on male or female movie stars, teachers, camp counselors, or boys. (Some still very enthusiastic about horses.) "Bobby-sox swooning reaction," parents report.

Boys now mention admiration for slightly older boys as well as for sports stars ("I touched Levi Jackson's jersey!"), or historical figures ("When I get stuck I think to myself 'What would John Adams have done?' "), or movie stars. This latter is more common in girls than in boys, however.

14 YEARS

Many girls now have established reciprocal friendships for boys. Others still have crushes on movie stars (male or female), teachers of either sex, camp counselors, or on other girls. Or on boys whom they do not actually know very well.

Some boys still admire sports stars. Few still have crush on movie stars.

15 YEARS

Some girls (perhaps immature) have crushes on teachers, counselors, or male movie stars or crooners.

Among our group of boys no crushes are mentioned, either for people they know or movie stars or sports figures.

16 YEARS

Many girls have intense relationships with other girls and may even wear "friendship wedding rings" to indicate that they are "going steady with their girl friend." However, these friendships as a rule do not enter the realm of crushes.

A very few girls, sometimes more masculine and not yet interested in boys, do appear to have crushes on each other. Similarly, an occasional immature boy, not yet interested in girls, may exhibit an almost worshipful attitude toward some slightly older boy companion.

Most emotions seem to be spent on someone of opposite sex and approximately the same age, without any crush aspect to the relationship other than is normally involved in heterosexual relations.

By now, some boys and girls are themselves the objects of crushes on the part of younger children—siblings of friends, or camp counselees.

8. PARTIES

10 YEARS

Not many boy-girl parties. At any which are given, games and food are the main interests. Not much relation between boys and girls, though some report that boys are beginning to be mischievous.

11 YEARS

Not a strong age for parties. The majority of those given are for "just girls" or "just boys."

12 YEARS

Quite a bit of enthusiasm for boy-girl parties, but they often do not turn out well. The boys either all gang together and ignore the girls, or else act very badly: they throw food and drink, act rough and "spoil the party."

A good deal of turning out of lights, which the boys consider a very racy thing to do.

13 YEARS

Parties a little calmer than at twelve, though there can be a good deal of throwing of food and drink and actual destruction of property. Also sometimes the boys are not "nice" to the girls.

However, with proper supervision, parties may turn out well. Things often get off to a very slow start, but once games and dancing have started may go fairly well. Refreshments still a very important part of the party.

Some girls still say, "Parties are better with just girls. More fun."

14 YEARS

Parties still improving, though still, unless well supervised, there can be a lot of throwing and destruction.

But girls and boys much more interested in each other than formerly, and this may improve general behavior.

15 YEARS

Parties may be quite successful now except that a few boys are beginning to drink and this may cause difficulty unless there is careful chaperonage. One girl comments, "Kids eat and neck and talk. Behave pretty well."

Girls and boys much interested in each other, and easier with each other than formerly.

16 YEARS

A big age for parties—punch parties, beach parties, informal or formal dancing parties. Many of these gatherings are formal, but more frequent are informal parties at which they "sing, drink, dance, listen to music, talk."

Some boys and girls go around with big "gangs" and these meet very frequently, especially in the summer, at parties of one kind or another.

Most parties go very smoothly, much more so than earlier. Eating and prank playing are of much less interest than they were. Real boy-girl interest causes most to behave reasonably well. Most have gotten over earlier stiffness (or too great lack of inhibition) and really enjoy themselves at parties. Trouble, if any, is apt to come from (a) uninvited guests who crash the party; (b) boys who have had too much to drink; (c) immature boys who can still, as earlier, be a disrupting influence.

CHAPTER SIXTEEN

Activities and Interests

THE HUMAN organism is a storer and distributor of energies, variously vigorous, subtle, intense, leisurely, and strenuous. Particularly so in the period of adolescent youth. The expenditure of recreational energy is more than a mere discharge or release of excess vitality. It is channelized and patterned by powerful cultural forces through a vast system of publications and communications, including, as of today, radio, television, cinema, comics, pictorial journalism, spectator and competitive sports, and a great array of organized group activities. The "interests and activities" of modern youth therefore reflect the complexion of our contemporary culture. But they also reflect the spontaneous reactions of the individual to the pressures which impinge upon him and to the opportunities which are open to him. His reactions are unmistakably influenced by his maturity.

Outdoor Activities. At the ten-year level free outdoor play is the most consuming interest. Ten plays so naturally and associates so easily with his playmates, running, racing, and bounding, that we can readily understand his sheer joy in gross motor activity. His growing skeletal musculature demands this exercise. He does not need a competitive urge to activate him. He takes pleasure in chasing, "fooling around," and "wrassling." Girls too are active, but not as rangy. They enjoy the more restricted pastimes of jumping rope, hopscotch, and roller skating. But they bicycle with the boys, and a girl may even be admitted to a scrub baseball team "if she's good." Sex lines still are readily crossed.

Imaginative outdoor play is at an elementary level. It includes running and hiding games, secret huts, cowboy and Wild West forays, verbalized "pretend" dramatics, and of course plain gunplay. But, already, there are precursor signs of the dawn of new interests; boys are beginning to give up gunplay. At eleven, cops and robbers, the wild frontier, and Davy Crockett are vanishing.

Eleven is still very active, but his activities are more diversified and more closely linked with a rising interest in people (as opposed to mere play) and a curiosity as to their activities. His multiple tensional outlets keep him almost incessantly restless and explorative. They accelerate rather than retard the output of conversation. He is most happy when he can go on a carefree walk with a listening companion and a mobile dog.

At the twelve-year level spontaneous gross motor activity is less marked and less general. In many instances it is replaced by a more or less lively "hanging around" or "just fooling around." In the period from fourteen to sixteen years this evolves into "hacking around," to "going places with friends," and to a growing spectator interest in sports. By twelve years there is an increasing differentiation of sports on the basis of sex preferences, and in accordance with athletic and non-athletic types. Swimming, however, is almost universally enjoyed.

Thirteen is wrapped up in sports and sometimes is even reputed to be "sports crazy," going to extreme lengths to perfect an athletic skill. At fourteen the outdoor activities are less isolated and concentrated; they form a more natural part of the pattern of daily living. Fifteen is more apt to restrict his field of activities, and he appears to be peculiarly in need of relaxation as well as exercise.

Girls of sixteen may show a decreasing interest in sports, and more inclination for social contacts and experiences. Boys of this age are proud of their growing muscular strength; and welcome opportunities to apply it.

The developmental changes in the choice of outdoor activities during the years from ten to sixteen are sufficient to suggest the importance of maturity factors in educational planning and procedures.

Indoor Activities. Collections constitute a favorite pastime throughout the years ten, eleven, and twelve. At about thirteen years of age this interest begins to decline. Collections of stamps, coins, and postcards are most likely to survive the ravages of time and of competing interests. The peak of passionate acquisitiveness comes at eleven, and the collections include everything from shells and stones to birds' nests and horse models. A boy's pocket becomes the repository for surplus miscellaneous items. At eleven the collecting zeal is reinforced by swapping and bartering. Eleven, being interested in people as well as things, likes the interpersonal aspect of such transactions. He has an eager, insistent method of approach which sometimes results in huge collections. Twelve takes a more reflective interest in his collections and gains an aesthetic pleasure from them.

Card and table games and puzzles are staple recreations from ten through twelve and into thirteen, when childish things are put aside (but not without lingering remnants). At thirteen, individual hobbies take shape in the arts and sciences. The hobbies are often foreshadowed in a previous year by an exploratory interest in photography, chemistry, microscopy, electricity, carpentry, and building of models.

At fourteen there is a shift from the intense hobby to more balanced interpersonal interests and social activities. There is an increase in person-to-person telephoning, and also in listening to musical records and in solitary reading. These trends gather depth and detail during years fifteen and sixteen. The boys go on with their mechanical and scientific tinkerings. By casual and concentrated reading they keep in touch with the world of sports, entertainment, and technology. There is an increase of creative activity especially in painting and drawing, on the part both of girls and boys. Girls also make special use of the creative possibilities of conversation. They do a vast amount of talking not only about boys but about allied subjects. Perhaps because of their inquisitiveness they gain a more penetrating insight into the world about which they talk. At any rate, talking may be set down as an important indoor activity. Even outdoors, girls enjoy talking combined with walking.

It is interesting to note that all these indoor and outdoor activities are extracurricular. They are methods of self-education. And they all have some significant relation to the process of growing up and becoming an adult. This is evident even in the charming behavior patterns of the child of ten. He likes best to be his own age, and he identifies best with children of his own age. But he also likes to read about famous grown-up people when they were once his age. With a touch of superiority, he likes to play with pets and younger siblings. He likes to settle down in a secret hut. He plays pretend games; he manfully carries and discharges a gun, the ultimate primitive weapon of adult man. Even Ten expresses disdain for outgrown activities.

Meanwhile, the 10-year-old girls play house, sew dresses to clothe their dolls, and create paper dolls, while their masculine age-mates create imaginative gadgets and invent jet rockets in secret rooms. At the eleven-year age level, girls, being more concerned with amenities, play dramatic games in the role of secretary, nurse, and librarian. Twelves begin to knit and sew for themselves and occasionally for dolls, because there is still a remnant of doll play. After thirteen there is increasing observation of the life and conduct of grownups and a progressive trend toward sharing in adult activities and interests. And there are imitations, identifications, and daydreams.

It thus appears that in adolescence as well as in childhood, play continues to serve its ancient biological function to prepare the young for maturity.

Clubs and Camps. Ten, whether a Cub Scout or a Brownie, takes a keen delight in the very notion of a club. He tingles with excitement at the thought of forming a new club where he meets with pals, to eat, to play games, and to talk. Later the members will decide to re-form this club and get a better motto. Or they will start a new mystery club with codes, which may branch out into an F.B.I. auxiliary for tracking down criminals. The clubs are transient and fluid. But the urge and the passion are strong; they spring from the instinctual levels of the action system.

The interest of Eleven remains strong, but is more critical and less amiably conforming. He is prone to do a lot of shifting in his self-organized clubs, giving much attention to election of officers, dues, and votes on projects. He stands firm on restricting membership to males.

Twelve is a favorable age for Scouts or for 4-H types of organization. Private clubs still flourish and show increased stability in organization and project programs; but the earlier club interest is losing its intensity. Secret clubs are on the wane at thirteen. Special purpose clubs take their place and continue to prosper at ages fourteen and fifteen. These private clubs include school and church organizations, 4-H and Y Teen clubs, and special clubs for music, dramatics, photography, science, badminton, music, and skating.

These trends show a steady shift toward adult areas and levels of interest. Sixteen is competent and eager to go along with adults on occasion, sharing in the fun and the activities.

As for summer camps, they span the nadir and the zenith of emotional satisfaction for the young camper—the nadir if he succumbs to homesick-ness, the zenith if he gets the right counselor and a good bunch of kids. It is not our task to appraise camps, but the homesickness reminds us that they serve invaluable functions in educating the morale of individual children and their parents.

Twelve proves to be an optimal age for many campers. Group spirit and sociability come naturally at this stage of maturity. Many Elevens enjoy camp and meet its demands; but others prefer the more flexible freedom of family life in a summer cottage.

Thirteen as an individualist may prefer to stay at home. Or he may really enjoy camp, "if they let you alone." Fourteen is more socially inclined but he makes a clear-cut choice as to whether or not he wishes to attend a camp, and parents tend to respect his decision. By sixteen or even fifteen he may choose to return as a counselor. This is further evidence that the summer camp in America is an important educational institution which provides a steppingstone opportunity to facilitate the process of growing up and achieving independence.

Reading, Looking, Listening. Under this triple heading we can briefly sketch the age trends of interest for books, comics, magazines, newspapers, phonograph, radio, movies, and television. These eight media are closely related historically and culturally. It is their immediate impact upon youth which concerns us. In terms of mass distribution the media are mainly designed for adults. The youth must adapt, select, reject, and appropriate as well as he can in a bewildering array of invitations to read, to listen, to look.

Among all the media, books remain the most fundamental, the most flexible, and the most diversified. Books are scarcely time-bound; they range over all the centuries and aeons that ever were and they penetrate into those yet to come. A book may be read any time of the day or night, in part or whole. It is portable in space as well as time. Regardless of place, it can set up a stage whereby author and reader may communicate with intimacy. Because of this interpersonal quality many books have been especially addressed to adolescents at various age levels. But even more significant is the adult literature, classic and otherwise, which most vitally assists a boy or girl toward achieving mental maturity.

Since such reading of prose and poetry combines these fundamental advantages most uniquely, books become a touchstone for evaluating the merits of competing and supplementary media. One judicious critic has already suggested that television is not likely to supplant books. "For the child, it may simply make them [the books] seem better."

The 9-year-old usually is on his way toward making use of his newly acquired skill of getting thought and feelings from the printed page. He may be punch-drunk with interest in "comics" but he is beginning to enjoy silent reading. Some 10-year-olds reportedly always have their nose in a book. But great individual variations appear in our group, at each age level. A minority never read; some read one book a week, others as many as five, eight, or ten a week. The amount read seems to depend more on the individuality of the reader than on ages. Girls read somewhat more than boys.

At the twelve-year level, reading becomes more discriminating and critical. There is more awareness of type of book and individuality of authors. Preferences include mystery, sports, adventures, classics, and "not love books." The previous interest in animal tales and the passionate absorption in dog and horse stories are lessening. Many Twelves make regular and effective use of library facilities. There is increasing interest in owning favorite volumes. There is also a growing interest in adult books, which continues through the following years. However, many of our subjects from fourteen through sixteen pleaded lack of time for reading.

Nevertheless, at thirteen, there is a general increase of reading interest and amount of reading. Avid readers read intensely, and Thirteen, true to character, does an additional amount of *re*-reading for pleasure and for profit. We should probably encourage such re-reading and a habit of contemplative reading.

Despite parental inhibitions comics are greatly read by 10-year-olds. Even a visit to the dentist is ameliorated if there are some new comics in the waiting room. But there are signs of release. Ten does not use his spending money as freely as before to increase his collections and rare items; there is less barter and borrowing. A few Elevens, however, may have from two to five hundred copies in their holdings, and two-thirds of our subjects still read comics with moderate to avid intensity. The comics reported in our survey consisted of the usual popular series published in newspapers or books, but did not include the abnormal types of horror and mutilation comics.

Two-thirds of our twelve-year group and only half of the thirteen-year group still read comics, but the interest is definitely decreasing, and at thirteen it is generally spasmodic. At fourteen only one-quarter read comics at all. The reading is occasional and skimming. No favorites are reported except *Classic Comics,* which is read in connection with book reviews at school. At fifteen- and sixteen-year levels there is almost no reading of comics (in our research group).

The reading of magazines and newspapers is marginal and is determined chiefly by what is available at home. Ten, Eleven, and Twelve read chiefly for pictures, comics, cartoons, and sketchily for headlines and sports. At thirteen and fourteen there is much more extensive and selective reading, including special features and sections, such as woman's page, Believe It or Not, and society column. Many subscribe to a teen-age magazine. By fifteen and sixteen the approach to the national and pictorial magazines becomes more adult. The reading is more thorough and purposeful. Boys read scientific and technical magazines. Girls elect a woman's magazine. Some of the readers at these age levels frankly say that they only read magazines, preferring them to books, which is a reminder that books may miss their mission because they are not as conveniently available as are journals.

The perennial problem is one of distribution—to get the right book to the right youth at the right time and place. The annual Book Week, book fairs, book lists which classify books in age groups, render a great service to parents, teachers, and children alike. The New York Public Library, for example, distributes an annual list of *Books for the Teen Age.* The current list is designed primarily for leisure-time reading. About 80 per cent of the 1,400 titles were chosen from adult publications, ranging over a hundred subjects from Adventure to Science and Stage and Screen. The books selected are constantly tried and tested with New York City readers aged thirteen to eighteen.*

* *Books for the Teen Age* is published in January of each year. Copies are 25 cents each by mail. Printed and issued by the New York Public Library, Fifth Avenue and 42nd Street, New York 18, New York.

The Teen Age Book Reviewers of the New York Public Library are a group of young people who read widely and express their honest opinions about what they read. Their reviews of books, old or new, are published periodically in their bulletin, *Back Talk about Books from the Teen Age.*

(If as a teen-ager you are interested in writing reviews—no matter where you live—send them with your name, address, and school to Room 107, the New York Public Library. Everyone who sends reviews is automatically a member of the Reviewers and receives a copy of the bulletin.)

Radio, television and movies are mass media. The phonograph record approximates more nearly the status of a book. The interesting current vogue of collecting era and folk records results in albums, shelves, and libraries. The role of sound in relation to sight varies with different media. It also depends upon individual differences in mental imagery preferences and capacities. Some youths are highly visual, others auditory; most are mixed in varying degrees. Some like the stillness and muteness of silent reading; others prefer background music. Some are better oriented in near as opposed to remoter space. Looking and listening, therefore, are subject to a vast variety of factors, in addition to timing, programming, and levels of maturity.

The age trends, in our group, for radio and television are briefly as follows: Some at ages ten and eleven prefer radio and may listen to thirty or forty set programs a week. Interest in after-dinner programs is rising; and some are already dropping Westerns and adventure series. At age twelve soap operas and give-away programs are out. Twelve lists general and adolescent comedies, murder mysteries, and jazz among his favorites. In the next year there is a marked reduction in listening and looking. Thirteen may substitute telephoning. Fourteen listens and views only occasionally. It is interesting to note that an appreciable number still prefer radio. At fifteen and sixteen the amount of time spent continues to fall off and becomes more incidental to other activities. Sixteen typically comments, "Most of the kids don't spend much time watching. We're forever on the go."

The interest in phonograph records, on the contrary, tends to increase with age and is a major interest for many 16-year-olds. Ten and Eleven listen with the family group, but with no excess of enthusiasm. At twelve and thirteen the interest of music lovers begins to assert itself. Self-initiated use of the phonograph increases. Jazz and classical music are preferred. Some girls like to dance alone to the record which they put on the turntable. By fourteen, about a quarter of our group play the phonograph consistently, and some almost constantly. There is great delight in certain records which are played time and again for relistening when the mood strikes. By fifteen the phonograph has become a consuming interest for a third of our subjects. They regard a favorite record as though it were a treasured book, and so it is in essence. They may buy the record from their own funds and possess it as part of a personal collection.

The cinema with its expansive screen and public setting contrasts sharply against the intimate individual impact of a book or a phonographic record. Its mass appeal limits its influence for the changing youth in the years from ten to sixteen. Most of our 10-, 11-, and 12-year-olds attend movies only occasionally. Some Twelves report that they prefer to play outdoors if the day is good. Ten is sensitive to "bad" parts of a film and protects himself by looking away or covering his eyes. Both at ten and eleven there are complaints of headache, bad dreams, stomach-ache, and smarting eyes. Parents try to offer protection from traumatic films but not always with success. Twelve, however, is also the age when a favorable film is selected and viewed repeatedly with home permission.

At thirteen and fourteen movie attendance tends to become more routine—once weekly or every other week. Choice of program becomes more selective. Most popular are musicals and comedies. Romantic films are favored by the girls; sport movies by boys. Heroes and heroines and star players are admired and idolized by the opposite sex. Considerable empathy (even to the point of tears) is displayed at sad pictures.

Fifteen and Sixteen are moving in the direction of adult practice. Many give up routine attendance; they are more selective. For the first time "grown-up" movies lead in the mention of favorites. By sixteen movie attendance has lessened considerably (the majority average one movie a month). There is much less emphasis on stars, more on musicals, comedies, historical and documentary films.

Sixteen is also beginning to appreciate the superior and unique power of the theater with its stage and living actors. It is an enriching experience to be a member of an alert theater audience and to share in the audience reactions to a dramatic performance. This is indeed a growing-up experience for Sixteen and a symptom of deepening maturity.

Our survey of adolescent interests and activities has indicated a wide range of individual differences and preferences. Despite these variables the over-all developmental trends reveal underlying maturity factors. The patterns of a youth's play and pastimes therefore afford some clue as to whether he is functioning at an immature level, or whether he gives evidence of latent talents and capacities.

Ideally the culture should place a premium upon the kinds of recreation which release the best potentials of its individual children, both average and gifted. Educators may feel some concern that the mechanization of entertainment will limit the development of individual initiative and expressions of creative imagination. With the disintegration of intimate community life, the whole problem of recreation and leisure in the adolescent years assumes increasing importance.

G R O W T H   G R A D I E N T S

1. OUTDOOR ACTIVITIES

10 YEARS
Bike riding very strong. Horseback riding (girls more than boys).
Baseball, catch, throwing ball against house.
Sledding, skating, swimming.
Building or playing in "secret huts." Climbing trees.
"Pretend" games—may involve activity or be just verbal.
Running and hiding games.
Playing with and caring for pets and younger siblings.
Nature interests (in a few).

Girls.   Jump rope, roller skates, hopscotch.

Boys.   Racing—plain, bicycle, three-legged.
Cowboys, Wild West, just plain "guns." (Some are outgrowing this.)
"Just fooling around," "wrassling."

11 YEARS
Bicycling. Horseback riding (girls more than boys).
Hiking, walking in the woods. Nature interests. Pets.
Dodge ball, tether ball, kickball.
Seasonal sports (boys more): baseball, football, basketball. Some tennis.
Skating, skiing, sledding, swimming. Some sailing.
Running and hiding games (still, in some)—especially in big fields, vacant lots, woods.

Girls.   Remnants of roller skating, hopscotch, jump rope.

Boys.   Building hideouts or tree huts.
Fishing and hunting. Some gardening.
Remnants of cops and robbers, Wild West.

12 YEARS
Many "just hang around" or "just fool around."
Swimming, sailing, skiing, skating, sledding.

Bicycling. Horseback riding (girls more).
Remnants of hide-and-seek, running games.
Helping in yard or garden (some enjoy this).
Walking in woods. Interest in nature. Pets.
Spectator sports.

Girls. Croquet. Non-athletic girls now losing interest in sports.

Boys. Climbing trees, tree forts. Hunting, shooting, fishing.
Seasonal sports: baseball, football, basketball, hockey.
Tournaments: tennis, badminton, boxing, bicycle races, fencing.

13 YEARS
Baseball. (This is declining in girls.)
Swimming and sailing. Skating and skiing. Tennis.
Horseback (declining).
Pets.

Girls. Walks or bicycle rides with friends. "Boys and baseball."
Outdoor interests are narrowing down more than boys' interests. Sports nearly
out except with the athletically inclined.

Boys. "Wrapped up in sports"—basketball, football, hockey, all other kinds.
Hunting, fishing, shooting.
Shoveling snow, raking leaves (enjoyed by some).
Golf and caddying.
Imaginary ballgames (played alone).

14 YEARS
"Hacking around."
Baseball—playing or watching.
Skating, skiing, hockey, sledding. Swimming and sailing. Tennis.
Bicycling and horseback riding (girls most for both).
Spectator sports.

Girls. Walking (mostly to store, movies, friend's house).

Boys. Some just say "sports." Football, basketball, golf.
Hunting, fishing, shooting.
"Fooling around" with automobiles, supervised driving.
Yard work.
More different outdoor activities than girls.

15 YEARS
"Going places with friends"—movies, beach, coke places. Dating.

Baseball or basketball. Swimming. Skiing.
Watching games.

Girls.   Horseback riding (less than before). Walking in woods.

Boys.   "Any sports." Football, hockey. Hunting, fishing.
Driving (under supervision), "hacking around" in friend's car.
More different outdoor activities than girls.

16 YEARS

The usual sports—baseball, basketball, swimming, tennis, sailing—in those who
   now care for sports.
Taking walks, going for rides.
Watching sports events.

Girls.   Shopping. Horseback riding.

Boys.   Shooting. Hunting and fishing. Golf.
"Just hanging around." Driving.

2. INDOOR ACTIVITIES

10 YEARS

Collecting: stamps, coins, china animals, dolls, postcards, trading cards, model
   airplanes, stones, shells, nature specimens, boxes, box tops.
Card and table games. Jigsaw puzzles. Scrapbooks.
Entertaining, especially reading to, younger siblings.
Pets.
Secret clubs.

Girls.   Doll play—playing house, sewing for dolls. Creating paper dolls. Drawing, painting, ceramics. Writing stories or plays, then dressing up and
   acting them.

Boys.   Drawing, designing, creating or imagining gadgets and inventions:
   secret rooms, jet rockets or planes, boats, etc.
Constructing model planes. Erector sets. Electric trains.
Chemistry sets. Beginning interest in photography.
Disdain is expressed for outgrown activities.

11 YEARS

Huge collections: stamps, coins, postcards, trading cards, baseball cards, horse
   models, china animals, dolls, shells, stones, birds' nests, boxes, model boats,
   toy guns.
Card games, table games, puzzles.

Secret clubs.
Playing piano or other instrument "just for fun."
Making up poems, plays, imaginative games.
Dancing school begins for some.

Girls. Cooking. Sewing, knitting, embroidering. Some can make a blouse or
skirt, or dolls' clothes. Some use sewing machine, some don't.
Putting on plays in costume. Sketching and painting.
Imaginative games as secretary or librarian take the place of playing house.
(Dolls and paper dolls mostly discarded.)
Phoning friends (much shrieking and squealing). Visiting friends overnight.

Boys. Drawing war pictures, planes, trains.
Making gadgets and inventions out of wood and wire.
Electric trains. Chemistry sets. Some interest in photography.
Shooting at a target.

12 YEARS

Collections: coins, stamps, postcards, rocks, shells, match covers, glass animals,
horse or dog pictures. "Not as vicious on this as I used to be."
Cards, table games as Monopoly, puzzles.
Drawing, painting, some creative writing.
Some writing to pen pals—often rather abortive.
"Fooling with printing press."
Dancing school.
Some playing of musical instrument for fun.
Just talking with friends (girls mostly).

Girls. Remnants of doll play in some, especially sewing for dolls.
Sewing for self, or knitting.
A little dressing up (stuffed halter and lipstick). Putting on plays.
Daydreaming.
Having friends in for the night.
Special lessons enjoyed by some.

Boys. Taking things apart and putting them together again (guns, clocks).
Photography. Using microscope. Chemistry. Electricity.
Making things out of wood, tin. Building models. Electric trains.
Gym.

13 YEARS

Interests beginning to narrow down: "Read and draw," or, "Listen to records
and read"; "Talk, go to the movies," or "Mostly sports."
Reading strong. Many prefer to be in own room alone in spare time.

Collections—stamps, coins, postcards, match covers—but decreasingly in most.
Individual hobbies. Photography. Some interested in science.
Cards, table games, puzzles. Ping-pong.
Creative activity—especially drawing and painting. Being in contests.
Playing musical instruments or listening to music.
Telephoning, talking things over, staying overnight with friends.
Dancing or other special lessons.

Girls.   Sewing and knitting. Writing letters.
Daydreaming about romantic activities. Talking about boys.

Boys.   Making models or designing cars and planes. Carpentry.
"Fooling around" with radio and electricity, or actually studying for ham
   license.
Gym.

14 YEARS

"Talk, play cards, go for a walk, go to a friend's house, hang around." Not
   the organized play of earlier years.
Reading, listening to music on radio or phonograph.
Dances, parties, dates.
Telephoning, talking with friends. "Kill time" or "Loll around."
Creative activity, especially drawing and painting.

Girls.   Talking about boys.
Trying on clothes. Sewing and knitting. Cooking.
Writing letters, keeping a diary.
Girls have more different indoor interests than do boys.

Boys.   Anything related to sports—reading about, watching on TV.
Special hobbies: photography, building radios, studying for ham license, still
   some carpentry or model building.

15 YEARS

Parties and dances. Dating.
Playing or listening to music, reading, radio, TV, movies.
Telephoning (girls mostly). Sitting around talking, arguing, discussing.

Girls.   Talking about boys. Dreaming and lying around.

Boys.   Sports—reading about sports, watching sports on TV.
Building radios, and related activities. Making things, tinkering with motors.

16 YEARS

Dating, dancing, going to parties. Church and "Y" clubs.

Reading. Listening to records. Playing musical instruments.

Girls. Talking with friends.

Boys. Working on radios or cars. Playing cards.

3. CLUBS AND CAMPS

10 YEARS

Clubs. Ten shows great pleasure in club activities. Most who belong think their clubs are *wonderful* and would do anything for them.

Brownies and Cub Scouts are extremely popular and much enjoyed. Boys may be a little rambunctious at Cub meetings, but can usually be managed easily because their enthusiasm for the organization is so great.

Much forming and re-forming of informal, often short-lived, "secret" clubs— sometimes with just two members, sometimes with more. Sharing secrets and meeting to eat, play games, and talk things over seem to be the main activities. But also important are mottoes ("Share Hardships Together"), rules ("No Sulking"), names ("U & R Club," "Mystery Club"), codes, purposes ("Tracking down criminals").

Camp. Reaction to camp very variable at ten. Not many of our group attend. Of those who do, some are ready for it and enjoy it; others are homesick and do not wish to stay or to return next year. Attendance may be most successful on a trial or short-term basis.

11 YEARS

Clubs. About a third of our group belongs to Brownies or Girl Scouts or Cubs or Boy Scouts. Most are enthusiastic, though some are both critical and hard to manage. Some boys say they will finish out Cubs, but won't shift to Boy Scouts. Criticisms include: "Infantile program," "boring," "keep on repeating the same things," "never do anything interesting." Many are most thrilled about these clubs just before they join.

Informal secret clubs ("Fatal Five"), sometimes short-lived, are still very strong with many. "Would give up anything for the club." Some "mostly talk and give off secrets." But others take active interest in organization, election of officers, payment of dues, exclusion and inclusion of members, planning and voting on projects. The clubhouse is very important to boys, and their groups are strictly masculine, giving much attention to excluding girls—not only from the clubhouse, but even from the premises. Some Elevens seem almost exclusively occupied with forming and re-forming of these clubs, which often do not hold together well.

Some show about equal enthusiasm for adult-organized groups and their own informal organizations.

Camp. Many have been to camp and like it very much. Others like it "O.K." —except counselors and food. Some prefer to go somewhere with the family (summer cottage), or even to stay at home.

Discipline can be a problem at camp; not too much group spirit prevails.

12 YEARS

Clubs. Twelve can be a strong age for Scouts and 4-H. However, some did not shift from Cubs to Scouts, and others drop out during the year. Parents and leaders do not understand why children make sweeping generalizations: "Boring"; "No one in our grade belongs"; "Everybody hates Scouts"; "We didn't do anything."

Among those who do stay in, and who remain enthusiastic, there may nevertheless be some battle for status between members and adult leaders. But those who like it are usually enthusiastic, vigorous, co-operative members.

Private clubs still prosper with some boys and girls, and now are better organized, have more continuity and more structure than earlier. May have projects and special activities beyond just meeting, electing officers, and excluding people, as earlier. These clubs are still very secret and exciting. Boys may have elaborate clubhouses (trap doors, etc.) and still enjoy keeping girls out. Girls may give parties and plays and earn money.

However, clubs are breaking up with many Twelves. There appears less need for the kind of strong exclusiveness and inclusiveness which they represent.

Camp. Many say they like camp and will probably go back next year. Twelve is a good age for camp. There tends to be great enthusiasm for this kind of vigorous group activity. Many want to be, and are, "good campers."

13 YEARS

Clubs. Scouts has declined in popularity with most girls, except when the leader is ingenious enough to change the program: "Last year all by the rules and no fun. Now we meet at different people's houses and have fun— knit, sew, talk, have refreshments." Of boys who still belong to Scouts, a few are still extremely enthusiastic. Apart from these, about equal numbers say Scouts are O.K. and say they are "no good." Some state, "I absolutely will not join." Personality of the leader as well as variety of program seems to be extremely important at thirteen. A strong and skillful leader may be able to keep up real interest.

4-H and Y Teen clubs usually hold up better than Scouts.

Secret private clubs are largely dropping out, and school (or church) activity clubs are increasing, more with girls than boys: clubs for music, dramatics, skating, badminton, photography, science, debating.

Camp. Thirteen is an individual age, with great differences between those who love camp and go every year, and those who won't go, or who have gone and won't return ("It's like a jail"). Some like a camp program with definite routine; others like a camp where they "let you alone."

14 YEARS

Clubs. 4-H and Y Teen clubs may flourish, but only a few boys and girls now belong to Scouts. Most either did not shift from Brownies or Cubs, never belonged, or gave up Scouts earlier. "No time," "leader treated us babyishly," "no fun," or friends dropped out.

School and church activity clubs include all those listed at thirteen, and increase in membership and interest.

The beginning of sororities and fraternities in schools which allow them.

Camp. Most are now very clear-cut about their preferences, either wanting to go to camp, or wanting not to go, and their preferences are usually respected by parents. Some love camp and wouldn't miss it. Others dislike it, would rather do other things, and think you miss too much by going to camp.

15–16 YEARS

Clubs. Attitudes toward adult-organized clubs are much as at fourteen, but with Fifteen's tendency to withdraw from adults, private clubs may again appear, in new forms, to rival school or church clubs. Sororities, fraternities, and loosely organized social clubs of boys and girls meet to talk, give plays or parties. Boys may call for girls at the end of girls' meetings.

However, school clubs continue strong with most, and center around real special interests: dramatics, writing, debating, foreign language, photography, sports, music. Those whose special skills are limited may serve on committees. Teachers may help, but do not boss.

Camp. Some still attend regular camp, though many now go as counselors. Others now attend special purpose camps: church camp, music camp, sailing camp, French camp.

4. READING

10 YEARS

Great personal variation in interest in reading appears. Some are "not much for reading." Others "love reading"—"my favorite thing," "nose always in a book."

Amount read varies from less than a book a week to five or more, and for
many reading time equals the amount of time spent on radio and TV.

May get books from library, school, or may own them.

Quite a number are good about reading to younger siblings.

Prefer: animal (especially horse or dog) stories, mysteries, girls' and boys'
adventure series, biographies.

Comic Books. Most read comics, many avidly, and some still collect them
avidly, though there is somewhat less collecting, swapping and borrowing
than earlier. Mothers mostly object and some forbid. Many favorites:
Disney, *Little Lulu, Looney Tunes, Supermouse, Bugs Bunny, Annie,*
Westerns, *Felix, Superman, Batman.*

Magazines. Very little magazine reading, except for looking at pictures and
cartoons in family's magazines. May subscribe to special children's magazines as *Jack and Jill.*

Newspapers. Minimal in most. Funnies and headlines are read most. Many
just skim through paper.

11 YEARS

Great individual variation, but most read at least some, even if only comic
books. Range from "Never read" or one book a month, to eight a week.
More girls than boys "love" to read.

In some it is the chief spare-time pursuit. Others claim they don't have time
to read.

Quality of book important: "Like it if it's something real good."

Like to tell in greatest detail plots of stories they have read.

Prefer: animal (especially horse) stories, mysteries, historical or biographical
books, Westerns, information books, classics (*Tom Sawyer,* etc.). Some
read, "Just horse books"; others, "Anything that's a book." Several say,
"No romantic stories," or, "No love!"

Comic books. Two-thirds of our subjects read comics, some still avidly. Most
read moderately and in some the interest is falling off. Comic reading is
under cover for some. A few still collect and barter, and may have two
hundred to five hundred copies, stacked around. Some do not buy them
but do read them. Favorites are about as at ten years.

Magazines. As at ten, most just look through or read cartoons. The favored
adult magazines—at eleven and every following age—include *Life, Time,
Saturday Evening Post,* and *The New Yorker.* Many name some variety of
children's magazine among their favorites.

Newspapers. Some never read newspapers but the majority at least look through them. Comics, news, and sports are read most, in that order. Many say, "Just the funnies." Preference for "articles about planes crashing," or "crimes and murders and robbers." A few boys express mild interest in politics. Some have to read for Current Events class.

12 YEARS

Great variation. Some never read or "just look at the pictures," others read five to ten books a week. Perhaps a little decline in reading, but amount read depends more on individuality than age.

Books must be "interesting." Adult books coming in more, and ones they have outgrown are described as "boring" or "silly."

Many use library regularly and well. Increased interest in owning books.

Less naming of specific books liked and more mention of type of book. Beginning of interest in special authors.

Prefer: mystery, sports, adventure, classics. "No love" and less interest in animal stories.

Comic books. About two-thirds of our subjects read comics, but few now read avidly. Some interest continues but is definitely decreasing in many. Little collecting. May not even buy them, reading only if they are available. Preferences less strong, and comics are not read and reread.

Magazines. Most look at magazines which parents buy or subscribe to, some read them. Besides the adult favorites, now including *Reader's Digest*, such boys' and girls' publications as *Boy's Life* or *Calling All Girls* are mentioned.

Newspapers. The number reading newspapers at all increases, though the number reading thoroughly does not. Parts read most are comics, news, and sports in that order.

13 YEARS

An increase in interest in reading and in amount read, though there are still many non-readers. Many read in every spare moment, reading and rereading favorite books.

Selective—likes "plot" or "action." Reading of adult novels is increasing, though some avoid emotional parts of books.

Preferences are very varied, but in general are: classics, detective stories, adult novels, some animal stories, adventure. Sports books and magazines very strong with boys.

Comic books. Only about half admit to reading these at all and virtually none read avidly or collect. Interest is generally slight and spasmodic. ("I don't

buy them—I read my sister's." "No longer. Stopped about a year ago.")
Fewer preferences though *Little Lulu, Looney Tunes, Classic Comics,
Famous Funnies,* and "romantic ones" are named.

Magazines.   Much more magazine reading. Many subscribe to teen-age magazines. Favorite also are sports and (by a few girls) screen magazines, in
addition to the adult magazines mentioned earlier.

Newspapers.   The majority now read the newspaper and a few read it thoroughly. Preference continues to be for comics, news, and sports, in that
order, but more different sections are read. Radio, TV, and movie news,
ads, lost and found, woman's page, Believe It or Not, society, and columns
are all mentioned by at least several.

14 YEARS

Great variability. Some never read, while many read "all the time"—ten to
fifteen books a week, some report. Others are reading less, or "have no time
for reading," though would like to if they had time.
Good use of library facilities. May by now be responsible about getting books
back on time.
Reading of sexy books by some boys, and others will now accept romance in
stories. Several mention the mood produced by different types of books.
Preferences: adult novels—especially classics, adventure, mysteries, sports
(boys), books about adolescents (girls), information and science books
(boys). Great interest in preferred authors.

Comic books.   Only a quarter of our subjects read comics at all, and this
reading is mostly slight and occasional. No collecting or swapping, virtually
no buying. No favorites reported except *Classic Comics,* used by some to
help with school book reviews.

Magazines.   Less reading than at thirteen, but more apt than earlier to read
text and not just look at pictures and cartoons. Selective—some do not like
"trashy" magazines. Science, sports, and movie magazines are preferred,
besides the adult magazines favored since eleven.

Newspapers.   Comics, news, and sports are still read most, but there is some
reading of nearly all other parts—the most reported to date.

15 YEARS

Those who like to read now read exhaustively—"anything I can get my hands
on." Some read a book an evening, or even ten or twelve books a week.
Some say reading is just about as much fun as anything. Some collect books and
will spend own money on them.
Conscientious girls feel guilty that they take time from studying to read.

Some boys will read if they think of it themselves but not if urged.

Boys interested in sexy books. Both boys and girls accept romance in the plot. Preferences are adult novels, classics, adventure, sports, historical, and mystery stories.

Comic books. There is almost no reading of comic books except as one is picked up if there is nothing else to do. "Used to, gave it up."

Magazines. Some prefer magazines to books, but there is more real reading, less just "looking through." Favorites are shifting. *Life* still leads, but science magazines come second. Then *Saturday Evening Post* and *Seventeen.* Women's magazines are read much more now (by girls) than earlier.

Newspapers. Some state that they *never* read the paper. Most do read it, but less reading is reported than at fourteen, and fewer parts are read—primarily comics, news, sports, and amusements.

16 YEARS

Probably less reading than at fifteen, even for the more enthusiastic readers. Many say they would like to but don't have time. Others would "rather DO something," and read only what is required for school. "Don't read for pleasure."

Preferences are expressed for adult novels, classics, sports, mystery, humor. However, some are too old for children's books and not quite ready for adult books.

Comic books. Virtually no reading of comics except "now and then," "I keep in touch with them."

Magazines. Several say that they are only magazine readers, preferring them to books. *Life, Time* and the *Post* are the favorites; *Reader's Digest* and *Collier's* come next. Girls increasingly read *Seventeen* and the women's magazines. Boys read magazines about science, cars, and radio.

Newspapers. Most read the paper at least a little and quite a few read it thoroughly. The front page is now reported as read most, followed by funnies, sports, editorials, classified ads, amusements, and the magazine section.

5. RADIO, TELEVISION, AND PHONOGRAPH

10 YEARS

Radio or TV listening is on the decline with some Tens, who listen not more than one or two hours a day. Others still listen "all day long," have thirty to forty set programs a week, and can and do list all, with times and stations. Their whole life may be regulated by radio.

The 5 to 6 P.M. programs (Westerns and adventures) are dropping out; after dinner programs stronger.

Some prefer radio, some prefer TV, some "love radio and love TV."

Programs preferred are general comedies, Western and adventure programs, murder mysteries, and adolescent comedies.

Relatively little interest in phonograph. May listen with family group. Some say phonograph is broken and nobody gets it fixed.

11 YEARS

The more immature listen systematically, often for several hours a day, but systematic, intensive listening is falling off in many. A large factor in amount of time spent on TV is its newness. The first incessant watching decreases eventually, but slowly, for many.

Most are bored with the 5 to 6 P.M. radio programs, no longer send away to get things or join clubs, and reject soap operas.

Listening time is mostly after dinner or before going to sleep.

Some prefer radio; some prefer TV. On both, the programs preferred are general comedies, murder mysteries, adolescent comedies. Last age for Westerns and adventure and some have already dropped these. Some "can adjust to most anything except those speeches."

About a third listen to phonograph though no extreme enthusiasm. May prefer songs from musical comedies. May like to have albums rather than single records. Less listening with family.

12 YEARS

Many have regular programs, but not the battery they had at ten years. Many listen to radio and/or TV one to two hours a day; for a few, "It goes on continually."

The 5 to 6 P.M. programs are now definitely out, with most weekday listening between 7 and 9 P.M. and after bedtime. Some like to have radio or TV on while they do their homework, often preferring radio because it combines more easily with the homework.

Questioned about favorites, some can list types or classes of program rather than listing specific ones. Preferred are general comedies, murder mysteries, adolescent comedies, and jazz. Soap operas, Western, and give-away programs are out, and many also say, "No LOVE!"

Individual differences marked in regard to phonograph. Music lovers—both popular and classical—play it a lot; others never do.

13 YEARS

A real drop in time spent just in listening to radio or TV occurs at this age, though music may be on as a background to reading or studying. Instead of following a schedule of favorite programs, Thirteen is more apt to tune in and see what is on. The time when he is free to listen (often 8 to 9 P.M.) may decide, as much as the program.

In some, telephoning has taken place of listening.

Many prefer TV, but some like radio equally well.

Some criticize their own tastes, as for murder mysteries. Murder and comedy are both decreasing in popularity, though both still rank among the favorite types of program: general comedy, jazz, murder mystery, theater, sports.

Use of the phonograph increases. Jazz and classical music are preferred. Girls like romantic popular music; boys do not. Some are beginning to buy own records. Some girls like to dance to music alone.

14 YEARS

Viewing and listening are mostly only occasional. Several say they can take radio (TV) or leave it alone—"Too much else to do."

Some boys interested in building radio, getting license, etc.

A few favorite programs are selected and followed, and music is still liked by some as an accompaniment to homework. May listen or view on weekends but not on week nights.

Some prefer TV, but an appreciable number still prefer radio.

Prefer: jazz, murder mysteries, comedies, sports and theater. Choice may now reflect personal taste, as in music, sports, theater.

About a quarter of our group play the phonograph a good deal, some almost constantly. Jazz preferred but also popular, romantic, and classical music. Many buy records, though some object to the expense. Phonograph listening exceeds radio in some. Great enthusiasm for certain records or certain bands.

15 YEARS

Amount of listening (viewing) is still falling off. "Not much time for it— Lucky if I listen three hours a week. Used to listen all the time." A few individuals, however, even now listen "constantly."

Some like radio as a general background, and still listen while studying, but many finish homework first. May just listen, or watch, to kill time when nothing else to do. Some listen secretly if at a boarding school where it is not allowed.

Jazz now the great favorite, followed by murder mysteries, news, sports, and classical music.

Phonograph a "real fad" in about a third of our subjects. These have marked personal preferences for classical or jazz music. May buy own records and may collect records.

16 YEARS

Radio listening and TV watching are still decreasing for most. The majority listen only while doing something else—homework, housework, reading, driving, getting ready for bed. It is the exceptional 16-year-old who plays the radio constantly.

Radio is played more than TV. Many neither have TV at home nor watch it elsewhere. "Most of the kids don't spend much time watching. We're forever on the go," is a typical comment.

Music is the favorite on radio, especially jazz. On both radio and TV, sports and news are favorites.

The phonograph is a great favorite with many. Many have own phonograph and own record collection, both popular and classical.

6. MOVIES

10 YEARS

Most report that they attend movies only occasionally. Many (girls more than boys) still go with their parents. The majority go with one friend of the same sex, usually on Saturday afternoon.

Ten is not very selective, will go to almost anything, though some emphasize preference for a "good" movie. Favorites mentioned are Westerns, comedies, cartoons, historical and horse movies, and plots are reported in endless detail. Both boys and girls choose men as well as women as favorite actors. Some, if allowed to, see the same movie several times.

Some "don't look if it's too bad." Others complain that movies give them headaches and bad dreams.

Most accept parents' refusal to let them attend at certain times or to let them see certain pictures.

11 YEARS

Most attend only occasionally—some prefer to play outdoors rather than attend movies. Some now go weekly or every two weeks, usually on Saturday afternoon, and usually with parents, siblings, or same-sex friends.

More definite preferences than at ten, and these include comedies, Westerns, musicals, "movies without fighting and murder," adventure movies. The peak age for endless recital of entire plot and action. Favorite actor may be of either sex.

Still accept parents' refusal to let them attend certain movies. Some like to see same movie several times.

Can "look" at entire picture now, even "bad" parts, but some get stomach-aches or headaches, or eyes hurt. Do not behave too well: "If movie is boring I talk and make a noise."

12 YEARS

The majority attend only occasionally and some still report preferring to play outdoors if it is a good day. More than earlier now attend weekly or every two weeks, and most no longer go with parents but with a same-sex friend, or friends. Less reporting of plot at home.

May see same film repeatedly if allowed—"Same movie eleven times," one reports. The strongest age for this.

Comedies are preferred, then Westerns, musicals, adventure. Many specify that they do *not* like romantic pictures. "A little bit of love is O.K. but all mush I hate." Favorite players may still be of either sex.

Many specify that the movie must be *good* or they won't go.

More complex emotional reactions reported: "I get a terrific *thrill* out of it," or, "It almost made me *sick* it was so wishy-washy," or, "I *hate* love movies." Some girls cry at sad parts.

A few (girls) read movie magazines.

13 YEARS

As many now report attending weekly or every two weeks as only occasionally. As at twelve, the majority go with a single friend of the same sex, or with several. Time of attendance is shifting, if it had not earlier, to Friday nights.

Favorite players for the first time (in many) are of the opposite sex only. Some girls definitely have crushes on male actors. Boys comment on attractive actresses but seem less involved.

Some who earlier were not, are becoming quite selective. Musicals lead as favorite type of program. Then come comedies and adventure stories, then Westerns. Many still specify "no romance," but others, girls especially, are beginning to accept romance or even to prefer it. Only a few now like to see same movie more than once.

Girls are apt to be very tearful at sad parts. Some read movie magazines.

Some go to movies hoping to attract some notice from opposite sex.

14 YEARS

Average attendance now is weekly; most often on Friday nights. The majority now attend with several friends of the same sex, some go with one same-sex friend. Quite a few now go with someone of the opposite sex or on a double date, or girls and boys go separately but sit together when there. Social aspects of going to the movies equal or exceed in importance the mere seeing of the picture.

Favorite players are mostly of the opposite sex. Some select more on the basis of the players than of title or plot. Favorite kinds of movies are musicals and comedies. Sports movies are favored by boys, and romantic movies by girls.

Some are very critical about quality of the movie. Some—boys especially—worry about the expense.

Considerable empathy—girls leave theater feeling like the actress. Many girls cry at sad pictures.

May behave very badly in theater. Much activity related to opposite sex; very noisy.

15 YEARS

Many have now given up routine weekly attendance. They may attend as often, but much more selectively—when they have a date or when there is a good movie. In fact, many speak scornfully of routine attendance: "I'm not the kind who goes every Friday night."

For the first time the majority attend with a friend of the opposite sex, usually on a double date, though some still go with one same-sex friend.

Favorite players may be of the same or opposite sex now. Girls especially "simply adore" certain actors. May choose movie by its star. Or from the reviews.

For the first time "grown-up" movies lead as favorites, followed by musicals, comedy, romance, and historical. Few now attend the same movie twice.

Even some boys now like emotional movies: "I like the ones that cause me to weep and cry. None of this lukewarm stuff."

Most behave better in theater than at fourteen.

16 YEARS

Movie attendance has considerably lessened and is mostly quite selective. Although some (especially if they are away at school) still attend weekly, the majority average only about one movie a month. "Sometimes I go just for the sake of going but that's rare. Mostly it has to be a *worthwhile* movie *and* someone good to go with."

The majority go on dates, single or double, though a good many go with a group of same-sex friends, and some with a single same-sex friend. The social aspect is strong—though few ordinarily see the same picture twice, they might if a friend hadn't seen it.

Little emphasis on special interest in the stars. Most now like a "good" or "worthwhile" movie—tastes are quite adult. Emphasis is on musicals, comedies, historical and documentary films.

Girls especially may identify with the heroine.

CHAPTER SEVENTEEN

School Life

▬▬▬

THE FAMILY has been a basic institution throughout the long history of man. It remains the most fundamental unit of modern culture. Even in an atomic age the household must serve as the cultural workshop for the transmission of cherished traditions and for guiding the child in the pathways of development. But as childhood merges into adolescent youth the school also becomes a cultural workshop of unique power. In a democracy this power is far-reaching because the school, whether private or public, is charged with the double task of educating its youth both as individuals and as future citizens. The school system thereby becomes the chief instrument by which society perpetuates and renews itself. Teachers become agents in transmitting our cultural heritage and defining the duties of citizenship. The adolescent boys and girls whom they teach are beneficiaries and participants. It is a vast mutual enterprise in which both the individual and the nation have a stake.

A notable report on Readjustment of High School Education * carries this statement: "We think schools should put equal emphasis on the *obligations* and the *privileges* of citizenship, for no government demands so much from its citizens as Democracy, and none gives so much in return." The recent White House Conference on Education with its two thousand delegates and 166 simultaneous discussion panels has dramatized the colossal scope of our educational problems.

These problems may be envisaged in terms of the growing individual

* A Report to the Citizens of New York State by the Regents Council on Readjustment of High School Education, The University of the State of New York, 1954, Albany.

449

or in terms of the community in which he lives. The claims of the individual and of the community are of course interdependent. The spirit and resources of the local community as a cultural unit are reflected in the educational provisions made available. The nature and the needs of the individual are manifested in his reactions to these provisions.

Our study of school life was especially concerned with the individual reactions of the research group of youths. We did not attempt any appraisal of the school practices but we were interested in the pupil attitudes and behavior patterns which came to light. Supplementary information was secured by direct consultation with teachers. On analyzing the data, maturity traits and trends became evident in the succession of years from ten to sixteen. Inasmuch as school organization is based on yearly units of age, it should be profitable to examine these developmental trends.

What follows is an informal survey of school behavior patterns which were more or less characteristic of the several age zones from ten years onward. It is of course recognized that the educability of a specific youth at a specific time is greatly influenced by his abilities and motivations. But these factors are in turn influenced by growth factors which reveal themselves when the advancing age groups are compared with each other. Learning and growth are closely allied. In the very nature of things growth forces permeate the whole educational process.

Ten. The ten-year age zone presents an instructive developmental picture, because ten is a nodal age. It marks the summit of childhood. "Ten" —we shall continue to use an age designation as a convenient demonstrative pronoun—Ten is educationally amenable and responsive. He usually likes his teacher and his schoolroom (vaguely he feels at home and may inadvertently address her as though she were his "mommy" or some adult friend). He expects teacher to schedule his activities; he likes to follow a schedule in detail. He likes to talk, to read, and to be read to, especially about other children like himself.

He is very fond of spot geography, of writing to dictation, of copying, of memorizing. He wants to learn facts—spot facts! He shows less interest and capacity in connecting the facts by associational thinking. He enjoys and needs abundant gross motor activity. He wants freedom of movement and communication within the schoolroom. He likes to sing. Let him sing! But avoid sissy songs, for he is beginning to feel twinges of manliness.

Eleven is in an active developmental transition, which contrasts with the relative equilibrium of the previous year. There is a restless, seething, and somewhat explosive quality about his schoolroom behavior. He wriggles in his seat. He has bursts and flurries of activity with intervals of pronounced fatigue. He fluctuates from a bad mood to vivid exuberance. Frequently he is literally excited by the act of learning, and teachers find him a challenging and rewarding subject on such occasions. His responses are radiant at the moment of acquiring a new thought and insight. Such a reaction is explosive; it is an explosion which bursts inward, and is the counterpart of some of his intense outward thrustings. For he is indeed an eager seeker after new episodes and experiences.

He is in a phase of growth which makes trouble for himself and teacher, but it is not a true state of belligerency. He can be very fond and even affectionate toward a teacher. His schoolmates are important to him too, and for the same reason: he has much to learn from them. He does it by contact, by nudging, poking, chasing, teasing. He joins a transient cluster of his pals and enters into their intrigues. He is highly competitive. His games call for supervision.

He needs the stimulus and outlet of non-academic activities which give scope to his natural spontaneity and latent creativeness—shop, music, arts, dramatics. His manifold versatility may make tensions for himself and his teacher. But she knows he can be exciting as well as exhausting. He thrives best under a patient, understanding teacher, who combines firm control with well-timed flexibility. And this is the kind of teacher he likes most.

Twelve can buckle down better than Eleven. He is more adaptable and has a longer span of sustained attention. He is less episodic, less restless. Still he can become fidgety with fatigue long before noon, and like Eleven he calms down with a snack. (It is easy to forget that in a growing organism food, energy, and education are interrelated.)

From the standpoint of educability, the cardinal trait of Twelve is enthusiasm. He often speaks of his teacher as wonderful, and shows a wide range of interest in his school subjects, including arithmetic ("just love decimals"), astronomy, and debating. The brighter boys and girls show a perceptible advance in ability to arrange, classify, and generalize. Social studies evoke lively comments.

The group is important to Twelve in a new way. He may easily lose his own identity and thus gets lost. But he greatly enjoys a group project, like planning a play and painting the scenery for the play. The sexes separate, but they are increasingly interested in each other.

Twelve is less dependent on his teacher and less involved. He does not join his mates to flock around her, as he did earlier. Yet the school group likes to include her in their undertakings. Usually there is a good reciprocal relationship between teacher and pupil. Twelve is curious and zealous to learn. Above all Twelve wants a teacher who can teach.

Thirteen is not as expansive as Twelve. He is more focalized in his intellectual and emotional processes. He shows a stronger tendency to evaluate what he observes and learns. His experiences are more inwardized; his thinking is somewhat deeper. It may take him longer to mobilize his attention and to settle down; he may even show a juvenile form of absent-mindedness. Yet he can also muster his forces and concentrate remarkably well. He is reputed to have periods of indifference and boredom when he does not apply himself. However, he is more in character when he sets to and delves into a problem. This is the aspect which delights his teachers and enlarges their influence.

He wants to feel rather independent of his teacher, although he really needs her help. He tends to be critical, and even belligerent, but he has genuine respect for the teacher who can serve an ample intellectual fare. He has a keen, many-sided curiosity and he brightens inwardly when he experiences a new thought and pursues its ramifications. There is a feeling side to intellect. Facts take on new meanings to the bright mind at moments of self-discovery. These are the high moments of the educative process in which the teacher has a vested interest.

With his appetite for knowledge, Thirteen enjoys discussion and debate at a somewhat higher analytic level. Often he writes better than he talks, although the reverse was true at eleven and ten. He likes to write stories about himself. He keeps up with pen pals. His handwriting may become small and uniform. On many counts he is in a very interesting educational phase.

Fourteen comes into a new phase of expansive enthusiasm. He is now more outgoing and less self-conscious. He is quieter within himself, even though he may be noisy in the school corridors because of sheer sociability. He uses the periods between classes to make social contacts. He intermingles well with his schoolmates, and is also more adjustable and respectful toward his elders. He is more aware of people as personalities. His interest in academic school work almost seems secondary to his propensity for socialization. Most of our research subjects felt sure they had too much homework. Nevertheless, "everybody likes school, but of course we complain."

The group has strong attractions for Fourteen. He likes to sit with his peers when they assemble. The group pressures are difficult to withstand. He enjoys association with his schoolmates; he thrives on educational club activities and group projects, dramatic and otherwise.

In these social activities he is prone to do a great deal of evaluating of his companions and of himself. He relates his interests in school life with those of the outside world. He is eager to know more about himself and human nature in general. His questionings and curiosity make this a favorable period for individual counseling and for incidental guidance by teachers. He is at the brink of senior high school and is looking toward the more distant horizon of his career. He is peculiarly in need of understanding. Educational arrangements should recognize and protect the many-sided new potentials which are unfolding at this particular stage of his development.

Fifteen is often an age of struggle and discouragement especially in the intellectual realm of school life. Poor orientation at fourteen may lead to uncertainty, confusion, and even outright hostility. A slump may descend to a drop-out. On the other hand, under happier conditions, the student may rise to excellent integrated form and to high achievement, expressed in talents and leadership. He is totally caught up in school and immersed in its various club and other activities. At the other extreme is the boy who seems to lack purpose, skills, and, most regrettably, a sense of belongingness. He yearns for an apprenticeship, a vocation, or a job.

Fifteen is characteristically susceptible to group influences. He definitely identifies with his compeers and with their doings. He imitates. He copies. He exhibits intense allegiance to his gang and to his athletic team. He may overemphasize a loyalty to the detriment of his studies. But he also responds to the group stimulus of panel discussion. Here he shows up at his best; he wants to think for himself—which is a good trait for any future citizen. He is capable of asking critical questions.

Fifteen tends to have a respect for the teacher who helps him to think straight. She may have to work against initial resistance and opinionated remarks; but she may make allowance for his naive intellectual rebellion against authority. A challenge is there. Much depends upon what Fifteen and his teacher think of each other.

Sixteen has more friendly attitudes toward his teachers, toward school, and toward himself. One youth summed it up: "I seem to like everyone better than in the past!" Sixteen is in general better integrated and in tune with the world. He has a more tolerant outlook on homework, and accepts responsibility for a reasonable amount of it. His adjustability shows that he has a broader outlook on the functions and program of the school. Accordingly, he is more responsive to its demands and "easier to teach."

He has a more mature awareness of the individual characteristics of his teachers, his friends, and probably also of himself. The teachers likewise become increasingly aware of the individual differences among their pupils—the slow learners, the fast learners, the slow readers, the mediocre, the leaders, the gifted in science, the arts, or technology, the maladjusted, and the ambitious who have set their sights on college. These differences in personality and ability take on added educational significance in the year prior to graduation from high school.

Educational Implications

The foregoing summary of maturity trends confirms the suggestion that the years from ten to sixteen constitute a distinctive cycle of development. Each year brings forth its own accents and maturity traits, which inevitably influence the complex processes and arrangements of education. Despite individual differences, it is possible to characterize these traits and to consider how they may affect the school life of youth and the professional task of the teacher. When the maturity trends are viewed in deep perspective the teacher-pupil relationship stands out as the most crucial factor in the day-to-day affairs of schoolroom education.

Teachers of wide experience become familiar with the conduct and learning characteristics of various ages and grades in the school system. Concretely they can describe the differences between a typical fifth grade and sixth grade. They are aware of the exuberance of the 12-year-old as compared with withdrawn 13-year-olds. Teachers can testify to the contrastive traits of high school sophomores and juniors. Discerning teachers appreciate the significance of various maturity factors. They usually acquire a preference for a favorite age or grade with which they would like to work. Ideally there should be a fair degree of compatibility between the teacher and her pupil group, because compatibility leads to mutual understanding.

Our data, gained directly from the pupils themselves, indicate that they generally prefer a teacher who knows how to teach and who is consistent in discipline. They are not looking for an indulgent teacher, although they prize a sense of humor. And they wish to be understood.

They try to understand themselves, but a perceptive and sympathetic teacher can give them much help through the very manner in which she conducts her work from day to day, and through the considerateness which she bestows on their patterns of maturity.

It is here that a developmental approach to the teaching task proves its merits. This approach does not rely upon rigid absolutes and remote goals, but fosters an awareness of the ever-present maturity factors which affect the behavior of the individual and the school group. The teacher finds it profitable to study the group forces, to identify the leaders, and to utilize them to advantage. Awareness of the maturity traits and trends of her age group also enables her to detect significant individual deviations. A developmentally minded teacher tends to gear her work to the developmental readiness of her pupils, and to adapt it to their creative energies. Above all their curiosity and gifts for self-expression must be kept alive to safeguard the kind of mental growth which promotes mental health.

Knowledge and skills are the proper aims of education, but not the exclusive goal. The full development of the individual demands that his inner life of feelings and attitudes should keep abreast of his attainments. This is the subtle and elusive realm of aesthetic, moral, and spiritual values, which are embedded in the literature and the humanities and the sciences which the youth are taught in school. To some extent these values are communicated by formal lessons and discussion.

But there is another kind of communication which is purely incidental, which depends upon the vitality of the teacher and the latent responsiveness of the group of individuals. A vital teacher is one who has a knack for reaching individuals without singling them out. She depends upon the spur of psychological moments to drop a hint, to make a shrewd suggestion, to add a dash of humor or friendly irony, and to register her own sincere reactions of surprise, wonderment, seriousness, and approval. Such a teacher demonstrates one of the profound paradoxes of psychological growth. Growth of mind and personality takes a long time; but this growth also incorporates brief moments of significant experience.

A vital schoolroom multiplies these moments. It has faith in the here and now. Citizenship remains the ultimate goal. But sufficient unto the day is the spirit of youth and "its immemorial ability to reaffirm the charm of existence."

GROWTH GRADIENTS

1. GENERAL

10 YEARS

Most Tens say that school is "O.K.," and indicate that on the whole they like school. But they tend to be restless, and attention span is short. Most "hate" some subjects, but rebellion is passive and individual, doesn't come to a head in open revolt. They rebel by withdrawing.

Social relationships are important, but generally not intense. Fairly easy acceptance of one sex by the other. Much note passing—often about the opposite sex, though notes are passed between members of the same sex. Some plan mean things to get other children into trouble. May discuss contemporaries not as whole people, but in terms of "his reading," "his arithmetic."

Beginning of a sophisticated self-consciousness in reciting or singing.

Most can get off for school on time without confusion and without losing or forgetting things.

11 YEARS

A turn for the worse often appears in school behavior. Elevens can be very fatiguable, show uneven performance, have frequent illnesses. Many become restless, careless, forgetful, daydreaming, dawdling, sprawling, boisterous. Attention span is very short. Still, school behavior is usually better than behavior at home.

Much interaction among children: notes, spitballs, teasing, chasing, hitting, etc. Boys and girls very aware of "the boys" and "the girls," but gauche in their approaches: push, pull, fool around, act silly to attract attention. Their reporting emphasizes relationship with peers more than with teacher.

Many keenly interested in their relative standing in the group, work for good grades, show self-satisfaction in doing well.

Often much commotion and flurry about getting off to school in the morning. Burst out of school when dismissed.

12 YEARS

Many show strong emotional reactions; they either love school or hate it. Some "would like to be free," not go to school. But many emerge from 11-year-old scatter into more smoothness. Nicer in class, more co-operative, more adaptable; less lazy, aggressive, and rebellious. Sudden spurts of energy, but these cannot be sustained and child grows restless. Still needs freedom to move about.

May act better as individuals than as a group. Group situation may foster note passing, shooting erasers and rulers, throwing chalk, hiding papers and property of others. Yet hard to establish a group structure, because all are trying to express themselves. The group is important to them but it is hard for them to subordinate themselves to it.

Girls stay with girls and boys with boys except for boy-girl fooling and teasing. Girls more interested in boys than boys in girls. Considerable sex and elimination joking in school; quick to note double meanings.

"Bad" classroom behavior is not necessarily a sign of dislike of school or teacher.

13 YEARS

Many are happier in school than earlier, think it is "better than last year," seem readier to learn. However, some go through an indifferent period: "Boring. No sense slaving."

Thirteen wishes to feel and to be independent. Some students may seek special projects and extra assignments. Time is now better organized, concentration more sustained, self-control and sense of responsibility more evident. But teachers and parents complain that some "don't apply themselves." Some seem so far inside themselves and so absent-minded that they don't hear instructions. Less readiness to recite and perform before others.

The group acts more as a unit; less separation in class of "the girls" and "the boys." Can be boisterous in the hall, but quieter now in class, though quite a bit of revolt. Group may play tricks on teacher.

Many like to get to school early and to settle in slowly.

14 YEARS

Many more Fourteens (in our group) say that they like than that they dislike school. Expansively enthusiastic, energetic, sociable, Fourteen may do well in school. But can become submerged and lost as a Freshman in a four-year high school.

Quite a few criticize the way the school is run: the system, the administration. But may admit, "Everybody likes it, but of course we complain."

A few now admit (though this occurs more at fifteen) that they don't work as hard as they should or "don't try."

Strong group feeling. May like to sit together as a group in assembly. Group pressure strong; some "might be bad just to go along with the group."

Girls much interested in the boys. Noisy, much interaction between boys and girls.

Fourteen thrives on a variety of program. Enjoys participation in extracurricular activities and clubs: athletic, scientific, dramatic, musical, etc.

15 YEARS

Fifteen's attitude toward school is often extreme: enthusiastic and whole-hearted or hostile, rebellious, and indifferent. School is wonderful or it is impossible—badly run, too much work, poor grades, awful teacher.

Many are extremely critical of the way school is run. Much talk about unfair-ness—of grading, of teacher, of the administration.

Many show a "15-year-old slump"—indifferent, don't work but don't know why not. May make a total rejection of school: "Boring," "everything is wrong." Others are "totally caught up" in school and very busy in its related clubs and activities.

Many would like to go away to school, and some do much better at school away from home. But even these may comment, "I like being away from home—but schools, of course, are just schools."

16 YEARS

Most seem to be getting on well. Typically: "I'm perfectly satisfied with school"; "Much better than it was"; though "It has its ups and downs." Several say they love school and even hate to think of graduating. Some object to school "just because it is school"; would rather be doing something else.

Much interest in how the school is run. Some are satisfied, but several feel it is run like a prison. However, many comment on how much feeling of school spirit or class feeling now exists.

Many are now getting better grades. Some are motivated toward better achieve-ment by promise of driving license or use of car. Distinguish between grades they deserve, those they expect, and those they get.

Outside activities now a major concern: student council, committees, band, school paper, debating, dramatics, managing teams, athletics, etc. Many are involved successfully in several of these activities.

2. SCHOOL SUBJECTS AND WORK

10 YEARS

Tens seem most interested in concrete learning experiences, and learning of specifics. Generally love to memorize, but don't generalize or correlate facts, or care what you do with knowledge. May like to know what a thing is called but have little interest in mechanism or source of material. Often enjoy "place" geography—names of states, capitals, etc.—but vague about actual geographic characteristics.

Like to talk and listen more than work. Often better with oral and pictorial presentation than with printed words. Like to take dictation; like oral arithmetic.

Not able to plan own work, need schedules. Usually not much homework assigned. What there is, they can usually manage by themselves with little help and without much complaint.

11 YEARS

Many Elevens are still excited about learning. Compared with Tens, may show even more enthusiasm but less organization. Seem to thrive on competition.

Most still seem better at rote learning of specific information than at generalization. Prefer a certain amount of routine. Want their work to be related to reality—may thus prefer current events to past history.

Strongest feelings are expressed about mathematics—it is both the best liked subject (by many) and the least liked (by others). Most prefer the mechanics of arithmetic to solution of problems.

Girls' favorites are art and math, sewing and cooking; their most disliked subjects are English and math. Boys prefer science, math, shop; dislike math and spelling. Great enthusiasm for gym and sports.

Homework may cause much trouble. Is left until the last minute. Elevens need, but repudiate, mother's help; whole family may become involved. However, many still say they don't have too much homework.

12 YEARS

Many are better able to arrange, classify, and generalize, and enjoy doing so.

Strongest feelings are still expressed about math—it is among the subjects most liked and the most disliked by both girls and boys. English is especially favored by girls, French very much disliked. More than earlier are ready for social studies.

Boys enjoy astronomy and experiments in science; dislike spelling.

Boys like shop; girls like home economics, and both sexes enjoy athletics.

Most think they have too much homework, and may rebel if they think it is really excessive. But they are a little more independent about doing homework than at eleven. Mother may need to get them started and to help some, but less of a battle and scramble than earlier.

13 YEARS

Thirteen may like certain subjects even though they consider them hard, or even though they dislike the teacher of the particular subject. Discussion periods are much enjoyed, and new subjects or new approaches are tried with interest.

Many Thirteens enjoy the broadened outlook on world affairs provided by social studies. Those who like English are likely to prefer reading and composition to grammar.

Boys prefer math, science—especially its experimental aspects, history, shop; often dislike English. Girls more often dislike math, prefer languages, art, home economics.

Thirteens often feel that they have too much homework, but many are quite conscientious, and some would "work all night" if parents would let them. Most can accept any help needed from parents more gracefully than earlier.

14 YEARS

Many enjoy evaluating subjects and teachers. Ease of achievement is not always a criterion of interest; some like subjects even though they do not do well in them.

Less interest than earlier in the broader social studies, but more in any with a psychological slant—subjects which tell them about themselves.

Girls most often prefer art and English; boys, math and science. Girls tend to dislike math; boys, Latin.

Most think there is too much homework. Though lazy about homework, usually need less help than earlier.

15 YEARS

A wide range of attitudes toward subjects appears, from resentment to indifference and apathy, to enjoyment of intellectual challenge. Many are stimulated by the chance to air their opinions and beliefs in the panel discussion type of class. And interest is often shown in whatever affects their own life, such as biology.

Girls most often like English and social studies, dislike math. Boys like math and science, dislike French.

Nearly all feel there is too much homework, and some say they just don't do their homework.

16 YEARS

Great individual variation appears. A few say, "I like all my subjects now."

English and math are the subjects most liked and also most disliked. Besides these two, boys tend to prefer Spanish, chemistry, physics, history; they especially dislike English. Likes and dislikes are less strongly expressed by girls.

Some still have trouble with "tool subjects"—reading, in particular.

Though "everybody gripes about homework—it's the thing to do," most have less trouble with it than they did. Some can nearly finish homework during study periods in school; others spend up to several hours a day at home on it. The responsibility for homework is mostly taken by Sixteens themselves.

3. TEACHER-CHILD RELATIONSHIPS

10 YEARS

Most Tens like and respect their teachers. May pay even more attention to teacher than to parents; "Teacher is God," one parent reports.

Critical analysis of teachers is just beginning. Most describe teacher as "nice" or "O.K." Describe in terms of physical characteristics: "A little bit fat and not too tall"; "Dyes her hair and small." Like to compare one teacher to another. Main demand is that teacher be fair. Beginning criticism of methods of teaching: "Monotonous," or, "Makes sense."

Express affection for and accept affection from teacher. Can be easily hurt and upset by criticism. However, respond well to firmness, seem to appreciate it. If there is to be punishment, they want it to be on the spot; can't stand long-term punishments.

11 YEARS

Elevens often are resentful and rebellious against teacher; may be quite difficult to manage. Very restless and active, though they say that if they are angry at a teacher, all they can do is "sit and take it," or "sit and sizzle." Or may mutter under breath, or write and pass notes about her.

Describe teacher less by appearance, more by behavior characteristics. Attributes they like: that she is fair, is patient, has no favorites, doesn't yell, is understanding, cracks jokes. Most disliked traits are that she is unfair, is too strict, is crabby, yells, or flies off the handle.

Some have a crush on teacher, like to do things for her. Though Elevens don't want to be held with an ironclad hand, they do prefer a tough teacher, one who can challenge them.

12 YEARS

Less dependent on teacher and less embroiled with her than at eleven. About equal numbers (in our group) say they like and say they dislike teacher.

Great enthusiasm for those they like: "Just about the wonderfullest person I ever met"; "Perfect in any way that I can figure." They like it when she is nice, humorous, understanding, "doesn't treat us like babies," "is a good teacher" (i.e., can communicate subject matter). Attributes disliked are that she is "not a good teacher" (in techniques and knowledge), not a good disciplinarian, unsympathetic, yells, plays favorites.

Can be challenged by teacher—ready to be held in line and demanded of. But much uproar in room if teacher is not a good disciplinarian. Teacher needs also to have patience with the considerable heterosexual interest and activity which appears.

13 YEARS

Less embroiled with teacher than earlier. Will give in on small points to keep the peace. Many Thirteens report that teacher is "better than last year." Most like some teachers, dislike others.

Many can now recognize a teacher as a good teacher, even though they may not like her personally. Much interest in whether teacher is strict or easy; usually prefer strict teachers if not too strict.

Attributes liked: interesting, good personality, humorous, understanding, can keep discipline. Disliked: too strict, doesn't know how to teach, too critical. Especially dislike criticism of their work.

Want to be free of teacher but actually need considerable help. Some actual revolt against teacher in the form of practical jokes. "We try to get away with things with the teacher. That's only human nature." May make faces at her if angry.

May now be quite critical of the principal.

14 YEARS

As at thirteen, most have several teachers, like some, dislike others. In general, quite a tolerant attitude toward them: "Most . . . are pretty nice. They can be unreasonable, but on the whole they're pretty nice."

Evaluations now quite detailed: "She doesn't have much personality; doesn't know how to keep us in order"; "Too dominating. I don't agree with her politics at all and I can't get a word in edgewise. Don't know if she realizes it or not."

Reasons for liking teachers: "Friendly," "kidding," "wonderful personality." Appreciate teachers who "try to figure out your personality, don't just think about your work."

Dislike teachers who are unsympathetic, unreasonable, too strict, unfair markers, too indifferent, not worldly, "scares you." May be very critical of the way teacher conducts class.

Principal also comes in for criticism: "She has the wrong idea on life altogether. I think she should consult the children and let them make the rules more."

15 YEARS

May be hostile and rebellious toward teachers. May show considerable resistance, argue, put up own ideas against teacher's. Some intellectually quite contemptuous of teacher. However, with a successful teacher, may be intellectually challenged, may identify with her. What teacher thinks of Fifteens is important.

May like a teacher who doesn't like them: "I think he's wonderful, but he doesn't think I am." Often show mixed feelings toward teachers: "Picks on me, but otherwise pretty nice." "Crazy. A lot of horse sense, though. A good teacher"; "A monster, but a marvelous teacher."

Reasons for liking: teaches well, knows a lot, down to earth, doesn't permit fooling, everybody respects her, "has a lot stronger personality than the rest—can handle anybody," "you have a wonderful time but you really learn."

Reasons for disliking: "I don't think the way she does," not fair, sarcastic, tells about her personal affairs, hard marker, doesn't like children, moody, can't teach.

If angry at teacher, they say, they "sit and take it," "give her a cold look."

16 YEARS

Much more friendly attitudes toward teachers, less trying to put things over on them. Many say teachers "are better this year" or "are all O.K. now."

Comment about which teachers like them, which don't. Some think they get better grades than they deserve because teacher likes them.

Interested in personalities of teachers and how well they teach. Most are tolerant even if teacher sometimes gets mad or "gets off the track." May say, "Nice teacher, though doesn't teach us much." But they do show most respect for those who keep discipline and who "teach us a lot."

CHAPTER EIGHTEEN

Ethical Sense

MANY a tract and tome has been written about and around the subject of this chapter. For the ethical sense of man has had a far-reaching effect upon his conduct and culture. The ethical sense is concerned with moral values and principles, with character and will, with guilt, conscience, justice, punishment; delinquency, war and crime, with the duties and motives of men. It is natural that a trait of such vast implications should figure prominently in the development of adolescent youth. It is amazing, however, to find that this development is so clearly prefigured in the first five years of life.

Even a 36-week-old infant will briefly respond to a monitory No-No! A 1-year-old will inhibit an action on a comparable cue. At 18 months he runs away and drops an object which he should not have taken. He shames at making a puddle, and by way of alibi blames the cat or some other member of the household. At two years he associates "good boy" and "bad boy" with routine duties well performed or not performed. At two and a half he is little influenced by adult approval and disapproval; but at three years he tries to please and conform. "Do it dis way?" he asks. At four years he begins to understand the meaning of rules. At five he respects the rules. He likes to stand in well with people, and even asks permission. He has a sense of "goodness" and "badness," in terms of concrete actions which his parents allow or forbid.

The foregoing outline gives a fair indication of how the ethical sense grows and organizes with advancing stages of maturity and of cultural sophistication. To a remarkable degree equivalents of these ethical stages

464

reappear in the cycle of years from five to ten; and emerge once more in the cycle from ten to sixteen. In a general way each of these cycles registers an improvement and broadening of ethical attitudes. The improvement is correlated with increase of intelligence; the broadening with an enrichment of interpersonal relationships. Feeling plays an important role in the perception of moral values; but the intellectual aspect is pre-eminent. The logic of life plays the primary role in shaping ethical attitudes. Piaget hinted as much in his epigram: "Logic is the morality of thought just as morality is the logic of action."

There is an unmistakable trend from the specific to the general and from the concrete to the abstract. Another trend shows increasing tolerance, a quality of judiciousness and a regard for the relativities of conduct. Most impressive is the consistent concern for fairness, which shows up at all the ages from ten to sixteen. For youth this seems to be a cardinal moral virtue, which progresses from fairness claimed for the individual self to fairness claimed also for others.

The lines of progress can be traced through a year-by-year review of the illustrative symptoms of the ethical sense, as manifested by the youths in our research group.

Ten. The preschool child makes concrete distinctions between "good" and "bad." The 10-year-old is just beginning to distinguish more abstractly between "right" and "wrong." A few in our ten-year group state that their conscience tells them "that it's wrong." One girl revealed an intermediate stage of differentiation: "My conscience usually tells me if it's wrong and then I wait till mummy bawls me out to see if it is." Characteristically Ten is concretely specific: "If I stepped in a brook and got my feet wet I know that was wrong." "I know if an example was right or wrong."

Ten tends to be more concerned about wrong than right; and somewhat more concerned about the wrong of others rather than of himself. One boy did not know what conscience is: "Is it something that tells you if you've forgotten something?" Others feel darting pricks of conscience. If Ten has told a lie he wants to make it right by confessing in private to his mother. He is somewhat naïvely susceptible to ethical teaching, and overreacts to it with what resembles a self-righteous attitude. He gets excessively concerned about swearing. He thinks cheating is "awful." Nevertheless, he himself is very strong at alibiing and pushing blame upon a sibling or someone else. "Someone else started it," he says.

In these various patterns of behavior, Ten displays transparently the persistence of childhood characteristics—the concreteness of his "moral" orientation and the simplicity of dependence shown toward his mother. With adolescence there will be reorientations, but in general they will be gradual rather than precipitous, and they will be governed by the growth of social intelligence and new attitudes toward his peers.

Eleven is beginning to steer his own course. He wants freedom to be a non-conformist. He is not as rigid and puritanic as he may have been at ten. He is influenced by his feelings in ethical situations, but he also approaches them somewhat experimentally. He argues intensely to score a triumph (not with father, but with mother). In matters of truthfulness he tends to think first of himself, for self-protection, and he can camouflage some forms of guilt by shifting the shafts of criticism upon others. If uncomfortable, he can resort to magic, crossing his fingers to ward off the evil of untruth. His conscience is by no means uniformly bland. He can waver agonizingly between two choices. If he makes the wrong choice, he sometimes seeks the balm of confession. He may be tempted to cheat at an examination; but he also waxes indignant at the very thought. With experimental intent, he may purposely do wrong in order to be mean (for a little while). He is sensitive to the taunts of his age-mates. In order not to be called a "yellow" weakling or a "chicken," he joins his pals in trespassing upon an open lot.

By such tokens Eleven gives evidence that he is entering a new phase in the development of his ethical attitudes. Because he is in the midst of new beginnings, he is greatly in need of guidance and understanding. Fortunately, the very intensities of his behavior—negative and positive— denote the vitality of his moral potentials. He goes to extremes of truthfulness and downright untruthfulness. His puzzlements suggest that he is trying to overcome or circumvent the contradictions of inner and outer dualisms.

His aspirations are summed up in a double column of DOS and DON'TS drawn from the secret files of a Secret Club of 11-year-olds, whose chief motto is or was: *Share Hardships Together.* Chief rule: *Have Will Power.*

D O S	*D O N ' T S*
1. Be brave	A. Don't tell lies
2. Be able to fight	B. Don't be vain
3. Be truthful	C. Don't start fights
4. Be strong	D. Don't brag
5. Be smart	E. Don't whine

D O S	*D O N ' T S*
6. Be kind	F. Don't be a baby
7. Have willpower	G. Don't be a stick-in-the-mud
8. Be a good sport	H. Don't be fussy
9. Be loyal	I. Don't be unneighborly
10. Be useful	J. Don't be fresh

Twelve. The turbulence of Eleven abates with maturity and experience. Twelve is much more level-headed in his approach to ethical problems. He is more realistic and he can deliberately weigh the pros and cons, and even figure the points, arithmetically, for and against a course of action. He is less apt to do the wrong thing as he frequently did at eleven. His conscience stands a more severe guard.

He is sensitive to the group opinion of his peers. He is socially, if not ethically, inclined to protect another person by a white lie; but generally Twelve spontaneously tells the truth. Out of a sense of fairness he does not want a friend to be wrongly accused.

Twelve tries to think out things for himself; he shows less dependence upon adults. But in his characteristic balancing way he makes his decision by combining what grownups tell him with what he himself thinks: he can argue an ethical issue calmly and with politeness, but he may also have fixed ideas not too open to reason. Personal considerations may enter into a moral judgment: "People wouldn't like me if I didn't take the blame when I do things"; "I do what mother wants me to, if I'm not mad at mother." All of which goes to show the complexity of ethical attitudes and the slowness of the growth which brings them to the full maturity of a moral adult.

Thirteen. Thirteen advances a step toward higher maturity by thinking about the significance of ethical conduct for others. He is now less apt to consider the advantages in terms of self alone. He takes more factors into account, and exercises what he calls "my judgment." With his inwardizing proclivities he likes to probe into these matters through his own thought processes. This does not prevent him from doing something slightly wrong, just for the experimental fun of it, to evoke a reaction from his teacher. He is responsible enough to take blame for a misdeed; but sometimes he blames others as a joke. Even the development of an ethical sense is not all somber and disciplinary. It has a lighter side in humor and in the reciprocal banter of personal relationships.

At this maturity level the group opinion is more exacting than the conscience of the individual. Thirteen feels the temptation of cheating, particularly at examination time; but would not think of reporting another's infraction, for he detests a squealer.

Thirteen often shows an intellectual interest in ethical questions. This makes him ready to argue and to discuss issues with his parents. Both boys and girls listen to reason, but at the same time they keep a tenacious hold on their own ideas. Says one boy, "They [the parents] can change my mind, but I still want to do it in my mind." One girl says, "They can change my mind pretty easily. If they're asking my opinion I can't change my opinion very well, but I would give in on what to do." Day by day the ethical sense organizes by resolving tensions which may arise between adult and youth.

Fourteen. Tensions are somewhat relaxed at this maturity level. The conscience of Fourteen tends to operate less dogmatically. He distinguishes between right and wrong with greater ease. He depends on natural instinct, on the feel of things, and also on common sense in arriving at judgments: "I just know." "I know it automatically." There are many individual differences, but his mind now seems to be moving toward the broader field of moral values.

The thinking of Fourteen is less focalized and more liberal. He takes arguing more lightly and makes it a kind of game to enjoy. One boy comments, "I'm pretty ethical. Not basically incorrigible." A girl of fourteen, with a dash of humor says, "If in a problem, I would ask mother. Then would allow myself about 5 per cent more freedom because I want to have fun; 5 per cent because she is old-fashioned, and 5 per cent 'cause I know she'll allow for my taking off. So I do about 85 per cent of what she says." Again we see what intricate and tenuous webs are woven while the ethical sense gathers force and form.

The mood of Fourteen becomes serious when he contemplates social injustice. He now considers with some earnestness public issues, such as minority rights, prison reform, juvenile delinquency, segregation, totalitarianism. This is a new kind of ethical awareness which is destined to expand in the oncoming years. It is taking him from a restricted self into the wide realm of moral values.

Fifteen. The trend toward broader and more abstract thinking is evident during this stage of development. Fifteen is more aware of the structure of society. He is beginning to apprehend the function of standards, manners and customs, principles and codes. This makes his thinking more conceptual. He may also perceive the safeguards of family life and the value of his parents' counsel in a new light. He himself is beginning to feel the *need* of ethical conduct: "I have to tell the truth, because people wouldn't trust me."

Broad and vague moral problems seem to challenge him. He turns them over in his mind and tries to think them through to a conclusion. This self-examination is one way in which, almost consciously, he builds up his ethical attitudes. It is in essence a growth process. Often he likes to argue his viewpoint. Perhaps he clings to it stubbornly, but in many instances it is a sincere defense of his moral outlook (for the time being).

At any rate, Fifteen has a more defined ethical sense than he has had in any previous year. It has become enriched and organized in much the same way that his general intelligence has developed. Both are subject to cultural influences; both depend upon innate and ordered growth potentials. Even our crude gradients reflect these potentials as they emerge into view throughout the years of youth.

Sixteen. At the sixteen-year level of maturity the ethical sense usually becomes both more flexible and more stable. This is a cardinal sign of relative maturity. Conscience is not obtrusive, because the judgment of Sixteen is often sure enough in itself. But the conscience is there if it needs to intervene. For ordinary and practical purposes, Sixteen knows almost instinctively what is right and what is wrong. He and she may even be surprised that their own ideas turn out to be so much like those of their parents.

The relationships between parent and youth rise to a higher plane and become more reciprocal. The footing is on a more equal and grown-up basis. Arguments are less importuning. A mature 16-year-old can discuss privileges and obligations in a candid vein, and he is able to take some account of the parent's point of view. He rather likes "a good healthy dispute."

The greater maturity of Sixteen colors his interpersonal attitudes. Problems of responsibility, decision, and conscience are less acute, for he has attained a wholesome self-assurance. He has achieved a sense of independence, which in its origins and ingredients is closely allied to his underlying, pervasive ethical sense. Far from being a metaphysical fiction, his ethical sense proves to be a growing reality which determines the structure and patterns of his character. It has taken sixteen years of development to bring it to its present level of functioning and there are many potentials yet to be realized.

In other words, the ethical sense is an intangible but unquestionable product of long-term growth. It has its perturbations and crises, but under favoring conditions and a favorable endowment it gradually and rather steadily takes form.

In panoramic retrospect, one can almost detect the movements of the mind toward a distant goal—stage by stage, as follows:

Infantile shame (*18 months*); disregard of approval and disapproval (*2½ years*); obedient conformance (*3 years*); respect for rules (*5 years*); turbulence (*year 6*); responsiveness to ethical appeal (*year 7*); strong insistence on fairness (*year 9*); childlike concreteness and amenability (*year 10*); strong, orderly trends toward deepened self-insight and considerateness for others (*the years from 10 to 16*).

Such in bare outline are the stages by which a youth attains an ethical outlook and moral standards of conduct. His ethical sense is in many ways the most complex attribute of his entire psychological make-up. Like other complex traits it is dependent upon hereditary aptitude and the interaction of constitutional and cultural factors. The underlying growth process which organizes all these factors operates fatefully for good or evil throughout childhood and very especially throughout the years of adolescence.

A Note on the Problem of Juvenile Delinquency

This book is almost entirely concerned with the relatively normal aspects of juvenile behavior. But a chapter on the growth of the ethical sense of youth demands some reference to the vast problem of juvenile delinquency. In the next twelve months, it is estimated that one million boys and girls under the age of twenty-one will commit "crimes" serious enough to be picked up by the police. (The criminal law of the State of New York defines an adult as a person sixteen years of age or older—the age group below sixteen being called *juvenile delinquents*. The group sixteen through twenty is called *youthful offenders*.) Recent statistics for New York State show a startling increase of delinquent acts by the younger boys, sixteen, seventeen, and eighteen years of age. (Boys outnumber girls four to one.)

From a developmental standpoint the age trends revealed by records of the FBI and the U.S. Children's Bureau are particularly significant. The majority of delinquent youths who come before juvenile courts are between fifteen and seventeen years of age. The age at which the largest number are first apprehended by the police or referred to court seems to be between thirteen and fifteen. Nine-tenths of these children had difficulty in adjusting to normal life before age eleven and more than a third of the total group showed "noticeable signs of becoming delinquent at the age of eight or younger."

These age trends strongly indicate the importance of a developmental approach to the problem of juvenile delinquency. Where shall we look for the origins of delinquent behavior with all its multiple facets? Broken homes, quarrelsome and neglectful parents, slum neighborhoods, inadequate school and recreation facilities, gangs, misadventures, and a host of environmental influences combine to precipitate acts of delinquency.

These influences, physical and interpersonal, make up the culture in which the child lives and has his being. But why is one child markedly susceptible to adverse circumstances and surroundings, while another adjusts and remains relatively stable? The difference is one of individual constitution. We should know more about the assets and liabilities of each child—his innate capacity to grow and his demonstrated patterns of development. His ways of growth offer a basic clue to the constitutional factors which underlie his conduct and his ability to adjust to the normal demands of life.

From the standpoint of long-range prevention and of timely guidance, the early detection of pre-delinquent traits is fundamental. We should reach the potentially delinquent child well before his first contact with a law-enforcing agency. This can be accomplished only by taking realistic account of constitutional, developmental factors. Cautiously and by progressive steps we should identify the individual child who needs very special consideration because of the immaturity and faulty organization of his total behavior equipment, including his ethical sense.

Ideally, the protection of child development demands provisions for the periodic diagnosis and supervision of physical and mental health needs. Preventive pediatrics and child psychiatry are already showing trends in this direction. The extraordinary progress of present-day medical and biological sciences suggests that the democratic concept of universal education will gradually broaden to include the general developmental welfare of the individual infant and the growing child. Education at all levels would then be more deeply concerned with the laws and mechanisms of growth, with growth potentials, and the conservation of favorable potentials. This concern would extend to all types of individuals, normal and atypical.

By safeguarding the individual, a socially oriented system of developmental supervision promotes the aims of democracy. This would shift the preventive problem of juvenile delinquency into the wide realm of public health, where it must eventually go if we wish to strike at root origins.

GROWTH GRADIENTS

1. RIGHT AND WRONG

10 YEARS

Distinguishing. A slight majority of our Tens—more girls than boys—report that they can tell right from wrong. But nearly as many (far more than at other ages) admit simply that they cannot. Nearly all are definite, one way or the other; responses are only rarely qualified ("Usually, but not always. I'm not really hot at that.")

Most say they distinguish by what their mothers tell them or what they learn in Sunday school, a few by conscience. ("Conscience usually tells me if it's wrong—and then I wait till mummy bawls me out to see if it is.")

More concerned about what is wrong than what is right, and very specific in their concepts: "I'd know if an example was wrong"; "If I stepped in a brook and got my feet wet . . ."; "If you wanted to chop down a tree, the first thing you'd use a saw and not an ax if great bunches of people were around."

Doing. Most report that they try to be good most of the time, and many that they succeed. Some try and fail. "Sometimes I do a few bad things, but I try to be a good boy."

Ten's standards for right and wrong acts of *others* are very high.

Conscience. Most girls say their conscience does bother them; boys either allow that it does, or expect that it would if they ever did wrong. Some mention that it depends on the deed. But most are not bothered excessively, "It's just there handy." A smaller number, mostly girls, are untroubled by conscience.

A few are not sure what conscience is: "Something that tells you when you've forgotten something?"

11 YEARS

Distinguishing. The majority state they can tell right from wrong. Fewer than at ten simply cannot tell, but many more can only "usually" tell. Some, girls especially, report more difficulty: "Right and wrong puzzles me"; "I don't think anybody knows."

The most still say they depend on the teachings of parents and Sunday school; some combine parents' ideas with their own. Conscience tells a few, and some try to figure things out for themselves.

Doing.   Boys claim to be better than girls do; by far the majority say they try to do right all the time—or nearly always. Most girls admit that they sometimes do wrong. "I know what's right, but I don't always *do* what's right."

Some Elevens say it is fun to do wrong sometimes, or "might do wrong on purpose if mad at mother." Several mention a relativity: might do wrong against someone they disliked. Some do wrong and ask friends to promise not to tell parents.

Conscience.   Though the majority, boys especially, say they are bothered by conscience when they do wrong, most qualify this: "If it was *really* wrong," "except when I'm really roaring mad."

But more than at other ages, and more girls, state that they are not bothered when they do wrong—either because they enjoy it ("usually sort of *glad* when I'm bad; sort of nice to let yourself go"), or "because I usually don't think it's wrong."

12 YEARS

Distinguishing.   Great variability. The most report they can, nearly as many "usually" can, but a sizable number still feel they can not tell right from wrong.

Less dependence on adult concepts is reported. More are now trying to figure things out for themselves, and decide by combining what grownups tell them with what they themselves think. Some, especially boys, say they "just know."

Doing.   Nearly half—again more girls than boys—admit to doing at least an occasional wrong, especially if it was just "slightly wrong." Some say they dislike children who are "too good."

Conscience.   Twelve seems bothered more by conscience than was Eleven. The great majority have "big" consciences—"My conscience is hard on me"; "It causes a lot of trouble." Many fewer are simply unconcerned by conscience, though with many it depends on the "badness" of what they have done. The extremes of both the nagging and the *laissez-faire* conscience are less evident.

13 YEARS

Distinguishing.   Few Thirteens feel simply unable to distinguish right and wrong; the majority conservatively state that they *usually* can do so. A few boys admit "a little bit of trouble in telling." Their own judgment is very important to them, and they may "figure it out," or (more often with boys) "just automatically know." Some are helped to figure by thinking what people (sometimes mother) *would* say.

Doing. A majority say they try to do right nearly always, though some do feel it is fun to be bad sometimes—especially in school. Boys' responses are more similar to those given by girls at twelve—about evenly divided between those who do right "nearly always," and those who admit to occasional wrongdoing.

Conscience. Thirteen tends to qualify his statements about conscience. An increasing number now make the hypothetical statement that conscience *would* bother them if they did wrong, and many others say it bothers them *sometimes*: "It depends—if I thought it was justified it wouldn't"; "Wouldn't bother if it was just something the *school* thought wrong."

A number of boys claim to be untroubled by conscience, while others, and especially girls, describe their consciences as very "firm" and several say they would *brood* if they did wrong.

14 YEARS

Distinguishing. Fourteen appears more definite than did Thirteen—many fewer say they *usually* can tell, but more, especially girls, say that they are unable to tell right from wrong. The uncertainty seems to arise from increasing dependence on their own judgment, and the discrepancy between this and their parents' ideas: "The way my mother would think I should do and the way I feel would be best are often two radically different things. I do what would work out best with the kids and then I sort of temper it down with my mother."

The attempts of both boys and girls to weigh alternatives ("Figure out who it would benefit and who it would harm") often result in strong emphasis on relativity, with things considered worse in some circumstances than others, or, "Wouldn't tell a *big* lie"; "Wouldn't do anything *very* wrong."

Doing. Wrongdoing in *little* things is admitted by a great many Fourteens— actually a majority of the boys. But most "wouldn't do *really* wrong, like stealing," and they themselves frequently do not think of what they do as actually wrong, but feel their parents would consider it so.

Conscience. The largest number are only potentially troubled by conscience ("It *would* bother me . . ."). A large minority of boys, feel "pretty hard-boiled," or have their consciences "pretty well trained." "It might bother; it depends. If I thought it was justified it wouldn't."

15 YEARS

Distinguishing. Fifteen again takes a more conservative path, less often stating that he can tell, or that he cannot, but saying "usually." Many are very much interested in problems of ethics, and girls especially have a great deal to say about it.

Most are trying to arrive at decisions for themselves, and say that parents' ideas are just one factor in deciding. But some realize that how they have been brought up is a strong influence, even when they feel they are thinking things out for themselves. They refer not to what parents *teach*, but to what they *have taught*.

And, as one mother says, "It is no longer black or white, but gray," as some Fifteens are beginning to think of behavior as "adequate," "thoughtful," "considerate," rather than right or wrong. Many now feel that they see the need for honesty and fairness better than they did earlier.

Doing. An increasing number is aware of at least occasional wrongdoing, often stating, "I *know* right, but don't always *do* it." Some say they do wrong "sort of unconsciously," or they "just don't think." But others sometimes have to "talk myself into it that something is right that is wrong."

As deciding factors, they mention they might do wrong if the punishment would not be too bad if discovered, or if the deed would not harm others.

Conscience. Fifteen shows less complete denial of conscience than Fourteen. Most have, or would have, a guilty conscience, though some vary or would feel guilty about important things only. Social concern is more strongly emphasized—it would bother them if the deed were going to hurt anyone. Boys are more likely to admit actual pain from conscience; girls more often say conscience would bother them if they did wrong.

16 YEARS

Distinguishing. None of our Sixteens say that they cannot tell right from wrong. A slight majority of boys state simply, yes, they can tell. Girls much more often say they *usually* can tell. Boys also more often say that they "just know instinctively," while girls are more aware of a reasoning process in deciding.

Girls say they are influenced by what their parents (especially mother) "and society" think. Several, in fact, specifically ask themselves, "Would mother approve?" when deciding. A few girls report a trial-and-error method—when in doubt they go ahead and do what they wanted; then if it turns out badly they know better next time.

Both boys and girls surprisingly often say that their own ideas and those of their parents now "go along together very well."

Doing. A majority of our Sixteens say they do right most of the time, or **try** to do so. Several, both boys and girls, say they wouldn't do anything they wouldn't do in front of their mothers, but many state, "I don't always do what's right."

Fewer girls than boys state flatly that they always *do* do right, and several realize they are swayed by their own desires, or influenced by their friends. A minority of boys, too, make such frank admissions as, "I don't go out of my way to do right."

Conscience. Sixteen seems to have conscience in hand reasonably well. Most say they have a conscience, but few say flatly that they are pained by it— the fewest of any age. Girls most often say they *would* be, if they did something wrong; boys most often say they *sometimes* are, depending on the misdeed. And several boys (no girls) say that conscience seldom **or** never bothers them.

2. SENSE OF FAIRNESS

10 YEARS

Fairness. In 10-year-olds' reporting, fairness is very important, and they are especially concerned that their parents treat them fairly.

Taking blame. Very few take blame if they can get out of it; nearly all will try to push it off onto a sibling or someone else. Alibiing is very strong— someone else always started any difficulty. Many Tens admit quite frankly, "I wouldn't bother taking the blame for something I did. Would say I didn't do it if they blamed my brother for something I did and he said I did it."

11 YEARS

Fairness. Eleven is very exacting that things must be fair. Especially he insists that parents should be fair to him—and is apt to think they are not, particularly in regard to siblings.

Taking blame. Most Elevens still at least try to blame someone else or to alibi. As at ten, "If they were blaming my sister for something I did, I would shut up. Even if they asked me outright, if they still had my sister blamed for it, I'd shut up." Girls take blame slightly better than do boys.
The high point for: "You always blame *me!*"

12 YEARS

Fairness. Twelves are quite exacting, boys perhaps more than girls, and many still report feeling that parents are not fair, especially with regard to siblings.

The viewpoint expressed still emphasizes that others should be (but are not) fair to them.

Taking blame. A real change occurs between eleven and twelve. Quite a few still do blame others, or vary, depending on how much trouble it may make for them. But now a majority say that they do take blame for things they have done. Some girls say, "People wouldn't like me if I didn't."

Rather than shifting blame, many are concerned with explaining *why* they did the thing.

13 YEARS

Fairness. Fairness at school is now an important concern. It is essential to Thirteen that teachers and principal be fair—and often he thinks they are not.

Taking blame. Much variation appears here—from child to child, and in one child from time to time. ("Depends on the situation. I think everybody hesitates a little bit before owning up to something.")

At least as many will now admit their own fault as try to blame others, and this is the first age at which some state definitely that they will *not* blame others. "Used to push the blame off on others, but now I try to do better."

14 YEARS

Fairness. As at thirteen, the unfairness most resented is any on the part of a teacher. More now show concern about whether people other than themselves are treated fairly, some even worrying about pupils' unfairness to a teacher.

Taking blame. Most report that they do take blame and do not blame others. Almost none now say they consistently blame siblings or others. Some, however, do not blame people but do blame situations—and may emphasize the wrong aspect of the situation.

15 YEARS

Fairness. Fairness is still a major concern with many. Some are spreading out to an interest in fairness not only for themselves and friends, but for minority groups and any individuals of lesser status.

Taking blame. Now nearly all take blame themselves, and make an effort not to blame others. "Against my principles to blame others—though I might." Some are reported as especially concerned with shouldering blame: "He almost goes too far in excusing others."

16 YEARS

Fairness.   Fairness to individuals with fewer advantages is a concern for many.

Taking blame.   As at fifteen, nearly all are good about taking blame themselves, and will not blame others—"Unless they are to blame." Many explain they don't blame others wrongly because they don't like to be wrongly blamed themselves. Some do say they "like a little company" if the offense was serious, and admit that their readiness to admit wrongdoing might depend on potential severity of punishment.

3. RESPONSE TO REASON

10 YEARS

Listening to reason.   Ten is reported to listen to reason customarily, or at least sometimes. Certainly Ten tries harder to be reasonable than do the ages to follow.

Arguing with parents.   About half our group admit to arguing sometimes. Most try to be polite, and most *try* to mind, but may sometimes ask, "Why do I have to?" Some get so MAD they can't help arguing. But if Ten does argue, it is to win his point, not just for the fun of it.

11 YEARS

Listening to reason.   Even according to his own reporting, Eleven is at a high point for not listening to reason: "Rather do what I plan; not easily convinced"; "Hard to persuade me. I put up quite a bit of resistance"; "I stick to my own way."

Arguing with parents.   The majority report that they argue sometimes—girls a little more often than boys, who may feel that arguing is a waste of time.

A differential response is sometimes reported: "Not with father but with mother."

The beginning of reports of arguing "sometimes for things I want, sometimes for the sake of arguing."

12 YEARS

Listening to reason.   Twelves still view themselves as quite stubborn, though most will at least sometimes listen to reason. Boys more stubborn than girls: "I stick to things. Not easy for people to change me."

Arguing with parents.   Well over half our subjects admit to arguing sometimes, though some (boys especially) say they "don't dare" because of the consequences. Fathers may be firmer with boys than with girls about this. Twelve may sometimes argue "for the fun of it," but the majority still argue primarily to win their point.

13 YEARS

Listening to reason. The most docile age, according to Thirteen's own reporting. Thus: "I can listen to reason. If the reason was better than my own I would change." However, "They can change my mind, but I still want to do it in my mind."

Arguing with parents. As at twelve, the majority admit that they argue—mostly to gain a point, but occasionally for the exercise involved.

14 YEARS

Listening to reason. Fourteen sees himself as much more resistant than did Thirteen. As many recognize that they do not listen to reason as feel they do. "They can't convince me—I'm hard to convince." Many are impatient with the adult point of view: "I sit there and wait till they finish, and then I tell them what I think . . . and I usually win."

Arguing with parents. Most argue at least sometimes. The fewest girls of any age say they do not. Arguing for the sake of argument is quite strong: "I argue just about anything cause it's fun to argue . . . Don't know if my parents think so."

15 YEARS

Listening to reason. More than do Fourteens, Fifteens describe themselves as open to reason—*if* they think the reason is a good one. But few are consistently reasonable ("Probably don't have too open a mind if my *family* reasoned with me"), and some say they would *listen* but would not change their minds.

Arguing with parents. Most argue at least sometimes, many a good deal of the time. Arguments often concern theoretical issues as much as practical ones. ("She should have been a lawyer.")

Though sometimes the subject and its outcome are of primary importance, many arguments occur just for love of the sport. Boys, even more than girls, find pleasure in argument. "I never accept anything my parents say as absolute truth." "It gives me great satisfaction to prove them wrong."

16 YEARS

Listening to reason. Most feel they listen to reason fairly well—boys somewhat less than girls. However, there is considerable disagreement in situations where they themselves hold strong opinions. Some say they can be swayed by the opinion of friends, but "have a front against my parents so mostly stick to my own way."

Arguing with parents.   Almost without exception, boys and girls in our group do argue with their parents. The more mature (or more intellectual) say that they "discuss more than argue," and that both they and their parents enjoy it.

As occurred earlier, however, many argue not for the sake of argument but to win their point. Arguments are more about privileges than about abstract issues. Many become very angry, and arguments may be bitter—even though most feel that arguing doesn't really do any good, because parents won't admit it when wrong.

4. HONESTY

10 YEARS

Cheating.   Ten has a strict code, and feels that "cheating is awful." Most Tens say specifically that they would not cheat, though a few report one or two children at school who do.

Stealing.   No children admit to stealing. Many comment that stealing is very bad. Some might be tempted, but many know they would feel "awful" if they did; others know the consequences would be too bad. Several say they know children who do steal, and remark on the badness of this.

Truthfulness.   Most Tens are described as "quite" or "usually" truthful, straying only sometimes, or telling just "white lies." Many say they *try* to tell the truth, but a large number—boys especially—"sometimes do and sometimes don't" tell the truth. A few more girls than boys are described as "strictly" truthful, but more girls are also described as untruthful. Several Tens themselves admit they are untruthful, and are described by mothers as telling "whoppers."

11 YEARS

Cheating.   Though stating that they themselves would not cheat, many Elevens show much concern (as did Six) about others who do. Most report that some of the children at school cheat, girls frequently saying that most boys cheat on exams.

Some say they used to cheat when younger, though they no longer do.

Stealing.   Most say that they never do, but that they know people (even own twin) who steal either from stores or from their mother's pocketbook.

Many are troubled about this, and most comment that it is a bad idea or wrong. One or two admit they used to, but say, "No longer."

From reports other than their own, it appears that more girls than boys are likely to be involved in an episode of pilfering at eleven.

Truthfulness. The majority are now, according to their mothers, "pretty truthful." Among boys, the groups showing the extremes of rigorous truthfulness and of downright untruthfulness (which appeared among girls at ten) now appear.

Standards for themselves appear to be high in a great many, even though they may not live up to these standards ("I'm not as truthful as George Washington, or anything"). Girls more often emphasize that they are truthful in the *big* things, boys that "it depends on how much of a jam I'm in."

12 YEARS

Cheating. Compared with Ten, Twelve shows a very casual attitude toward cheating. Many say they would not cheat, but others say they might if they had to, and quite a few say that they do ("All the kids do—we help each other out").

Stealing. A similar change appears. Most say that they themselves do not steal. But a few—boys more than girls—admit to occasional stealing, several mentioning the "fun" of it. A great many say they "know kids" who steal, mostly from ten-cent stores, and may add, "They charge too much anyway."

Some seem mildly admiring of others who steal.

Truthfulness. The majority are "quite truthful," or "medium," and may vary from time to time. Many say that they try to be, or are, in the big things, and that they tell a "reasonable amount" of truth, but "sometimes you have to tell lies if you have a good reason."

13 YEARS

Cheating. Thirteen reports that a few classmates cheat, but most do not. Most 13-year-olds disapprove of others' cheating, and do not admit to doing so themselves—unless there is some good reason.

Stealing. Pilfering from stores is less frequently reported—even in Thirteen's mention of "the other kids." The thrill element is somewhat discounted: "What's the use of going and lifting little whistles?"

Truthfulness. According to Thirteens' own reports, they seem to be less truthful than earlier. This may be partly a matter of greater accuracy (and truthfulness) in reporting, rather than an actual decline in truthfulness, though parents tend to concur in reporting fewer Thirteens as strictly veracious.

The change is not to complete falsity, but to a recognition of partial truth: "I don't always tell the *whole* thing"; "Might embroider the truth a little." Most departures from the truth are either to save someone's feelings, or to gloss things over (e.g., bad grades).

A few parents do report, "He's much too honest—much too ethical."

14 YEARS

Cheating. Boys and girls have more to say about cheating now than they did earlier. Most feel that there is not too much cheating at school: "I think most kids are pretty honest. A few will cheat if they have the advantage." But the situation clearly differs from school to school, and even from class to class. Some report that "75 to 80 per cent of the kids" cheat; others that school is run on the honor system, and almost no one cheats.

In their own practices, a slightly qualified honesty seems to prevail—some are honest *except* ("except in Latin") and others are honest *if* (if they respect the teacher). Some say it is confusing because some teachers allow you to check your work with other pupils more than others do.

Stealing. As usual, they do not admit to stealing themselves. When discussing others' stealing, Fourteen no longer appears shocked (as at ten) or slightly admiring (as at twelve), but rather understanding: "I think it's something she'll grow out of."

Truthfulness. The great majority are "usually" or "reasonably" truthful, though this seems to allow quite a lot of leeway. Fewer boys than girls admit to real untruths, but nearly all admit that they exaggerate, tell white lies, or lie in unimportant situations. Though a few admit to being downright untruthful, Fourteen seems to feel it is better to be truthful, in general, and a few girls say they "feel queer" if they are not.

15 YEARS

Cheating. Fifteen seems to feel more strongly about cheating. Most say that they themselves do not cheat, and some say they would rather flunk than cheat. Nearly all state that a few in their class do, but all seem to think this wrong. "I will not help a person who wants an answer."

Stealing. Most of our subjects say not only that they do not steal, but that they do not know anyone who does. Increasingly cited is the concept that it really doesn't pay, because if you do steal people don't trust you.

The power of the social group is shown in one response, however: "I wouldn't unless you had to do it to get in good with your clique."

Truthfulness. As at fourteen, by far the majority feel they are "reasonably" truthful. Several comment that it is best to tell the truth, because then people can count on you. As earlier, most might shade the truth if the truth would hurt someone, but they try to "keep as close to the truth as possible."

16 YEARS

Cheating. All our Sixteens say they would not cheat in any situation, except perhaps examinations. Here they differ widely. Some say, "Oh, we all cheat in exams," others say they don't know anybody who cheats. Still others say there is no point in cheating except getting better marks, so it's not worth it since "cheating isn't you."

Stealing. As at fifteen, no stealing is reported by our subjects, either by themselves or by acquaintances.

Truthfulness. Nearly all the boys we interviewed at sixteen, and about half the girls, are "medium" or "usually" truthful. A sizable group of girls, and a few boys, are extremely truthful, however. These report that the truth "just comes naturally"—"I can't possibly tell a lie, even if I plan to." A few of the boys say they are truthful "because if I get caught telling a lie the results are too bad."

The majority, usually truthful, occasionally tell a white or social lie, or might exaggerate a little "if telling my adventures to a friend." And several say they do not lie to their parents, but just neglect to tell about some things.

5. SWEARING, DRINKING, AND SMOKING

10 YEARS

Swearing. Most Tens consider that it is "bad" or "not nice" to swear, and "feel awful" if they do. Some say, "I don't, but sometimes I'd like to," and a few profligates say, "I do, but I shouldn't."

Nearly all feel that grownups, especially their own parents, should not swear.

Drinking. Some feel that it is all right for adults to drink if they don't drink too much, but some are extremely critical of any drinking by adults.

Smoking. No girl mentions having tried smoking. An occasional boy is discovered by his parents smoking, or having smoked, but the activity is at a purely experimental level.

11 YEARS

Swearing. Eleven is frequently against swearing—"I don't like it and I don't do it." Some also don't like to hear it, and may even cover their ears when anyone does.

Though most try not to, some do swear, but are particular about not doing so in front of certain people. "Boys in our room don't swear when girls are around," or, "Not in front of other boys." A few think it is fun—"sounds real group-up."

Some who swear use as an excuse that their parents do. However, a great many report that swearing is "bad for anyone, but worse for grownups," since it sets a bad example for children.

Drinking. The majority feel that it is all right for adults to drink, if they don't drink too much, or if they drink "just beer," or "just cocktails."

Smoking. Smoking is not reported by any girls. Boys who smoke secretly do not admit it to adults, and it is not, in our group, reported by mothers. Such smoking as does occur is extremely sporadic.

12 YEARS

Swearing. Several Twelves admit that they do occasionally swear, usually when angry, though most feel they ought not to. Several think that it is all right for children ("All the kids do at school") but wrong for grown-ups, as it sets a bad example. This may be varied somewhat: "For grown-up women it's bad. For men it's not as bad because they're men." Boys as well as girls are extremely sensitive about their parents' swearing, and think it "sounds awful."

Drinking. The majority continue to say it is all right for adults, provided they don't drink too much. (Most are far more permissive about adults' drinking than about their swearing.)

Smoking. Girls still do not report smoking, and most boys have not smoked except on rare occasion. The general attitude is typified by: "I wouldn't smoke because I don't like the taste of it and it gives me hay fever, but I don't object to anyone else doing it."

13 YEARS

Swearing. Some are more critical of swearing, in children or adults, than at twelve. These feel that it is "horrible" or "ill-bred," though they may admit that it is "excusable" under certain circumstances.

Some report that though others swear they try not to, or do so only under their breaths.

Some boys, however, say they do swear—some have to be "one of the gang." And a few are often very profane, or even obscene, even in talk with their mothers.

Drinking. Though a few are much against drinking, most still are willing for adults to drink if they do not drink "too much."

Most girls do not drink at all; most boys do not drink beyond an occasional glass of beer—this mostly at home.

Smoking. Most girls simply say they do not smoke. Many boys say they have smoked occasionally, but don't make a habit of it. Some say they do it "just to go along with the gang."

14 YEARS

Swearing. "I don't think you should, but I do," is a most characteristic comment. Many report that "all" their friends swear, or "everybody does except ministers." The words used matter to some, who permit *damn* and *hell* but not naming of the Deity.

Most feel that it is not right for children to swear, but that grownups (men) may if they want to. Some girls feel that it is O.K. for boys, but not for girls and parents. Especially, they do not want their mothers to swear.

Drinking. In discussing drinking, most now spontaneously refer to the practices of contemporaries, rather than of adults. Drinking or not drinking has become a contemporary problem.

Girls most often say that they and their friends do not drink yet, but that some of the boys do at parties—and most feel that this is all right, if they can "hold their liquor."

Boys either say they do not, or admit to drinking an occasional beer.

Smoking. Many girls say they have smoked, or do smoke occasionally, but not regularly, giving such justifications as: "Something to do with your hands"; "People would think I was a baby if I didn't." Girls report that many of the girls at school smoke—"To show off, I'm sure, but they speak of it as if it were their very existence."

Some boys smoke, though none say that they do it regularly. Many report that "all the boys at school smoke."

15 YEARS

Swearing. The majority of our subjects admit to swearing sometimes. Most no longer think of it as absolutely "wrong," just as something that doesn't sound nice.

Much greater tolerance is expressed for the swearing of others (except their mothers)—"If others do, it's their business, not mine." However, most still feel that adults' swearing is a poor example for children.

Both the words and the amount used seem quite important—*darn, damn,* and *hell* are considered innocuous, though even these should not be used to excess.

Drinking. Though more interested in discussing the drinking of contemporaries, most still say it is all right for adults to drink in moderation, but are critical of overindulgence. ("We went from one party to another, and sat around and watched the other kids' parents get drunk. Took a girl home and her father was pie-eyed.")

Most girls say they do not drink, though some report beginning to have one drink at parties. "The girls drink a little when there's a party, not too much. Some of the boys drink too much, but not many. No real problem."

About half the boys in our group say they do not drink—think they are too young. Others mostly admit to some beer, and an occasional whiskey. Many say, "Just enough to be sociable." Boys report that there is drinking at parties, but usually not enough to cause any trouble.

Smoking. Quite a few of the girls now admit to smoking occasionally, but almost none do so regularly. Most who say they smoke do so at home— mother would rather know about it.

Some boys now smoke quite a bit, but the majority do not report that they smoke regularly.

16 YEARS

Swearing. Most are now tolerant of swearing, feeling that it is a "part of everyday life," and that "at times nothing else will suffice." However, most also feel that you should not swear too much and that there are times and places where it is not acceptable.

Some of the more immature are trying not to swear.

Drinking. Concern about adults' drinking is no longer expressed, only about that of contemporaries.

Fewer than half our girls drink, even on occasion. Of those who do, it is usually "just one drink to be polite." Most report of girl friends and acquaintances, "Very few drink, and almost no girls that I know drink too much."

Of the boys in our group, half report that they do not drink anything. Of the rest, most drink "only beer" or "beer, mostly." Very few report drinking gin or whiskey. However, many report that "lots of the kids drink." Several say that some of the senior boys "get tanked."

Smoking. More than half our boys actually do not smoke: they are on an athletic team, have bargained with father not to, just don't care about it, or "did but gave it up."

As many girls smoke as boys, though almost none do so extensively. Several also report that about half the girls they know smoke. Of those who smoke, most know that their parents do not favor it, so they try to limit the amount. One girl comments of friends who smoke, "They start doing it to show off, but then they get into the habit."

CHAPTER NINETEEN

Philosophic Outlook

PHILOSOPHY is systematized knowledge. It is concerned with the nature of man and his relations to the universe in which he lives. Philosophy had its primitive beginnings in the remote past when man began to utter words and to link them with his thoughts and desires. After immense ages he was able to arrange his language and ideas in more or less rational sequences. His philosophic outlook continues to change with every advance and setback in his civilization. His philosophies reflect his evolution.

By similar token the philosophies of children and youth reflect the mental growth of the individual. The young child makes no intellectual distinction between subjective and objective, between his inner life and the outer world. The outer world with its trees and earth, clouds and houses, is regarded as a virtual extension of himself. Nature is endowed with his own feelings and purposes. Even his imaginary playmates are real like himself (be careful not to sit on them!). Five and Six believe that anything which moves must be alive. Seven shows great interest in magic, wishing stones, and tricks. Nine may have a strong faith in luck and superstitions; but he also displays an emerging capacity for framing critical judgments.

During the ensuing years from ten to sixteen this capacity shows a steady increase in the form of conceptual thinking. Knowledge becomes more systematized and abstract. Words are employed as tools to define ideas and feelings. This does not mean that a youth now deliberately sets out to build and perfect a system of concepts. **Nevertheless, his daily** experiences yield an implicit philosophy which takes changing shape under the influence of spontaneous growth impulses. To characterize his philosophy at any given age, it would be necessary to consider the significant maturity traits which he manifested in various behavior fields —interpersonal, ethical, emotional; school life; interests and activities and also the domain of the growing self.

Philosophic outlook depends upon attitudes as well as upon intellectual content. We found an impressive degree of interest in philosophic questions on the part of our research group. For many of our young subjects this was the favorite area of discussion during the interview session. In the eagerness of exchange the questions were often redirected back to the interviewer. Our explorations were informal rather than systematic. We selected as key topics "Time and Space" and "Death and Deity." These themes lie at opposite poles of impersonality and personal interest, but they fall in the domain of philosophy. They at least offer a challenge to the intellect which is undergoing a surge of development in this period of adolescence. To obtain a direct glimpse of the mental operations we shall freely quote the exact language used by our subjects. Their very own words will testify to the spirited effort of their striving minds.

Space has priority over time in development. Space is a form of awareness which derives from the outside; it is an outer experience. Time, on the contrary, originates from within; it is an inner experience. The adult philosopher may combine the two forms of experience. But the infant is space-minded: he uses space words like "up" and "down," "in" and "out," and "turn around" as early as the age of two. By three years of age he distinguishes the three aspects of time: past, present, and future, and makes remarkably fast progress in using basic time words such as "tomorrow," "pretty soon," "It's time." At eight years of age he can tell time and distinguishes right and left in spatial situations. Orientations of time and space organize under the joint influences of maturity and experience. The practical capacity to manage time and space undergoes correlated changes.

What Is Time?

Ten—What is time?—Ten's concept is typically static, specific, and concrete. "It is something that the watch tells." "Time means the clock." "A clock tells time." Some statements are more dynamic: "Time is something that passes." "Time is an excuse because you can always find time. So it is always really an excuse." "Time is days past or future; time is seasons, time is centuries." The characteristic concreteness of Ten is evident in these formulations.

Eleven has a more dynamic sense of time. He feels its inevitable, relentless passing. "No one can stop it, even if you break all the clocks." Eleven adds a truly philosophic observation: "Time never goes backward." "All the time, time is going by."

Both Ten and Eleven are fairly responsible in meeting the demands of time. Yet time may drag or fly too fast on occasion. Ten is a split-minute precisionist in terminating the period of time assigned for piano practice.

Twelve has interesting and somewhat revealing difficulties in defining time. Time is referred to persons or places and it is linked with spaces. "A period of, well, time. Well, it's a space of moments of different phases which goes on, never ending. . . . Sometimes I want to do more things than I have time for; sometimes I dawdle but very rarely." The foregoing was by a boy; this by a girl: "It means the whole span of life on earth. Apt to be in sort of a rush; too much to do . . . usually time for dates. School sometimes I'm a little late, not really late but not there early."

Thirteen. His concept tends to be less fluid. His definitions are more static. Time is a space, a period, or an interval *between* two happenings. "It marks spaces in life, I guess." "Time is still my enemy." "Never enough time." He is prone to be caught in a last-minute rush—"those decisive five minutes."

Fourteen seems to sense the complexity and variety of time factors. He may take a global view and remark that, "The world is run by time." "It is how long it takes for the earth to go around the sun." "Time means a period of hours or any other measure." "Things grow, things die; anything can happen." Some statements suggest that time produces events. "Just the passing of events, and if you are in a dark cell with four walls and ceiling and floor (making six) and staring at a dark wall all your life, you don't have any time."

Fifteen. Definitions again take on a static formulation, in an effort to be more profound and abstract. There are flashes of adult insight, mixed with simple ingenuousness. "Time is stable. It's what we don't have too much of. It's what we try to pattern to. . . . It's one thing that is *unchangeable*. It can't be made." "Time to me is the extent of space filled up by various doings." "Time is sort of like an interval of space." "Time is the thing that controls the fates of all men."

Sixteen apparently has a more fluent and adaptable sense of time. He defines it in terms of action and process, with emphasis on its forward movement from the past into the future. "The passing of generations, people, and events, happenings." "The interval between one occasion and another." "It is the dimension through which we move from birth to death."

The sense of time and the attitude toward time are highly subjective phenomena. They vary enormously with individuality. Personal and even moral factors may influence the manner in which a given youth utilizes and habitually manages his time. But maturity factors also play a role as shown by the recorded interviews. The concreteness and specificity of Ten ("time is the clock") give way to the dynamic and abstract concepts of the succeeding ages.

What Is Space?

The concept of space, although more fundamental than that of time, is less intriguing. The interview responses show less variety in definitions. At almost every age space is simply defined as "nothing" or "the place where there is nothing."

Ten reveals his concreteness by relating space to air. "Space is an empty piece of something." *Eleven* elaborates. "Lots of kinds of space. Space in the room. Space where the universe is. Space between a word on the typewriter. Space—I don't think I could get lost in New Haven." A more abstract statement vaguely links it with time: "Space is a noth-ingness that goes on forever." *Twelve* finds space as difficult to explain as time. "Well, air or nothing. Just sort of blank. Plain. Of course plain things don't have to be space, but space is plain." "Something where there isn't anything else." A more personal approach yielded this generalization: "Oh, space is what we live and sleep and eat and die in." *Thirteen* favors the concept of "nothingness"; but also amplifies the idea with far-flung references: "past the sun and stars, vastness, atmosphere, distance." "Space is a vastness." "Space is all around us; and between all the planets and stars. In it minute particles of matter float endlessly."

Fourteen comments even more on the all-inclusiveness of space. "Space is everything. Space is eternity." "Well, it's a place where there is nothing, no air, nothing. Really isn't even a place. Just sort of like eternity." Others are positive that space is something: "Something that occurs between objects." *Fifteen* recognizes the logical antithesis between something and nothing. He likes to discuss a paradox, utilizing knowledge that he has learned. "Space is a vast expanse of gaseous matter." "Space is a vast emptiness though usually filled with the normal aspects of life." "I think that space and time are hooked up, but I don't understand Einstein." "Space is something where nothing is. Though it couldn't really be said to be something. Just nothing—period! How could you have nothing I wonder. How could nothing go on forever? And if it ended what is beyond the end?" *Sixteen* pursues the subject in a freer vein, with more diverse angles of approach. One girl referred to the "loneliness of space." It is "something you can't see or feel." "An element of nature." "A limitless vacuum." "A tremendous expanse of absolute nothing. Out of human comprehension." "All I can say is infinity."

The foregoing verbatim records tell us something of how the mind of the adolescent operates. To read these records in their developmental order is to gain a glimpse of the underlying process of maturation which serves to shape his ideas and experience. Note again the concreteness of Ten compared with the concepts of Sixteen. Ten: "Space is an empty piece of something." Sixteen: "Space is a limitless vacuum."

Death

The problems of death and deity are infinitely more personal and intimate than those of time and space. The comments on these problems are of course influenced emotionally by individual experience and by environmental factors. But they also reflect developmental phases which are based upon the growth of intelligence and other maturity factors. Because of the complexity of the subject we limit ourselves to a sketchy summary of age trends.

Ten is concrete and matter-of-fact. What do you think happens after you die? One out of four replies, "You get buried." About the same number say, "You go to heaven." Others indicate that they have not been there, so wouldn't know. Not much concern is manifested.

Eleven may show what looks like indifference; but he reacts sensitively to the death of a pet dog and is affected by immediate experiences. There are varied ideas as to the fate of the dead. They stay in a "long sleep," "their souls keep on going," they may be reincarnated. By coming back to earth the death process is reversed.

Twelve is generally more concerned. He may shudder with passing dread, or is surmounting an earlier fear. He wants to grapple with the problem; he looks heavenward with awe and wonder and with mixed feelings of fear and love. He asks theoretical questions about afterlife.

Thirteen is more rationalistic in attitude. Many (in our group) show skepticism, neutrality, or indifference. The tendency to theorize about heaven and hell is strong. Death is too remote and inevitable to be dreaded. "Death is the end."

Fourteen is less skeptical; tends if anything to be more concerned about life as the opposite of death. He wants "to live a whole life," but fully accepts the inevitability of death. Is frankly unknowing about life after death.

Fifteen is a skeptical age. Many disbelieve in heaven. They are more earth-bound and may prefer to think that when you die your spirit lives on in those who remember us; but it is "beyond us to know." Fifteen tries to accept death, yet beneath his nonchalance there may be some lingering dread.

Sixteen may not give much thought to death and heaven; but is deeply moved by an experience of death. Speculates rather critically about afterlife. Tends to think that life on earth carries its own inherent retributions and rewards.

Deity

The interview conversations about death and afterlife naturally led to discussions of deity. Here again the concepts pertaining to deity show a marked trend toward increased abstractness in the years from ten to sixteen. More striking developmental changes take place in the period from five to ten. The earlier notions of God are amazingly concrete and animistic. A 5-year-old may believe that when a child falls, it was God who pushed him. This God also pushes the clouds in the sky. The concept of God derives from the child's own father. He thinks of Him as being a man like his father. The identification is so literal that it has been described as the "paternalization" of deity. The 10-year-old retains vestiges of this idea.

Ten does not do much thinking about God. He imagines him, if at all, as an invisible man. Earlier he used to blame God for misfortunes, and even now he may seek God's help to find a lost object. He treats Him as a person, someone to talk to. A few pray. *Eleven* regards Him as "a spirit." The majority (in our group) express a belief in God. They vaguely begin to feel that what happens to you is determined by your acts. Perhaps you lost the prized object if you didn't believe in Him. Eleven prays when he really wants something. *Twelve* relates God to earthly affairs and may define Him as "half spirit, half idea," "half man, half spirit." Twelves may do a great deal of thinking about God and religion, with varying degrees of emotion. They may end up with doubt or a vague certainty, "something that you cannot explain," but reason tells them there is "something controlling everything." There are outright disbelievers who shock their believing friends. *Thirteen* is skeptical, but not necessarily agnostic. He gives thoughtful definitions of God; he wavers between belief and disbelief, and may even be shocked by his own lack of faith. Confirmation makes this an age of decision. He prays. The seat of conflict and doubt shifts to his inner self and the responsibilities of his own life. *Fourteen*. Convictions are now more positive and definitely stated. Again the majority are avowed believers. Their concepts of God are becoming more abstract: "A power over us"; "An idea in people's minds." It is impossible to explain God: "It's just something there, you can't define it." *Fifteen*. Fewer now express a flat disbelief in God. There is more searching amidst uncertainty, rather than rejection. "I half believe, half don't." May think of God as a power or a person. *Sixteen* displays a heightened belief in a Supreme Being but has not built up a continuing relationship with God. He thinks of Him variously as a divine power, as a guiding ruler, as a personal force "neither man nor spirit," as just a feeling. Sixteen has difficulty in putting his idea into words. "It's a mystery to me." "I don't have a concept that satisfies me." "If I had a definite concept He would not be a deity."

Using the word philosophy in a free, non-technical sense, we are justified in concluding that the adolescent is a philosopher of sorts. He may not always be in love with wisdom, but he cannot escape the cumulative consequences of his thoughts, his language, and his maturity. Whether articulate or not, he acquires an outlook upon life and the world about him. The essence and net sum of his impressions and interpretations constitute a philosophy in the making. The net sum keeps changing with the development of his insights and interests.

Our brief examination of his ideas of time, space, death, and deity has shown that he tries to meet the challenge of philosophic problems. He has a latent desire for concepts which clarify or idealize and help him to evaluate. He feels the need of broad ideas and principles which have an integrating effect upon his thinking and conduct.

It has often occurred to us that development is a key concept which has significance for the adolescent as well as for the adult. Perhaps the significance is mutual and interacting.

And so we conclude with a brief postscript addressed directly to any youth who may be interested. The postscript aims to suggest the value of a philosophy of growth during the years of adolescence.

A Postscript Addressed to Youth

The Value of a Philosophy of Growth

WE HAVE not, in this book, spoken directly to the youths themselves by way of precept or advice. But neither have we written anything that we would want to withhold from them. Curiosity may prompt some to read certain sections or chapters, for adolescent boys and girls have a natural interest in the psychology of human behavior, including their own. Perhaps such a reading may even cast light on certain personal problems, for this book deals with the patterns and sequences of psychological growth. A sharpened appreciation of basic behavior traits which mark the stages of growing up can result in improved self-understanding.

A concept of growth may have some value for an adolescent youth. He is in a crucial period of his development as an individual. He may find a source of strength in a philosophy that looks ahead, that brings into awareness the silent, unceasing process of growth and the potentials of growth. With a longer range perspective view of his own growth cycle, he can better safeguard these potentials. This orientation may help him to make right choices along the way. Right choices place a premium on decisions and attitudes which protect his future development.

Although human growth is governed by deep-seated laws of nature, the ultimate achievements of personal growth lie within the individual. He must do his own growing. The finest achievements are won through self-mastery based on self-discovery.

So we would like to address this postscript directly to you as an adolescent youth. We are reasonably certain that a philosophy of growth is useful to your parents, teachers, and counselors because it tends to place mutual problems in perspective. You have already had some experience in the realm of growth, and can begin to build up a philosophy of your own growth. This will help you to achieve a sense of perspective, both in terms of the present and the future. Such a philosophy will mature as you mature.

495

G R O W T H   G R A D I E N T S

1. TIME AND SPACE

10 YEARS
Time.   For Ten, time is "something the clock tells." His definition is related
to some specific units—minutes, hours, months, centuries.

He senses that there can be differences in how long these units *seem*, however:
"Good things go fast; bad things go slowly."

Space.   Conceptually, Ten is most likely to define space as *nothing*—"Just sort
of nothing"; "Just nothingness." Some refer to *air* or *place between things*.

Dealing with space more behaviorally, getting around in it himself, Ten can
often manage bus trips downtown. Some can do so if they are meeting an
adult, others can go and return unaccompanied on simple errands, even
going to the dentist alone. A few, however, are still not allowed to cross
busy streets.

11 YEARS
Time.   A sense of movement appears in Eleven's definitions of time, which
stress the *passing* of something—"The passing of days, minutes, hours."

As at ten, the subjective relativity of time is sensed—"Goes faster when you're
doing something that is fun," or, "I'm on time for good things, late for
bad."

Space.   Like Ten, Eleven tends to define space as *nothing*, or as a *place between objects, room*. A number refer to planets and stars, the solar system,
outer space.

Many have considerable control over immediate space and can go downtown
alone on the bus, even travel on the train, if they do not have to change
trains.

12 YEARS
Time.   Twelve feels less confident that he can exactly state his idea of time,
and his definitions show greater variety. Most characteristic is definition
in terms of *durations* or spans ("A period of—well, time"; "The length
between something and something else"; "The whole span of life on
earth"). Related to these definitions, and also frequent, are those which
define time as a *measurement*: "Time is what you measure life in."

Space.   Twelve's ideas of space are, like his ideas about time, hard for him
to explain, and a number cannot do so at all. For many, space is still

nothing, or *air*. Others solve the problem by giving multiple definitions: "Air, space in the room, gravity, atmosphere."

Immediate space seems well under control—virtually all can go downtown alone by bus, shop or go to the dentist alone. And more distant space is increasingly in hand. Many now travel alone on the train, can find their way in strange cities, asking a policeman or others. Considerable interest in foreign travel is expressed.

13 YEARS

Time. Thirteen's definitions tend to be static. Time is seen as a *period* or interval—"Space between one event and another"; "Period from one happening to another happening."

Space. *Nothing* is still the outstanding part of Thirteen's definition of space, but this "nothing" is often amplified—with descriptions (vast, endless, infinite), or with reference to atmosphere, planets, and stars.

Now parents describe children as going to Boston or New York alone, rather than "downtown" as at ten. But 13-year-olds express less interest in travel than they did at twelve. Some say they like to be alone when they travel, not talk to people.

14 YEARS

Time. Fourteen most often defines time in terms of *action* and movement: "The passing of events"; "The world is run by time"; "Things grow; things die."

A variety of individual definitions show Fourteen's ideas of the complexity of the subject ("Time is rather indefinable, unless you want to be awfully unabridged about it").

His responses often show a feeling for balance: "Sometimes I have too much time; sometimes too little."

Space. At fourteen, space may be "nothing," "something," "everything"—with more emphasis on a positive *something* then at other ages. Fourteen describes it in terms of *endlessness* or *vastness*.

Nearly all now arrive at some definition of space, frequently by the use of *multiple concepts*—"Just the air where nothing is and the stars and the moon". Or, "An area between something and nothing."

Concepts, rather than personal experiences, increasingly dominate Fourteen's discussions of space—ability to get around in space is taken more for granted. Many 14-year-olds travel independently now without difficulty.

15 YEARS

Time. Definitions at fifteen again take on a more static quality. Most are phrased in terms of a space, a lapse, or a period. Some 15-year-olds describe time rather than defining it. Even these descriptions emphasize static aspects: "Time is stable, unchangeable."

Space. Emphasis on the *vastness* and *endlessness* of *nothingness* appears frequently in Fifteen's definitions—"Space is a vast emptiness." Relations to distance, the universe, even to time may appear, sometimes in multiple definitions.

Many Fifteens are not satisfied with their own definitions, and shift courses or argue with themselves about them. Many like to emphasize paradoxical aspects of their definitions.

16 YEARS

Time. At sixteen, the largest number of definitions are again in terms of action and processes: "The moving onward of things"; "The passing of generations, people, and events"; or, "Life slipping away."

But a wide variety of other definitions is given. Many, as at fifteen, conceive of time as a lapse, period, or space between events. Others give as definitions "fourth dimension," "measurement of events," and "way of recording passing of events."

Space. Space is thought of as *something* as well as *nothing, vast and endless,* and the concept of *things being contained* within other things plays an outstanding role in definitions: "Just everything with everything in it"; "Just a vast, empty vacuum filled with nothing"; "Just something in which something is contained"; "Infinite distance with nothing in it."

2. DEATH AND DEITY

10 YEARS

Death. Ten's concrete, down-to-earth quality is well expressed by his answering the question, "What do you think happens after you die?" with the simple, factual reply, "You get buried," sometimes adding a mention of the funeral or disintegration of the body. The more theoretical ideas about death expressed in the teens are largely absent at ten. Also characteristic is Ten's spontaneous comment that he hopes his parents won't die.

Some of our group (about a quarter) say that after death the good go to heaven, and a number of these feel that the bad must go too. Some say they wonder what heaven is like. Many, however, express doubt, ignorance, or unconcern about heaven ("I don't know, and I don't think about it much").

Deity. A belief in God is expressed positively by a majority of our subjects. A large minority, however, say they do not believe, question His existence, or are "less interested" than formerly.

God is conceived of as "a spirit" by most, as "a man" by some. Few believe that "God makes things happen to you" (though more do than at later ages), but more feel they are influenced by thoughts of God. Prayers are said by a small number—including some who say they do not believe in God.

A majority of our subjects attend Sunday school regularly, while a few say they have never attended. Of those who go, most say they enjoy going ("The family likes to have me go, but it's fun anyway"). A smaller number attends but does not enjoy it, a few saying their families make them go. And quite a few admit that they and other children—especially the others —act badly in Sunday school.

11 YEARS

Death. Comment about burial and eventual disintegration continues to be frequent, but theorizing about what happens after death increases. Though a simple "you go to heaven" response occurs less often, ideas about other possibilities—reincarnation, "a long sleep," "fading away"—are entertained by a few. Where some Tens hoped their parents would not die, Eleven ranges more widely and comments about relatives and friends who have died.

Deity. Eleven's beliefs do not differ strikingly from Ten's: the majority express a belief in God, and most of the rest say they question God's existence or say they are "less interested."

God is defined as "a spirit" by most believers, as a "man" by some, and a few definitions are more abstract than this. Thus: "God is just goodness"; "A goal, an idea."

About as many Elevens attend Sunday school regularly as at ten, but the number that enjoys attending has decreased and more go only because the family insists. This is the peak age for admitting to acting badly in Sunday school.

12 YEARS

Death. Great skepticism is expressed, though in many Twelves this actually reflects a concern with the problems of religion. Few believe you go to heaven, and the largest number for any age expresses doubt or lack of interest. Nevertheless, most of the group, including many of the "unconcerned," do hold theories—traditional or more personal—about after death. The most for any age spontaneously mention reincarnation, a few see death as a long sleep, a few as "the end."

Typical of Twelve's "all black or all white" thinking is his belief that only the good go to heaven. Those who believe in a heaven believe too in a hell, and none will admit the possibility that the bad might go to heaven.

Deity. Beliefs have not changed markedly since eleven, though at this outgoing age prayers are said by the fewest of any age. Only a few conceive of God as other than a "spirit" or "a man," though some combine the two for a double definition: "half spirit and half man."

Fewer Twelves attend Sunday school than earlier (though still more than half our group do), and a substantial number does not attend even occasionally. More express themselves as not enjoying Sunday school, going only because of family insistence. For the first time, a few attend church quite regularly, either instead of or in addition to Sunday school. An appreciable number state that in their opinion a belief in God—not attending church or Sunday school—is the important thing.

Practically none report acting badly at Sunday school. Perhaps at eleven those who would not conform were still required to go; by twelve they either do conform, or are not required to go.

13 YEARS

Death. In discussing death, Thirteen makes little mention of such immediate, concrete aspects as burial. More than at other ages believe that we go to heaven, though skepticism is still more frequent. Speculating about other possibilities occurs in a number. As we might expect at this static age, the prevailing theory is that "death is the end."

A personal concern about others is shown. Friends or relatives who have died are mentioned, and Thirteen comments on the sadness of those left behind. Concern with whether both good and bad go to heaven, or only the good, is again mentioned. And for the first time the comment is made, "Sometimes I wish I were dead."

Deity. Much skepticism is expressed at thirteen—more than at any other age. Most of our subjects express some degree of disbelief in God. The majority are dubious, some are "uninterested," and the rest flatly disbelieve. For the first time, no subjects believe that God gives them actual proof of His existence.

More mature and thoughtful definitions of God are now replacing the earlier, simpler acceptance. Subjects are thinking things out for themselves. And despite the prevalent skepticism, more at thirteen than earlier do say prayers. A few (more at this age than any other) are described by their families as being very religious.

As many attend Sunday school as at twelve, but still more (for the first time a majority) do not enjoy it. In many, church or choir attendance is taking the place of (or being added to) regular Sunday school attendance. Thirteen is the main age for Confirmation. Young People's Sunday Night Service is attended by just a few (most churches set a minimum age limit for such groups).

This is the last age for any self-admitted "bad behavior" in Sunday school.

14 YEARS

Death. Fourteen is more variable in response. Many believe we go to heaven, others present a variety of alternative beliefs, and the group which expresses skepticism is smaller than previously.

A few 14-year-olds say that they are "scared of death," but one of the strongest trends is stress on the inevitability of death, generally coupled with matter-of-fact acceptance of this inevitability.

Deity. Beliefs at fourteen seem more definite. Again a majority of our subjects believe in God, while on the other hand many state flatly that they do not believe. Fewer simply question His existence.

Being personally influenced by thoughts of God is reported by fewer than at other ages, and several more impersonal concepts appear—that there must be a God, because there are too many things that science does not explain—that the concept of God is a "good idea," "useful for keeping people in line."

Fourteen is the last age when more than half our subjects attend Sunday school with any regularity. For the first time an appreciable number attends church or choir, or Young People's Evening Services, and many attend no form of service.

Though fewer attend Sunday school than formerly, those who attend do so because they enjoy it. For many this is a peak age of enthusiasm for religious activities, and some regularly attend Sunday school, church, and Young People's, devoting the major part of Sunday to these activities. A few even belong to—or at least attend—two different churches.

15 YEARS

Death. Fifteen seems more earth-bound. By far the fewest of those interviewed now believe you go to heaven when you die. A few speculate about what happens—some believing that our spirits live on in those who remember us. Several mention that any punishment for badness occurs in life, not after death. And a few say they just don't like to think about it. The large majority disbelieve in heaven, are dubious, or are unconcerned.

As at fourteen, some stress the inevitability of death, and some are frightened by the idea.

Deity. Fewer at fifteen express flat disbelief in God. Some question, rather than disbelieve—"I half believe, half don't." In some ways, fifteen seems a more devout age, in that more state that they are influenced personally by thoughts of God, and many say prayers. But belief does not seem strong, or a matter of more than intellectual concern for many.

Sunday school attendance is sharply reduced at fifteen, but many more attend church, choir, or Young People's, usually with considerable enthusiasm. However, a majority of our group attends no religious services. It is striking that those attending Sunday school do so because they enjoy the services, not because their families want them to go, or because it is the thing to do.

16 YEARS

Death. Many more Sixteens than Fifteens believe in a heaven, a place or state of reward for the good. Most conceptions of heaven are more complex than they were earlier, however. Thus: "Not a *place*, but two *conditions* of life— one for the good and one for the bad." On the other hand, more critical concern occurs at sixteen than at any other age. Many think seriously about death, and some who have been extremely devout now comment, "I don't know *what* to believe now," or, "My religion teaches what I should believe, but I don't know. I suppose it's possible that we go to heaven, but it doesn't seem probable."

Inevitability of death is mentioned by many: "Afraid of it, but when you gotta go you gotta go," or, "Not afraid of it—I know it's gonna come."

Deity. Sixteen shows belief in a divinity more than at any preceding age. The great majority of our group believe in some sort of power greater than man. But the Deity is conceived as being less human-like in form than earlier. Some define God simply as "a spirit," but the largest number give a more complex definition, involving some kind of power, force, feeling, "intangible Being," or "something eternal."

While most believe that "there is something," many are less certain than earlier what the "something" is ("Don't have a concept that satisfies me"; "It's a mystery to me"); and definitions are qualified, "probably" used frequently (*"Probably* something, but it's glorified more by the religious. They have kind of played it up a bit"). Only a third of those who believe feel directly influenced personally by the belief.

The great majority of those who now attend any service attend church. Most feel that they are too old for Sunday school, though a few Sixteens do still attend, generally willingly. Nearly half the churchgoers attend regularly, but many only because they have to. Many Sixteens (about a quarter of our subjects), including several boys, attend Young People's Services— usually because they enjoy it, but in a few cases simply because they are officers.

Appendix A. Subjects and Methods

1. SAMPLING OF SUBJECTS

Subject Contacts

Though our method of study required a group of subjects who would return yearly for our tests and interviews, inevitably families moved, subjects became ill or could find no time for research appointments. The resulting sample, then, was an overlapping sample, but not a pure longitudinal one.

Altogether we saw a total of 165 different subjects—eighty-three boys and eighty-two girls. Of these, 115 constituted a "core group," seen multiple times in adolescence (more than four separate times, on the average). The remaining fifty, each seen once only, served to increase the range of material at a particular age but did not allow for inter-age comparisons. (Even these subjects were not strangers to us. For example, four of the eight 16-year-olds seen just once in adolescence had been members of a group of infants filmed and studied intensively from four weeks of age.)

For any particular age we had a total of sixty to eighty-eight subjects. At least two-thirds of these had been seen at the immediately preceding age; at

Table 1

Distribution of Subjects
Number of Subjects Seen at Each Age and Each Pair of Ages

Age	Number seen at age	Seen also at age:					
		11	12	13	14	15	16
10	76	57	52	47	46	29	20
11	85		65	59	57	38	27
12	83			58	57	38	26
13	82				61	39	31
14	88					61	45
15	71						49
16	60						

Number of subjects in core group: 115
Number of subjects seen once only: 50
Total number of different subjects: 165
Total number of yearly contacts: 545

503

least two-thirds were seen at the immediately following age. With increasing distance between ages the proportion of overlap dropped. Even so, a third of our 16-year-olds had been seen as Tens.

Table 1 presents the number of subjects seen—for all or part of our battery—at each age, and at each pairing of ages. Each subject is counted only once for any one year, even though some paid us several visits within a year.

Socio-Economic Distribution

An estimate of the social backgrounds of the subjects is afforded by their distribution on the Minnesota Scale of Paternal Occupations.* Table 2 presents this distribution—by individuals and by total contacts—for our sample, and for

* Institute of Child Welfare. *The Minnesota Scale for Paternal Occupations.* Minneapolis: University of Minnesota, 1950.

Table 2

Socio-Economic Distribution

Classification of Subjects' Fathers on
the Minnesota Scale of Paternal Occupations

Number and Percentage of Individuals and of Contacts,
Compared with U.S. Urban Population *

	Adolescent Study				U.S. Urban Population
Occupation	Different individuals		Total contacts		Percentage
	N	%	N	%	
I. Professional	86	52%	312	57%	6.2%
II. Semi-professional, managerial	49	30	152	28	13.1
III. Clerical, skilled trades, retail business	18	11	48	9	28.9
IV. Farmers	0	—	0	—	.4
V. Semi-skilled, minor clerical, minor business	7	4	17	3	29.4
VI. Slightly skilled	5	3	16	3	13.6
VII. Day laborers	0	—	0	—	8.4
Total	165	100%	545	100%	100.0%

* Data reclassified from 1950 Census: Employed, urban males. (*Urban* defined as residing in towns of 2,500 or more; 64% of the total U.S. population is so classified.)

the total United States urban population. The restriction in family background is clear.

Intelligence Test Distribution

Intelligence test scores were available for all but 5 per cent of our subjects. These were Wechsler-Bellevue scores, or occasionally Stanford-Binet scores, obtained in our own examinations. A test score was not obtained in a small number of cases. This lack could be supplemented in a few cases by reports of group tests given by the schools which the subjects attended.

To assess the comparability of the sample at the different ages, the mean and standard deviation of IQ's were computed for each age separately. Each child was not tested at every age, however. Our purpose was not an investigation of the tests themselves. A single test score was assigned to each subject, and entered at each age to which he contributed other data. (When a subject had several IQ scores the average was used.)

Table 3 presents the intelligence test results. As would be expected from the amount of overlap, the means are extremely stable from age to age. However, even between ten and sixteen—the ages showing least overlap—the difference between the means is only one IQ point.

A greater change is evident in the dispersion of scores than in the central tendencies. After age twelve there appears a small but steady decrease in the standard deviation, apparently reflecting an increasing homogeneity in the sample with the continuing selection and drop-out process.

Table 3

Intelligence Test Results

Test * Means and Standard Deviations at Each Age

Age	% having IQ data	IQ	
		mean	SD
10	91%	117.3	13.4
11	97	117.3	13.1
12	94	118.2	13.6
13	95	118.1	12.7
14	99	117.8	11.8
15	96	118.3	11.1
16	93	118.4	10.7

* Test scores reported:

Wechsler-Bellevue	88%
Stanford-Binet	8%
Other	4%

2. OUTLINE OF SOURCES OF INFORMATION

I. DEVELOPMENTAL EVALUATION

A. *Developmental Examination*
1. Naturalistic observations: response to examiner and examination, behavioral adjustments, posture, tensional outlets, etc.
2. Organization and consistency of performance of simple tasks: writing name, address, date, numbers, writing name with non-dominant hand; copying plane and solid geometric forms, drawing forms from memory, completing incomplete drawing of a person; following simple and complex directions of right and left orientation.
3. Standardized psychometric tests: Wechsler-Bellevue Scale of Adult Intelligence, Verbal and Performance Subscales; Five-figure formboard (Pintner-Paterson), Healy Pictorial Completion Test 2.
4. Projective techniques: Rorschach Ink-Blots, Lowenfeld Mosaic Test, Thematic Apperception Test.

B. *Visual Examination*
1. Case history: subject report on school, outdoor, and home interests; visual symptoms, headaches; reaction to wearing glasses or to visual training.
2. Visual analysis: visual acuity with and without glasses; ophthalmoscopy; modified Optometric Extension Program's Twenty-One-Point Visual Examination (including lateral phorias, retinoscopy, subjective evaluation, adduction, fusional reserves, amplitude of accommodation, etc.)
3. Visual skills: amplitude of triangulation; pursuit fixations in various directions; stereopsis; retinoscopy while reading; modified Keystone Visual-Skills Test.

C. *Physical Growth Evaluation* *
1. Observations of response to situation.
2. Standard physical growth measures: height, weight, grip strength.
3. Standardized physique photographs: for somatotype estimates and maturity status evaluations.

---

* Our findings in this area have been checked against, and in some areas supplemented by, the published research findings. Particularly helpful were the studies of the following workers: Bayley, Greulich, Jones, Kinsey, Pryor, Ramsey, Schonfeld, Shock, Shuttleworth, Stoltz and Stoltz, and Stuart.

II. Subject Interview

An informal discussion of subject's behaviors and attitudes in many life situations. Topics and sequence varied with subjects, but generally covered at least the following subjects and approximated the following order:

1. *Emotions*
   Anger, worries, fears
   Disposition, happiness, humor, sadness, crying
   Competition, jealousy, pride, revenge
   Expression of moods, of hurt feelings

2. *Sense of Self*
   Self-evaluation: assets, faults, problems, diary
   Wishes, likes, dislikes
   Desire to grow up, best age
   College, career, marriage

3. *Interpersonal Relationships*
   Family, mother, father, siblings
   Same- and opposite-sex friends, parties

4. *Activities and Interests*
   Outdoor activities, sports
   Clubs, camp
   Indoor activities
   Reading, radio, phonograph, movies, TV

5. *Self-Care and Routines*
   Eating: appetite, preferences, refusals, snacks, manners, cooking
   Sleep: bedtime, night, dreams, waking
   Bath, care of hair
   Clothes, care of room
   Money, work

6. *Action System*
   Health, tensional outlets

7. *School*
   General, subjects, teachers

8. *Ethical Sense*
   Right and wrong: distinguishing, doing, conscience
   Fairness, taking blame
   Listening to reason, arguing
   Cheating, stealing, lying
   Swearing, drinking, smoking

9. *Philosophical Outlook*
   Time, space
   Death, deity, church

III. Parent Interview

Still more informal than subject interview, but generally covered the same topics, plus a few additional topics such as impact of subject upon family group, observed and inferred sex behavior, general summary of subject's personality, etc.

IV. Teacher Interview

Discussions with a number of teachers concerning youths' behavior in school settings. Interviewees were not teachers of subjects in this study, but groups of teachers selected as especially insightful and successful by superintendents in several parts of the country.

3. METHODS OF ANALYSIS

As has already been described (Chapter 1), analysis of the data fell into two parts. In the first stage, records were sorted by age, and the most characteristic patterns for each age were defined. (These findings arranged by topics are reported in the *gradients of growth.*) In the second stage, the patterns discerned in the stricter age groupings were further investigated, with individuals grouped according to patterns of behavior shown rather than by chronological age. (Results from this stage appear in the double-column *maturity traits* under each age.) The procedure of composing the growth gradients can be described here briefly.

After records were sorted by age and sex, the personal and parent interviews and our own observations were read for classification of responses under the nine areas of behavior considered here (see Chapter 1). The classification was facilitated by the fact that the interviews tended to take up the questions under a particular topic together. Naturally, however, subjects discussed interpersonal relations when being asked about emotions, etc. The responses under each topic were considered for items which could be classified or counted; that is, for responses which appeared as if they might be made by a number of subjects, for example: Attributes desired in spouse, Food preferences, Behavior (reported) when angry. These were listed at length, and the particular responses of every child were tabulated under appropriate age and sex groups. Specific items could then be grouped, or dropped if infrequent, and the larger tabulations could be summarized. Tables 4 to 7, which follow, are examples of four kinds of summary tables, and are presented here to show various types of analysis used for different topics. In every case they are much less detailed than the tables actually used in analysis. Additional help in analysis was often found in graphic treatment of the data. The findings of Table 4 are shown in graphic form in Figure 1.

Further tables are not presented here, because they would give a misleading emphasis on statistical precision. No single table stood alone in the composition of the gradients; the total picture was derived from many sources of information. The trends in each table were cross-checked with other, related tables and with less formal material.

Finally, the gradients themselves were composed only after a rereading of the actual subject responses in light of the tabular trends. Thus descriptions could be formulated to illustrate both the predominant trends and some individual variations, and apt examples of actual statements could be chosen.

Table 4

Anger

Question: What do you usually do when you get angry?

Percentage of Subjects Reporting Each Type of Response at Each Age [*]

	Age:	10	11	12	13	14	15
	Number Reporting:	60	70	57	52	50	50
Physical violence [†]							
(hit, kick, bite, etc.)		42%	61%	53%	19%	16%	12%
Emotional violence							
(explode, cry, etc.)		38	41	26	23	20	12
Leave room, go to own room		20	33	30	45	34	30
Verbal response:		22	44	39	29	34	36
Verbal violence (scream)		18%	23%	19%	8%	22%	14%
Verbal retort		2	21	16	21	6	18
Other verbal		2	0	4	0	6	4

[*] Data for age sixteen not reported, since question often was not appropriate to type of interview conducted and the more informal coverage did not lend itself to the same sort of analysis.

[†] Percentages overlap, since one subject may show several responses.

Table 5

Wishes

Question: If you could have three wishes, what would they be?

Percentage of Individuals Making Most Frequently Occurring Wishes at Each Age

---

10 Years

Material possessions *	48%
(bicycle, 19%)	
Health	22
Happiness (for self or others)	16
To be better, smarter, nicer	16
"All the wishes I want."	15
To live on a farm	14
To have a baby in the family	10

11 Years

Material possessions (horse 22%; dog, 13%; house, 11%; bike, 11%)	53%
Health	23
To live on a farm	17
To be better, smarter, nicer	16
Happiness (for self)	10
No wishes	14

12 Years

Material possessions (horse, 16%)	46%
Re profession	25
To be better, smarter, nicer	19
Happiness (for self or others)	18

13 Years

Material possessions (horse, 13%; house, 10%)	24%
Peace	20
"All the wishes I want"	17
Happiness (for self or others)	16
To be smarter, better, nicer	15
Re profession	15
Two wishes, no third	25

14 Years

Peace	32%
Re profession	22
Happiness (for self or others)	20
Material possessions (varied)	18
To be smarter in school	15
Money	15
Betterment of others	9

15 Years

To be better, smarter, nicer	23%
Happiness (for self or others)	17
Peace	14
Material possessions	13
Good personality	12
To be popular	11
Re profession	11

16 Years

Betterment of others	29%
Material possessions (car, 20%)	28
Peace	25
Happiness (for self or others)	21
To be better, smarter, nicer	18

* Tabulated only once for any one individual; thus means "Percentage making one or more wishes for material possessions." The specific possessions wished for were, of course, also tabulated separately.

Table 6

Marriage

Question: Do you plan to get married someday?

Percentages of Boys and Girls Responding to Question and Spontaneously Adding Further Comments

		10 Years			11 Years			12 Years			13 Years			14 Years			15 Years			16 Years		
Age: Sex:		G	B	All	G	B	All	G	B	All	G	B	All	G	B	All	G	B	All	G	B	All
Number reporting:		26	20	46	33	29	62	20	20	40	17	16	33	22	14	36	20	16	36	20	27	47
Responses																						
Going to marry		81%	50%	67%	91%	52%	73%	85%	55%	70%	94%	75%	85%	100%	43%	78%	100%	75%	89%	80%	19%	45%
Not going to marry		4	0	2	0	0	0	0	15	8	0	6	3	0	14	6	0	19	8	0	7	4
Don't know		15	50	30	9	48	27	15	30	23	6	19	12	0	43	17	0	6	3	20	74	51
Spontaneous Additions																						
Emphasizes spouse		31%	20%	26%	45%	14%	31%	45%	15%	30%	29%	13%	21%	36%	7%	25%	40%	31%	36%	10%	4%	6%
Emphasizes children		65	20	46	60	31	47	60	20	40	82	19	52	36	14	28	35	38	36	35	4	17
Gives desired number of children		65	10	41	54	28	42	45	15	30	53	6	30	14	0	8	35	25	30	0	0	11
"Somebody picked out"		4	5	4	0	3	2	0	10	5	0	0	0	0	0	0	0	0	0	0	0	0
"Nobody picked out yet"		8	25	17	6	14	10	5	5	5	6	38	21	5	0	3	0	13	6	0	0	0

Table 7

Religious Services: Attendance and Attitudes

Question: Do you go to Sunday school? Church? Go because you want to?

	Age:	10	11	12	13	14	15	16
	Number Reporting:	38	51	45	39	39	35	30
Attendance * (Percentage of total number)								
Sunday school		68%	69%	60%	64%	54%	23%	17%
Young People's		0	0	0	8	26	31	23
Church or Choir		0	0	7	10	26	26	80
Do not attend services:		32	31	36	20	21	26	7
Never have attended		11	12	7	5	3	3	0
Went to SS earlier		21	18	29	15	31	53	50
Attitudes toward Sunday school (Percentage of no. who attend)								
Enjoy going		66%	57%	60%	44%	67%	100%	81%
Do not enjoy:		34	43	40	51	33	0	19
Go because parents insist			12	27	30	20	24	0
"Thing to do"		0	0	11	4	10	0	0
Report others' misbehavior		19	34	3	16	0	0	0

* Percentages may overlap, since some attend more than one kind of service.

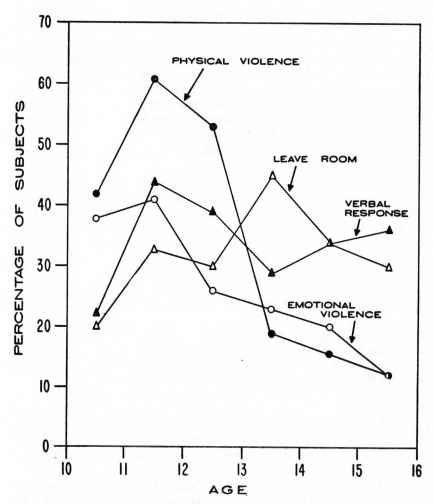

FIGURE 1. Anger Responses Reported by Subjects

Appendix B. Age Standards and Eligibilities

I. LEGAL

General:

Employment: Broadly speaking, sixteen is the minimum age at which children may leave school for full-time employment. Although there are State variations, the over-all effect of State child-labor and school-attendance laws and of the Federal Fair Labor Standards Act is a sixteen year minimum age for most employment during school hours and for most factory employment.

The Federal law and some State laws set an eighteen year minimum age for certain hazardous jobs. Both Federal and State laws permit some employment outside school hours at fourteen and fifteen; in some States and for some occupations this minimum is lower.

Juvenile Courts: By 1919, all states but three had some kind of a Juvenile Court system.

Family Allowances in Canada: The Dominion Government since 1945 has provided family allowances which are spent directly for the welfare of young children. A Canadian mother receives a total of $1,128 between a child's birth and its sixteenth birthday. The allowances vary with the age of the child. The monthly payments are as follows: Under six, $5; six through nine, $6; ten through twelve, $7; thirteen through fifteen, $8.

Connecticut: (Provisions selected from current statutes)

Juvenile Court: All children under sixteen years of age, and those under eighteen who are transferred from the jurisdiction of another court, are under the jurisdiction of the Juvenile Court. This court has "exclusive, original jurisdiction" over all proceedings, concerning children except for guardianship matters, adoption proceedings, and property matters. In the case of temporary detention, the judge has the power to assign the child to the care of any agent he deems fit (usually the parents) until the time of the hearing.

A child cannot be sent to jail under the age of sixteen. If, in the judge's opinion, the child needs the discipline of a state commitment, he can send the child only to an institution which is permitted by law to care for children. These commitments are indeterminate and can be reopened twice a year by the parents for review. If the judge so decides, the child may be kept in a detention center until the age of twenty-one.

Employment and School Attendance: School attendance is compulsory over seven years of age and under sixteen, without equivalent instruction. A "leaving certificate" may be obtained between the ages of fourteen and sixteen with the parents' consent and a physical examination. A child may not be employed by anyone between the ages of fourteen and sixteen without this leaving certificate. In practice, however, the occupations for which a child may obtain a leaving certificate are very few, since most occupations are prohibited until the age of sixteen. Some of the possible ones are agriculture, domestic service, and work at home.

No child under the age of sixteen can be employed in any manufacturing, mercantile, theatrical, or restaurant industry, or in any bowling alley, barbershop, or shoeshine establishment. No child under the age of eighteen may be employed in any hazardous industry.

No child under eighteen may be employed in any establishment or industry without a certificate from the state. The hours and conditions of employment between the ages of sixteen and eighteen are strictly regulated. No night work is permitted under eighteen. About the only occupations not covered by these regulations are domestic service, agriculture, and street trades. Thus a working certificate is needed for almost all occupations up until the age of eighteen.

Automobile Licenses: Over the age of sixteen, a vehicle may be operated for thirty days when a licensed driver is present. After this a license may be obtained. This license is rather probationary until the age of eighteen, since the parents' or guardian's permission must be filed and the license can be "recalled" by the authorities at their discretion.

Liquor: Under the age of twenty-one, no person can be employed or loiter in a room where liquor is served at a bar. No person under twenty-one can purchase liquor or be served liquor in any public establishment.

Tobacco: Tobacco cannot be sold, given, or delivered to anyone under the age of sixteen. There is evidently no penalty for the child himself, but only for the agent from whom he received the tobacco.

Other Licenses: A license to hunt or trap in the company of an adult can be obtained between the ages of twelve and sixteen. Otherwise, all licenses can be obtained after sixteen.

Credit: A child who is still a student cannot obtain credit under the age of twenty-one.

II. RELIGIOUS

Catholic: A child attends Sunday school from the time that he enters school. Confirmation does not confer a change in status, but is an affirmation of faith. This usually takes place, after appropriate instruction, anytime between eleven and fourteen years of age. It varies according to when the individual churches hold Confirmation services.

Jewish: A coming-of-age ceremony is held, for boys only, at the age of thirteen. The child demonstrates his religious knowledge and is henceforth permitted to attend synagogue and is considered an adult in the eyes of the religion.

Protestant: Ages for starting Sunday school are very variable. In some churches a child joins the church formally at about twelve or thirteen.

III. SCOUTING ORGANIZATIONS

Boy Scouts:

A boy may join, as a Cub Scout, at the age of eight. He may become a Boy Scout at eleven, but under some circumstances may remain in the Cub Scouts until he is eleven and a half. At the age of fourteen he is called an Explorer and he may remain as an Explorer in his Boy Scout Troop, or he may elect to leave the Troop and join a unit consisting of boys age fourteen and over. These units are called Explorer Posts.

The groups that the boys work in are largely determined, beyond these regulations, by the number of boys in any particular area who are Scouts. If there are enough for several groups, they are divided into age groups. If not, the groups will range from eight to eleven, and from eleven to fourteen and over. Ages of earning badges are very variable. The National Director of Research Service of B.S.A. reports that a sampled group reached Eagle Scout rank at the average age of 14.6 years.

Girl Scouts:

A girl can join, as a Brownie, at the age of seven or when she is in the second grade. She remains a Brownie until the age of ten or when she is in the fifth grade. She then becomes an intermediate Scout, and remains in this group until the age of fourteen or when she is in the ninth grade. She becomes a Senior Scout at the age of fourteen or when she is in the ninth grade and remains in this group until she is seventeen or finishes high school.

Like the Boy Scouts, groupings beyond the above depend upon the number of Scouts in any one area.

Campfire Girls:

A girl may join, as a Blue Bird, when in the second grade. She remains a Blue Bird until she is ten, or in the fifth grade, when she becomes a Campfire Girl. There is an older group, the Horizon Club, which she may join when she is fifteen or in the ninth grade. This group contains girls from fifteen to seventeen, or ninth grade through high school.

A girl cannot earn the highest rank in Campfire until she is fifteen. Otherwise there are no limitations on badge and rank earning.

IV. ARMED SERVICES

A boy may join the Army, Navy, or Marine Corps at the age of seventeen with his parents' permission. At eighteen, parents' consent is no longer necessary. To become a jet pilot trainee one must be from nineteen to twenty-six-and-a-half years of age.

Appendix C. Readings and References

1. READINGS FOR PARENTS AND RESEARCH REFERENCES

Ames, Louise B. et al. *Rorschach Responses in Adolescence*. New York: Hoeber, in preparation.

Ames, Louise B. et al. *Mosaic Test Responses from Two to Sixteen Years*. In preparation.

Arlitt, Ada Hart. *Adolescent Psychology*. New York: American Book Co., 1933, x + 250.

Ausubel, David P. *Theory and Problems of Adolescent Development*. New York: Grune & Stratton, 1954, xviii + 580.

Bayley, N. & Tuddenham, R. Adolescent changes in body build. *43rd Yearbook, Nat'l. Soc. Study Ed.*, 1944, 33–55.

Blos, Peter. *The Adolescent Personality. A Study of Individual Behavior*. New York: Appleton-Century-Crofts, 1941, 517 pp.

Breckenridge, Marian E. & Vincent, E. L. *Child Development: Physical and Psychological Growth Through the School Years*. Philadelphia & London: W. B. Saunders Co., 1943, ix + 592.

Cole, Luella. *Psychology of Adolescence*. New York: Farrar & Rinehart, 1936, xvi + 503.

Conklin, Edmund S. *Principles of Adolescent Psychology*. New York: Henry Holt, 1935, ix + 437.

Dennis, Wayne. The adolescent. In L. Carmichael (Ed.), *Manual of Child Psychology*. New York: Wiley, 1946, Chap. 12.

Dimick, Hedley S. *Rediscovering the Adolescent*. New York: Association Press, 1937, xx + 287.

Duvall, Evelyn Millis. Keeping up with teen-agers. *Public Affairs Pamphlet No. 127*, 31 pp.

Fine, Benjamin. *1,000,000 Delinquents*. New York: World Publishing Co., 1955, 377 pp.

Farnham, Marynia F. *The Adolescent*. New York: Harper, 1951, ix + 243.

Fleming, Charles M. *Adolescence: Its social psychology*. London: Routledge & Kegan Paul, 1949, vii + 262.

Frank, Lawrence K. *Individual Development*. Garden City: Doubleday & Co., 1955.

Freud, S. *An Outline of Psychoanalysis*. New York: Norton, 1949, 127 pp.

Gallagher, J. R. *Understanding Your Son's Adolescence*. Boston: Little, Brown, 1951, viii + 212.

Gardner, G. E. The mental health of normal adolescents. *Mental Hygiene*, 1947, Vol. xxxi, No. 4, 529–40.

517

Garrison, Karl C. *The Psychology of Adolescence.* New York: Prentice-Hall, 1946, xx + 355.

Gesell, Arnold. *Studies in Child Development.* New York: Harper, 1948, x + 224.

Gesell, Arnold & Ilg, Frances L. *Infant and Child in the Culture of Today.* New York: Harper, 1943, xii + 399.

Gesell, Arnold & Ilg, Frances L. *The Child from Five to Ten.* New York: Harper, 1946, xii + 475.

Gesell, Arnold & Ilg, Frances L. & Bullis, Glenna E. *Vision: Its development in infant and child.* New York: Hoeber, 1949, xvi + 329.

Gesell, Arnold & Thompson, Helen. Twins T and C from infancy to adolescence: a biogenetic study of individual differences by the method of co-twin control. *Genet. Psychol. Monog.,* 1941, 24, 3–121.

Grayson, Alice Barr. *Do You Know Your Daughter?* New York: Appleton-Century-Crofts, 1944, xiv + 306.

Greulich, W. W., Day, H. G., Lachman, S. E., Wolfe, J. B., & Shuttleworth, F. K. A handbook of methods for the study of adolescent children. *Monogr. Soc. Res. Child Dev.,* 1938, 3, No. 2.

Greulich, W. W. et al. Somatic and endocrine studies of puberal and adolescent boys. *Monog. Soc. Res. Child Develpm.,* 1942, 7, No. 3.

Hall, G. Stanley. *Adolescence.* Vols. I and II. New York: Appleton, 1904, xx + 589, vi + 784.

Havighurst, Robert J. & Taba, H. *Adolescent Character and Personality.* New York: Wiley, 1949, x + 315.

Healy, W., Bronner, Augusta F., & Bowers, Anna M. *The Structure and Meaning of Psychoanalysis.* New York: Knopf, 1930, xx + 482.

Hellersberg, Elizabeth. *Adolescence: A Time of Transition.* Unpublished.

Hellersberg, Elizabeth. The Horn-Hellersberg test and adjustment to reality. *Amer. J. Orthopsychiat.,* 1945, 15, 690–710.

Hollingshead, August B. *Elmtown's Youth: The Impact of Social Classes on Adolescents.* New York: Wiley, 1949, xi + 480.

Hurlock, Elizabeth B. *Adolescent Development.* New York: McGraw-Hill, 1949, x + 566.

Jones, Ernest. *The Life and Work of Sigmund Freud.* New York: Basic Books Inc., 1953 and 1955, Volume 1, xiv + 428; Volume 2, 512 pp.

Jones, H. E. & Bayley, Nancy. The Berkeley growth study. *Child Develpm.,* 1941, 12, 167–73.

Jones, Harold E. *Development in Adolescence.* New York: Appleton-Century-Crofts, 1943, vii + 166.

Kinsey, A. C., Pomeroy, W. B., & Martin, C. E. *Sexual Behavior in the Human Male.* Philadelphia: W. B. Saunders, 1948, xv + 804.

Kinsey, A. C. et al. *Sexual Behavior in the Human Female.* Philadelphia: W. B. Saunders, 1953, 842 pp.

Kuhlen, R. G. & Kuhlen, A. M. Age differences in religious beliefs and problems during adolescence. *J. genet. Psychol.,* 1944, 65, 291–300.

Kuhlen, R. G. *The Psychology of Adolescent Development*. New York: Harper, 1952.

Landis, Paul H. *Understanding Teen-Agers*. New York: Appleton-Century-Crofts, 1955, 246 pp.

Lawton, Shailer. *The Sexual Conduct of the Teen-Ager*. New York: Greenberg, 1951, ix + 180.

Levine, M. I. & Seligmann, J. H. *Helping Boys and Girls Understand Their Sex Roles*. Chicago: Science Research Associates, 1953, 48 pp.

MacFarlane, Jean W., Allen, Lucile, & Honzik, Marjorie P. *A Developmental Study of the Behavior Problems of Normal Children Between Twenty-one Months and Fourteen Years*. University of California Publications in Child Development, Vol. 2. Berkeley & Los Angeles: Univ. California Press, 1954, vii + 221.

Mead, Margaret. *From the South Seas: Studies of Adolescence and Sex in Primitive Societies*. (Includes *Coming of Age in Samoa*, *Growing up in New Guinea*, and *Sex and Temperament in Three Primitive Societies*.) New York: Wm. Morrow, 1939, 304 + 384 + 335 pp.

National Society for the Study of Education. *Adolescence*. Forty-third Yearbook, Part I. Chicago: Univ. of Chicago, 1944, 185 pp.

Neisser, Edith. *Brothers and Sisters*. New York: Harper, 1951, x + 241.

Nervous Child. *Difficulties of the Adolescent Girl*. Volume 4, No. 1, 1944–45. (Symposium)

Nervous Child. *Difficulties of Adolescence in the Boy*. Vol. 4, No. 2, 1944–45. (Symposium)

Prescott, Daniel A. *Helping Teachers to Understand Children*. Washington, D.C.: American Council on Education, 1945, xv + 468.

Pryor, Helen B. Certain physical and physiological aspects of adolescent development in girls. *J. Pediat.*, 1936, 8, 52–64.

Ramsey, Glenn V. The sexual development of boys. *Amer. J. Psychol.*, 1943, 56, 217–34.

Ramsey, Glenn V. The sex information of younger boys. *Amer. J. Orthopsychiat.*, 1943, 13, 347–53.

Redlich, Fritz & Bingham, Jane. *The Inside Story—Psychiatry and Everyday Life*. New York: Knopf, 1953, xiv + 280.

Richardson, Frank Howard. *How To Get Along With Children*. Atlanta: Tupper & Love, 1954, xii + 172.

Scheinfeld, Amram. *You and Heredity*. New York: Stokes, 1939, xvii + 434.

Schonfeld, W. A. Primary and secondary sexual characteristics: Study of their development in males from birth through maturity. *Amer. J. Dis. Child.*, 1943, 65, 535–49.

Schonfeld, W. A. & Beebe, G. W. Normal growth and variation in the male genitalia from birth to maturity. *J. Urology*, 1942, 48, 759–79.

Seidman, Jerome et al. *The Adolescent: A Book of Readings*. New York: Dryden, 1953, xviii + 798.

Sheldon, William H. *The Varieties of Human Physique*. New York: Harper, 1940, xii + 347.

Sheldon, William H. (in collaboration with S. S. Stevens). *The Varieties of Temperament: A Psychology of Constitutional Differences.* New York: Harper, 1942, x + 520.

Sheldon, William H. et al. *Varieties of Delinquent Youth: An Introduction to Constitutional Psychology.* New York: Harper, 1949, 899 pp.

Sheldon, William H. *Atlas of Men: A Guide for Somatotyping the Adult Male at all Ages.* New York: Harper, 1954, xvi + 357.

Sherif, M. & Cantril, H. *The Psychology of Ego-Involvements.* New York: Wiley, 1947, viii + 525.

Shock, Nathan W. Physiological changes in adolescence. *Nat'l. Soc. Study Educ.,* 43rd Yearbook, Part I: Adolescence, Chap. 4, 1944.

Shuttleworth, F. K. The adolescent period: A graphic atlas. *Monog. Soc. Res. Child Devlpm.,* 1951, 14, No. 1.

Simmons, Katherine. Physical growth and development. *Soc. Res. Child Devlpm. Monog.* Washington, National Research Council, 1943. 87 pp.

Stolz, Herbert R. *Somatic Development of Adolescent Boys.* New York: Macmillan, 1955, xxxiv + 557.

Stuart, Harold C. Physical growth during adolescence. *Amer. J. Dis. Child.,* 1947, 74, 495–502.

"Sub-deb clubs." *Life,* April 2, 1945, 18, No. 14, 87–93.

"Teen-age Boys." *Life,* June 11, 1945, 18, No. 24, 91–97.

"Teen-age Girls." *Life,* December 11, 1944, 17, No. 24, 91–99.

Thompson, Helen. *Manual of Child Psychology.* Chapter 5, Physical Growth. New York: Wiley, 1946, pp. 255–294.

Tryon, Caroline M. Evaluations of adolescent personality by adolescents. *Monog. Soc. Res. Child Devlpm.,* 1939, 4, No. 4.

Ullman, Frances. *Getting Along with Brothers and Sisters.* Chicago: Science Research Associates, 1950, 48 pp.

VanRiper, C. *Teaching Your Child to Talk.* New York: Harper, 1950, v + 141.

Wittenberg, Rudolph. *On Call for Youth: How to Understand and Help Young People.* New York: Association Press, 1955, xiv + 241.

Zachry, Caroline B. (in collaboration with M. Lighty). *Emotions and Conduct in Adolescence.* New York: Appleton-Century-Crofts, 1940, 563 pp.

2. Readings for Teen-Agers

Beck, Lester F. *Human Growth.* New York: Harcourt, Brace, 1949.

Beery, Mary. *Manners Made Easy.* New York: McGraw-Hill, 1954, xiii + 333.

Bryant, Bernice. *Miss Behavior: Popularity, Poise and Personality for the Teen Age Girl.* New York: Bobbs-Merrill, 1948.

Daly, Maureen. *Smarter and Smoother.* New York: Dodd, Mead, 1944.

Fedder, Ruth. *A Girl Grows Up.* New York: McGraw-Hill, 1939, xix + 235.

Fishback, Mary. *Safe Conduct—How to Behave and Why.* New York: Harcourt, Brace, 1938.

Jenkins, Gladys G., Bauer, W. W. & Shacter, Helen S. *Guidebook for Teen-Agers.* New York: Scott, Foresman, 1955, 288 pp.

Menninger, William C. et al. *How To Be a Successful Teen-Ager*. New York: Sterling, 1955, 256 pp.

Pemberton, Lois. *The Stork Didn't Bring You*. New York: Hermitage Press, 1948, xii + 213.

Richardson, Frank H. *For Boys Only*. Atlanta, Ga.: Tupper & Love, 1952, x + 91.

Richardson, Frank H. *For Girls Only*. Atlanta, Ga.: Tupper & Love, 1954, xii + 98.

Scholastic Magazines. Teen Age Book Club, 351 Fourth Avenue, New York, New York.

Shacter, Helen, Jenkins, Gladys G., & Bauer, W. W. *Into Your Teens*. New York: Scott, Foresman, 1951, 352 pp.

Shacter, Helen, Jenkins, Gladys G., & Bauer, W. W. *You're Growing Up*. New York: Scott, Foresman, 1950, 320 pp.

Strain, Frances Bruce. *But You Don't Understand*. New York: Appleton-Century-Crofts, 1950, xi + 217.

Stratton, Dorothy C. & Schleman, Helen B. *Your Best Foot Forward*. New York: McGraw-Hill, 1955, x + 244.

3. Youth in Fiction and Biography

(The books in the following list present portraits, fictional and biographic, of individuals between ten and sixteen years of age. Artists have recognized the crucial importance of the adolescent period in human development, and the literature is correspondingly extensive. Since we could not even attempt to be exhaustive in our listing, we have instead sampled a variety of different approaches. The works, ranging from light humor to serious studies, differ widely in literary merit. Some of the youths depicted are seen for only a few days out of their lives; others can be viewed in the years preceding age ten and for years after age sixteen. The youths themselves were not selected as being especially typical. Each is distinctively individual—as are their counterparts in real life. But each, in one way or another, gives us a glimpse of events or problems or relationships common to the period. The techniques of the artist can often serve far better than those of the scientist to convey the feelings and sensations that accompany the process of growing up.)

Anderson, Sherwood. *Tar; a Midwest Childhood*. New York: Boni & Liveright, 1926, xviii + 346.

Barker, A. L. *Innocents*. New York: Scribner, 1947, 204 pp.

Benson, Sally. *Junior Miss*. New York: Random House, 1941, 214 pp.

Brincourt, Andre. *The Paradise Below the Stairs*. (Translated by Herma Briffault) New York: Duell, Sloan & Pearce, 1952, 292 pp.

Burt, Nathaniel. *Scotland's Burning*. Boston: Little, Brown, 1954, 300 pp.

Childs, Marquis W. *The Cabin*. New York: Harper, 1944, 243 pp.

Cronin, A. J. *The Green Years*. Boston: Little, Brown, 1944, 347 pp.

Davis, Clyde B. *The Newcomer*. New York: Lippincott, 1954, 216 pp.

De La Roche, Mazo. *Growth of a Man.* Boston: Little, Brown, 1938, 380 pp.
Farrell, James T. *Studs Lonigan.* New York: Vanguard, 1935, xii + 1113. (3 Vols.)
Farrell, James T. *No Star Is Lost.* New York: Vanguard, 1938, 637 pp.
Farrell, James T. *Father and Son.* New York: Vanguard, 1940, 616 pp.
Faulkner, William. *The Unvanquished.* New York: Random House, 1938, 293 pp.
Fisher, Dorothy Canfield. *The Deepening Stream.* New York: Harcourt, Brace, 1930, 393 pp.
Frank, Anne. *The Dairy of a Young Girl.* New York: Doubleday, 1952, 285 pp.
Harriman, John. *Winter Term.* New York: Howell, Soskin, 1940, 373 pp.
Herbert, F. H. *Meet Corliss Archer.* New York: Random House, 1944, 275 pp.
Hughes, Richard. *The Innocent Voyage.* New York: Harper, 1929, 399 pp.
Jackson, Charles R. *The Sunnier Side.* New York: Farrar, Straus, 1950, 311 pp.
Jackson, Charles T. *The Buffalo Wallow.* Indianapolis: Bobbs-Merrill, 1954.
Keun, Irmgard. *The Bad Example.* (Translated by L. Berg and R. Baer) New York: Harcourt, Brace, 1955, 182 pp.
L'Engle, Madelaine. *The Small Rain.* New York: Vanguard, 1945, 371 pp.
Mann, Thomas. *Stories of Three Decades* (see the fight between Jappe and Do Escobar, "Tonio Kroeger"). (Translated by H. T. Lowe-Porter) New York: Knopf, 1938, 567 pp.
Manning-Sanders, Ruth. *The Growing Trees.* London: Morrow, 1931, 370 pp.
Maugham, Somerset. *Of Human Bondage.* New York: Doran, 1915, 648 pp.
Maxwell, William. *The Folded Leaf.* New York: Harper, 1945, 310 pp.
McCauley, Rose. *The World My Wilderness.* Boston: Little, Brown, 1950, pp. 244.
Mitchell, William O. *Who Has Seen the Wind?* Boston: Little, Brown, 1947, 300 pp.
Moody, Ralph. *Man of the Family.* New York: Norton, 1951, pp. 272.
Moody, Ralph. *The Fields of Home.* New York: Norton, 1953, 335 pp.
Moravia, Alberto. *Two Adolescents.* New York: Farrar, Straus, 1950, 268 pp.
Newby, P. H. *The Young May Moon.* New York: Knopf, 1951, 320 pp.
Plagemann, Bentz. *This Is Goggle.* New York: McGraw-Hill, 1955, 243 pp.
Pratt, Theodore. *Valley Boy.* New York: Duell, Sloan & Pearce, 1946, 331 pp.
Rawlings, Marjorie K. *The Yearling.* New York: Scribner, 1938, 428 pp.
Rölvaag, Ole E. *Peder Victorious.* New York: Harper, 1921.
Rossi, Jean B. *Awakening.* New York: Harper, 1952, 244 pp.
Salinger, J. D. *The Catcher in the Rye.* Boston: Little, Brown, 1951, 277 pp.
Sandburg, Carl. *Always the Young Strangers.* New York: Harcourt, Brace, 1953, 445 pp.
Santee, Ross. *Dog Days.* New York: Scribner, 1955, 244 pp.
Smith, Betty. *A Tree Grows in Brooklyn.* New York: Harper, 1943, 443 pp.
Skinner, Cornelia Otis. *Soap Behind the Ears.* New York: Dodd, Mead, 1941.
Spring, Howard. *My Son, My Son!* New York: Viking, 1938, 649 pp.
Stafford, Jean. *The Mountain Lion.* New York: Harcourt, Brace, 1947, 231 pp.

Tarkington, Booth. *The Fighting Littles.* New York: Doubleday, 1941, 304 pp.

Tarkington, Booth. *Penrod, His Complete Story.* New York: Grosset & Dunlap, 1914, 345 pp.

Tarkington, Booth. *Seventeen.* New York: Harper, 1916, 328 pp.

Wescott, Glenway. *The Apple of the Eye.* New York: Dial, 1924, 292 pp.

West, Jessamyn. *Cress Delahanty.* New York: Harcourt, Brace, 1953, 311 pp.

Westheimer, David. *The Magic Fallacy.* New York: Macmillan, 1950, 96 pp.

Wouk, Herman. *City Boy.* New York: Simon & Schuster, 1948, 306 pp.

Willans, G. & Searle, Ronald. *Down with Skool.* New York: Vanguard, 1954.

Index

Stripped p. 362